Special Edition

Using Corel WordPerfect® Suite 8

Written by Bill Bruck with

Read Gilgen • Joyce Nielsen

QUE®

Special Edition Using Corel WordPerfect® Suite 8

Library of Congress Catalog No.: 97-67459

ISBN: 0-7897-1328-4

99 98 6 5 4 3

Interpretation of the printing code: the rightmost double-digit number is the year of the book's printing; the rightmost single-digit number, the number of the book's printing. For example, a printing code of 97-1 shows that the first printing of the book occurred in 1997.

Screen reproductions in this book were created using Collage Plus from Inner Media, Inc., Hollis, NH.

Contents at a Glance

Table of Contents

V | Using Internet Applications

VII Integrating and Customizing Corel WordPerfect Suite 8

Credits

PRESIDENT
Roland Elgey

SENIOR VICE PRESIDENT/PUBLISHER
Don Fowley

PUBLISHER
Joseph B. Wikert

PUBLISHING DIRECTOR
Karen Reinisch

GENERAL MANAGER
Joe Muldoon

MANAGER OF PUBLISHING OPERATIONS
Linda H. Buehler

EDITORIAL SERVICES DIRECTOR
Carla Hall

MANAGING EDITOR
Thomas F. Hayes

DIRECTOR OF ACQUISITIONS
Cheryl D. Willoughby

ACQUISITIONS EDITOR
Don Essig

SENIOR PRODUCT DIRECTOR
Lisa D. Wagner

PRODUCT DIRECTORS
Melanie Palaisa
Nancy D. Warner
Carolyn Kiefer
Robin Drake

PRODUCTION EDITOR
Lori A. Lyons

EDITORS
Lisa Gebken
Tom Lamoureux

PRODUCT MARKETING MANAGER
Kourtnaye Sturgeon

ASSISTANT PRODUCT MARKETING MANAGER
Gretchen Schlesinger

TECHNICAL EDITORS
Kurt Barthelmess
Robert Hartley
Lorrie Maughan
Darralyn McCall
Christine Peterson

MEDIA DEVELOPMENT SPECIALIST
David Garratt

ACQUISITIONS COORDINATORS
Tracy M. Williams
Michelle R. Newcomb

SOFTWARE RELATIONS COORDINATOR
Susan D. Gallagher

EDITORIAL ASSISTANTS
Jennifer L. Chisolm
Virginia Stoller

BOOK DESIGNER
Ruth Harvey

COVER DESIGNER
Dan Armstrong

PRODUCTION TEAM
Heather Howell
Laura A. Knox
Lisa Stumpf
Donna Wright

INDEXER
Tim Tate

Composed in *Century Old Style* and *ITC Franklin Gothic* by Que Corporation.

About the Authors

Bill Bruck, Ph.D., is a consultant specializing in helping organizations prepare for the 21st century using today's computer technology. His company, Bill Bruck & Associates, can be found at **www.bruck.com** and delivers customized training and performance consulting services to clients nationwide.

A psychologist and WordPerfect Certified Instructor, Bill comes from academia, having taught at the University of Florida, Seattle University, and West Georgia College. He is currently a professor of psychology at Marymount University in Arlington, Virginia. Bill is also the author of several other Macmillan books on WordPerfect, GroupWise, and PerfectOffice.

Read Gilgen is Director of Learning Support Services at the University of Wisconsin, Madison. He holds a Ph.D. in Latin American Literature. His professional interests include support of higher education, especially foreign language education. He has taught and written extensively on DOS and WordPerfect. He is author of *Que's WordPerfect for Windows Hot Tips*, and contributing author to *Que's Using WordPerfect for Windows*, SE series, and a frequent contributor to *WordPerfect for Windows Magazine*.

Joyce J. Nielsen is an independent computer consultant, specializing in writing and developing books based on microcomputer software applications. Prior to her work as a consultant, Joyce was a Senior Product Development Specialist for Que Corporation. She is the author or coauthor of over 20 computer books, including Que's *Special Edition Using 1-2-3 97 for Windows 95*, *Microsoft Office 97 Quick Reference*, and *Word for Windows 95 Visual Quick Reference*. Nielsen also worked as a Research Analyst for a shopping mall developer, where she developed and documented computer applications used nationwide. She received a Bachelor of Science degree in Quantitative Business Analysis from Indiana University. You may contact her via CompuServe at **76507,2712** or via the Internet at **jnielsen@iquest.net**.

Acknowledgments

I would like to extend my thanks and acknowledgment to my coauthors, Read Gilgen and Joyce Nielson; and to the coauthors of the first editions of this book, Judy Felfe, Steve Mann, Sue Plumley, Patrice-Anne Rutledge, and Brian Underdahl. Their hard work formed the basis for this edition.

Special thanks to Michelle Murphy Croteau, Publishing Programs Coordinator at Corel; and thanks to various anonymous Corel technical support staff who have been uniformly courteous, knowledgeable, and helpful with a variety of questions and concerns.

Thanks to technical editors Kurt Barthelmess, Robert Hartley, Lorrie Maughan, Darralyn McCall, and Christine Peterson, and to Que staff, including Don Essig, Melanie Palaisa, Nancy Warner, Lori Lyons, and Michelle Newcomb for their support and the work they have put in to get this book to press.

Finally, my deepest appreciation to my wife, Anita Bruck, for her support, encouragement, and vitamins I received during this project.

We'd Like to Hear from You!

QUE Corporation has a long-standing reputation for high-quality books and products. To ensure your continued satisfaction, we also understand the importance of customer service and support.

Tech Support

If you need assistance with the information in this book or with a CD/disk accompanying the book, please access Macmillan Computer Publishing's online Knowledge Base at:

http://www.superlibrary.com/general/support

Our most Frequently Asked Questions are answered there. If you do not find the answer to your questions on our Web site, you may contact Macmillan Technical Support by phone at **317/581-3833** or via e-mail at **support@mcp.com**.

Also be sure to visit QUE's Desktop Applications and Operating Systems team Web resource center for all the latest information, enhancements, errata, downloads, and more:

http://www.quecorp.com/desktop_os/

Orders, Catalogs, and Customer Service

To order other QUE or Macmillan Computer Publishing books, catalogs, or products, please contact our Customer Service Department:

Phone: 800/428-5331
Fax: 800/835-3202
International Fax: 317/228-4400

Or visit our online bookstore:

http://www.mcp.com/

Comments and Suggestions

We want you to let us know what you like or dislike most about this book or other QUE products. Your comments will help us to continue publishing the best books available on computer topics in today's market.

Melanie Palaisa
Product Director
QUE Corporation
201 West 103rd Street, 4B
Indianapolis, Indiana 46290 USA

Fax: 317/581-4663
E-mail: **mpalaisa@mcp.que.com**

Please be sure to include the book's title and author, as well as your name and phone or fax number.

We will carefully review your comments and share them with the author. Please note that due to the high volume of mail we receive, we may not be able to reply to every message.

Thank you for choosing QUE!

Introduction

Corel WordPerfect Suite 8 is the most popular retail software suite of desktop applications you can buy. Its powerful, integrated software set includes many best-of-class applications, including the latest versions of WordPerfect for word processing, Quattro Pro for spreadsheet analysis, and Presentations for drawing and presentation graphics. In addition, you receive tools such as fonts, clip art, Photo House, QuickFinder, and Envoy to help integrate and publish your work.

With the power of Corel WordPerfect Suite 8 comes both ease of use and sophisticated features. Individuals can load it on their stand-alone machines at home and let PerfectExpert guide them through sending correspondence, making family budgets, and maintaining a Christmas list. Multinational corporations can load the Corel WordPerfect Suite 8 on LANs, and conduct enterprise computing via the Internet and corporate intranets through the Suite's built-in Internet features. Businesses can also maintain corporate documents electronically through Envoy, keep corporate financial spreadsheets in Quattro Pro, and create custom interfaces and automated tasks. ■

Who Should Use This Book?

Corel has created an easy-to-use and easy-to-learn product in WordPerfect Suite 8. However, the sheer number of included applications, richness of features, variety of shortcuts, and power of its automation functions imply that both the new and experienced user will not be able to take full advantage of the suite by mere experimentation. This book can increase understanding and decrease learning time for everyone using Corel WordPerfect Suite 8.

For newcomers, this book offers a conceptual overview of the suite, step-by-step instructions for common functionality, and a thorough introduction to each of the included applications.

More experienced users will appreciate coverage of the new features offered by suite applications, along with the sections on suite customization and integration. Discussion of creating and moving files from and onto the Internet will also be of great value.

Many readers will find that they use one application extensively, and the others occasionally. For these users, this book will be their only point of reference for those applications used occasionally. It will also serve as a first point of reference for their major application.

How This Book Is Organized

This book is organized into eight major parts that take you from the basic design of WordPerfect Suite 8, through using each application, and into advanced integration and customization of the suite:

Part I: Working with Corel WordPerfect Suite 8

Part II: Using Corel WordPerfect

Part III: Using Corel Quattro Pro

Part IV: Using Corel Presentations

Part V: Using Internet Applications

Part VI: Web Publishing with Corel WordPerfect Suite 8

Part VII: Using the Bonus Applications

Part VIII: Integrating and Customizing Corel WordPerfect Suite 8

Part I, "Working with Corel WordPerfect Suite 8," provides a conceptual overview of the suite. It shows you how to perform simple functions, explains how common tools such as the Desktop Application Director and help system work, and discusses common file management issues.

Parts II through IV are devoted to the specific applications that make up Corel WordPerfect Suite 8. You can turn directly to these sections if you have specific questions to answer or tasks to accomplish.

If you will be working with the Internet, Parts V and VI are for you. You'll learn all about how the Internet works, how to use Netscape Navigator to browse the Web, and how to publish documents on the Web from each of the main suite applications.

Part VII discusses the bonus applications. In it, you'll learn how to use Envoy to electronically publish documents, use Address Book to maintain your contact list, and use Photo House to touch up and edit your photographs.

Part VIII, "Integrating and Customizing Corel WordPerfect Suite 8," discusses ways in which individual applications work together. You find out more about using PerfectExpert projects to perform common functions, how to transfer data between applications, and how to create and edit toolbars and custom menus.

Conventions Used in This Book

The conventions used in this book have been developed to help you learn to use Corel WordPerfect Suite 8 quickly and easily. Most commands can be entered with a mouse, the keyboard, or toolbar buttons. Commands are written in a way that enables you to choose the method you prefer. For example, if the instruction says "Choose File, Open," you can click the File menu, and then click the Open option. Alternatively, you can press Alt+F to access the File menu, and then press O; or use the arrow keys to highlight Open, and then press Enter. Finally, you can use the mouse to click the Open file button on the toolbar.

When you need to hold down the first key while you press a second key, a plus sign (+) is used for the combination:

> Alt+F or Ctrl+M

The Shift, Ctrl, and Alt keys must all be used in this way.

When two keys are pressed in sequence, they are separated with a comma. For instance, the Home key is never held down while pressing another key, but it is often pressed before pressing another key. "Press Home, up arrow" means to press and release the Home key, then press and release the up-arrow key.

When a letter in a menu or dialog box is underlined, it indicates that you can press the Alt key plus that letter (or that letter alone in submenus and dialog boxes) to choose that command. In "Choose File, Open" you can access the menu by pressing Alt+F; then with the File menu selected, you can choose Open by pressing the letter O. Often, the underlined letter is the first letter in the word; at other times it is not. For instance, to choose Tools, Settings, you would press the Alt key and hold it down while you press T, then you would press the N key (for Settings).

If there are two common ways to invoke a command, they are separated with a semicolon (;). For instance, you can access the Print dialog box in two ways, as indicated by these instructions: "Choose File, Print; or press Ctrl+P."

Many times, the quickest way to access a feature is with a button on the toolbar. In this case, the appropriate toolbar button is shown in the margin next to the instructions.

Bold text is used to indicate text you are asked to type. *Italic* text is used for new terms. UPPERCASE letters are used to distinguish file names. On-screen messages appear in `monospace` type.

NOTE Notes provide additional information that might help you avoid problems or offer advice or general information related to the current topic.

TIP Tips provide extra information that supplements the current topic. Often, tips offer shortcuts or alternative methods for accomplishing a task.

CAUTION

Cautions warn you if a procedure or description in the topic could lead to unexpected results or even data loss or damage to your system. If you see a caution, proceed carefully.

TROUBLESHOOTING

I'm having a specific problem with a WordPerfect feature. Look for troubleshooting elements to help you identify and resolve specific problems you might be having with WordPerfect, your system, or network.

What About Sidebars?

Sidebars are sprinkled throughout the book to give you the author's insight into a particular topic. The information in a sidebar supplements the material in the chapter.

Cross-references like the following direct you to related information in other parts of the book.

▶ **See** "Starting Quattro Pro," **p. 214**

Internet references such as the following point you to sites on the Internet where you can find additional information about a topic being discussed:

ON THE WEB

You can access Corel's Internet Web Site at:

http://www.corel.com

We, the authors, hope you enjoy using *Special Edition Using Corel WordPerfect Suite 8*, and hope that you find this book to be a valuable tool, as well as an ongoing reference to assist you in the learning process.

PART I

Working with Corel WordPerfect Suite 8

CHAPTER 1

Introducing Corel WordPerfect Suite 8

Suite applications

Find out what applications are contained within the Suite.

Desktop Application Director

Learn to use the Desktop Application Director (DAD) to easily start Corel WordPerfect Suite 8 programs from the Windows 95 task bar.

Extend your desktop

Find out how Corel WordPerfect Suite 8 integrates with your network, corporate intranet, or the Internet.

With Corel WordPerfect Suite 8, you have purchased the latest version of the world's best retail-selling word processor, Corel WordPerfect, and a collection of other best-of-class applications, including Corel Quattro Pro and Corel Presentations. But the Corel WordPerfect Suite 8 is much more than a collection of applications. It is a true integrated suite of products aimed at making tasks you do at the office or at home easier. ■

What Is Corel WordPerfect Suite 8?

Corel WordPerfect Suite 8 is a collection of applications for common home and office tasks, integrated with the Desktop Application Director, that includes a scripting language for cross-program applications.

What's Included in the Suite?

The Corel WordPerfect Suite 8 is designed for the Windows 95 operating environment, and it ships with the following applications:

- Corel WordPerfect 8
- Corel Quattro Pro 8
- Corel Presentations 8
- Corel Photo House 1.0

In addition, you get a number of bonus applications with the suite, including:

- Envoy 7 Viewer
- Netscape Navigator 3.0
- Desktop Application Director
- Address Book 8
- Fonts
- Clipart and Photos

Corel also publishes Corel WordPerfect Suite 8 Professional, which is targeted to a more specialized audience. The Professional Suite includes the same core applications as the standard version and adds applications, such as Paradox, targeted towards business users.

You can use *Special Edition Using Corel WordPerfect Suite 8* to learn the core applications common to both the Standard and the Professional versions.

What Are the Operating Requirements?

To use Corel WordPerfect Suite 8, Corel recommends the following minimum system requirements:

- Windows 95 or Windows NT 4.0
- 486/66 processor
- 8M RAM (16 recommended)

- 80M hard disk space
- CD-ROM
- VGA or higher monitor

Understanding the Design Goals

The WordPerfect Suite isn't just a bunch of stand-alone applications bundled and marketed together. It is a true *suite* of products that are integrated together and aimed at home and business functionality.

Thus, understanding WordPerfect Suite 8 isn't merely a matter of learning the features of individual applications. In fact, before you learn about the functions of all the applications, it's important to understand the basic design goals of WordPerfect Suite. These may be divided into the following areas:

- Ease of learning and use
- Integrated working environment
- Extension of your desktop

Understanding Ease of Use Features

The WordPerfect Suite 8 has been developed with extensive input from Corel WordPerfect's usability testing procedures. Two features that have been incorporated into the Suite as a result of this research are a *consistent user interface* and the extensive availability of *help in a variety of formats.*

Consistent Interface A consistent interface means that the way you work in one application should parallel how you work in another. In WordPerfect Suite, this can be seen in several areas:

- *Menu similarity.* As you can see in Figure 1.1, menus are similar in WordPerfect Suite 8 applications. Not only are the names on the menu bar similar, the selections within each menu item parallel each other as much as possible, taking into consideration the differences in each application's features.
- *Toolbar similarity.* In menus that are parallel within each application, the same buttons are used for basic tools across applications. These buttons are shown in Table 1.1.
- *Dialog box similarity.* In addition, similar dialog boxes are used wherever possible throughout WordPerfect Suite. For instance, the same Open dialog box is used in WordPerfect, Quattro Pro, and Presentations.

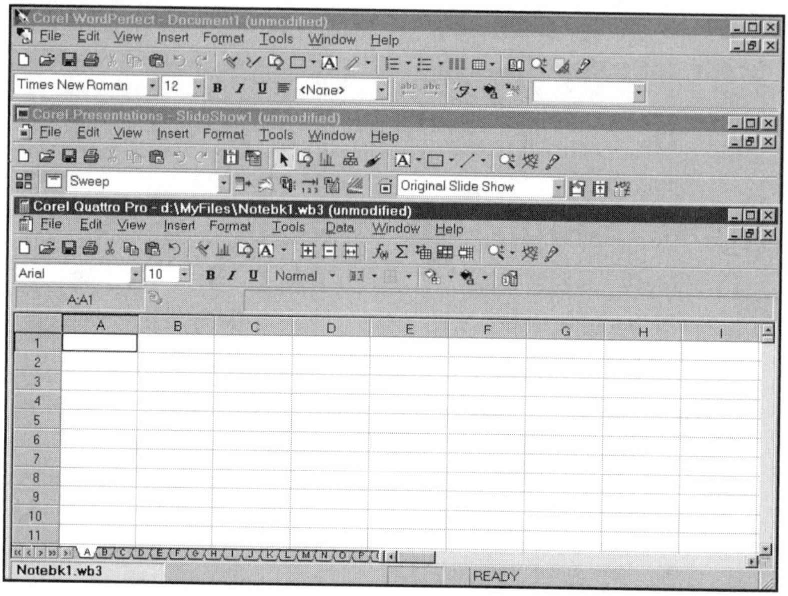

FIG. 1.1
Menus are similar in WordPerfect Suite applications.

Table 1.1 Common Corel WordPerfect Suite 8 Buttons

Icon	Name	Function
	New Blank Document	Creates a blank document in a new window
	Open	Opens an existing document into a new window
	Save	Saves the current document
	Print	Prints the current document
	Cut	Moves the selection to the Clipboard
	Copy	Copies the selection to the Clipboard
	Paste	Inserts the Clipboard contents at the insertion point
	Undo	Reverses the last change
	Bold	Turns on/off bold

Icon	Name	Function
	Italic	Turns on/off italic
	Underline	Turns on/off underline
	Web Browser	Launches your default Web browser
	PerfectExpert	Displays the PerfectExpert for assistance

PerfectExpert WordPerfect Suite's PerfectExpert helps you do everyday tasks in a number of ways.

PerfectExpert provides help. There is a PerfectExpert tab in the Help Topics dialog box. In this tab, you can ask questions in plain English, and the PerfectExpert will find the help topics most closely related to your request. For example, Figure 1.2 shows the question "How do I create page numbers?" PerfectExpert shows the help topics most likely to relate to the question. You see this dialog box when you choose Help, Ask the PerfectExpert.

▶ **See** "Ask the PerfectExpert," **p. 25**

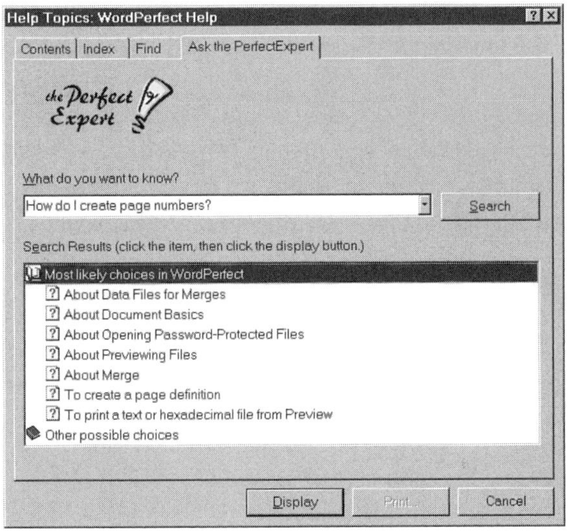

FIG. 1.2
The Help Topics dialog box contains a PerfectExpert tab that permits you to ask your questions in everyday English.

PerfectExpert guides you through tasks. When you display the PerfectExpert pane in suite applications, you see buttons for common tasks that apply to the type of document you are working on. For example, Figure 1.3 shows the PerfectExpert pane in a normal

WordPerfect document. Buttons take you through everything from prewriting tasks (such as creating an outline) to finishing tasks (such as saving, faxing, or printing your document).

FIG. 1.3
The PerfectExpert pane in WordPerfect provides assistance for every phase of creating a document.

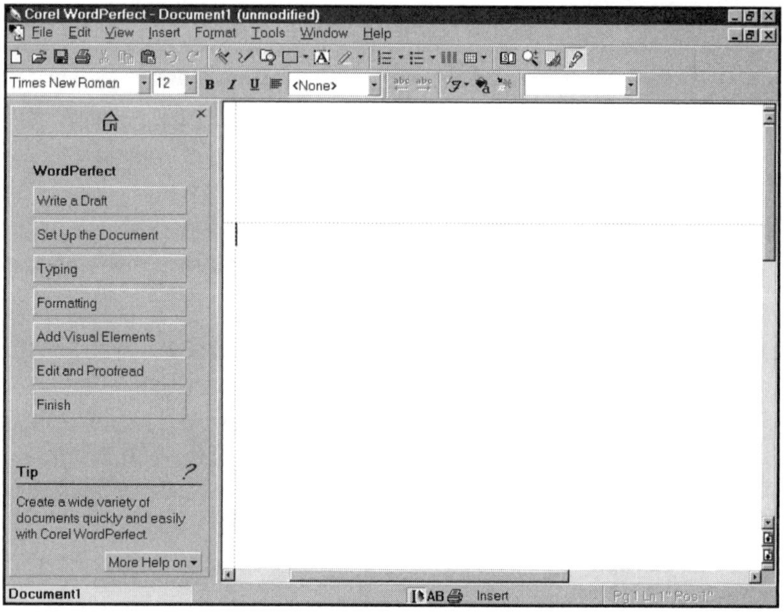

PerfectExpert has predesigned projects. The PerfectExpert pane in Figure 1.3 shows the steps for creating a simple WordPerfect document. Creating a simple WordPerfect document is a *project*. Projects are included for WordPerfect, Quattro Pro, Presentations, and Photo House. These range from creating simple documents and spreadsheets to complex projects that assist you in calculating seven-year balloon payments in Quattro Pro, or making a calendar in WordPerfect. You can see a partial list of projects in Figure 1.4.

▶ **See** "Using Projects," **p. 110**

▶ **See** "Managing PerfectExpert Projects," **p. 610**

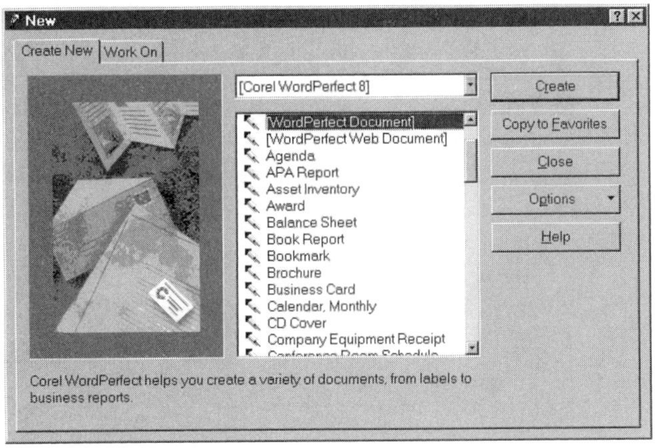

FIG. 1.4
PerfectExpert projects assist you in accomplishing even sophisticated tasks like creating a calendar or an asset inventory.

Understanding the Integrated Working Environment

Perhaps WordPerfect Suite 8's most powerful feature is the integrated working environment it provides. With WordPerfect Suite 8, you can concentrate more on the tasks you need to do and less on the application(s) in which you need to do them.

Of course, part of an integrated working environment is the common look and feel of applications. However, with WordPerfect Suite 8, this is only the beginning. WordPerfect Suite 8 offers features that include:

- PerfectExpert Projects (discussed in the previous section)
- Common tools for file management and writing
- The Desktop Application Director (DAD)

Common File Management Tools File management is the art of creating an electronic filing system that enables you to store files securely and find files quickly. WordPerfect Suite 8 offers you tools to assist you in your electronic filing tasks:

- *Common file management dialog boxes.* WordPerfect Suite applications have common file management dialog boxes (see Figure 1.5). These dialog boxes all have file management capabilities built in. From these dialog boxes, you can copy, move, rename, print and change file attributes, plus create, remove, and rename folders.
- *QuickFinder.* WordPerfect Suite 8 also includes the powerful QuickFinder indexing program. It enables you to build indexes of your data files. Using these indexes, you can search for files with specific words in them (for example, "Wilson Accounting Group"). Almost immediately, all files with these words are listed. You can even search for files containing synonyms of target words (accounting, budgeting), word forms (account, accounted, accounting), and common misspellings (acount).

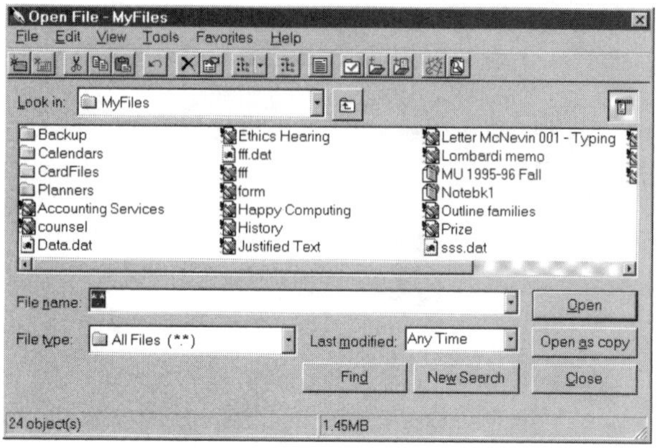

FIG. 1.5
WordPerfect Suite applications use common file management dialog boxes for file management.

You can access QuickFinder from any suite file management dialog box. It is also available to you from any Corel or non-Corel application by clicking the Start button on the taskbar, and then choosing Corel WordPerfect Suite 8, Tools, QuickFinder Searcher.

See "Using QuickFinder," **p. 50**

Common Writing Tools WordPerfect Suite 8 also provides you with writing tools that make the art of writing easier, and make your document more professional-looking. These tools are not only available in WordPerfect, but also in Presentations. They include:

- *Speller.* The speller (also available in Quattro Pro) will correct common spelling errors and catch irregular capitalization, words containing numbers, and repeated words. The speller will also remember words you have told it to ignore in a document so that future spelling checks of that document will continue to ignore the words.

  See "Checking Spelling," **p. 114**

- *Thesaurus.* The thesaurus provides you with synonyms and antonyms of selected words. It groups synonyms according to the word's meaning and part of speech (noun, adjective, verb).

  See "Using the Thesaurus," **p. 119**

- *Grammatik.* Grammatik is WordPerfect Suite's grammar checker. Not only does it flag more than a dozen types of errors, it will actually rewrite sentences for you! You can select from among predefined checking styles, depending on the style of writing you use, or you can create your own.

  See "Checking Grammar," **p. 121**

- *QuickCorrect.* Would you like for WordPerfect Suite to correct your spelling as you type? Would you like common abbreviations like LKSB to automatically expand as you type your firm's name of Luskin, Brankowitsch, Serrandello, and Buskin?

QuickCorrect is for you! Not only can QuickCorrect correct spelling and abbreviations, it can also automatically capitalize the first word of sentences, correct irregular capitalization, and place the correct number of spaces between sentences. QuickCorrect is also available in Quattro Pro.

▶ **See** "Using QuickWords Abbreviations," **p. 118**

Because these writing tools are used most when you are using a word processing program, they are discussed in the Using WordPerfect section. However, they work similarly throughout the WordPerfect Suite.

DAD DAD, the Desktop Application Director, provides convenient access to the WordPerfect Suite 8 applications. DAD installs application icons, called the Tool Tray, right on the Windows 95 taskbar (see Figure 1.6).

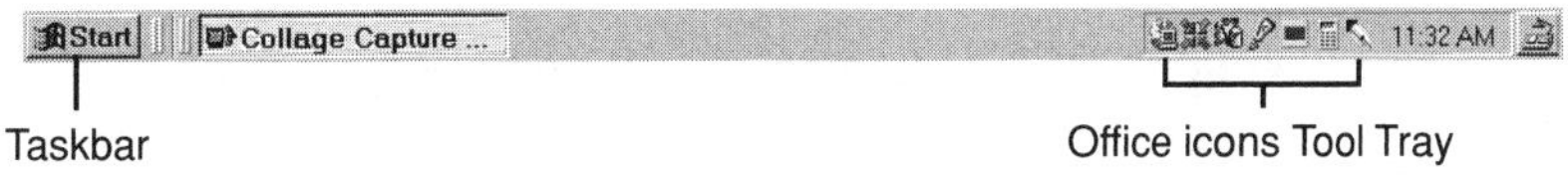

FIG. 1.6
DAD allows you to access WordPerfect Suite applications from the Tool Tray.

You can read more about DAD Bars in Chapter 2, "Getting Started with Corel WordPerfect Suite 8."

Extending Your Desktop

While Corel WordPerfect Suite 8 is a powerful desktop tool, its power is increased when you *extend your desktop* to your network, corporate intranet, or the Internet. The Suite's capability to extend your desktop can be seen in many areas, including:

- Performing common network tasks within applications
- Publishing documents with Envoy
- Internet Integration
- Data sharing
- Integrated code

Perform Common Network Tasks Whether you are running Novell, Banyan, Windows 95, Windows NT, or another common network operating system, WordPerfect Suite 8 enables you to perform common network tasks, such as attaching to file servers, from any file management dialog box.

Document Publishing As time goes on, companies are publishing more and more documents electronically. For instance, master copies of personnel manuals or technical manuals can be maintained electronically on a corporate intranet. They can then be updated as needed by responsible parties, and the updated information is available instantly to all users.

WordPerfect Suite 8 includes Envoy—a powerful document-publishing application that allows you to distribute documents across LANs, intranets, the Internet, or on disk. Files can contain bookmarks and hypertext links to assist users in jumping to areas of interest. Documents are "bonded" so that users cannot change them but can highlight or add notes to areas of interest. Envoy even includes a runtime viewer, so that documents can be read and annotated by others who don't have Envoy on their computer.

The Suite also includes Corel's Barista technology. Barista enables you to create documents that can be published on the World Wide Web, by making Java applets out of them. This enables the documents to include much more sophisticated formatting than is usually supported in HTML—the "lingua franca" of the Web.

Internet Integration WordPerfect, Quattro Pro, and Presentations are all able to convert files directly to HTML format for publishing on the World Wide Web. You can add links to Internet files in your documents so that a reader can click them and go immediately to a related file on the Internet. The Suite even extends the Help system to access help files that are maintained by Corel on the Internet.

In addition, the Suite comes with Netscape Navigator for browsing the Web, sending and receiving Internet e-mail, and a news reader for participating in group discussions on the Internet.

Data Sharing You can also extend your desktop by sharing data between applications with three WordPerfect Suite applications. Data sharing features include:

- *Shared file formats.* Whether you need to bring a WordPerfect outline into a Presentations slide, or clip a memo graphic from Presentations and insert it into a Quattro Pro notebook, you will find it easy to do.
- *OLE 2.0.* The latest version of Microsoft's Object Linking and Embedding (OLE) is available in WordPerfect, Quattro Pro, and Presentations. OLE 2.0 enables you to drag-and-drop objects such as drawings or charts from one application window to another. It also enables you to edit objects like Presentations drawings from within WordPerfect by merely double-clicking the object.

▶ **See** "Learning Techniques for Linking and Embedding," **p. 620**

Code Integration The Corel WordPerfect Suite 8 uses the concept of shared code to maximize performance and minimize use of system resources. Common tools such as the Speller, Thesaurus, Grammatik, QuickCorrect, and QuickFinder are shared between applications, thus saving disk space. Moreover, no matter which application calls them, they are only loaded once, saving system resources.

CHAPTER 2

Getting Started with Corel WordPerfect Suite 8

Well, here you are. You have Corel WordPerfect Suite 8 loaded and you're ready to get started. In this chapter, you learn about those elements of WordPerfect Suite that are similar throughout the Suite and make the it easy to learn and use.

Desktop Application Director (DAD)

Learn to use the Desktop Application Director to quickly launch Corel WordPerfect Suite programs from the Windows 95 task bar.

Understand common window elements

See how all the WordPerfect Suite applications have common menus, toolbars, Power Bars, and QuickMenus to make using several applications easier.

Use help systems

Learn about the tremendous variety of help systems WordPerfect Suite offers, from traditional Windows help, through Web-based help, on-line manuals, and the PerfectExpert.

Introducing DAD

DAD is the Desktop Application Director that enables you to launch Corel WordPerfect Suite 8 programs easily from the taskbar. In learning to use the WordPerfect Suite, it is appropriate that you start by learning how to use DAD to launch the Suite applications. Using DAD involves three aspects:

- Ensuring that DAD appears on your taskbar
- Launching applications with DAD
- Adding or removing applications from DAD

Displaying DAD

When DAD is installed, you see icons for various WordPerfect Suite tools in the Tool Tray area of your taskbar, as shown in Figure 2.1.

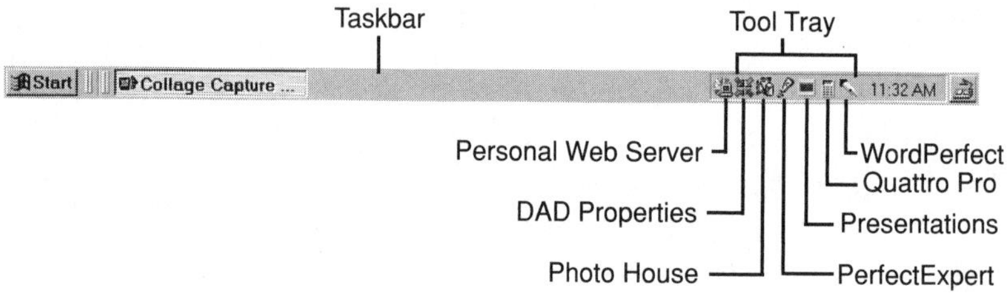

FIG. 2.1 The installation of Corel WordPerfect Suite puts DAD icons in the notification area of your Windows 95 taskbar.

If you do not see any of these icons, DAD is probably not installed or isn't in the startup folder.

TROUBLESHOOTING

I know that the Suite is on my machine, but the DAD icons do not appear on the Windows 95 taskbar. Someone has removed the necessary files from the Startup folder in the Windows directory. Start DAD from the Windows menu to see the icons on the tool tray.

Starting DAD If the DAD icons don't appear on the taskbar and you want to start DAD, click the Start button on the taskbar, and then click Corel WordPerfect Suite 8, Accessories, Corel Desktop Application Director 8. The WordPerfect Suite DAD icons appear on the taskbar.

If you want to ensure that DAD starts automatically whenever you start Windows 95, do the following:

1. Start DAD as described in the previous paragraph.
2. Right-click any DAD icon.
3. Choose Display DAD on Startup.

The next time you start Windows 95, DAD will be loaded automatically.

Exiting DAD Under normal circumstances, you should never need to close DAD. You will need to close DAD, however, if you want to add or remove WordPerfect Suite components using the Suite's Setup program.

To close DAD, do the following:

1. Right-click one of the WordPerfect Suite icons on the Windows 95 taskbar.
2. Choose Exit DAD from the pop-up menu shown in Figure 2.2. The Suite icons disappear from the taskbar, and you have exited DAD.

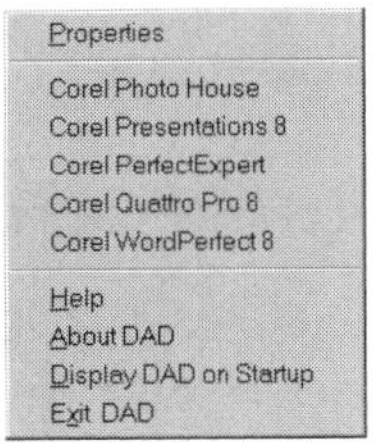

FIG. 2.2
Exit DAD by right-clicking a WordPerfect Suite application on the Windows 95 taskbar.

Launching Applications with DAD

To launch a WordPerfect Suite application from DAD, click the appropriate icon for the desired application on the Windows 95 taskbar.

TIP Occasionally, you may not know what application a button will launch. If you rest your mouse pointer on an icon for more than a second or so, you will see a pop-up QuickTip that tells you the name of the application.

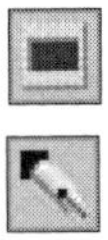

You can also use DAD to switch between Suite applications that are already open. For instance, if you click the WordPerfect icon on the DAD Bar, and then click the Presentations icon, both WordPerfect and Presentations will be open. If you click the WordPerfect icon again, you will switch back to WordPerfect.

Adding and Removing Applications from DAD

You can easily add or remove WordPerfect Suite icons from the taskbar by following these steps:

1. Right-click any WordPerfect Suite icon you see on the taskbar, and then choose Properties. You see the DAD Properties dialog box shown in Figure 2.3.

FIG. 2.3
Add or remove WordPerfect Suite applications from the taskbar with the DAD Properties dialog box.

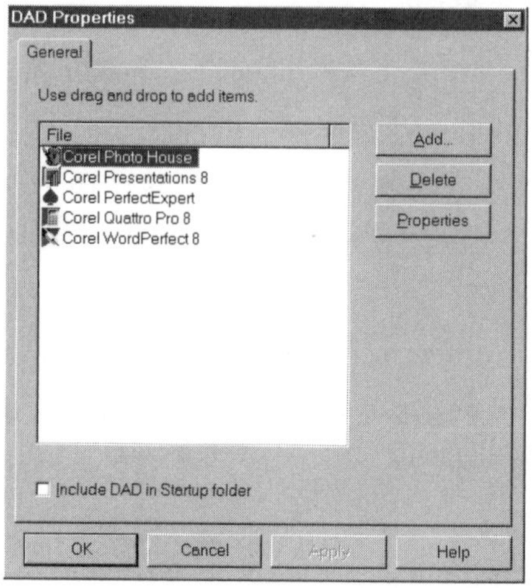

2. To add an application, choose Add. You see the Open dialog box. Double-click the application to be added.
3. To remove an application, highlight it and then choose Delete. The application is removed from the application list.
4. Click OK. You return to the Windows desktop and see the changed set of icons on the taskbar.

Using Help

The WordPerfect Suite offers many different ways to provide help to you, including:

- Help Topics
- The PerfectExpert system
- Upgrade help
- Help online
- Context-sensitive help
- Reference manuals

Using Help Topics

WordPerfect Suite uses a standard Windows 95 help system; in other words, WordPerfect Suite Help works the same way as it does in any other Windows 95 application.

To access the Help system, choose Help Topics from the Help menu; or press F1. What you see differs somewhat depending on the application you are in, but is similar to the WordPerfect Help dialog box shown in Figure 2.4. Four different types of help are offered: Contents, Index, Find, and Ask the PerfectExpert.

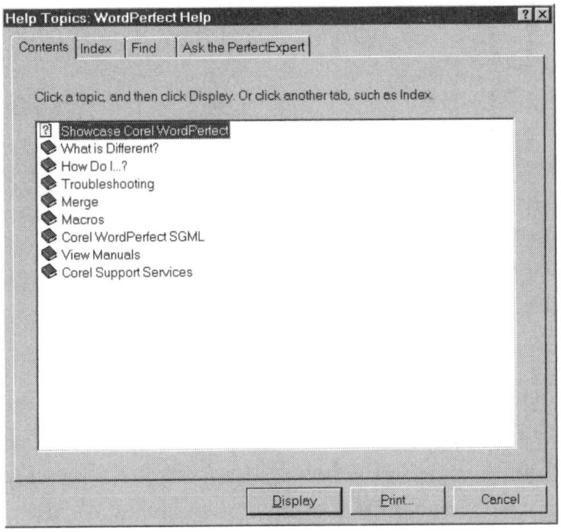

FIG. 2.4 The Help Topics: WordPerfect Help dialog box provides tabs offering four different types of help.

NOTE There are some slight differences between the help features in the main suite applications and the bonus applications. If you understand the Help options in this section, however, you will easily be able to obtain help in the other applications.

Contents The Contents tab of the Help dialog box acts like a table of contents for your help system, displaying major categories of help topics. For instance, as shown in Figure 2.5, What is Different shows you what's new and what old features have been eliminated from WordPerfect. The How Do I section shows a list of common tasks in the program. You also see help for Merge and help for Macros, which provide specialized help with creating merges, recording macros, and programming them in WordPerfect.

To use the Contents, do the following:

1. Choose Help, Help Topics, and make sure that you are in the Contents tab.
2. Double-click the major topic (like How Do I), and then double-click the desired subtopic (like Create Documents).

3. You may see further subtopics (denoted by a book icon), or help documents (pieces of paper with a question mark on them). Double-click on the subtopic or document you want to see.

FIG. 2.5
How Do I, which is available in the Help Topics: WordPerfect Help dialog box, lists common tasks you perform in the application.

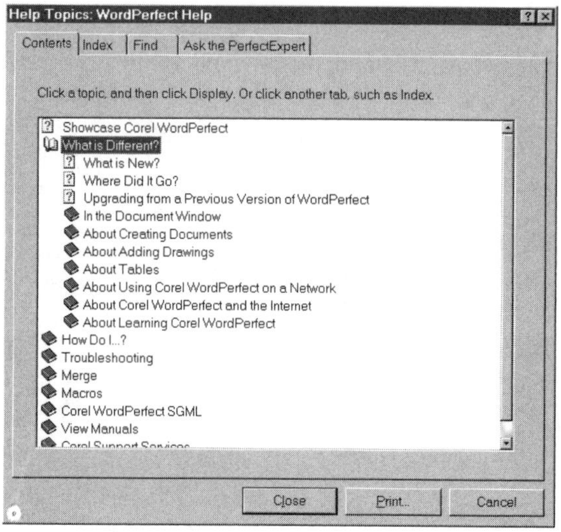

Index If the Contents tab is like a table of contents for your help system that lists major topics, the Index tab works like the index you might find in the back of a book. It lists key words that you find throughout the help system and enables you to quickly go to the help you need, even if it isn't a major help topic. The Index for WordPerfect is shown in Figure 2.6.

FIG. 2.6
The Help Index alphabetically lists all the keywords in the help system of each application, like the one shown here for WordPerfect.

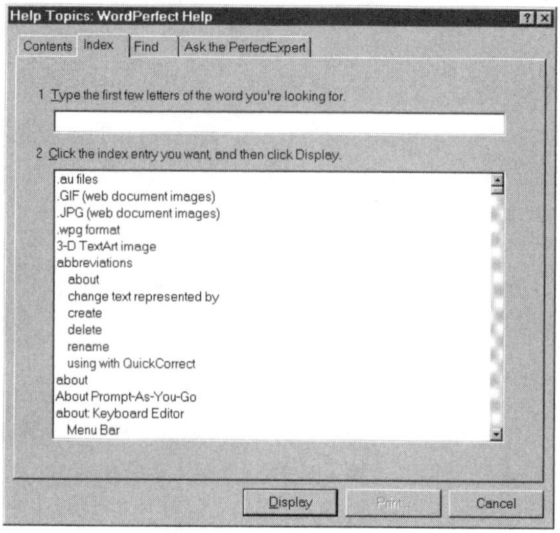

To use the index feature, choose Help, Help Topics, and make sure that you are in the Index tab. Type the word you're looking for in the Type The First Few Letters of the Word You're Looking for box. You see topics related to the desired term in the Index Entry box. Select the appropriate term, and then click Display.

Find The Find tab uses another Windows 95 help feature—an indexed list of every word in the help system. The first time you use the Find feature, a Wizard asks you a few questions, then all the words in the help file are indexed. After this is done, a word list is created, and you can search for *any* word in the help file—not just the ones the help file authors included in the index. The WordPerfect Help Find tab is shown in Figure 2.7.

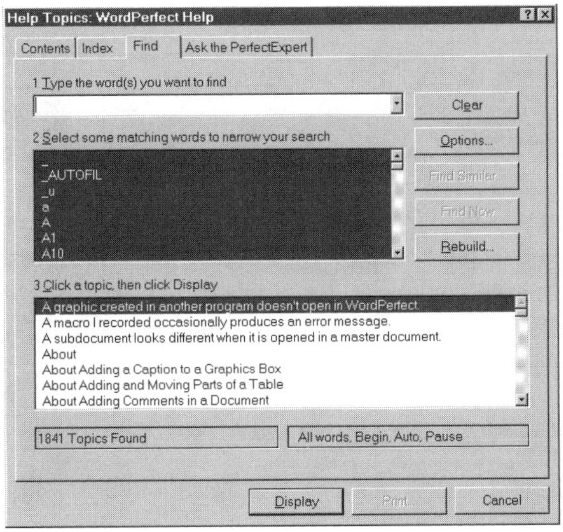

FIG. 2.7
Use the Find tab in your application's Help Topics dialog box when the topic you want is not in the Contents or Index.

To use Find, choose Help, Help Topics, and make sure that you are in the Find tab. Type the word you want to find in the Type the Word(s) You Want to Find box, and then select the term that best fits what you're looking for. You see a list of related topics in the Topic box. Select the most appropriate topic, and then click Display.

Ask the PerfectExpert

The Ask the PerfectExpert feature allows you to formulate queries in plain English. The PerfectExpert will interpret your question and display a number of help topics that may assist you.

To use the PerfectExpert, choose Help, Help Topics, and then select the Ask the PerfectExpert tab; or select Help, Ask the PerfectExpert from the Help menu. You see the PerfectExpert tab (see Figure 2.8).

FIG. 2.8
PerfectExpert allows you to frame queries in plain English in the Ask the PerfectExpert dialog box.

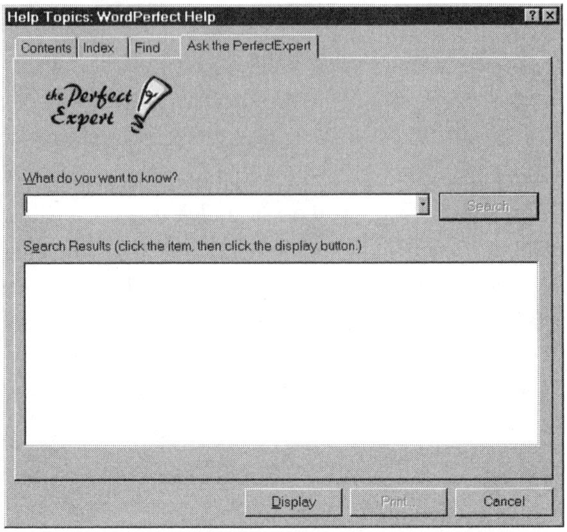

Type your question in the What Do You Want To Know box just as you would ask a help desk person. For example, type **How do I create page numbers?** When you click the Search button, you see a number of topics that may assist you, as displayed at the bottom of the dialog box in Figure 2.9. Select the one that addresses your question most directly, and then choose Display.

FIG. 2.9
After you ask the PerfectExpert your question, you see a number of topics that may assist you.

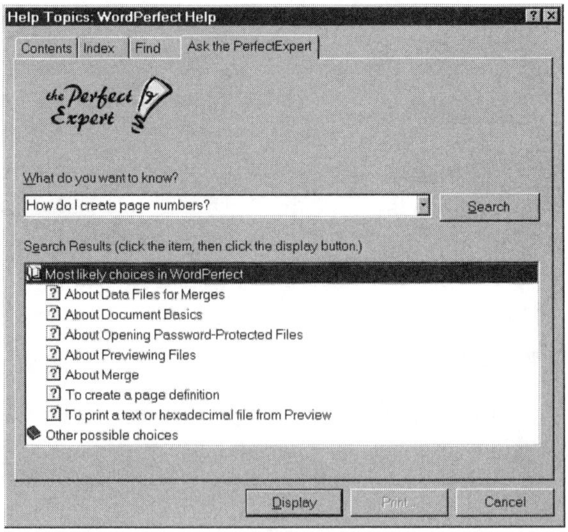

Upgrade Help

If you are upgrading from a previous version of WordPerfect, Quattro Pro, or Presentations, or from a competitive product, you may find the Upgrading from a Previous Version very useful. Access upgrade help by choosing Help, Help Topics. In the Contents tab, choose What is Different? Then choose Upgrading From a Previous Version.

Choose the product from which you are upgrading. You see a list of features. Click the feature you want to find help on, and you see help in the text box on the right of the dialog box.

Corel Web Site

You can immediately access the Corel documentation site on the Internet or the WordPerfect forum on CompuServe Information Services by choosing Help, Corel Web Site.

The Corel Internet site contains links to the Reference Center, from which you can download manuals and system administration information. You can also follow links to Corel Technical Information Documents, as well as tips and tricks for using the WordPerfect Suite effectively. To link to the Corel Internet site, you must have an Internet connection via your network or a dial-up connection, and a Web browser such as Netscape Navigator (included with the Suite).

The CompuServe connection takes you to the users' forums that discuss the use of Corel WordPerfect Suite 8. To link to CompuServe, you must have a CompuServe account and the WinCIM software that connects you to CompuServe.

TIP If you are attached to a network that has an ISDN or T1 connection to the Internet, you will find Help Online especially valuable, as you can access it almost as quickly and easily as the Help files that are on your local hard disk or network.

To access Help Online, do the following:

1. Choose Help, Corel Web Site. You see the Help Online dialog box (see Figure 2.10).

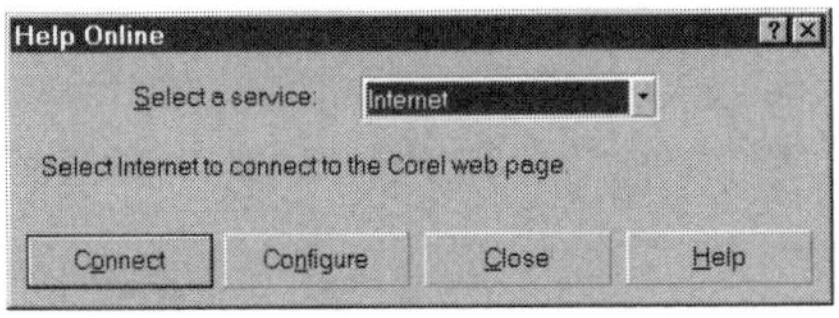

FIG. 2.10
You can choose to connect to the Internet or CompuServe for help online in the Help Online dialog box.

2. Choose Configure to automatically configure your system for the available Internet or CompuServe services.
3. Choose Internet or CompuServe in the Select a Service box.
4. Choose Connect. Your Web browser or CompuServe software starts, and you are connected to the appropriate online service, such as the Netscape connection to Corel's Web site.

Using Context-Sensitive Help

Context-sensitive help is available throughout the WordPerfect Suite applications. In many dialog boxes, you will see a Help button like the one shown in the WordPerfect Style List dialog box in Figure 2.11.

FIG. 2.11
Help buttons appear in many dialog boxes.

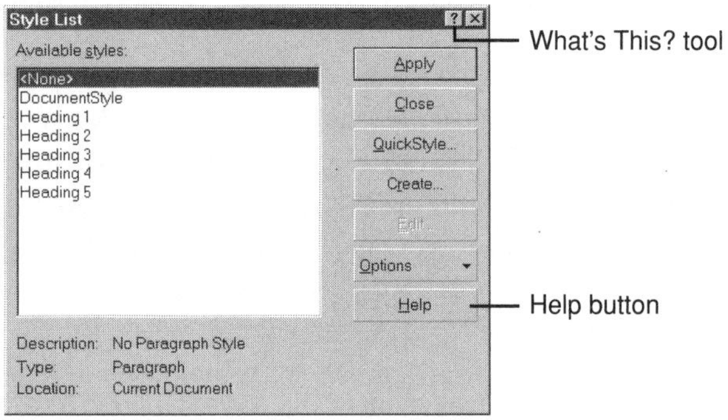

Choosing Help displays assistance for the function you are working on. In addition, even when there is no Help button, you can often receive context-sensitive help by pressing the Help key (F1).

Many dialog boxes also have a What's This? tool. If you click this tool, your mouse pointer changes to a pointer with a question mark. You can point at different objects in the active window or dialog box and click them to receive help on that specific object.

NOTE One other way that you can get context-sensitive help when you are not in a dialog box is to right-click an area of the active window to bring up the QuickMenu. The QuickMenu often has a What's This? choice.

Reference Manuals

If you loaded Corel WordPerfect Suite 8 from the CD, you have reference manuals online, in the *Reference Center*. You may have even installed them to your local hard drive or network workspace.

To access the Reference Center, put the Corel CD in your drive if you didn't install the Reference Center to your hard drive, and choose Start, Corel WordPerfect Suite 8, Setup & Notes, Reference Center. You see the Corel Reference Center dialog box shown in Figure 2.12.

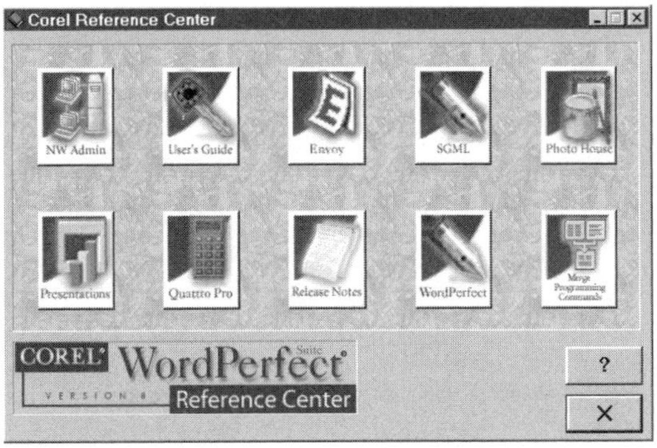

FIG. 2.12
The Reference Center provides reference materials for Suite applications.

Double-click any icon. The reference book is brought up in the Envoy viewer. You can click items in the table of contents to go to the area of interest, read the book cover to cover (if you do that sort of thing), or even search for specific keywords throughout the electronic manual.

See "Viewing and Annotating Envoy Files," **p. 545**

Using the IntelliMouse

The suite is compatible with the Microsoft IntelliMouse. The IntelliMouse looks like a regular two-button mouse. But it has a small wheel located between the two buttons. You can turn the wheel or click it.

If you are at the main editing window of a Suite application and see a vertical scroll bar, when you turn the wheel, the scroll down function is performed. In other words, turning the wheel is like clicking and holding the mouse button on the up or down arrow of the vertical scroll bar.

If you click the wheel, the vertical scroll bar changes its appearance, like the one shown in Figure 2.13.

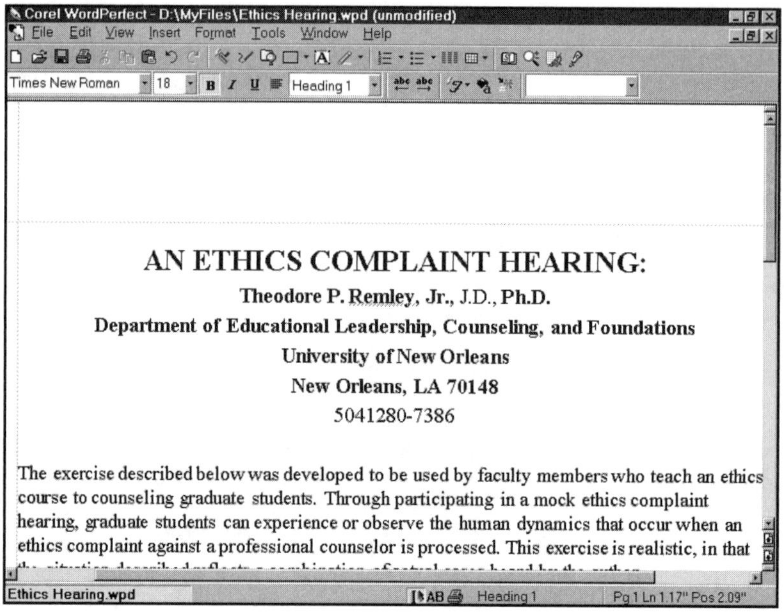

FIG. 2.13
When you click the IntelliMouse wheel, you can move the mouse up and down to scroll your document.

As you move your mouse up and down, your document scrolls smoothly. Stop moving the mouse to stop scrolling the document, and click the wheel again to return to the normal mode of operation.

TIP You must install the IntelliMouse software that comes with the mouse for the wheel to work. This software also provides many other options for efficiently using the mouse. Access these options by choosing Start, Settings, Control Panel, and then double-clicking the Mouse icon.

CHAPTER 3

Managing Files

Basic file management

Find out how to do basic file management operations such as saving, opening, and closing files.

Manage your electronic filing system

Create, rename, and remove folders; also copy, move, rename, delete, print, and assign attributes to files.

Find files

Find files quickly using Favorites and QuickFinder.

Can you imagine an administrative assistant who stacks all correspondence, outgoing letters, internal memos, and other paperwork in one large drawer? What would happen if everyone in a department did this using a large, common box? We can predict that this organization would not be able to function effectively!

Yet, many of us maintain our electronic files in an equivalent shambles. In this chapter, you learn how to use tools that enable you to create an effective electronic filing system. ■

Saving, Opening, and Closing Files

When you create a Corel WordPerfect document, Corel Quattro Pro spreadsheet, or Corel Presentations slide show, you are working with a *file*. Files can exist in your computer's memory and on disks. You can think of these electronic files like their paper counterparts.

Your computer's memory is like the surface of a desk that, for security reasons, is cleared off at the end of the day and everything on it is put into the shredder. You can work on files while they are on your desktop. You can create files, add information to them, or send them to other people. But at the end of the day, unless you put them away, they will be destroyed. In many companies, paper files can't stay on the desktop after hours. Similarly, electronic files are destroyed when you turn off your computer, or exit the program that creates them.

NOTE For those of you who aren't computer "techies," *memory* is the working area of your computer. Memory is also the generic term for Random Access Memory, or RAM. When you are using programs, they are loaded into memory. When you open a file, it is loaded into memory. The programs and data that are in memory are lost when you turn off your computer.

Disks, whether they are floppy disks, local (in your own computer) hard disks, or network drives, are storage areas. You do not "run" programs from the disk. You load a program from the disk into memory when you open it. Then, when it is in memory, you can use it. Similarly, you load data from your disk into memory to access it. Data on disks is maintained even when you turn off your computer.

Your disk is like your file cabinet. You can keep files in it indefinitely—until it gets full. Then, you can add another file cabinet, until your office gets full of cabinets! The better idea is to purge files in your file cabinet periodically, so that you only keep the ones you need. However, until you take a file from the file drawer and put it on your desk, you can't work on it. Similarly, electronic files can stay on a disk indefinitely, but until you load them into memory, you can't work on them.

In fact, the analogy can be carried further; you can think of each disk drive as a file cabinet. Each disk can contain folders—like file cabinets contain file drawers. Each drawer can contain hanging folders or loose sheets of paper, while electronic folders can contain subfolders or files. Each hanging folder can contain manila folders or sheets of paper, while electronic subfolders can contain other subfolders or files.

NOTE In Windows 95, the term "directories" that was used in previous versions of Windows and DOS has been changed to "folders." Users of previous versions can think of folders just as they used to think about directories.

Thus, whether you are working in WordPerfect, Quattro Pro, Presentations, or other Corel WordPerfect Suite 8 applications, you need to save your work if you want to be able to access it after you turn off your computer. You also need to be able to retrieve it from the disk into memory when you want to edit it again.

NOTE In most applications, files exist only in memory until they are saved. If you add 100 rows of information to a spreadsheet without saving your work and then the power goes off, you will lose that work. This is true in WordPerfect, Presentations, and Quattro Pro. Databases work somewhat differently. Once the database is created, each record is saved on the disk as it is created or edited. Thus, the most information you would lose in a power failure would be changes to the current record. CorelCentral and Paradox are databases. Each record is saved as it is created or edited.

Saving Files

Saving a file is like taking a copy of it from your desktop and putting it into a file drawer. To save a file means storing it on a disk—either a floppy disk, your local hard drive, or a network drive. After you save a file, it exists in two places—in memory and on the disk, until the program you used to create it is exited or the machine is turned off. Then you only have the file that you have saved.

In all Corel WordPerfect Suite 8 applications, you can save the file you are working on by choosing File, Save. If the toolbar is displayed, you can also click the Save button.

NOTE A path plus a file name (the drive, folder, and file name) can be up to 255 characters long and can have an optional extension of up to three characters. The name can contain any combination of letters and numbers except the following:

“ / \ : * ? < > | ”

Don't use any other special characters, such as commas or backslashes. Also, don't use any of the following names, which are reserved by DOS for its own use: CLOCK$, COM1, COM2, COM3, COM4, CON, AUX, LPT1, LPT2, LPT3, LPT4, NUL, or PRN.

CAUTION

Be careful in using long file names. Many network operating systems do not support file names longer than eight characters. Consider using no more than eight characters in your file names and no spaces, if you are using such a network.

The first time you save a file, you see a Save dialog box like the Presentations one shown in Figure 3.1. Type the name of the file in the File Name box and click Save to save your work.

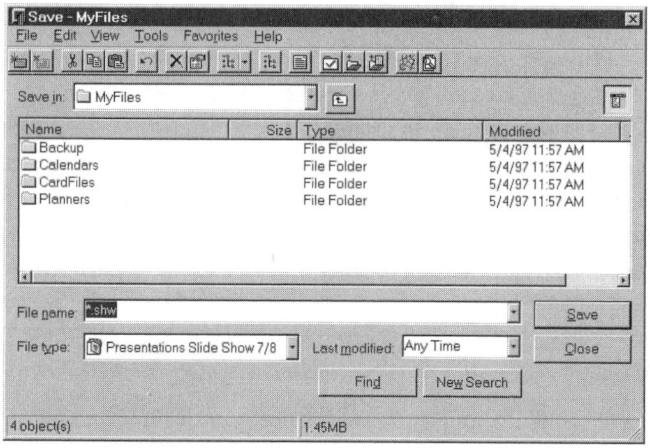

FIG. 3.1
The first time you save a file, you see the Save dialog box, enabling you to give the file a name.

TIP As you start saving more and more files, you will want to create electronic folders to organize your files. If you don't choose a folder, your files are saved in the default folder at first. If you change the folder you are saving your files in, additional files will continue to be saved to that new folder until you exit the application. Then, the next time you open the application, files will be saved in the default folder again.

You can also save the file on a different drive or in a different folder as explained in the section, "Using File Management Dialog Boxes," later in this chapter.

When you continue working in the same document and want to save your work again, choose File, Save, or click the Save button on the toolbar again. You do not see a dialog box. The operation happens immediately. When you re-save your work in this way, the first version is replaced on the disk by the second; thus, the earlier file is gone.

To save both versions, you need to either save the second one with a different name, or in a different folder. You cannot have two files with the same name in the same folder. Choose File, Save As to rename the latter version. You will see the Save As dialog box, and you can rename the document or specify a different folder prior to saving it.

Opening Files

Opening a file is like taking a copy of it from your file drawer and putting it on your desk. It then exists in two places—in the file drawer and on your desk. When you make changes to it, the original is still safely in the file drawer. The original copy in the file drawer is only changed when you save the edited version again.

Thus, when you open a file, you are retrieving a copy of the file from the disk to your computer's memory. In all Corel WordPerfect Suite 8 applications, you can open a file by choosing File, Open. If the toolbar is displayed, you may also click the Open button. In either case, you see an Open File dialog box similar to the one shown in Figure 3.2. Instructions for choosing files from this dialog box are found in the section "Using File Management Dialog Boxes" later in this chapter.

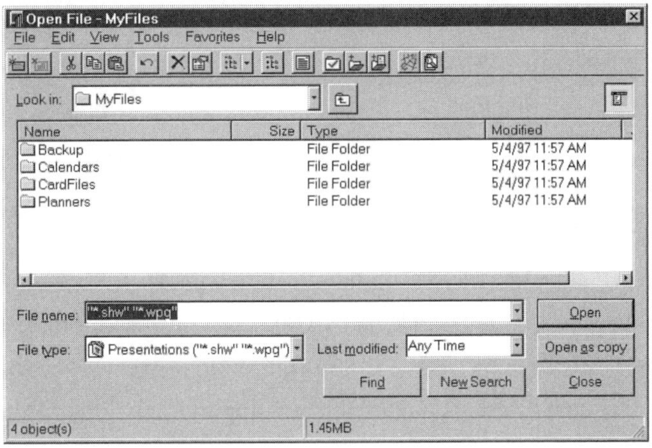

FIG. 3.2
Choose files to open from the Open File dialog box, which also provides many file management capabilities.

NOTE The title bar of file management dialog boxes includes the current folder name, Open File - MyFiles or Save File - Backup. What you see on the title bar will depend on what your default folder is. Furthermore, WordPerfect and Presentations use the name Save for the save dialog box, while Quattro Pro uses Save File. To prevent confusion, this book refers to file management dialog boxes only by their function, for example, Open File or Save File.

Closing Files

Closing a file is like taking it off of your desktop and shredding it. If you have saved it prior to closing it, it is in your file cabinet (or electronically, on your disk). Otherwise, it is gone for good.

Thus, when you close a file, you are erasing it from your computer's memory. In Corel WordPerfect Suite 8 applications, you close a file by choosing File, Close. If the file has been edited since it was last saved, you will be prompted to save it prior to closing it. Unless you want to lose your work, it's a good idea to do so.

NOTE When you close an application, you will also close any open files in that application. Thus, when you close an application that has modified, open files, you will be prompted to save them before the application closes.

TROUBLESHOOTING

Why isn't there a button to close a file like there is to save or open a file? There is—but it's not on the toolbar. The Close button is the button with the X on it in the upper-right corner of the menu bar. You can also put a button on your toolbar to close a document in most Corel WordPerfect Suite 8 applications.

See "Creating and Editing Toolbars and Menu Bars," **p. 635**

Creating a File Management System

File management dialog boxes allow you to manipulate files and folders with ease. Before learning *how* to do this, however, it's a good idea to start by understanding *what* you might want to do.

In creating an electronic filing system, it's important to think through several issues:

- Which drive you should save your files on
- What folders you should have
- How you should name your files

Choosing a Drive

You will generally have up to four choices for types of disk drives to save your files on: the floppy drive(s), local hard drive(s) (the hard drive(s) in your computer), network drives (if you're on a network), and the Internet or a corporate intranet (if you are so connected).

Floppy Drives In the past, most people saved their work on floppy disks. Many people are still used to doing this. It seems reasonable; you use a different floppy disk for each subject, and it's easy to stay organized. If someone else needs the file, you hand them the disk. This process keeps the hard disk from filling up.

A piece of advice: *Stop thinking this way.*

If you exchange files often, you should be working on a network. Hard disks hold 10 to 20 times more than they used to; if your hard disk keeps filling up, you should either have a high capacity hard disk, or better yet, archive and purge your files periodically like you do with your paper filing system. If you want to stay organized, use folders on your hard drives rather than individual floppies.

There are several reasons to use hard drives rather than floppy drives, which are explained in the sections that follow. Floppy drives are good in three circumstances:

- Taking files off-site to work on them
- Archiving old files when you don't have access to a tape backup or other mass storage devices for archiving purposes
- Creating backup copies of critical data that can be stored elsewhere and retrieved if necessary in a disaster recovery situation

Local Hard Drives A local hard drive operates 10 to 20 times faster than a floppy, and has the advantage that all your files are available whenever you want them. As you start to become more familiar with working electronically, this latter advantage becomes more important. You will find yourself bringing up old files often, and cutting pieces out of them for your new work. Or, you may use them as the basis for template and style creation. You can also use your old files as a knowledge base, accessing work done by yourself or others in your workgroup to learn from what you've done before, or to track the history of a project.

The other reason you will want to save your work on a hard drive is that the QuickFinder indexing system discussed later will then index all of your files, so that you can immediately find all documents by specifying any text that is in them—no matter what folder you have put them in on your hard drive.

Local hard drives are an excellent place to store documents when:

- You are working on a stand-alone computer
- Your network administrator limits the amount of storage you have for documents
- The files are ones that only you will use, and you regularly back up your hard drive

Network Drives Saving files on network drives has all the advantages of saving them on local hard drives, but there are a couple other considerations that must be taken into account.

First, the network almost invariably is backed up regularly, often daily. (Ask your system administrator for details.) Because most people don't back up their local drive regularly, this may be reason enough to save files on the network.

Second, if you work in a workgroup, saving files on a network is the best way to start creating a "learning organization"—a team of people who can build on each others' work.

There are three disadvantages to saving files on the network. First, if the network goes down, you will not have access to your files. Second, if you don't archive and purge your files regularly, the network drive will fill up rapidly. Third, some companies' network drive purge policies are time-based, meaning that if a certain file has not been actively used for a certain time period, that file is archived. If it is archived, it may still be accessible by request, but may require time or paper work for you to have the network administrator retrieve it; you will not have direct access to it.

TIP Saving files to a shared workspace on a network is one of the best ways of getting workgroups to start sharing files electronically.

Internet Servers You can also save files on an Internet Server, if you have a Web site and sufficient permissions. This gives people throughout the world access to the files.

The Corel WordPerfect Suite 8 can assist you in creating Web pages (files that can be viewed with Web browsers such as Netscape Navigator); however, the Suite does not have programs designed for uploading such files to the Internet.

▶ **See** "Publishing to the World Wide Web," **p. 494**
▶ **See** "Publishing Corel Quattro Pro Files," **p. 514**
▶ **See** "Uploading Your Presentation," **p. 539**

Ask your Internet Service Provider or Network Administrator for procedures to be used in uploading your files to the Internet. Be aware, however, that when you upload files to an Internet Service Provider there may be fees attached for storage of those files.

Understanding Electronic Filing Systems

Once you have decided which drive(s) to save your files on, you will want to create a filing system—a set of folders and subfolders—in which to save your files.

If you are saving files on a network drive, you will have a workspace that contains only your data files. If you are working on a stand-alone computer, consider creating a main folder for all your data files. When you install the WordPerfect Suite, the folder MyFiles is created. This can serve admirably as a main folder. If all your other folders are created as subfolders of MyFiles, you can easily back up your data files because they are all in one place. You can also keep all your data files separate from program folders so that you can more easily search them.

NOTE Your electronic filing system should mimic your paper filing system. Thus, if you have different filing cabinets or file drawers that are organized by type of business, client, or employee, your main subfolders should be organized the same way.

Create subfolders under the main subfolders that mimic your hanging files, and if needed, create an additional layer of subfolders that mimic your manila files. You probably don't want to have more than four or five layers of folders, because navigating through them becomes time-consuming. Coordinate your folders with your file-naming conventions, as described in the next section.

Setting File-Naming Conventions

Just as you wouldn't want your office manager or employees to randomly put stickers on manila folders, you will also want to systematically think about how to name your files. Keep in mind that you can now make use of long file names with spaces.

Consider the following when creating file-naming conventions:

- *Agree on file-naming conventions within the office.* Assign one person to be responsible for periodically checking file names in public workspaces, renaming files as needed, and notifying the owner of the file that the name has been changed. Create a document that outlines the file-naming conventions and distribute it to present and new employees.
- *Coordinate file names with folders.* If you have a folder for each client, with subfolders for letters, briefs, and legal memos, you do not need to have the word "letter" or the client name in the file name, because a letter will be saved in the appropriate client folder and letters subfolder.
- *Remember alphabetization.* Have the first word(s) of the file name be key words that you will want to alphabetize your files by. This may be type of file (letter), client name (Smith John), or subject.

A typical file management dialog box is shown in Figure 3.3. In this case, the filing system is set up in such a way that all letters (to anyone) are in a Letters folder. Thus, the file-naming convention calls for the client's last name, followed by the number of the letter, followed by a few words describing the subject of the letter.

FIG. 3.3
A good file-naming system allows anyone in your office to quickly find a file you have saved.

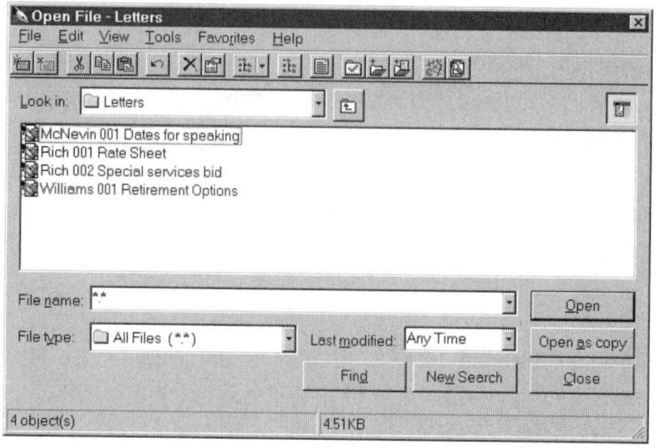

Using File Management Dialog Boxes

Corel WordPerfect Suite 8 offers extremely powerful file management features through *file management dialog boxes.* You see a file management dialog box whenever you use any feature that offers you options while saving or retrieving files (for example, File Open, File Save As, Insert File, Insert Object, and so on). In fact, any time you can select a file using a Browse button, you will be taken to a file management dialog box, like the Save File dialog box shown in Figure 3.4.

FIG. 3.4
All file management dialog boxes have options similar to the file management options shown in this Save File dialog box.

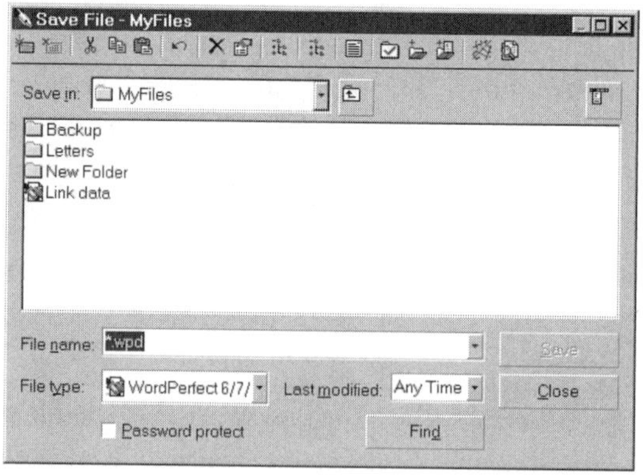

NOTE Your dialog box may not resemble the one shown, because the way files may be displayed is determined by options you can set, as explained in the next section.

File management dialog boxes allow you to quickly navigate throughout your filing system. More importantly, however, they allow you to manage your drives, folders, and files.

Setting File Management Dialog Box Options

Depending on their function, file management dialog boxes have slightly different options. However, you will see common options in all file management dialog boxes.

The toolbar is an excellent way to set dialog box display options. If the toolbar is not displayed, choose View, Toolbar. A check mark appears by the Toolbar entry (see Figure 3.5).

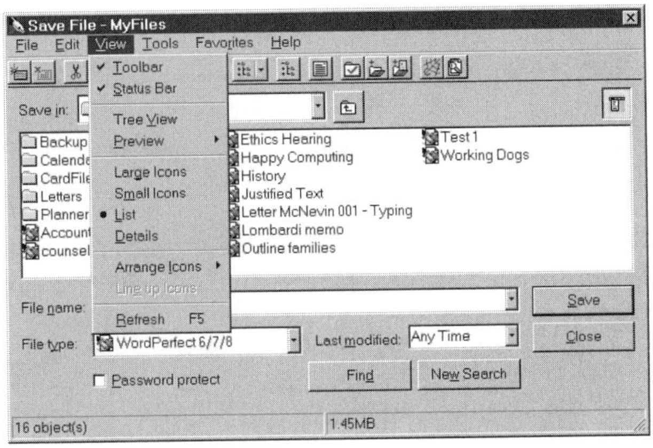

FIG. 3.5
File management dialog boxes have their own toolbars that you can display or hide.

You can split the main window that shows your folders and files into two or three separate windows:

- If you click the Tree View icon, you see your folders in the left window and the subfolders and files contained in the selected folder in the window to its right. Using the Tree View is the easiest way to navigate through your filing system.

- If you click the Preview icon, you see a window on the right that shows you the contents of the selected file.

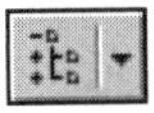

- You can also display the files in the selected folder in four ways: as large icons, small icons, a list of file names, or a single list of file names with details.

  Large and small icons show you what type of file each file is (Quattro Pro, WordPerfect, and so on). They are not terribly useful if you only store files of one type in a folder. Moreover, they don't permit as much of the file name to show.

  The file name list can be a very useful view because you see several columns of files in one screen, and can often locate your file much more quickly. The details view shows only one column of file names, but it does display the file size and date it was last saved, which some users prefer to see.

TIP When you are viewing file details, click a column such as file name or modified to put the files in alphabetical order based on that column. Click again for descending alphabetical order.

Navigating the Filing System

After you've used the Suite for a while, you will want to put your files in different folders to organize them. You can switch between drives and folders, and select one or more files with file management dialog boxes.

Switching Between Drives and Folders You will navigate through your filing system in two directions: up and down. Navigating down is easy; the subfolders of the currently selected folder will display in the window. For example, if the MyFiles folder has a subfolder called Letters, the Letters subfolder will display if the MyFiles folder is selected.

To navigate down to a subfolder, double-click it. For example, to navigate from the MyFiles folder shown in Figure 3.6 to the Letters subfolder, you would double-click it.

FIG. 3.6
Navigate down to a subfolder like Letters in the example shown by double-clicking it.

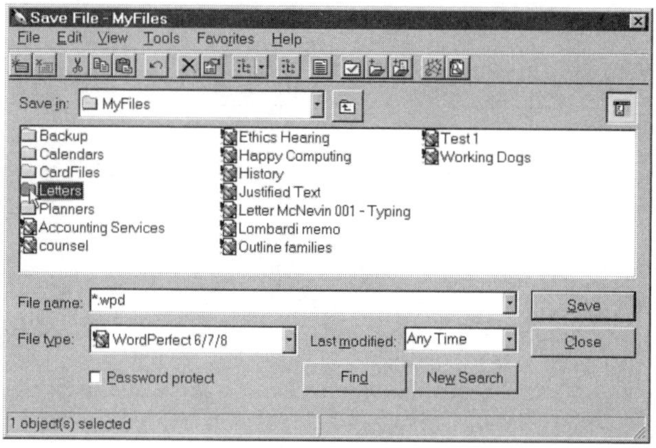

If you want to go to a folder that is not a subfolder of the currently selected folder, you'll need to navigate up, then (possibly) down again, by navigating up to a common point.

For example, say the MyFiles folder has several subfolders, including Letters and Memos. You are in the Letters subfolder and want to go to the Memos subfolder. You must first navigate up to the common folder, MyFiles, and then back down to the Memos subfolder. It may sound complicated, but it's actually quite easy once you've done it a few times.

If you continue to navigate up, you will reach the drive itself. One level up from the drive is My Computer. From My Computer you can see all the drives on the computer, as well as folders for the Control Panel and Printers.

One level up from My Computer is the Desktop, from which you can see your computer, the Network Neighborhood, Recycle Bin, and your Briefcase (if it is installed).

To see the folder, drive, or computer above the selected object, click the Up One Level button. For example, to navigate from a local hard drive to a network drive, you will continue to click the Up One Level icon until you reach the Desktop. Double-click Network Neighborhood, and then double-click the appropriate workgroup and the network computer you are navigating to.

Selecting Files Once you have navigated to the appropriate folder, you can type in the name of the file to be saved, or double-click the file to be opened.

On occasion, however, you will want to select more than one file—either to open multiple files or to perform file management tasks.

To select multiple adjacent files, click the first file to be selected, then hold down the Shift key and click the last file. To select non-adjacent files, click the first file to be selected, then hold down the Ctrl key while you click any additional files. The selected files are highlighted, as shown in Figure 3.7.

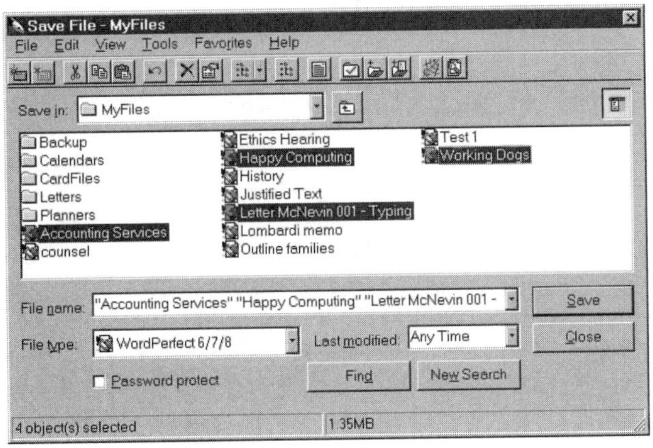

FIG. 3.7
You can select multiple files, whether they are adjacent to each other or not, as shown in this example.

Managing Drives

You can map and disconnect network drives from Corel WordPerfect Suite 8 file management dialog boxes. This can be very useful if you work on a large network, and are not normally connected to all the available servers. When you need to open a file on a server you are not connected to, you can map to that server, then disconnect from it when you are done.

TIP Mapping to a network drive assigns a letter to the drive. This makes the drive accessible to opening and saving files, and makes it possible to log on to the drive.

To map to a network drive, access any file management dialog box. Click the Map Network Drive button. You see the Map Network Drive dialog box shown in Figure 3.8. Select the letter for the Drive you want to map to, then type the Path to the drive and click OK.

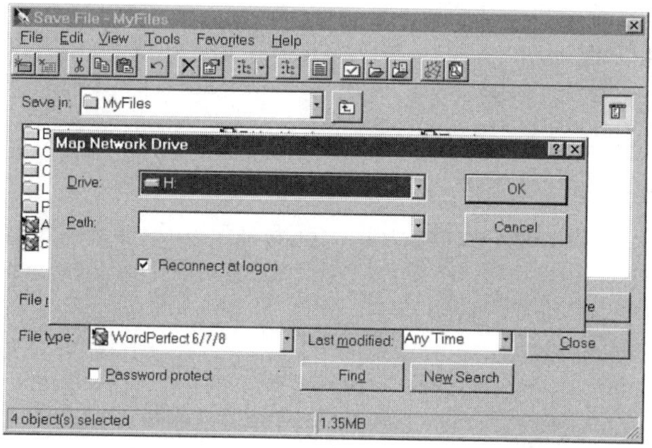

FIG. 3.8
You can map to network drives from the Map Network Drive dialog box, which can be accessed through any file management dialog box.

When you've finished, you can disconnect from the drive using the Disconnect Net Drive button.

TIP The Reconnect at Logon option causes Windows to automatically remap the specified drive when you log into the system the next time. This is handy if you use your network drive frequently. Keep in mind, though, that other people might have access to this information; check with your Network Administrator.

Managing Folders

If you remember our original analogy, folders and subfolders are like the drawers, hanging folders, and manila folders in a file cabinet (disk drive). They are used to organize your work, and enable you to create a system for maintaining your files.

In order to manage the directories that make up your electronic filing system, you need to be able to create, remove (delete), and rename directories (folders). To create a new folder, do the following:

1. Access a file management dialog box.
2. Navigate to the folder that will be the parent of the new folder.

3. Click the Toggle Menu On/Off button, if menus are not displayed. Choose File, New, Folder. You see the new folder named New Folder under the original folder, with its name highlighted, as shown in Figure 3.9.
4. Type the name for the new folder and press Enter.

FIG. 3.9
You can create new folders in any file management dialog box.

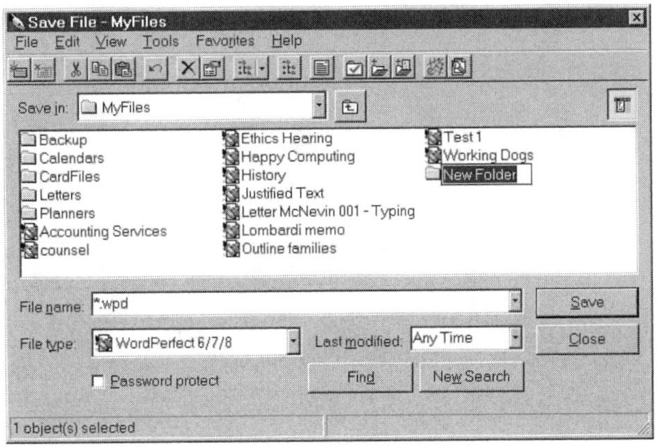

TIP You can access these options to manage folders via a QuickMenu by right-clicking the directory list.

To rename a folder, select it, then choose File, Rename. The folder name is highlighted; type the new name and press Enter.

To remove a folder, select it, then choose File, Delete. The folder and its contents are deleted, and its contents are moved to the Recycle Bin.

CAUTION

Removing a directory with files in it deletes the files from the disk and puts them in the Recycle Bin. While they can be recovered, they will not automatically be put back into the right folder, even if you recreate it. Use this command with care.

You can also view and set the properties for a folder, including whether it is hidden, read-only, or shared (on a Microsoft network). To do so, select the folder, then right-click and choose Properties from the context menu. You see the Letters Properties dialog box shown in Figure 3.10.

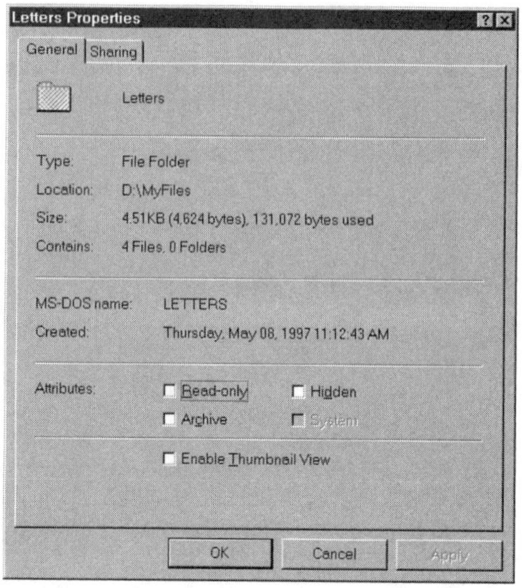

FIG. 3.10
You can view or set properties and file sharing options of a file from file management dialog boxes.

Managing Files

When you have the backbone of your filing system—the folders—created, you can finish creating your filing system by renaming and moving files into your new filing system. Periodically, you should archive and purge your filing system by moving files out of the folders and onto floppy disks or a tape backup unit.

With Corel WordPerfect Suite 8 dialog boxes, you can do these tasks and more. You can copy, move, rename, and delete files, and you can set their properties.

TIP If you hold down the Shift key while you delete a file, it will not go into the Recycle Bin. However, once a file is deleted in this way, it is gone and the safety provided by the Recycle Bin is not there.

Copying and Moving Files The easiest way to copy and move files is by using the Tree View. In this view, you can copy and move files just as you would using Windows 95 Explorer.

From any file management dialog box, click the Tree View button. Navigate through the folders in the left window until you see the folder containing the source file(s) you want. Double-click this folder, if necessary, so that you see the desired file(s) in the right window.

Navigate to the destination folder until you can see it in the left window. If you need to open folders to see subfolders, click the plus sign to the left of the folder icon rather than double-clicking the folder itself. This will ensure that the contents of the right window do not change.

When you can see the destination folder in the left window, select the file(s) you want to move or copy in the right window. Drag them from the right window to the icon for the destination folder in the left window.

Dragging files from one folder to another on the same drive moves them, by default. Dragging files from a folder in one drive to a different drive copies them, by default. To copy files instead of moving them from one folder to another on the same drive, hold down the Ctrl key while you drag them. You see a plus sign on the icon as they are moved, as shown in Figure 3.11, indicating that the files are being copied.

FIG. 3.11
Holding down the Ctrl key while dragging files is indicated by a plus sign in a box next to the cursor, and forces the files to be copied rather than moved.

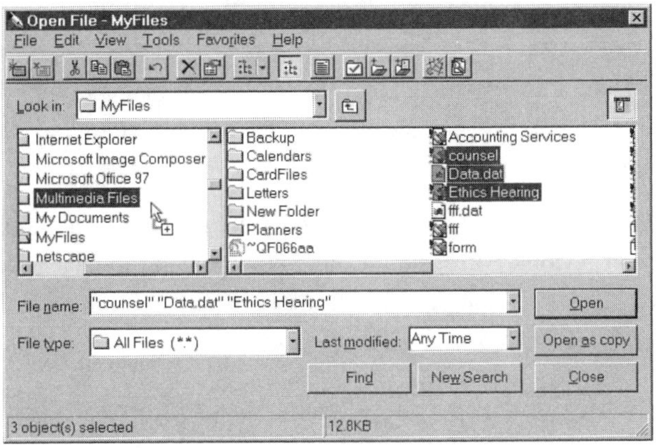

NOTE To move files from one drive to another, drag them using the right mouse button rather than the left. When you have dragged the file to the new drive, you will see a pop-up menu, and can choose whether to move or copy the file.

You can also move or copy files by selecting them, then choosing Edit, Cut or Edit, Copy. Then navigate to the destination folder and choose Edit, Paste. If you copy a file to the same directory, its name will have "Copy of" appended to the front of it.

Setting File Attributes You can make a file hidden, read-only, or see when it was created, last modified, and last accessed. To do so, select the file, then choose File, Properties; alternatively, right-click the file and choose Properties. You see the Accounting Services Properties dialog box shown in Figure 3.12. Set the properties as desired, then click OK.

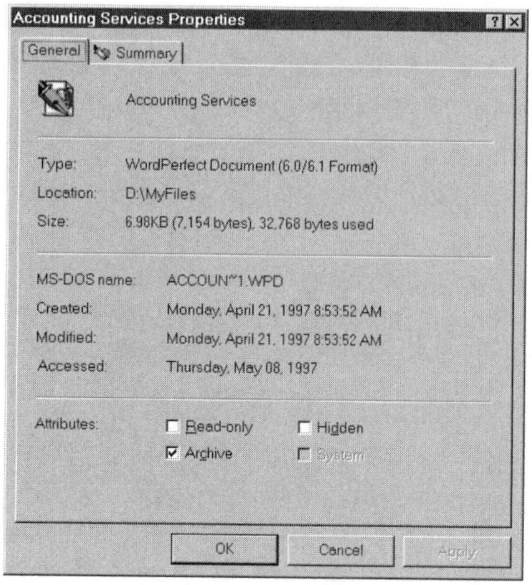

FIG. 3.12
You can set file properties or see when a file was created, modified, or last accessed in the file's Properties dialog box.

Renaming Files To rename a file, select it in a file management dialog box, then choose File, Rename; alternatively, you can right-click the file, then choose Rename. The file name is highlighted with a box around it. Type the new name and press Enter.

Deleting Files To delete one or more files, select them in a file management dialog box, as described previously. Press the Delete key or click the Delete button. You see the Confirm File Delete dialog box shown in Figure 3.13. Confirm that you want to delete the files, and they are moved to the Recycle Bin.

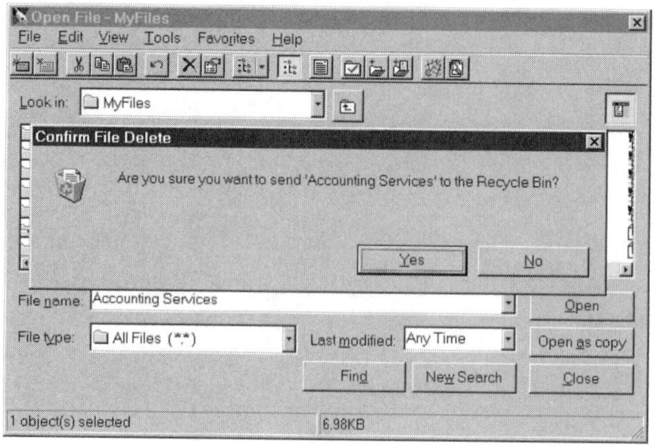

FIG. 3.13
When you delete files, they go to the Recycle Bin, where you can undelete them if you need to.

Finding Files

Sometimes, even with the powerful file management tools at your disposal, you forget where you have filed an important document. Or, someone else in your office comes to you and says, "Can you get that memo that I did sometime last month? It was about Providence National Bank." In the past, this could have been a full-day job, but not anymore!

Corel provides you with two powerful tools to make finding files a snap: Favorites and QuickFinder.

CAUTION

Your files might not go to the Recycle Bin if the Recycle Bin properties have been modified. To check your Recycle Bin settings, right-click the Recycle Bin icon on the desktop, then choose Properties.

Using Favorites

The Corel WordPerfect Suite 8 integrates tightly with the Favorites folder contained in Windows 95.

The Favorites folder contains shortcuts to your most used folders and files. The Favorites folder is common to all Windows 95 applications, so if you add a file to your Favorites folder while you are in a non-Corel application, you will see it when you access Favorites in Corel Suite applications as well.

NOTE A shortcut is a small file that, as the name implies, is a shortcut to another folder or file. It merely tells Windows 95 where the actual folder or file is located. When you double-click a shortcut, it has the same effect as double-clicking the actual folder or file.

To access your Favorites folder, you can be in any file management dialog box. Click the Go To/From Favorites button. You see the contents of the Favorites folder. If you click the button again, you return to the folder you were previously in.

To add an item to the Favorites folder, select it, then click the Add Selected Item(s) to Favorites button. You will be given the choice of adding the selected item, or the folder in which it resides.

To delete an item from the Favorites folder, go to the Favorites folder, select the item, press the Delete key, and confirm the deletion.

NOTE Deleting an item from the Favorites folder merely deletes the shortcut to the item that resides in the Favorites folder and leaves the item itself untouched.

Using QuickFinder

QuickFinder, as the name implies, is a utility that helps you quickly find the files you need. It can look through every file on your disk and find just the files that contain the words you specify. This can be a life saver when you can't remember what you named a file. It can also enable you to create *knowledge bases* by saving old documents that you can quickly look through to find other work on a subject of interest.

QuickFinder can even *index* your files by examining them during off hours, and making a list (index) of words that your files contain. That way, when you look for files containing "providence," you find them virtually instantly!

You can access QuickFinder from any file management dialog box by clicking the Find button. When you click the Find button, you see QuickFinder Search Results in the Look In box, as shown in Figure 3.14.

FIG. 3.14
QuickFinder is used to index your files, allowing you to search for files by the text they contain, and finding resulting files almost instantly.

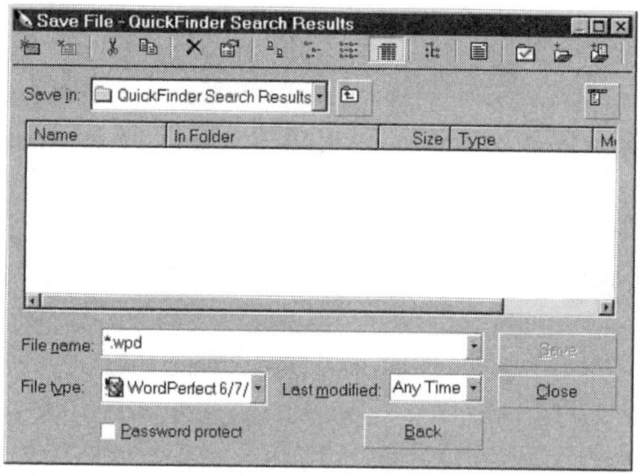

Before you start conducting searches, however, you should configure the QuickFinder to create index files of the folders you commonly store documents in.

Configuring QuickFinder QuickFinder can search for files in two ways. If you configure QuickFinder to index specific folders, an index file is created containing an alphabetical list of words and the files they are in. Then, when you search for text, QuickFinder searches this index and finds appropriate files very rapidly. This is called a Fast Search. If an index is not created, QuickFinder searches through files one by one, which is a very slow process.

To configure QuickFinder, do the following:

1. Choose Start, Corel WordPerfect Suite 8, Tools, QuickFinder Manager 8. You see the QuickFinder Manager dialog box shown in Figure 3.15.

FIG. 3.15
Configure QuickFinder in the QuickFinder Manager dialog box to do Fast Searches on your documents.

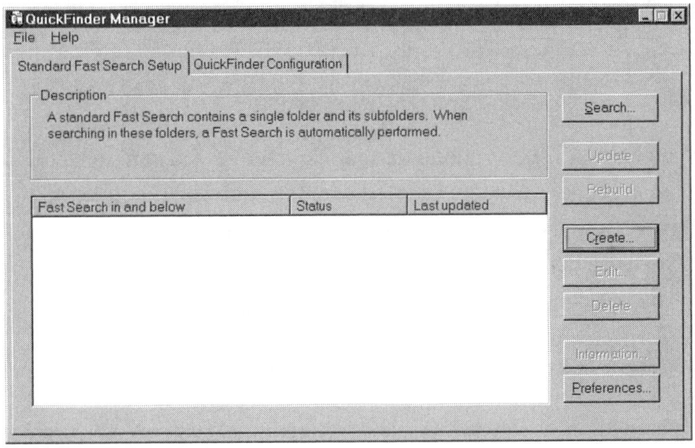

2. Any QuickFinder Fast Searches (indexes) are listed in the QuickFinder Manager dialog box. If you would like to index additional drives or folders, click the Create button. You see the QuickFinder Standard Fast Search dialog box shown in Figure 3.16.

FIG. 3.16
Configure QuickFinder to search through multiple drives or folders by creating new indexes in the QuickFinder Standard Fast Search dialog box.

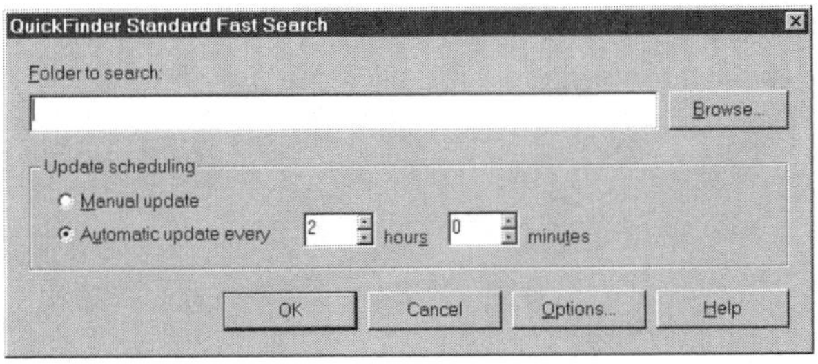

3. Type in the drive and folder you want to search; or click the Browse button, navigate to the desired folder, then double-click it.
4. Choose Manual Update, or choose Automate Update Every, and specify how often the index should be updated. If you choose Automatic Update, you will see a warning dialog box informing you that automatic update is disabled by default. Confirm that you want to enable Automatic Update before proceeding.

5. Click the Options button to specify whether the search should include the full document or just the document summary; then choose OK to return to the QuickFinder Standard Fast Search dialog box.

 TIP Automatic updating is most convenient, but it may slow down your computer dramatically during the time it takes to update the index.

6. Close the dialog box when you've finished.

If you have set your options for manual update, you can update a Fast Search by accessing the QuickFinder Manager dialog box, highlighting the index to be updated, and choosing Update. Periodically, you will want to delete your index and reconstruct it completely. This makes sure that you don't get false "hits" from files that have been deleted. You can do this by selecting an index and clicking Rebuild instead of Update.

 TIP You can edit a Fast Search to change the schedule by which it is updated, or delete one entirely, if desired.

Finding Files You can find files by using the QuickFinder from any Open dialog box, or by choosing Start, Corel WordPerfect Suite 8, Tools, QuickFinder Searcher.

To search for a file with a specified word or phrase in it, access an Open dialog box. Type the text you want to find in the File Name box, and specify the folder you want to look in in the Look In box. Click the Find button. The files containing the desired text appear in the file list, and you see QuickFinder Search Results in the Look In box.

To toggle back to your original file list, click the Back button. ●

PART II

Using Corel WordPerfect

CHAPTER 4

Getting Started with Corel WordPerfect

Understand the WordPerfect screen

This chapter identifies items on the WordPerfect screen that provide you both document information and shortcuts for common tasks.

Enter text

Learn the differences between entering text with WordPerfect and with a typewriter.

Edit text

WordPerfect makes it simple to add new text, delete unwanted text, and move or copy text from one place to another.

Save, close, and open documents

Learn to save your finished work on the disk and open stored files for further editing.

Of all the applications included with Corel WordPerfect Suite 8, Corel WordPerfect may be the one you use most. Besides producing letters and envelopes like an ordinary word processor, WordPerfect also creates memos, fax cover sheets, reports, newsletters, mailing labels, brochures, World Wide Web pages, and many other types of documents.

WordPerfect offers many features that help you complete your work quickly and easily. There are features that correct errors automatically, features that add visual interest to your documents, and features that help you organize and manage long documents. WordPerfect provides easy graphics handling, outlining, calculations of data in tables, the capability to create a mailing list, list sorting, and efficient file management. You can perform desktop publishing tasks such as formatting fonts, inserting drop caps, adding graphic borders, and adding shading. You can even prepare documents to be published on the Internet or a corporate intranet.

When you use WordPerfect, you're sharing a common look and feel with other applications in the

WordPerfect Suite 8. Switching to Quattro Pro for spreadsheets is easily accomplished without drastically changing your work environment. You can even integrate and edit data from another application while remaining in WordPerfect.

For example, when you embed a Quattro Pro spreadsheet in a WordPerfect document, you can edit the spreadsheet after double-clicking the embedded object in your WordPerfect document. Then, when you finish editing the spreadsheet, you can return to the WordPerfect document by choosing File, Exit and Return.

This chapter presents you with an overview of the WordPerfect program. In this book, you learn how to utilize WordPerfect as a word processor for common business tasks. ■

Understanding the WordPerfect Screen

When starting WordPerfect, you see certain screen elements (as shown in Figure 4.1), including the title bar, menu bar, the WordPerfect 8 toolbar, the Property Bar, guidelines, the Application Bar, and the scroll bars.

▶ **See** "Using Help," **p. 22**

FIG. 4.1
Using WordPerfect's screen elements can help you complete tasks quickly and efficiently.

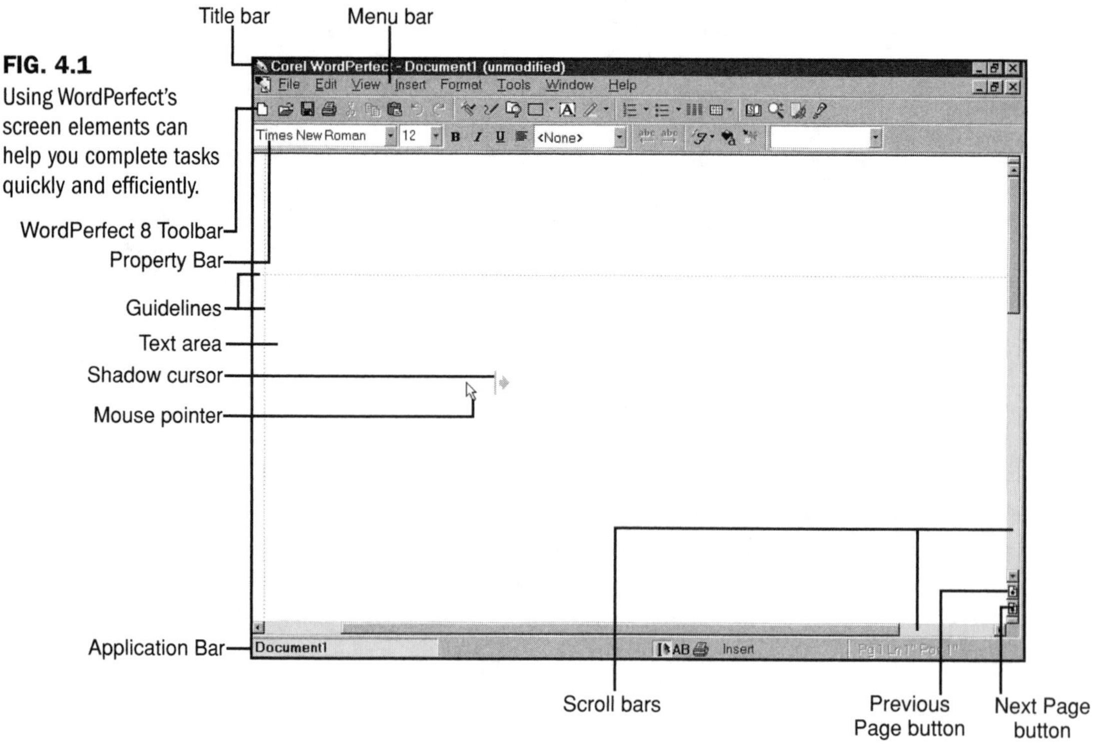

Screen elements provide information on your document and allow you to quickly complete common tasks.

- *Title bar.* The title bar identifies the WordPerfect application window and the name of the document in the current document window.
- *Menu bar.* The menu bar gives you access to the most commonly used WordPerfect features. Each menu contains a specialized list of related commands. Choose commands from the Format menu, for example, to specify fonts, change margins, create a header or footer, and so on.
- *Toolbars.* By default, the WordPerfect 8 toolbar is displayed just beneath the menu bar. When you point to a button, its name is displayed beneath the pointer and its function is described in the pop-up Quick Tip window. Toolbars contain buttons you can use to perform common tasks, such as opening an existing document, saving a document, copying text, and spell checking. When scroll arrows are displayed at the right end of the toolbar, you can use them to see other buttons. You can switch between toolbars whenever you like, and even choose where they will appear on the screen.
- *Property Bar.* The Property Bar consists of a series of buttons that give you easy access to common text editing and text layout features. When performing specialized tasks, a specialized Property Bar designed to help you with that task will appear. For example, when you're working with a table and have a cell selected, you will see the Table Cell Selected Property Bar.

  ▶ **See** "Customizing Toolbars," **p. 628**

- *Margin Guidelines.* Guidelines are the blue lines you see on-screen that indicate where your margins are. You will see other guidelines from time to time in addition to the blue guidelines you see when you first enter WordPerfect. You will see guidelines around headers and footers, around cells in tables, and around columns. Not only do these nonprinting guidelines show you where various elements will appear, you can drag them to change the element's formatting. For instance, you can drag the blue guidelines to set margins in your document.
- *Text area.* The text area consists of a blank "page" in which you can enter text or place pictures, graphics, and so on. By default, the text area is displayed in Page Mode—or, as it would appear on the printed page—including the margin space at the top of the page (depending on the zoom percentage, you may not see a full page of text at once). The insertion point is a blinking vertical line that indicates the position where text would be inserted if you were to type text.

NOTE You can switch between ways of looking at your document, called views. The Page Mode is most commonly used; it shows the page as it will print. The Draft Mode hides headers, footers, and watermarks. Because it does not show a space between one page and the next, some people prefer to use this view when reading long text documents. The Two Page Mode shows two complete pages, and is useful when examining your entire page layout. The Web Page Mode shows how the document would look if it were converted into a Web page. Switch between views by choosing View, then selecting Draft, Page, or Two Pages, or Web Page.

- *Application Bar.* The Application Bar informs you of the status of many WordPerfect features. Use it to quickly identify whether you are in Insert or Typeover mode, to note the currently selected printer, and to locate the page, line, and position of your insertion point. You can also use the Application Bar to turn the display of the Shadow Cursor or Caps Lock on or off, and to print your document. The names of all open documents display as buttons on the Application Bar, and you can easily switch between documents by clicking the appropriate button.
- *Scroll bars.* Use the scroll bars to move quickly to another area of the document. Previous Page and Next Page buttons appear at the bottom of the vertical scroll bar and are used to move to the previous or next printed page of the document.
- *Shadow Cursor.* As you move your mouse pointer over white space in your document, a blue bar with an arrow appears. This is called the shadow cursor, and it indicates where your insertion point will be if you click the mouse button.

You can display or hide many of these elements to suit your working style. To display or hide the toolbar, Property Bar, or Application Bar, do the following:

1. Choose View, Toolbars. You see the Toolbars dialog box shown in Figure 4.2.

FIG. 4.2
You can easily display or hide screen elements to provide more assistance, or give you the "clean screen" look.

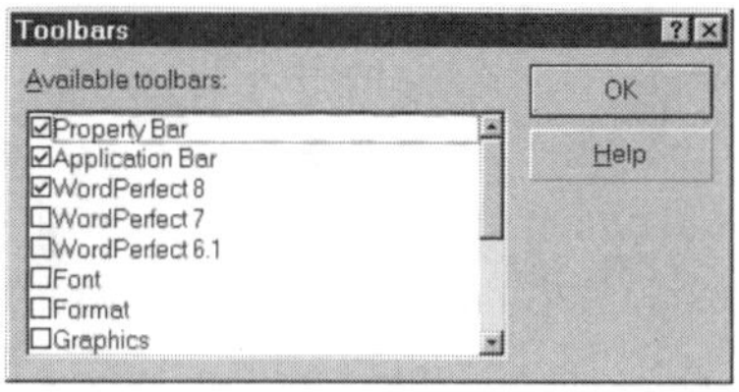

2. Check or uncheck the appropriate element to display or hide it.
3. Click OK.

TIP You can quickly hide the display of the Property Bar and Application Bar by right-clicking them, and then choosing Hide Property Bar or Hide Application Bar. You can hide the display of various toolbars by right-clicking a toolbar, and then clicking the check-marked toolbar on the menu that appears.

To change the display properties of the scroll bars or the shadow cursor, do the following:

1. Choose Tools, Settings, Display, and then choose the Document tab. You see the Display Settings dialog box shown in Figure 4.3.
2. Check Vertical or Horizontal to display the appropriate scroll bar, and choose Show Always or When Required to determine when the horizontal scroll bar will display.
3. Select shadow cursor options from the Shadow Cursor group as described in the following note.
4. Click OK, and then choose Close when you've finished.

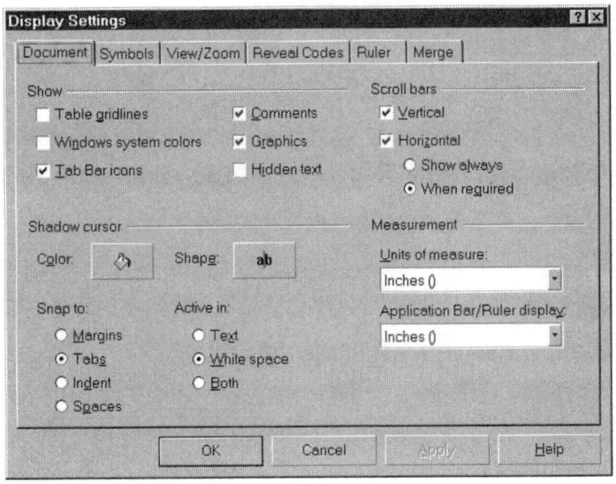

FIG. 4.3 You can change the display of scroll bars and the shadow cursor to suit your working style.

NOTE You can change the way the shadow cursor operates, to give you more or less assistance with placing your insertion point. From the Display Settings dialog box, choose whether you want your shadow cursor to be Active in the Text, Active in White Space, or Active In Both. The shadow cursor will automatically move the nearest margin, tab, indent, or space, depending on which option you select. This is called *snapping to* the element. You can also choose the Color or Shape of the shadow cursor.

Entering Text

When starting WordPerfect, you are supplied with a new, empty document window named `Document1` in the title bar. You can begin to type at the blinking insertion point, initially positioned just below the top margin. As you type, text is entered at the insertion point.

This section describes the basic techniques of entering text, moving through a document, and selecting text for editing.

Typing Text

When typing text, type as you would in any word processor. WordPerfect automatically wraps the text at the end of a line, so you don't have to press Enter to begin a new line. It does so by inserting a *soft return* at the end of the line. A soft return is a line break that appears as needed.

Press Enter only to start a new paragraph or create a blank line. Pressing Enter inserts a *hard return* into your document. A hard return is a line break that stays where you put it, even if the line of text does not extend to the right margin. WordPerfect defines a paragraph as text that ends with a hard return, a hard page break, or a hard column break.

As you type, certain keys that you press—such as Enter, Tab, and space bar—create nonprinting characters at the insertion point. You can view these nonprinting characters by choosing View, Show ¶.

Figure 4.4 illustrates nonprinting characters, with a document containing lines that wrap with hard returns and lines that wrap with automatic word wrap.

The words underlined in red are words the "Spell as you go" feature doesn't have in its dictionary, and are seen by WordPerfect as misspelled words. Words underlined in green are flagged as possible grammatical errors.

FIG. 4.4
Paragraph marks and spaces are nonprinting characters; they do not print, whether or not they are displayed.

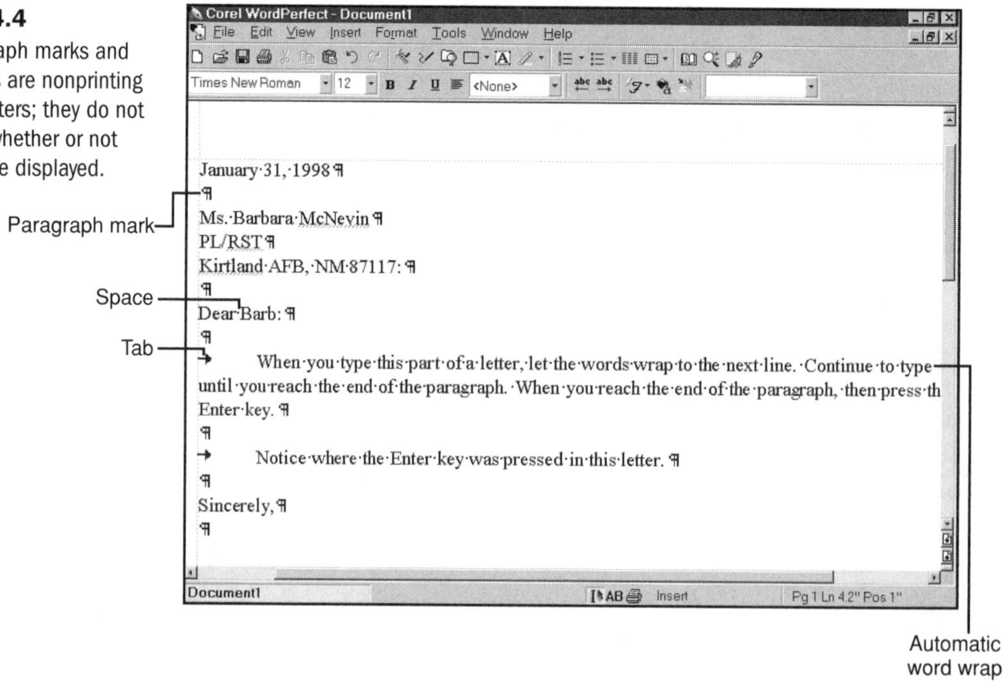

As you type, follow these guidelines:

- If you make a mistake, press the Backspace key to erase the character immediately preceding the insertion point.
- Alternatively, you may press the Delete key to remove the character immediately following the insertion point.
- When you're typing a sentence or phrase that extends past the end of the line, let the words wrap to the next line automatically (do not press Enter when you get to the end of the line, but rather only when you get to the end of the paragraph).
- Use the Tab key to indent the first line of a paragraph; don't use the space bar.
- Press the Insert key to use Typeover mode, in which the text you type replaces existing text. Press Insert again to switch from Typeover mode to Insert mode. You can tell whether Typeover or Insert mode is active by looking at the Application Bar at the bottom of the screen.

Positioning the Insertion Point

To move the insertion point, move the mouse pointer to the new location, noting the position of the shadow cursor as you move the mouse. When the shadow cursor is where you want it, click the left mouse button. You can position the insertion point anywhere in the text area, but not past the end of the text.

TIP If you don't see the shadow cursor, choose View, Shadow Cursor to make it visible.

To move the insertion point to a place that you don't see on-screen, use the scroll bar(s) to move to a new location. When the new location is visible on-screen, place the mouse pointer where you want to position the insertion point and click the left mouse button.

Another way to move the insertion point is by pressing keys on the keyboard. Sometimes, especially when you're already using the keyboard to type text, it's easier and faster to move the insertion point by pressing the cursor-movement keys than by using the mouse. Table 4.1 lists common keys that you can use to move around in your document.

Table 4.1 Keyboard Keys to Easily Move Around in a Document

Key	Moves Insertion Point
→/←	Next/Previous character
↑/↓	One line up/down

continues

Table 4.1 Continued

Key	Moves Insertion Point
PgUp/PgDn	One screen up/down
Ctrl+→/←	One word to the right or left
Home/End	Beginning or end of line
Ctrl+Home/End	Beginning or end of document

Selecting Text

After you enter text, you may want to delete a word, sentence, paragraph, or other section of text, or you may want to boldface the text or change its font or size. Before you can perform many formatting or editing actions on existing text, you first must select the text. Selecting the text shows WordPerfect where to perform the action.

You can select text with the mouse, the keyboard, or a combination of both. Some of the most useful ways to select text include the following:

- To select a section of text of any length, click and drag over the text.
- To select a word, position the shadow cursor anywhere in the word and double-click.
- To select a sentence, position the shadow cursor anywhere in the sentence and triple-click.
- To select a paragraph, position the shadow cursor anywhere in the paragraph and quadruple-click.
- To select a sentence, position the mouse pointer in the left margin area. When you point the mouse in the left margin area, the pointer changes to a right-pointing hollow arrow, as shown in Figure 4.5. Click to select a single sentence; to select multiple sentences, keep holding down the left mouse button after you click and drag through the sentences or drag the mouse pointer in the left margin.
- To select a paragraph, position the arrow pointer next to the paragraph in the left margin area. The arrow pointer should be pointing to the right. If it is not, move it further into the left margin area until it points to the right. Double-click to select the paragraph. To select multiple paragraphs, keep holding down the left mouse button after you click and drag through the paragraphs.
- For multiple selection options, position the right-pointing arrow pointer in the left margin area and right-click. Next, make a choice from selection options on the QuickMenu.

- To select a section of text of any length, position the insertion point at one end of the text. Next, position the shadow cursor at the other end of the text and hold down Shift while you left-click.
- To select text with the keyboard, position the insertion point at the beginning of the text, and then press and hold down the Shift key while you press the appropriate cursor-movement keys. To select from the insertion point to the end of the line, for example, hold down Shift while you press End. To select the character immediately following the insertion point, hold down Shift while you press the right-arrow key.

FIG. 4.5
To select text, position the mouse pointer in the left margin and click once.

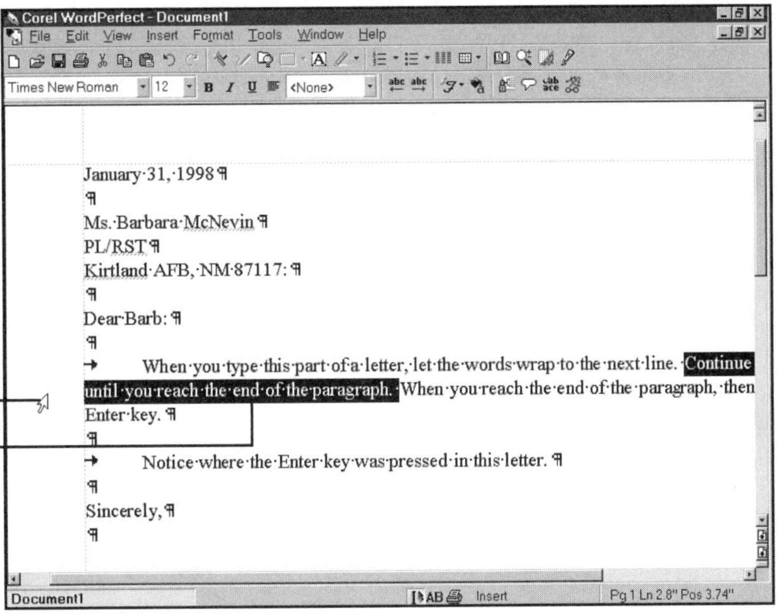

Mouse pointer

Selected sentence

TROUBLESHOOTING

I began typing the text, but it didn't appear where I expected it to appear. Text that you type appears at the insertion point, not at the mouse pointer. Before you type text, position the insertion point by clicking where you want the text to appear.

I have trouble controlling the selection when I drag through text with the mouse. It takes practice to control the mouse when you select text by dragging through it. Consider using this method only when all the text you want to select is visible on-screen. When it is not, click at the

continues

continued

start of the selection, use the scroll bars to move to the end of the selection, and then hold down the Shift key while you click at the end of the selection for maximum control.

I selected some text and made it bold, but when I started typing afterward the text disappeared. When text is selected, whatever you type replaces the selected text. It's a good idea to deselect text as soon as you finish performing any action(s) on the selection. To deselect text, click anywhere in the typing area. To recover your "lost" text, choose Edit, Undo.

NOTE You can use the Shift key to extend (or shrink) a selection. Hold down Shift while you press an arrow key to extend (or shrink) the selection. To deselect text, click the mouse anywhere in the text area, or press any of the arrow keys.

Editing Text

You can easily make changes and corrections to your document. You can select any text and delete it, copy it, or move it. You can even undelete text you accidentally deleted, or undo other editing operations you do by accident. This section shows you how to make basic editing changes quickly and easily.

Deleting Text

To delete a small amount of text to the right of the insertion point, press the Delete key. Hold the Delete key to continue deleting text. Similarly, to delete a small amount of text to the left of the insertion point, press the Backspace key. Hold the Backspace key to continue deleting text.

To delete larger amounts of text, select it as described above, and then press the Delete key.

TIP If you delete text by mistake, you can restore it using the Undelete or Undo commands.

Copying and Moving Text

One task you'll do frequently as you edit documents is copying and moving text. Copying text leaves the text in its original location, but makes a copy of it in another place. When you move text, it is deleted from the original location and inserted at the new location.

If you're going to copy or move the text to another location, you can use one of two methods: the "cut-and-paste" method or the "drag-and-drop" method.

Using the Cut-and-Paste Method To copy or move text from one area of the document to another area that is not visible on-screen, it is easiest to use the three-step, cut-and-paste method.

In the first step, you select the text, and then move or copy the text to the Windows Clipboard. Moving the text to the Windows Clipboard deletes it from its original location, and is thus called *cutting* the text. The text stays in the Windows Clipboard until you exit Windows or place something else in the Clipboard. (Thus, you can paste text from the Clipboard into your document any number of times, until you put something else in the Clipboard.)

To cut selected text, choose Edit, Cut, or press Ctrl+X. Alternatively, click the Cut button. To copy selected text, choose Edit, Copy, or press Ctrl+C. Alternatively, click the Copy button. The text is placed in the Windows Clipboard.

TIP You can also right-click the selected text, and then choose Cut or Copy from the QuickMenu.

After you move text to the Clipboard, show WordPerfect where you want to place the text by clicking where you want the text to appear in your document.

Paste the text from the Clipboard to the document by choosing Edit, Paste, or pressing Ctrl+V. Alternatively, click the Paste button. The text is copied from the Windows Clipboard to your document.

NOTE Copying text—or other elements in your documents, such as pictures and charts—is a way to share data between applications. The Windows Clipboard is common to all applications running under Windows. You can, for example, create text in WordPerfect, copy it, and paste it in Presentations. You can also copy a spreadsheet from Corel Quattro Pro and paste it into WordPerfect.

▶ **See** "Understanding Moving and Copying," **p. 616**

Drag-and-Drop Editing Another technique for moving and copying text is called drag and drop. Drag and drop is especially handy for moving or copying selected text a short distance—a location, say, that is already visible on-screen. Drag and drop can also be used to move graphics.

To move or copy text using drag and drop, take the following steps:

1. Select the text you want to move.
2. Point to the selected text and hold down the left mouse button.
3. Drag the pointer until the insertion point is at the new location. The drag-and-drop pointer shown in Figure 4.6 appears. When you are at the new location, release the mouse button.

TIP To copy the text instead of moving it, hold down the Ctrl key before you release the mouse button at the new location. When you hold down Ctrl, the drag-and-drop pointer includes a plus (+) sign.

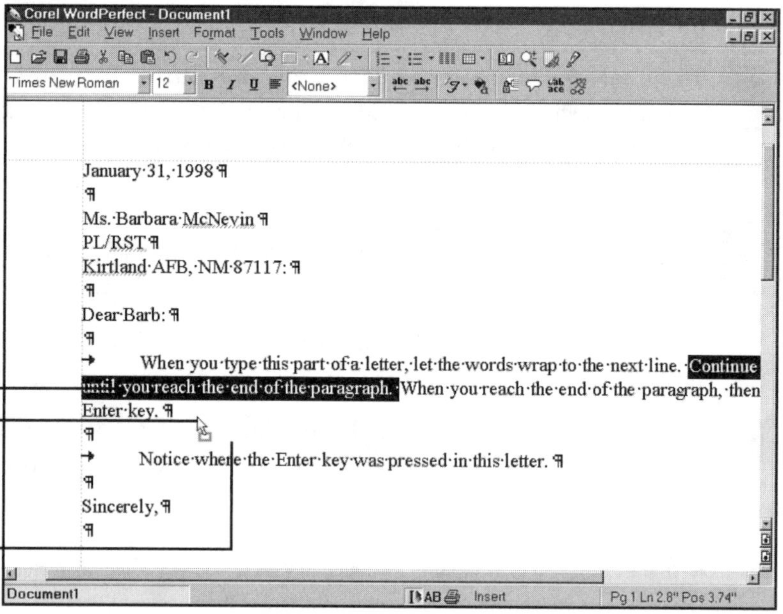

FIG. 4.6
Use the drag-and-drop pointer to drag the selected text or graphic to a new location. When the insertion point is correctly placed, release the mouse button.

Converting Case

WordPerfect includes a useful command that you can use to change the case of selected text. Suppose you type a heading with initial caps at the beginning of each word and then decide that it would look better in all uppercase. You can use Convert Case to convert it to uppercase.

To change the case of existing text, follow these steps:

1. Select the text.

2. Choose Edit, Convert Case.
3. Choose Lowercase, Uppercase, or Initial Capitals.

Correcting Mistakes

Unless you're one of those people who fills out crossword puzzles with a pen, you'll find the Undo command one of your best friends.

Many mistakes can be reversed with the Undo command. Suppose that you move text to the wrong place. You can undo the move operation with Undo. Click the Undo button on the WordPerfect 8 Toolbar to undo your most recent action, or choose Edit, Undo. Click the Undo button or choose Edit, Undo repeatedly to undo previous actions.

WordPerfect also provides a Redo command that you can use to reverse the last Undo. Click the Redo button on the WordPerfect 8 Toolbar to reverse your most recent undo action, or choose Edit, Redo.

WordPerfect provides a history of your edits and Undo actions. You can undo a series of actions by choosing Edit, Undo/Redo History.

Figure 4.7 shows the Undo/Redo History dialog box displaying the most recent actions. To undo the last four actions, click the fourth item from the top of the Undo list (this selects all of the first four items that are listed in the illustration) and then choose Undo.

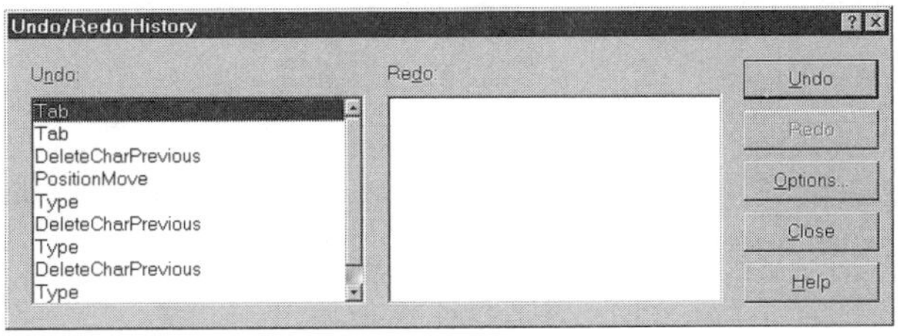

FIG. 4.7 The Undo/Redo History lists a series of the most recent actions that you can undo (or redo).

TROUBLESHOOTING

I accidentally deleted text that I didn't mean to delete. Restore the text by choosing Edit, Undo.

I pasted text in the wrong place. Before you place anything else in the Clipboard, click the Undo button, and then position the insertion point in the correct location and press Ctrl+V, or choose Edit, Paste.

continues

continued

I accidentally get the drag-and-drop pointer when I don't want it. Press Esc before you release the mouse button. If it's too late, and the text has already been moved, use the Undo command to correct the mistake.

I tried to move selected text to another page with drag-and-drop, but it was very cumbersome to position the insertion point while dragging the selection. Try using cut and paste rather than drag and drop when moving or copying to a distant location.

Saving, Closing, and Opening a Document

As you work on your document, you'll want to save it to the disk so that your work won't be lost if you turn off your computer or lose power. This section shows you how to save and close a document, open an existing document, and start a new one.

▶ **See** "Saving, Opening, and Closing Files," **p. 32**

Saving a Document

As in other WordPerfect Suite 8 programs, you save a WordPerfect document by assigning it a name and a location in your drive and folder list. After naming the file, you can save changes to the document without renaming it, or rename it to save both the original and new versions.

Naming a Document You can save a file to a hard drive, floppy drive, or network drive, and give your file a name that has up to 255 characters and includes spaces. If you need to exchange files with someone using a different word processor, you can even save your file in another format (such as WordPerfect 5.1 or Microsoft Word).

CAUTION

Some programs and versions of network operating systems cannot use long file names. You need to think about where this file will be going in the future. If there is any chance that the document might be going through or to a system that doesn't handle long names, you might consider using the older "8.3" file-naming conventions: Keep your file name to eight characters or less, with an optional period and up to three more characters; and don't use spaces in the file name.

When you're ready to save your document for the first time, do the following:

1. Choose File, Save; press Ctrl + S; or press the Save button on the toolbar. WordPerfect displays the Save File dialog box shown in Figure 4.8.

FIG. 4.8
The Save File dialog box allows you to save your file to the disk.

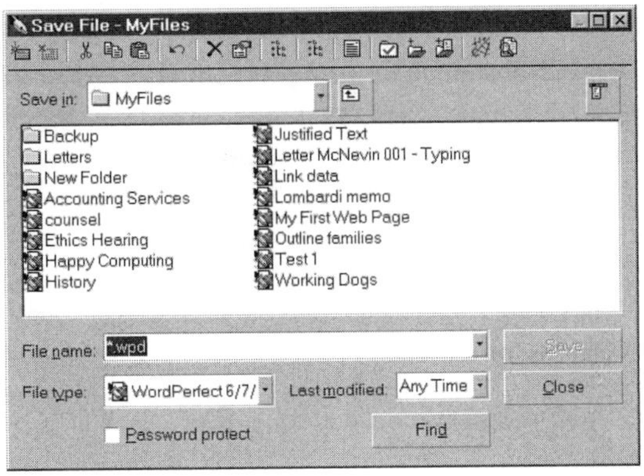

2. If you do not want to save your document in the default folder, navigate to the appropriate drive and folder by clicking the Save In box, and then select the drive and folder you want.
3. If you want to save your file in another format, click the File Type box, and pick the desired format.
4. Type the name of the file in the File Name box, and then click the Save button. Your file is saved, and you return to the editing window. Notice that the title bar displays the file's location, name, and that it is unmodified.

▶ **See** "Using File Management Dialog Boxes," **p. 40**

Part II Ch 4

NOTE You can specify the default folder in which your documents are stored and the default filename extension. To do so, choose Tools, Settings, Files, and then select the Document tab. Enter the default folder in the Default Document Folder box. To use a default extension, check the Use Default Extension on Open and Save box, and then enter the appropriate extension. Click OK, and then choose Close when you finish.

▶ **See** "Customizing File Settings," **p. 136**

Saving Changes to a Named Document When you've saved your document by assigning it a name and a location on the disk, you can continue to work on it. The changes you make are not saved, however, unless you tell WordPerfect to save them.

After modifying or editing an already-named document, choose File, Save, or click the Save button on the WordPerfect 8 toolbar. WordPerfect saves the changes and you are ready to proceed.

TIP Consider clicking the Save button whenever you are using your mouse to click a button on the toolbar. It's a particularly good idea to save your document before doing large-scale editing like a global search and replace.

Renaming a Document Occasionally, you will want to rename your document. This is particularly useful when you are making a new document (such as a proposal or a letter to a customer) that is based on an old one. In this case, you will want to keep both the old and new documents, so they need separate names.

TIP In previous versions of WordPerfect, you would also rename documents to keep track of *versions* of the file. In WordPerfect 8, you will do this with the version control feature.

To rename your document, do the following:

1. With the document on-screen, choose File, Save As. You see the Save As dialog box shown in Figure 4.9.

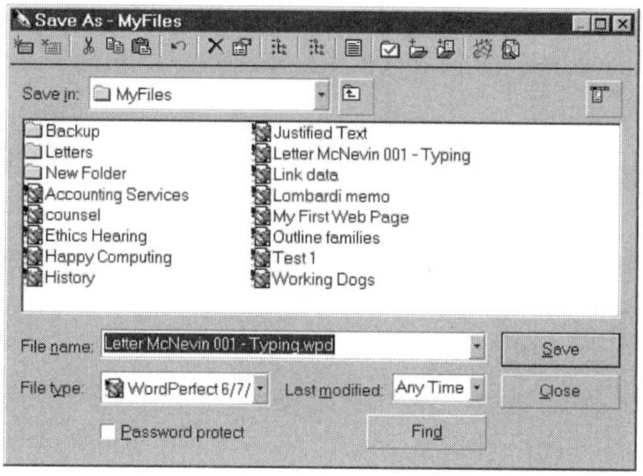

FIG. 4.9
You can rename your document using the Save As dialog box.

2. If you do not want to save your document in the default folder, navigate to the appropriate drive and folder by clicking the Save In box, and then select the drive and folder you want.
3. If you want to save your file in another format, click the File Type box, and pick the desired format.
4. If you want to change the name of your document, type the new name of the file in the File Name box.
5. Click the Save button. Your file is saved, and you return to the editing window. Notice that the title bar displays the file's location and name and that it is unmodified.

Closing a Document

When you finish working with a document, you can choose File, Close. The document is removed from the screen. If there are changes that haven't been saved, WordPerfect asks if you want to save them before closing the document.

If you intend to exit WordPerfect after working on the document, you do not need to close the document first. The document will be closed automatically when you exit WordPerfect, and you will be prompted to save the document if there are unsaved editing changes.

Opening a Document

When you open a document, a working copy of it is made from the disk onto the screen and your computer's memory. You can open up to nine documents at once, which can be very helpful when you need to bring information from several old documents into a new document.

If you prefer, you can open the document as a *copy*. If you do this, the document opens as a read-only file, and you will be unable to accidentally modify the original document. You will still be able to save the document, however, if you rename it.

> **TIP** If you open a document that has been saved in another format, such as WordPerfect 5.1 or Word 6.0, the document will be converted automatically.

To open a document, do the following:

1. Choose File, Open, or click the Open button on the WordPerfect 8 toolbar. WordPerfect displays the Open File dialog box shown in Figure 4.10.

FIG. 4.10
The Open file dialog box is where you select the file from the list of files, and then choose Open to open the document.

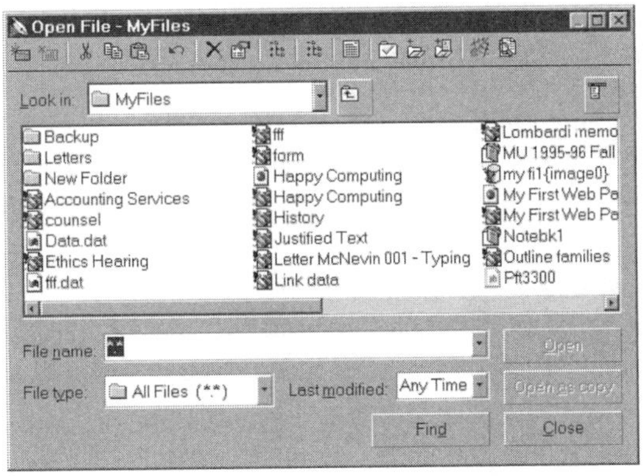

2. In the Open File dialog box, select the file name from the list of files, if you saved it in the default folder. Otherwise, you can change the drive and folder by clicking the Look In box to navigate to the desired folder, and then select the appropriate file name.
3. Click the Open button or the Open As Copy button, as desired; or double-click a file name from the list. You see the document in the editing window, with its name on the title bar.

TIP To open several files at once, hold the Ctrl key down while selecting each file you want to open. To open several adjacent files, click the first file, and then hold the Shift key and click the last one.

TIP If the file you want to open was recently edited, it will be listed at the bottom of the File menu when you choose File. You can select it from the File menu without accessing the Open dialog box.

Starting a New Document

All documents are based on *templates*. A template is a master document that contains formatting information, and can also contain text, macros, styles, and keyboard definitions. The *standard template* is where you save default formatting settings for future documents. The Standard template has the following characteristics:

- Uses an 8 1/2 by 11-inch portrait-oriented page
- Includes 1-inch top and bottom margins and 1-inch left and right margins
- Uses the initial printer font for the currently selected printer
- Uses left justification
- Supplies five heading styles that can be used to format different levels of headings in your document

Starting a New, Blank Document You can start a new document at any time. To start a new, blank document based on the standard template, click the New Blank Document button, or press Ctrl+N. You see a new, blank document in the editing window.

NOTE You do not need to close your old document before starting a new document because WordPerfect can have up to nine documents open at once. If you cannot create a new document, check to see if the maximum number of documents is already open, or if your insertion point is currently in a substructure such as a graphics box.

Starting a Document and Specifying a Template A *template* is a basic document design that can include text as well as formatting. You can save time and work by using templates for your standardized documents, such as letters, memos, and fax forms. Many templates prompt you for information when you use them; this saves you the work of positioning the insertion point manually to fill in the information. Many templates for common office tasks ship with WordPerfect.

See "Introducing Templates and Projects," **p. 110**

TROUBLESHOOTING

I wanted to save a file with a new name, but when I clicked the Save button, I didn't have a chance to change the name. To change the name, storage location, or file type of the document in the active document window, choose File, Save As. In the Save As dialog box, you can change any of these options.

I wanted to save a file in a different folder, but that folder isn't listed in the folder list. You may need to select a folder above the selected folder before you can see the desired folder name. For example, if C:\Myfiles\WPDOCS is the selected folder and you want to look at the files in C:\Myfiles\MEMOS, first you must select C:\Myfiles. Then, you can see (and select) the C:\Myfiles\MEMOS folder. Remember that you should double-click a folder to select it.

I opened a document that was created in another file format, and now I want to save it. Choose File, Save As. WordPerfect displays the Save File dialog box.

I can't open a file; in fact, New and Open are grayed out on the File menu. You already have nine documents open, the maximum WordPerfect allows at once. Close an open document, and then try again. If this isn't the problem, your insertion point may currently be in a substructure such as a header, footer, or graphics box. Click in the main body of the document, and then try again.

CHAPTER 5

Formatting Text and Documents

Change the appearance of your screen

The WordPerfect screen can be customized in many ways. Learn about the three views of your document, how to zoom your screen, and how to display and hide screen features.

Work with the Reveal Codes window

See how to use WordPerfect's famous Reveal Codes window to examine and modify the codes that make your document appear the way it does.

Format your text

See how you can easily specify fonts, size, appearance attributes, and the color of the text you print.

Format your paragraphs

Learn how to specify line spacing, indents, margins, justification, and tab settings.

Format your page

Create headers and footers, print page numbers, choose paper size and orientation, and shrink your document to fit perfectly on one piece of paper.

Many Corel WordPerfect Suite 8 features enable you to change the appearance of your documents by formatting your documents. You can boldface or italicize text, you can adjust the spacing between lines, or you can choose from many other formatting features to make your documents more readable and more attractive.

WordPerfect makes formatting quick and easy. You can use toolbar buttons and menu commands to make an ordinary business document eye-catching and readable.

NOTE When you format a document, WordPerfect records your commands in the form of embedded codes. You can avoid formatting problems if you remember to check the position of the insertion point before you make a formatting change. Unless you want to remove specific formatting manually (by removing the code that causes the formatting—discussed later in this chapter), you don't need to concern yourself with embedded codes. You can, however, see embedded codes whenever you want by choosing View, Reveal Codes. ■

In this chapter, you learn how to format text, lines, paragraphs, and pages using the easiest and fastest methods. ■

Changing Screen Appearance

WordPerfect enables you to change your screen appearance in several ways to suit your working style. These include:

- Displaying or hiding screen elements
- Specifying viewing modes
- Setting the screen magnification
- Working with the Reveal Codes window

The display or removal of screen elements, view modes, and magnification options are all set from the View menu. To select your view mode, choose View, and then select Draft, Page, or Two Pages. To work with the Reveal Codes window on, choose View, Reveal Codes.

Displaying Screen Elements

You can remove or display various screen elements, such as the toolbar, Property Bar, Ruler, Application Bar, and display of nonprinting characters to customize the way your screen appears.

To remove or display the toolbar, Property Bar, or Application Bar, choose View, Toolbars. You see the Toolbars dialog box shown in Figure 5.1. Check the elements you want to display, and then choose OK. To toggle the display of the Ruler, choose View, Ruler. The Ruler will display when there is a check mark next to Ruler in the View menu.

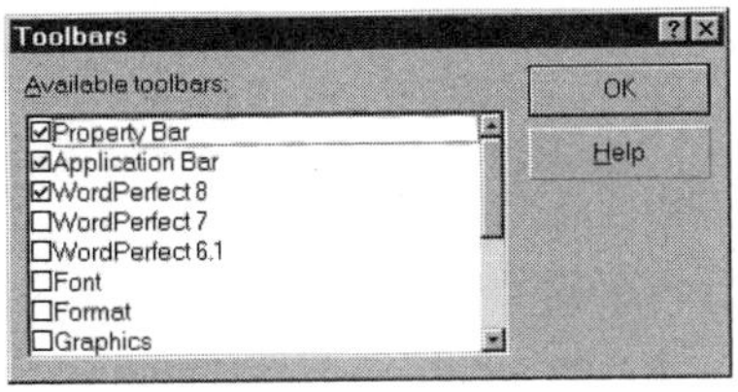

FIG. 5.1
You can display or remove screen elements to customize the look of WordPerfect in the Toolbars dialog box.

To provide a totally "clean screen" look and remove all bars (including scroll bars and the title bar), do the following:

1. Choose View, Hide Bars. Unless the display of this dialog box has been suppressed, you see a Hide Bars Information dialog box that tells you the effect of this command and how to restore the screen to its original look.
2. Suppress the future display of this dialog box, if desired, by checking Do Not Show This Message Next Time I Hide Bars.
3. Choose OK. Your screen will look like the one in Figure 5.2.
4. Press the Esc key to restore the original look of the screen.

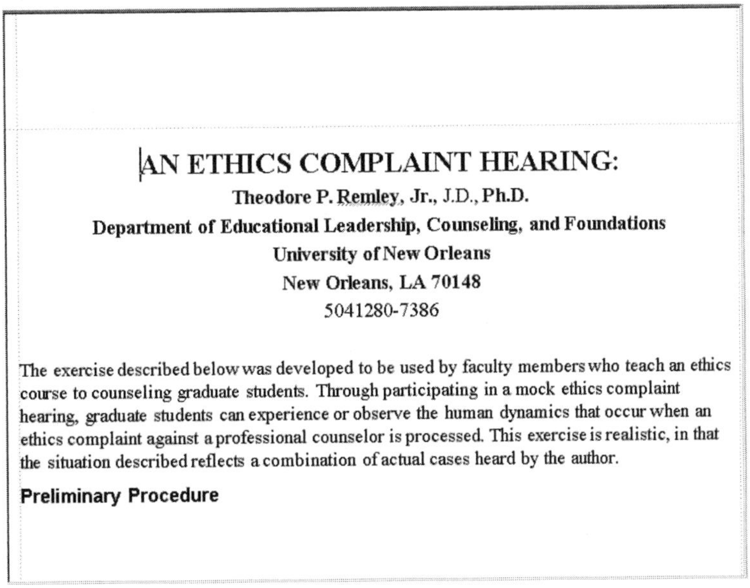
AN ETHICS COMPLAINT HEARING:
Theodore P. Remley, Jr., J.D., Ph.D.
Department of Educational Leadership, Counseling, and Foundations
University of New Orleans
New Orleans, LA 70148
5041280-7386

The exercise described below was developed to be used by faculty members who teach an ethics course to counseling graduate students. Through participating in a mock ethics complaint hearing, graduate students can experience or observe the human dynamics that occur when an ethics complaint against a professional counselor is processed. This exercise is realistic, in that the situation described reflects a combination of actual cases heard by the author.

Preliminary Procedure

FIG. 5.2
You can produce a completely clean screen look by choosing View, Hide Bars.

You can also modify the viewing options to display nonprinting characters, such as spaces, hard returns, tabs, indents, and so forth, on the current and new document. You may not want these characters to show on-screen, as they can become quite distracting and take your eye away from the text you are typing. On occasion, however, it may be useful to know where spaces and tabs are—especially at the "blank" end of a line. To show these elements, use the following steps:

1. Choose Tools, Settings, Display.
2. Select the Symbols tab. You see the Display Settings dialog box (see Figure 5.3).

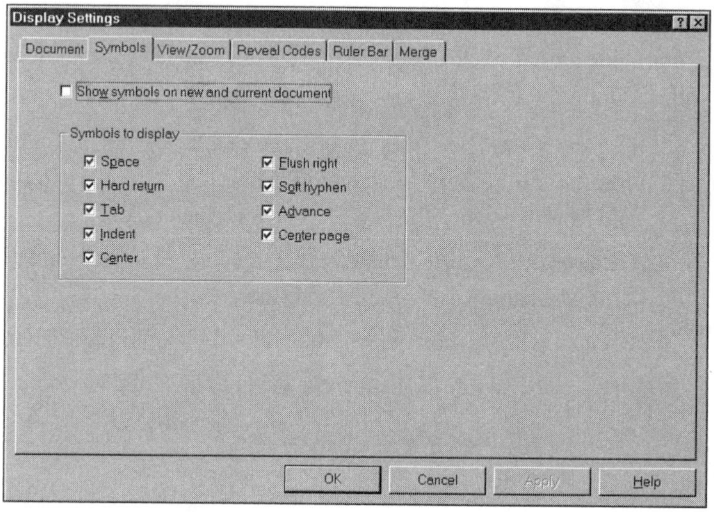

FIG. 5.3
You can specify which nonprinting characters should display on your screen in the Display Settings dialog box on the Symbols tab.

3. Check Show Symbols on New and Current Documents, and then check the specific symbols you want to display.
4. Click OK to exit the Display Settings dialog box.
5. Click Close to exit the Settings dialog box and return to your document.

Using View Modes

TIP To quickly toggle the display of nonprinting characters, choose View, Show ¶.

WordPerfect offers three different viewing modes that you can use while you are editing your document: Page view, Draft view, or Two Page view. Each view offers its own advantages for text editing and formatting. Changing the view affects the on-screen appearance of the document; it doesn't affect the actual formatting of the document or the way it will print out.

When you work in a document, you're working in Page view by default. You can use the View menu to switch to another view whenever it suits you.

TIP You can modify the viewing options to change the default view from Page view to Draft or Two Page view by choosing Tools, Settings, Display, and selecting the View/Zoom tab. Select the desired view, click OK, and then choose Close to return to your document.

Page View In Page view, you see on-screen the page just as it will print, as shown in Figure 5.4. This is a true WYSIWYG (What You See Is What You Get) view of your document. Page view displays headers, footers, page borders, top and bottom margins, and footnotes. Page view is well-suited for applying finishing touches to the text and page layout, although many people like to use this view for entering and editing text as well. Working in Page view is slightly slower than working in Draft view; on faster computers, however, this difference may be imperceptible.

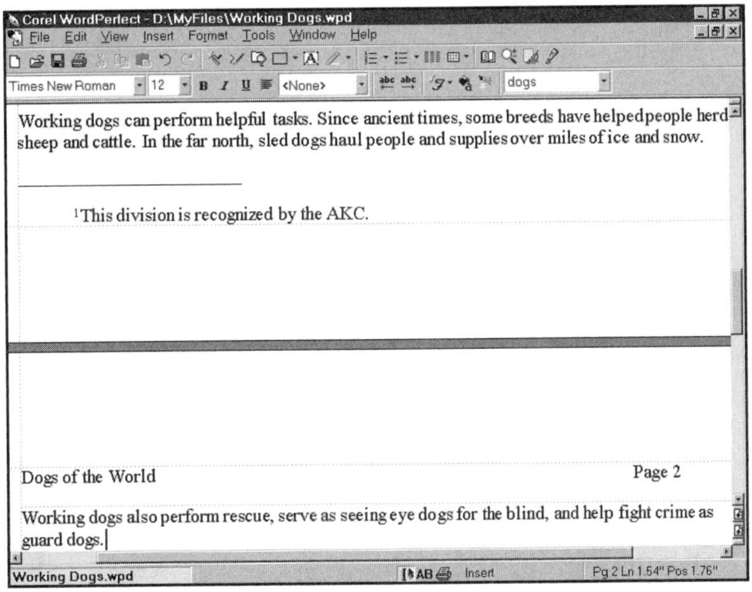

FIG. 5.4
Page view shows you everything on the page just as it will print; this is a true WYSIWYG view.

Draft View Entering and editing text is faster and easier when you work in Draft view. In Draft view, you see text just as it will print, including variations in font face, font size, and graphics elements, as shown in Figure 5.5. You can scroll smoothly from the bottom of one page to the top of the next page without jumping past the gap between the bottom margin of one page and the top margin of the next page. Whenever you want to see *everything* on the page just as it will print, including margin space, headers, footers, page numbering, and page borders, you can switch from Draft view to Page view.

FIG. 5.5
Draft view enables you to enter and edit text smoothly and easily.

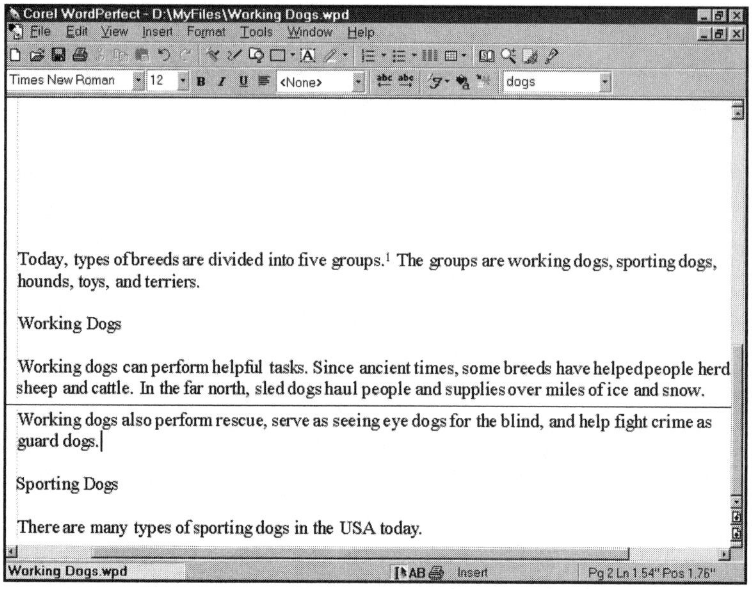

Two Page View Use Two Page view when you want to see two pages on-screen at the same time. Two Page view is best suited for looking at facing pages (when you're printing on both sides of the paper) and for seeing more of the document layout than you can see in Page view. You can see where text will fit on a page best with the Two Page view and determine how much white space exists on each page.

You can edit your document in Two Page view just as you can edit it in Draft view or Page view, although the text is extremely small. Working in Two Page view is even slower than working in Page view.

Changing the View Magnification

In addition to the choice of views, WordPerfect provides various magnification options for viewing a document. You can adjust the view magnification from 25 to 400 percent when you are in Draft or Page view. If you have a 15-inch or larger monitor, you may want to use a smaller magnification. The letters on the screen will still be readable, but you will be able to see more of the page.

Setting magnification does not affect the way the document is formatted or how it will print out; it only affects its on-screen display.

To change magnification, click the Zoom button on the toolbar. You see a drop-down menu like the one in Figure 5.6. Choose your zoom setting from the menu, or select Other to select a setting that does not appear.

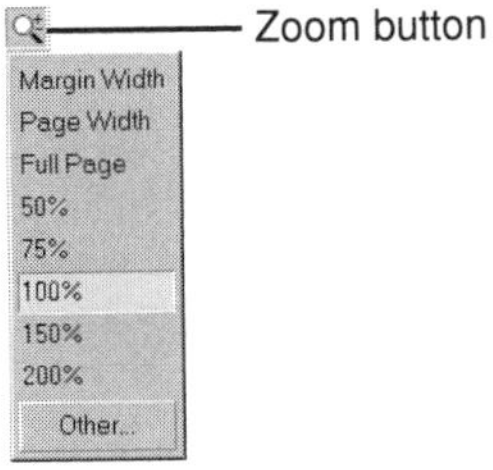

FIG. 5.6
Using the Zoom button on the toolbar, you can change the magnification of the screen without affecting the document format or the way it prints out.

When you select Other, the Zoom dialog box will appear, as in Figure 5.7. This same dialog box appears when you choose View, Zoom from the menu bar. You can click one of the preset magnification levels in the box, or you can set your own level from 25 to 400 percent by clicking the up or down arrows in the spin box at the bottom of the Zoom dialog box.

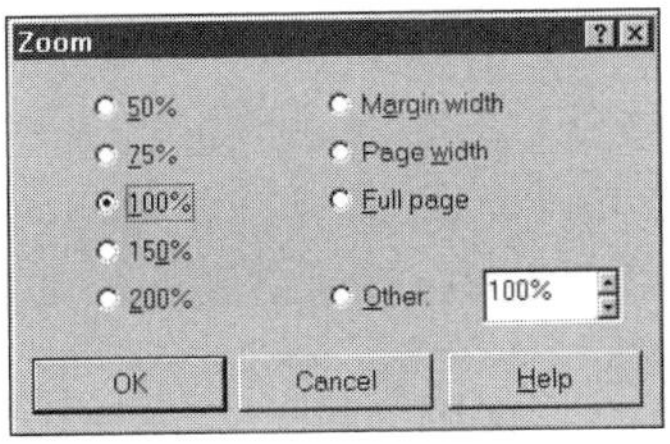

FIG. 5.7
In the Zoom dialog box, you can change the magnification factor of the screen to preset levels or set your own level.

TROUBLESHOOTING

I can't see all of the text on a line on-screen at once. Change the level of magnification with the Zoom button or after choosing View, Zoom. Experiment with 100 percent, Margin Width, and Page Width to see what best suits the situation.

It takes too long to scroll through a document. Maximize the speed at which you're working by using Draft view mode (open the View menu to change the view mode).

When I scroll from the bottom of one page to the top of the next page, the screen takes a big jump and it's difficult to get a continuous view of the text from one page to the next. Choose View, Draft to change from Page view to Draft view.

Working with the Reveal Codes Window

The Reveal Codes window gives you a behind-the-scenes look at your document. Unless you have formatting problems, there is no need to look at the Reveal Codes window. Working with Reveal Codes turned on, however, is an excellent method of becoming familiar with codes and formatting. That way, when something does appear on-screen differently than you expected, you will be able to spot the problem code immediately. Remember that WordPerfect records your formatting commands in the form of embedded codes. The Reveal Codes window shows you those embedded codes along with your text. Sometimes, the most efficient way to solve a formatting problem is by working in the Reveal Codes window and by removing the code that causes a problem. This section shows you how to work in the Reveal Codes window.

Accessing the Reveal Codes Window The position of the insertion point determines the placement of codes and where their formatting takes effect. When you select a subtitle and make it bold, for example, bold codes are embedded at both ends of the subtitle. When you change tab settings anywhere in a paragraph, however, a tab set code is embedded at the *beginning* of that paragraph.

To display the Reveal Codes window, choose View, Reveal Codes; press Alt+F3; or drag one of the Reveal Codes bars up or down. The editing screen is split into two windows, as shown in Figure 5.8.

FIG. 5.8
Formatting codes are visible in the Reveal Codes window at the bottom of the screen.

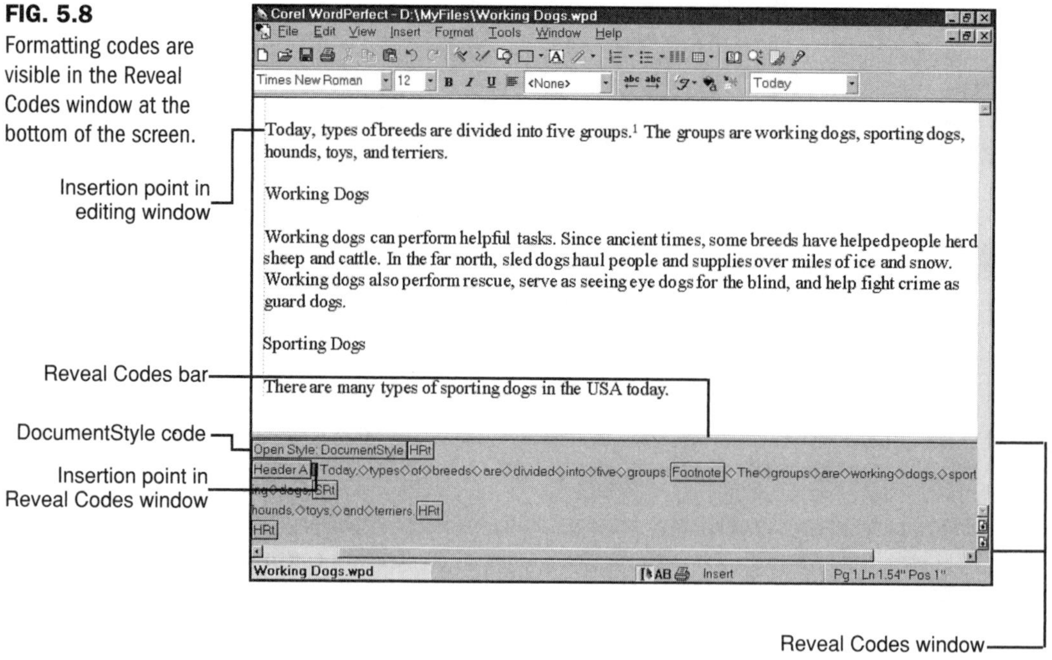

NOTE Every document contains an `Open Style: DocumentStyle` code at its beginning. This code cannot be removed, but it can be edited. Formatting in the DocumentStyle is a reflection of formatting in the DocumentStyle for the current template.

The following pointers will help you work in Reveal Codes:

- To remove a code, drag it out of the Reveal Codes window, or position the insertion point in front of the code and press Delete.
- There are two kinds of codes: open and paired. Open codes are contained in rectangular boxes. Paired codes are contained in boxes with points at the right (for a Start code) or left (for an End code). Open and paired codes are discussed more fully in the following section.
- To edit a code (so you can change the value it contains), double-click the code in the Reveal Codes window. To edit a margin code, for example, double-click the code. You are taken to the Margins dialog box, where you can specify a new value.

Open and Paired Codes Most character formatting commands are inserted as *paired codes*—they always have a Start and an End code—for example, a Start Bold and End Bold code. When you select text and then apply the formatting, you are inserting a Start code at the beginning of the block and an End code at the end of it. When you set your insertion point without selecting text and then apply the formatting, you are inserting a Start code immediately followed by an End code, with your insertion point between them. The End code is pushed ahead as you type new text, and the specified formatting attribute is applied to the new text.

Some formatting codes, like typeface and size, are *open codes*. If you set your insertion point and apply the formatting without selecting text, an Open code is placed in the document, and all text from then on takes that attribute. If you select text before inserting one of these open codes, WordPerfect puts the open typeface or size code at the beginning of your blocked text, and then automatically also puts an open code for the original typeface or size at the end of that text. Thus, the text after the selected text returns to the original typeface or size.

Formatting Characters

With WordPerfect, you can format your text with a variety of font attributes such as font face, size, and appearance. The most frequently used features can be easily accessed via the WordPerfect toolbar and the Property Bar.

TIP Another way to format characters is with the WordPerfect Style feature, discussed in Chapter 8, "Organizing and Formatting Large Documents."

Font Attributes

Font attributes that you can specify include the following:

- *Font Face*. The font face is the typeface of text. Common faces are Times New Roman and Courier. Choose the font face that suits your work. For an informal flyer, you could choose a light italic font, such as Brush. For a more formal effect, you could choose Shelley or Caslon Openface.
- *Font Size*. Font size is measured in points. A smaller point size results in a smaller print; a larger point size results in a larger print. All text you enter in a new document that is based on the Standard template is in your printer's initial typeface and size. Most font faces are scaleable, meaning that you can change the font size.

NOTE Font size points and picas are typesetter's measurements used for measuring spacing, line thickness, and other font attributes. There are 12 points to a pica and 6 picas to an inch; therefore, there are 72 points to an inch. Standard 12-point text has 6 lines per inch—the same as a normal typewriter.

- *Appearance*. WordPerfect allows you to specify common appearance attributes such as bold, italic, underlined, and double-underlined. You can also specify attributes including outline (letters appear with a clear fill), shadow, small caps, redline (for new text), strikeout, and hidden (text that will not normally appear when the document is printed).
- *Position*. Text can be normal, superscript (text set slightly above the line—r^2 for example), or subscript (text set slightly below the line, as with H_2O).
- *Relative Size*. You can specify that text be normal, large, extra large, small, or fine. This will enlarge or reduce the text proportionally to the base font size you have selected.
- *Text Color*. You can choose the color of the text. It will display in color and, if you have a color printer, also print in color; although the display color and the printer color shade or tone may be somewhat different from each other.
- *Shading*. You can also specify the darkness of the color you have chosen. 100 percent black is black; 50 percent black is gray.
- *Underline Options*. You can specify whether the underline feature underlines spaces and tabs, or just the words.

You can apply formatting commands via the toolbar and Property Bar, or via the Font dialog box.

Formatting Existing Text The easiest way to change the appearance of existing text is to select it, and then click the Bold, Italic, or Underline buttons on the Property Bar; or click the Font Face or Font Size buttons on the Property Bar. Selecting a font face is shown in Figure 5.9.

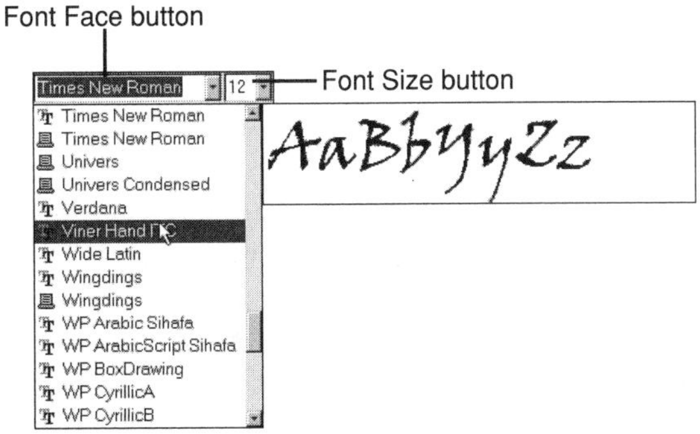

FIG. 5.9
Selecting a font face may be done through the Font Face pull-down menu.

If you need more control over your text appearance, or to access features that are not on the toolbar and Property Bar, select the desired text, and then access the Font dialog box by choosing Format, Font. You see the Font dialog box shown in Figure 5.10.

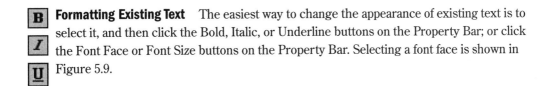

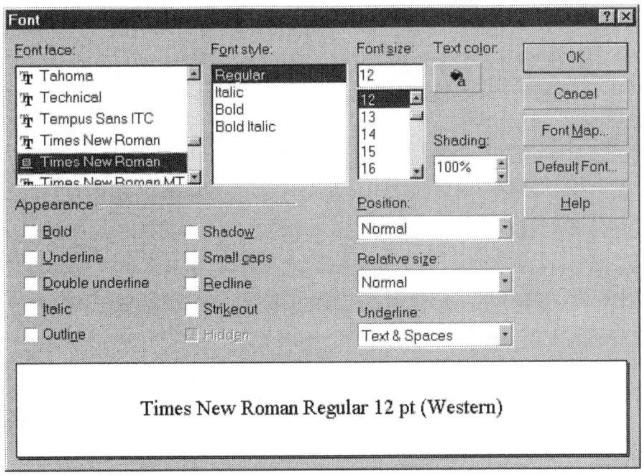

FIG. 5.10
You can set a variety of text appearance attributes using the Font dialog box.

Formatting New Text You format *new* text by positioning the insertion point, making the formatting changes with the toolbar or Font dialog box, and then typing the text. All text typed from that point on will be formatted according to your specifications, until you change the formatting again. In addition, if you change the typeface or size, the old text starting from the insertion point will take on the new attributes you specify.

When you format text, you put hidden control codes in your document. You can see these by selecting View, Reveal Codes.

TROUBLESHOOTING

I just changed the font and font size of the text, and now I want to return it to its original format. Choose Edit, Undo repeatedly to undo the changes.

Choosing the Document Default Font

To select the font that you want for all elements of a document, including headers, footers, footnotes, and graphic box captions, do the following:

1. Choose Format, Font, and then click the Default Font button in the Font dialog box.
2. Make your selections in the Document Default Font dialog box (see Figure 5.11.)
3. Click OK to return to the Font dialog box, and then click OK to return to the main editing window.

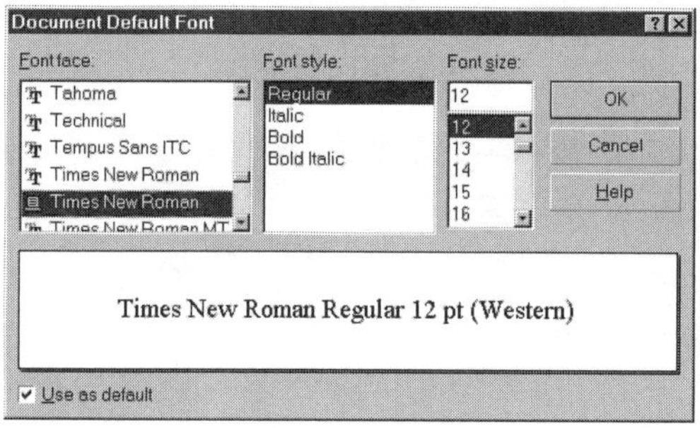

FIG. 5.11
Set a variety of text appearance attributes using the Document Default Font dialog box.

You can change the document default font for the selected printer while you are in the Document Default Font dialog box by selecting the desired font, and then checking the Use as Default check box. When you change the default font for the selected printer, that font becomes the default font for the standard template, and will thus be the default font for all new documents created based on the standard template.

TIP

An easy way to reuse font attributes you have recently used is by selecting the text to be changed, and then clicking the QuickFonts button. The last fonts you have used, along with their appearance attributes, are saved on the QuickFonts list; you can pick the one you want to reuse.

Formatting Lines and Paragraphs

Use Line and Paragraph formatting features for many of the appearance changes that you want to make in a document. For example, you can change line spacing, center text on a line, indent paragraphs, or change margins and justification.

Line and paragraph formatting features are available through the Format menu, and some additional ones are also available on the Property Bar and the WordPerfect 8 toolbar. If you're going to be doing a lot of document formatting, however, you may want to display the Format toolbar. It provides many other options for formatting the lines and paragraphs. To do so, right-click the toolbar, and then choose Format from the drop-down menu. You see the Format toolbar pictured in Figure 5.12. The use of buttons from this toolbar are discussed throughout this section.

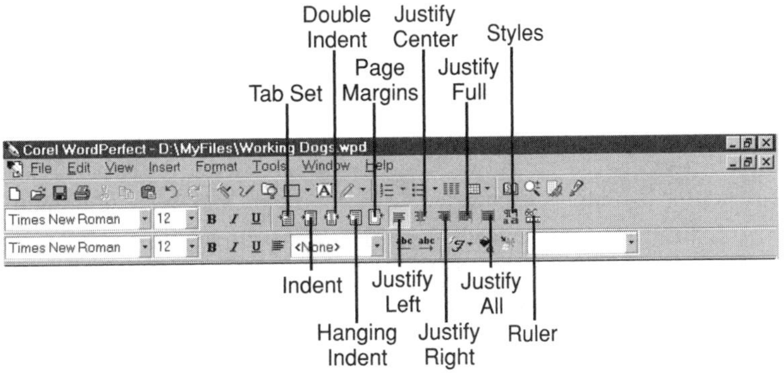

FIG. 5.12
The Format toolbar provides buttons for many paragraph and line formatting tasks.

TIP Use QuickFormat to quickly copy text formats, as discussed later in the section "Copying Formats."

Adjusting Spacing

You can adjust the spacing between lines of text within a paragraph when it suits your work, or you can adjust the spacing between paragraphs. Unless you change the defaults, or unless you're using a specialized template, you'll be using single spacing between lines and between paragraphs.

Line Spacing Line spacing refers to the space between the baseline of one line of text and the baseline of an adjacent line of text, as shown in Figure 5.13. WordPerfect adjusts line spacing automatically to allow for the height of the largest font on a line (the line height). Enough extra white space is added to make the text readable.

FIG. 5.13
Line spacing affects readability and page design.

Single line spacing

One-and-one-half line spacing

Double line spacing

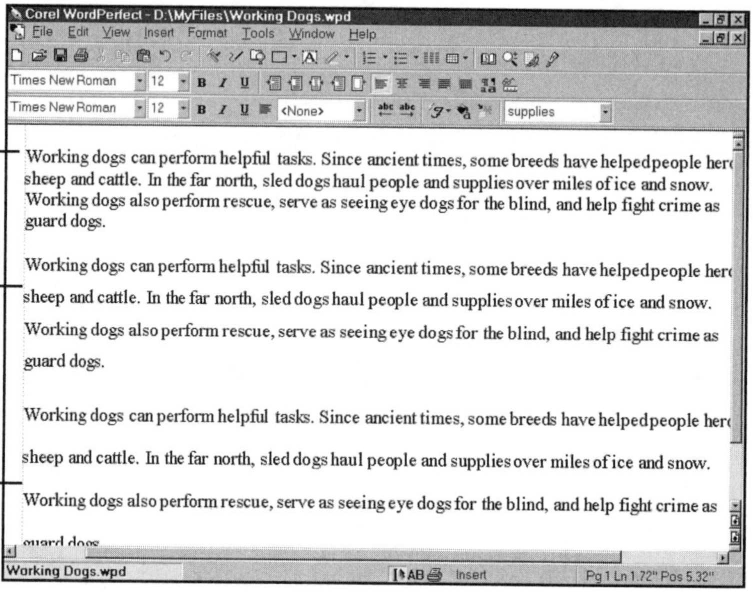

WordPerfect's default line spacing is set to single spacing. When you specify a new number for the line spacing value, the current line height is multiplied by that number. If you choose a value of 1.5 for line spacing, for example, the height of a single-spaced line is multiplied by 1.5.

NOTE Line spacing refers to the spacing between lines that are separated by automatic word wrap. Paragraph spacing (discussed later) refers to lines that are separated by a hard return (an Enter keystroke).

To adjust line spacing, do the following:

1. Place your insertion point where the new line spacing should begin, or select the text to which it should be applied.
2. Choose Format, Line, Spacing. You see the Line Spacing dialog box shown in Figure 5.14.

FIG. 5.14
Change the line spacing in the Line Spacing dialog box.

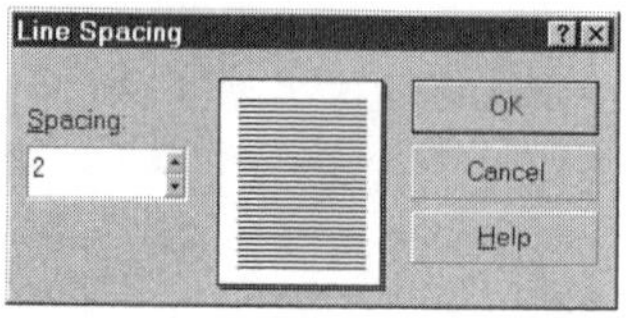

3. In the Line Spacing dialog box, enter a new value in the Spacing text box.
4. After entering the value you want for line spacing, choose OK.

TIP You can specify the line spacing to two decimal accuracy (for example, .98 or .35) for total control of your document appearance.

NOTE Line spacing is inserted as a paired code if text is selected and as an open code otherwise.

Paragraph Spacing Adjust the spacing between paragraphs rather than lines when you want to adjust the white space between paragraphs (wherever there is an Enter keystroke). In single-spaced text, for example, paragraphs are often separated by a blank line. This appearance can be produced by pressing Enter twice. However, when you set paragraph spacing to 2.0 and press Enter (once) at the end of the paragraph, you achieve the same effect. Not only does this save keystrokes, but you can ensure consistency in your document's appearance because all paragraphs will have the same spacing.

To adjust the spacing between paragraphs, choose Format, Paragraph, Format. The Paragraph Format dialog box appears (see Figure 5.15). Enter a new value for Spacing Between Paragraphs and choose OK. You see the way the paragraph will look in the sample box within the dialog box. Text with paragraph spacing adjusted to 1.5 is shown in Figure 5.16.

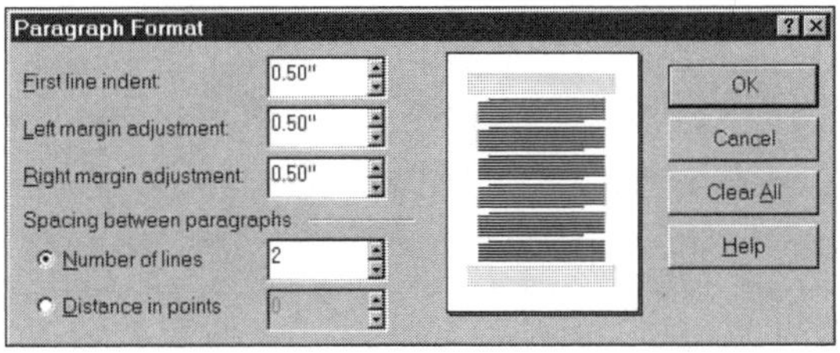

FIG. 5.15
In the Paragraph Format dialog box, add extra spacing between paragraphs for readability.

Centering and Flush Right

You can position specific text on a single line with the Center or Flush Right command. Centered text is centered between the left and right margins. Title lines are commonly centered. Text that is flush right aligns at the right margin; it extends "backward" to the left.

FIG. 5.16
With paragraph spacing set at 1.5 in the Paragraph Format dialog box, you just press Enter once between paragraphs to get a result that looks like this.

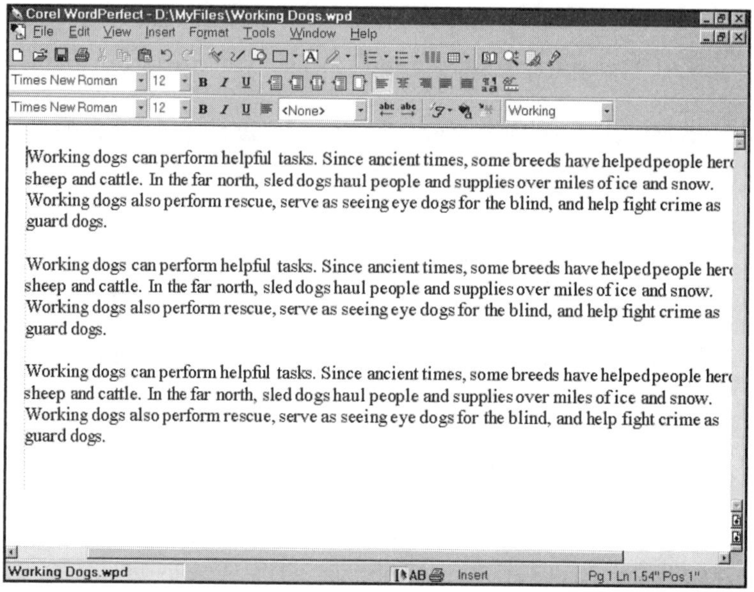

To apply Center or Flush Right, follow these steps:

1. Position the insertion point immediately before the text that is to be centered or flush right. (To center or flush right the entire line, position the insertion point at the beginning of the line.)
2. Right-click with the mouse, and then choose Center or Flush Right from the QuickMenu.

   ▶ **See** "Using Context-Sensitive Help," **p. 28**

When you apply Center or Flush Right, text following the insertion point is formatted with that feature. Thus, you can easily have some text on the same line that is at the left of the line, another few words that are centered, and some others that are flush right. To do so, you would position your insertion point before the text to be centered, choose the Center command, position your insertion point before the text to be flush right, and then choose the Flush Right command.

TIP To create text that is centered or flush right with a dot leader (a series of dots) before it, apply the Center or Flush Right command twice.

The Center and Flush Right commands apply only to text on a single line. To make all text after the insertion point centered or flush right, use the Justification button on the Property Bar.

For more information on aligning text, see the later section "Setting Justification."

Indenting Text

You can indent one or more paragraphs to emphasize the text, format a long quotation, or create subordinate levels. There are four common types of indents that you can see in Figure 5.17.

FIG. 5.17
You can emphasize text with four types of indents.

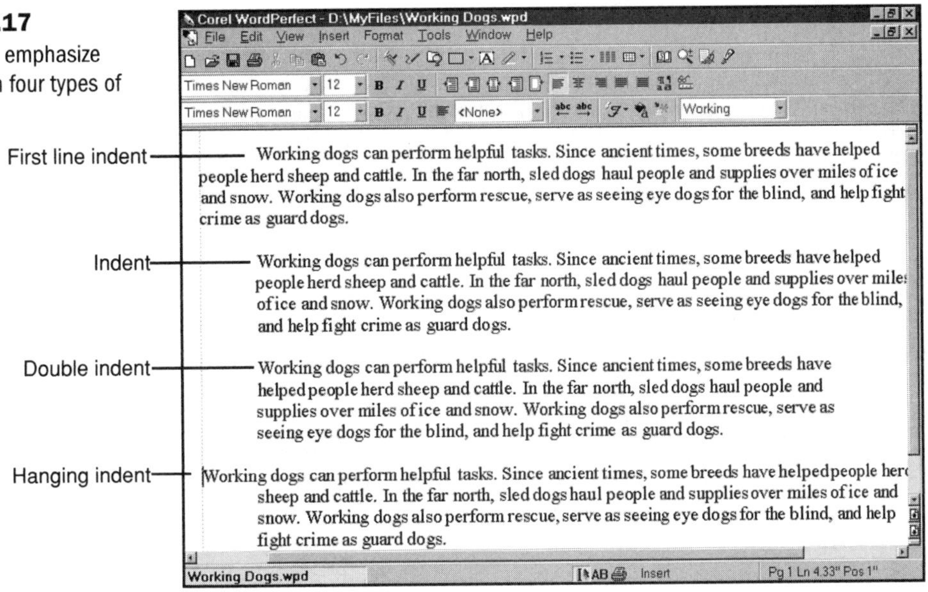

- *First line indent.* The first line of text is indented one tab stop from the left, as when you press the Tab key at the beginning of a paragraph. This is most often used for double-spaced text.

- *Indent.* This is WordPerfect's term for moving the entire paragraph one tab stop in from the left. This is often used to set off points you are making.

- *Double Indent.* The entire paragraph is moved in one tab stop from both the left and from the right. This is often used for long quotations.

- *Hanging Indent.* The first line extends to the left margin, but successive lines are indented in from the left by one tab stop. This is often used in bibliographies.

All of these indents affect the text from the insertion point, through the end of the paragraph.

To create a first line indent, you can press the Tab key at the beginning of each paragraph. You can automate this process by using the paragraph formatting feature; this is often done in conjunction with setting paragraph spacing. This will ensure that all your paragraphs look the same and have the same first line indent. Do so by positioning your insertion point before the paragraphs to be indented, then choose Format, Paragraph, Format. The Paragraph Format dialog box appears (refer to Figure 5.15). Enter a new value for First Line Indent, such as .5, and choose OK.

NOTE Remember that a paragraph ends with a hard return (an Enter keystroke).

TIP You can further automate this process by creating a *style* that automatically indents each paragraph. For more information see "Using Styles" in Chapter 8.

To indent several paragraphs at once, first select the paragraphs, and then follow the steps for indenting a single paragraph.

TIP Indenting is such a common task that you may want to remember the hotkey for it—F7.

CAUTION

Don't try to align paragraphs on-screen with the space bar or Enter key. It probably won't look lined up when you print the document, even if it does look okay on-screen.

Setting and Using Tabs

Unlike indents, which affect all text lines until the next hard return, tabs affect only the current line of text. Tabs are used primarily to indent the first line of a paragraph, to indent one-line paragraphs, and to line up columns of text or numbers.

By default, tabs are set at half-inch intervals across the page. When you use a feature that positions text at the next tab stop (Tab, Indent, Hanging Indent, or Double Indent), the insertion point moves to the next tab stop to the right. You can customize tab stops to suit your work. For example, if you want less space between the bullets in a bulleted list and the text following the bullets, move the tab stop that aligns the text closer to the bullet. You can also set customized tabs to type in columns of text or numbers.

NOTE By default, tabs are measured relative to the left margin, not from the left edge of the page. This means that when the left margin is changed, tab settings remain at the same distance from the margin. You can optionally set tabs in absolute measurements, from the left edge of the paper. This feature is used primarily to maintain compatibility with past versions of WordPerfect.

Another way to align columns of text or numbers is with a table. Tables make it easy to align text, and there are many formatting features that you can use to enhance the appearance of tables.

▶ **See** "Working with Tables," **p. 162**

Setting Tabs with the Ruler You can quickly set tabs using the Ruler. New tab settings take effect at the beginning of the current paragraph. If you have selected text, the new tab settings apply only to the selection. If you have not, new tab settings apply to all text from the paragraph the insertion point is in until a different tab setting code is reached. Be sure to position the insertion point properly (or to select the text for which you want customized tab settings) before you adjust tab settings.

For more information about displaying the Ruler, see the earlier section "Displaying Screen Elements."

Tab settings on the Ruler are indicated by markers that hang down in the bottom area of the Ruler. The shape of the marker indicates the type of alignment (left, center, right align, decimal align) and whether the tab stop has a dot leader. Figure 5.18 shows the Ruler with customized tab settings for several types of alignment.

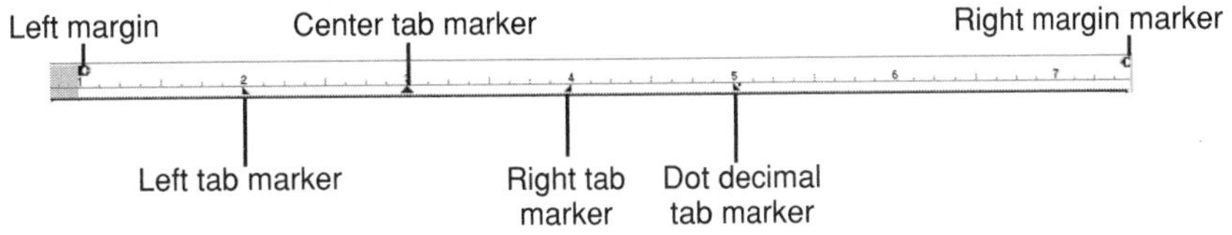

FIG. 5.18 Setting different types of tabs is easy on the Ruler. Just drag a tab to a new position to move it, or drag a tab below the Ruler to remove it.

Important items to remember about setting tabs include:

- Before you set new tabs, position the insertion point and clear all existing tab stops by right-clicking the bottom of the Ruler and choosing Clear All Tabs.
- To move a tab, drag it to a new position. As you drag, the original position is indicated on the Application Bar.
- To insert a new tab (of the current type), click in the Tab area of the Ruler, beneath the numbered ruler scale where you want the marker to appear.

- To set a different type of tab, right-click in the Tab area on the bottom portion of the ruler and choose a type from the QuickMenu. For example, to set a tab that aligns a column of numbers, first right-click in the Tab area. Choose Decimal, and then left-click at the desired position on the ruler scale.
- To remove a tab, drag it below the ruler. To remove all tabs, right-click in the Tab area and choose Clear All Tabs from the QuickMenu.

Setting Tabs from the Tab Set Dialog Box The Tab Set dialog box enables you to set tabs precisely and to specify options that aren't available from the Ruler. Before you adjust tabs, be sure to position the insertion point in the paragraph where you want the new tab stops to take effect, or select the text that you want formatted with new tab stops.

To display the Tab Set dialog box, choose Format, Line, Tab Set, or right-click in the Ruler and choose Tab Set. WordPerfect displays the Tab Set dialog box (see Figure 5.19).

FIG. 5.19
After positioning the insertion point, use the Tab Set dialog box to position tabs in precise positions. Positions in this box and on the Ruler are set in inches by default.

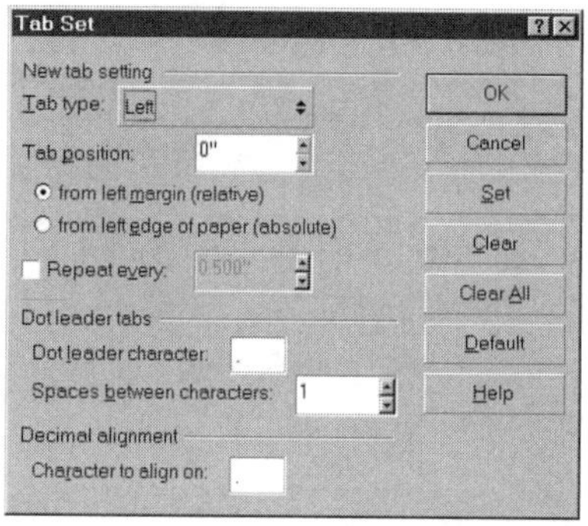

It is best to clear out old tabs before setting the new ones.

To clear a single tab setting, specify the setting in the Tab Position text box, and then choose Clear or Clear All to clear all tabs. To clear existing tab stops and restore the default tabs, choose Default.

To set a tab using the Tab Set dialog box, take the following steps:

1. Select a tab type from the Tab Type drop-down list.
2. Specify a position (in fractions of inches) that you want in the Tab Position box.
3. Choose Set.

Click OK when you finish working in the Tab Set dialog box.

▶ **See** "Outlining a Document," **p. 146**
▶ **See** "Using Styles," **p. 151**

Setting Margins

You can change the margins at any point in a document. You may want to make the left and right margins smaller to add more room for text in columns, or you may want to set one-half inch top and bottom margins when you use page headers and footers. WordPerfect's Standard template uses 1-inch top and bottom margins and 1-inch left and right margins. Left and right margins can be set by dragging margin markers on the Ruler; all four margins can be set from the Margins dialog box or with the guidelines, as described in the next section.

▶ **See** "Using Headers and Footers," **p. 101**

NOTE To make your margin change affect all elements of the document–including text, page headers, and footers–choose Format, Styles. Within the Style List dialog box, highlight DocumentStyle and click Edit. Within the Styles Editor dialog box, choose Format, Margins, and set the Margins you want. Click OK. Click the Use as Default check box before you click OK to close the Styles Editor, then click Close to close the Style List dialog box.

If no text is selected when you set left and right margins, changes take place from the beginning of the current paragraph. Similarly, when you set top and bottom margins, changes take place from the beginning of the current page. Margin changes apply to all following text until another margin code is reached. Alternatively, if text is selected when you change margins, margin changes apply only to selected text.

Setting Margins Using Guidelines You can optionally see gray lines in your editing window that show you where the margins are. They are called guidelines. You can turn the display of guidelines on and off by choosing View, Guidelines.

You can quickly adjust all four of the margins using the guidelines, as follows:

1. Select text or position your insertion point as needed.
2. To adjust the left or right margin, drag the appropriate guideline to the desired position. As you drag the guideline, you will see the margin setting in a tiny pop-up window, as shown in Figure 5.20.

Setting Margins with the Ruler If you prefer, you can also quickly adjust left and right margins using the Ruler:

1. Select text or position your insertion point as needed.
2. If it is not already displayed, choose View, Ruler to display the Ruler.
3. To adjust the left or right margin, drag the appropriate margin marker to the desired position (symbols for the margin markers are identified earlier in Figure 5.19). The left margin marker is the outside marker at the left end of the white space in the

Ruler. The right margin marker is the outside marker at the right end of the white space. As you drag a marker, its position is indicated on the Application Bar and a vertical dotted line marks its position.

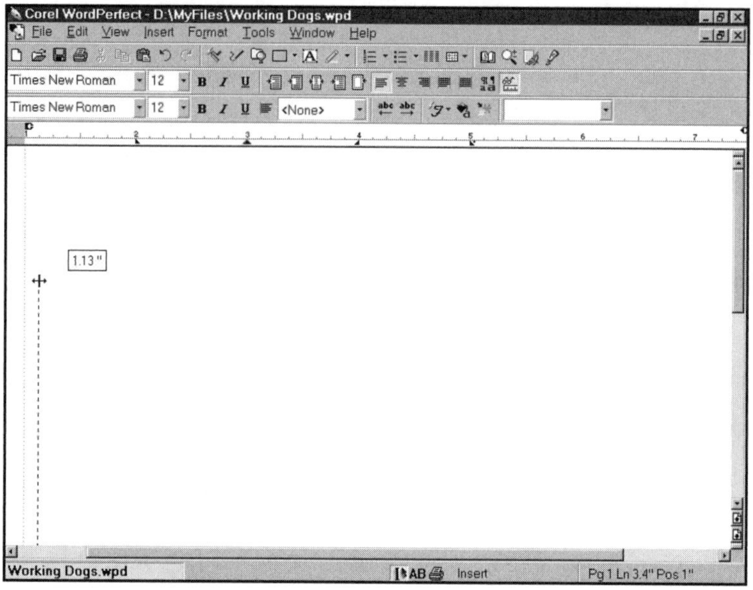

FIG. 5.20
You can drag the guidelines to set margins. When you do, the margin setting appears in a small pop-up window.

Setting Margins from the Page Setup Dialog Box You can specify precise margins from the Page Setup dialog box using the following steps:

1. Select text or position your insertion point as needed.
2. To access the Page Setup dialog box, choose Format, Margins. You see the Page Margins tab (see Figure 5.21).
3. Enter the new settings in the appropriate text box areas.
4. When you finish adjusting margins, choose OK.

Setting Justification

Justification is the way that text is aligned relative to the left and right margins on the page. The way you justify text can make the text easy to read, decorative, eye-catching, formal and sophisticated, or casual and flexible. WordPerfect provides five main types of justification: Left (the default), Center, Right, Full, and All (see Figure 5.22).

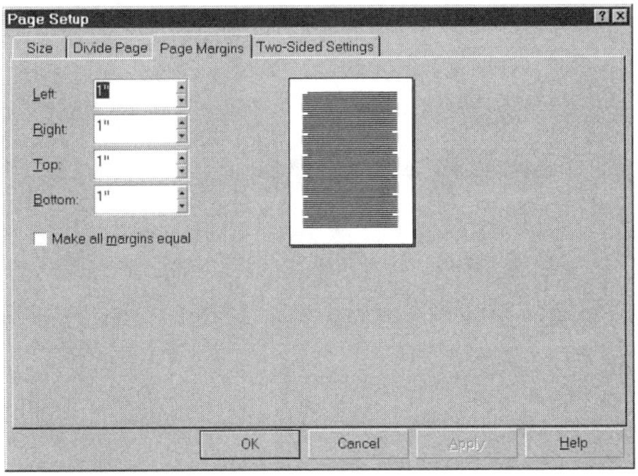

FIG. 5.21
Specify precise margins from the Page Setup dialog box.

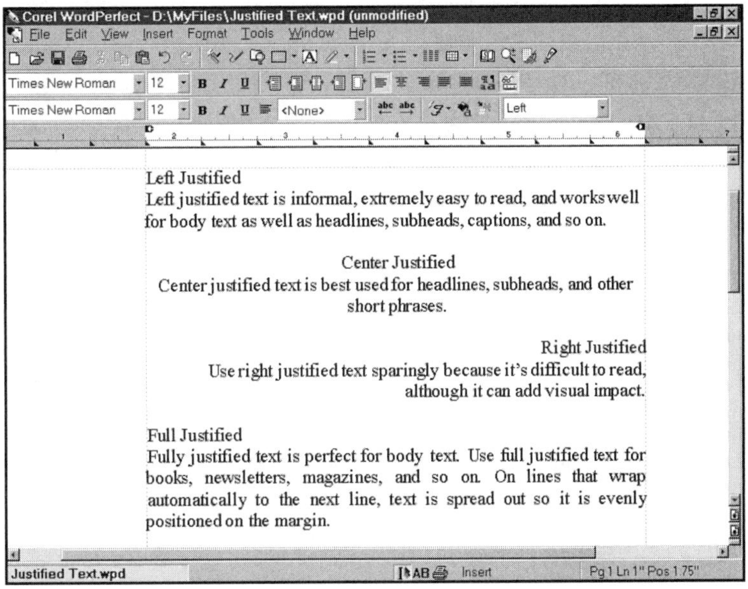

FIG. 5.22
WordPerfect offers five types of justification: Left, Center, Right, and Full are pictured here.

NOTE Full and All both produce text that is aligned with both the left and right margins. The difference is in how spaces are inserted. Full justification inserts spaces between words; All inserts spaces between words and between letters within words. All also aligns all lines of text including the last line, which ends with a hard return.

If you have text selected when you set justification, the justification will apply only to the selected text. Otherwise, it will apply from the paragraph the insertion point is in until it reaches another justification command. To set justification, follow these steps:

1. Select text or position your insertion point as needed.
2. Click the Justification button on the Property Bar, and choose the justification style you desire.

NOTE If you want all your new documents to use a justification that is different from the default, change the default justification. Choose Format, Styles. Within the Style List dialog box, highlight DocumentStyle and click Edit. Within the Styles Editor dialog box, choose Format, Justification, and select the justification that you want. Click the Use as Default check box before you click OK to close the Styles Editor. Click Close to close the Style List dialog box.

TROUBLESHOOTING

I used a Double Indent to indent a quotation in my document, but I want the text to go further in from the margins. Position the insertion point in front of the indented text and create another Double Indent. This indents the text by one more tab stop.

I set customized tab stops for columns of text and now, at the end of the document, my bulleted list doesn't look right. Position the insertion point at the end of the columns of text and restore the default tab settings (choose Format, Line, Tab Set, Default, OK).

I tried to adjust the customized tab settings that I created for columns of text, but now the columns don't line up evenly. You can undo the damage with the Undo button. Before you adjust tab settings again, be sure to position the insertion point on the first line of the text that you want to adjust.

I used full justification in my document, and now there are big gaps between words. Try using All rather than Full justification, because All will put spaces between letters as well as between words. Another way to alleviate the problem is to turn on Hyphenation by choosing Tools, Language, Hyphenation, Turn Hyphenation On. For more information on using hyphenation, see Hyphenation in the WordPerfect online Help.

Copying Formats

QuickFormat makes it easy to copy formats from already formatted text without respecifying each format instruction. Suppose that you took pains to apply several font changes to a subtitle to make it look just right. Now you want to give the same look to other subtitles. Just show QuickFormat where to copy the formats, and it does all of the work for you. When you choose to format headings, WordPerfect automatically updates all related headings formatted with QuickFormat. If you change your mind about the typeface in your heading, for example, you can change the font in one of the headings, and your change is instantly reflected in the others.

N O T E You can apply more than one set of QuickFormat formats in the same document. ▪

To use QuickFormat, first select the text that contains the formats that you want to copy, or place the insertion point in the paragraph whose formats you want to copy. Next, click the QuickFormat button on the WordPerfect 8 toolbar, or choose Format, QuickFormat. The QuickFormat dialog box appears (see Figure 5.23).

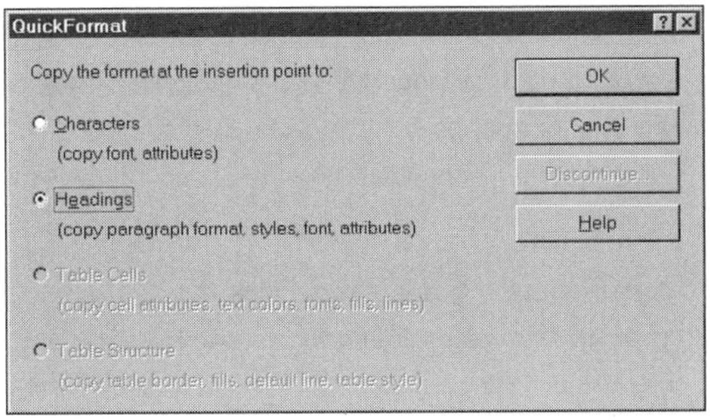

FIG. 5.23
Choose Headings from the QuickFormat dialog box to copy paragraph formatting as well as fonts and attributes. Choose Characters to copy fonts and attributes only.

Select Headings to copy fonts and attributes as well as paragraph formatting. When you choose OK, the mouse pointer changes to a paint roller or a paint brush, depending on whether you chose to format characters (brush) or headings (roller). Figure 5.24 shows you the paint roller pointer while QuickFormat is active.

Part
II
Ch
5

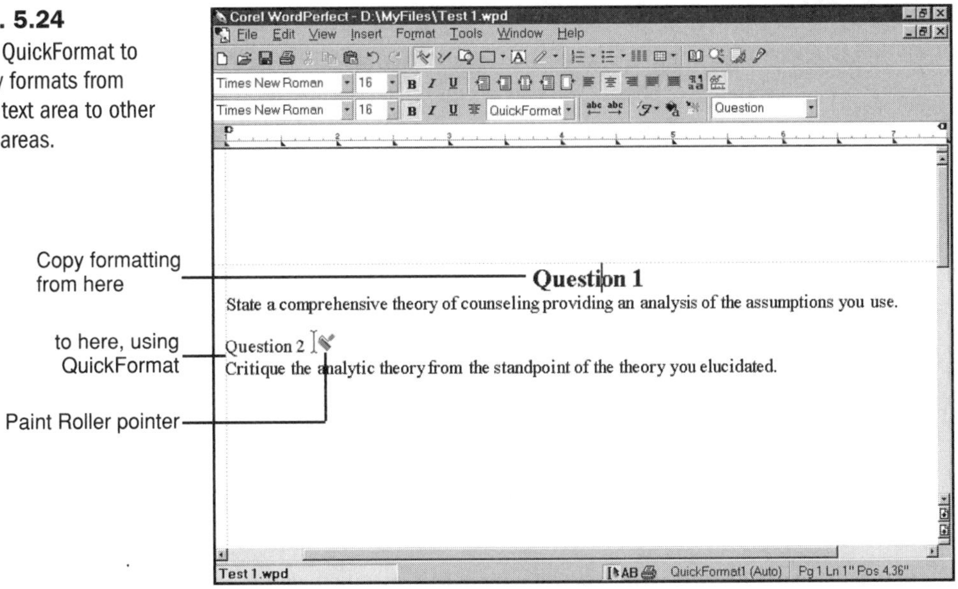

FIG. 5.24
Use QuickFormat to copy formats from one text area to other text areas.

Copy formatting from here

to here, using QuickFormat

Paint Roller pointer

While QuickFormat is active, select any text to which you want to copy formats, or click in a paragraph to which you want to copy formats. Repeat this step as often as desired. When you finish copying formats, click the QuickFormat button to deactivate the feature. The new format is applied to all of the selected paragraphs and the pointer returns to its I-beam appearance.

TROUBLESHOOTING

I indented a paragraph, but it doesn't look right. Remember that you should only use Indent once at the beginning of the paragraph to indent the entire paragraph. If you used Indent again anywhere else in the paragraph, this may be what caused your problem. Either delete the paragraph and retype it, or remove any extraneous `[Hd Left Ind]` codes (choose View, Reveal Codes to turn on Reveal Codes).

I used QuickFormat to copy formats to text in several locations, but after I finished, I accidentally copied them to an extra place. When you choose Headings at the QuickFormat dialog box, it's easy to copy formats; simply click in the paragraph that you want to format. However, it's also easy to click inadvertently and to format text unintentionally before you remember to turn off QuickFormat. The damage is easily reversed by clicking the Undo button, even after you've turned off QuickFormat.

Formatting the Page

When you work with multiple-page documents, you may be concerned with the position of page breaks. You also probably want to use page headers or footers, and you might want to number pages. These topics can all be thought of as elements of page formatting. Page Size is also an element of page formatting, although this topic can just as easily apply to a single-page document as to a multiple-page document.

WordPerfect's page-formatting features are flexible and easy to use. You can change the appearance of the page to fit your text so that you present the most professional-looking document possible.

Working with Page Breaks

WordPerfect automatically divides your document into pages based on the formatting choices you make. These automatic page breaks are called soft page breaks. The position of a soft page break adjusts automatically as you edit a document and cannot be deleted.

Because it's often important to break a page at a specific location, WordPerfect offers ways to control where pages are divided. The simplest method for ensuring that a page break falls where you want it to fall, regardless of format changes, is to use the Page Break feature. A page break created with the Page Break feature is called a hard page break.

To create a hard page break, position the insertion point at the beginning of the first line that is to start on a new page, and press Ctrl+Enter, or choose Insert, New Page. All text following a hard page break automatically repaginates.

In Draft view, a hard page break appears as a double line across the screen; a soft page break appears as a single line across the screen. In Page view, soft page breaks and hard page breaks look exactly alike; each appears as a heavy line across the page.

NOTE When you remove hard page breaks from a document, start at the beginning of the document and work your way toward the end of the document. When you remove a page break, all text from that position on repaginates automatically, and you can adjust subsequent page breaks accordingly.

CAUTION

When you use hard page breaks too often, your document cannot easily be edited, because the page breaks wind up in the wrong position. Use hard page breaks only when pages should always end at the hard page break—at the end of chapters, for example.

A hard page break can be removed. To remove a hard page break, position the insertion point just in front of the page break and press Delete, or position the insertion point just after the page break and press Backspace. The Make It Fit feature is a good way to avoid using hard page breaks (see "Using Making It Fit" later in this chapter).

Using Headers and Footers

A header or footer is information that appears at the top or bottom of every page (or just on odd or even pages). You can save yourself a lot of work by creating headers and footers in multiple-page documents.

WordPerfect's headers and footers are easy to use and very flexible. A header or footer can include one or more lines of text, automatic page numbers, the document path and file name, graphic lines, and other graphic elements, as well as formatting such as tables or columns.

The amount of white space at the top or bottom of the page changes only when you change the top or bottom margin, not when you use headers or footers. When you use headers and footers, there is less room on the page for body text. Soft page breaks adjust automatically to allow room for headers and footers.

Headers and footers are visible on-screen in Page view or Two Page view. Even though you can't see a header or footer on-screen in Draft view, it will print.

WordPerfect provides two headers, Header A and Header B, and two footers, Footer A and Footer B, in case you want different headers or footers on odd and even pages. Unless you're printing on both sides of the paper, you only need one header or footer. The instructions that follow refer to Header A, but are the same as the instructions for Header B, Footer A, or Footer B. To create Header A, perform the following steps:

1. Position the insertion point on the page where you want the header to begin.
2. Right-click in the top margin, and then choose Header/Footer; or Choose Insert, Header/Footer. The Headers/Footers dialog box is displayed. Select Header A, if it's not already selected.
3. Choose Create. You are placed in a special editing screen for Header A (indicated in the title bar at the top of the screen). The Header/Footer Property Bar replaces the Main Property Bar that you usually see, and provides extra features for creating your header. If you're working in Page view or Two Page view, you can see the body text on-screen while you're working with your header. The insertion point is placed at the beginning of the header area, as shown in Figure 5.25.

FIG. 5.25
WordPerfect provides tools that make it easy to create and format headers and footers.

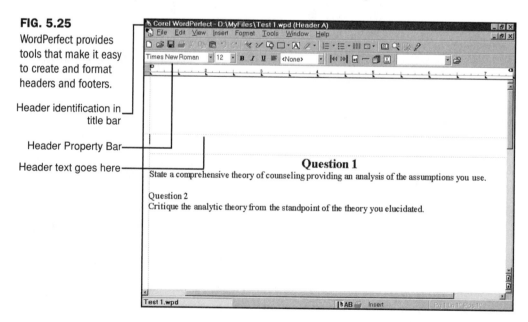

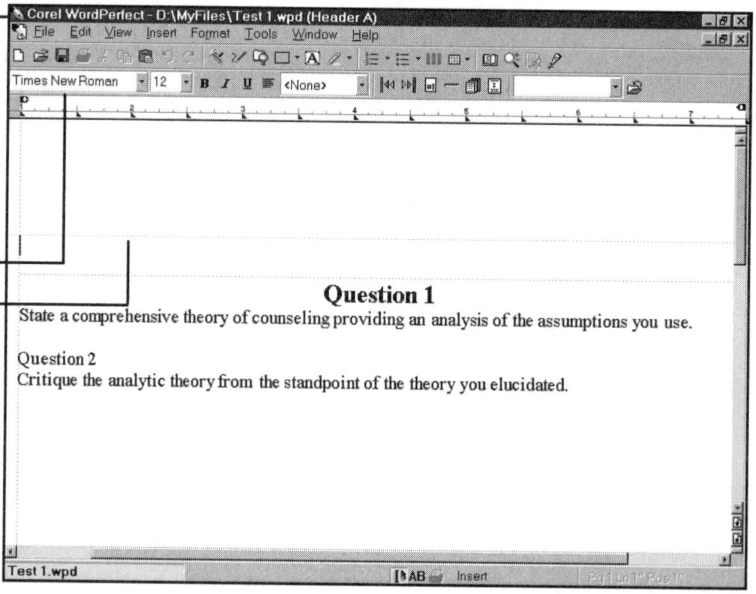

While you are creating a header or footer, you can insert a number of codes that provide information about your document:

- Choose Insert, Other, Path and Filename to insert the path and file name.
- Use the Center or Flush Right feature to place information appropriately within the header by clicking before the text, then choosing Format, Line, Center or Format, Line, Flush Right.
- To insert the current date, choose Insert, Date/Time. You see the Date/Time dialog box. Highlight the Date/Time format you prefer. To insert a date that always displays the current date, check Automatic Update. Click Insert to insert the date in your header.

- Click the Page Numbering button, then choose Page Number to insert automatic page numbers at the insertion point.

- Click the Horizontal Line button to insert a horizontal graphics line that extends from margin to margin at the baseline of text on the current line.

- Click the Header/Footer Placement button on the Property Bar to specify whether the header or footer should be on odd pages, even pages, or all pages.

- Click the Header/Footer Distance button on the Property Bar to adjust the distance between text in the header and text on the page.

- Click the Header/Footer Prev button on the Property Bar to edit the previous header or footer, if there is one.

- Click the Header/Footer Next button on the Property Bar to edit the next header or footer if there is one.

4. Use the WordPerfect menu bar, the toolbar, and the Property Bar as needed to format and edit your header.
5. When you finish working in the header editing screen, click the Close button on the feature bar.

NOTE To edit a header or footer, switch to Page view by choosing View, Page. You will be able to see the header or footer at the top or bottom of the page. Click in the header or footer to edit it, or delete the text in it to delete it.

Numbering Pages

Although you can insert page numbers in headers or footers, you also have the capability to number pages with the Page Numbering feature. The page number prints in the top or bottom line of the text area. WordPerfect inserts a blank line to separate the number from other text on the page. In Page view, page numbering is visible on-screen. To suppress page numbering, see the later section "Suppressing Headers, Footers, and Page Numbering."

Choosing a Page Number Format To use the Page Numbering feature, you must specify a format for the numbering. Choose Format, Page, Numbering. The Select Page Numbering Format dialog box appears. Figure 5.26 illustrates the Select Page Numbering Format dialog box with Bottom Center as the selected position. Dashes can be added on either side of the number by selecting the appropriate format in the Page Numbering Format box. Choose OK to close the dialog box.

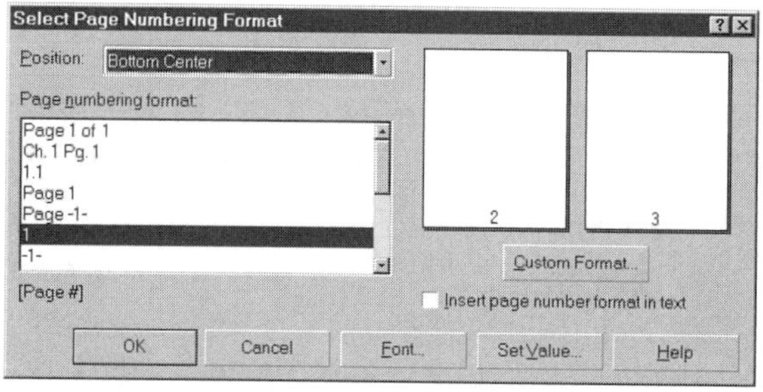

FIG. 5.26
Add page numbers to your document with the Page Numbering Format feature.

Changing the Page Number Value By default, WordPerfect uses the physical page number as the page number value. The page number value is the number that will print, whether you ask for page numbering in a header or footer or whether you ask for it with the Page Numbering feature. When you have a title page at the beginning of your document, you need to change the page number value on the first page of body text so that WordPerfect thinks of that page as page 1.

This feature is useful for documents that will be interleaved with other documents—such as charts, maps—to create a presentation, annual report, and more. The pages of the WordPerfect document may end up being numbered 1, 5-12, 27-38, 74, for example, and the user can specify where to start numbering each time.

To change the page number value, position the insertion point on the page to be renumbered, then choose Format, Page, Numbering to display the Select Page Numbering Format dialog box. Click Set Value to display the Values dialog box (see Figure 5.27). In the Page tab, set the page number, and then click OK to close the Values dialog box. Click OK again to return to the main editing window.

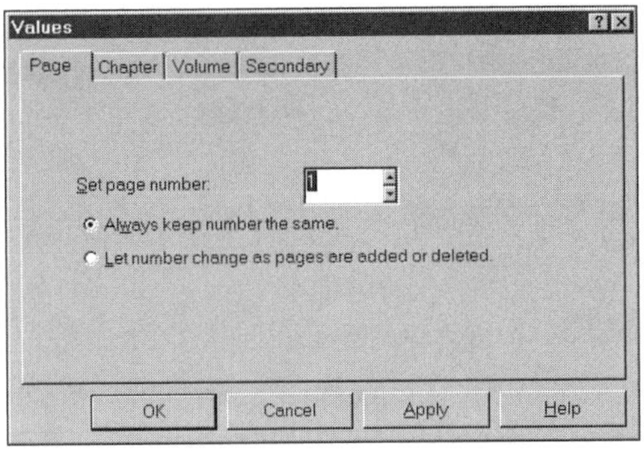

FIG. 5.27 You can change the initial page number to account for title pages and tables of contents in the Values dialog box.

NOTE You can also set the number of your chapter, volume, or secondary pages using this dialog box. This can be useful when creating large manuscripts or books. You can insert your chapter, volume, or secondary page number from the Select Page Numbering Format dialog box by choosing Format, Page, Numbering.

Suppressing Headers, Footers, and Page Numbering

To keep a header, footer, or page number from printing on a specific page, use WordPerfect's Suppress feature. A header or footer typically is created on the first page of body text, although it may be suppressed on that page. Headers and footers are usually suppressed on title pages at the beginning of new sections in a long document.

To suppress headers, footers, and page numbering, perform the following steps:

1. Position the insertion point on the page where you want to suppress the header/ footer page numbering.
2. Choose Format, Page, Suppress. The Suppress dialog box shown in Figure 5.28 is displayed.

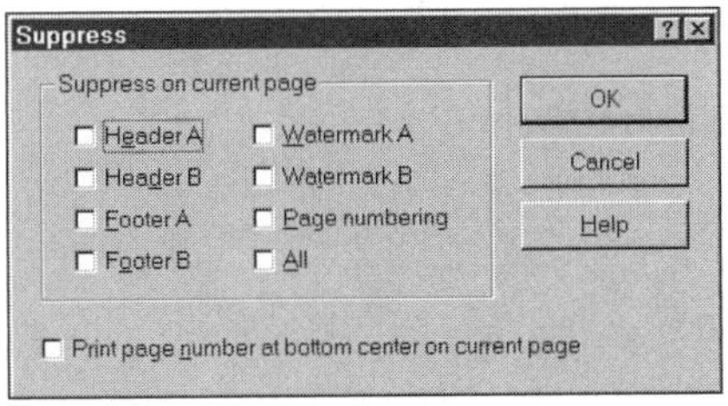

FIG. 5.28 Suppress headers, footers, or page numbering on the current page in the Suppress dialog box.

3. Click beside the features that you want to suppress on the current page.
4. Choose OK.

NOTE WordPerfect's Delay Codes feature provides you with a method for delaying the effects of headers and footers (and other types of formatting) for a specified number of pages. Use Delay Codes by choosing Format, Page, Delay Codes. Specify the number of pages to delay in the Delay Codes dialog box, and then choose OK. Insert codes such as headers and footers, and then click Close on the Delay Codes Feature Bar.

Changing the Page Size

Whenever you start a new, empty document with the Standard template, you're using the Letter page size (8 1/2×11-inch paper in a portrait orientation). To use a different physical size or a different orientation, specify another page size with WordPerfect's Page Size feature. For example, if you need a lot of page width for a table with many columns, you could choose Letter Landscape as your page size.

CAUTION

Your printer must be able to use the size paper you select and print that size paper in the orientation you select, or you may get unpredictable results.

To change the Page Size, follow these steps:

1. Position the insertion point on the first page where you want to specify a page size.
2. Choose Format, Page, Page Setup. Ensure that the Size tab is selected. The Page Setup dialog box appears (see Figure 5.29).

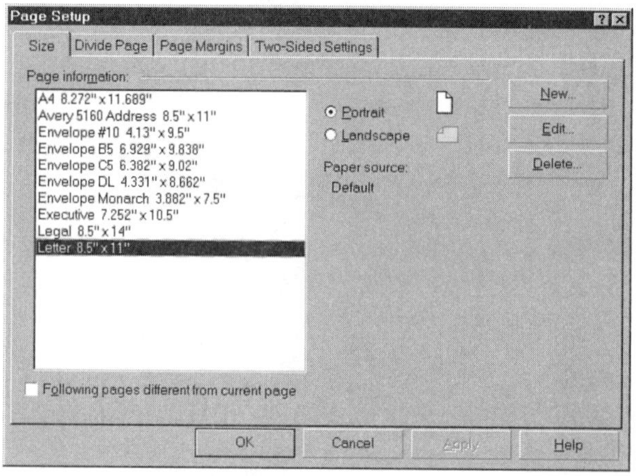

FIG. 5.29
Select your page definition in the Page Setup dialog box.

3. Select the paper size that you want from a list of predefined page definitions.
4. Choose OK. The selected page size takes effect on the current page.

TROUBLESHOOTING

I created a hard page break, but now I have too many page breaks. Make sure you're working in Draft view so that you can see which page breaks are hard page breaks (you can't remove a soft page break). Position the insertion point just in front of a hard page break and press Delete to remove it. Alternatively, turn on Reveal Codes so that you can delete the code (see the previous section, "Working with the Reveal Codes Window," in this chapter).

I asked for Page Numbering on the first page where I wanted it, and the number that prints is not 1. Unless you change the page number value, the number that prints is the same as the physical page number. Position the insertion point on the page that you want numbered with a 1, and change the page number value to 1 (after choosing Format, Page, Numbering, Set Value).

Using Make It Fit

It's easy to make a document fit on the page when you use the Make It Fit feature. Instead of making endless trial-and-error adjustments to margins, font size, and line spacing, let Make It Fit do it all for you. You get a perfect fit every time. You tell WordPerfect what kind of adjustments to make; if you don't like the results, Undo them and try Make It Fit with another set of specifications.

To use Make It Fit, take the following steps:

1. In an open document, choose Format, Make It Fit. The Make It Fit dialog box is displayed (see Figure 5.30).

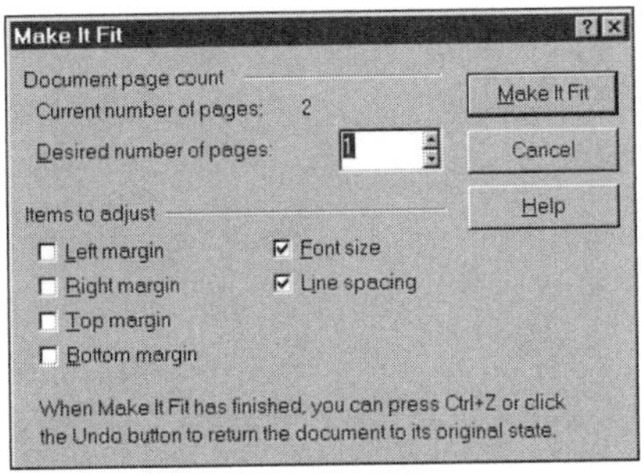

FIG. 5.30
The Make It Fit feature contracts or expands a document to a specified number of pages.

2. Specify the number of pages you want the finished document to be in the Desired Number of Pages box. For example, to make a document that is just barely too long for a single page fit on one page, specify 1 as the number of pages to fill.
3. Check the options that you want adjusted in the Items to Adjust area.

4. Choose Make It Fit.
5. Check the results to see if they're satisfactory. Remember that you can zoom back and forth from a Full Page view with the Zoom button. If you don't like the results, click Undo and repeat these steps with different adjustments.

CHAPTER 6

Using Writing Tools and Printing

Corel WordPerfect supplies a variety of tools that make it easy to create professionally finished documents without errors. By simply selecting a project and filling in the blanks, you can quickly create fax forms, memos, daily planners, and many other standard documents. In addition to supplying you with preformatted documents, Corel WordPerfect provides a variety of powerful proofreading tools. You can check spelling and correct errors automatically. You can keep your text from being monotonous and repetitive by finding alternative words with the Thesaurus. You can use the grammar checker to suggest improvements to your writing style.

With all of these writing tools at your fingertips, you can create error-free, well-written documents that look as though they were created by a professional editor. Corel WordPerfect takes care of much of the tiresome detail work of formatting, manual proofreading, and evaluating your writing style.

Once you finish your document, you can print it. Corel WordPerfect provides features that make it easy to print envelopes and mailing labels as well as documents. ■

Use projects and templates

Learn about templates and PerfectExpert projects that automate the preparation of many types of business documents.

Check your spelling

See how Corel WordPerfect offers sophisticated spell checking, including automatic correction of common errors, and an indicator that shows you misspellings as you type.

Use the Thesaurus

Corel WordPerfect's Thesaurus doesn't just provide synonyms. Use this complete dictionary to define common words.

Check your grammar

Learn to select the writing style you want, and let Corel WordPerfect tell you how you're doing.

Print your document, envelopes, and labels

Understand how to easily print part or all of your document to any available printer, as well as envelopes for your letters and Avery labels.

Introducing Templates and Projects

Every new document that you create is based on a template. A *template* is a master document that contains formatting codes that your new document will be based on. It can also contain standard text for the document, macros, styles, keyboard definitions, and anything else that any other WordPerfect document can.

When you create a new document by choosing File, New, you see a list of common documents. Projects you have recently used appear at the top of the project list.

These documents are based on different WordPerfect templates. Many of them also contain further PerfectScript programming commands that provide help in building the document; remember your preferences for previous documents.

Because these templates are often augmented with additional features, Corel has given them a special name. They are called *PerfectExpert projects.*

In fact, no matter what WordPerfect Office Suite application you are in, you see the same list of projects when you choose File, New. In WordPerfect, the WordPerfect projects are initially selected, while in Quattro Pro, at first you see the Quattro Pro projects. However, you can select projects from any suite application, or see the entire list of them.

You can also access the project list by clicking the Corel PerfectExpert button on the taskbar.

NOTE Projects consist of a combination of templates with what were termed *experts* and *coaches* in previous versions of WordPerfect.

Using Projects

There are a number of different projects supplied with WordPerfect: projects related to business, education, legal documents, personal documents, publishing, and Web documents.

Some projects are further automated with dialog boxes that ask you a series of questions before constructing your document. That way, you can customize the document to your tastes and needs.

Using projects can be an easy and even fun way to create great-looking documents, once you've started using them. To demonstrate how easy they are, the following steps show you how to use a common project—preparing a memo:

1. Choose File, New. You see the New dialog box shown in Figure 6.1.
2. Ensure that the [Corel WordPerfect 8] group is selected, and then select Memo in the list box.

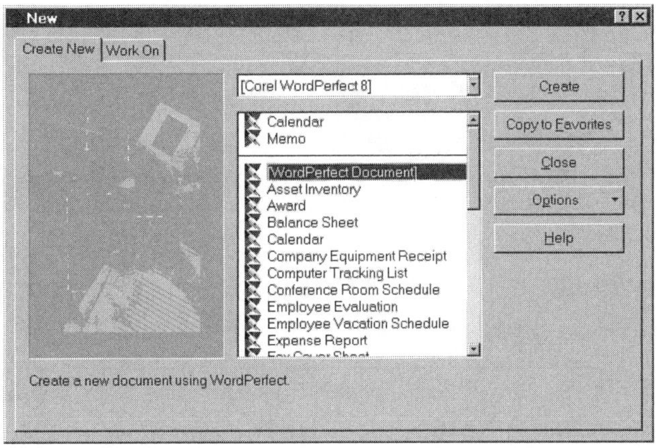

FIG. 6.1 WordPerfect comes with projects to help you create many different types of documents.

TIP The first time you use a template, you see the Personalize Your Templates dialog box that allows you to enter personal information about yourself and your organization. This is discussed in Chapter 28, "Using Corel Address Book 8."

3. Assuming you have entered your personal information, after a few seconds, you see the formatted memo in the background and the PerfectExpert window pane at the left, as shown in Figure 6.2.

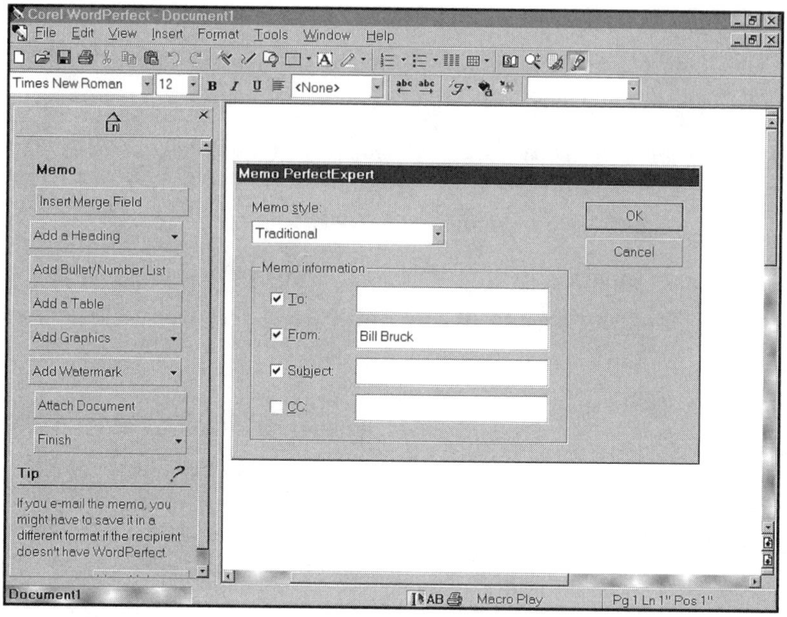

FIG. 6.2
The Memo project allows you to modify various elements of the memo you are creating.

4. Choose the style for your memo in the Memo Style drop-down list box.
5. Fill out the To, From, Subject, and the CC: boxes.

TIP You can also use the Address Book for this information in some projects, as discussed in Chapter 28, "Using Corel Address Book 8."

6. Choose OK. The memo is created as shown in Figure 6.3, and you can add text to it and edit it as needed.
7. Use the buttons in the PerfectExpert pane to complete additional tasks, such as inserting merge fields, attaching documents to your memo, or finishing it by spell checking, printing, faxing, or e-mailing it.

Once you've used the Memo project, using other projects is simple. Merely choose File, New, pick the category of your project, then select the project you want to use. You'll be prompted for certain information, then your document will be created. It's that simple.

For example, creating a calendar is easy with a PerfectExpert project. To do so, choose File, New. Select the WordPerfect group, then choose Calendar. You see the Calendar PerfectExpert dialog box shown in Figure 6.4.

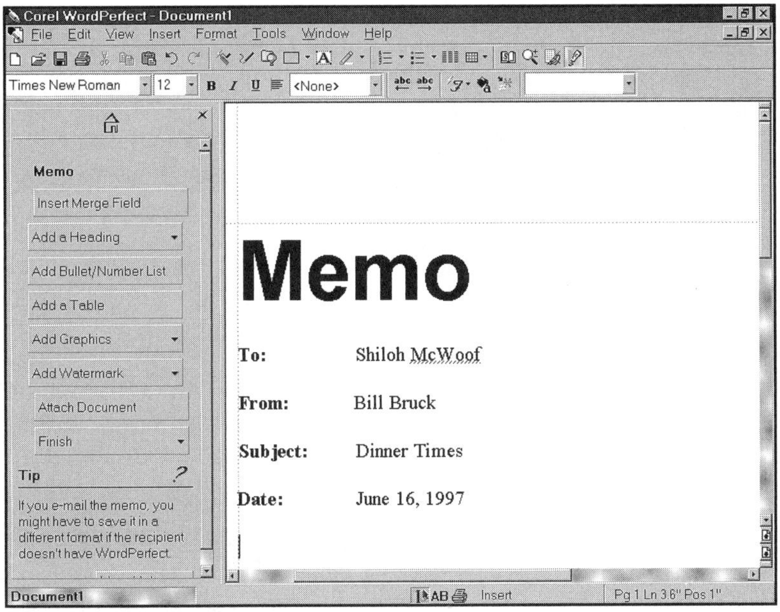

FIG. 6.3
Your memo is created using the information you have provided.

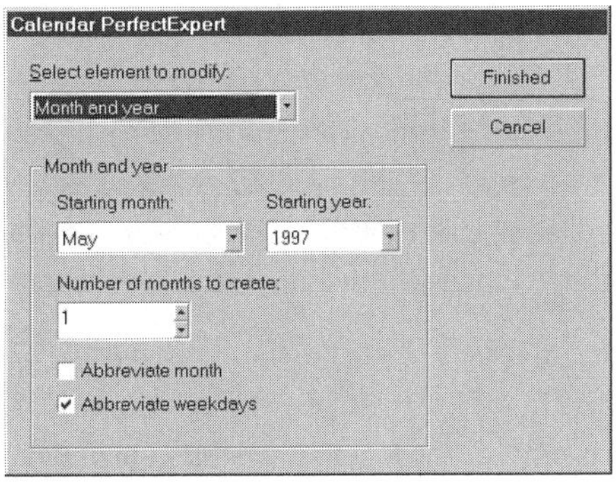

FIG. 6.4
Many projects use a template information dialog box, which allows you to enter information that will be placed in the document you create.

After you enter the information and choose OK, you see the calendar, like the one shown in Figure 6.5.

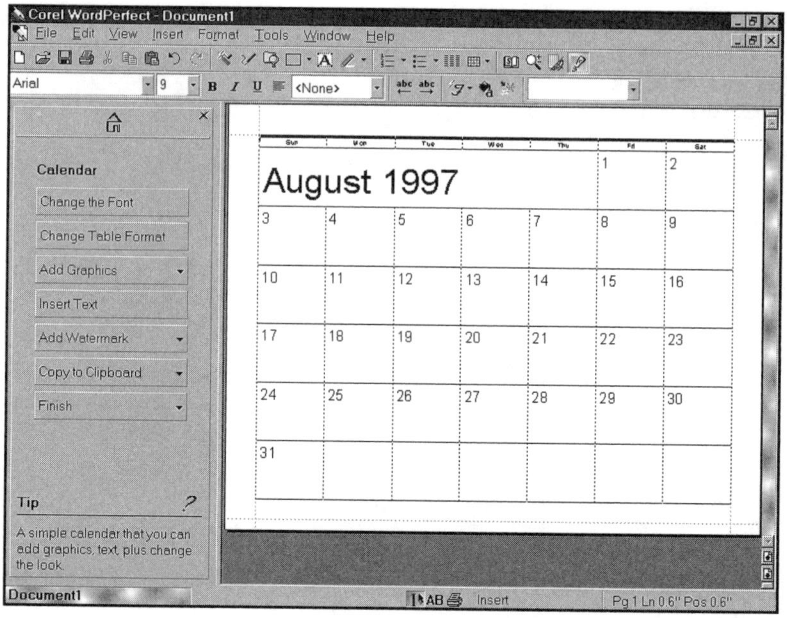

FIG. 6.5
You can create a calendar with a project.

Checking Spelling

The *Spell Checker* is the single most important proofreading tool you can use. No matter how long or short a document is, using the Spell Checker is well worth the time it takes. Just think, "How do you feel about the person who sends you a letter with a typo or a spelling error?" Don't let this happen when someone else receives your letter.

The Spell Checker looks for misspelled words, duplicate words, and irregular capitalization. When it finds a word with one of these problems, it stops and offers suggestions. You can choose to replace the problem word, skip to the next problem, or select one of several other options for each word where the WordPerfect dictionary finds an inconsistency.

WordPerfect includes two additional features that help you with your spelling. *Spell-As-You-Go* shows your spelling errors as you type; *QuickCorrect* corrects spelling mistakes as you make them.

Using Spell-As-You-Go

If Spell-As-You-Go is selected, spelling errors will be shown to you as you type. As soon as you press the space bar after misspelling a word, the misspelled word will appear with a red wavy underline.

To activate the Spell-As-You-Go feature, choose Tools, Proofread, Spell-As-You-Go.

You can easily correct the word immediately by right-clicking it. You see a pop-up menu that provides alternate spelling choices, as shown in Figure 6.6.

FIG. 6.6
When you right-click a misspelled word, you see alternate spellings and other correction option choices.

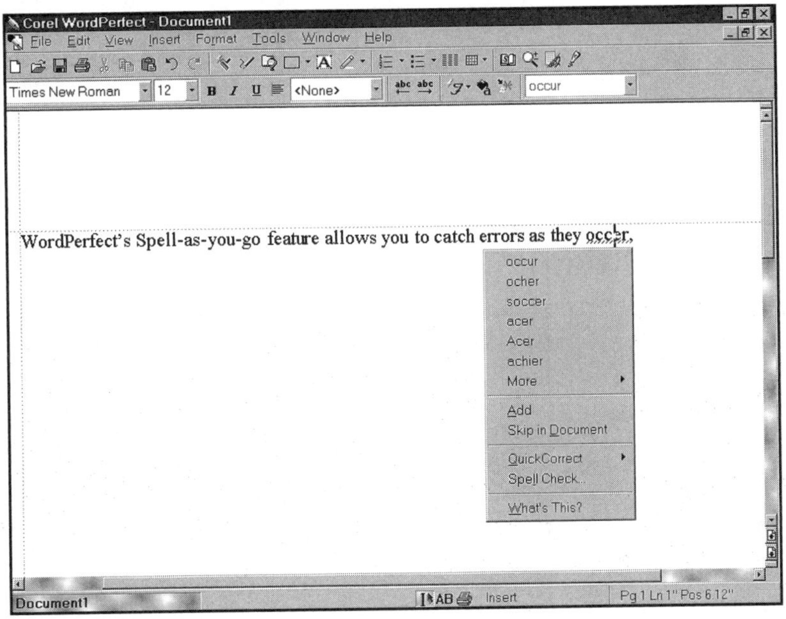

You can use the following options for the misspelled word:

- Click any alternate word choice to replace the misspelled word with a correctly spelled one.
- Choose Add to add the word to your spelling dictionary. It will never be marked as misspelled again.

CAUTION

Be careful in adding words to your dictionary. Don't add acronyms that would prevent the dictionary from finding a commonly misspelled word, and try not to add hundreds of words (such as names you'll only use infrequently) that can slow down your spell checking.

- Choose Skip in Document to ignore future occurrences of the misspelled word in the current document.
- Choose Spell Check to start the spell checker (see the upcoming section "Using the Spell Checker").

Using the Spell Checker

To start the Spell Checker, click the Spell Check button, or choose Tools, Spell Check and confirm that the Spell Checker tab is selected. The Spell Checker dialog box tab shown in Figure 6.7 appears. The first problem found is both selected in the text and displayed in the dialog box, with a list of suggestions for replacement. Table 6.1 describes options in the Spell Checker dialog box.

FIG. 6.7
Select a word in the Replacements list, or enter the correct word in the Replace With box to correct the mistake in the text.

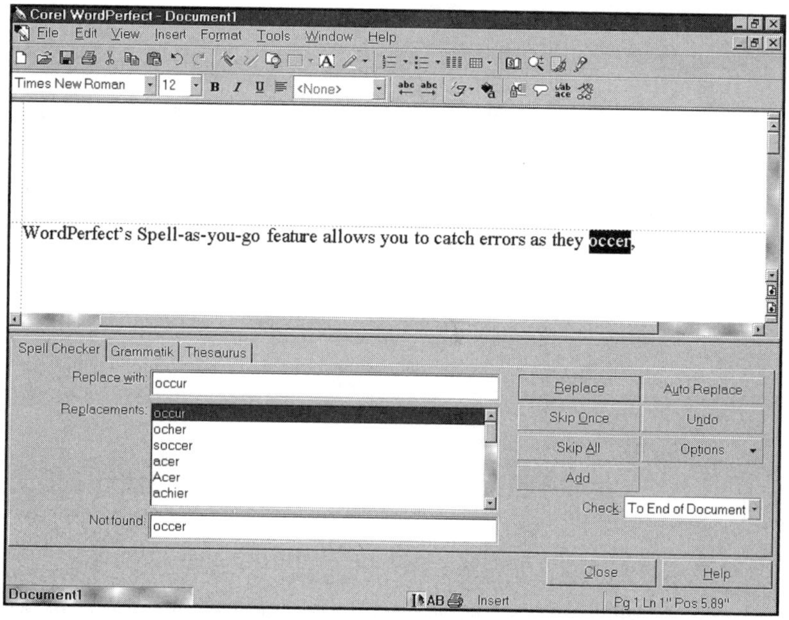

Table 6.1 Spell Checker Options

Option	Description
Not Found	Displays the word in question.
Replace With	Displays the selected suggested spelling. If this is incorrect, enter correct spelling in this text box.
Replacements	Selects a word to replace the misspelled word. After clicking the correct word, it will then appear in the Replace With box.
Replace	Replaces the word in the Not Found box with the text specified in the Replace With box.
Skip Once	Skips this occurrence and moves to the next problem.
Skip All	Skips all occurrences of this word in this spell check session.

Option	Description
AutoReplace	Replaces the word with the word in the Replace With box, and adds the error and the replacement word to the QuickCorrect list. (See the following section "Using QuickCorrect" for more information.)
Undo	Undoes the last correction.
Add	Adds the word to the default supplemental dictionary. Use this option to add frequently used proper nouns (like your name or street address) so the Spell Checker won't stop on them again.
Options	Customizes spell checking options.
Check	Specifies the portion of the document to be spell checked.
Close	Closes the Spell Checker.

If the problem word contains a capitalization error, WordPerfect displays a Capitalization box instead of the Not Found box. Select the correct suggestion, or type it into the Replace With box, then choose Replace.

If the problem word is a duplicate word, WordPerfect displays a Duplicate Words box instead of a Not Found box, and suggests that you replace the duplicate word with a single word. You can replace or skip to the next problem.

TIP If you select text before starting the Spell Checker, only the selected text is spell-checked.

Using QuickCorrect

QuickCorrect saves time and effort by correcting common spelling errors as you make them. QuickCorrect replaces the error with the correct spelling (or the correct capitalization) as soon as you move past the misspelled word. If, for example, you often type **teh** instead of **the**, QuickCorrect corrects the word as soon as you press the space bar, or as soon as you press another punctuation key (such as a comma, period, or semicolon). In addition to correcting spelling errors, QuickCorrect can automatically correct other problems, like double spacing between words. You can also program QuickCorrect to replace open and close quotes with typesetter-style quotes called *SmartQuotes.*

QuickCorrect has a built-in list of common misspellings and their correct spellings. You can add your own common misspellings to the list. QuickCorrect is just one of WordPerfect's many features that can be customized for the way you work.

To add items to the list of common misspellings and their corrections, or to change QuickCorrect options, choose Tools, QuickCorrect. The QuickCorrect dialog box is displayed as shown in Figure 6.8.

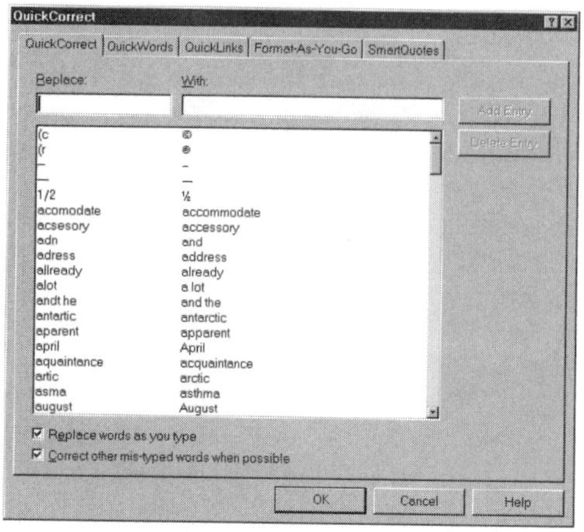

FIG. 6.8
The QuickCorrect dialog box is used to identify the common spelling errors that will be automatically corrected and their replacements.

Add an entry by typing what you want to correct in the Replace box, typing what you want the correction to be in the With box, and then choosing Add Entry.

TROUBLESHOOTING

I have a lot of words that contain numbers, such as measurements, in my document. I want the Spell Checker to skip these words. Choose Options from the Spell Checker dialog box, then deselect Check Words with Numbers.

I want to remove a word that I inadvertently added to my dictionary. From the Spell Checker dialog box, choose Options, User Word Lists. Highlight the appropriate word list, then highlight the appropriate entry in the Word List Contents group. Choose Delete Entry, and then click Close to return to the Spell Checker dialog box.

Using QuickWords Abbreviations

If you like to do work efficiently, *QuickWords* abbreviations are for you. With QuickWords, you can define an abbreviation for words or phrases that you type often. As you type the abbreviation, it expands automatically—saving you time and keystrokes.

To create a QuickWord, do the following:

1. Type the expanded text for the abbreviation in your document.
2. Select the expanded text.
3. Choose Tools, QuickWords. You see the QuickWords tab of the QuickCorrect dialog box shown in Figure 6.9.

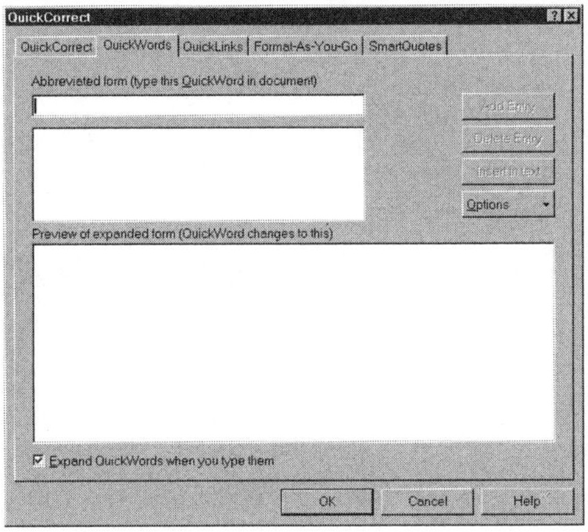

FIG. 6.9
Add abbreviations for frequently typed words with QuickWords.

4. Type the abbreviation in the Abbreviated Form (Type This QuickWord in Document) list box.
5. Choose Add Entry. You return to your document, and the abbreviation is added to the QuickWords list.

To use your new abbreviation, just type it in the document.

TIP Sometimes, short abbreviations like **b** will expand when you don't want them to. To avoid this, precede them with a period–such as **.b**–because this letter combination doesn't usually occur in documents.

You can easily delete or rename a QuickWord. To do so, access the QuickWords tab of the QuickCorrect dialog box by choosing Tools, QuickWords. Then do the following:

- To delete a QuickWord abbreviation, highlight it, then click Delete Entry.
- To rename it, choose Options, Rename Entry, then type the new name in the Rename QuickWord dialog box and click OK.

Using the Thesaurus

WordPerfect's Thesaurus can help you improve your composition skills. When you can't think of the word that means exactly what you want to say, or you think that you've used the same word too often, let the Thesaurus help you. The Thesaurus supplies a variety of alternatives (synonyms and antonyms) for the word you're looking up. You can choose the word you want from the list of alternatives and ask the Thesaurus to provide a replacement.

To find a synonym for a word:

1. Place the insertion point in the word.
2. Choose Tools, Thesaurus. The Thesaurus dialog box tab appears, as shown in Figure 6.10.

FIG. 6.10
Find alternate words or definitions with the Thesaurus.

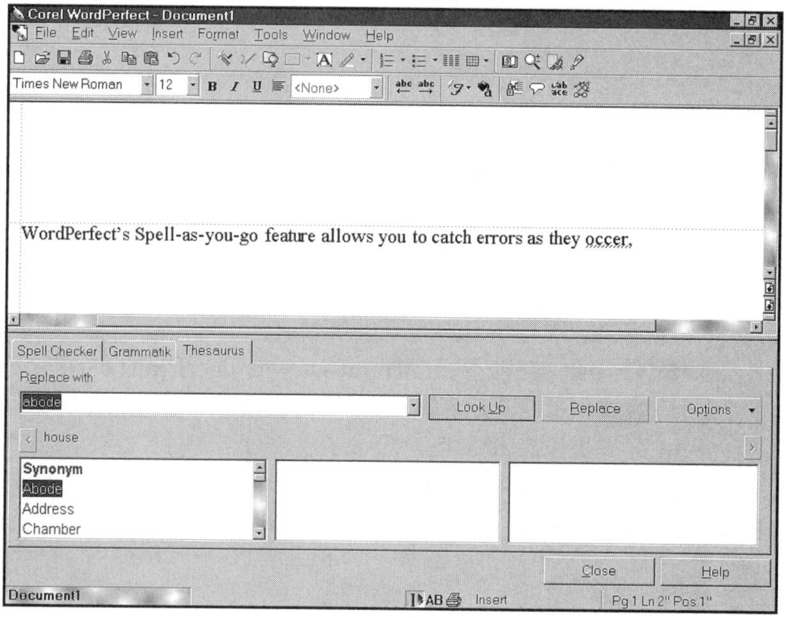

If available, synonyms and antonyms for the word appear in the leftmost column. The alternatives are divided into categories, such as Synonym, Related Words, and Antonym. (Use the scroll bars along each side of the box to see alternatives that are not visible.) Scroll through this box to view alternative definitions.

3. To look up synonyms for the displayed alternatives, double-click them.
4. Select the replacement you want to use, and then choose Replace. If you decide not to make a replacement, choose Close.

TROUBLESHOOTING

I looked up several meanings, and now I want to go back to the original word I looked up in the Thesaurus. Use the Replace With drop-down list to see the previous words you have looked up, then select the original word.

While I was using the Thesaurus, I thought of a different word that I wanted to look up. Can I do it without closing the Thesaurus and typing the word into the document? Type the word that you want to look up in the Replace With box, and then choose Look Up.

Checking Grammar

Grammatik is yet another proofreading feature that WordPerfect provides for you. Grammatik is a built-in grammar checker that checks your document for correct grammar, style, punctuation, and word usage, and thus catches many errors that would be bypassed by the Spell Checker. Grammatik checks both grammar and spelling; so you actually take care of grammar problems and spelling problems all at once.

Even if you don't think you have problems with your writing style, Grammatik may help you. When Grammatik points out a potential problem and explains the logic behind the problem, you may realize that its suggestions offer real improvement.

When Grammatik reports a potential grammar problem, you can review the error and suggestion, then decide whether to change the text.

To proofread your document with Grammatik, choose Tools, Grammatik. Proofreading begins and the first item for review brings up the Grammatik dialog box tab, as shown in Figure 6.11.

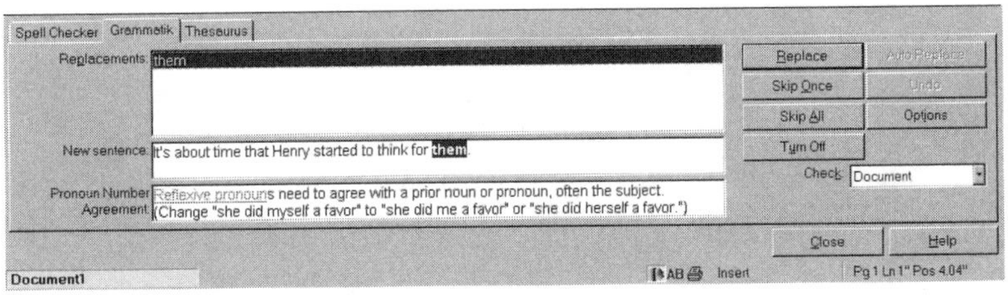

FIG. 6.11
Grammatik checks your word usage, punctuation, and sentence structure, as well as your spelling.

Correcting Errors

When Grammatik stops on a problem, you see information in the four boxes shown previously in Figure 6.11. The dialog box is dynamic, so the boxes and buttons will change slightly depending on the error that is found:

- The Replacements box shows choices for a new suggested word or phrase.
- The New Sentence box shows the new sentence as it will look.

- The bottom box shows information on the grammatical rule that is being applied. This box will change depending on the error found.
- The Check box shows you the area of the document that is being checked.

When Grammatik finds an error, you can respond with the options described in Table 6.2.

Table 6.2 Grammatik Options

Option	Description
Resume	This option appears after you pause Grammatik to edit the document. Click Resume to resume proofreading.
Replace	Replace the problem word or phrase with the suggested replacement that is listed in the New Sentence box.
Skip Once	Ignore the highlighted problem and move on to the next problem.
Skip All	Ignore the highlighted problem for the rest of this proofreading session.
Turn Off	Turn off the current rule.
Add	Add the word to the selected dictionary.
Auto Replace	Add the misspelled word and its replacement to the QuickCorrect list.
Undo	Undo your last replacement.
Options	Change Grammatik options, including the checking style.
Close	End the proofreading session.

In some cases, the grammatical problem might require manual editing. When this occurs, click in the document window and, using the scroll bar if necessary, edit the problem in the document window. When you finish your manual editing, choose Resume on the Grammatik tab.

Changing the Checking Style

The Grammatik checking style determines what is identified as a potential problem. For example, in a formal checking style, a contraction (such as `won't`) is identified as a potential problem. You can change the checking style to one that's best for your work.

To change the checking style for this session and future sessions:

1. Choose Options from the Grammatik dialog box.
2. Choose Checking Styles. You see the Checking Styles dialog box in Figure 6.12.

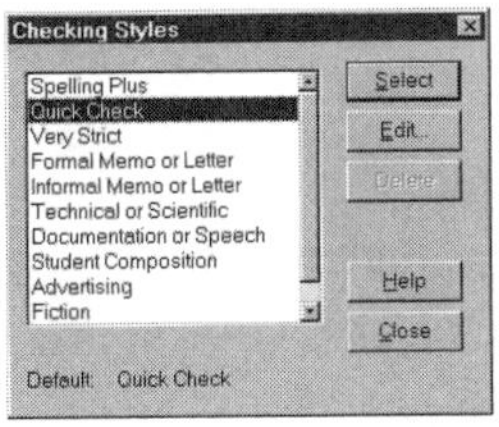

FIG. 6.12
Choose the checking style most appropriate for your writing style and the style of the document being checked.

3. To examine the rules for any style or to edit the style, select the checking style and choose Edit. You see the Edit Checking Styles dialog box shown in Figure 6.13.

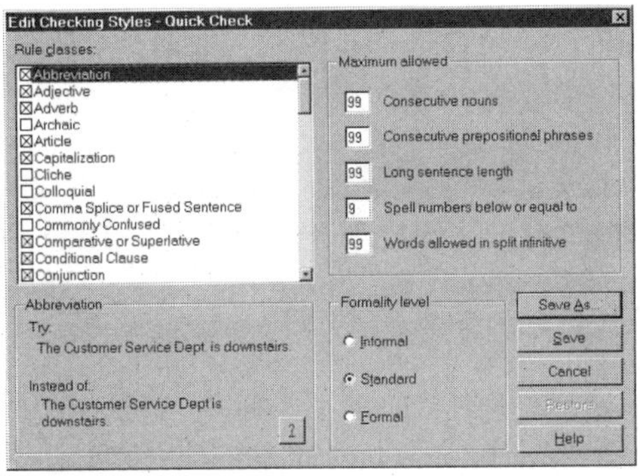

FIG. 6.13
Each editing style has different rules that are applied to the text being checked.

4. In the Edit Checking Styles dialog box, you can see which rule classes are selected for the style and other rules that apply to the style. To edit the style:
   - Check or uncheck the rule classes you want to use.
   - You may also select the numbers in any of the boxes in the Maximum Allowed section and type in new numbers.
   - Click the button of the Formality Level based on the type of document being checked and your writing style.
5. Save your changes with Save (to keep the same style name) or with Save As (to give the edited style a new name). You return to the Checking Styles dialog box.
6. Choose Close to return to the Grammatik tab.

Analyzing Your Writing

Grammatik can analyze your writing in a number of ways. If you choose Options, Analysis from the Grammatik tab, you can choose to parse the selected sentence, show which part of speech each word in the selected sentence is, or show how many words, sentences, and so on are in your document. You can even compare the readability of your document to an IRS form, a Hemingway short story, or the Gettysburg Address.

TROUBLESHOOTING

Grammatik keeps stopping on contractions (won't, you're, and so on) and I want it to skip them. You can either change the checking style to a less formal style, or you can turn off the rule with the Turn Off button located on the Grammatik tab.

Printing

Whether you use WordPerfect to create simple documents or desktop publishing masterpieces, printing is a task that you perform often. Because you are working in a WYSIWYG environment, what you print is not the mystery it was a few short years ago. If you're working in Draft view, you can see almost everything just as it will print. You can click the Page/Zoom Full button to get a quick look at a full page in Page view. Alternatively, you can use the View menu to switch to Page view.

Printing a Document

To print the document in the active window, click the Print button, or choose File, Print. The Print dialog box is displayed, as shown in Figure 6.14.

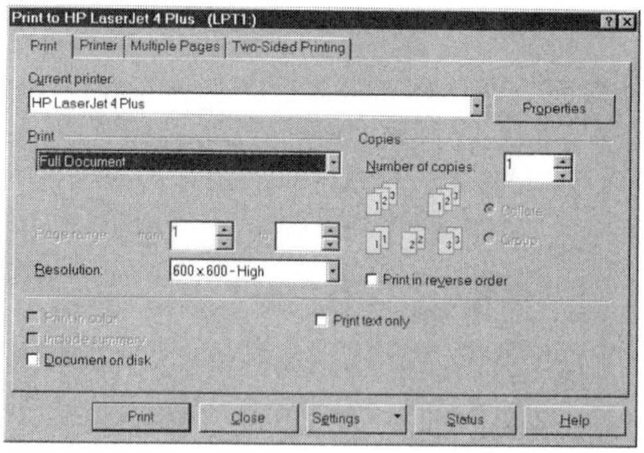

FIG. 6.14
You can set all the print options in the Print dialog box.

When you print a document, most often you will print using the default options in the Print dialog box, which print one copy of all the pages in the document. Switch between the Print, Printer, Multiple Pages, and Two-Sided Printer tabs of the dialog box to see all the print options. Table 6.3 describes options in the Print dialog box.

NOTE The exact tabs in this dialog box will vary according to the type of printer you have. Similarly, the options in Table 6.3 will vary.

Table 6.3 Important Print Options in the Print Dialog Box

Option	Description
Print	Select which parts of the document to print (Full Document, Current Page, Multiple Pages, Print Pages).
Resolution	Choose from available resolutions for your printer.
Print in Color	Use the color printing capability of your printer (if available).
Include Summary	Print the document summary as well as the document.
Document on Disk	Print a document on the disk rather than the document on the screen.
Number of Copies	Specify the number of copies.
Collate or Group	Print all pages of one copy together (versus print all copies of each page together).
Print in Reverse Order	This option is useful for some printers that cannot collate copies or which print "face up" output.
Print Text Only	Speed up printing by not printing graphics.

TIP You can print several files directly from the disk. Select all the files to be printed in the Open dialog box. Right-click them, and then choose Print.

NOTE If you have more than one printer on your system, you can choose which printer to use in the Printer tab of the Print dialog box.

The Multiple Pages tab allows you to specify exactly which pages will be printed. You can also use this tab to indicate that certain chapters or volumes of the document will be printed.

The Two-Sided Printing tab allows you to set two-sided printing options. If your printer supports two-sided (duplex) printing, you can set options for this here. If it doesn't, you can still manually print two-sided documents by specifying that the printer print the odd, then the even pages. Also use this tab to set options for binding *offsets* (the white space on the inside margin of the document).

The Settings button allows you to name and save printer settings, and to specify one set of printer settings as the default for this application. This can be useful if you prefer to have Quattro Pro or Presentations print landscape by default, or if you want to have a named setting for printing on both sides of the paper.

Printing an Envelope

WordPerfect's Envelope feature automatically formats and addresses your envelope for you. If you have already typed the inside address into a letter and you want an envelope for the letter, just choose Format, Envelope.

To address an envelope after typing a letter, follow these steps:

1. Choose Format, Envelope to open the Envelope dialog box shown in Figure 6.15.

FIG. 6.15
Corel WordPerfect's Envelope feature automatically formats and addresses your envelope.

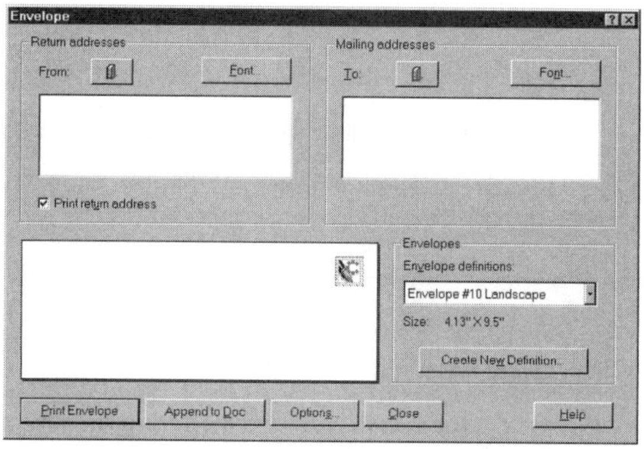

2. Check Print Return Address, then type your return address in the From box.
3. To change the font face or size used in the return address, choose the Font button in the return address section.

NOTE The font on an envelope is automatically taken from the document initial font (Format, Font, Initial Font). To save yourself the work of changing fonts twice—once in the document text and once in the envelope window—make sure that the document initial font is what you want both for the letter and the envelope.

4. To enter mailing address (if the mailing address is not automatically selected), type the recipient's name in the To box.

TIP You can also click the Address Book button to choose the return or mailing address from Corel Address Book. Using Corel Address Book is discussed further in Chapter 28.

5. As with the return address, you can change the font face or font size used in the mailing address.
6. Select the envelope size from the Envelope Definitions drop-down box.

7. If you want a USPS bar code printed on the envelope, or to change the vertical or horizontal position of the mailing address and/or return address, click the Options button and make the appropriate selections.
8. To print the envelope immediately, choose Print Envelope; to add the envelope to the document, choose Append to Doc.

TIP Choose Create New Definition to display the New Page Size dialog box. You can define a new envelope type, including its name, size, and orientation, in this dialog box. This is great for printing on odd-sized envelopes.

Printing Labels

WordPerfect makes it easy to print labels by showing you each label on-screen exactly as it will appear on the printed sheet. All you have to do is find and select the brand name and item number on WordPerfect's list of label types and then enter the names and addresses.

If you're printing three-across labels, you probably want to select a font that is smaller than the font you usually use for your documents; otherwise, long names and addresses may not fit on your labels.

Choosing a Label Definition To choose a label definition, take the following steps:

1. Place the insertion point at the beginning of an empty document or on a blank page.
2. Choose Format, Labels to open the Labels dialog box shown in Figure 6.16.

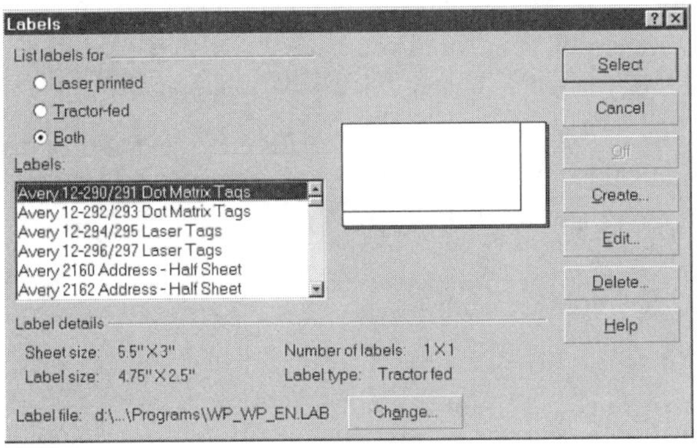

FIG. 6.16
Select the labels you want to print from WordPerfect's list of label types.

3. In the Labels list, choose the definition you want to use, then choose Select. An empty label is displayed on-screen.

Centering Text on Labels To center the name and address information vertically on each label so that it doesn't start at the top edge of the label, use Corel WordPerfect's Center Page feature.

To center all names and addresses between the top and bottom of each label:

1. Position the insertion point at the beginning of an empty document, or on the first label.
2. Choose Format, Page, Center.
3. In the Center Page(s) dialog box, choose Current and Subsequent Pages.
4. Choose OK.

Entering Text on Labels To understand how the Labels feature works, imagine that each separate label is a page, although there may be many labels on a single sheet of paper. Each label is treated as a logical page, although it may not be a physical page. This means that you can print page headers on each label, you can apply the Center Page(s) feature to all labels, and you can (and need to) create hard page breaks between labels. After choosing a label definition and determining if you want the labels centered:

1. Type the name and address as you want it to appear on the printed label.
2. At the end of each line, press Enter to move to the next line, but only if there are more lines to be typed for this label. If the line you just typed is the last line for this label, press Ctrl+Enter to create a hard page break.
3. Continue typing names and addresses (or other label text) and inserting hard page breaks after each label, until you have typed all the labels that you want to print. As you add each label, it appears on-screen exactly as it will print. Be careful not to press Enter after you type the last line of each label; this adds an unnecessary blank line and distorts the vertical centering. After you add several names and addresses, your screen may look like Figure 6.17.

FIG. 6.17
See your labels on-screen just as they will print. Lines are ended by pressing the Enter key; labels are separated by hard page breaks.

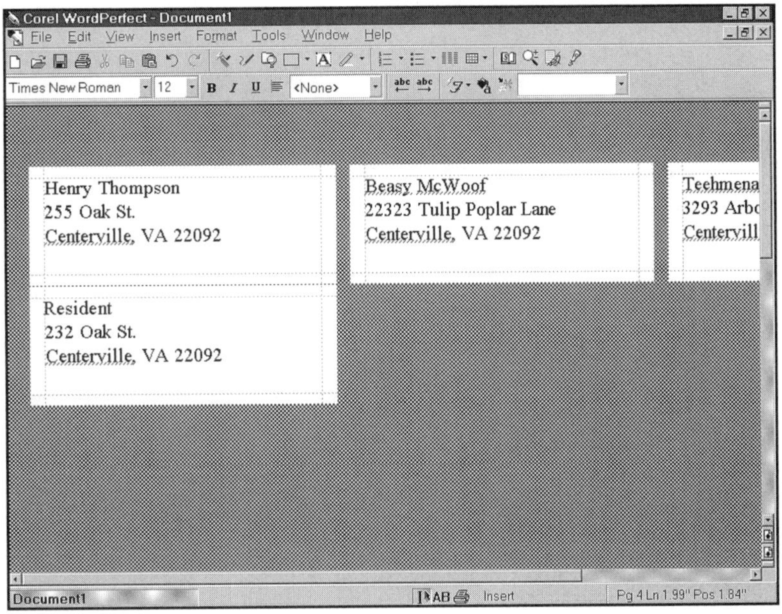

TROUBLESHOOTING

I have several lines of text that overflow to the second page of my document, and I'd like them to be on the first page. Choose Format, Make It Fit. At the Make It Fit dialog box, pick the options that you want adjusted and choose Make It Fit.

After I typed a letter, I told WordPerfect to create an envelope, but the inside address didn't appear in the mailing address area. If your letter isn't in a standard business format, WordPerfect may not be able to find the address inside of it and copy it to the mailing address. If this happens, close the Envelope dialog box, select the inside address, and access the Envelope dialog box again. When you select a name and address before using the Envelope feature, the selected information appears automatically in the mailing address on the envelope.

Some of my labels aren't centered vertically, even though I used the Center on Page feature. If you add extra Enters at the bottom of your labels, you may distort the vertical centering. Look in Reveal Codes for extra hard returns and eliminate them.

CHAPTER 7

Customizing Corel WordPerfect

- **Customize the screen display**

  Learn how to choose which view and zoom percentage you see by default in new documents.

- **Customize the environment**

  Understand how to set user information about yourself, as well as options for setting QuickMarks that take you to where you were in the document when you last closed it.

- **Customize the location of files**

  Learn about specifying where files will be stored and about default file extensions.

- **Customize document summaries**

  See how to tell Corel WordPerfect to prompt you for document summary information when saving your file, as well as specify which fields the document summary should contain.

Corel WordPerfect is flexible and can be customized in many ways to suit your working habits and settings. Customizing the program involves changing any of its default settings, after which your new settings remain in effect until you change them again.

Many types of settings are customized through the Settings dialog box. To customize the screen display, for example, you first access Settings. Other settings are customized through the particular feature being customized. When you choose a default initial font for the selected printer, for example, you choose it through the Font Map feature. When you customize the writing style that Grammatik uses to evaluate your writing, you customize it through the Grammatik feature.

This chapter introduces you to some of the ways that you can customize Corel WordPerfect and tailor it to your own personal working habits. ■

Using the Settings Dialog Box

Because many of the features you will learn to customize are accessed from one starting point—the Settings dialog box—let's begin by looking at this dialog box. Choose Tools, Settings. You see the Settings dialog box (see Figure 7.1).

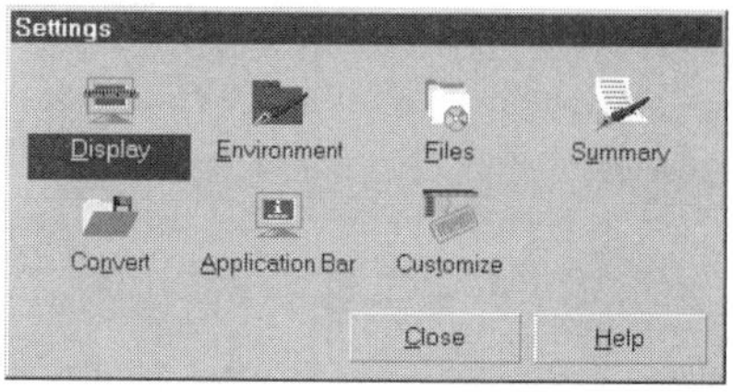

FIG. 7.1
Customize WordPerfect to suit your taste by using the Settings dialog box.

TIP Right-click the toolbar, Property Bar, Application Bar, or either scroll bar and choose Settings from the QuickMenu; you'll go directly to the Settings dialog box for that screen element.

Starting from the Settings dialog box, you can customize Display Settings, Environment Settings, File Settings, and Summary Settings. These subjects are covered in detail in the following sections. Customizing toolbars, the Property Bar, the Application Bar, the keyboard, the menu bar, and file conversions are summarized under "Customizing Other Settings," later in this chapter.

Customizing Display Settings

Use Display Settings to customize the way various screen elements are displayed onscreen. Choose Tools, Settings, Display to open the Display Settings dialog box. Figure 7.2 illustrates the Document tab of the Display Settings dialog box.

The selected tab (Document, Symbols, View/Zoom, and so on) determines the options that are available in the lower portion of the dialog box. When you select View/Zoom, for example, the available options involve the Default View mode and the Default Zoom percentage. Figure 7.3 illustrates the Display Settings dialog box with the View/Zoom tab selected. Set the Default View to Draft view to hide the display of the top and bottom margins, along with any footers, headers, footnotes, and page borders.

See "Using View Modes," **p. 78**

Most users will never need to change most of these settings. However, some of the options that you can change through Display Settings will speed up your work. As you increase the graphics display on-screen, you slow down the screen refresh rate; whatever you do to reduce graphical display will make your work go faster.

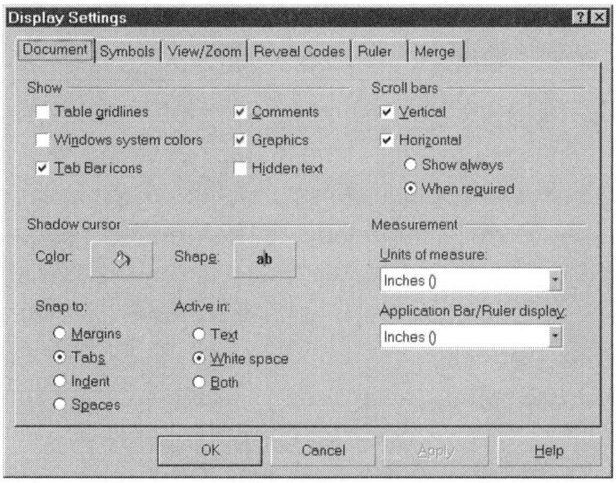

FIG. 7.2
Document options are displayed in the Display Settings dialog box.

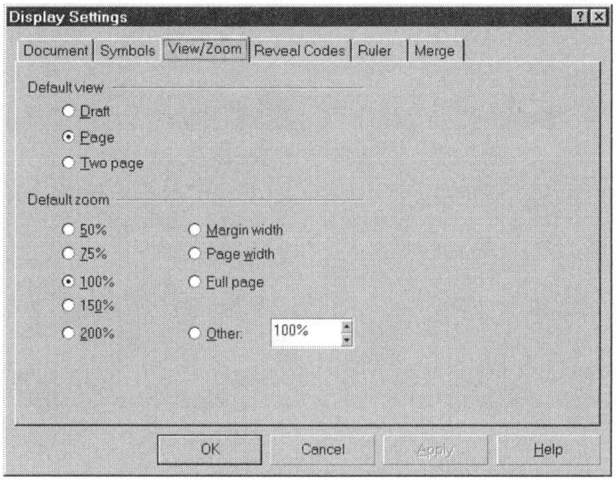

FIG. 7.3
View/Zoom options are displayed in the Display Settings dialog box.

Display settings you can select to speed up your work include:

- Choose Draft view rather than Page or Two Page view (View/Zoom tab).
- Deselect Graphics to suppress the display of graphics in the editing window (Document tab); when Graphics is deselected, an empty box is used as a placeholder.
- Deselect the Horizontal check box in the Scroll Bars section of the Document tab if you don't want to display the horizontal scroll bar on-screen.

You can also temporarily change many display settings from the View menu. If you've told WordPerfect to work in Draft view by default, you can always use View, Page menu selection to switch to Page view when you want to see headers, footers, and page borders. If you've told WordPerfect to show table gridlines in your Display Settings, you can use the View, Table Gridlines menu selection to see lines and fill styles in a table. When speed is not a priority, you can use the View, Graphics menu selection to display graphics.

View, Show ¶ options can help by showing you what keys you've pressed (you won't have to look in Reveal Codes). Although showing nonprinting characters as symbols (spaces, hard returns, tabs, and so on) adds clutter to the screen, many of us can benefit from seeing these symbols. For example, if you can't tell by looking whether you pressed the space bar once or twice, you'd know for sure by the number of dot symbols that represent spaces. Then, you can easily position the insertion point in the correct location and delete an unneeded symbol. You can also choose to show these symbols all the time on new and current documents by selecting the Show Symbols or New and Current Document check box in the Symbols tab of the Display Settings dialog box (see Figure 7.4).

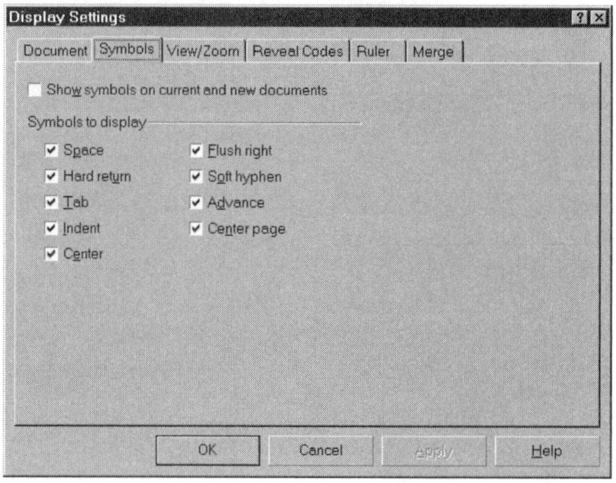

FIG. 7.4
You can tell WordPerfect that you want to display nonprinting characters and choose which characters you want to display as symbols from the Symbols tab of the Display Settings dialog box.

You can determine what suits you best only when you know what options are available. After you know what your options are, you can think about how the various choices affect your work.

TIP See the online Help system for the functions of infrequently used Display Settings options.

TROUBLESHOOTING

I changed my Settings to display table gridlines and now when I format my table with table lines, they're not there. Your table lines are there; you'll see them when you choose View, Table

Gridlines (to turn off the gridlines and display any defined table lines), or when you print the document.

I'd like to have my Ruler on-screen all the time without having to ask for it. Just choose View, Ruler to display the ruler.

Customizing Environment Settings

The first time that you access Environment Settings by choosing Tools, Settings, Environment, you should see the name you entered during installation in the Name text box (see Figure 7.5). Enter your correct name (if it's not already entered correctly), your initials, and select a personal color. What you enter in the User Info for Comments and Summary area will be applied in document comments or summaries.

TIP All comments you make will display in your personal color. If several reviewers make comments on a document, it is helpful if they have different personal colors.

FIG. 7.5
Customize User Info, Language options, Beep On options, and other environment options through the Environment Settings dialog box.

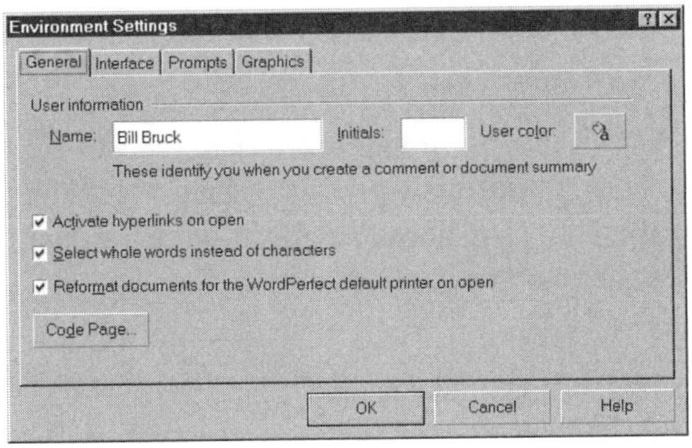

Commonly used options in this dialog box include the following:

- *General Tab.* When Select Whole Words Instead of Characters is selected, entire words are selected automatically as you drag through text with the mouse (you can still hold down the Shift key and press an arrow key to adjust the selection on a character-by-character basis).

  Hypertext links allow you to jump to another location in the same document or a different document, or to execute a macro. When Activate Hypertext Links on Open is enabled, all hypertext links in your documents are automatically activated (although Hypertext still can be activated on an as-needed basis).

▶ **See** "Using Hypertext Web Links," **p. 494**

- *Interface Tab.* The Save workspace options can be especially handy if you frequently want to work on the same document(s) that you were working on during your last work session in WordPerfect. You can, for example, exit WordPerfect while a particular document is still open, then start WordPerfect and automatically open the same document all at once.

  Menu options are also listed in the Interface tab. You may want to check Display Shortcut Keys so that these keys will display on the menu. This makes it easier to learn them.

  If you have purchased another language version of WordPerfect and you want to use that language's formatting conventions, select the appropriate language from the Interface Language drop-down list.

- *Prompts.* You can specify conditions under which WordPerfect beeps at you in the Prompts tab. For example, if you want to be beeped when a find operation is unsuccessful, select the Find failure option.

  In the Prompts tab, you can tell WordPerfect whether you want to confirm the deletion of formatting codes and to note the position of these codes. Leave Confirm Deletion of Table Formulas selected to help you guard against the accidental deletion of table formulas.

  ▶ **See** "Formatting the Page," **p. 100**

- *Graphics.* When you create or import a graphic, WordPerfect just puts it on the current page near the insertion point by default. Instead, you may prefer to check Drag To Create New Graphics Boxes. If you do so, you can drag with the mouse to size and position your graphic.

Customizing File Settings

The Files Settings dialog box, accessed by choosing Tools, Settings, Files, includes options about where and how you save or access various types of files. Figure 7.6 shows the Document tab of the Files Settings dialog box. Important settings in this tab include Default Save File Format. If you are sharing many files with users of earlier versions of WordPerfect, you may want to save your document as a WordPerfect 6/7/8 or WordPerfect 5.1/5.2 file. The Default Document Folder option allows you to specify where your documents will be saved by default.

The Use Default Extension On Open And Save box has been selected, and the default extension is specified as wpd. Files Settings also includes choices on the default extension for new documents and on automatic backup options.

WordPerfect expects to back up any open documents every 10 minutes; you can adjust the interval, but it's not a good idea to deselect the Timed Document Backup option. If your system freezes and you haven't saved changes, the timed backup can spare you a lot of grief.

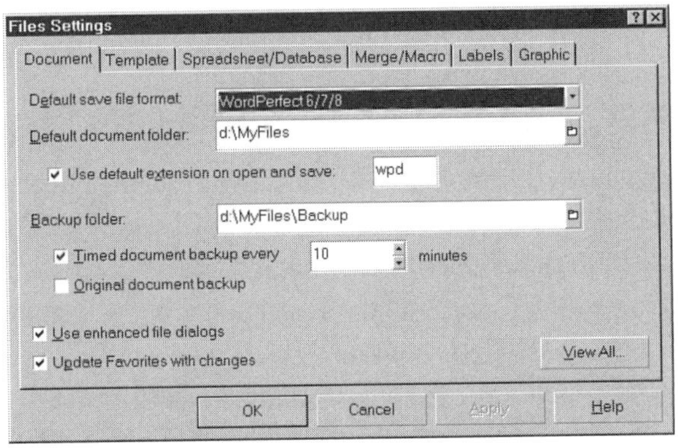

FIG. 7.6 Tell WordPerfect where you want to save and access files using the File Settings dialog box.

When you install WordPerfect on your computer, the location of files is defined for you by default (you can, however, specify your own locations during installation by using Custom Install rather than Traditional Install). Documents are stored in one location, templates in another location, and graphics in another location. This normally works exactly the way you want, so you probably wouldn't want to change these Settings, although you can change them if desired. When you're working with Files Settings, you can see where a particular type of file is stored by selecting that file type (Document, Template, Spreadsheet/Database, and so on), or you can see all of the default storage locations at once by clicking the View All button. The Update Favorites With Changes option tells WordPerfect whether or not to update the Favorites list of folder names in directory dialog boxes, such as the Open dialog box.

▶ **See** "Saving Files," **p. 33**

CAUTION

Even though WordPerfect backs up open documents for you, do not wait until you finish working on a document to save it. Save your work at regular intervals—every 10 minutes, for example. Automatic backup is a disaster recovery feature; it is not a substitute for regular file save operations.

Just as with Display Settings and Environment Settings, you can easily customize your Files Settings to suit the way you work. Through Files Settings, you can specify whether to use automatic file name extensions for documents (and for merge files); you can also change default storage locations and customize backup options.

Customizing Document Summaries

Would you like to include a general overview of a document with the document, or other reference information such as keywords that are used in the file? If the answer to either one of these questions is yes, then customize WordPerfect's document summary Settings.

▶ **See** "Using QuickFinder," **p. 50**

Including Summary Information with Individual Documents

Even if you don't customize summary Settings, you can include summary information with individual documents through the File menu. Choose File, Properties to enter or change summary information for an individual document. The Properties dialog box appears (see Figure 7.7). Any summary information that you enter is saved with the document when you save the document.

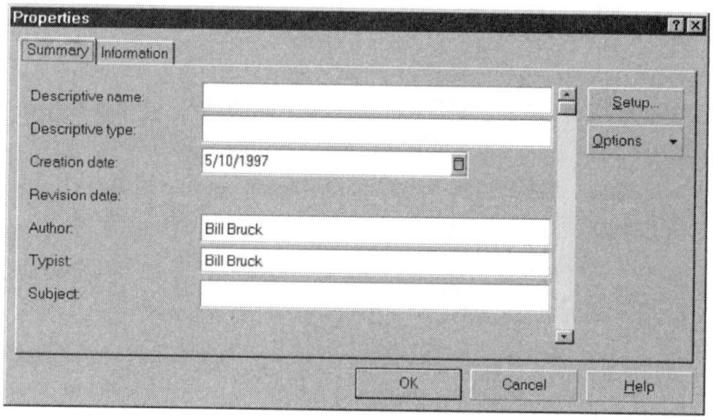

FIG. 7.7
Enter or change summary information for a document, or change the configuration for summaries, in the Properties dialog box. Use the scroll bar to see other summary fields.

TIP Click the Options button in the Properties dialog box to specify which fields to use in summaries and the order in which the fields appear.

To customize your Summary Settings for all documents, choose Tools, Settings, Summary. The Document Summary Settings dialog box appears (see Figure 7.8). By default, all three check box options are deselected; in this example, summary Settings have already been customized so that options are selected. You can use the Subject Search Text option to tell WordPerfect how to identify a document subject. For example, when RE: is the specified subject search text, any text following RE: is automatically inserted in the Subject field in the document summary.

FIG. 7.8
Create summary information by default by customizing your Document Summary Settings.

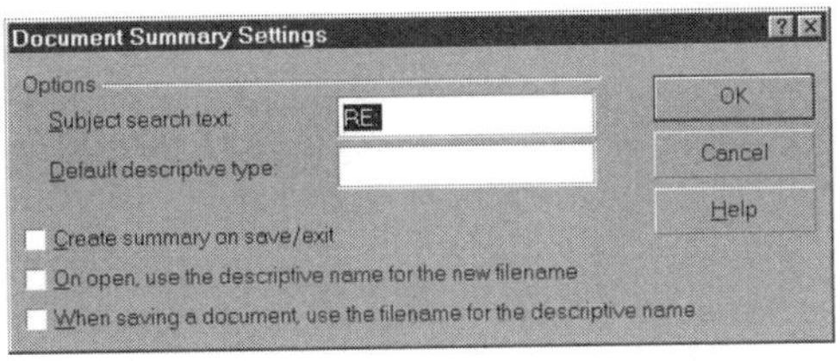

Creating Summaries on Save/Exit

When you specify that you want to Create Summary on Save/Exit in the Document Summary Settings dialog box, WordPerfect automatically asks for summary information when you save a document for the first time. Although this might seem like a nuisance when you don't want to enter summary information, it only takes a single click (OK) or keystroke (Enter) to get past the request. This feature can be helpful when you are in a workgroup environment, and people use keywords when saving their documents.

TROUBLESHOOTING

I want to include a document number in my summaries, but there isn't a place to do it. Choose File, Properties, Setup. You see the Document Summary Setup dialog box. Check Document number in the Select Fields list, and then choose OK twice.

I'd like to print the document summary for my document. Choose File, Print, and then select Document Summary in the Print dialog box.

Customizing Other Settings

You can customize Display Settings, Environment Settings, File Settings, and Summary Settings; you can also customize Settings for toolbars, the Property Bar, the Application Bar, the keyboard, the menu bar, writing tools, printing, and file conversions.

This section summarizes some of the changes you can make for each of these other types of Settings. See Chapter 32, "Customizing Toolbars, Property Bars, and Menus," for more information.

TIP Double-click any Application Bar item to either toggle the action or open its related dialog box. Clicking the date or time item will add the date or time text to your document.

The following list summarizes some of the changes you can make for Settings that are not covered previously in this chapter. Customize settings for toolbars, Property Bars, menus, and keyboards by choosing Tools, Settings, Customize. The Customize dialog box appears with the following tabs:

- *Toolbars.* Use Options to customize the appearance or location of toolbars; you can display text on toolbar buttons, a picture, or both. You can also specify the maximum number of rows to be used for displaying a toolbar (displaying two rows takes more screen space but lets you display more buttons at once). You can also edit the toolbar to add, remove, or rearrange buttons.
- *Property Bars.* Edit and reset property bars to their original defaults.
- *Menu.* Display, create, or manage another predefined menu bar, including any that you have created.
- *Keyboard.* Display, create, or manage another keyboard, including any customized keyboard that you have created for special-purpose work.

TROUBLESHOOTING

Help! I experimented with customizing the Application Bar, and now I'd like to put it back the way it was. Choose Tools, Settings to display the Settings dialog box. Select Application Bar, and choose Reset.

I frequently import database files in an ASCII-delimited format, and I'd like to have quotation marks stripped when the file is imported. Choose Tools, Settings to see the Settings dialog box. Choose Convert to see the Convert Settings dialog box. Specify Quotations marks as characters to be stripped.

You can also specify default delimiters, encapsulation characters, and characters to strip for ASCII text files (options that are most commonly used or referenced when merging with database data files). Choose Tools, Settings, Convert, and select options from the Convert Settings dialog box shown in Figure 7.9.

FIG. 7.9
Specify which characters define delimited text files in the Convert Settings dialog box.

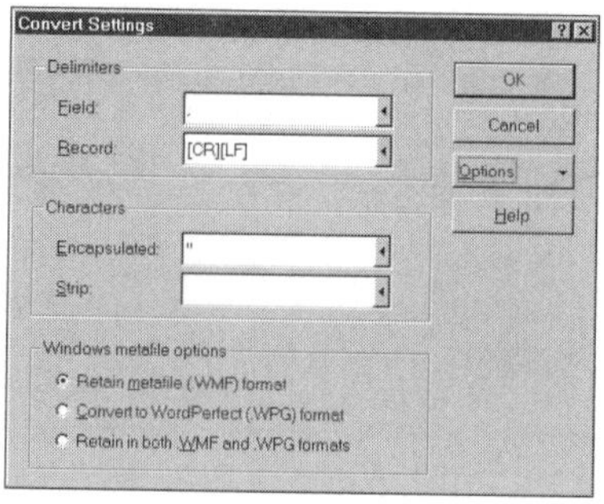

Customizing the Default Settings for New Documents

Whenever you open a new, empty document, you accept default settings that are associated with the standard template. Many other formatting defaults are included in these settings, including margin settings, the justification setting, and tab settings. If you prefer to work with settings that are not the same as these defaults, you can change the defaults for these other settings for new documents through the Document Initial Codes Style. This section shows you how to change the default settings for new documents that are based on the standard template.

▶ **See** "Using Styles," **p. 151**

To change the default settings for new documents that are based on the standard template, follow these steps:

1. Choose Format, Styles.
2. Highlight the DocumentStyle style, and then choose Edit. The Styles Editor dialog box appears (see Figure 7.10).

FIG. 7.10
Customize formatting for new documents in the Styles Editor dialog box.

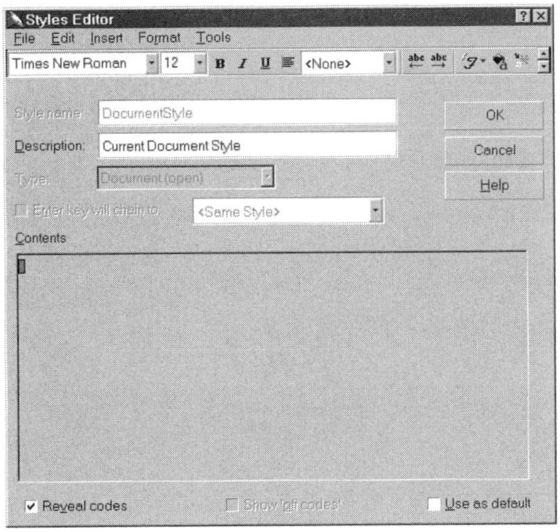

3. In the style Contents area, insert any format settings that you want as defaults for all new documents based on the standard template. For example, if you prefer to work with full justification rather than left justification, insert a formatting code for Full justification by selecting Format, Justification, Full in the menu bar of the Styles dialog box.

4. Check Use As Default.
5. Click OK.

After you customize the Initial Codes Style and specify that the formatting should be used as a default, all new documents based on the standard template will use the customized settings. An illustration of the Initial Codes Style with customized settings is shown in Figure 7.11. The Use As Default check box option has been selected.

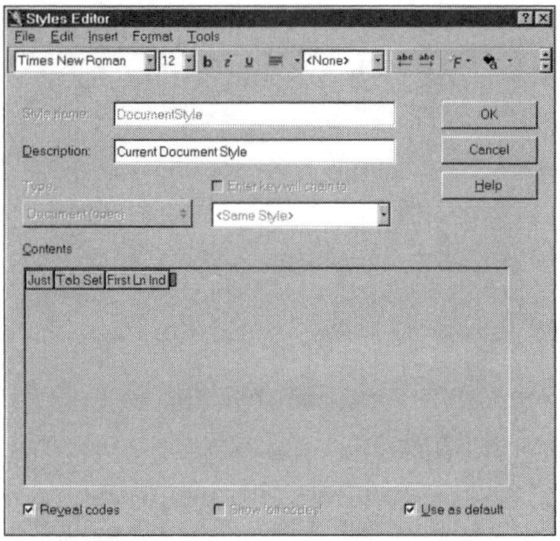

FIG. 7.11
When you customize formatting for new documents in the Styles Editor dialog box, make sure to select the Use As Default check box.

CHAPTER 8

Organizing and Formatting Large Documents

When you produce long documents—sometimes with hundreds of pages—you need special organizational and managerial techniques. Corel WordPerfect provides a number of features that help you manage long documents. You can use these features for short documents as well.

One organizational feature you can use in a large document is *outlining*. An *outline* gives you an overview of a document by organizing topics into a list that can have as many as eight different levels. The outline helps you determine what topics you want to cover and in what order the topics should be presented.

WordPerfect's Styles feature helps you format long documents consistently and easily. With a single operation, you can apply a style that includes preformatted fonts, attributes, and even text. ■

Organizing a simple list with bullets or numbers

One of the best ways to organize points you are making is with bulleted and numbered lists. Learn how to create these easily with Corel WordPerfect.

Using Corel WordPerfect's outline feature

Understand how you can use WordPerfect as a thinking tool to organize your thoughts in outline form, then open just the part(s) of the outline that you are working on.

Using Corel WordPerfect's built-in styles to format a document

Use WordPerfect's built-in styles to easily format titles, headings, and body text, thus ensuring consistency of appearance and saving time and effort.

Creating and editing your own styles

Once you start using WordPerfect's styles, you'll want to create your own. This section shows you how to do so quickly and easily.

Using Bullets & Numbers

Corel WordPerfect's Bullets & Numbers feature gives you a quick and easy way to create an outline in a simplified format. Use the Bullets & Numbers feature to create lists like the ones shown in Figure 8.1. A bullet or number appears at the left margin, followed by an indent. Numbers increase automatically with each item in the list.

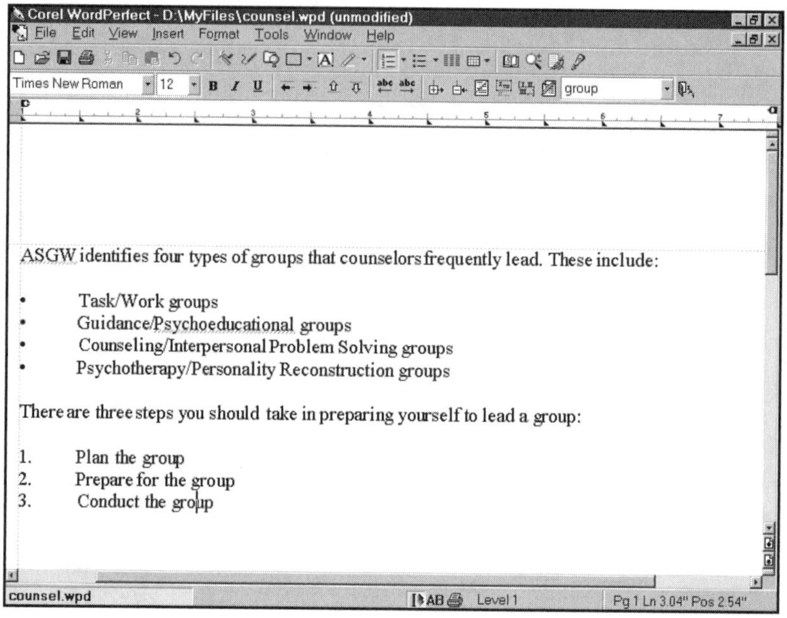

FIG. 8.1
Create bulleted and numbered lists easily with the Bullets & Numbers feature.

Take the following steps to create a simple list:

1. Position the insertion point at the left margin of the first line in the list.
2. Choose Insert, Outline/Bullets & Numbering. You see the Bullets & Numbering dialog box shown in Figure 8.2.
3. Select the style that you want for your list.
4. Click OK. WordPerfect inserts the first bullet (or number) followed by an indent into your document.
5. Type your text and press Enter.
6. You see the next bullet or number. Continue typing text and pressing Enter until you finish typing the list. To enter a blank line, press the Enter key twice. Use the Backspace key to remove the extra bullet or number at the end of the list and to stop the sequence.

FIG. 8.2
Making a selection at the Bullets & Numbering dialog box produces a number with an indent.

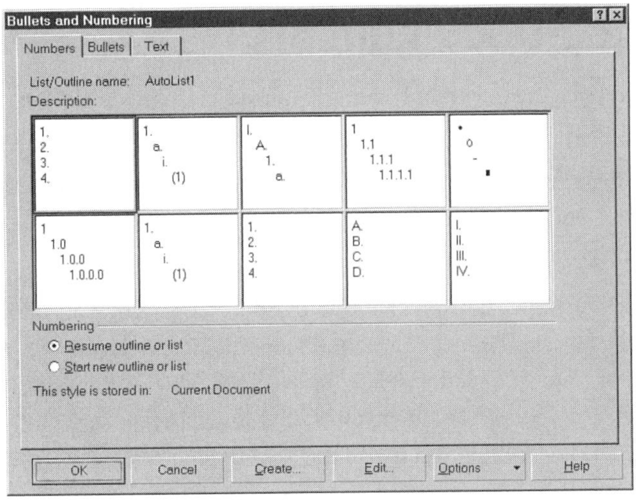

TIP Use the Bullets or Numbering buttons to quickly create another bullet or number.

NOTE WordPerfect gives you a choice of 10 types of bullet styles and 9 types of number styles with its Bullets & Numbers feature. There are also three predefined Text styles that insert predefined text at the beginning of each paragraph. You can customize any of the predefined styles. You can, for example, use a different WordPerfect character as a bullet by editing one of the predefined styles and replacing the bullet character with the character of your choice.

TROUBLESHOOTING

I created a numbered list and now I'd rather have a bulleted list. Select the entire list, click the Numbering button to removing the numbering, and then click the Bullets button to insert bullets.

I created a numbered list, and I want to add another item to the list. Insert the item using the Numbering button to create a number at the beginning of the item. Numbers will resequence automatically.

I typed a list of items without bullets, and now I'd like to add bullets at the beginning of each item. Select the entire list and click the Bullet button.

When I'm typing a bulleted list, sometimes I want to add a line without bullets. Press Shift+Enter and the new line will not have a bullet. When you press Enter again, the next line will have a bullet.

Outlining a Document

Whenever you create a numbered list you are creating an *outline*—not just a numbered list.

A WordPerfect outline is more than numbers that are typed in at the beginning of each new topic. Once you start an outline, the numerals, if there are any, are created and sequenced automatically.

When you change your mind about the order of topics in your outline, you can easily rearrange topics. The rest of the topics resequence automatically when you rearrange topics—or when you add or delete topics. If you change your mind about the style of the outline, place the insertion point anywhere in the outline and choose a different style. To see only the most important topics in your outline, collapse the outline down to the first level.

Before you work with outlines, it helps to familiarize yourself with outline concepts and terminology and with the Outline Property Bar.

Understanding Outline Concepts and Terminology

The following concepts and terminology will help you work with outlines:

- An outline is a series of paragraphs, called *outline items*, in which each paragraph has an optional number or letter and a hierarchical level. The level number or letter type generally corresponds to the number of tabs or indents that separate the beginning of the topic from the left margin.
- An outline can include body text. Body text does not have a number, and may not have the same level of indentation as the portions of the outline that surround it.
- An *outline family* is a group of related material consisting of all the numbered paragraphs and body text that are sub-items of the first item in the group.
- An *outline style* is a formatting style that uniquely defines the appearance of the number and text for each level of an outline.

Understanding the Outline Property Bar

The Outline Property Bar shown in Figure 8.3 is your gateway to the commands that you use when you work with outlines. This section introduces you to the Outline Property Bar. Table 8.1 describes individual buttons on the Property Bar.

FIG. 8.3
The Outline Property Bar provides one-button access to Outline's capabilities.

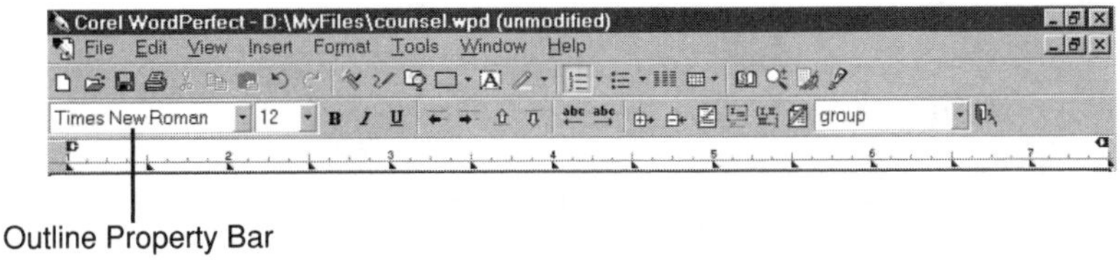

Table 8.1 Buttons on the Outline Property Bar

Button	Name	Function
	Promote	Changes the current outline item to the previous level. Decreases an outline item's level number or letter by 1 (same as Shift+Tab).
	Demote	Changes the current outline level to the next level. Increases an outline item's level number or letter by one (same as pressing Tab).
	Move Up	Moves the current or selected family or item up; keeps the same level. Moves the outline item or selection text up one item without changing its level letter or number.
	Move Down	Moves the current or selected family or item down; keeps the same level. Moves the outline item or selection text down one item without changing its level letter or number.
	QuickFind Previous	Finds the previously selected element of the document.
	QuickFind Next	Finds the next selected element of the document.
	Show Family	Shows all levels of the outline family. Shows/redisplays the collapsed family that is below the current outline item.
	Hide Family	Hides all but the current level of the outline family. Hides/collapses the family that is below the current outline item.
	Show/Hide Body Text	Toggles the display of non-outline items.
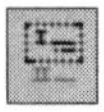	Show Levels	Specifies how many levels of the outline should display.

continues

Table 8.1 Continued

Button	Name	Function
	Set Paragraph Number	Allows you to manually set the paragraph number of the current paragraph.
	Modify	Selects an outline format. You see the Create Format dialog box that allows you to create or edit your outline style.

Creating an Outline

The general steps for creating an outline are as follows:

1. Position the insertion point at the left margin of the line that will be the first line in the outline.

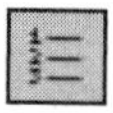

2. Click the Numbering button on the toolbar, or type **1.** and press the Tab key. The Outline Property Bar appears.
3. If the style of the inserted outline number is not the one you want, use the down arrow on the right side of the Numbering button to select another style, or choose Insert, Outline/Bullets & Numbering and select a different style from the Bullets and Numbering dialog box.
4. Type the text, and then press Enter. The insertion point is automatically positioned at the same level to enter the text for the next item.

5. To change the level of an outline item, click anywhere in the item, then click the Promote or the Demote button. Note that the Property Bar displays the outline level of the current paragraph.
6. To add body text to the outline, press the Backspace key to delete the paragraph number. You see the Outline Property Bar change to the Text Property Bar. To resume the outline numbering, click the Numbering button at the beginning of a paragraph. You see the next consecutive number.
7. To complete the outline and start typing text again, press the Backspace key at the beginning of a new paragraph to delete the outline number. You see the Outline Property Bar change to the Text Property Bar.

NOTE If you accidentally delete an outline number, either Undo the action, or Backspace to the end of the previous item and press Enter.

Collapsing and Expanding Portions of an Outline

WordPerfect makes it easy to work with a portion of your outline by letting you display only the portion in which you're currently interested.

When you're displaying just the portion that you want to work with, it's easy to edit (or reorganize) outline items. Because outline items are just normal text with automatic numbering applied to them, you edit text in outline items just as you do any other text.

Figure 8.4 is an example for the hiding and showing techniques that follow.

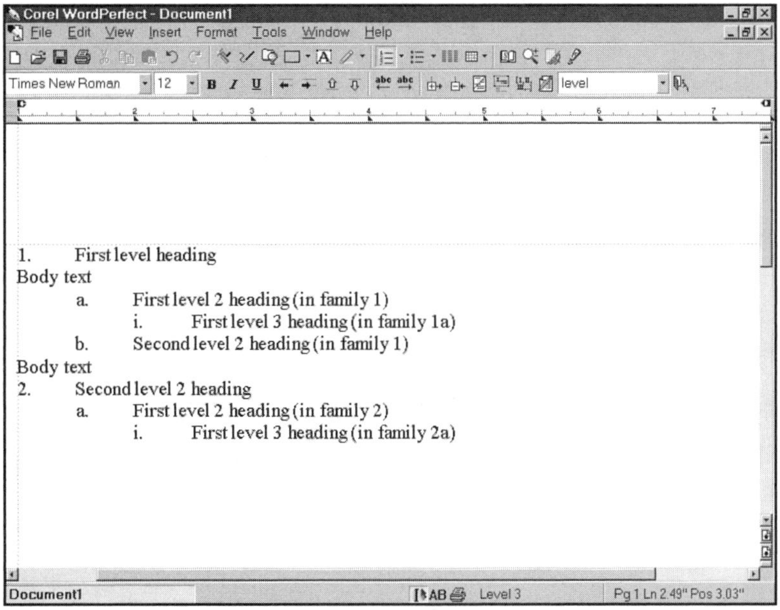

FIG. 8.4
The complete outline used in the hiding and showing examples.

Using the Outline Property Bar, you have the following methods to control what portion of an outline is displayed:

- To hide an outline family—that is, to collapse the family so only its first-level item is visible—click in the first level of the family and click the Hide Family button.

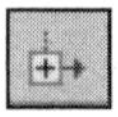

- To show a collapsed outline family, place the insertion point in the visible outline item and click the Show Family button.

- To hide the body text and leave only the outline, click the Show/Hide Body Text button. The body text is hidden. To redisplay body text, click the Show/Hide Body Text button again.

Figure 8.5 shows the result of hiding elements of the outline.

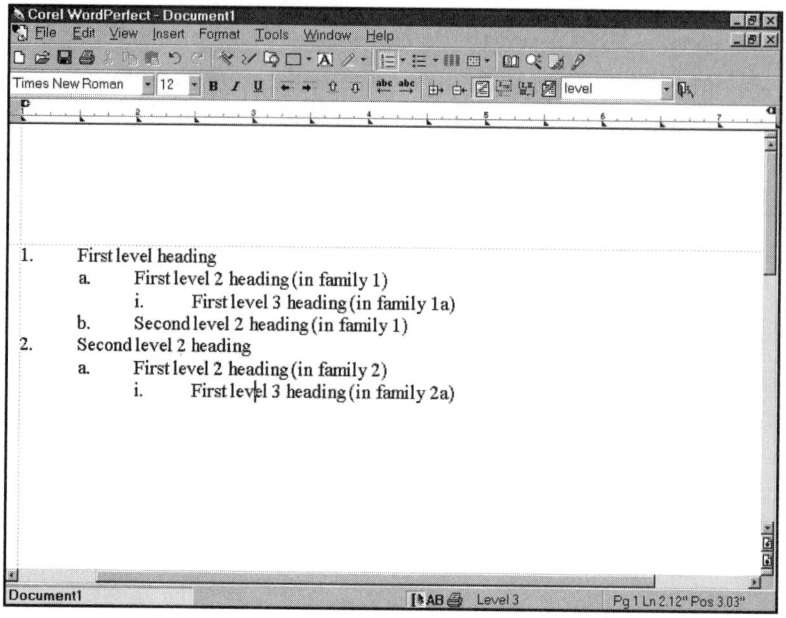

FIG. 8.5
The same outline is shown with body text hidden.

Modifying an Outline's Structure

You can modify an outline's structure by rearranging items and families, inserting new families, or deleting families. You can also switch an outline item to body text or vice versa. WordPerfect automatically adjusts the numbering of the outline.

Adjusting Levels Levels of the outline can be adjusted according to the following options:

- To increase the level of an outline item, position the insertion point anywhere in the item and choose the Promote button.

- To decrease the level of an outline item, position the insertion point anywhere in the item and click the Demote button.

To increase or decrease several items at once, select the desired items, then click the Promote or Demote button.

Changing To and from Body Text To change an outline item to body text, click at the beginning of the item and press the Backspace key to delete the outline number. The text is placed at the left margin. You may want to adjust its indentation with Tab or Indent (F7).

To change body text back to an outline item, place the insertion point anywhere in the body text and click the Numbering button.

Changing an Outline's Style

You can select from among several different predefined outline numbering styles. To change an outline's style, take the following steps:

1. Position the insertion point anywhere in the outline.

2. Click the down arrow at the right of the Numbering button. You see several choices for numbering styles.
3. Select your preferred numbering style. The outline numbering changes accordingly.

Using Styles

Use styles to format your documents and templates easily and quickly, and to give them a consistent and professional look. Styles are an extraordinarily powerful formatting tool. Instead of applying several separate formatting changes to a subtitle in a long document, you can apply them all at once with a style. You can apply the same style over and over again to every subtitle in the document. If you change your mind about any of the formatting, you have only one change to make—to the style itself. Styles are readily available for use in other documents; see the section "Sharing Styles Between Documents" later in this chapter for more information.

Because styles can incorporate nearly any WordPerfect formatting feature—as well as text, graphics, and even other styles—their potential is nearly unlimited. You can save a great deal of time and work by learning to use styles, especially when you work with long documents.

TIP Chapter 9, "Using Tables and Graphics," also covers working with graphics lines and creating paragraph and page borders, drop caps, graphics boxes for figures and text, special text effects with text art, and watermarks.

Considering Types of Styles

Styles are classified in three ways: by who creates them, by their location, and by their type.

Styles that are part of the WordPerfect program are called *system styles*. When you first access the style list in a new document, immediately after installation of the program (see Figure 8.6), you see a style list that displays the built-in system styles. When you create a new style, it is added to the style list. The styles that you create are called *user styles*.

Another way to classify styles is by their location. Styles can be saved in the document, in a separate style file, or in the template that the document is based on.

FIG. 8.6
WordPerfect comes with styles for five levels of headings.

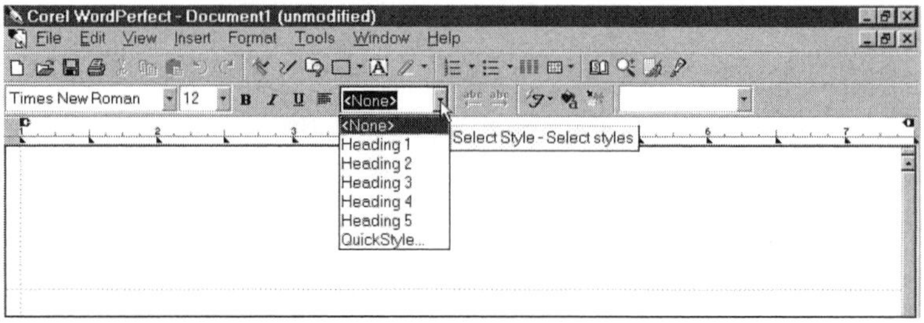

In addition, there are five types of styles:

- *Character Style.* The formatting in a Character style takes effect at a specified character, and it ends at another character. Characters following the character style revert to their previous formatting. Character styles are especially good for applying multiple character formatting attributes to individual words or letters. For instance, if you need to print certain words in bold small caps, a character style would be very useful.
- *Automatic Character Style.* Thistype of style is like the Character style, except that formatting in the style is automatically updated when you change any paragraph that is formatted with the style. Thus, if you change the character formatting style of one paragraph, all other paragraphs in the document with that style will change as well.
- *Paragraph Style.* The formatting in a Paragraph style affects the current paragraph (or a series of selected paragraphs). A Paragraph style is ideal for formatting one-line titles and headings.
- *Automatic Paragraph Style.* This type of style is like the Paragraph style, except that formatting in the style is automatically updated when you change any paragraph that is formatted with the style. Thus, if you change the style of one paragraph, all other paragraphs in the document with that style will change as well.
- *Document (open).* A Document style applies a formatting command from the insertion point until the end of the document, unless overridden by another formatting command. This can be useful when you want to change margins, the base font, or a paper orientation for the remainder of the document.

WordPerfect's styles are much more powerful than those of competing word processing programs that can only include formatting codes in styles. With WordPerfect, you can also include text and graphics in your styles. Thus, you could have a style that inserts your company logo, or a style that even inserts text for you.

Using System Styles

The easiest way to learn about styles is to start using the built-in System Styles to format headings in your document. To do so, create or click a document heading, then click in the Styles list box, and choose Heading 1 through Heading 5 for the paragraph, as shown in Figure 8.7.

FIG. 8.7
This document is using several heading styles; the Styles list box open.

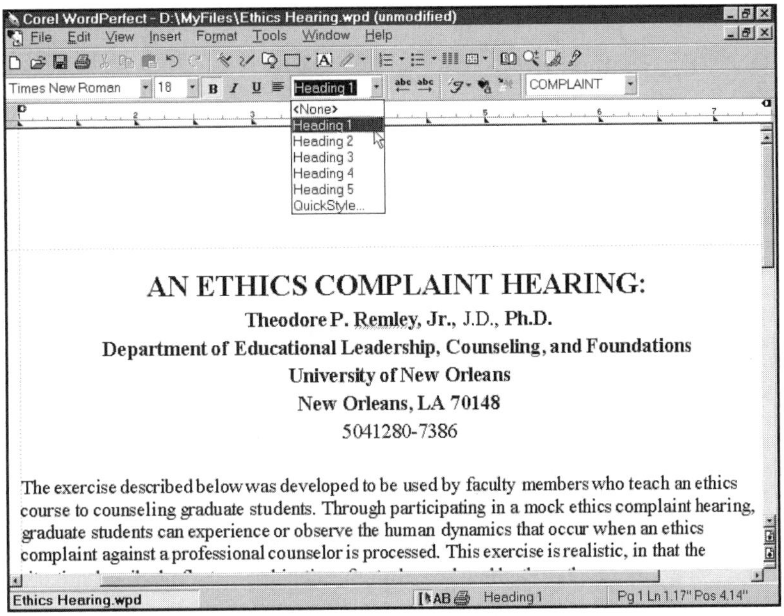

To understand styles a little bit more, it's helpful to open the Style List dialog box shown in Figure 8.8. Do so by choosing Format, Styles.

FIG. 8.8
The Style List dialog box shows the styles saved in the standard template.

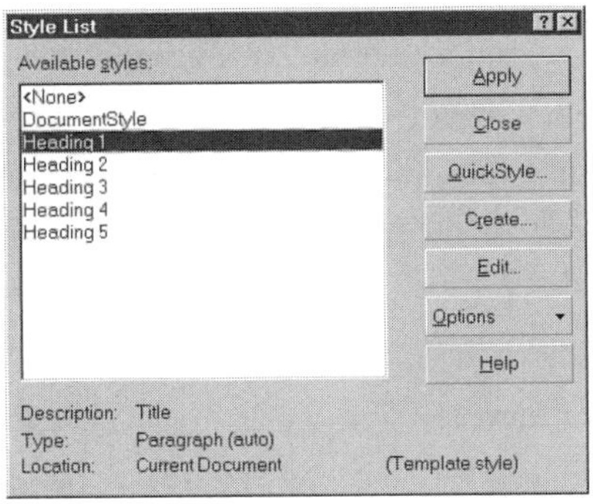

In the Style List dialog box, you can highlight each style name on the list and see the description and other information about that style below the list.

The DocumentStyle sets formatting defaults that affect the entire document. The Heading styles are designed to format the title and various levels of headings in a document; these styles contain font changes, centering, and Table of Contents markings. The number and bullet styles (if present) contain formatting for Bullets & Numbers styles.

Creating and Using Your Own Styles

When you see and feel the power of styles, you'll be willing to put in some extra time and work learning how to create your own styles. Although the use of styles adds a level of complexity to your work, the results are well worth it. You'll save time formatting; your documents will have a professional, consistent appearance; and you'll be able to make global formatting adjustments quickly and easily.

TIP To learn more about styles, explore WordPerfect's templates. Create a document based on a template as discussed in Chapter 6, "Using Writing Tools and Printing," then access the Style List dialog box, select a style, and choose Edit to see what codes it contains.

Creating a Style with QuickStyle An easy way to create a style is to format some text as you want it to look, and then use the QuickStyle feature to copy the formatting into a style. With QuickStyle, you can create a Paragraph style that contains all of the formatting codes and font attributes in an existing paragraph; or, you can create a Character style that contains all the font attributes on an existing character.

To create a style with QuickStyle, complete the following steps:

1. Format a section of text or a paragraph with the features that you want included in the style.
2. Click anywhere in the paragraph to create a Paragraph style, or select the formatted text to create a Character style.
3. Click the Styles button, and then choose QuickStyle; or, choose Format, Styles, QuickStyle. The QuickStyle dialog box is displayed, shown in Figure 8.9.
4. Enter a name for the style.
5. Enter a description for the style.
6. Select the Paragraph or Character Style type.
7. Click OK. The style is created, and you are returned to the document window or the Style List dialog box.

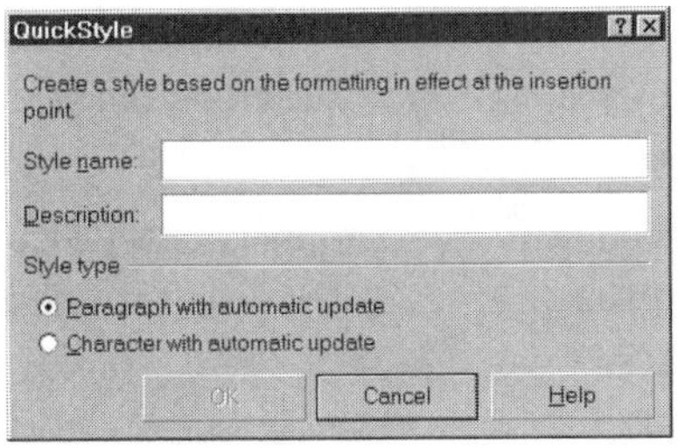

FIG. 8.9
Format text as you want it to look, then use the QuickStyle dialog box to copy the formatting into a style.

Creating a Style from Scratch Maximize the power of styles by creating your own styles with exactly the formatting, text, graphics, and even other styles that suit your work.

To create a style from scratch, you need to enter formatting codes (and any other contents for the style) in the Styles Editor window. Follow these steps to create a style from scratch:

1. Choose Format, Styles. The Style List dialog box appears.
2. Choose Create. The Styles Editor window is displayed like the one shown in Figure 8.10.

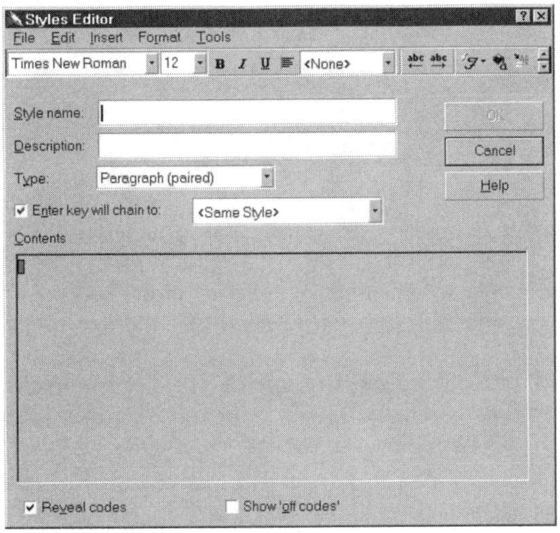

FIG. 8.10
A paragraph style named Body, used to format the body text for a report, is shown in the Styles Editor dialog box.

3. Enter a name for the style in the Style Name box.
4. Enter a description for the style in the Description box. It's helpful to describe the formatting used in the style or the purpose for which it will be used.
5. Change the style type, if desired, from the Type drop-down list.

6. For a Paragraph or Character style, program the Enter key, if desired. The Enter key can be programmed to make the *next* paragraph the same style, another style that you specify, or no style at all.
7. Click in the Contents area and enter formatting codes, text, or graphics that should be included in the style. (Inserting graphics is discussed further in Chapter 9, "Using Tables and Graphics.")
8. If the style type is Paragraph or Character, you can specify formatting and text that takes effect after the text that is included in the style. For example, you might want to insert a graphics line after a heading that is formatted with the style. To do so, check Show 'Off Codes'. You see a comment in the Contents box that says `Codes to the left are ON - Codes to the right are OFF`. Click to the right of this comment, then put the text or formatting you want to have take effect after the style, like the paragraph border code in Figure 8.11.

FIG. 8.11
You can include elements like graphics lines that should be inserted after the style is turned off.

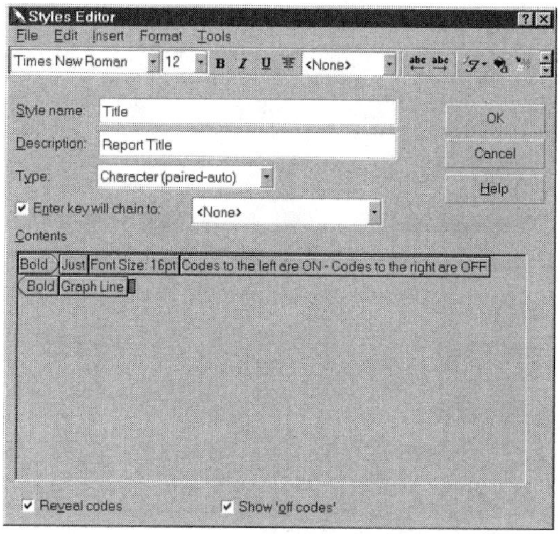

9. Click OK, and then click Close to return to the document window.

Applying a Style You can apply a style either to existing text or to new text.

TIP If the style type is Character or Paragraph (Automatic), you don't have to edit a style with the Styles Editor. When you change any paragraph that is formatted with the style, the changes are automatically reflected in the style.

To apply a style to new text, complete the following steps:

1. Click at the end of the document.
2. Click the Styles button on the Power Bar to display the style list.
3. Select the style that you want to apply.
4. If the style being applied is a Document type or a Paragraph type, you have finished applying the style.

   If the new text is at the end of the document and the style being applied is a Character style, type the text that is to be affected by the style, then pull down the style list again and select None or another style from the list. This turns off the first style.

To apply a style to existing text, complete the following steps:

1. If the style being applied is a Document style, position the insertion point where you want its effects to begin.

   If the style being applied is a Paragraph style, position the insertion point in the paragraph to be affected, or select the paragraphs to be affected.

   If the style being applied is a Character style, select the text to be affected.
2. Click the Styles button and select the style.

Editing a Style Once you create and apply a style, you may change your mind about formatting in the style. Styles are very flexible; as soon as you change the style, the changes take effect wherever that style is applied.

To make any changes that should apply to the document as a whole (except for the Document Initial Font), edit the Document Style. Every document contains the Document Style code at the beginning of its text (you can't remove the code). When you edit the Document Style, therefore, your formatting takes effect at the beginning of the document. Because the Document Style is a Document (open) style, its formatting stays in effect for the rest of the document, or until it is overridden by other formatting of the same type. You might, for example, insert justification and margin codes in the Document Style.

NOTE Formatting codes that appear in the body of a document, or in other styles that are applied in the document, override similar formatting in the Document Style.

To edit a Character (auto) or Paragraph (auto) style, merely edit text in your document that has that style applied to it. The changes will be automatically reflected in the style and in other text that has that style applied to it.

To edit other types of styles:

1. Choose Format, Style to open the Style List dialog box.
2. Select the style you want to edit and choose Edit. The Styles Editor window appears.
3. Make any desired changes, then click OK and Close.

Sharing Styles Between Documents When you create a new document, it contains all the styles that the template upon which it is based has. Additionally, you can specify an Additional Objects template that contains other styles that you use frequently.

TIP Often, the Additional Objects template is used for your office or workgroup templates, such as a letterhead. Specify the Additional Objects Template in the File Settings dialog box by choosing Tools, Settings, Files, Template.

Styles are automatically saved with the document containing them. They are not, however, saved in the template unless you specify this as described in this section.

When you work on an existing document, your style list may thus contain system styles (saved in the Default template), styles from the template upon which the document was based, styles from the Additional Objects template, and styles previously created and saved in the document.

When you want to use your styles in a new document, the easiest way to do it is by saving the current document's style list in a separate file that only contains the style list. Then you can retrieve the style file into the style list of another document.

If you want customized styles to be available in *all* new documents based on a particular template, copy the styles to the template, or create the styles while you edit the template.

You can save and retrieve styles in the following ways:

- To save styles in the current document to a separate style file, access the Style List dialog box. Choose Options, Save As. Type a name for the style file in the resulting Save Styles To dialog box. Choose whether to save the User Styles, the System Styles, or Both; then click OK.
- To save a style in the current document to the current template, display the Style List dialog box; select the style name; choose Options, Copy. Click Default Template in the Styles Copy dialog box; and then click OK.
- To retrieve styles from a style file (or from another document), display the Style List dialog box; choose Options, Retrieve; enter a file name (and path); and choose OK. You are asked whether you want to overwrite current styles (with incoming styles that have the same names). Answer Yes or No to complete the retrieve operation.

You can also click the folder icon to the right of the block for path to the styles. This will show a browse dialog box from which you can choose a template by clicking the file name and clicking Select.

TROUBLESHOOTING

I created a style to format the company name, but when I apply it, it formats the entire paragraph. Change the style type from Paragraph to Character.

I want to use the styles I created in my Report file in a new document. With the new document on-screen, access the Style List dialog box. Choose Options, Retrieve, and then enter the file name (and path) of your Report file and choose OK. When asked whether you want to overwrite current styles, answer Yes. The retrieve operation will then be completed.

I want to add Table of Contents markings to a style, but I can't figure out how to do it. You can add Table of Contents markings to any paired style. At the Styles Editor window, select the Show 'Off Codes' check box option. Select only the comment code `[Codes to the left...]`. Choose Tools, Reference, Table of Contents. Choose the level you want by choosing one of the Mark buttons on the Table of Contents dialog box that appears at the bottom of the screen. `[Mrk Txt ToC]` codes now surround the comment, and will surround any text that is formatted with the style.

CHAPTER 9

Using Tables and Graphics

Create a table

Make tables to display information in your documents, or create attractive forms for data entry.

Create graphics lines and add borders to paragraphs, columns, and pages

Create graphics lines and borders to set off headers and footers, section headings, or other design elements in your documents.

Create and edit graphics boxes that contain pictures or charts

Include clip art, charts, and drawings in your documents.

Use drop caps and watermarks

Create drop caps and watermarks that make your documents stand out in the crowd as something special.

Now that you've learned how to create WordPerfect documents, format them, and work with long documents, you may want to "spice up" your documents with elements like tables, clip art, and watermarks.

Corel WordPerfect provides simple ways to include these design features in your documents. You will also find many features that ship with WordPerfect, including attractively designed lines, borders, and pictures that can also be used to enhance your documents.

Working with Tables

Corel WordPerfect's Tables feature offers many practical uses. Tables can illustrate, define, and explain text; they can enhance your documents and make them more effective.

A table also gives you a convenient way to organize text. Use a table to organize columns of numbers, produce forms, or add spreadsheets to your documents. There are many formatting options you can apply to a table to make it visually appealing. WordPerfect even provides a Table SpeedFormat to let you preview and apply a table style (a set of formats) to your table all at once.

A table consists of columns and rows that form a grid of cells. You can fill cells with text or graphics. When you type text into a cell, the text wraps automatically from one line to the next, and the cell expands vertically to accommodate your text.

TIP Several PerfectExpert Projects, including the calendar and the Balance Sheet, are based on tables.

An example of a WordPerfect table is shown in Figure 9.1.

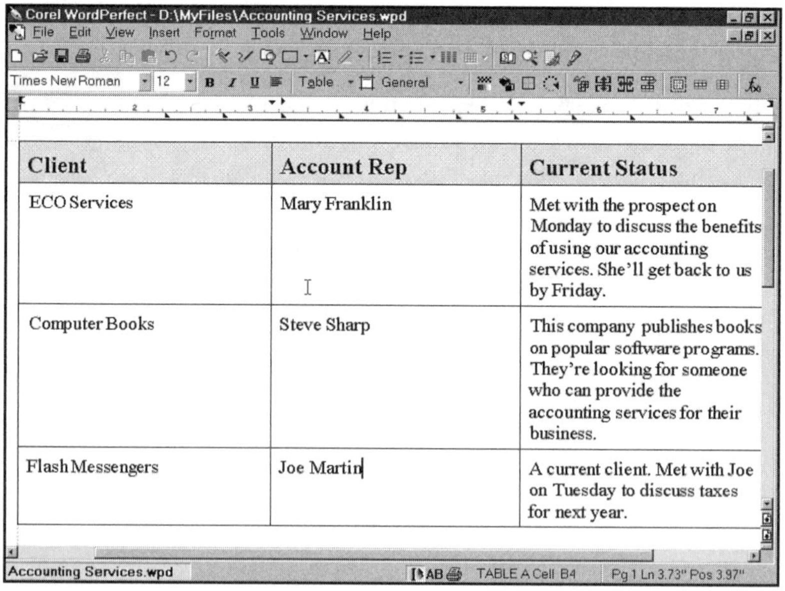
Corel WordPerfect - D:\MyFiles\Accounting Services.wpd
File Edit View Insert Format Tools Window Help
Times New Roman
12
Table
General
Client
Account Rep
Current Status
ECO Services
Mary Franklin
Met with the prospect on Monday to discuss the benefits of using our accounting services. She'll get back to us by Friday.
Computer Books
Steve Sharp
This company publishes books on popular software programs. They're looking for someone who can provide the accounting services for their business.
Flash Messengers
Joe Martin
A current client. Met with Joe on Tuesday to discuss taxes for next year.
Accounting Services.wpd
TABLE A Cell B4
Pg 1 Ln 3.73" Pos 3.97"

FIG. 9.1
Enter columns of text with automatic word wrap by placing the text in a WordPerfect table.

Creating a Table

A table can be inserted at any point in a document. You can create a table either by choosing Insert, Table or with the Table QuickCreate button on the toolbar.

NOTE The quickest way to create a table is by pulling down a grid from the Table QuickCreate button on the toolbar, and dragging through the number of columns and rows that you want for your table. The size of the grid doesn't limit the size of your table; the grid expands as you drag past its edge.

To create a table from the menu, take the following steps:

TIP It's a good idea to already have your margins set before creating a table. When you change margins after you've created the table, it tends to mess up the column widths.

1. Position the insertion point where you want the table to begin.

2. Choose Insert, Table or click the Table QuickCreate button on the toolbar. The Create Table dialog box is displayed, as shown in Figure 9.2.

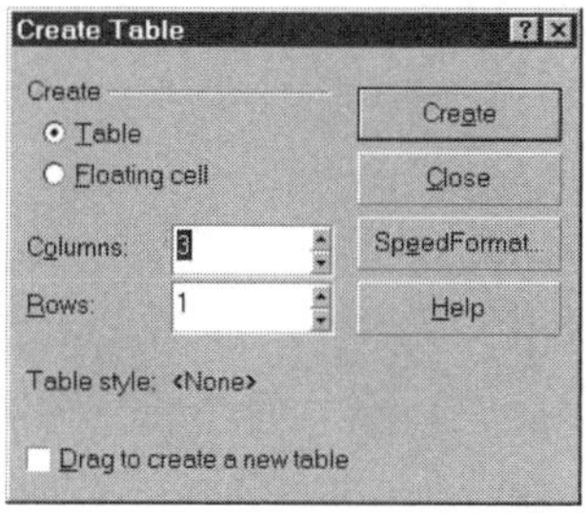

FIG. 9.2 Specify the number of columns and rows when you create a table.

TIP You can also create a floating cell with this dialog box, which is a 1×1 table. Floating cells are useful because they can be linked to Quattro Pro notebooks to present dynamically changing information in the middle of a paragraph.

3. Enter the number of Columns and Rows that you want.
4. Choose a style for your table, if desired, with the SpeedFormat button. For information on using this feature, see the section "Using Table SpeedFormat to Enhance a Table," later in this chapter.

NOTE It's easy to add rows to a table after you create it. See the section "Inserting and Deleting Columns and Rows," later in this chapter.

5. Click Create. A table with the specified number of columns and rows (and predefined style, if any) is inserted in your document. The table spans the width between the left and right margins. All columns have the same width.

Moving Within a Table The easiest way to move within a table is to use the scroll bars until the part of the table you want is visible on-screen, and then click with the mouse in the desired cell.

TIP When the insertion point is positioned in a table, WordPerfect automatically displays the Tables Property Bar for you.

You can also move within a table using the keyboard, as shown in Table 9.1.

Table 9.1 Keyboard Commands for Moving in a Table

Command	Result
Tab or Alt+Right Arrow (→)	Next cell
Shift+Tab or Alt+Left Arrow (←)	Previous cell
Alt+Up Arrow (↑)	Up one row
Alt+Down Arrow (↓)	Down one row

Entering Text Within a Table As you enter text into your table, consider each cell a miniature document with its own margins and formatting. As you enter text, words wrap automatically to a new line and the row increases in depth. Press Enter only when you need to force words to wrap to the next line.

▶ **See** "Typing Text," **p. 60**

When you have completed entering text for a cell, press Tab to move to the next cell. When you reach the last cell of the table, pressing Tab will create a new row so that you can continue entering data.

Editing Table Design

A table has a very flexible structure. When you first create a table, it has a specified number of columns and rows, and every column has the same width. While you work with the table, you can adjust the column width to suit your taste, and you can add or delete columns and rows. You can even join cells to create a single cell, or you can split a cell into rows or columns.

When your insertion point is in a table, you see the Tables Property Bar. If you have one or more cells selected, you see the Table Cell Selected Property Bar instead. These toolbars have a number of buttons that make editing your table design a snap.

> **TIP** You can also access most table formatting commands by right-clicking in the table to display the QuickMenu.

Selecting Table Cells Many editing operations can be performed more quickly if you select the group of rows, columns, or cells that you want them to apply to. Follow these guidelines for selecting table elements:

- Turn on row/column indicators by clicking the Table button on the Property Bar, and then choosing Row/Col Indicators on the drop-down menu.
- To select a *single cell*, position the mouse pointer against any edge of the cell so that it becomes a white arrow as shown in Figure 9.3, and then click the mouse button. The entire cell should be highlighted.

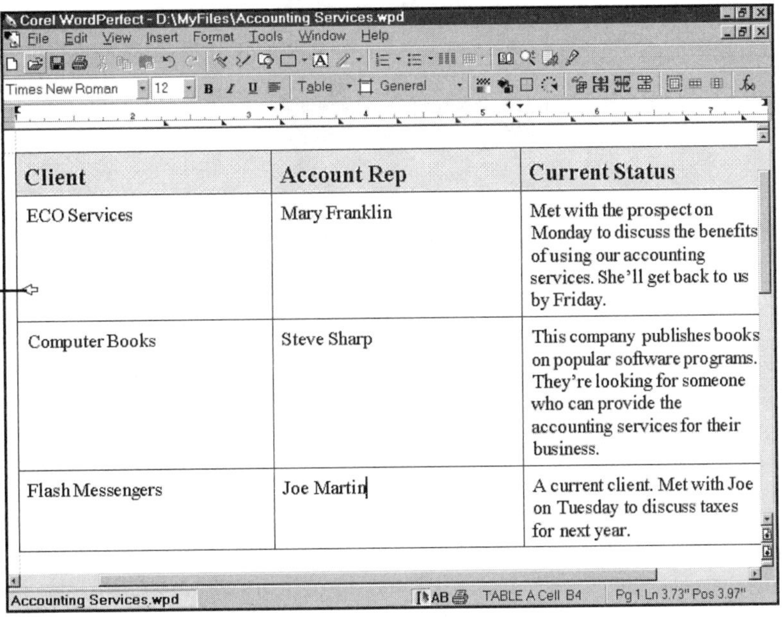

Corel WordPerfect - D:\MyFiles\Accounting Services.wpd
File Edit View Insert Format Tools Window Help
Times New Roman
12
Table
General
Client
Account Rep
Current Status
ECO Services
Mary Franklin
Met with the prospect on Monday to discuss the benefits of using our accounting services. She'll get back to us by Friday.
Computer Books
Steve Sharp
This company publishes books on popular software programs. They're looking for someone who can provide the accounting services for their business.
Flash Messengers
Joe Martin
A current client. Met with Joe on Tuesday to discuss taxes for next year.
Accounting Services.wpd
TABLE A Cell B4
Pg 1 Ln 3.73" Pos 3.97"
White arrow pointer

FIG. 9.3 You can select a cell to change the formatting of all the text in that cell all at once.

- To select *several cells*, position the mouse pointer in the cell that is in the upper-left corner of all the cells that you want to select. Drag through the cells that you want to select. The cells should be entirely highlighted.

- To select *columns or rows* if the row and column indicators are displayed, click or drag in the row/column indicators. The columns or rows in your selection should be entirely highlighted.
- To select *columns or rows* if the indicators are not displayed, position the mouse pointer against the top edge of the top cell in a column, or the left edge of the left cell in a row, so that it becomes a white arrow. Double-click to select the entire column or row.

Figure 9.4 illustrates a table after column A has been selected. Row/column indicators have been turned on (from the Tables toolbar) to make selection easier.

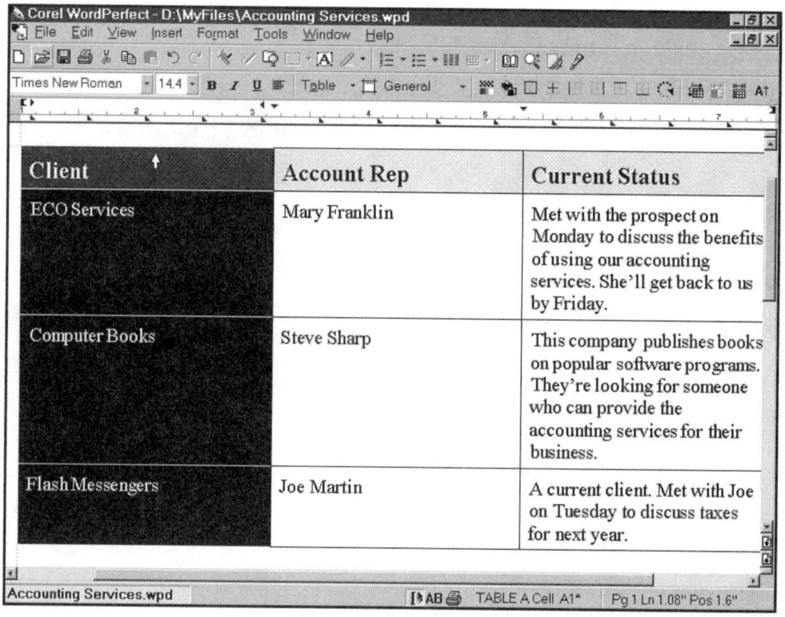

FIG. 9.4
You should select table cells before formatting those cells.

Changing Column Width To change the column width in a table, you can use the Size Column to Fit button or drag the column border. To use the Size Column To Fit button, select one or more cells in the column(s) to be resized. Click the Table button on the Property Bar, and then choose Size Column to Fit.

To adjust column width by dragging a column border, take the following steps:

1. Position the mouse pointer against the right edge of the column you want to adjust, so that the pointer becomes a cross with horizontal arrowheads.

TIP It's a good idea to start with the leftmost column that you're going to adjust and work your way to the right.

2. Drag the border to a new position. As you drag, a dotted vertical line appears and the exact position is indicated in a small pop-up window (see Figure 9.5).

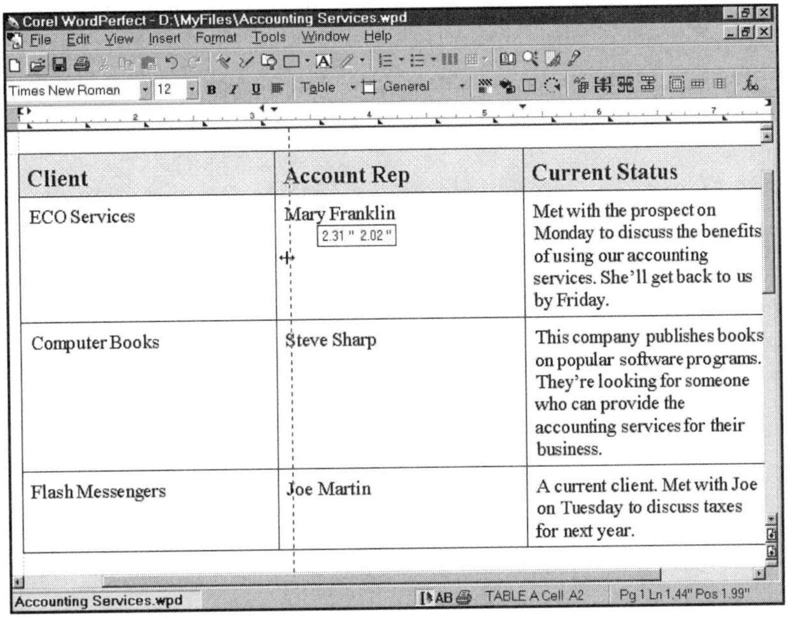

FIG. 9.5
Drag a column border to adjust the column's width.

TIP Alternatively, you can drag a Column Break icon on the Ruler to adjust the width of a table column.

NOTE You can also set a number of columns to have an equal width. Select one or more cells in each column to be resized, click the Table button, and then choose Equal Column Widths.

Inserting and Deleting Columns and Rows What if you enter several rows of information in your table and you realize that you need a new row in the middle of the table? No problem. You can insert a row anywhere in the table without disturbing what's already there.

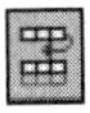

To do so, click in the row below the row to be inserted, and then click the Insert Row button on the Table Property Bar. You can add a new row at the bottom of a table with the Tab key. Position the insertion point in the last cell of the table and press Tab to create a new row. If you're entering a list of names and addresses into your table, you can press Tab to add a new row just before you add the next name and address.

You can also insert new rows or columns by using the Table menu and following these steps:

1. Position the insertion point in the row or column next to where you want a new row or column.
2. Click the Table button on the Table Property Bar, and then choose Insert. You see the Insert Columns/Rows dialog box (see Figure 9.6).

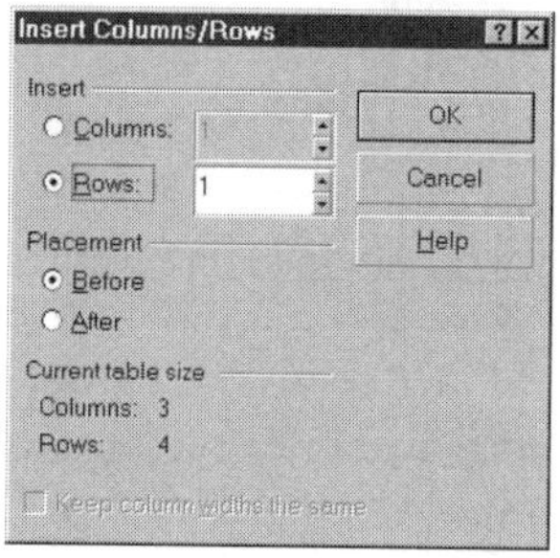

FIG. 9.6
Use the Insert Columns/Rows dialog box to indicate how many rows or columns to insert before the current column or row.

3. Choose Columns or Rows, and then specify how many to insert.
4. If desired, adjust the Placement from Before to After.
5. Click OK.

NOTE New rows and columns will contain the same formatting as the current row (or column).

TIP Insert a row just above the current row by pressing Alt+Insert. Delete the current row by pressing Alt+Delete.

You can delete rows and columns just as you can easily insert them by following these steps:

1. Position the insertion point in the row or column that you want to delete, or select the rows or columns that you want to delete (see the section "Selecting Table Cells," earlier in this chapter).
2. Click the Table button on the Table Property Bar, and then choose Delete. The Delete dialog box is displayed, as shown in Figure 9.7.
3. Choose Columns or Rows. If you selected rows or columns before accessing the Delete dialog box, click OK. If you positioned the insertion point before accessing the Delete dialog box, you can specify how many rows or columns to delete, and then click OK.

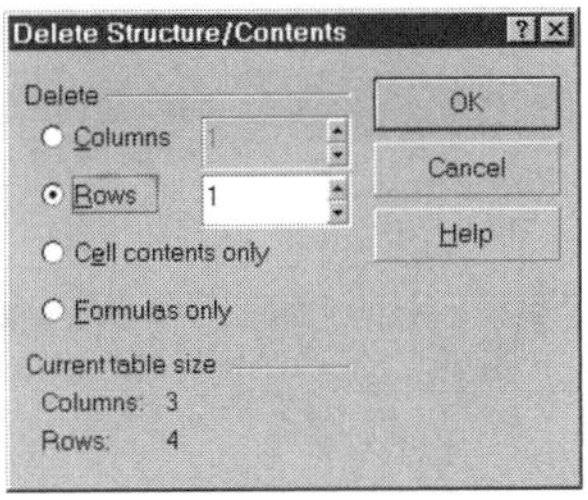

FIG. 9.7
Delete selected rows or columns with the Delete dialog box.

> **TIP** You can also delete cell contents or cell formulas using the Delete dialog box.

Joining and Splitting Cells What do you do when you want a title centered between the left and right edges of your table? You join table cells. When you first create a table, it has the same number of cells in every row and in every column. It doesn't have to stay that way; you can select the cells that you want to join and tell WordPerfect to join them. The top row of the table shown in Figure 9.8 has a single cell that was created by joining adjacent cells.

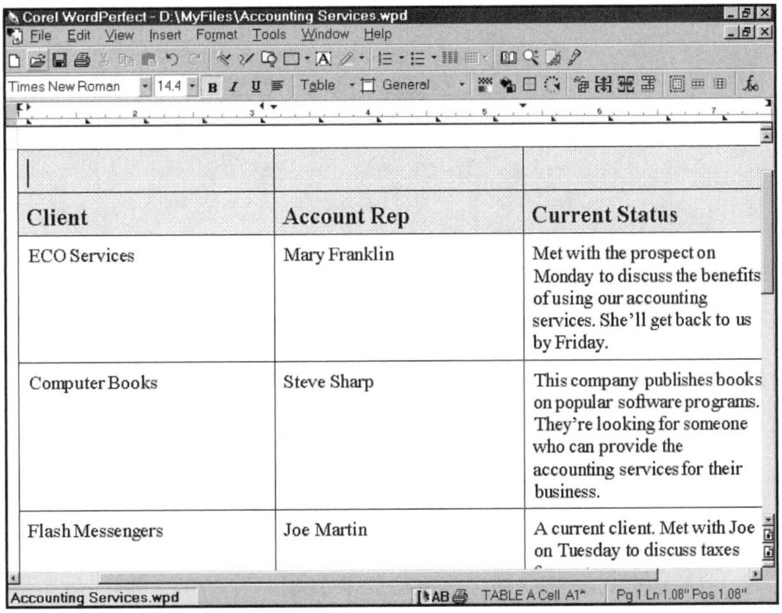

FIG. 9.8
Join cells in the top row to create an attractive title row.

To join table cells, click the QuickJoin button on the Table Property Bar. Drag across the appropriate cells to join them. Click on the QuickJoin button again to deselect it.

On occasion, you may find it useful to split cells. You can split a cell into two or more cells either vertically or horizontally. The second row of the table shown in Figure 9.9 has a single cell that was split into three cells.

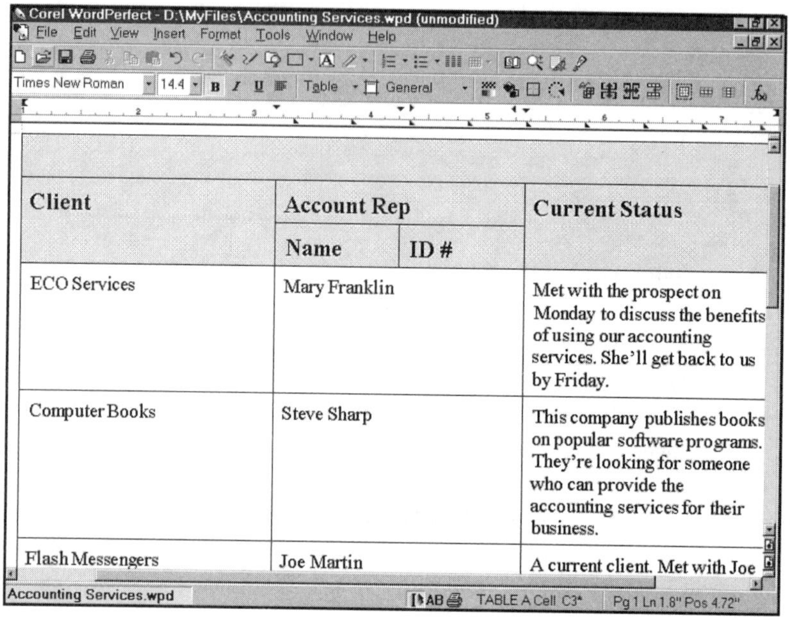
Corel WordPerfect - D:\MyFiles\Accounting Services.wpd (unmodified)
File Edit View Insert Format Tools Window Help
Times New Roman
14.4
Table
General
Client
Account Rep
Current Status
Name
ID #
ECO Services
Mary Franklin
Met with the prospect on Monday to discuss the benefits of using our accounting services. She'll get back to us by Friday.
Computer Books
Steve Sharp
This company publishes books on popular software programs. They're looking for someone who can provide the accounting services for their business.
Flash Messengers
Joe Martin
A current client. Met with Joe
Accounting Services.wpd
TABLE A Cell C3*
Pg 1 Ln 1.8" Pos 4.72"

FIG. 9.9
Split cells to create multiple cells where needed.

To split table cells, follow these steps:

1. Select the cells that you want to split.
2. Click the Table button, and then choose Split. Select Cell, Table, QuickSplit Column, or QuickSplit Row.
3. Select whether you want to split the cell into Rows or Columns and the number of cells that should be created.
4. Click OK to split the cells.

Alternatively, if no cells are selected, click the QuickSplit Row or QuickSplit Column button. When the QuickSplit feature is active the pointer becomes a dotted line in the direction of the split, with arrows pointing out at 90-degree angles to the dotted line. Click in the cell to be split, and then click the button again to deselect it.

Formatting a Table

Use Table Format options to specify justification, text attributes, column margins, and so on for table cells. You can specify formatting either before or after you enter text in cells; in either case, the text is formatted according to the cell format.

NOTE A table format is overridden by a column format; a column format is overridden by a cell format. You could, for example, format an entire column for decimal alignment and the cell at the top of the column for center alignment.

Formatting cells could be a matter of changing the alignment in the cells, applying attributes such as bold or underline to text in cells, of specifying header rows within the table. In this section, formatting table cells is used to mean formatting that is applied to any table element, whether that element is a cell, column, row, or the entire table.

Many common cell formatting tasks can be done quickly and easily using the toolbar and Property Bar. Select the appropriate cell(s), and then click the Font Face, Font Size, Bold, Italic, Underline, or Justification buttons to change the cell format. There are other specialized buttons that you can use as well:

Button	Button Name	Description
General	Numeric	Shows a list of numeric formats you can apply to numbers in your table
	Cell Fill	Sets the background color for cells
	Foreground Fill Color	Sets the color for the foreground when you are using patterns that have two colors
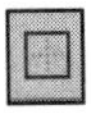	Change Outside Line	Allows you to specify type of line that goes around the outside of your table
	Rotate Cell	Rotates the text 90 degrees each time you click it; this only works if there is text in a cell

You can also format cells from the Properties for Table Format dialog box. To do so, follow these steps:

1. Select the cell(s) or column(s) that you want to format; or to format the entire table click anywhere in the table.
2. Open the Properties for Table Format dialog box by clicking the Table button and choosing Format; or click the Table Format button if cells are selected. Figure 9.10

illustrates the Format dialog box with Table format options displayed as tabs (types of format options are Cell, Column, Row, and Table).

FIG. 9.10
The Properties for Table Format dialog box with Table format options displayed.

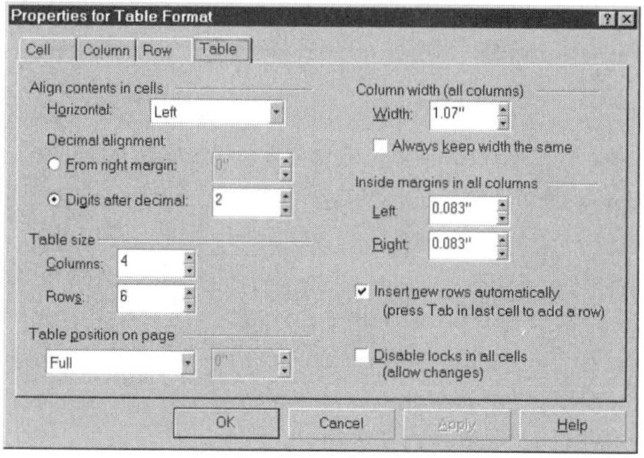

3. Choose the tab for the option type that you want to format: Cell, Column, Row, or Table.
4. Make the desired formatting changes. Your changes might include items in the following list:
   - When you format cells or columns, you can adjust the alignment with the Horizontal option. Cells containing numbers should be decimal-aligned.
   - When you format cells, you can lock cells to keep the insertion point from moving into the cells. You can also set vertical alignment, rotation, and place diagonal lines in cells.
   - When you format cells, you can specify that cell contents will be ignored in calculations (you might have to do this if you're adding a column that has a number in its column header).
   - When you format the table, you can adjust the Table Position relative to the page margins.
   - When you format rows, you can designate the selected row to be a header row if desired. When a table spans a page break, header rows print at the top of each page.
   - When you format rows, you can specify a fixed row height. This feature is useful when you create a table with "boxes" (cells) that should have a fixed height, regardless of any text they contain—for example, when you create a calendar. Unless you specify a fixed row height, the row height is a function of the number of text lines in the row.

5. Click OK to exit the Format dialog box and apply the specified changes to your table.

Changing Borders, Lines, and Shading in a Table

Give your tables visual appeal by changing table borders and lines and adding shading to cells. Your "desktop publishing" efforts can make the table more attractive and easier to read. For example, when you shade every other row in a table, it's easy to read across a row.

The lines around a table are called its *border.* Lines around cells are called *lines.* By default, tables have no border and single lines around each cell. Borders and lines are created and formatted separately, and borders mask lines. Thus, if you have single lines around each cell but a double-lined border, you will see the double line around the table, not the single line.

In addition to formatting table borders and lines, you can apply a fill style to table cells. Fill styles range all the way from standard gray shading to gradient patterns with blended colors.

You can use Table SpeedFormat to apply a set of changes for you, or you can make your own changes to table borders, lines, and shading.

Using Table SpeedFormat to Enhance a Table The fastest and easiest way to make changes to borders, lines, and shading in a table is to apply a table style (a set of changes) all at once with Table SpeedFormat.

TIP You can Undo the effects after you apply a table style with Table SpeedFormat by choosing Edit, Undo, or clicking the Undo button.

To use Table SpeedFormat, take the following steps:

1. Position the insertion point anywhere in the table.
2. Click the Table button, and then choose SpeedFormat. The Table SpeedFormat dialog box appears (see Figure 9.11).
3. Examine the available styles, if desired, by selecting a style and looking at the preview area.
4. Select the style you want to apply.

TIP To set the current table style as a default style for all new tables, access the Table SpeedFormat dialog box, choose Use as Default, and then choose Yes.

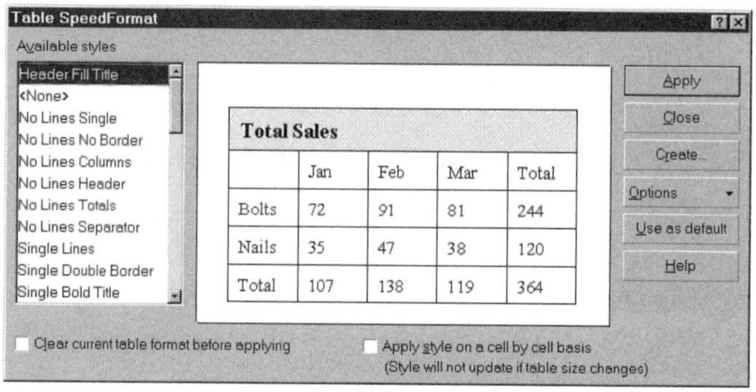

FIG. 9.11
Apply a set of formats to your table in the Table SpeedFormat dialog box.

5. If you have already applied changes to borders, lines, or shading, you may want to check the Clear Current Table Format Before Applying check box.
6. When you finish making selections in the Table SpeedFormat dialog box, choose Apply.

Making Your Own Table Enhancements You can make many changes to table borders, lines, or shading from the Property Bar. To do so, select the cells to be formatted, and then click the Change Left Line, Change Right Line, Change Top Line, Change Bottom Line, Change Inside Line, or Change Outside Line button on the Cell Selected Table Property Bar.

Alternatively, you can use the Table Lines/Fill dialog box to make formatting changes as follows:

1. Select the cells for which you want to change borders or lines or add shading.
2. Click the Table button, and then select Borders/Fill. The Table Borders/Fill dialog box is displayed.
3. If you want changes to affect the entire table, select the Table tab at the top of the dialog box. Figure 9.12 illustrates the Properties for Table Borders/Fill dialog box with the Table options displayed.
4. Select the border for the table by displaying the Border palette of border styles. To add a table border, choose any border style other than <None>. Change the default cell lines in the Table tab as well by changing the Line and Color options in the Default Cell Lines group.
5. To format lines or shading for selected cells, choose the Cell tab. Options in the dialog box now apply to the current selection, as shown in Figure 9.13.

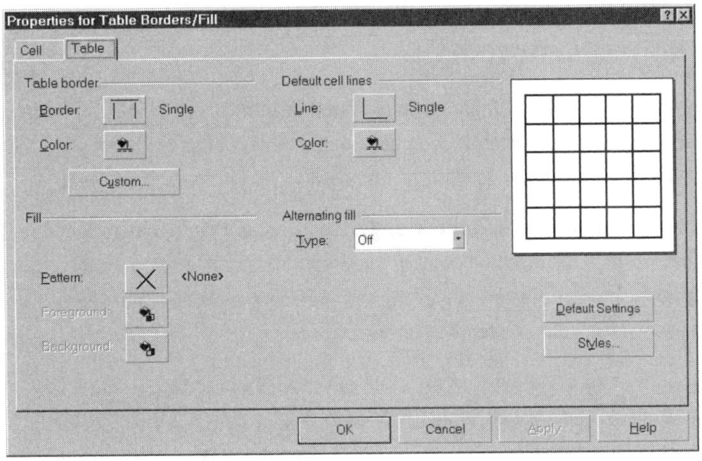

FIG. 9.12
The Properties for Table Borders/Fill dialog box with Table options displayed.

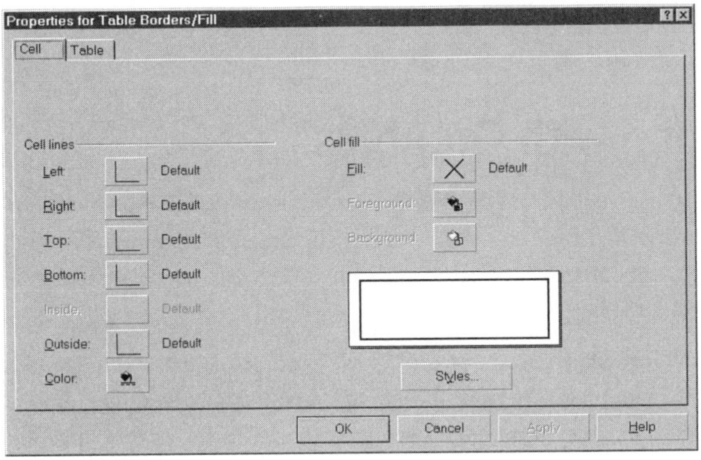

FIG. 9.13
The Properties for Table Borders/Fill dialog box with the Cell tab displayed.

6. Change the line style for the sides you want to change (left, right, top, bottom, or outside) from the pull-down palette of line styles.
7. With either the Table or Cell tab displayed, you can display a palette of fill styles and select a style. If the selected fill style has only one color, select a Foreground color, if desired. If the selected fill style has two colors, you can choose Foreground and Background colors.
8. Click OK to return to the table.

TROUBLESHOOTING

My table has cells with paragraphs of text in them. One row has an extra blank line at the bottom and I don't know how to get rid of it. Turn on the display of nonprinting characters by choosing View, Show +. Look for a + somewhere in the row and delete it.

I inserted several rows in the wrong place. Click the Undo button to remove the unwanted rows. Then position the insertion point in a row right next to where you want a new row or rows. Choose Table, Insert. Specify how many rows you want and make sure that you choose the correct placement (before or after the current row).

I removed all of the lines in my table and now it's hard to tell which part of the table I'm working in. Choose View, Table Gridlines to display dotted gridlines at the edges of cells. When table gridlines are displayed, you see gridlines at the edges of cells, regardless if any lines are defined for the cells. To view the table again as it will print (without the gridlines but with any defined lines or shading), choose View, Table Gridlines again.

Working with Graphics

Take advantage of WordPerfect's graphics features to add visual pizzazz to your documents. You can add lines, borders, shading, and pictures. Use graphics to call attention to your document, break the monotony of straight text, emphasize text, and pique the reader's interest.

You can add a line above (or below) headings to make them stand out or to help divide information on the page. Create a box with a border and enter text in the box, or add clip art to make a document more interesting. Use the Drop Cap feature to enlarge and emphasize the first letter in a paragraph. Use the Watermark feature to add a logo or clip art image or text behind the printed document text.

Working with Graphics Lines

The easiest way to insert horizontal or vertical graphics lines is through buttons on the Graphics toolbar. To display the Graphics toolbar, right-click the toolbar and select Graphics.

The default graphics lines are thin lines that extend from margin to margin (left to right, or top to bottom). You can tell WordPerfect how thick to make the line, what the color should be, how long it should be, or exactly where it should be on the page. Alternatively, you can use the mouse to adjust the thickness, length, and position of the line.

NOTE You can also insert lines and shapes by choosing Insert, Shape.

Figure 9.14 illustrates the use of a default horizontal graphics line to separate headings in a memo from the body of the memo.

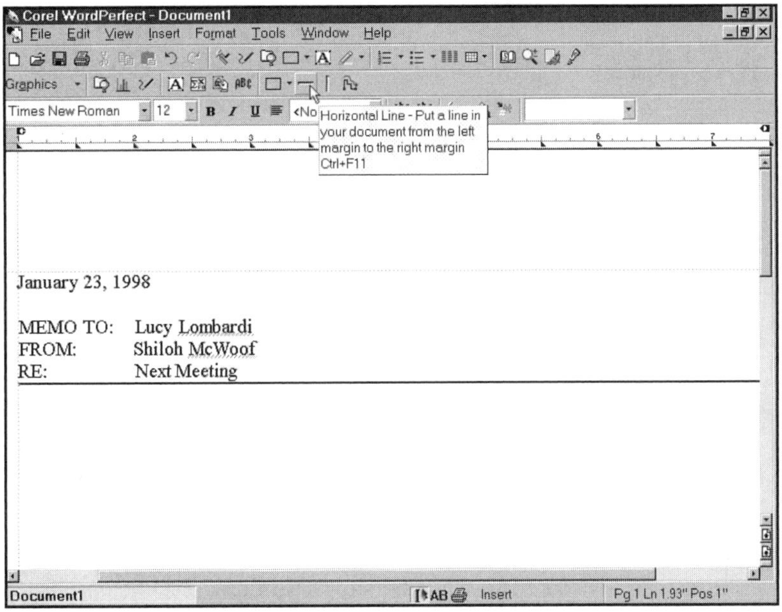

FIG. 9.14
Click the Horizontal Line button to create a horizontal graphics line that effectively separates the headings in a memo from the body of the memo.

Creating Instant Lines You can instantly create a horizontal graphics line by clicking the Horizontal Line button on the Graphics toolbar. The result is a thin line that extends from margin to margin at the baseline of text on the current line.

Correspondingly, you can instantly create a vertical graphics line by clicking the Vertical Line button on the Graphics toolbar. The result is a thin vertical line that is placed at the insertion point and extends from the top margin to the bottom margin.

NOTE WordPerfect won't insert a vertical line in the middle of centered text. It puts the line to the left of the text instead.

Creating a Custom Line To create a custom line, follow these steps:

1. If the line is to be a horizontal line, position the insertion point where you want the horizontal line. If you want the line to be placed slightly below a line of text, insert a hard return between the text and the horizontal line.

2. Click the Custom Line button. The Edit Graphics Line dialog box is displayed, as shown in Figure 9.15.

FIG. 9.15
Customize a graphics line in the Edit Graphics Line dialog box (or in the Edit Graphics Line dialog box).

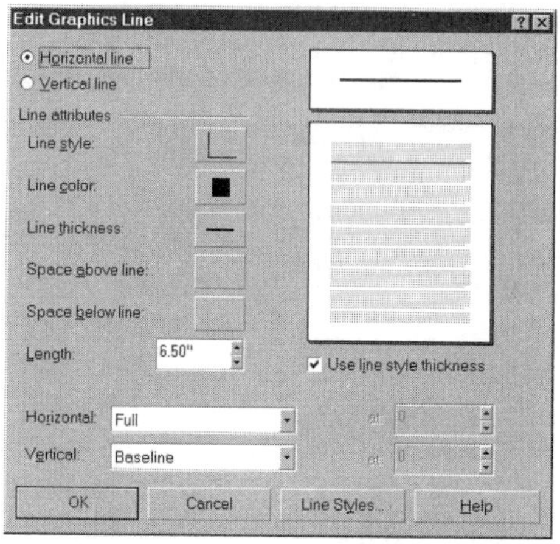

3. Adjust settings for the line as desired. For example, use the Position Horizontal option to adjust the length of the line. When you finish adjusting settings, click OK.
4. If the line you created is a horizontal line, you probably want to insert a hard return after the line.

NOTE The Create Graphics Line dialog box becomes the Edit Graphics Line dialog box when you edit a line.

Editing a Graphics Line Edit a graphics line either with the mouse or through the Edit Graphics Line dialog box. The mouse is quick and easy to use, but not as precise as the dialog box.

To edit a graphics line with the Edit Graphics Line dialog box, take the following steps:

1. Click the line to select it. You see small square dots called *handles* around the selected line, and you see the Horizontal/Vertical Line Property Bar.

2. Click the Line Graphic Edit button. The Edit Graphics Line dialog box appears (it looks like the Create Graphics Line dialog box shown earlier).

TIP You can also access the Edit Graphics Line dialog box by double-clicking the selected line or right-clicking the line and choosing Edit Horizontal (or Vertical) Line from the QuickMenu.

3. Change any settings as desired and click OK.

To edit a line with the mouse, select the line first. To move the line, place the mouse pointer against the line so that the pointer becomes a four-headed hollow arrow. Then drag the line to a new position. To adjust the thickness or length of the line, position the mouse pointer against a selection handle so that the mouse pointer becomes a two-headed hollow arrow. Then drag the handle to adjust the thickness or length.

Creating Borders

A graphics border is a box that surrounds text, emphasizes your message, separates text, or adds pizzazz to the page. You can use a paragraph border to call attention to one particular paragraph of text in a letter, for example; or you can add a page border to each page of a report to guide the reader and to create consistency within the report.

TIP You can use a variety of line styles and thickness with page and paragraph borders.

Figure 9.16 illustrates a newsletter with a paragraph border, a page border, and a column border.

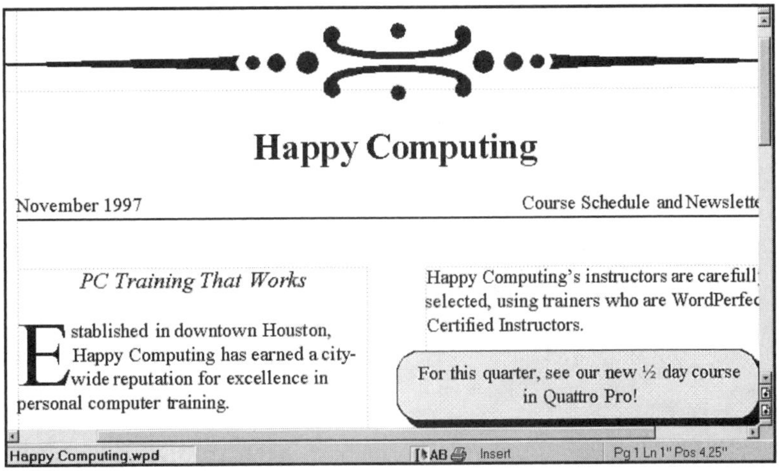

FIG. 9.16
The page border dresses up the page. The paragraph border emphasizes the announcement about what's new.

Creating Paragraph Borders A paragraph border is a frame that surrounds an individual paragraph or selected paragraphs. The border can include a fill style. WordPerfect gives you a choice of many border styles and fill styles.

To add a paragraph border to your document, follow these steps:

1. Place the insertion point in the paragraph to which you want to apply a border, or select the paragraphs to which you want to apply a border.
2. Choose Format, Paragraph, Border/Fill. The Paragraph Border/Fill dialog box appears, as shown in Figure 9.17.

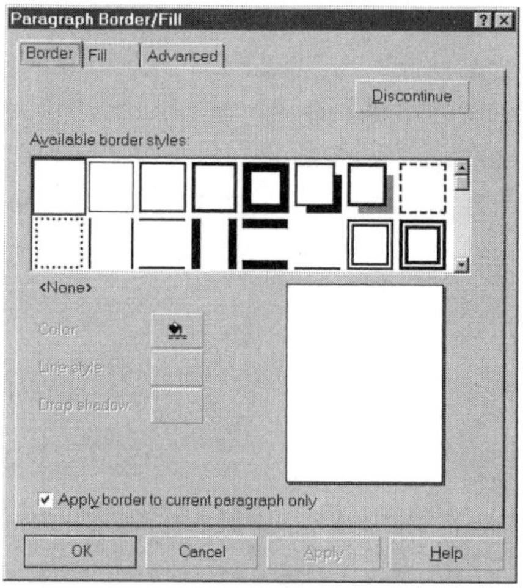

FIG. 9.17
Use the Paragraph Border/Fill dialog box to add a paragraph border (and a fill, if desired) that calls attention to specific text.

3. In the Border tab, choose an available Border Style to put a border around the selection, and select a Color, Line Style, and Drop Shadow if desired.
4. To frame the current paragraph and not all subsequent paragraphs, ensure that the Apply Border to Current Paragraph Only check box is not selected.
5. To add a fill to your border, choose the Fill tab, and then pick a style from the Available Fill Styles. Choose a Foreground color, a Background color, and a Pattern if desired.
6. Click OK.

Creating Page Borders A page border can add style to any document. Usually, you repeat the page border on all pages of a document, but you can choose to apply it to the current page only.

TIP Use Page view to see page borders on-screen; you can't see them in Draft view.

To add a page border to your document, do the following:

1. Position the insertion point on the first page where you want to apply a page border.
2. Choose Format, Page, Border/Fill. The Page Border/Fill dialog box is displayed, as shown in Figure 9.18.

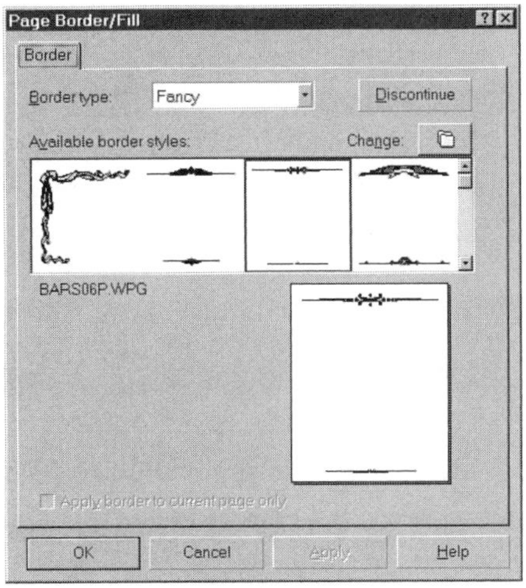

FIG. 9.18
Select the available border styles and you can see what the actual page will look like in the accompanying page border preview.

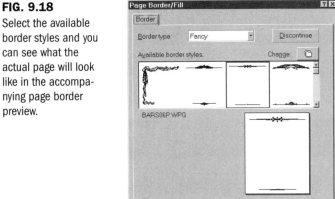

3. Select Fancy or Line as the Border Type.
4. In the Available Border Styles area, select a border style.
5. Click OK.

NOTE To remove a page border, place the insertion point on the page where the page border begins. Open the Page Border dialog box and choose Discontinue.

Inserting Graphic Objects

You can insert a number of different types of graphic objects in your WordPerfect documents. These objects are contained in *graphics boxes.*

A graphics box is a box that holds an image—for example, clip art, a drawing, a chart, an equation, or a table or text—like the pull quotes you see in newsletters. The contents of the document are adjusted to make room for the box. The box can be selected and moved or resized. A graphics box has its own contents and its own border; a paragraph or page border, on the other hand, is simply an ornamental frame surrounding text that is already in your document.

Adding graphics boxes to your documents illustrates the text, draws attention to the message, and adds interest to the document. Images, for example, help the reader understand the text, while text callouts attract the reader's attention to the text and break up "gray space" on the page. WordPerfect enables you to add several types of graphics boxes to your documents, each with a style and purpose of its own.

Understanding Graphics Box Styles Each of WordPerfect's graphics box styles is designed to work best with one particular type of image or text. For example, the Image, Figure, and User styles work well with graphics images; the Text Box and User styles work well with text. Any box, however, can hold any type of image, text, table, equation, and so on. The box style is simply a suggestion for the box's use. Each type of graphics box has a default line style (width and type of border line). Other aspects of the box style include its placement (how it is attached or anchored to the document), its caption style, and the amount of space allowed both outside and inside the box. When you choose a box style, you choose the default settings for that box style. The style of an individual box, however, can be customized.

An example of a graphics box containing an image is shown in Figure 9.19.

FIG. 9.19
Add graphics boxes to your document for visual interest.

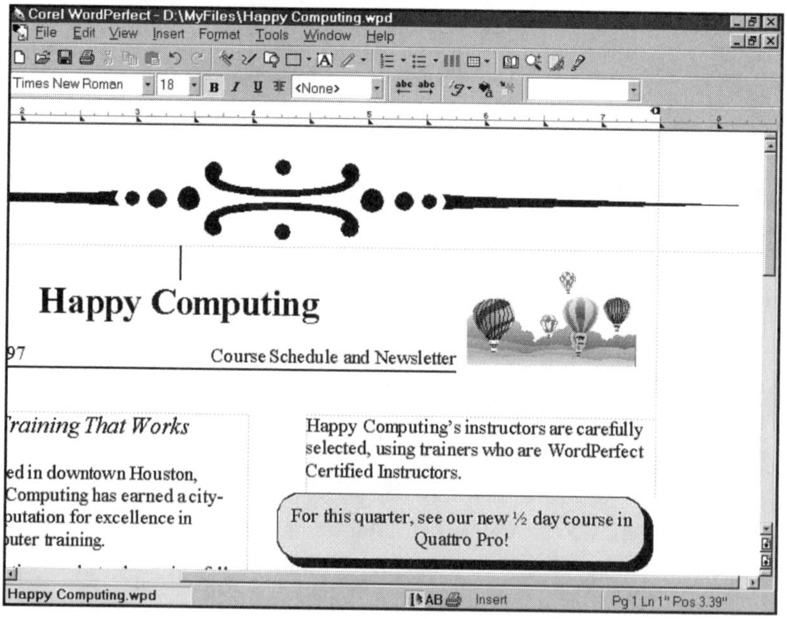

Graphics boxes are *attached* to the document in three ways: paragraph, character, or page. The way the box is attached to the document determines whether and how it will move when the document is edited. Table 9.2 describes how each type of placement works and for what it is suited.

Table 9.2 Graphics Placement

Attach Box To	How It Works	Suitable For
Paragraph	The box stays with the paragraph that contains it.	Boxes that are associated with text in the same area.
Character	The box is treated like a single character on a particular line of text.	Very small boxes that are associated with a line of text.
Page	The box stays in a fixed position on the page, regardless of editing changes to the text.	Boxes that are meant to stay in the same place on the page, such as a masthead at the top of a newsletter page.

Understanding Graphics Objects You can insert a number of different types of graphics objects into your WordPerfect document. Some of these are files on your disk. You create others like charts using applications that are common throughout the WordPerfect Suite. Graphics objects include:

- *Clipart.* Artwork that ships with WordPerfect
- *TextArt.* Fancy shaped text, used for logos and titles
- *Pictures.* Artwork that you create with Suite drawing tools
- *Charts.* Pie charts, histograms, and so on
- *Acquired Images.* Images that you scan in

For more information about graphics, see Chapter 20, "Adding and Enhancing Objects."

Creating a Graphics Box By default, WordPerfect inserts the graphics box close to where the insertion point is. After it is inserted, you can move or size the box.

TIP If you prefer to be able to click and drag with the mouse to position and size your box when it is created, choose Tools, Settings, Environment, Graphics, and check the Drag to Create New Graphic Boxes check box.

To create a graphics box, follow these steps:

1. Click in the document where you want the graphic box to appear.
2. Choose Insert, Graphics, and then select the type of box you want: Clipart, From File, TextArt, Draw Picture, Chart, or Custom Box.
3. What you see next depends on the type of box you selected:

TIP If you want to insert clipart or a text box into your WordPerfect document, you can quickly do so by clicking the Clipart or Text Box buttons.

- If you chose Clipart, you see the Scrapbook dialog box shown in Figure 9.20. Double-click the image you want to insert in your document.

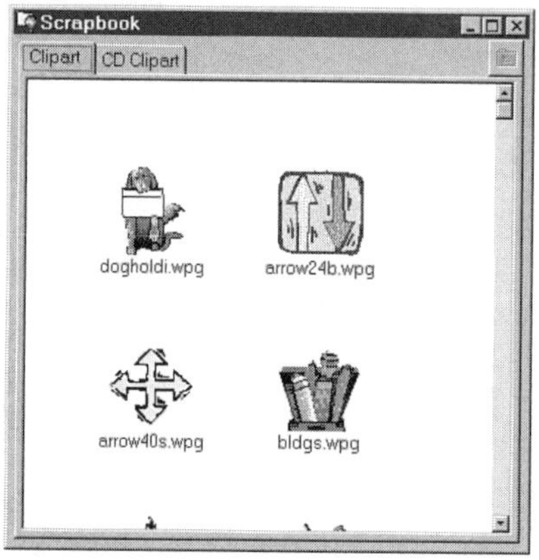

FIG. 9.20
WordPerfect comes with clipart images that you can include in your document.

- If you chose TextArt, you see the Corel TextArt 8.0 dialog box. Create the text art as described in "Creating TextArt" in Chapter 20, and then click OK to insert it in your document.
- If you chose Draw Picture, you see the Presentation toolbars and menu. You can use Presentation's drawing tools to create the image as discussed in Chapter 20. Click outside the selected object to return to WordPerfect.
- If you chose Chart, you see the Chart module of Presentations. Create the chart as described in "Creating a Data Chart" in Chapter 19. Click outside the chart to return to WordPerfect.
- If you chose Acquire Image, what you see will depend on the type of scanner you have installed. Follow your usual steps for scanning and image. (You will not see this entry unless you have a scanner attached to your computer.)

4. Adjust the size or position of the box by ensuring that the graphics box is still selected (has handles around it). Then use the two-headed sizing pointer or the four-headed moving pointer to size or move it.

To edit a graphics box, ensure that it is selected, and then click the Image Tools button on the Property Bar. You see the Image Tools floating dialog box (see Figure 9.21), which contains a variety of tools to edit the graphics box. When you finish working with the graphics box, deselect it by clicking outside the box.

FIG. 9.21
The floating Image Tools dialog box allows you to change how the graphics box appears in the document.

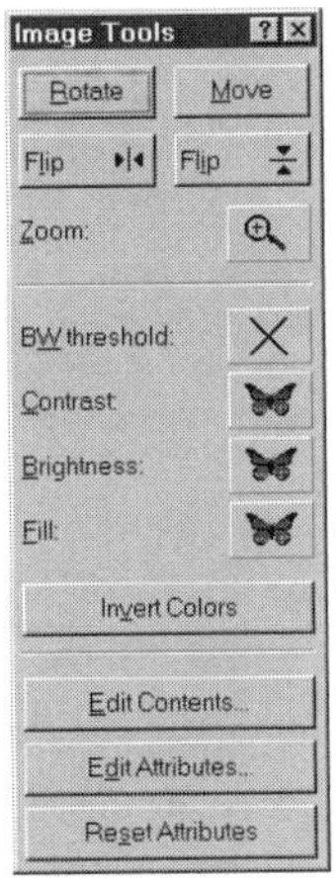

There are a number of things you can do to enhance the appearance of the image in your document:

- To contour text around the image in a box, click the Wrap button on the Property Bar.
- To quickly edit the text or the actual image in a graphics box, double-click the box.
- To remove a graphics box, select it and then press the Delete key.
- Choose Insert, Graphics, Custom Box to select a style for a box before you create the box. The box is created using default formatting options for your selected style.
- Double-clicking a graphic allows you to edit the graphic image using Corel Presentations.

Creating Drawings

You can include drawings in your WordPerfect document to illustrate points, or use drawing objects to call attention to important points. You can use all of Presentation's tools to draw your picture, or you can add simple drawing shapes directly from WordPerfect.

To use Presentation's tools to draw a picture, do the following:

1. Click where you want the picture to appear.

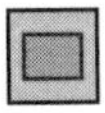

2. Choose Insert, Graphics, Draw Picture or click the Draw Picture button. Your menu and toolbar change to Presentations, and the title bar indicates that you are in the Presentations Drawing mode, as shown in Figure 9.22.

FIG. 9.22
When inserting a complex drawing, you can use all the power of Presentations' drawing tools.

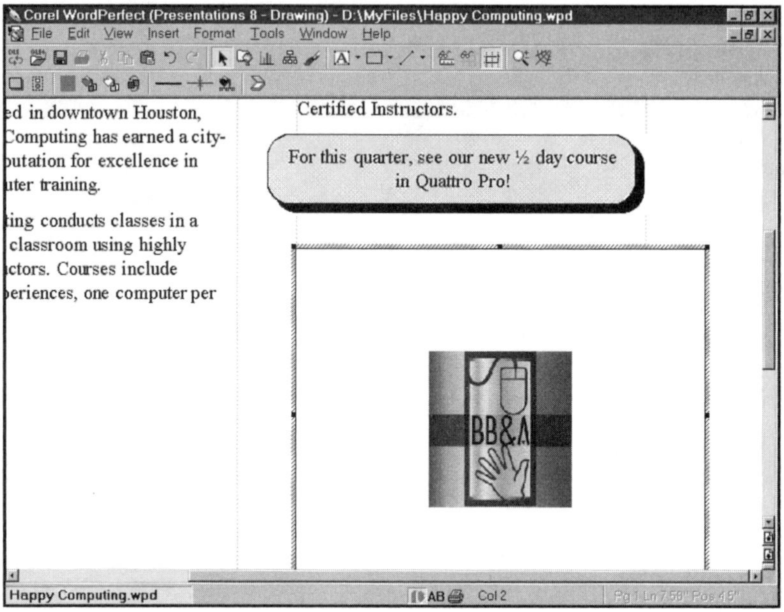

3. Draw the picture using Presentations drawing tools, as described in the section "Using Drawing Tools" in Chapter 20.
4. Click outside the object to return to WordPerfect.
5. Adjust the size or position of the graphics box by ensuring that the graphics box is still selected (has handles around it). Then use the two-headed sizing pointer or the four-headed moving pointer to size or move it.

Alternatively, if you merely want to place a simple object like a rectangle or circle in your document, it may be easier to do this directly within WordPerfect, as follows:

1. Click the down arrow to the right of the Draw Object button, and then click on the shape you want to draw.
2. Move your mouse pointer into the document and notice that the pointer is now a crosshair.
3. Click and drag over the area where the object should appear. The object appears with handles around it.
4. Move or size the object using the fill handles as needed.
5. Click outside the object to deselect it.

Using Drawing Layers

When you insert graphic objects in your WordPerfect document, they are *layered*. In other words, they appear over top of each other and can thus obscure one another. You can specify which objects go in front of each other very easily, however.

To do so, click the desired graphic object. You see selection handles and the Graphics Property Bar. Click the Object(s) Back One button to move the object one level back and the Object(s) Forward One button to move it toward the front of the stack of objects.

Creating Drop Caps

WordPerfect's Drop Caps feature puts desktop publishing within everyone's reach. Now it's easy to add visual interest to your text by creating an oversized character at the beginning of a paragraph, like the one in Figure 9.23.

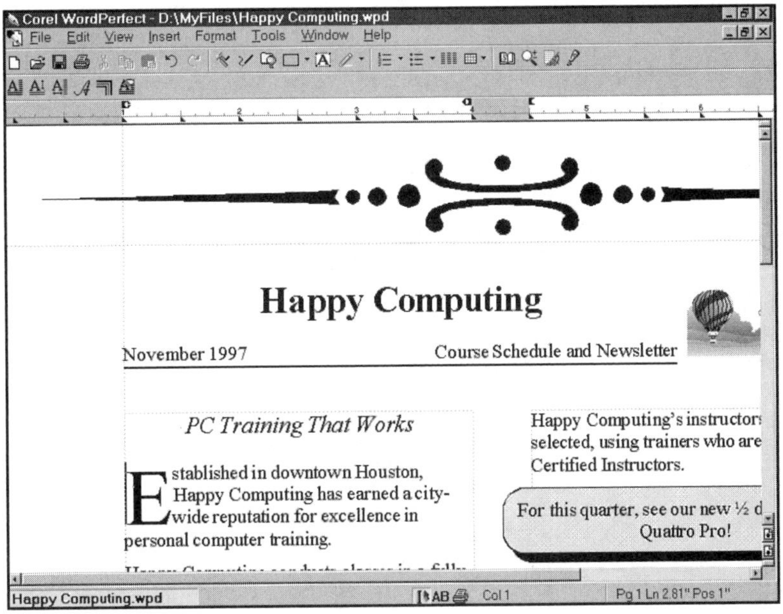

FIG. 9.23
Drop Caps add interest and visual appeal to text.

To create a drop cap, take the following steps:

1. Position the insertion point in the paragraph in which you want a drop cap.
2. Choose Format, Paragraph, Drop Cap. WordPerfect creates a drop cap three lines deep using the first character in the paragraph and displays the Drop Cap Property Bar.

3. Adjust the drop cap, if desired, by using buttons on the Property Bar. For example, if you want the drop cap to drop down through four lines of text instead of three, click the Size button, and then select 4 Lines High.
4. Begin to type your paragraph. The first letter you type is put into the drop cap format you selected.

Creating Watermarks

A *watermark* is a special type of graphics box that contains either text or graphics but prints in the background. The watermark prints lightly so that the text you enter in the foreground is readable.

There are many uses for watermarks. You can dress up a letter to a client with your company logo, you can add text ("Draft") to the background of reports, and so on. You can use any of WordPerfect's watermark files, create your own images or text to use as watermarks, or use images and text from other applications.

Using a Text Watermark Most of WordPerfect's watermark files consist of text that has been saved as a graphics image. You can use WordPerfect's watermark text, or you can create your own text (it doesn't have to be saved as a graphics image). Figure 9.24 illustrates using your own text (`Draft`) as a watermark in a draft copy of a newsletter.

FIG. 9.24
You can place a watermark with text to indicate the nature of your document.

Using Images as Watermarks You can use images created in other applications, or you can use any of the images in WordPerfect's Graphics folder as a watermark image. The image you use doesn't have to be designed specifically as a watermark image. Figure 9.25 illustrates one of WordPerfect's image files (ROSE.WPG) used as a watermark in a newsletter.

FIG. 9.25
You can also use an image, such as a rose, for your watermark.

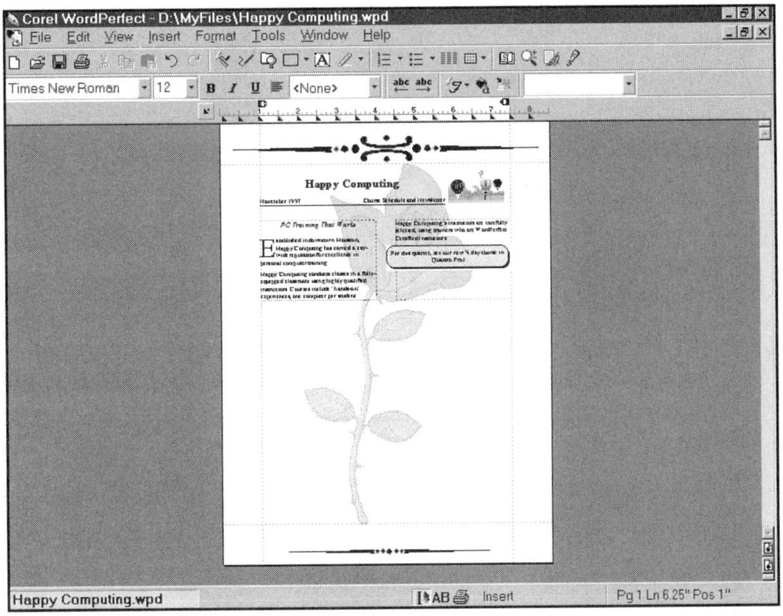

Creating a Watermark Before creating a watermark, enter and format all document text. When the watermark appears on-screen, text editing slows considerably. To add a watermark to a document, follow these steps:

1. Position the insertion point on the first page that is to have a watermark (the watermark will appear on that page and on every subsequent page).
2. Choose Insert, Watermark. In the Watermark dialog box, choose Create. You are placed in the Watermark A editing screen shown in Figure 9.26. The Watermark Property Bar appears above the text area at the top of the screen.
3. If you're going to create a watermark from text, you can type the text directly on the screen. You'll probably want an extremely large font size, however. Type (and format) the text that you want as a watermark. Then click the Close button on the Watermark Property Bar to return to your document.
4. To create a watermark that contains an image, click the Insert File button on the Watermark Property Bar and choose an image. The image you choose is automati-

cally sized to fill the entire page. If you want to edit the image, right-click the image, and then choose Edit Image from the QuickMenu. Click the Close button on the Watermark Property Bar to return to your document.

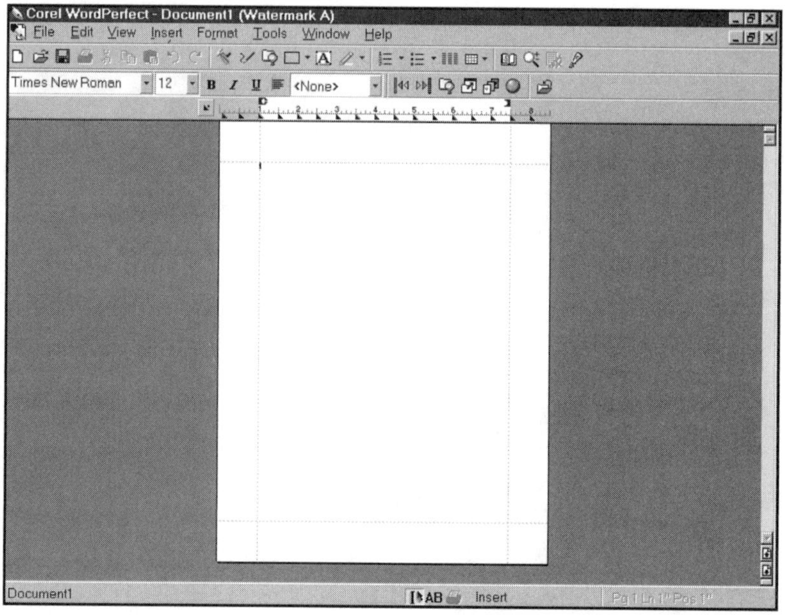

FIG. 9.26
You can create watermarks that appear behind the text on each page.

TROUBLESHOOTING

I keep creating a page border, but no matter what I do I can't see it on-screen. Change the view from Draft view to Page view by choosing View, Page.

My page border only prints on the first page, and I have to specify it again and again on every page. When you create the page border on the first page, be sure that the Apply Border to Current Page check box is not selected.

My watermark is too dark. Edit your watermark by choosing Insert, Watermark, Edit. Click the Shading button to display the Watermark Shading dialog box. Adjust the percent of the text or image shading as needed and choose OK. Click the Close button on the Watermark Property Bar to return to your document.

I created a box and placed an image in it, and now I'd like to change the border lines. Right-click your graphic and choose Border/Fill from the QuickMenu. Make whatever changes you want at the Box Border/Fill Styles dialog box, and click OK. Click outside of the box to deselect it.

CHAPTER 10

Automating with Macros and Merge

Corel WordPerfect supplies many features that enable you to complete your work quickly and efficiently. Two of these features are Macros and Merge. Both features save you time by automating your work.

You can automate your work with macros, or mini-programs, by recording your keystrokes and commands, saving the recording, and then playing back the recording any time you need to repeat the same keystrokes and commands.

WordPerfect's Merge feature also saves you time and work. If you ever have to send the same letter to a number of people, you know how much work this can be. WordPerfect enables you to merge (combine) fixed information (the text in the letter) with variable information (the names and addresses). The form letters are produced all at once in a single merge operation.

Play a macro

Macros automate repetitive keystrokes and commands. Learn to play macros that are supplied with Corel WordPerfect.

Create your own macros by recording keystrokes and commands

When you're comfortable with using macros, you'll want to learn how to create your own.

Discover the power of Merge

See how you can use Corel WordPerfect's Merge feature to send out mass mailings, address envelopes or labels, or customize messages to any number of people. You can even fill out forms with it.

Fill in forms

You can use the Keyboard Merge feature to create forms that can be quickly filled in by users.

Using Macros

Macros can save you time by performing repetitive tasks automatically. You can, for example, record a macro that types a closure to a letter. You can use macros to speed everyday formatting and editing, to automate an elaborate set of tasks, or to combine several commands into one (the one that plays the macro).

In addition to using macros you create yourself, you can use macros that WordPerfect provides for you. Macros that WordPerfect provides include: CLOSEALL.WCM, which closes all open documents; PLEADING.WCM, which creates a sample pleading for legal offices; and WATERMRK.WCM, which prompts you for text or a graphic and creates a watermark out of it.

TIP To see a description of the macros included with WordPerfect, choose Help, then look up Macro in the index, and select Macros Included with WordPerfect.

This section introduces you to playing macros, recording macros, and making simple editing changes to macros.

NOTE WordPerfect enables you to save macros inside templates, or as files on the disk. In the former case, they are saved as part of the template file, and are available only when you are using the appropriate template. In the latter case, they are saved as stand-alone files and are always accessible.

Template macros are accessed by choosing Tools, Template Macro; the other macros are accessed by choosing Tools, Macro. Other than the location in which they are saved, they work the same way. The remainder of this chapter discusses macros saved as files, but the discussion applies as well to template macros.

Playing a Macro

When you play a macro, you execute the keystrokes and commands that are saved in the macro. The macro may type in text. It may perform formatting functions. It may even ask for your input and then perform certain steps depending upon your input.

TIP Once you have played macros, you can play recently played macros again easily. Choose Tools, Macro, and then choose a recently played macro listed at the bottom of the Macro menu.

To play a macro, take the following steps:

1. Choose Tools, Macro, Play. The Play Macro dialog box appears (see Figure 10.1).

FIG. 10.1
Select a macro to play in the Play Macro dialog box.

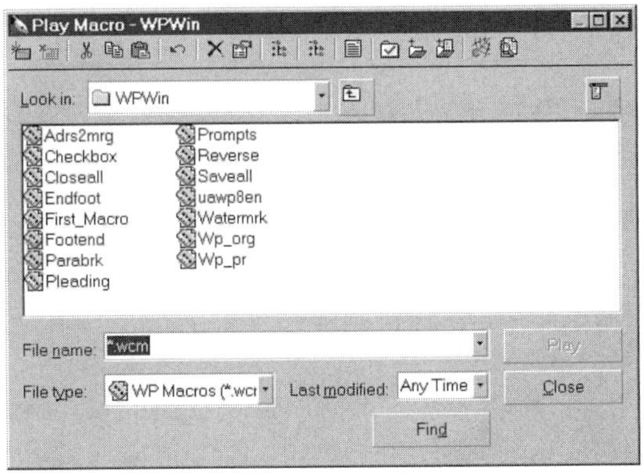

NOTE WordPerfect automatically lists macros in the default directory specified for macros through File Preferences. To change this directory, choose Tools, Settings, Files, Merge/Macro, Default Macro Folder.

2. Select the desired macro.
3. Choose Play. If this is the first time that you have played the macro, it compiles before it plays, and it takes a little extra time to get going.

Stopping a Macro

When you're testing a macro, it's a good idea to save any open documents before you play the macro. If something goes wrong during playback (for instance, if the macro adds text to the wrong part of your document), you'll want to cancel macro execution. You can usually stop a macro during playback by pressing the Esc key; however, the Esc key could be disabled or assigned to a specific function by the macro. After you cancel macro execution, you can always close all open documents without saving and then reopen them.

Creating a Macro

Creating a macro is simply a matter of starting the macro recorder, performing the actions that you want recorded, and ending the recording session.

To record a macro, follow these steps:

1. Choose Tools, Macro, Record. The Record Macro dialog box appears (see Figure 10.2).
2. Enter a name for your macro. WordPerfect assigns a WCM extension to the name.
3. Choose Record. The macro recorder is activated and the Macro Property Bar is displayed at the top of the screen (see Figure 10.3) `Macro Record` is also displayed on the Application Bar.

FIG. 10.2
Enter a name for your macro in the Record Macro dialog box.

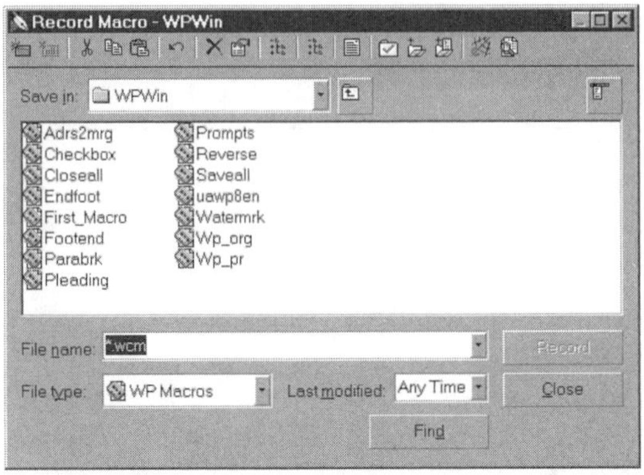

FIG. 10.3
The Macro Property Bar displays while a macro is being recorded.

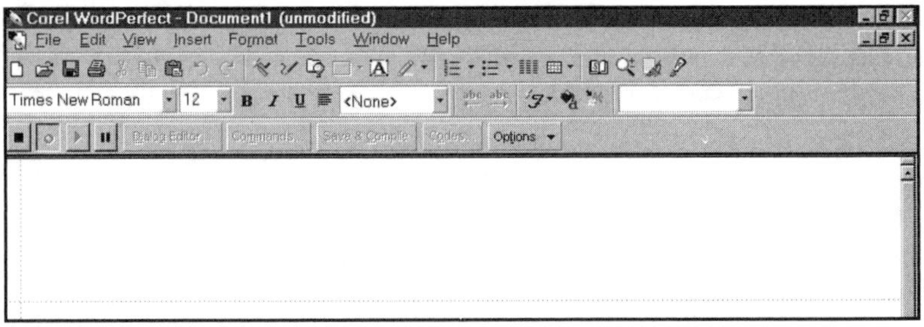

4. Perform the actions that you want the macro to record. You can enter text from the keyboard, and you can choose commands from menus (with the keyboard or the mouse). Use Shift + arrow key to select items because you cannot use the mouse to move the insertion point or to select text while the macro recorder is active.

5. To finish recording, click the Stop Record button on the Macro Property Bar; or choose Tools, Macro, Record. The Macro Record message disappears from the Application Bar and the macro is saved to disk. You can close the document window without saving changes after you end recording, because the macro was saved when you ended recording.

Making Simple Editing Changes to a Macro

Don't be afraid to make simple editing changes to a macro. If you decide that you want to add a middle initial to a closure that is typed by a macro, for example, you can add the text without having to learn macro syntax and commands.

To make simple editing changes to a macro, do the following:

1. Choose Tools, Macro, Edit. The Edit Macro dialog box appears (it looks similar to the Record Macro dialog box).

2. Select the macro that you want to edit, and then choose Edit. The macro file is opened into an editing window and the Macro Property Bar appears just above the text window, like the macro being edited in Figure 10.4.

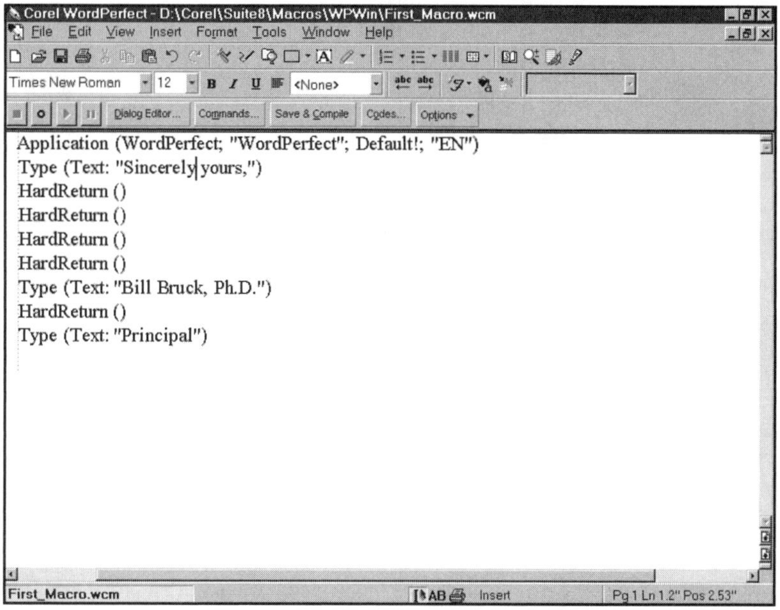

FIG. 10.4
You can edit macros like you would edit any other WordPerfect document.

Part II Ch 10

3. Use normal editing techniques to make simple editing changes.

   For example, to add a middle initial to the signature in the First_Macro.wcm macro, insert the middle initial in the appropriate place in the `Type` command. To remove one of the blank lines before the signature line, select a `HardReturn()` command and press Delete. To add a blank line above the signature line, type the command **HardReturn()**, or copy and paste a `HardReturn()` command.

   While you're editing the macro, you can press Enter (or Tab or the space bar) to separate commands. This formats the macro so that it's easier to read, but it doesn't affect what happens when you play the macro.

CAUTION

Be careful, however, not to press Enter when the insertion point is positioned in the middle of a command; the Enter key signals the end of a macro command.

4. When you finish editing the macro, click the Save & Compile button on the Macro Property Bar. The save and compile process begins. If there are no errors, the process is completed and the macro remains on-screen. If WordPerfect detects

errors during compilation, a dialog box appears describing the error and its location. You can then cancel compilation, correct the error, and try the save and compile operation again.

5. After the macro successfully saves and compiles, choose Options, Close Macro to close the document window.

NOTE WordPerfect provides extensive on-screen help information about macros. For help with a specific macro command, choose Help, Help Topics. In the Contents tab, choose Macros, Macro Programming. You can also refer to the Reference Center if you installed it from your CD.

TIP Make your macros easy to use by adding them to the toolbar. See "Adding Macros to Toolbar Buttons" in Chapter 32.

TROUBLESHOOTING

I'm recording a macro to move the insertion point and select text; however, I can't use the mouse to move the cursor within the text. The macro recorder cannot record mouse actions within document text, such as selecting text. Use the keyboard to record these actions.

I'd like to type some commands into my macro when I'm editing it, but I don't know the syntax. While you're editing a macro, you can click the Begin Record button on the Macro Property Bar and record commands (this is easier than looking up the syntax and typing in the command). When you turn on the macro recorder, you access a new document window where you can choose the commands you want to record in the macro, either through the menu, the toolbar, or the Property Bar. When you finish recording, click the Stop Record button on the Macro Property Bar to return to the editing window for the macro. The steps you performed while recording are added to the macro at the insertion point. You can also press Ctrl+M while you are editing your macro to see a dialog box of macro commands.

Using Merge

Using WordPerfect's Merge feature, you can mass-produce letters, envelopes, mailing labels, and other documents. When you merge a form letter with a list of names and addresses, each resulting document contains a different name, address, and company name. The process of merging a form letter with names and addresses is sometimes referred to as a *mail merge*. Because the names and addresses are saved in a separate file (the data file), you only have to enter them once—when you create the data file. You can use that same data file over and over again when you perform a merge.

Not only can you perform a merge in WordPerfect using a data file, but you can also perform a keyboard merge. A *keyboard merge* merges a form file with input from the keyboard rather than from a data file. The result of a keyboard merge is a single, filled-in form document.

What Is a Merge?

A *merge* is the process of combining fixed information and variable information. The fixed information—a form letter, for example—is in a file referred to as a *form file*. Every merge has a form file. The variable information can come from another file (referred to as a *data file*) or it can come from user input at the keyboard. A data file could be a WordPerfect data file or it could be a file from a database program such as Paradox, dBASE, or Access.

To create a merge data file or form file, or to perform a merge, access the Merge dialog box. Choose Tools, Merge. You see the Merge dialog box shown in Figure 10.5.

FIG. 10.5
Create a merge file or perform a merge in the Merge dialog box.

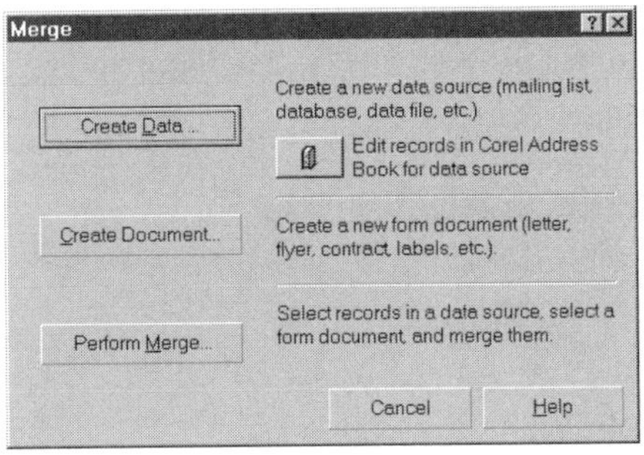

Performing a simple merge is a matter of creating a data file with variable information, creating a form file that asks for information from the data file, and performing the merge.

In the following sections, you learn to create the data file and form file that are used to perform a merge. You also learn to create the form file for a keyboard merge and to perform a keyboard merge.

Creating a Data File

When you create a data file through the Merge dialog box, WordPerfect guides you through the process of creating the file.

A WordPerfect data file can be either a text file or a table. In either form, the data file is organized into fields and records. A *field* is one category of information; for example, a field is a name or a phone number. A *record* contains all of the information about one person and is comprised of a complete set of fields.

To create a data file, take the following steps:

1. In an empty document window, choose Tools, Merge. The Merge dialog box appears (refer to Figure 10.5).

TIP If you already have a table that is formatted as a list, you can use the table as a data file. You can also click the Address Book icon to use your Address Book as the data file for the merge.

NOTE If you have text in the active document window when you choose Create Data, WordPerfect displays a Create Merge File dialog box that asks if you want to use the file in the active window or open a new document window to create the data file. Choose New Document Window if you want to create the data file from scratch.

2. Choose Create Data. Once WordPerfect knows that you want to create a data file, the Create Data File dialog box appears.
3. In the Create Data File dialog box, create a field name list by typing each field name and pressing Enter to add the name to the list. Figure 10.6 illustrates the Create Data File dialog box after field names have been defined.

FIG. 10.6
Define field names in the Create Data File dialog box.

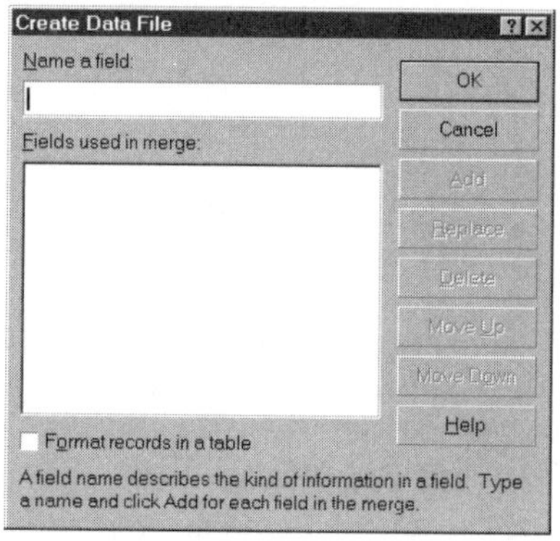

4. After you finish creating the field name list, click OK to close the Create Data File dialog box and open the Quick Data Entry dialog box.
5. At the Quick Data Entry dialog box, enter the data for each record, pressing Enter between each field and record. Figure 10.7 illustrates the Quick Data Entry dialog box with a filled-in record.

FIG. 10.7
Enter data records in the Quick Data Entry dialog box.

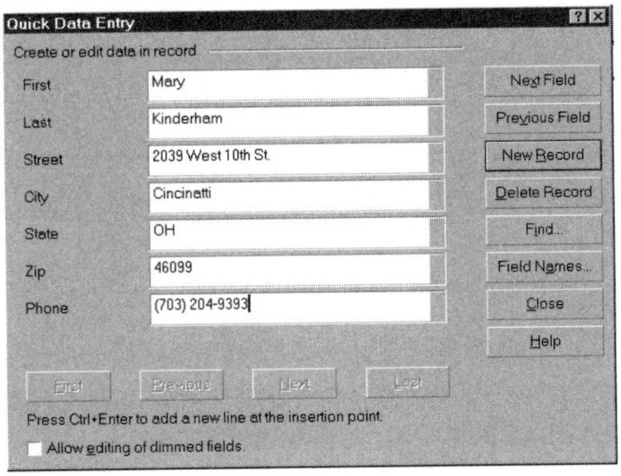

NOTE A field can have more than one line. An address field, for example, could have one or more lines for the street address and a line for the city, state, and zip code. In general, though, it's easier to sort and select records when fields are broken down into small categories. If you do want to enter more than one line of data in a field, press Ctrl+Enter before each subsequent line. Scroll arrows at the right end of the field box let you see different lines in the field.

6. Choose Close after you finish entering records. WordPerfect then prompts you to save the data file. You don't have to type an extension for the file name unless you want to. WordPerfect automatically supplies a DAT extension.
7. Choose Yes to save the data file. Then specify a file name and click Save. If your data file is in a text format (rather than a table format), you see something like the illustration shown in Figure 10.8. At the top of the data file are the field names, followed by a page break. The end of each field is marked with an `ENDFIELD` code, even if the field is empty (the phone field in the second record is empty). The end of each record is marked with an `ENDRECORD` code and a hard page break. The Merge Property Bar is displayed at the top of the screen.

Editing and Printing a Data File

You can edit your data file after creating it to add more records or to change existing data. You may want to print the data for verification. To edit a data file if it's not already in the active window, open it like any other file. When WordPerfect opens the file, it recognizes it as a data file and displays the Merge Property Bar at the top of the screen.

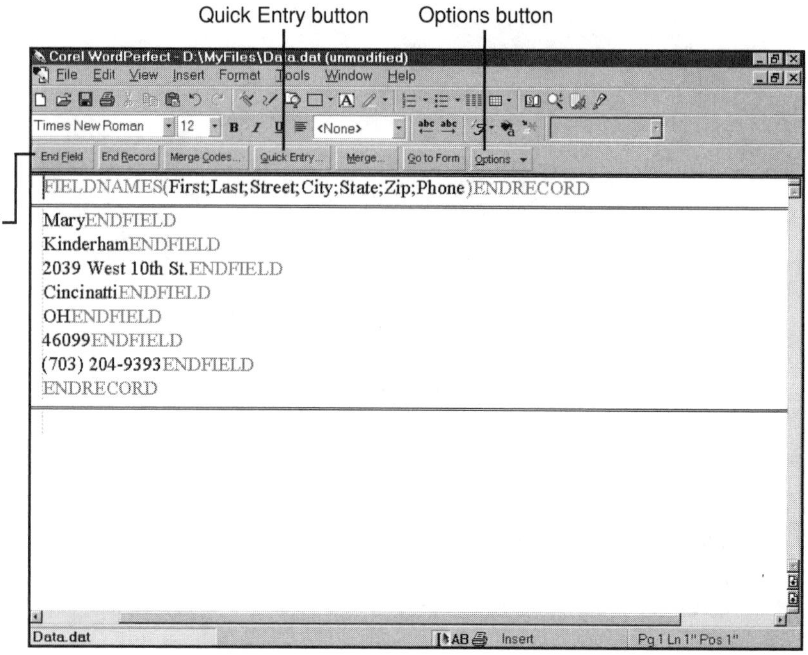

FIG. 10.8
A text data file with records created in the Quick Entry dialog box.

Adding Records

When you don't have time to enter all of your data file records at once, or you don't have all of the information when you create the data file, you'll want to reopen the file later and add records.

To add more records to the data file in the active window, follow these steps:

1. Choose Quick Entry on the Property Bar.
2. In the Quick Entry dialog box, choose New Record if one is not already displayed. An empty record form appears.
3. Enter new records until you've finished, and then choose Close.
4. When WordPerfect prompts you to save your file, answer Yes and then save it to its existing name.

TIP It's easier to read the data on-screen if you choose Options on the Property Bar, and then select Hide Codes.

Editing Records

When you need to update the information in your data file—for example, when someone's address changes—reopen the data file and take the following steps:

1. Position the insertion point anywhere in the first record that you want to change, and then choose Quick Entry; or position the insertion point at the beginning of the document and choose Quick Entry.
2. If the record that you want to change isn't displayed in the Quick Entry dialog box, choose Find. A Find Text dialog box appears. Enter the text that you want to find and choose Find Next. The first record that contains matching text is displayed in the Quick Entry data form (you may have to perform more than one find operation).
3. When the record you want to edit appears in the data form, make the desired changes and choose Close.

Printing the Data File

It's often helpful to have a printout of your data file. WordPerfect makes it easy to print your data in a readable format. To print your data, follow these steps:

1. With the data file that you want to print on-screen, choose Options. To suppress the display of codes in the printout, make sure that Hide Codes is selected.
2. From the Options menu, choose Print. WordPerfect asks you to confirm that you want to print with no page breaks between records.
3. Click OK; the data file is printed.

Creating a Form File

Every merge has to have a form file; the form file controls the merge. The form file contains merge codes that ask for information from another source. It should also contain any text, formatting, and graphics that you want in the final merged documents. When the merge is executed, the text, formatting, and graphics, if any, in the form file appear in every merged document. Merge codes in the form file are replaced by information from the data file or from the keyboard.

To create a form file, take the following steps:

1. If you already have a document with the fixed information for your form file, open the document.

2. Choose Tools, Merge. The Merge dialog box appears (refer to Figure 10.5).
3. Choose Create Document. WordPerfect asks whether you want to use the current document window for your form file, or whether you want to create the form file in a new, empty window. Make the appropriate choice.
4. WordPerfect then prompts you for the name of the data file to associate with your form file, as shown in Figure 10.9. The associated data file is the file that is merged with the form file. Enter a name for the data file, or select it after clicking the list button to the right of the text box.

FIG. 10.9
Associate a data file with your form file in the Create a Form File dialog box.

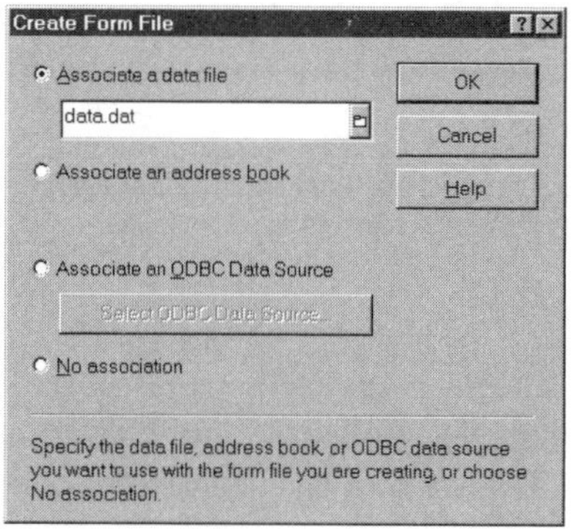

5. Alternatively, if you are in your Data Source file, to create a form file click the Go to Form button on the Property Bar. You see the Associate dialog box shown in Figure 10.10. Choose Create to create a form file.

FIG. 10.10
The Associate dialog box allows you to create or open a form file to associate with the data file.

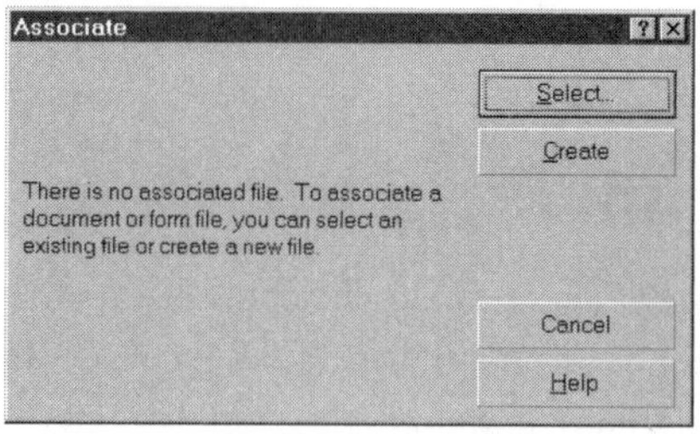

6. Type, edit, and format any text that should appear in your form file. Formatting text is described further in Chapter 5, "Formatting Text and Documents."
7. Position the insertion point where you want to insert the first merge code. If the form file is a form letter, for example, you might want to merge in the computer date at the top of the letter.
8. To insert a Date merge code, choose the Date button.

9. To insert a Field merge code, choose the Insert Field button. The Insert Field Name or Number dialog box appears, displaying a list of field names from the associated data file. Select the desired field name and choose Insert. The field merge code is inserted in the document and the dialog box is still on-screen. Figure 10.11 shows a form file just after inserting a date merge code and the first field merge code.

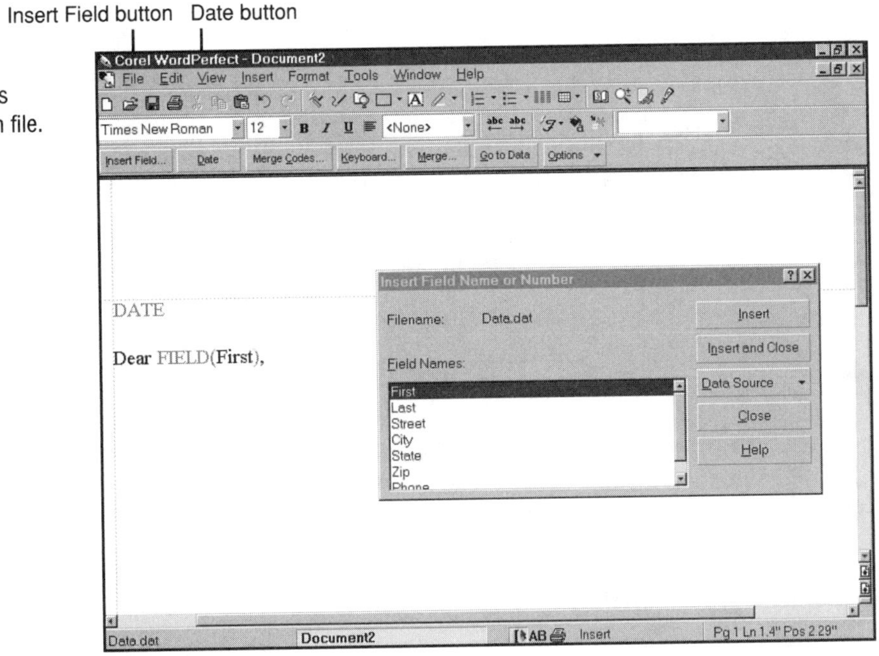

FIG. 10.11 The merge code is inserted in a form file.

10. Position the insertion point where you want another merge code; or type, edit, and format text until the insertion point is where you want to insert the next merge code. Place commas and spaces between merge codes on the same line as appropriate. For example, if you have just inserted a Field code for the City in the inside address of a form letter, press the comma key and then the space bar.

TIP If the Insert Field Name or Number dialog box obscures your view of the form file, drag it to a new position.

11. When the insertion point is positioned where you want another merge code, select it from the list and choose Insert.

12. Repeat steps 10 and 11 until you have entered all of the merge codes that you want to enter. When you finish, close the Insert Field Name or Number dialog box. You can insert the last field and close the dialog box at the same time by clicking Insert and Close. The finished result may appear as illustrated in Figure 10.12.

FIG. 10.12
A sample form file includes the form letter and the inserted fields.

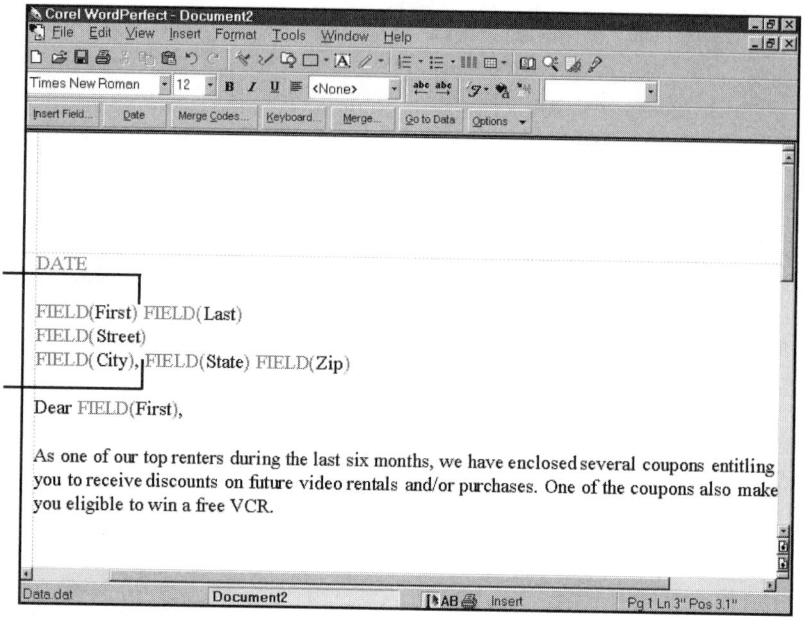

13. Save and close the form file as you would any document. You don't have to type a file name extension; WordPerfect automatically adds an FRM extension to the file name.

Performing the Merge

When you have a form file and a data file, you have the ingredients for a merge. To perform a merge, follow these steps:

1. If you are not in the Form or Data file, choose Tools, Merge, and then choose Perform Merge from the Merge dialog box. If you are in the Form or Data file, select Merge from the Property Bar. The Perform Merge dialog box appears (see Figure 10.13).

FIG. 10.13
The Perform Merge dialog box allows you to specify options for the merge.

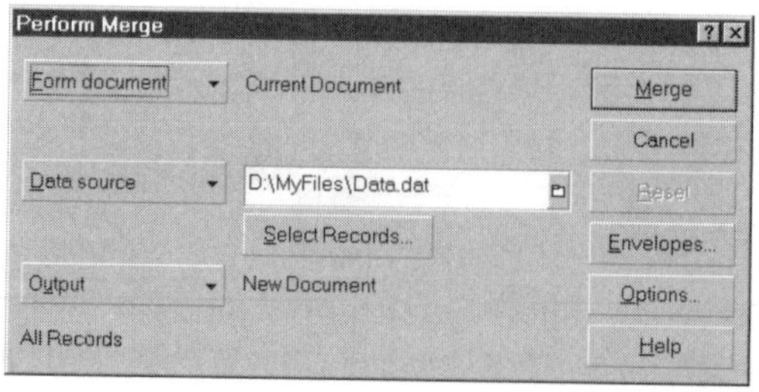

2. If they do not already appear, enter the names of your form file and data file, or use the list button for each option to select the name from a list.

NOTE To create merged envelopes at the same time that you create merged form letters, see the next section, "Creating Envelopes."

TIP You can select specific records from your data file or address book for your merge. See Records (merge), Select in the WordPerfect Help Index.

3. Choose Merge to perform the merge. When the merge has been completed, the insertion point is positioned at the end of the last merged document. Page breaks separate each document.
4. Scroll through the merged documents to verify the success of the merge. If there are any problems, close the window containing the merged documents (don't save), edit the file that is causing the problem (either the form file or the data file), resave the corrected file, and perform the merge again.
5. When the merge has completed without problems, you can save the results, if desired, and print the merged documents all at once.

Creating Envelopes

WordPerfect simplifies a merge by making it possible to create merged letters and envelopes all at once. When the merge is completed, both the form letters and the envelopes are in the active document window, ready to print.

To create merged envelopes and form letters in a single merge operation, perform the following steps:

1. Enter the names of the form file and data file in the Perform Merge dialog box (see the previous section).
2. Choose Envelopes. The Envelope dialog box is displayed.
3. Place your insertion point in the Mailing Address box, delete any data that appears there, then click the Field button. Select the field you want to insert and choose Insert and Close. Position the insertion point for the next field, and then repeat this step until you have added all fields for your envelope. A completed Envelope dialog box is shown in Figure 10.14.
4. Add a bar code, if desired, through the Options button.

NOTE Adding a bar code speeds the delivery of your mail.

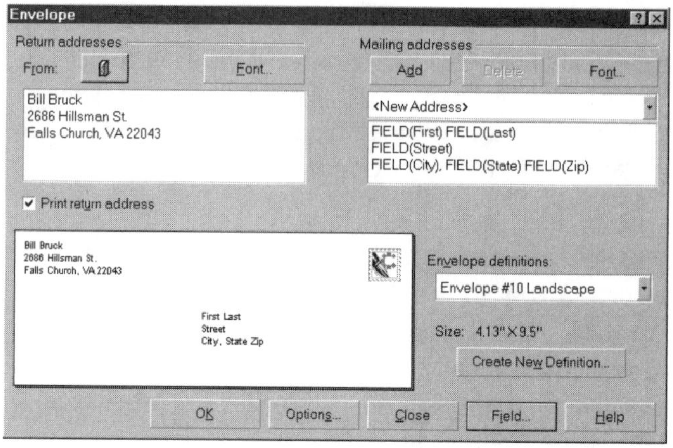

FIG. 10.14
To create merged envelopes, enter field merge codes in the Mailing Addresses area.

5. Specify a return address, if desired. You can pick your return address from the Address Book by clicking the Address Book button.
6. When you finish working in the Envelope dialog box, click OK to return to the Perform Merge dialog box.
7. Choose Merge to perform the merge. Merged letters and envelopes are created in the designated output file (usually a new document). The insertion point is positioned at the end of the last letter; the envelopes are below the letters.
8. As with any merge, check the results before printing or saving. If there are problems, close the current window (don't save), edit and resave the problem file (it could be either the form file or the data file), and perform the merge again.
9. When the results are successful, you can save the output file, if desired, and print it all at once.

Filling in a Form with a Keyboard Merge

You can pause the merge operation to fill in information that is unique to each record. You can even create a form file that has no references to data file fields, but only has pauses for you to enter information. Creating and merging such a file is called a ***keyboard merge***.

TIP Many of WordPerfect's templates are automated merge forms. The fax expert, for example, prompts you for keyboard input and then places your input in appropriate places on the fax form.

You can use this technique to quickly create forms that require you to enter text in specific areas. All you have to do is start a merge and enter information as prompted. You don't have to move the insertion point to the next place that needs input; WordPerfect does it for you. You even get help on what to input (from the prompt that is associated with each keyboard merge code).

Creating a Form File for a Keyboard Merge

When you create a form file for a keyboard merge, it's usually easier to create the document text first and add the merge codes later. You can, however, add the merge codes while you create the text.

To create a form file for a keyboard merge, do the following:

1. Create a boilerplate document containing all of the fixed information and formatting that should appear in every merged document.

TIP *Boilerplate* is the term for unchanging text in a document. For example, a collections letter may use the same text every time it's sent out, with only the recipient's name and the amount owed changing.

2. Choose Tools, Merge. In the Merge dialog box, choose Create Document. In the Create Merge File dialog box, choose Use File in Active Window. Click OK.
3. At the Associate Form and Data dialog box, choose No Association (to indicate that there is no associated data file), and then click OK.
4. In your form file, position the insertion point where you want input from the keyboard. Choose Keyboard. The Insert Merge Code dialog box appears (this dialog box appears whenever you insert a merge code that requires additional information, such as a prompt).
5. Enter a prompt for the user to see when he inputs information at this specific place on the form. An example of the Insert Merge Code dialog box with a filled-in prompt is shown in Figure 10.15. When you finish entering the prompt, click OK.

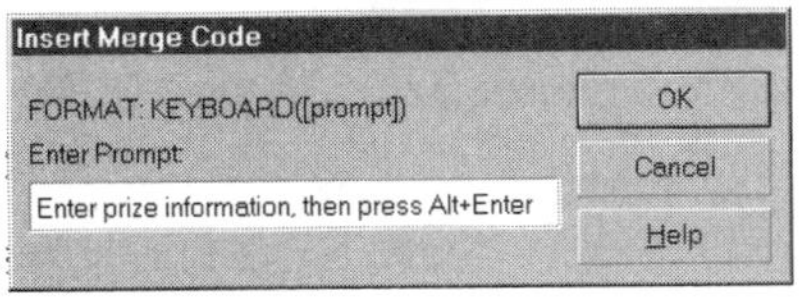

FIG. 10.15 Remind the user what he should do while filling in variable information from the keyboard.

NOTE It's helpful to tell the user which keystrokes to press to continue the merge after filling in data at the current location. For example, include the prompt **Type recipient's name, then press Alt+Enter to continue.**

6. Continue to enter keyboard merge codes wherever you want input from the keyboard. A completed form might look like the illustration shown in Figure 10.16.

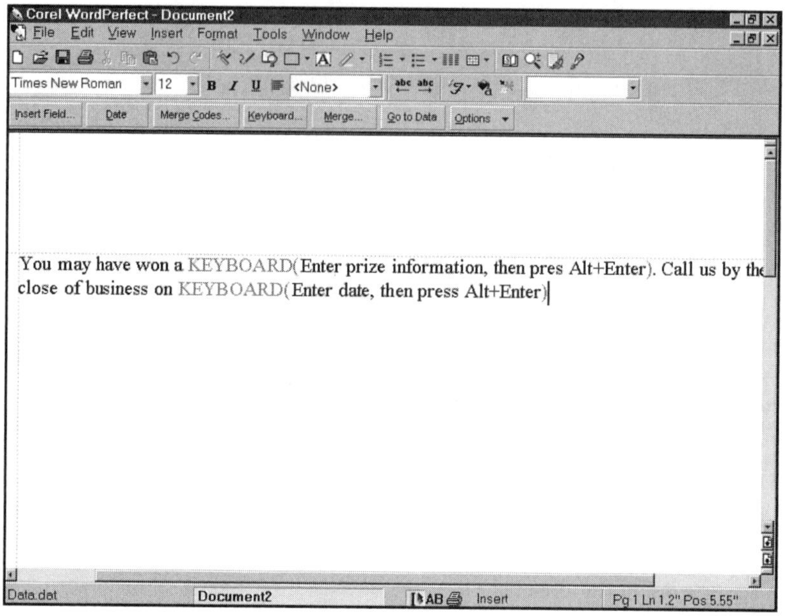

FIG. 10.16 This is a completed form file for a keyboard merge.

7. Save and replace the completed form file.

Performing a Keyboard Merge

When you perform a keyboard merge, you fill in the blanks in your form file from the keyboard while the merge occurs. The result is a single merged document. After the form is filled in, you can print the results and save them.

To perform a keyboard merge, take the following steps:

1. In an empty document window, choose Tools, Merge. In the Merge dialog box, choose Perform Merge. In the Perform Merge dialog box, specify a form file, and then make sure that the Data Source text box is empty. Choose Merge to begin the merge.
2. A merge Property Bar appears at the top of the screen. When the merge pauses at the first keyboard merge code (see Figure 10.17), the prompt that is associated with that particular keyboard code appears in the center of the screen. Type the appropriate information. When you finish typing, press Alt+Enter or choose Continue from the Property Bar. This tells WordPerfect that you have finished entering information here and that you are ready for the merge to move on.

FIG. 10.17
A merge paused for input at a Keyboard merge code. What you type is entered at the insertion point.

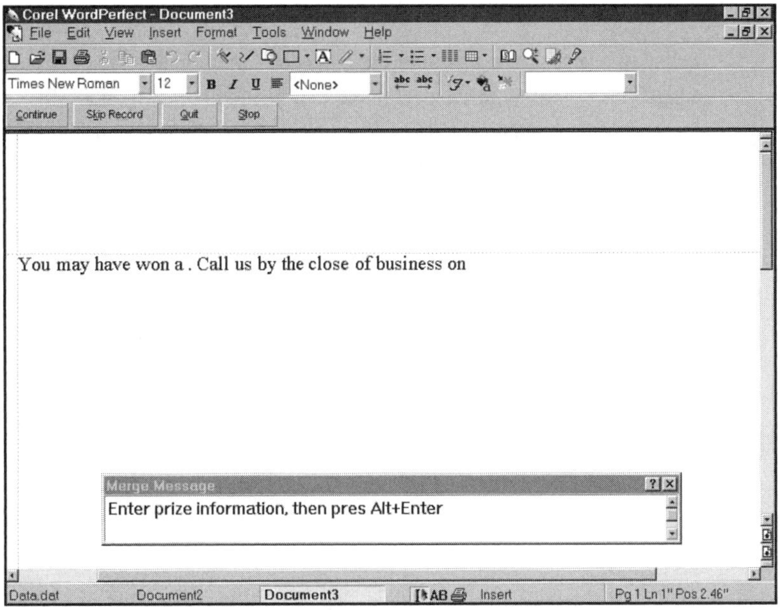

3. The merge moves to the next keyboard code, if there is one, and prompts you for input. As long as you are being prompted for input, the merge is in process. You must tell WordPerfect to move on from each Keyboard merge code, whether or not you type input at that code.

TIP You can type as many lines as necessary at a keyboard prompt. You can also add or correct any formatting on previous entries.

4. When the merge is complete, you can print the document on-screen and save it, if desired.

TROUBLESHOOTING

I created a data file and a form file and then I performed a mail merge, but the city, state, and zip code are all jammed together in the inside address. In a normal letter, you have a comma and a space separating the city and the state in an inside address. In a form file, you need the same text (a comma and a space) between the Field code for the city and the Field code for the state. Correspondingly, you need spaces between the state and zip code fields.

I performed a merge and asked for envelopes, but they're not there. When a merge completes, the insertion point is beneath the last form letter but above the envelopes. Scroll downward to see the envelopes after you perform the merge.

continues

continued

I created a keyboard merge form file but when I performed a merge, I pressed Enter and the merge didn't move on to the next place that needed keyboard input. Then I didn't know what to do. When you get into a mess like this, the best solution is to cancel the merge (click Stop), close the document window without saving, and start again. The only way you will move on from the current Keyboard merge code during a merge is by choosing Continue or by pressing Alt+Enter. You must repeat this action for every Keyboard merge code in the form file in order for the merge operation to come to a normal termination.

PART III

Using Corel Quattro Pro

CHAPTER 11

Getting Started with Corel Quattro Pro 8

Understand Corel Quattro Pro

This chapter shows you what Corel Quattro Pro adds to your Corel WordPerfect Suite 8 toolbox.

Access the correct commands

Learn how to save hours of work by knowing where to find the most often used and helpful commands.

Learn about important shortcuts

Learn about Quattro Pro's many shortcuts that will enable you to perform tasks quickly with simple keystrokes or a few clicks with your mouse.

Get expert help from within Corel Quattro Pro

See how you can use the built-in Experts to make learning and using Quattro Pro easy and even fun.

Corel Quattro Pro 8 is the spreadsheet component of the Corel WordPerfect Suite 8. This chapter introduces Corel Quattro Pro 8 and prepares you to begin using this powerful tool quickly to analyze data, prepare reports, and graph results. After you learn the basics, you'll be ready to apply your skills to creating your own Quattro Pro spreadsheets.

This chapter assumes that you are familiar with standard Windows techniques and file-management operations. If you are not comfortable with your knowledge in these areas, please read Part I, "Working with Corel WordPerfect Suite 8," before continuing. ■

Understanding Corel Quattro Pro

Corel Quattro Pro is a *spreadsheet* program. You might like to think of a spreadsheet program as an electronic notebook, one which can quickly calculate the results of any formulas you enter. Quattro Pro is a very capable electronic notebook, with hundreds of built-in features designed to make creating your spreadsheets as easy as possible.

What Can You Do with Corel Quattro Pro?

Even the most powerful tool is useless if you don't know what it can do and how to use it. Fortunately, even though Quattro Pro is one of the most advanced spreadsheet programs available, it is also very easy to understand and use. You don't have to be an accountant or a computer whiz to use Quattro Pro. In only a short time, you'll be able to create Quattro Pro notebooks that solve some of your problems with ease.

A typical, traditional use for a spreadsheet is to prepare reports that summarize data. By automatically performing a report's calculations with complete accuracy, a spreadsheet makes quick work of the task. If you run a small business, you probably perform many different calculations on a daily basis. You might, for example, want to keep track of the receipts for a video rental business you recently began. To know whether the new business is worthwhile, you probably want to know whether you're making a profit after paying for the new movies, plus your utilities and other expenses, and maybe even the cost of hiring someone to help keep the store open in the evenings.

You also may want to calculate the cost of refinancing your mortgage and determine how long it will take to make up for the fees your lender may charge. In addition, it would be useful to know which products you sell bring the highest profits, and when those products are most likely to be sold. Finally, suppose you needed to calculate the cost of building permits which were based on many different combinations of features for each property. Wouldn't it be nice to just enter the proposed building's size, type, and quantity of fixtures, and have a totally accurate bill printed instantly?

These are but a small sample of the things you can do with Quattro Pro.

Starting Corel Quattro Pro

When you start Quattro Pro, a new, blank notebook named NOTEBK1.WB3 appears (see Figure 11.1). This new notebook is your starting point for creating your own applications. You can use a more descriptive name when you save your notebook in a file on disk.

Each Quattro Pro notebook provides a very large workspace—much larger than you can see on-screen at one time. Each notebook has 256 sheets, and each sheet includes 256 columns and 8,192 rows. The intersection of each row and column on each sheet is a *cell*, the place where you store data, formulas, or labels. A Quattro Pro notebook has an incredible 536,870,912 cells—many more than you will ever need no matter how complex a report you want to produce.

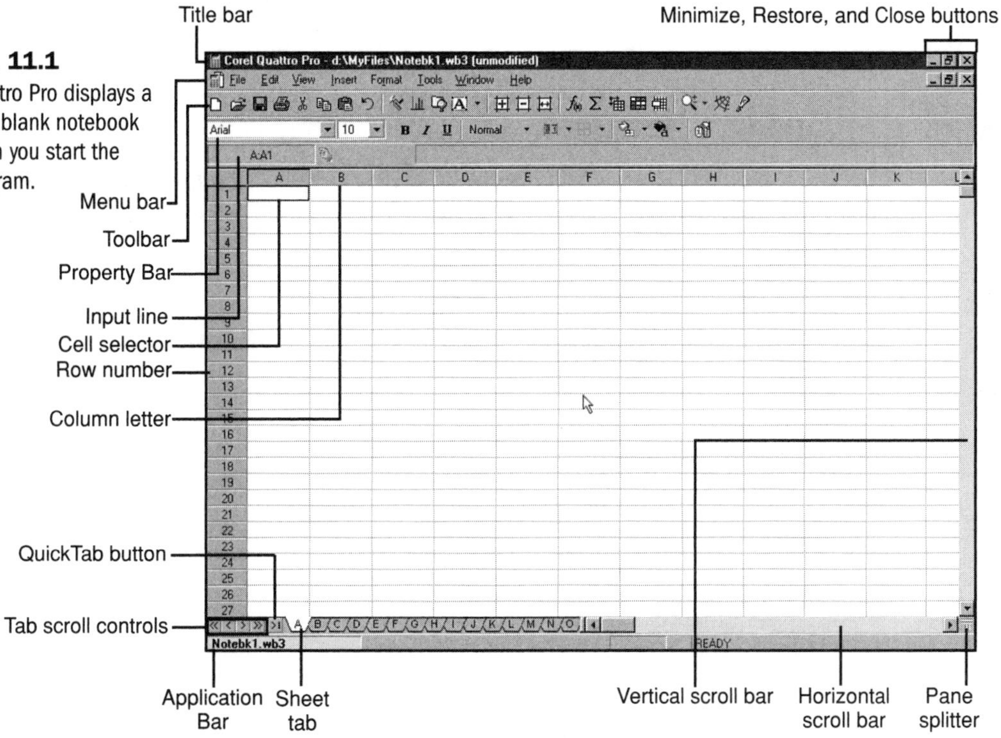

FIG. 11.1
Quattro Pro displays a new, blank notebook when you start the program.

Cells are identified by the sheet letter, followed by a colon, the column letter, and row number. The cell in the first row of the first column on the first sheet of a notebook is designated by the cell address A:A1. If you're referring to a cell on the current sheet, you don't have to include the sheet letter or colon, but can instead refer to this same cell address as simply A1.

The location of the current, or *active* cell is indicated by the *cell selector*—a darker outline around the cell. In Figure 11.1, the cell selector is in cell A:A1, making this the active cell. You can only place data, formulas, or labels in the active cell. To place anything in a different cell, you first must make the new cell the active cell by clicking it with the mouse. The address of the active cell appears in the cell indicator box at the left end of the input line. The column letter and row number in the notebook frame also indicate which cell is active, because they appear to be depressed, or selected.

TROUBLESHOOTING

My screen shows NOTEBK2.WB3 instead of NOTEBK1.WB3. Quattro Pro starts new notebooks using sequential numbers. If you create a new notebook, it automatically is named NOTEBK*xx*.WB3, with *xx* replaced by the next higher number. When you save the notebook, you'll be prompted for a new name.

Moving Around in a Notebook

When you want to enter data, formulas, or labels in a cell, you first must move to that cell. There are several methods you can use to move around in a notebook, and the best method often depends on your destination.

You can use the arrow keys, as well as the PgUp, PgDn, Home, and End keys to move the cell selector between cells. Table 11.1 describes the functioning of these navigational keys.

Table 11.1 The Navigation Keys

Key(s)	Action(s)
→ or ←	Moves right or left one cell
↑ or ↓	Moves up or down one cell
Ctrl+←	Moves left one screen
Ctrl+→	Moves right one screen
Ctrl+F6	Makes the next open notebook window active, if multiple notebooks are open
Ctrl+Home	Moves to cell A1 on the first sheet of the current notebook
Ctrl+PgDn	Moves to the notebook sheet immediately below the current sheet (from sheet A to sheet B)
Ctrl+PgUp	Moves to the notebook sheet immediately above the current sheet (from sheet B to sheet A)
End+→ or End+←	Moves right or left to a cell that contains data and is next to a blank cell
End+↑ or End+↓	Moves up or down to a cell that contains data and is next to a blank cell
End+Ctrl+Home	Moves to the lower-right corner of the active area on the last active sheet

Key(s)	Action(s)
End+Home	Moves to the lower-right corner of the active area on the current sheet
F5 (Go to)	Moves to the cell you specify
Home	Moves to cell A1 of the active sheet
PgUp or PgDn	Moves up or down one screen on the current notebook sheet

It is often quicker and easier to perform tasks such as moving the cell selector using the mouse instead of the navigation keys. For example, to move from cell A1 to cell C4, you could press the right-arrow key twice and then the down-arrow key three times, or you could simply point to cell C4 and click the left mouse button. Of course, if you hold down an arrow key instead of quickly pressing and releasing it, the cell selector will move several rows or columns instead of just one. Even so, a single mouse click is often much faster than the equivalent keystrokes. Moving between sheets with the mouse is even faster—just click the appropriate sheet tab. Use the tab scroll controls to display different sheet tabs if necessary.

You can also use the scroll bars at the right edge or bottom edge of a notebook to view other parts of the current notebook sheet. Click the scroll bar or drag the scroll box to bring a different part of the sheet into view.

TROUBLESHOOTING

The cell selector disappears when I use the scroll bars. The scroll bars change only the portion of the sheet that is visible. To move the cell selector, first use the scroll bars to display the destination cell, and then click the destination cell to make it the current cell.

Using the Menus

Many tasks you perform in Quattro Pro require use of a command. Commands help you analyze and organize data effectively, copy and move data, chart and format data, sort and manipulate databases, open and close notebooks, and use colors and fonts to customize notebooks.

The Quattro Pro menu appears on the menu bar near the top of the screen. If you use the mouse to select commands, just click the command you want to use. To access a command on the menu bar with the keyboard, you first must activate the menu by pressing the Alt key. A reverse video highlight, the ***menu pointer***, appears in the menu bar when you choose a command menu by highlighting it with the arrow keys. You can also simply press the Alt key and the underlined letter of the command name.

TIP Learn Quattro Pro's commands by moving the menu pointer through the menus. A description of the command appears in a yellow tip box next to the menu. This box is called a *QuickTip*; it also appears when you point to other parts of the screen, such as toolbar buttons.

TIP Commands which are dimmed are currently unavailable.

Quattro Pro has several different menus. The menus change depending upon the type of task you're performing. For example, when you work with normal data in a notebook the main menu appears. If you create or modify a chart, the menu changes to include commands appropriate to charts. Most of the time, however, you see the main menu.

NOTE If you have used earlier versions of Quattro Pro, you'll notice that the menu structure and dialog boxes have been streamlined in Quattro Pro 8. These improvements to the interface will make your work easier because related commands and options are now more closely grouped.

If you prefer to use the familiar menus and dialog boxes from Quattro Pro 7 (until you have time to learn the new Quattro Pro 8 commands), you can easily switch to the Quattro Pro 7 menu. Right-click the menu bar, and then click <QP7 Menu>. If you are switching from Microsoft Excel to Quattro Pro 8, you can use the same method to switch to the Microsoft Excel menu. Just right-click the menu bar and choose the <Excel Menu> option.

Learning the Shortcuts

In any field, the most productive people are usually those who know the fastest way to get things done—the shortcuts. Quattro Pro provides many different shortcuts you can learn and use to get things done more quickly. You don't have to learn all of them, but you will find some that you'll use quite often.

Using Toolbar Buttons The Quattro Pro toolbar contains many useful buttons you'll find very helpful as you build your notebooks (see Figure 11.2). Table 11.2 describes the buttons on the main Notebook toolbar, which we'll use later in this and several following chapters. For more information on the complete range of toolbar buttons, choose Help, Help Topics and see the topic "toolbars" on the Index tab of Quattro Pro's online help.

Table 11.2 Notebook Toolbar Buttons and Their Functions

Button	Function
	Opens a new notebook
	Opens an existing notebook into a new window
	Saves the current notebook
	Prints a notebook or chart
	Moves the selection to the Clipboard
	Copies the selection to the Clipboard
	Inserts the Clipboard contents into the notebook
	Reverses the last change made
	Pastes the format from the current selection to all subsequent selections (until QuickFormat is turned off)
	Creates a floating chart on the notebook sheet
	Imports clip art and other graphics files
	Inserts a drawing object or shape
	Inserts cells, rows, columns, or sheets
	Deletes cells, rows, columns, or sheets
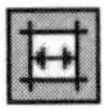	Adjusts a column's width to its widest cell entry
	Builds complex formulas with @functions
	Totals values in the selection

continues

Table 11.2 Continued

Button	Function
	Fills blank cells in the selection
	Applies a predefined format to the selection
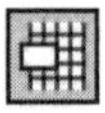	Joins and centers cells
	Zooms the sheet by a specified percentage
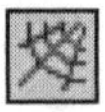	Gets Help from Documentation and Technical Support on the Web
	Displays the PerfectExpert

FIG. 11.2
Toolbar and Property Bar buttons are another way to access the tools you need to create powerful notebook sheets.

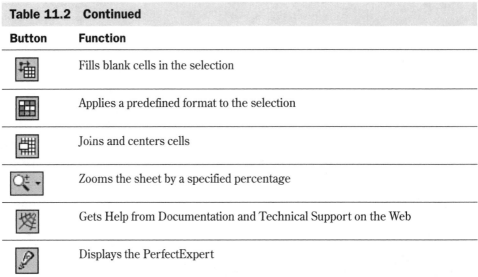

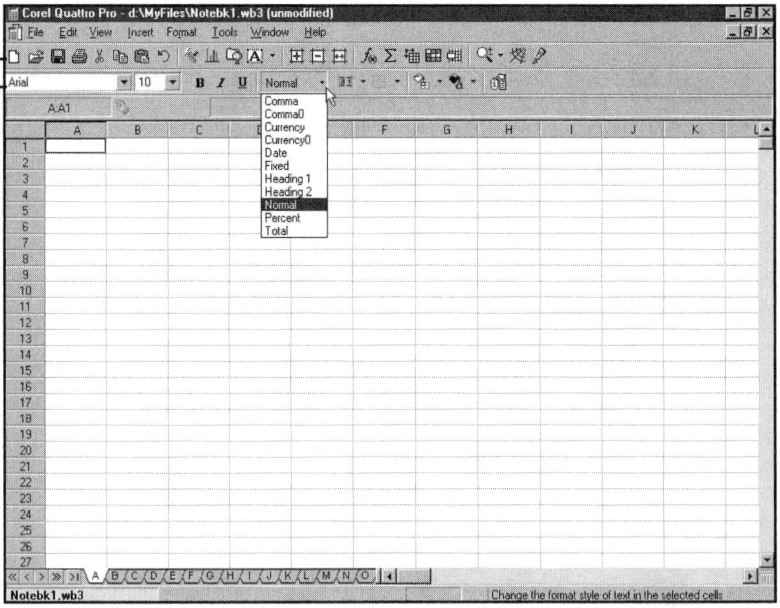

Using QuickMenus and Dialog Boxes In Quattro Pro, almost everything you see is an *object*—something that has properties you can change. But instead of requiring you to search through Quattro Pro's menus to find the commands necessary to change an object's properties, Quattro Pro gives you another choice. When you point to an object with the mouse pointer and click the right mouse button, you will see either a dialog box or a *QuickMenu* associated with the object. The dialog boxes contain all of the property settings for the object. QuickMenus are short command menus containing only those commands most appropriate for the selected object. QuickMenus always include a Properties selection at the bottom of the menu, which displays the dialog box for the selected object.

If you have not used them before, QuickMenus and dialog boxes may be a little confusing at first. After you begin using them, however, you'll find them to be very helpful. Figure 11.3 shows the QuickMenu that appears when you right-click a notebook cell. The commands on this menu are also available if you search through several of Quattro Pro's standard menus, but the QuickMenu has gathered several of the most frequently used commands that you might want to apply to a cell in one convenient place.

FIG. 11.3
QuickMenus gather commands from several menus into one convenient menu.

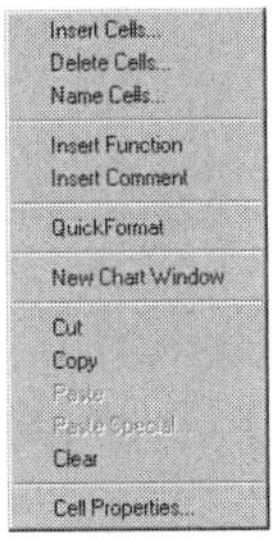

Notice the last item on the QuickMenu, Cell Properties. If you select this item, the Active Cells dialog box appears (see Figure 11.4). You can also use the F12 shortcut key to display the Active Cells dialog box directly. This dialog box contains six tabs that have every possible setting for a cell (or block of cells). In Figure 11.4, the tab labeled Cell Font is selected, so the dialog box displays all possible font settings. As you select different options, or a different tab, such as Numeric Format, the dialog box changes and displays the available options.

FIG. 11.4
Dialog boxes enable you to adjust object properties.

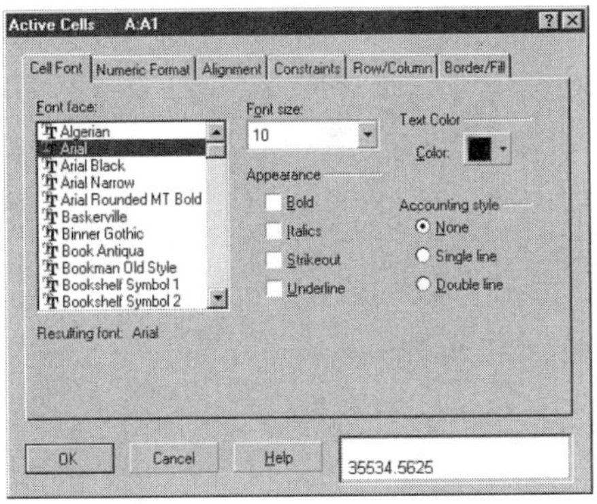

If you change a property setting, such as changing the font from Arial to Times New Roman, the name of the changed property tab will be displayed in blue letters rather than black—as long as the dialog box is open—so that you can tell what changes you have made. You can adjust more than one property while the dialog box is active. Click OK when you've made all of your changes, or click Cancel if you decide you don't want to apply the changes. When you re-enter the dialog box the next time, all of the tabs will again be black, regardless of whether the change was accepted or canceled.

Table 11.3 shows some of the Quattro Pro objects (other than individual cells) that you can adjust by right-clicking them.

Table 11.3 Corel Quattro Pro Objects

Object	Action
Blocks of cells	Right-click in the selected area.
Notebook sheets	Right-click the sheet tab.
Notebook	Right-click the notebook title bar if the notebook is in a window and not maximized.
Toolbar	Right-click the toolbar.
Chart objects	Right-click the object including drawn objects, titles, data series, and the chart background objects.
Quattro Pro itself	Right-click the Quattro Pro title bar.

Important Shortcut Keys Table 11.4 describes many of the more useful Quattro Pro shortcut keys. To learn about even more shortcut keys, see the topic "key shortcuts" in the Quattro Pro online help system.

Table 11.4 Important Quattro Pro Shortcut Keys

Key(s)	Action(s)
F1	Displays a Help topic
F2	Places Quattro Pro in EDIT mode so that you can edit an entry
Alt+F2	Displays the Play Macro dialog box
F3	Displays the Save File dialog box
Alt+F3	Displays a list of functions
Ctrl+F3	Displays the Cell Names dialog box if pressed while a group of cells is selected

Key(s)	Action(s)
F4	Toggles formulas from relative to absolute and vice versa as you are entering formulas or when you edit formulas in the Input line
Alt+F4	Closes Quattro Pro 8 for Windows or a dialog box
F5	Displays the Go To dialog box
F6	Moves the cell selector between panes
Ctrl+F6	Displays the next open window
F9	In READY mode, recalculates formulas; in EDIT or VALUE mode, converts a formula to its current value
F10	Activates the menu bar
F11	Displays the current chart
F12	Displays dialog box for the selected object
Alt+F12	Displays the Application dialog box
Shift+F12	Displays the Active Notebook dialog box
Alt+Tab	Switches from one Windows application to another
Ctrl+*letter*	Same as choosing Tools, Macro, Play; executes a macro in Quattro Pro
Ctrl+Break	Exits from a macro and returns to Ready mode
Ctrl+Esc	Activates the Start menu on the taskbar for Windows 95

TROUBLESHOOTING

Some Ctrl+*letter* shortcut keys don't perform the proper shortcut procedure. If you create macros that use the Ctrl+*letter* naming convention, Quattro Pro runs the macro instead of using the key combination to run the shortcut. If the shortcut is one you use often, consider renaming the macro to restore the default shortcut.

Using Experts

Quattro Pro includes some specialized tools—*Experts*—that can ease your way through learning Quattro Pro and executing difficult tasks. In this section, we'll take a quick look at the Experts.

Computer-based training isn't new; programs have included tutorials for years. But Quattro Pro's Experts use a different approach to completing tasks. Instead of using a carefully preselected data set unrelated to the data you want to enter (as many tutorials do), the Experts allow you to use your own data. Not only that, but the Experts also allow you to save your work in a Quattro Pro notebook. When you complete a task, the notebook contains your data.

Experts provide the expertise to solve complex problems while you provide the data. These Experts cover a broad range of topics. Table 11.5 provides a brief description of Quattro Pro's Experts.

Table 11.5 Corel Quattro Pro's Experts

Expert	Description
Analysis	Helps you use the Analysis Tools (choose Tools, Numeric Tools, Analysis)
Budget	Helps you create and manage home and small business budgets (choose Tools, Numeric Tools, Budget)
Chart	Helps you create charts (choose Insert, Chart)
Map	Helps you create maps of your data (choose Insert, Graphics, Map)
Slide Show	Helps you create professional-looking slide shows (choose Tools, Slide Show, New)
Consolidate	Helps you combine data from different sources, such as different stores or company divisions (choose Tools, Consolidate, New)
Scenario	Helps you create and manage scenarios—multiple groups of related data that enable easy what-if analysis (choose Tools, Scenario, New)
What-If	Helps you generate what-if scenarios (choose Tools, Numeric Tools, What-If, Expert)

TIP Part IV, "Using Corel Presentations," shows you how to create slide shows using a tool specifically designed for the task.

For example, the Chart Expert leads you through the steps necessary to create powerful business graphics that will present your data in a highly effective visual manner. You don't have to be a graphics expert yourself; all you need to do is answer some questions and make a few selections along the way. The Budget Expert shown in Figure 11.5 is another tool you'll probably find quite useful. Everyone knows the importance of a budget, especially in running a small business. The Budget Expert helps you prepare a Quattro Pro notebook containing an individualized budget specific to your needs. You can access the Budget Expert by choosing Tools, Numeric Tools, Budget.

FIG. 11.5
Use the Budget Expert to simplify creating a budget for your home or small business.

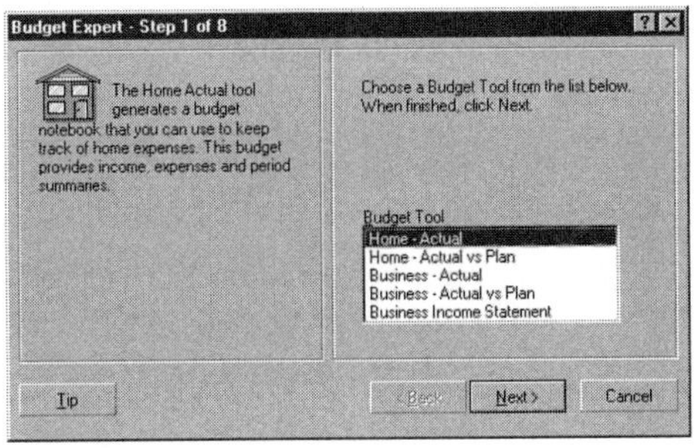

CHAPTER 12

Learning Spreadsheet Basics

This chapter presents information you need to use Corel Quattro Pro notebooks. If you are new to electronic spreadsheets, this chapter helps you learn to use a spreadsheet for basic data analysis. If you have used other spreadsheet programs, this chapter is valuable for learning the conventions and features of Quattro Pro. ■

Work with single and multiple notebook sheets

Understand the three-dimensional arrangement of Corel Quattro Pro to help organize your work and make your spreadsheets much easier to use.

Link notebooks

See how to link Quattro Pro notebooks so you can efficiently use data that comes from many different sources.

Enter and edit data

Learn how to enter and edit different types of data properly so that Quattro Pro recognizes the data correctly.

Document formulas, numbers, and data

Learn how proper documentation techniques will help you remember why you created complex formulas and understand the assumptions used to create your models.

Use the Undo feature

Learn to use the Undo feature to correct mistakes easily.

Understanding Notebooks and Files

In Corel Quattro Pro, a single spreadsheet is called a *sheet*—a two-dimensional grid of columns and rows. A file that contains 256 sheets and an Objects sheet in a three-dimensional arrangement is called a ***notebook***. Besides working with a single notebook, you also can work with several notebooks at the same time, and you can link notebooks by writing formulas that refer to cells in another notebook.

Using 3-D Notebooks

You will often need only a single sheet to analyze and store data. You can organize simple reports effectively on a single sheet without the added complication of including sheet references in your formulas. Sheet references are necessary, though, for accessing data that spreads across several sheets.

Some situations, however, are well-suited to multiple notebook sheets. Reports that consolidate data from several departments often work well as multiple-sheet reports. You also can use multiple sheets to separate different kinds of data effectively. You might place data input areas on one sheet, macros on another, constants on another, and the finished report on yet another sheet. This technique can provide some assurance that a spreadsheet isn't damaged by an inadvertent error. For example, a data-entry error can write over formulas, or the insertion or deletion of a row or column can destroy macros or data tables contained on the same sheet. Building your notebook by using several sheets provides some protection against these all-too-common problems.

TIP Protect important formulas and macros by placing them on separate notebook sheets.

Quattro Pro notebooks are automatically 3-D notebooks, whether you have data on one sheet or multiple sheets. You don't have to manually add sheets to a Quattro Pro notebook as you do with most other spreadsheet programs.

Naming Notebook Sheets One good way to use multiple notebook sheets is to place each month's data on a separate sheet and use a 13th sheet for the yearly totals. Because Quattro Pro enables you to name individual notebook sheets, you can name each sheet for one month so that you can locate the correct sheet easily. Figure 12.1 shows a notebook that uses named sheets to hold each month's sales data separately.

You can name a notebook sheet by pointing to the sheet tab and double-clicking the left mouse button. Simply type the new name directly on the tab after you double-click it. Alternatively, you can display the Active Sheet dialog box and select the Name tab. To display the Active Sheet dialog box, right-click the sheet tab and choose Sheet Properties.

Click the Name tab (see Figure 12.2). Type the new name for the sheet in the Sheet Name text box, or click Reset to restore the original sheet letter.

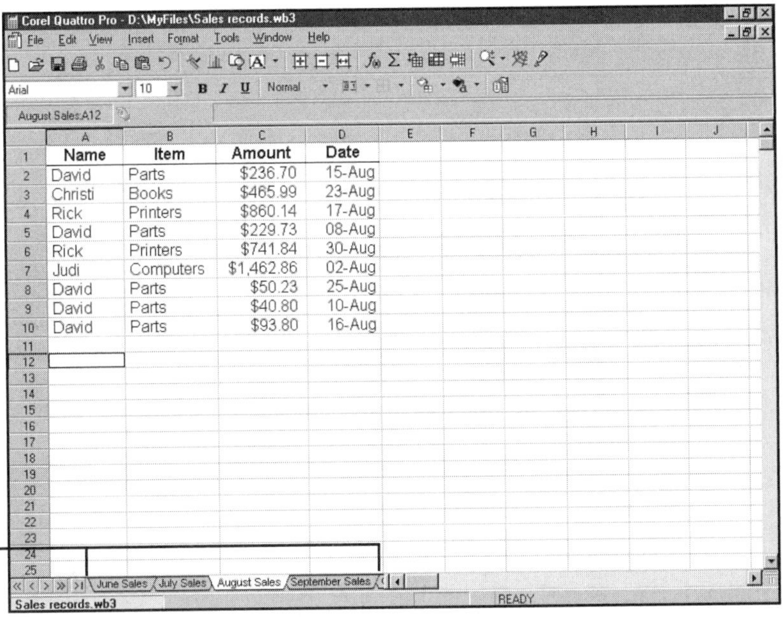

FIG. 12.1
Name notebook sheets to indicate their purpose.

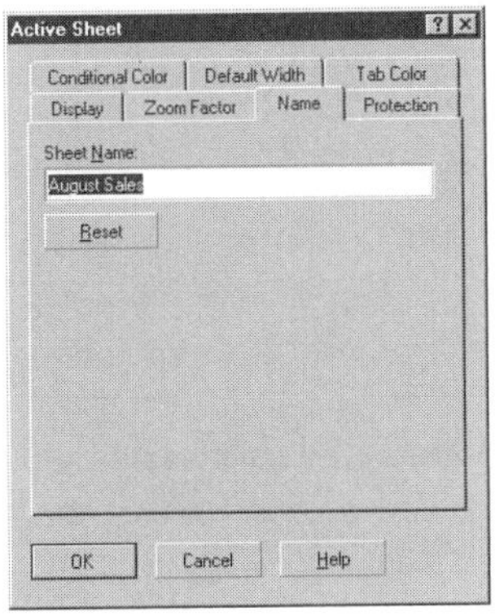

FIG. 12.2
You can use the Active Sheet dialog box to name a notebook sheet.

Sheet names can be up to 63 characters in length, but longer sheet names allow fewer sheet tabs to appear on-screen. You can use both letters and numbers in sheet names, as well as spaces and several special characters. If you have grouped notebook sheets, you cannot use the same name for a notebook sheet and a group.

NOTE You group notebook sheets so that any changes you make to one sheet, such as applying formatting, affect all sheets in the group. To group sheets, hold down the Shift key while you click the sheet tabs for the first and last sheets you want to group. A line appears under the sheet tabs of grouped sheets. To ungroup the sheets, click any sheet tab except the current sheet tab.

TIP You can also name blocks of data. Learn more about this in the "Naming Blocks" section of Chapter 13.

Moving Between Sheets Multiple notebook sheets wouldn't be of much value if there wasn't a quick way to move between sheets. You have already learned that the key combinations of Ctrl+Page Down and Ctrl+Page Up allow you to move through the notebook one sheet at a time. In addition, you can click a sheet tab to move to that sheet.

Sometimes, though, you may want to move to a sheet that has a tab not currently visible, such as a sheet far removed from the current sheet. The best method for moving to a distant notebook sheet is to use the Edit, Go To command (or press the shortcut key, F5) to display the Go To dialog box (see Figure 12.3). Select the sheet in the Sheets list box, and click OK.

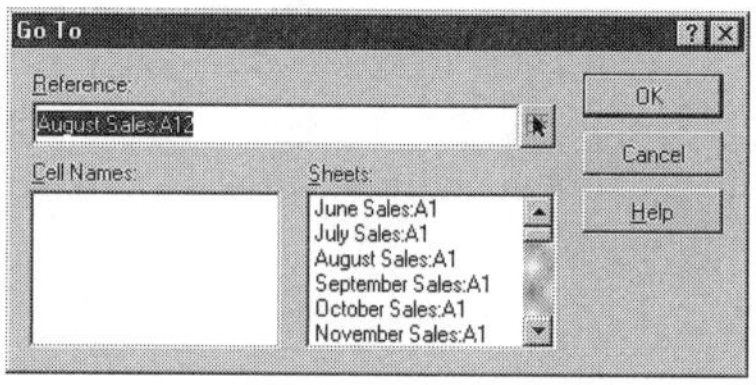

FIG. 12.3 Use the Go To dialog box to move to a distant notebook sheet.

TROUBLESHOOTING

Selecting a sheet by using the Edit, Go To command always moves the cell selector to cell A1 on the selected sheet. Create a block name (see the section "Naming Blocks" in the next chapter) and select the named block in the Cell Names list box as the destination. The cell selector will then move to the upper-left corner of the named block.

Linking Notebooks

A single notebook, whether it uses multiple sheets or is contained on a single sheet, is not always the best solution for storing data. Linking multiple notebook files with formulas is often a better solution than using a single notebook. Consolidating data from several departments or company locations may be easier when using multiple notebooks, especially if several people are producing the individual reports. The person producing the consolidated report can create a notebook that uses formula links to consolidate the data from each notebook.

TIP Link notebooks with formulas rather than combining all the data into a single notebook.

When you work with data from several notebook files, you enter a formula in one notebook cell that refers to cells in another notebook. This technique is called *linking*. With this capability you can easily consolidate data from separate notebook files. A consolidation notebook can use formulas to combine the data from each notebook.

Figure 12.4 shows the notebook CONSRPT.WB3, which is used to consolidate data from three other notebooks: CARSRPT.WB3, RENORPT.WB3, and SPARRPT.WB3. Formulas link the notebooks. The formula in cell A:B5 of CONSRPT.WB3, for example, is:

```
+[CARSRPT]A:B5+[RENORPT]A:B5+[SPARRPT]A:B5
```

FIG. 12.4
You can use formulas to link to data in other notebooks.

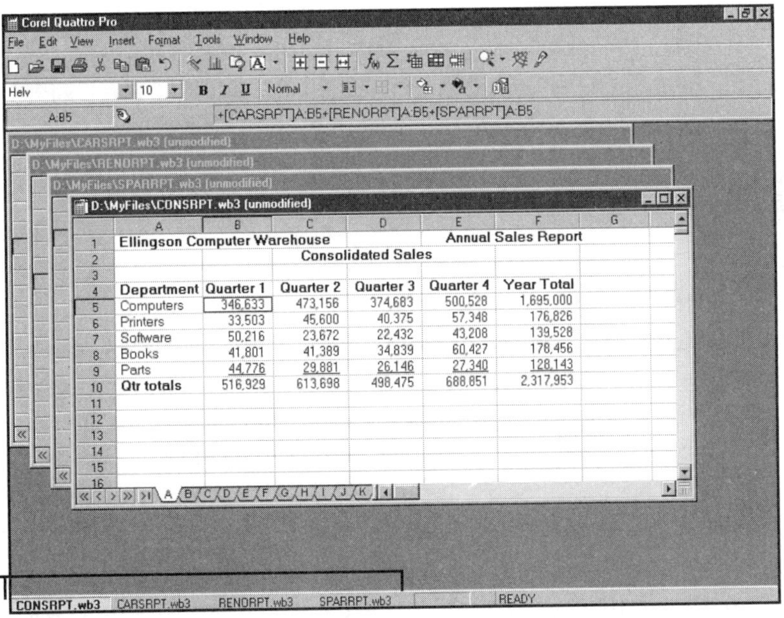

File names of open notebooks

This formula, as shown in the input line of Figure 12.4, tells Quattro Pro to add together the values in cell A:B5 of CARSRPT.WB3, cell A:B5 of RENORPT.WB3, and cell A:B5 of SPARRPT.WB3. In this case, the same cell in each notebook supplies the data for the formula, but that is not a requirement. You could, for example, create a linking formula, which adds values from cell A:A1 in one notebook and cell D: AA216 in another notebook. In most cases, it is less confusing if each linked notebook uses a similar structure. However, when taking data from different departments or companies, you may not always have control over their spreadsheet structure development.

Linking formulas can refer to notebooks that are open or closed. Quattro Pro maintains the formula links even after the supporting notebooks are closed, but must be able to locate the supporting notebooks when the notebook containing the formula links is opened. If the supporting notebooks are not available, Quattro Pro will not be able to determine a value for the linking formulas and will display NA (Not Available) instead of a value in the open notebook.

TIP Use full path names to make certain Quattro Pro can find the linked notebook.

When you open a notebook containing formula links to closed notebooks, Quattro Pro displays a Hotlinks dialog box that offers three options: Open Supporting, Update References, or None. If you select None, Quattro Pro changes the linking formula values to NA, but you can use the Edit, Links, Open Links or Edit, Links, Refresh Links commands to later update your linking formulas. See the section "Entering Formulas" later in this chapter for more information on creating formulas to link notebooks.

TIP If you don't need to see the values of linking formulas, select None when you open notebooks containing linking formulas. The linked notebook will open much faster.

Using Workspaces

Figure 12.4 showed four different Quattro Pro notebooks open at the same time. If you are using notebooks that are linked, it may be convenient to open all of the linked notebooks, especially if you need to create additional formula links or enter data in more than one of the notebooks. When you work with multiple notebooks it is often handy to create a standard window arrangement, such as the cascaded windows in Figure 12.4, so you always know where to find each notebook.

Quattro Pro has two commands—File, Workspace, Save and File, Workspace, Restore—that enable you to save the current notebook layout and then restore that same layout at a later time. When you use File, Workspace, Save, Quattro Pro saves the current screen layout in a file with a WBS extension. You use File, Workspace, Restore to open the same group of notebook files and restore their screen layout in a single command. When restoring a workspace that has linked files, select Update References when the Hotlinks dialog box appears. If you select Open Supporting, the files will be opened full screen.

CAUTION

The File, Workspace, Save command does not save the notebook files, only their current screen layout. You must also save the individual notebook files to save any changes they may contain.

Entering Data for the First Time

You can enter data only in the currently active cell, so to begin entering data you first must move the cell selector to the target cell. Then, type the data and press Enter. As you type, the data appears in the input line and also in the current cell. If you enter data in a cell that already contains an entry, the new data replaces the existing entry.

TIP Always make certain the cell selector is in the correct cell before you begin entering data.

If you are entering a column of data, the cell selector automatically moves down one row in the same column when you press Enter. If the cell selector does not move when you press Enter, you need to select this option. Right-click the Quattro Pro title bar and select Application Properties, or press Alt+F12. Then click the General tab and select Move Cell Selector on Enter Key. This setting makes entering columnar data much faster and easier.

Editing Cell Entries

You can edit cell entries several different ways. If you want to completely replace a cell entry, just retype the entire entry (first make certain the cell selector is in the correct cell). When you press Enter or move the cell selector to another cell, your new entry replaces the existing entry. To cancel the new entry, press Esc before you press Enter or move the cell selector.

To replace part of a cell's current contents, select the cell and press F2 (Edit), or double-click the cell with the left mouse button. You can then use the mouse pointer or the arrow keys to place the insertion point where you want to insert or delete characters. Or, you can select the characters you want to replace by dragging over them, and typing the new characters. Press Enter or click another cell to confirm your edits. To cancel any edits before you press Enter, press Esc. To reverse the edits if you have already pressed Enter, immediately choose Edit, Undo Entry.

Understanding the Kinds of Data You Can Enter

If you plan to enter labels or values in more than one cell, you do not need to press Enter after each entry. Instead, you can enter the data, and then move the cell selector to the new cell with an arrow key to complete the entry and move the cell selector in a single step. This technique does not work if you are entering formulas.

You can create two kinds of cell entries: labels or values. A *label* (or string) is a text entry, and a *value* is a number or formula. Quattro Pro usually determines the kind of entry from the first character you type. The program always treats the entry as a value (a number or a formula) if you begin with one of the following characters:

+ – (@ # . $

If you begin an entry with a number, Quattro Pro assumes you are entering a value unless you include any non-numeric character other than a single period. If you begin by typing any other character, Quattro Pro treats the entry as a label.

Entering Labels

Labels make the numbers and formulas in a notebook understandable. In Figure 12.4, shown earlier, labels identify the departments and the time periods that generated the displayed results. Without labels, the numbers are meaningless.

In Quattro Pro, you can place up to 1,022 characters in a single cell. Although this allows you to create very long labels, remember that you will probably not be able to display nearly that many characters on-screen nor in a single line of a report.

As mentioned in the previous section, Quattro Pro determines the kind of entry from the first character you type in a cell. You can override this, however, by adding a *label prefix*—a punctuation mark that controls the label's alignment in the cell—to the cell entry. The label prefix is not displayed in the spreadsheet. You can change the way a label is aligned by using one of the following label prefixes:

'	Left-aligned (default)
"	Right-aligned
^	Centered
\	Repeating (the same characters repeat as many times as necessary to fill the column width)
|	Nonprinting (if the label is in the leftmost column of the print block)

NOTE Quattro Pro allows you to enter labels that begin with numbers. You only need to use a label prefix if you want to make a number by itself into a label, such as a ZIP code.

Regardless of the label prefix you enter, any label longer than the column width is displayed as a left-aligned label. If a label is longer than the cell width, the label appears across empty cells to the right. A label that is too long to display on-screen appears in its entirety in the input line when you edit the cell.

If the cells to the right of a cell that contains a long label are not blank, Quattro Pro cuts off the entry display at the nonblank cell border. The complete entry is still stored in the cell, however. To display more of the label in the spreadsheet, you can insert new columns to the right of the cell that contains the long label. Alternatively, you can widen the column by moving the cell selector to the cell that contains the long label and clicking the Adjust Column's Width To Its Widest Cell Entry button on the toolbar.

You can also use the Wrap Text option on the Alignment tab of the Active Cells dialog box to make text fit within the column width. (Press F12 or right-click the cell and select Cell Properties to display the Active Cells dialog box.) If you select this option, however, the row height may automatically increase when the text wraps in the cell.

See "Inserting Columns, Rows, or Sheets," **p. 284**

TIP You can also adjust column width by dragging the right border between the column letters when the mouse pointer changes to a double-headed arrow. To automatically fit the column to the widest entry in that column, double-click the border between the column letters.

Entering Numbers

Spreadsheets originally were designed to make calculation less time consuming and easier to do. Most calculations involve numbers, so numbers will represent a large portion of the data you enter in your Quattro Pro notebooks. When you enter a number, you type the number and certain other characters according to the following rules:

- A number can start with a plus sign (+), but the plus sign is not stored when you press Enter. For example, **+302** is stored and displayed as `302`.
- If you start a number with a minus sign (-), the number is stored as a negative number. Negative numbers are usually displayed with the minus sign, but some numeric formats display negative numbers in parentheses. Therefore, **-302** may be displayed as `-302` or `(302)`.
- Numbers can include only one decimal point and no spaces.

- If you enter a number with commas, you must include the correct number of digits following the comma if you want Quattro Pro to recognize the entry as a number. That is, the entry **12,000** is recognized as a number, but **12,00** is recognized as a label.
- If you include a currency symbol, such as a dollar sign ($), Quattro Pro displays the currency symbol in the cell.
- If you end a number with a percent sign (%), the number is divided by 100, and the number appears as a percent.
- Numbers are stored with up to 15 significant digits. If you enter a number with more significant digits, the number is rounded and stored in scientific notation; that is, only 15 digits are retained, and any extra digits are dropped. Scientific notation uses powers of 10 to display very large or small numbers.

The appearance of a number in the notebook depends on the cell's format, font, and column width. If the number is too long to fit in the cell, Quattro Pro tries to show as much of the number as possible. If the cell uses the default General format and the integer portion of the number does not fit in the cell, Quattro Pro displays the number in scientific notation.

TROUBLESHOOTING

Quattro Pro displays asterisks instead of the number entered in a cell. If the cell uses a format other than General or Scientific, or if the cell width is too narrow to display in scientific notation and the number cannot fit in the cell width, Quattro Pro displays asterisks instead of the number. Use the Adjust column's width to its widest cell entry button on the toolbar to change the column width, select a different numeric format, or change the font to a smaller size.

Entering Formulas

Formulas are the real power of a spreadsheet program like Quattro Pro. Formulas enable the program to calculate results and analyze data. As you change or add new data to a spreadsheet, Quattro Pro recalculates the new results. With little effort, you can quickly see the effects of changing information on the end results.

Formulas can operate on numbers, labels, or the results of other formulas. A formula can contain up to 1,022 characters and can include numbers, text, operators, cell and block addresses, block names, and functions. A formula cannot contain spaces except in a block name, a quoted text string, or a note (see the section "Adding Reference Notes," later in this chapter).

NOTE Operators are symbols that represent mathematical operations, such as the plus sign (+) to indicate addition, the asterisk (*) to indicate multiplication, or the forward slash (/) to indicate division.

You can use Quattro Pro as a calculator by typing numbers directly into a formula, as in **123+456**, but doing so ignores the real power of Quattro Pro formulas. A more useful formula uses cell references or block names in the calculation. Figure 12.5 demonstrates this capability.

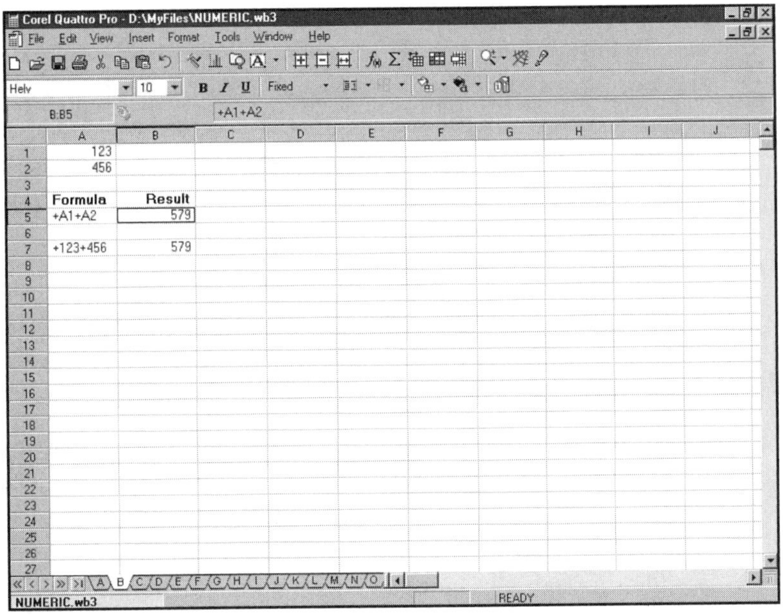

FIG. 12.5
Use cell references instead of the numbers in formulas.

In this figure, the values 123 and 456 are placed in cells A1 and A2, respectively. In cell A5, the listed formula +A1+A2, which refers to these two cells, produces the same result as the formula 123+456 listed in cell A7—the value 579. (Notice that the formula in cell B5 begins with a plus sign—if the formula begins with a letter, not a plus sign, Quattro Pro assumes that you are entering a label and performs no calculations.) Suppose, however, that the data changes and you discover the first value should be 124, not 123. If you used the cell reference formula, you just type **124** in cell A1 and the formula recalculates the new value of 580. If you used the formula with numeric values rather than the cell reference formula, you must edit or retype the formula to change the data and obtain the new result.

Quattro Pro uses four kinds of formulas: numeric, string, logical, and function. The following sections briefly describe each type of formula.

Using Numeric Formulas Numeric formulas are instructions to Quattro Pro to perform mathematical calculations. You use *operators* to specify the mathematical operations and the order in which they should be performed. You use operators for addition, subtraction, multiplication, division, and exponentiation (raising a number to a power).

NOTE Because Quattro Pro attempts to evaluate simple numeric formulas that use division, such as 6/26, as a date entry, you must begin such formulas with a plus sign (**+6/26**). This tells Quattro Pro you want to perform a calculation rather than trying to use the entry as a date.

Quattro Pro evaluates formulas according to a set of defined operator preferences. That is, exponentiation is performed before multiplication or division, and all three are performed before any addition or subtraction. If the formula includes two operators of the same precedence, this portion of the equation is evaluated left to right. You can control a formula's evaluation order by placing portions of a formula within parentheses, because Quattro Pro always evaluates items within a set of parentheses first.

For example, the formula 5+3*2 results in a value of 11, while the formula (5+3)*2 results in a value of 16. In the first formula, Quattro Pro multiplies 3 times 2 and adds the result, 6, to 5. In the second formula, Quattro Pro adds 5 and 3, and multiplies the result, 8, by 2. As you can see, a very small change in the formula produces quite different results.

Using String Formulas A *string* is a label or the result of a string formula; it is text rather than numbers. Only two string formula operators exist: the plus sign (+), which repeats a string, and the ampersand (&), which *concatenate*s (joins) two or more strings. String formulas use different rules than numeric formulas. String formulas always begin with the plus sign but cannot include more than one plus sign. To add two strings, you concatenate them by using the ampersand.

Figure 12.6 shows several examples of string formulas. In the figure, cell C10 shows the results when the plus sign is used to repeat a string value. The formula to repeat a string or a numeric value is the same. C11 shows the result of concatenating two strings. Notice that no spaces exist between the two concatenated values. C12 and C13 demonstrate how to include spaces and commas in quoted strings to produce better looking results.

If you attempt to add two strings using the plus sign rather than the ampersand, Quattro Pro treats the formula as a numeric formula rather than a string formula. A cell that contains a label has a numeric value of 0 (zero), so the formula +B4+B5 in C14 returns a value of 0. You can use the ampersand only in string formulas. Also, if you use any numeric operators (after the plus sign at the beginning) in a formula that contains an ampersand, the formula results in ERR.

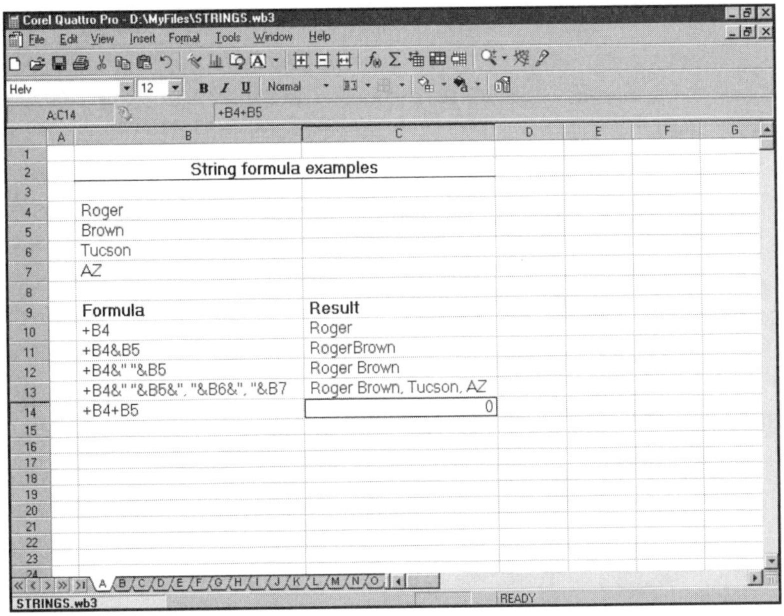

FIG. 12.6
Use string formulas to join text, such as first and last names.

Using Logical Formulas *Logical formulas* are true/false tests. A logical formula returns a value of `1` if the test is true and a value of `0` if the test is false. Logical formulas often are used in database criteria tables and also to construct the tests used with the @IF function, discussed in the next section, "Using Function Formulas."

Part III Ch 12

TIP Logical formulas are also called Boolean formulas.

Logical formulas provide a shortcut method of performing conditional calculations. Suppose that you want to include the value contained in cell A1 only if this value is greater than 100. The logical formula +A1*(A1>100) returns the result you want. In this formula, the logical test, A1>100, evaluates as 0 unless the value in A1 is greater than 100. If A1 contains a value over 100, the logical test evaluates to 1. Because any value multiplied by 0 equals 0, and any value multiplied by 1 is the original value, the logical formula returns the result you want.

Using Function Formulas Although you can build many formulas by using the numeric, string, or logical operators, some calculations are simply too complex to create with these simple operators. For example, if you want to calculate the interest due on a loan payment, you can simply multiply the beginning balance by the periodic interest rate. It's much more difficult, however, to calculate the actual payment amount necessary to pay off a loan in a series of equal payments.

TIP Quattro Pro provides a number of built-in *projects* (sometimes referred to as *templates*) that can help you when setting up notebooks that calculate loan payments, budgets, expense reports, and so on. To access these projects, choose File, New; then select a project from the list, and click Create.

Fortunately, Quattro Pro provides a large number of built-in *functions*—preconstructed formulas that handle a broad range of complex calculations. You will learn how to use these functions in Chapter 13. These functions enable you to perform many different types of calculations by simply supplying the raw data. For example, to determine the payments on a loan, you can use the @PAYMT function. You supply the necessary data—the interest rate, number of payments, and the loan amount—and Quattro Pro solves the problem.

Quattro Pro includes nearly 500 powerful, built-in functions you can use in your formulas. Figure 12.7 shows an example of how the @PAYMT function calculates the loan payment on a slightly more complex loan, one with a balloon payment due at the end of the loan. In this case, a borrower wants to know the monthly payments on a loan with the following terms:

Principal	$100,000
Annual interest rate	9%
Term	15 years
Balance due at end of loan (balloon)	$10,000

In this case, because the payments are made monthly, but the interest rate and term are stated in yearly amounts, the term must be multiplied by 12, and the rate must be divided by 12 to obtain the term in months, and the monthly interest rate. The monthly loan payment, $987.84, is automatically adjusted if any of the raw data in cells B4..B7 is changed.

TIP See the @Function Reference item on the Contents tab of the Quattro Pro online help system for a complete listing of all built-in functions.

When you create formulas in a Quattro Pro notebook, you can often combine functions with numeric, logical, and string formulas to produce the results you need. The next chapter provides much more information on functions.

▶ **See** "Using Functions," **p. 270**z

Creating Formulas by Pointing to Cells Most formulas you create will contain operators and cell references. One way to enter a cell reference in a formula is to just type the cell address itself. However, you can also point to the cell by clicking the cell, or moving the cell selector to the cell with the navigation keys. When you move the cell selector as you are entering a formula, the mode indicator at the right edge of the Application Bar changes from VALUE to POINT, and the address of the cell selector appears in the input line (see Figure 12.8).

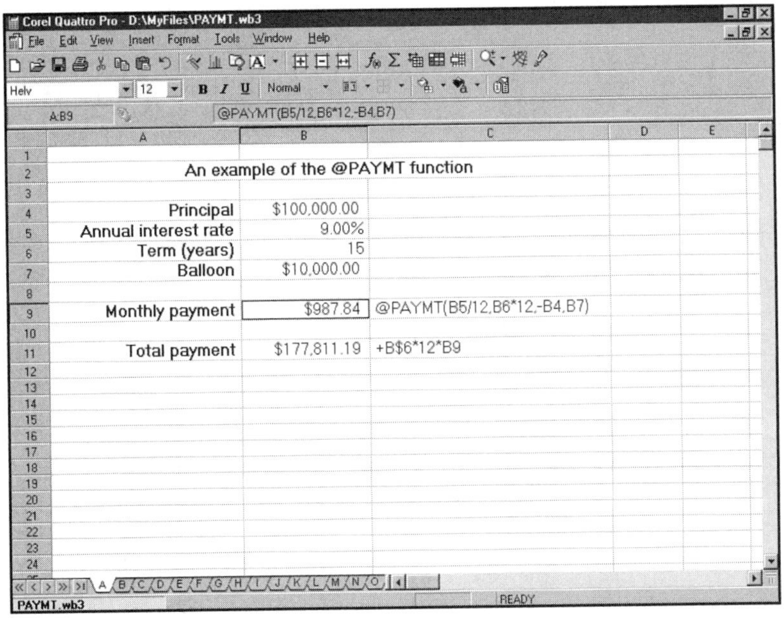

FIG. 12.7
Function formulas quickly perform complex calculations by using your data.

If the formula requires additional entries, type the next operator and continue entering *arguments*—the information you must supply to complete the formula—until you finish. Press Enter or click the Confirm button (the blue check mark at the left of the input line) to place the formula in the notebook (see Figure 12.8). You can combine pointing and typing cell addresses—the result is the same.

To refer to a cell on another notebook sheet, include the sheet letter or name, followed by a colon and the cell address. To include the value of cell A14 from a sheet named EXPENSES, for example, type **+EXPENSES:A14**. To point to a cell on another sheet, click the sheet tab with the mouse and then point to the cell. You also can type + and then use the navigation keys, including Ctrl+Page Down and Ctrl+Page Up, to move the cell selector to other sheets.

Finding Formula Errors Sometimes you may find your formulas display ERR or NA instead of the value you expected. ERR means the formula contains an erroneous calculation, such as dividing by zero. This can result from missing data or even from an error in entering a cell address. NA means some of the necessary information is currently not available, and can result from including a reference to a cell containing the @NA function or from linking formulas that were not updated when the notebook was opened. Finding the source of such errors can prove difficult, especially in a complex formula. Quattro Pro enables you to track down such errors using two different methods.

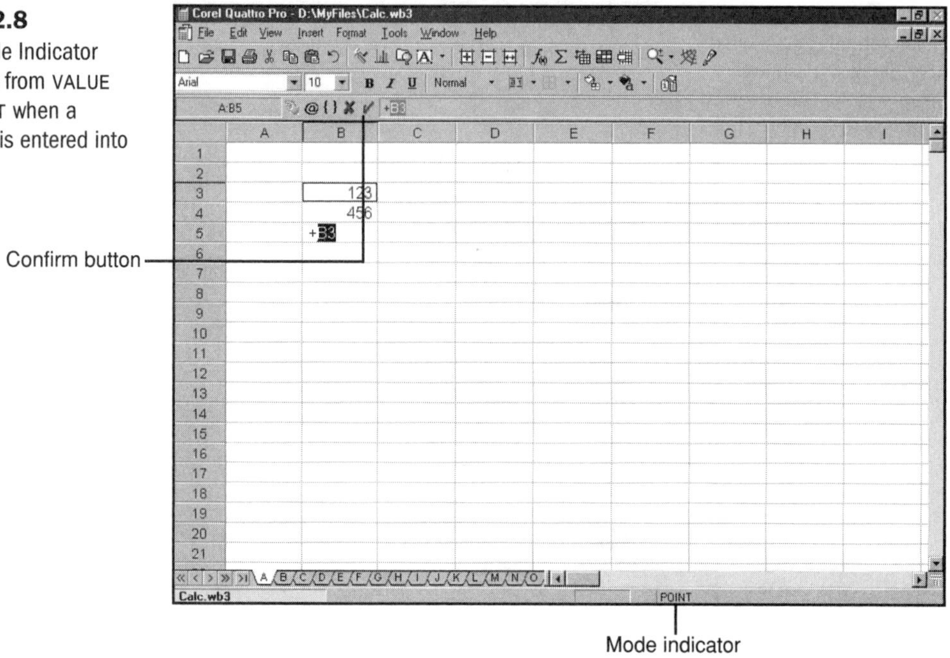

FIG. 12.8
The Mode Indicator changes from VALUE to POINT when a formula is entered into the cell.

TIP Use the F5 (Go To) key to quickly move the cell selector.

To quickly find the source of an ERR or NA value, use the Go To feature. First, move the cell selector to the cell displaying ERR or NA, and then press F5 (Go To) or choose Edit, Go To. Do not change the destination in the Reference text box; instead, just click OK, and the cell selector will move to the cell that is the source of the error. If the cell selector is already on the cell that is the source of the error, it will remain in the current cell.

To understand how this works, imagine that cell A5 contains the formula **+1/A1**, cell A10 contains the formula **+A5**, and cell A1 is empty. ERR will be displayed in both A5 and A10. If you select cell A10, press F5 (Go To), and press Enter, the cell selector will move to A5, because cell A5 contains the original formula that generated the error. If you select cell A5, press F5 (Go To), and press Enter, the cell selector will remain in A5, telling you that no other formula is contributing to the error.

Adding Reference Notes

Documentation is always important, and it is even more important when you create complex formulas that may be difficult to understand. It's pretty easy to forget why you built a formula exactly as you did, but even a brief note is often all you need to remind yourself. Quattro Pro makes documenting formulas and values easy by allowing you to add notes to cell entries.

These reference notes don't appear when you print a report, but as Figure 12.9 shows, the notes appear on-screen in the input line when you move the cell selector to a cell that contains a note. You can press F2 (Edit) or double-click the cell to see the note in the current cell (see Figure 12.9); use this option if the note is too long to appear in the input line when you select the cell.

FIG. 12.9
Add notes to formulas to provide valuable documentation.

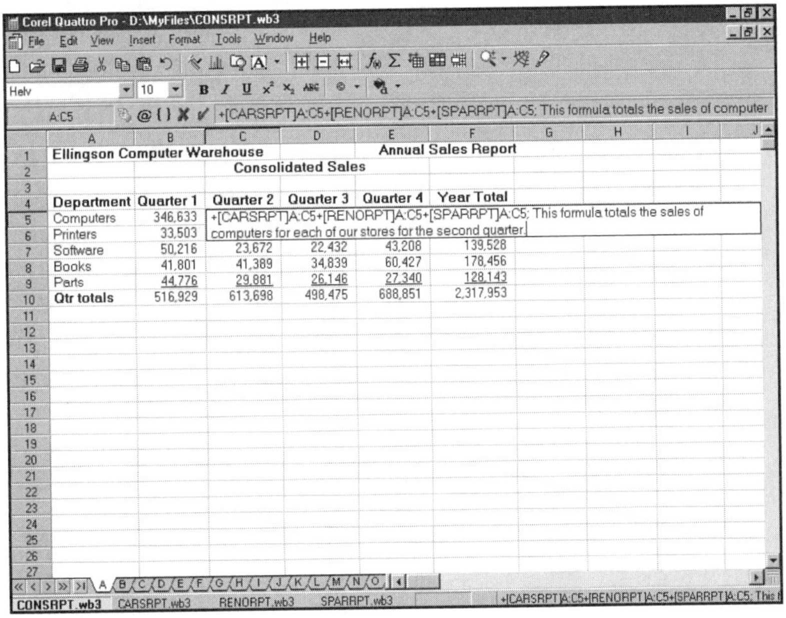

The note attached to the formula in cell C5 in Figure 12.9 clearly states the purpose of the formula—to show the combined total of sales of computers in each store during the second quarter.

To attach a note to a cell containing data, type a semicolon immediately following the formula or value—don't leave any spaces before the semicolon—then type the note. You can include up to 1,022 characters in a cell, including the length of the formula or value and the note. Because these notes won't have any effect on your printed reports, they are a good method of creating internal documentation that will always remain with the notebook.

TIP To print the notes attached to formulas, choose File, Page Setup, click the Options tab, select Cell Formulas, and click Print.

Correcting Errors with Undo

When you type an entry, edit a cell, or issue a command (such as Edit, Delete), you make changes in the notebook. If you make a change in error, you can usually choose the Edit, Undo command (or press Ctrl+Z) to reverse the previous change. You can also use the Undo button on the toolbar. If you type over an entry in error, you can undo the new entry to restore the previous entry. The Undo feature undoes only the last action performed, whether you were entering data, using a command, running a macro, or using Undo.

The Undo feature is powerful, and using it can be a little tricky. To use Undo properly, you first must understand what Quattro Pro considers to be a change that can be undone. A change occurs between the time Quattro Pro leaves READY mode and the time it returns to READY mode. If you press F2 (Edit), Quattro Pro enters EDIT mode. After you press Enter to confirm the edits, Quattro Pro returns to READY mode. If you choose Edit, Undo or click the Undo button, Quattro Pro restores the cell contents that existed before you pressed F2 (Edit). To restore the last change that was undone, choose Edit, Redo (which replaces Edit, Undo until you make another change that can be undone), or click the Undo button again. If a single command makes the change, the Undo feature can undo changes (such as Edit, Delete) made to an entire block of cells or even an entire notebook.

NOTE The Edit, Undo and Edit, Redo commands inform you of the action which can be undone or redone by including a one-word description that changes with each type of action that follows the command. If you make an entry in a cell, for example, the command appears as "Edit, Undo Entry." If you use the Edit, Undo Entry command, the command then changes to "Edit, Redo Entry."

Quattro Pro cannot undo some commands. Moving the cell selector, saving a notebook, and the effects of recalculating formulas are examples of commands that cannot be undone. Before you make a serious change to an important file, always save the work to protect against errors that Undo may not reverse.

Quattro Pro has two levels of Undo command functionality. To ensure that the full Undo feature is available, make sure that the Undo Enabled check box in the General tab of the Application dialog box is checked (see Figure 12.10). To access this dialog box, right-click the Quattro Pro title bar or press Alt+F12. If you don't enable the full Undo command, you will still be able to undo certain actions, such as entering data into a cell or changing a chart type or a chart title.

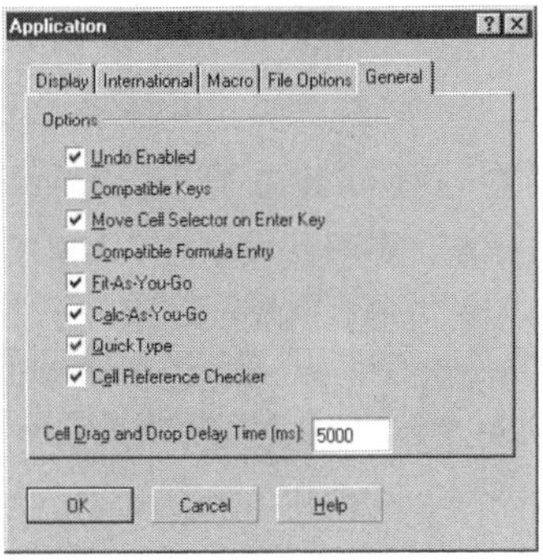

FIG. 12.10
Select Undo Enabled to ensure that the full Undo feature is available.

Saving Your Work

When you create a Quattro Pro notebook, it first exists only in your computer's volatile memory—RAM. To make the notebook available for future use, you must also save the notebook in a file on disk. If you don't save new notebooks or changes before you quit Quattro Pro, you lose your work. You must also save a notebook in a disk file if you want to share the notebook with other people. The notebook file remains on disk after you quit Quattro Pro or turn off the computer.

Saving Notebook Files

To save your work, choose File, Save or File, Save As, or click the Save button on the toolbar. If you have not yet saved the notebook, Quattro Pro suggests a default name, such as NOTEBK1.WB3. When you use File, New to open new blank notebooks, Quattro Pro increases the numerical portion of the file name. The second new notebook is NOTEBK2.WB3, and so on.

If you already have saved the active notebook and assigned a name, File, Save saves the active notebook to disk using the assigned name. If you choose File, Save As, Quattro Pro saves the active notebook using a name you specify in the Save File dialog box (see Figure 12.11).

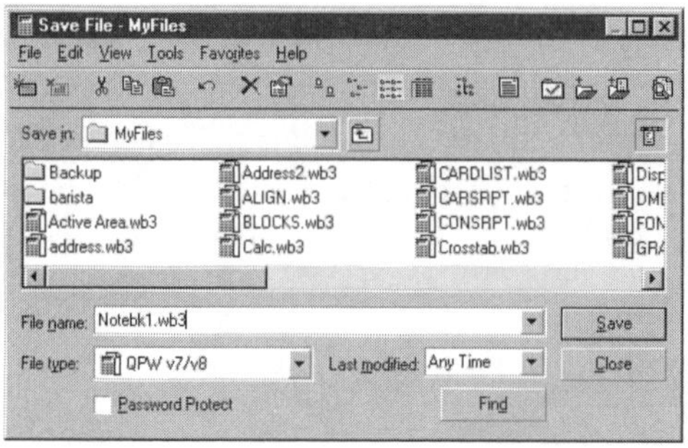

FIG. 12.11
Use the Save File dialog box to name your notebook files.

The standard extension for Quattro Pro notebooks is WB3, but you can open or save notebook files in many different formats by selecting the appropriate type in the File Type list box in Figure 12.11. The standard extension for Quattro Pro workspace files is WBS. When you type a notebook or workspace name to save, type only the descriptive part of the name. Quattro Pro adds the appropriate file extension for you.

Protecting Files with Passwords When you save a Quattro Pro notebook in a disk file, anyone with access to your computer can open the file. While this isn't a problem in most instances, you may have some files that should remain confidential and restricted. To prevent unauthorized access to certain notebook files, you can apply a password to them when you save them. When a notebook is protected by a password, you must know the correct password before Quattro Pro permits you to retrieve or open the notebook.

To apply a password to a notebook file you are saving, select the Password Protect check box in the Save File dialog box, type a file name, and select Save. In the Password text box, type a password of up to 15 characters. As you enter characters, Quattro Pro displays number signs (#) rather than the password. After you click OK to confirm the dialog box, Quattro Pro displays a dialog box with a Verify Password text box. Retype the password using the same combination of uppercase and lowercase characters. Passwords are case-sensitive. Click OK to confirm the dialog box.

TROUBLESHOOTING

Quattro Pro reports that I used the wrong password when I attempted to open a password-protected notebook file. Passwords are case-sensitive and can be very tricky to use. **BRIAN** is not the same as **brian** or **Brian**. Try entering the password again with the case reversed (press the Caps Lock key before entering the password) or with only the first letter of the word capitalized.

Saving Files in Other Formats Quattro Pro can read and save files in many popular formats, including Lotus 1-2-3 for DOS, Lotus 1-2-3 for Windows, Quattro Pro for DOS, Excel, Paradox, dBASE, ASCII text, and HTML. If you want to save a Quattro Pro notebook in another format, select the correct file extension in the File Type drop-down list box in the Save File dialog box (refer to Figure 12.11). To save a notebook as a Lotus 1-2-3 for Windows file, for example, select 1-2-3 v4 or 5.

TIP Unless you need to share a notebook file with someone who does not have Quattro Pro, always save notebooks using the QPW v7/v8 file format.

If you save a notebook in any type other than the default "QPW v7/v8" format, any features unique to the newest version of Quattro Pro will be lost. For example, because Lotus 1-2-3 Release 2.x spreadsheets cannot have multiple sheets, only the first notebook sheet is retained if you save the file by using the 1-2-3 v2.x file type.

Making Space on Your Disk Each time you create a file, you use space on a disk—usually your hard disk. Eventually, you'll run out of disk space if you don't occasionally erase old, unneeded files from the disk. Even if you have disk space left, too many files make it difficult to search through the file list for a specific file.

Before you delete old files, consider saving them to a floppy disk in case you need them again. Quattro Pro notebook files are quite space efficient, and you can store a large number of files on a single floppy disk. Quattro Pro has no command for deleting files. You can use the Windows Explorer to delete old, unneeded files.

Using Automatic Backups

Many different types of problems can cause you to lose the results of your work. If there is a power failure, for example, any changes to a Quattro Pro notebook that haven't been saved to disk will be lost. If a program crashes and locks up your system, the same thing may occur. There's always the problem of the over-confident user, too. Have you ever lost work because you thought you already saved it, but then realized you hadn't because you were distracted? These are only a few of the many problems that present a danger to your notebooks and your data.

Saving your work frequently is the best insurance against losing a notebook or data to any of these problems. Unfortunately, it's pretty easy to forget to save your work often enough. When you're under deadline pressure, who remembers to select File, Save?

Fortunately, Quattro Pro can quickly save your notebooks automatically at intervals you specify. That way, if a problem occurs, your notebook file on disk isn't too far behind and you won't lose too much work.

To activate the automatic backup feature, right-click the Quattro Pro title bar and select Application Properties or press Alt+F12 to display the Application dialog box. Select the File Options tab (see Figure 12.12). Use the Timed Document Backup Every option to specify how often you want Quattro Pro to automatically back up your notebook files. Select the Timed Document Backup Every check box to enable the automatic backup feature. Click OK to save the change and close the dialog box.

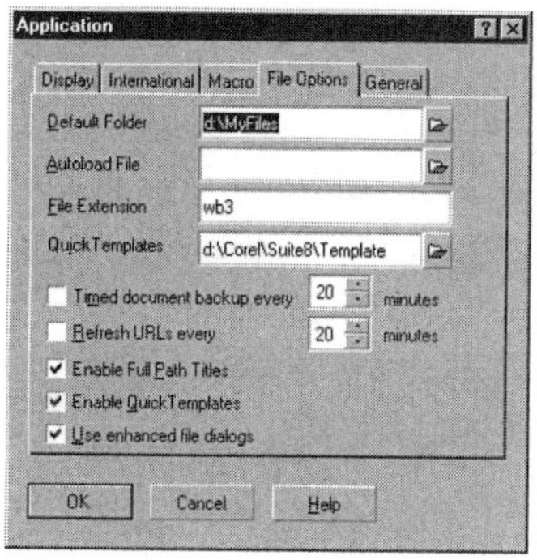

FIG. 12.12
Use the automatic backup feature to automatically save your notebook files at specified intervals.

How often should you have Quattro Pro save your files? The best answer to that question is another question: "How much work are you willing to do over?" Most notebook files can be saved quite quickly, so there isn't much of a delay as they save. A setting of 10 minutes between backups is probably a good compromise, but you can adjust the setting to one that suits your work style. ●

CHAPTER 13

Building a Spreadsheet

Use basic Corel Quattro Pro commands

Learn which commands will help you perform the tasks necessary to create spreadsheet models that accomplish your goals.

Use blocks of cells as a unit

Save time by telling Quattro Pro to perform the same actions on numerous cells at the same time.

Copy and move data

Learn how to use the same data in more than one place, or move data to more appropriate locations to make your spreadsheets far more useable.

Automatically fill blocks of cells with useful data

Quattro Pro can easily automate the process of entering data, and it will enter many types of data for you.

Use built-in functions

Use built-in functions to leverage the power of Quattro Pro in your notebooks and easily perform complex calculations.

If you're new to Corel Quattro Pro, you may think that building a spreadsheet is quite a task. It's true that some models can be pretty complex, but most of the time you'll find them quite simple. Remember, you don't have to build a complete, complex masterpiece all at once. You don't even have to start with very complicated models, either. The best way to learn to build Quattro Pro spreadsheet models is to start small, and then work your way up.

This chapter covers some of the basic subjects that will help you begin building your models. Don't be confused if you see the terms *spreadsheet*, *model*, *worksheet*, and *notebook* used interchangeably; they all refer to the same thing unless noted otherwise. ■

Choosing Commands from Menus

Commands are used for almost everything you do in Corel Quattro Pro. Commands tell Quattro Pro to perform a task, change the basic operation of Quattro Pro, or operate on a notebook, a notebook sheet, a block of cells, or individual cells. Some commands are general enough to apply to all notebooks; still others are specialized and apply to individual objects such as blocks or cells.

The Quattro Pro main menu includes eight options. Each option leads to a drop-down menu.

Each drop-down menu provides a series of commands you can use to accomplish specific types of tasks. You'll save quite a bit of time if you understand the basic purpose of each main menu selection, because you won't spend so much time hunting for the correct command. Let's have a quick look at the main menu options:

- The File commands enable you to save and open notebooks, print reports, set up your printer, send reports directly from Quattro Pro to others via e-mail, and quit Quattro Pro.
- The Edit commands enable you to undo commands; use the Windows Clipboard to copy, cut, and paste information; convert formulas to unchanging values; create links to other Windows applications; delete cells, rows, columns, and sheets; fill blocks with data and define customized fill series; and search and replace.
- The View commands enable you to zoom in or out; control the display of screen elements; group sheets; split the notebook into horizontal or vertical panes; lock rows or columns on-screen; and switch between the notebook draft view, notebook page view, and the Objects sheet.
- The Insert commands enable you to insert cells, rows, columns, and sheets; name blocks of cells; add a QuickButton onto a sheet; query, link to, or import external databases; use the Database Desktop utility; add functions to cells; add charts, images, or other objects to a notebook; and insert comments and page breaks.
- The Format commands enable you to create and modify styles; modify styles of blocks, sheets, and notebooks; reformat text; apply SpeedFormats; use QuickFit; and adjust the position of objects added to a sheet.
- The Tools commands enable you to check spelling and use QuickCorrect; create, run, and debug macros; use QuickFilter and sort to organize data; use Scenario Manager; perform what-if analyses, data regression, and matrix manipulation; use the Consolidator, Optimizer, and Solve For utilities; create your own dialog boxes and toolbars; customize Quattro Pro's default settings; create geographical maps; and create on-screen slide shows.

- The Window commands enable you to cascade or tile windows; create additional views of your notebooks; control the display of open windows; and select a window.
- The Help commands enable you to access the Quattro Pro Help system; use the PerfectExpert; access help on the Internet; and display product and license information.

For more detailed information on Quattro Pro's menus, you can use the Help, Help Topics command. You can also press F1 (Help) when a command is selected for context-sensitive help that explains how to perform the selected task.

TROUBLESHOOTING

Sometimes it's difficult to determine where to find the command necessary to perform a task. Try choosing Help, Ask the PerfectExpert for help on how to perform a task. The PerfectExpert will show you a number of topics relating to the task, and you can select the topic you want.

Using Blocks

A *block* is usually a rectangular group of cells in a notebook. In Quattro Pro, a block also can contain several groups of cells defined by collections of rectangular blocks. In other words, a single named block does not have to be rectangular, but can contain several smaller rectangular blocks. Figure 13.1, for example, shows one rectangular block in cells A1..B3; a nonrectangular block including B5..B6, B7..D9, and E7..F7; and a noncontiguous block that includes C14..D15 and E17..F18 (the blocks are shaded gray to make them easier to see).

TIP Blocks are called *ranges* in Excel and Lotus 1-2-3.

You specify a block address (usually in a text box of a dialog box) by using cell addresses of any two diagonally opposite corners of the block. You separate the cell addresses with one or two periods and separate each rectangular block with commas. You can specify the nonrectangular block shown in Figure 13.1 by typing **B5..B6,B7..D9,E7..F7**, for example. You also can specify this block in several other ways, as long as you separate each rectangular block with commas.

A block can also span two or more notebook sheets. This *three-dimensional* block includes the same cells on each sheet. When you use a three-dimensional block, you must include the sheet letter or sheet name with the cell addresses. For example, to extend the rectangular block in Figure 13.1 to a three-dimensional block, type **A:A1..C:B3**.

FIG. 13.1
You can create several different kinds of Quattro Pro blocks on one page.

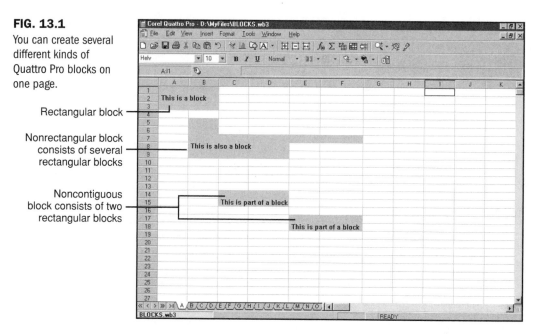

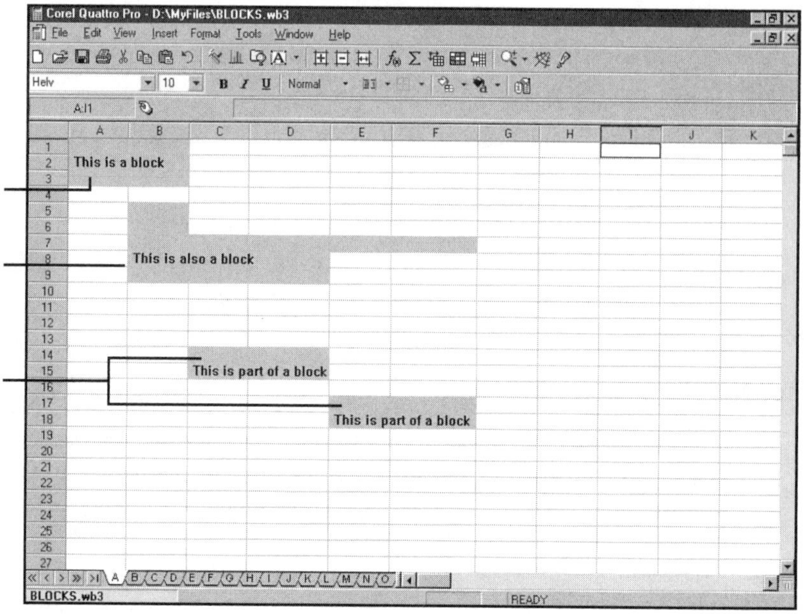

Selecting Blocks

Many commands act on blocks. The Edit, Copy Cells command, for example, displays a dialog box asking for a From and a To block. To enter a block, you can type the address of the block, select the block with the mouse or the keyboard before or after you choose the command, or type the block name (to learn about creating a name, see "Naming Blocks" later in this chapter).

TIP You can specify a rectangular block address using any two diagonally opposite cells.

Typing the Block Addresses If you want to type a block address, type the addresses of cells diagonally opposite in a rectangular block, separating each cell with one or two periods. If the block is nonrectangular, you must specify each rectangular block and separate each block with a comma. To specify the block A1..C4, for example, you type either **A1..C4, A1.C4, A4..C1,** or **A4.C1.** Quattro Pro regards each of these addresses the same as A1..C4.

Selecting Blocks The easiest method of specifying a block's cell addresses is usually selecting the block by pointing with the mouse or the keyboard. You can select a block before or after you issue a command. In a formula, however, you must select the block after you begin typing the formula. If you select a block before you issue a command, the block remains selected, allowing you to use the same block with more than one command without reselecting the block. To use the mouse to select a block, simply hold down the left mouse button as you drag the mouse across the block.

TIP If you use the keyboard to select a block, you can use the Shift+F7 keyboard shortcut as a method of anchoring a block selection. To *anchor* means to retain the location of the active cell, as you extend the highlight to include other cells in the block. You can also anchor a block selection by pressing and holding down the Shift key while moving the cell selector.

When you preselect a block, the address automatically appears in the text boxes of any command dialog boxes. Some dialog boxes, however, require you to specify more than one block. For example, if you use the Edit, Copy Cells command, you must specify both a From (source) and a To (destination) block. If you have selected a block before you issue the command, the From text box will show the selected block. You can use the mouse or press Tab and Shift+Tab to move the highlight between the text boxes. Then enter the second block by typing its address or block name, or by pointing.

In some dialog boxes, a button with an arrow appears beside text boxes. This means that you can click the arrow button to select a cell or block directly in the sheet; the dialog box changes to show only the title bar, enabling you to see more of the sheet. After you've finished selecting the cell or block, click the Maximize button in the dialog box title bar to return to the dialog box. The address of the cell or block you selected in the sheet now appears in the text box of the dialog box.

Specifying a Block with a Name You also can specify a block in a dialog box by using a name you assign to the block (see "Naming Blocks," later in this chapter). Whenever Quattro Pro expects the address of a cell or a block, you can specify a block name. You can enter a block name in the Go To dialog box, for example, and Quattro Pro moves the cell selector to the upper-left corner of the named block.

You gain a number of advantages by using block names:

- Block names are easier to remember than block addresses—especially if a block is noncontiguous.
- Typing a block name usually is easier than pointing to a block in another part of the notebook.
- Macros that use block names rather than cell addresses automatically adjust after you move a block.
- Block names also make formulas easier to understand. The formula +QTR_1_TOTAL (using the block name QTR_1_TOTAL) is easier to understand than the formula +B10.

Extending Block Selections Extending a block selection to include a three-dimensional block or a group of blocks allows you to include more than a single two-dimensional block in a command or a block name. These extended blocks make some operations easier and faster because one command can replace a series of commands, such as applying numeric formats, adding shading, and choosing a text font.

TIP Hold down the Ctrl key when selecting noncontiguous blocks.

Selecting noncontiguous blocks (when you want to change the formatting of multiple blocks in a sheet, for example) using the mouse is much easier than selecting noncontiguous blocks using the keyboard. You can select noncontiguous blocks using the mouse before or after you choose a command; but to select noncontiguous blocks using the keyboard, you must select the block after choosing a command.

If you use the mouse to extend a block selection that includes noncontiguous blocks, you can select the blocks before or after you choose a command. Use the following procedure:

1. Select the first rectangular block.
2. Press and hold down the Ctrl key.
3. Select each additional rectangular block.
4. Release the Ctrl key.

TIP To work on noncontiguous blocks using the keyboard, choose the command first, and then select the block.

To use the keyboard to extend a block selection that includes noncontiguous blocks, perform the following steps:

1. Choose the command in which you want to use the noncontiguous blocks.
2. Select the appropriate block text box by pressing the Tab key or, if the text box has an underlined letter, by pressing Alt plus the underlined letter.
3. Enter the block addresses by typing the addresses of rectangular blocks and separating each block with a comma. You also can point to the first cell of each rectangular block, press the period key to anchor the selection, and use the navigation keys to select the block. Enter a comma and continue selecting rectangular blocks until you have selected each block.

Naming Blocks

Block addresses can be difficult to remember, and it's easy to type the wrong set of cell addresses when specifying a block. Quattro Pro provides a very good solution to this problem: ***block names***. If you name blocks, you can always substitute the block name for the block's cell addresses in commands and formulas, ensuring the correct block will be affected by the command or formula. Block names also make formulas much easier to read and understand, because Quattro Pro will always substitute block names where appropriate in formulas—even if you didn't use block names when you created the formula.

TIP Quattro Pro does not distinguish between uppercase and lowercase letters; Block_1, block_1, and BLOCK_1 are equivalent block names.

You should follow certain rules and cautions when creating block names:

- You can use up to 63 characters to name a block.
- You can use block names in formulas, functions, commands, and macros.
- Don't use the following characters in block names:

    + - * / & > < @ # ^ $ ( )

- Although block names that start with numbers are valid, try to avoid starting block names with numbers because they may cause problems in formulas.
- Don't create block names that also are cell addresses, column letters, or row numbers (such as A1, AA, or 199), names of keys (such as Edit), function names (such as @AVG), or macro commands (such as WRITE).
- Use descriptive block names.
- Join parts of block names together with the underscore (such as QTR_1_TOTALS) rather than spaces.
- If you share spreadsheet files with users of other spreadsheet programs (such as Microsoft Excel, Lotus 1-2-3, or even older versions of Quattro Pro), limit block names to 15 characters to ensure compatibility.

Quattro Pro provides several methods of creating block names. Each method uses the Insert, Name, Cells command (Ctrl+F3) to first display the Cell Names dialog box (see Figure 13.2). The following sections describe the block naming options available through this dialog box.

CAUTION

Don't confuse the Insert, Cells and Insert, Name, Cells commands. The Insert, Cells command adds a rectangular block of cells to a notebook sheet, thus moving other cells down or to the right. The Insert, Name, Cells command creates block names.

FIG. 13.2
The Cell Names dialog box provides several block-naming options.

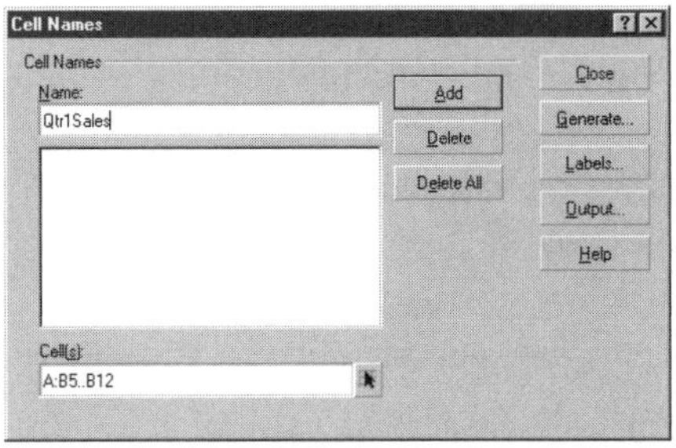

Creating Block Names with Insert, Name, Cells, Add You can use the Insert, Name, Cells, Add command to assign a name to a cell or a block. To create a block name using this command, follow these steps:

1. Select the cell or block you want to name.
2. Choose Insert, Name, Cells (or press Ctrl+F3). The Cell Names dialog box shown in Figure 13.2 appears.
3. Type the block name in the Name text box, and then click Add.
4. Click Close.

If you want to add more than one block name, repeat step 3 as necessary.

Creating Block Names with Insert, Name, Cells, Generate You can also create block names automatically using the Insert, Name, Cells, Generate command. This command can generate block names for a row, a column, or for every cell in a selected block, using labels in the block. To create block names using this command, follow these steps:

1. Select the cell or block you want to name.
2. Choose Insert, Name, Cells (or press Ctrl+F3).
3. Click Generate to display the Generate Cell Names dialog box (see Figure 13.3).

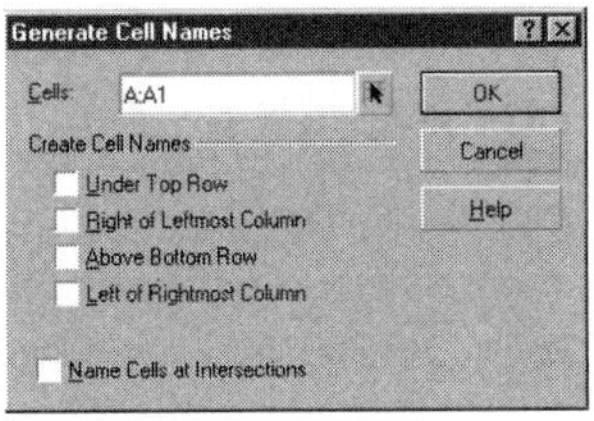

FIG. 13.3
You can create block names automatically using the Generate Cell Names dialog box.

4. The check boxes in this dialog box determine which cells (in the selected block) the labels identify. Choose Under Top Row, Right of Leftmost Column, Above Bottom Row, or Left of Rightmost Column. For example, you might use labels to identify product lines and time periods.
5. To name all cells in the block using the label cells in combination, select Name Cells at Intersections.
6. Click OK to return to the Cell Names dialog box.

The Name Cells at Intersections option creates block names by concatenating (joining) the column label, an underscore, and the row label. For example, if the column label is "Year Total" and the row label is "Software," the name generated for the intersecting cell is Year Total_Software.

Creating Block Names with Insert, Name, Cells, Labels You also can use the Insert, Name, Cells, Labels command to create block names. With this command, you use labels already typed on a notebook sheet as block names for adjacent cells, such as to identify cells where users will input data. To create block names using this command, follow these steps:

1. Select the cell or block you want to name.
2. Choose Insert, Name, Cells (or press Ctrl+F3).
3. Click Labels to display the Create Names From Labels dialog box (see Figure 13.4).

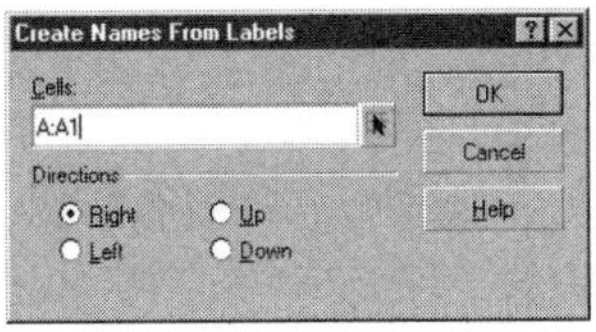

FIG. 13.4
The Create Names From Labels dialog box is useful for creating block names.

4. The Directions option buttons determine which cells are named using the labels. Select the appropriate direction, Right, Left, Up, or Down.
5. Click OK to return to the Cell Names dialog box.

The Insert, Name, Cells, Labels command ignores blank cells in the label block as it creates single-cell blocks. If you need to create multiple-cell blocks, you must use the Insert, Name, Cells, Add command.

Listing Block Names A table of block names serves as important notebook documentation. Quattro Pro creates a two-column table of block names and addresses using the Insert, Name, Cells, Output command. When you choose this command, select an area with enough room for the block name table, because the table overwrites any existing data without warning.

TROUBLESHOOTING

The block name table doesn't seem to show the correct addresses for some blocks. If you change the definition of a block name, or add or delete block names, the block name table is not updated automatically. You must issue the Insert, Name, Cells, Output command again to update the table.

Some formulas don't show the correct results even though they appear to contain correct block names. Make certain your block names don't contain any mathematical operators, such as a plus or minus sign. Quattro Pro may be confused if you include these operators in block names that appear in formulas.

Deleting Block Names There's usually little reason to remove block names from a Quattro Pro notebook. Block names don't use much memory, and the documentation they provide can be invaluable. Still, if you want to delete existing block names, Quattro Pro has two commands that delete block names from the notebook. Use the Insert, Name, Cells, Delete command to delete a single block name or several block names. You can delete all block names at one time using the Insert, Name, Cells, Delete All command.

Copying and Moving Information

Few Quattro Pro notebooks are masterpieces when first created. Most often, it's useful to copy or move data from one place to another. You might, for example, want to duplicate the appearance of an existing report, or you might simply find it's awkward to enter data correctly in the notebook's initial layout. Whatever your reason, you'll discover that Quattro Pro offers several different methods of copying and moving data.

TIP Chapter 14, "Changing the Display and Appearance of Data," shows you how to make your Quattro Pro notebooks look as good as they should.

The three primary methods of moving and copying data in Quattro Pro are:

- The Edit, Cut; Edit, Copy; Edit, Paste; and Edit, Paste Special commands, which all use the Windows Clipboard
- The Edit, Copy Cells command, which does not use the Clipboard
- The mouse

NOTE The Edit, Move Block command that appeared in earlier versions of Quattro Pro is no longer available in Quattro Pro 8; you must use the Windows Clipboard method or the mouse to move data.

In the following sections, you'll learn the advantages and disadvantages of each method, and why each method is important to you. You'll also learn the different ways to copy formulas.

Copying and Moving Using the Clipboard

The Windows Clipboard is a feature shared by most Windows applications. Data stored on the Clipboard is available to any Windows program that knows how to use the data. When you place data on the Clipboard, it remains there until new data replaces it, or until you exit from Windows. This permits you to make multiple copies of the same data without having to copy the data to the Clipboard each time (as long as you don't use another command that places new data on the Clipboard).

Using Edit, Cut The Edit, Cut command removes—or *cuts*—data from the notebook and places the data on the Clipboard. Any existing Clipboard data is lost unless it has been saved elsewhere. When you place data on the Clipboard, you can make as many copies of the data as you want using Edit, Paste.

CAUTION

The Edit, Cut command replaces any existing Clipboard data with new data. You cannot recover the old data; so be sure to use Edit, Paste to save the old data, if you will need it in the future, before you use the Edit, Cut command on the new data.

You can place any selectable object on the Clipboard. If you select a single cell, the Edit, Cut command removes the data from the selected cell and places the data on the Clipboard. If you select a block of cells, the entire block is removed from the notebook and placed on the Clipboard. You can also use Edit, Cut to place other types of objects, such as charts or drawn objects, on the Clipboard. Any object placed on the Clipboard using Quattro Pro's Edit, Cut command can later be returned to the notebook using Edit, Paste, but other Windows applications may not be able to accept all types of Quattro Pro objects.

To use Edit, Cut, first select the object you want to cut, and then choose Edit, Cut (Ctrl+X), or click the Cut button on the toolbar. The selected object will disappear from the Quattro Pro notebook. If you cut an object in error, immediately choose Edit, Undo before selecting any other commands.

Edit, Cut places any numeric formatting, alignment, or other object properties on the Clipboard along with the data. If you've used the dialog boxes to modify any of the properties for the selected object, these properties will be removed from the notebook along with the object and placed on the Clipboard for possible use later.

Using Edit, Copy The Edit, Copy command works very much like the Edit, Cut command, but there is one very important difference. When you use Edit, Copy, the selected object remains in your Quattro Pro notebook, and an exact duplicate is created on the Clipboard. This duplicate shares all of the original object's properties, including any numeric formatting, alignment, and so on. After the duplicate is placed on the Clipboard, however, the two objects—the original and the duplicate—are totally independent of each other. In other words, any changes you make to the original object in your notebook are not reflected in the duplicate on the Clipboard. If you want the duplicate to match the changed original, choose Edit, Copy again to create an updated duplicate.

TIP Edit, Copy adds a copy of the object to the Clipboard. You need to use Edit, Paste to add the copy to your notebook.

It's easy to become confused by the title of the Edit, Copy command. Although you might expect this command to make a copy of an object, the copy it produces isn't visible to you. The copy of the selected object only exists on the Windows Clipboard—ready to be pasted into another location in your Quattro Pro notebook or into another document created in another Windows application.

To use Edit, Copy, first select the object you want to copy, and then choose Edit, Copy (Ctrl+C), or click the Copy button on the toolbar. You won't see any change in the notebook, but the Clipboard will now contain an exact duplicate of the selected object.

NOTE Objects placed on the Windows Clipboard are stored in your computer's memory until you choose Edit, Cut or Edit, Copy to replace them with another object, or until you exit from Windows. Very large objects, such as bitmaps or sound files, can use quite a large portion of your system's memory, making your system operate at an unusually slow pace (especially if your notebook has lots of complex calculations). If you have copied a very large object to the Clipboard, but no longer need to store the object there, copy a single notebook cell to the Clipboard to free the memory for other uses.

Using Edit, Paste The Edit, Paste command places a copy of data contained on the Clipboard into your Quattro Pro notebook. The object on the Clipboard is unaffected by this command, and can be pasted into more than one location using additional Edit, Paste commands. Quattro Pro notebooks can contain most types of objects that can be placed on the Clipboard.

To use the Edit, Paste command, first choose Edit, Copy or Edit, Cut to place the object on the Clipboard. Next, position the cell selector at the location where you want to place a copy of the data, and select Edit, Paste (Ctrl+V) or click the Paste button on the toolbar.

The following guidelines enable you to determine the number and type of copies that will be created:

- If the data placed in the Clipboard with the Edit, Copy or Edit, Cut command was from a single cell, one copy of the data will be added to each selected cell after you choose Edit, Paste.
- If the data moved to the Clipboard with the Edit, Copy or Edit, Cut command was from several rows in a single column, one copy of the data will be added to each selected column after you choose Edit, Paste.
- If the data moved to the Clipboard with the Edit, Copy or Edit, Cut command was from several columns in a single row, one copy of the data will be added to each selected row after you choose Edit, Paste.
- If the data moved to the Clipboard with the Edit, Copy or Edit, Cut command was from several rows and several columns, one copy of the data will be added to the sheet starting at the selected cell after you choose Edit, Paste.

Three-dimensional data always creates a three-dimensional copy. If the source or destination data block includes more than one sheet, the same rules that apply to rows and columns also apply to the sheet dimension.

If you want additional copies of the same data, just reposition the cell selector and select Edit, Paste. Don't use any additional Edit, Copy or Edit, Cut commands if you want additional copies of the same data, because the Clipboard holds the most recent Edit, Copy or Edit, Cut contents.

CAUTION

If you paste data to a block that already contains data, Quattro Pro replaces the existing data with the new data. Use care with Edit, Paste to avoid pasting data into cells that contain formulas or other data you don't want to lose.

Copying Data Using the Edit, Copy Cells Command

Quattro Pro includes another command you can use to copy data from one place in the notebook to another. Edit, Copy Cells copies data directly within the notebook without using the Clipboard. Quattro Pro 8 doesn't include a comparable command to move cells; you must use the Clipboard method or the mouse to move cell data.

Because this command doesn't use the Clipboard, any objects you've already placed on the Clipboard aren't affected by the Edit, Copy Cells command. You can still use Edit, Paste to make copies of the unchanged Clipboard contents even after you use Edit, Copy Cells.

When you copy data, the copy contains the same labels, values, formatting, and style properties as the original data. The data in the original location remains unchanged.

You can copy a single cell or a block to another part of the same notebook sheet, to another notebook sheet, or to another open notebook. You can make a single copy or multiple copies at the same time. To copy data with the Edit, Copy Cells command, follow these steps:

1. Select the cell or block you want to copy. If you preselect a block, it appears in the From text box.
2. Choose Edit, Copy Cells. The Copy Cells dialog box shown in Figure 13.5 appears.

FIG. 13.5
You can use the Copy Cells dialog box to copy a single cell or a block of cells.

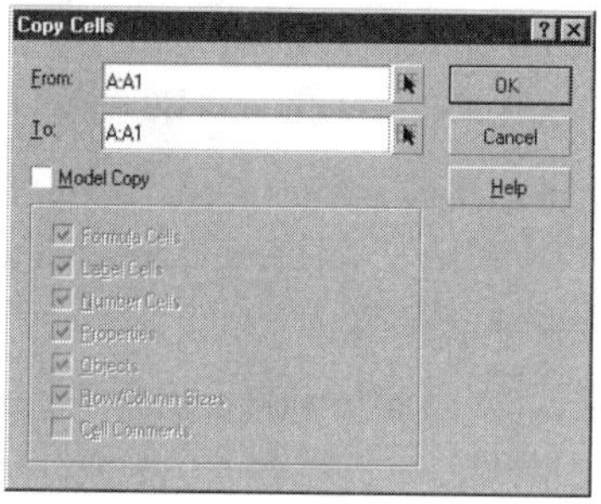

3. Press Tab to select the To text box.
4. Type the destination address, or use the mouse or navigation keys to select the destination block.
5. Click OK to confirm the dialog box and copy the block.

Quattro Pro copies the data, overwriting any existing data in the destination block.

You can use the Model Copy option to make a copy that uses the From block as a model for the To block. If you check Model Copy, formula references—even absolute references—adjust to fit the To block (see "Copying Formulas" later in this chapter for more information on formula references). In addition, if you check Model Copy, you can specify whether to copy Formula Cells, Label Cells, Number Cells, Properties, Objects, Row/Column Sizes, or Cell Comments.

Copying and Moving Data Using the Mouse

Quattro Pro offers yet another method of moving or copying data—one that takes advantage of the graphical nature of the Windows environment. This method, called *drag and drop*, uses the mouse and is by far the easiest way to move data short distances within a Quattro Pro notebook.

To move data using the drag-and-drop method, perform the following steps:

1. Make sure the destination block—where the data is to be moved—does not contain any information of value, as it will be deleted by the block move.
2. Select the block of data you want to move. The block can be any size, including a single cell.
3. Point to a border of the selected block until the mouse pointer changes to a four-headed arrow.
4. Hold down the left mouse button and drag the selected block to the new location. As you move the mouse pointer, Quattro Pro displays an outline the size of the selected block. Any existing data within this outline will be overwritten.
5. Release the mouse button to drop the block of data in the new location.

To copy, rather than move, the selected block of data, hold down the Ctrl key when you point to the block in step 3. When you hold down the left mouse button, a plus sign appears next to a hand-shaped mouse pointer when you are copying, rather than moving, data.

If the mouse pointer changes too quickly when you are selecting a block, you can adjust the delay time. Right-click the Quattro Pro title bar and choose Application Properties, or press Alt+F12 to display the Application dialog box. Select the General pane (see Figure 13.6). To increase the delay time, type a higher number in the Cell Drag and Drop Delay Time text box.

FIG. 13.6
The Application dialog box is where the Cell drag-and-drop delay time may be changed.

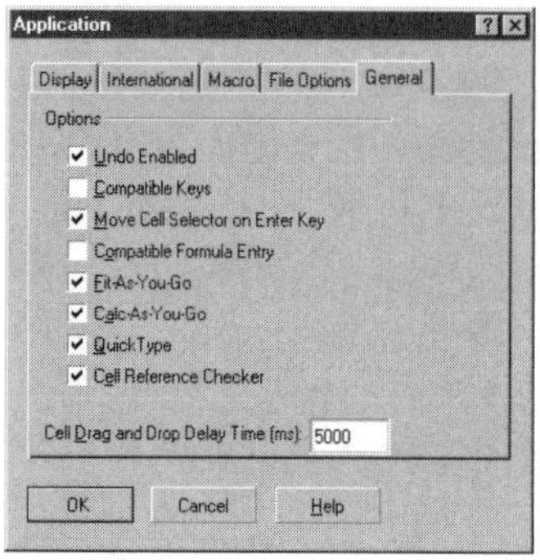

Copying Formulas

Copying formulas in Quattro Pro is more complex than copying data because of the way the program stores addresses in formulas. Addresses may be:

- *Relative.* Refers to column, row, and sheet *offsets*—distances measured in columns, rows, or sheets—from the formula cell.
- *Absolute.* Always referring to a specific cell.
- *Mixed.* A combination of relative and absolute.

Relative Addressing If you enter the formula **+B2** in cell C5, Quattro Pro does not store the formula quite the way you may expect. The formula tells Quattro Pro to add the value of the cell one column to the left and three rows above C5. When you copy this formula from C5 to D6, Quattro Pro uses the same relative formula but displays the formula as +C3. This method of storing cell references is called *relative addressing*. After you copy a formula that uses relative addressing, Quattro Pro automatically adjusts the new formula so that its cell references are in the same relative location as they were in the original location.

Absolute Addressing Sometimes you do not want a formula to address new locations after you copy the formula. You may, for example, create a formula that refers to data in a single cell, such as an interest rate or a growth factor percentage. Formulas that always refer to the same cell address, regardless of where you place the copy of the formula, use *absolute addressing*.

TIP You can use the F4 key to toggle cell addresses in a formula between relative and absolute modes.

To specify an absolute address, type a dollar sign ($) in the formula before each part of the address you want to remain absolutely the same. The formula +$B:$C$10, for example, always refers to cell C10 on notebook sheet B regardless of where you place the copy of the formula.

Mixed Addressing You also can create formulas that use *mixed addressing*, in which some elements of the cell addresses are absolute and other elements are relative. You can create a formula, for example, that always refers to the same row but adjusts its column reference as you copy the formula to another column. To create a mixed address, use a dollar sign to indicate the absolute address portions of the formula, leaving off the dollar sign for relative addresses. The formula +$B1, for example, always refers to column B on the current notebook sheet, but adjusts the row reference relative to the current row.

Filling Blocks

Creating Quattro Pro notebooks can seem like quite a task, especially if the model you want to build requires you to enter a series of data in a large number of consecutive cells. For example, a notebook based on an incrementing time series, such as a loan amortization schedule, may require you to include dates in monthly intervals. A notebook tracking results from each of your company's locations may require you to enter the location names, possibly in several different places. Entering the same data numerous times seems like a lot of work, doesn't it? Wouldn't it be nice if you could get someone else to do that sort of thing for you?

TIP Let Quattro Pro do the work for you by automatically filling in data.

Fortunately, there is one thing computers are very good at—doing repetitive work. Quattro Pro takes this concept a step further by providing easy-to-use methods of filling blocks automatically with either a number series or groups of related labels. In the following sections, you'll learn how to use two types of block-filling options.

Using Edit, Fill

You use the Edit, Fill, Fill Series command to fill a block with numeric values. This command offers a large range of options, as shown in Figure 13.7. These commands are suitable for almost any instance needing an incrementing number series, such as a series of interest rates or budget percentages.

FIG. 13.7
The Fill Series dialog box is used to fill blocks with numeric values.

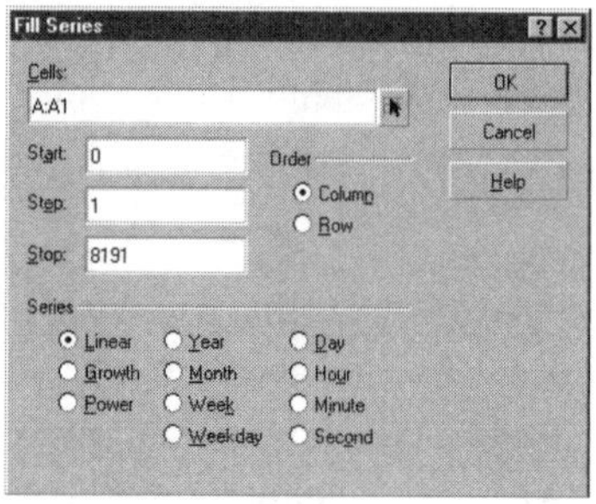

To use the Edit, Fill, Fill Series command, follow these steps:

1. Select the block you want to fill.
2. Choose Edit, Fill, Fill Series. The Fill Series dialog box appears (refer to Figure 13.7).
3. Enter the Start, Step (or increment), and Stop values in the appropriate text boxes.
4. If the block spans multiple rows and multiple columns, choose Column to begin filling the block in the first column, then the second column, and so on; choose Row to fill the first row, then the second row, and so on.
5. In the Series field, choose the type of fill. Table 13.1 summarizes the fill options.
6. Click OK to confirm the dialog box and fill the block.

Table 13.1 Data Fill Types

Series	Type of Fill
Linear	Step value is added to start value.
Growth	Step value is used as a multiplier.
Power	Step value is used as an exponent.
Year	Step value is in years and is added to start value.
Month	Step value is in months and is added to start value.
Week	Step value is in weeks and is added to start value.
Weekday	Step value is in days with weekend days skipped and is added to start value.
Day	Step value is in days and is added to start value.
Hour	Step value is in hours and is added to start value.
Minute	Step value is in minutes and is added to start value.
Second	Step value is in seconds and is added to start value.

By default, Quattro Pro uses 0 for the start number, 1 for the step (or increment), and 8191 as the stop number. Be sure to adjust these values to fit your needs. When filling a block, Quattro Pro stops entering additional values when the specified block is filled or the stop number is reached.

TIP If you specify a start value larger than the stop value, no values enter the block.

If you want to fill a block with a sequence of dates, it's important to understand how Quattro Pro enters date values. Quattro Pro uses *date serial numbers* to determine dates. Date serial numbers increment by one for each day, starting with 1 for December 31, 1899.

NOTE For compatibility with Lotus 1-2-3 and Microsoft Excel, Quattro Pro uses the value 61 for March 1, 1900, even though the year 1900 was not a leap year. Dates prior to March 1, 1900 are incorrect in Lotus 1-2-3 and Microsoft Excel. Dates prior to January 1, 1900, and dates after December 31, 2099, are not allowed in Lotus 1-2-3. Dates prior to January 1, 1900, and dates after December 31, 2078 are not allowed in Excel. Quattro Pro correctly determines dates in the entire range of January 1, 1600, through December 31, 3199, using negative date serial numbers for dates prior to December 30, 1899.

Because date serial numbers increment by one each day, the default Stop value is too small for most useful dates. For example, you cannot use Edit, Fill, Fill Series to enter a date such as June 26, 1997, which has a serial number of 35607, unless you remember to increase the stop value to a number at least as high as the serial number of the ending date you want.

Using QuickFill

Another Quattro Pro option for filling blocks is *QuickFill*. Unlike Edit, Fill, Fill Series, QuickFill can fill a selected block with a set of labels, such as month names or store locations. You activate the QuickFill feature either by clicking the QuickFill button on the toolbar, or by choosing Edit, Fill, QuickFill.

The QuickFill option functions two different ways, depending on whether the block you select already has sample values. If the block has sample values, these values are used as a pattern for filling the block. If the block is empty, QuickFill presents a list of predefined fill series for selection.

Filling a Block Using Sample Values To fill a block based on sample values you enter in the block (such as Jan, Feb, Mar, or Qtr 1, Qtr 2, Qtr 3), follow these steps:

1. First enter some sample values in the top-left corner of the block that you want to fill. If the first sample value is enough to define the series, you only have to enter one value. If you want to use an increment other than 1, you must enter at least two sample values.
2. Select the block you want to fill (remember to include the cells containing the sample values you entered in Step 1).
3. Click the QuickFill button.

Filling a Block Using a QuickFill Series You can also use a predefined series to fill a block. To fill a block based on a predefined series, follow these steps:

1. Select the block you want to fill. The block should not contain any sample values.
2. Click the QuickFill button to display the QuickFill dialog box (see Figure 13.8).

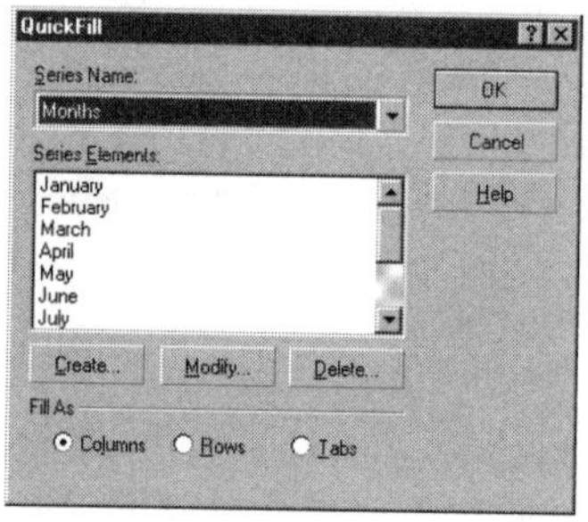

FIG. 13.8
The QuickFill dialog box is used to fill a block based on a predefined series.

3. Select the series you want in the Series Name list box.
4. If necessary, select Columns, Rows, or Tabs; then click OK.

TROUBLESHOOTING

The Tabs option doesn't appear in the QuickFill dialog box, so I can't use QuickFill to name sheet tabs. The Tabs option will appear only if an empty, single-cell block is selected when you click the QuickFill button. The same also applies to the Columns and Rows options. If the selected block consists of multiple cells in a single row or a single column, none of these options are available.

Creating a Custom QuickFill Series Quattro Pro includes several predefined QuickFill series for entering months, quarters, and days, but this limited set of options is really only a sampling of what you can do with QuickFill. This tool can really make the task of creating a Quattro Pro notebook much easier by automatically entering any series of labels you want.

Imagine, for example, that you work for a company with 20 stores, and that you're often asked to create new analyses of sales data, advertising costs, or any other factors that affect your business' bottom line. Each time you create a new notebook, you have to enter each of the store's names, the sales representative's names, or even the region names associated with store groupings. Sounds like quite a job, doesn't it? Fortunately, by creating a custom QuickFill series, you can do the job once and, except for occasional modifications, simply use QuickFill to automatically enter the same series into any new notebooks.

TIP Create custom QuickFill series for data you must enter often.

Creating a custom QuickFill series is rather easy. You can enter the series as a set of labels in a dialog box, or you can even use a series of labels you've already entered in a notebook block. Modifying or deleting an existing series is just as easy. To create or modify a custom series, follow these steps:

1. Choose Edit, Fill, Define QuickFill to display the Define Fill Series dialog box (see Figure 13.9).

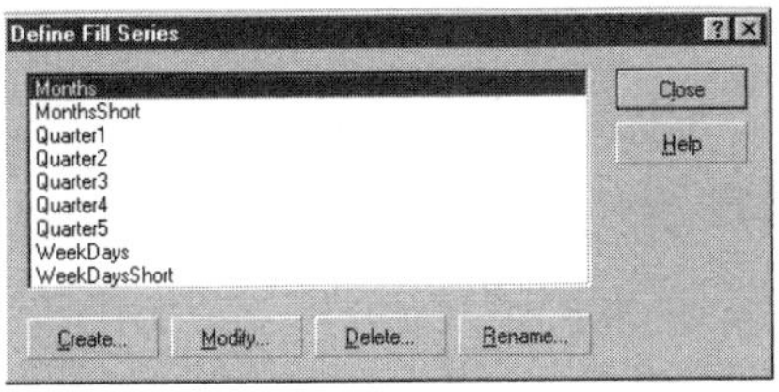

FIG. 13.9 The Define Fill Series dialog box makes using existing series to fill blocks easy.

2. Select the Create or Modify button to display the Create Series or Modify Series dialog box. Figure 13.10 shows the Create Series dialog box.

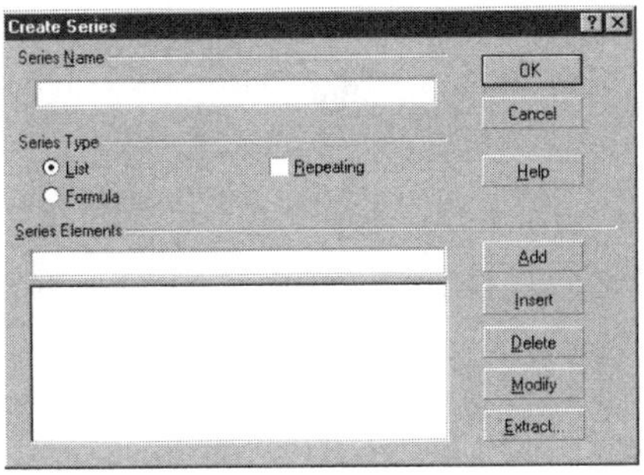

FIG. 13.10 Use the Create Series dialog box to easily create a customized series for filling blocks.

3. Use the options in the Create Series or Modify Series dialog boxes to customize the fill series to suit your needs. For example, to create a custom series that automatically fills in the locations of your company's stores, enter each location in the Series Elements text box, and then click Add. Continue until you have completed the series. Be sure to use a descriptive Series Name in the Create Series dialog box.
4. Click OK to confirm the dialog box.

NOTE If the selected block is empty, you can also access the Create Series or Modify Series dialog boxes using the Create or Modify buttons in the QuickFill dialog box. If you use this method to access the Create Series or Modify Series dialog boxes, you can immediately use the new or modified series when you return to the QuickFill dialog box following step 4.

To use an existing series of labels in the Create Series or Modify Series dialog boxes, select Extract in step 3 and then specify the notebook block containing the labels you want to save as a custom QuickFill series. For example, if you already have the set of store names in cells A1..A20, select Edit, Fill, Define QuickFill, Create, Extract and specify **A1..A20** as the block to use.

Use custom QuickFill series to make repetitive notebook entries, even if the fill series is not an incrementing series. When you create a custom QuickFill series, it will then be available for use in all of your Quattro Pro notebooks. You don't have to save the custom QuickFill series—it is automatically saved for you.

Using Functions

As you learned in the previous chapter, the real power of a Quattro Pro notebook is its capability to perform calculations. You can create many different types of formulas and perform many different types of calculations quickly and easily in Quattro Pro. Using the built-in functions can make your formulas even more powerful, permitting you to perform calculations far too complex to build using simple arithmetic operators.

Understanding Functions

When electronic spreadsheets were first introduced in the late 1970s, the programs included a few, limited, built-in functions. The calculations you could perform using these functions were fairly simple. When Lotus 1-2-3 made spreadsheets a standard business tool in the early 1980s, the program offered nearly 100 different functions covering a wide range of calculations. Still, there were gaps in what the built-in functions offered, and PC users with specialized needs often had to resort to complex contortions, or had to turn to third-party developers to solve demanding equations.

Quattro Pro sets a new standard in spreadsheets by offering nearly 500 built-in functions, covering the bases with specialized functions for many unique types of calculations. Some of these functions perform sophisticated financial calculations; others conduct engineering calculations, execute various statistical analyses, or analyze database records. The following sections briefly summarize the function categories included in Quattro Pro.

TIP See the @Function Reference on the Contents tab of online help for a complete listing of the functions. You can view the function information by category or as a comprehensive alphabetical listing.

Understanding Database Functions You use database functions to perform statistical calculations and queries on a database. Each database function has an equivalent statistical function. Database functions differ from statistical functions in a very important way—database functions calculate values that meet criteria you specify, while statistical functions calculate all values in a block.

For example, @DAVG finds the average value in a field in a database, but only for records that meet specified criteria. @AVG finds the average value of all cells in a block.

Understanding Date and Time Functions You use the date and time functions to perform date and time arithmetic. These functions enable you to easily calculate differences between dates or times, sort by dates or times, and compare a range of dates or times. Date and time arithmetic uses date/time serial numbers.

For example, to convert a date into a date/time serial number, you can use the @DATE function to convert a date given as a year, month, and day into a date/time serial number. You can then use this serial number in additional calculations. To find the number of business days between two dates, you can use the @BDAYS function.

Understanding Engineering Functions You use the engineering functions to perform calculations for solving complex engineering problems; perform binary, octal, decimal, and hexadecimal number manipulations; work with imaginary numbers; convert between numbering systems; and test results. The engineering functions return modified Bessel functions; join, compare, and shift values at the bit level; convert or modify a complex number (a number whose square is a negative real number); and return error functions or test the relationship of two numeric values.

For example, you use the @BASE function to convert a decimal number to another numbering system. You can use the @CONVERT function to convert between different systems of measurement, such as from miles to kilometers.

Understanding Financial Functions You use the financial functions to discount cash flow, calculate depreciation, and analyze the return on an investment. These functions greatly ease the burden of complex financial and accounting calculations. They also provide tools allowing the average user to perform less complex, everyday financial computations.

For example, you can use the @AMPMTI function to calculate the interest portion of the *n*th periodic payment of an amortized loan. You can use the @PRICEDISC function to calculate the price per $100 face value of a security that pays periodic interest.

Chapter 15, "Analyzing Data," provides a look at some additional Quattro Pro analysis tools.

Understanding Logical Functions You use the logical functions to add standard true/false logic to the spreadsheet. The logical functions evaluate Boolean expressions, which are either true (returning a value of 1) or false (returning a value of 0). These functions can help to prevent errors that may occur if a cell used in a formula contains the wrong data, to test for the values ERR (error) or NA (not available), or to determine whether a specified file exists. These functions are important for decision making when conditions elsewhere in the spreadsheet lead to different answers in the function results. Logical functions also control the operations of advanced macro programs.

For example, you can use the @IF function to select between different results based upon evaluation of an expression, such as including a value only if it is positive.

Understanding Mathematical Functions You use the mathematical functions to perform a variety of standard arithmetic operations, such as adding and rounding values or calculating square roots.

For example, you can use the @CEILING function to round a number up to the nearest integer, @RANDBETWEEN to generate a random number between two values, and @LN to calculate the natural logarithm of a number.

Understanding Miscellaneous Functions You use the miscellaneous functions to determine information about notebooks and cell attributes, current command settings, system memory, object properties, and Quattro Pro's version number. You also use the miscellaneous functions to perform table lookups.

For example, you can use @CELL to determine whether a given cell is blank, contains a label, or contains a numeric value. You can determine the value contained in a given cell in a block using @INDEX. A single @ARRAY function can perform a series of calculations, producing many different results from a single formula.

Understanding Statistical Functions You use the statistical functions to perform all standard statistical calculations on your notebook data, such as aggregation, counting, and analysis operations on a group of values.

For example, you can use the @AVG function to determine the average of all numeric values in a list and @COUNT to determine the number of nonblank cells in the list. You can use @CONFIDENCE to compute the confidence interval around the mean for a given sample size, using the normal distribution function.

Understanding String Functions You use the string functions to manipulate text. You can use string functions to repeat text characters, convert letters in a string to upper- or lowercase, change strings to numbers, and change numbers to strings. You also can use string functions to locate, extract, or replace characters. String functions can be important also when you need to convert data for use by other programs. They are invaluable when you need to read or write directly to ASCII text files.

@PROPER, for example, converts to uppercase the first letter of each word in a string and converts the rest to lowercase. @REPLACE changes specified characters in a string to different characters. @STRING changes a numeric value into a string, making it possible to use the value in a string formula.

Using the Formula Composer

If these short descriptions of Quattro Pro's function categories have whetted your interest in using functions, you're probably wondering how you can ever build your own function formulas, especially with nearly 500 functions to select from. After all, a comprehensive description of each function, especially one with examples, would fill a complete book all by itself. How can you possibly get started, and how can you use the functions effectively in your formulas?

One answer to learning and using Quattro Pro's many functions is to turn to the *Formula Composer*—a calculator-like tool that helps you include functions in your formulas. Using this tool, you build formulas one step at a time, adding functions and supplying arguments as necessary. As you build a formula, you can even see an outline of the formula, so you can make certain you're creating exactly what you need to solve a problem.

To use the Formula Composer, click the Formula Composer button on the toolbar. This displays the Formula Composer dialog box (see Figure 13.11). You use this dialog box to build your formula.

The Formula Composer functions like a sophisticated scientific calculator but has capabilities far beyond any calculator you can buy. If you want to use one of the Quattro Pro built-in functions, simply click the @ button in the Formula Composer dialog box toolbar. Select the function you want to use, and the Formula Composer adds it to the formula. When you select a function, the right pane of the Formula Composer dialog box describes the selected function as well as any arguments.

FIG. 13.11
Use the Formula Composer dialog box to more easily create formulas.

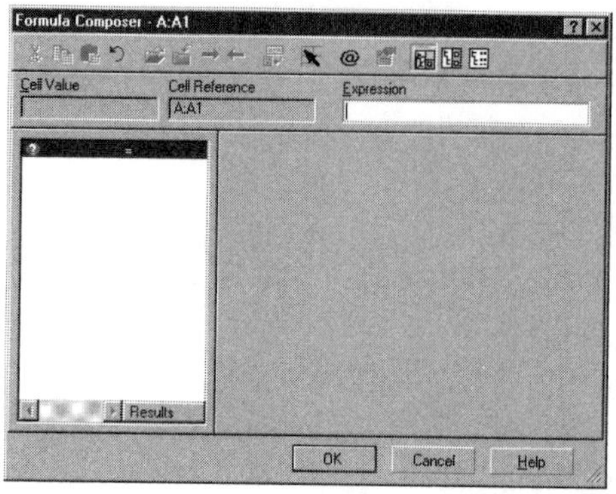

For example, suppose you want to enter a formula in cell A1 that calculates the number of business days between June 26, 1997 and December 25, 1997. To make your formula flexible—to allow you to use the same formula to determine the number of business days between any other two dates—you place the two dates in cells A2 and A3. This enables you to replace the dates in these two cells and instantly calculate new formula results. To begin building your formula, follow these steps:

1. Select cell A1, and then click the Formula Composer button on the toolbar.
2. Click the @ button in the Formula Composer dialog box toolbar.
3. The Functions dialog box appears. Select Date in the Function Category list box and then BDAYS in the Function list box. As you select a function, the description pane at the bottom of the dialog box describes the selected function (see Figure 13.12).

FIG. 13.12
Use the Functions dialog box to select the function you want to use in the formula.

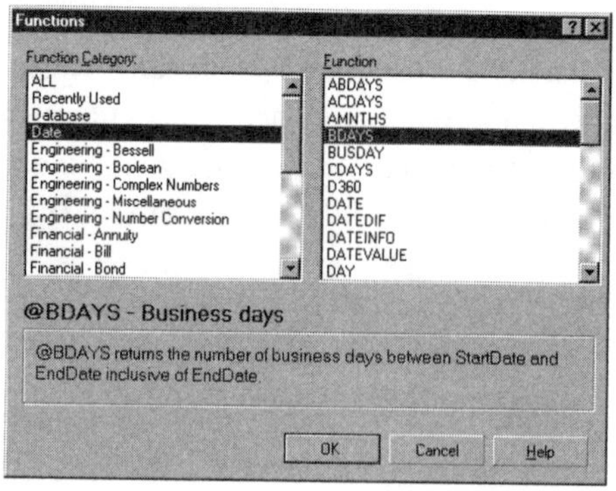

4. Press Enter or click OK to return to the Formula Composer dialog box. The dialog box changes to display the function pane and describes the selected function, as well as its arguments (see Figure 13.13).

FIG. 13.13
After you select a function, the Formula Composer dialog box displays the function pane where you fill in the required arguments.

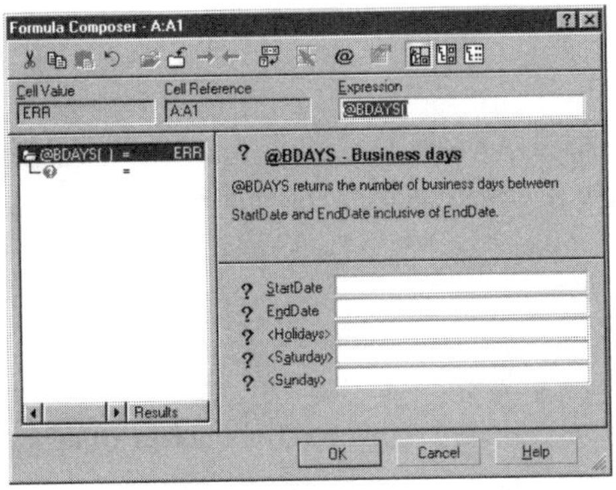

5. Fill in each argument by selecting the argument's text box and then pointing to the notebook cell containing the argument. When you have entered the minimum required set of arguments, the dialog box displays the results of the calculation (see Figure 13.14). In this case, Holidays, Saturday, and Sunday are optional arguments and do not require an entry.

FIG. 13.14
After you specify all required arguments, the Formula Composer dialog box displays the result in the Cell Value box.

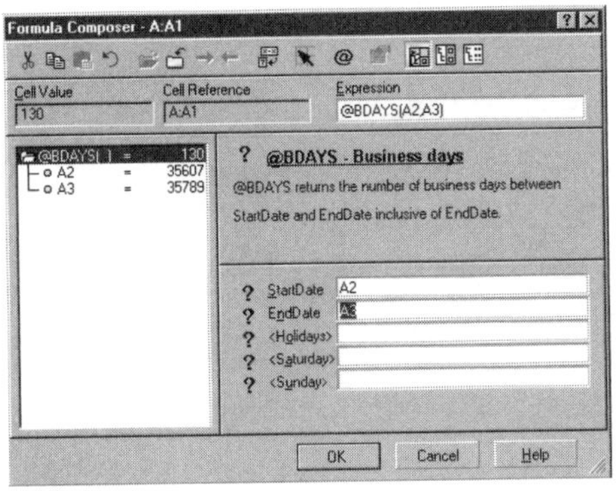

6. Click the OK button to return to the notebook and enter the formula in the cell.

To enter any of the required or optional arguments in step 5, you can point to the cell containing the argument or you can type an address or block name. If you want to use another function to specify the value for an argument, click the @ button.

TROUBLESHOOTING

It's often difficult to remember which cells hold each of the function arguments. Enter labels in the notebook to identify the arguments, and then use the Insert, Name, Cells, Labels command to name the cells. You can then use the block names instead of cell addresses in your formulas, making the formulas much easier to understand.

Functions really unlock the power of Quattro Pro. The brief descriptions provided in these sections on using functions have only touched the surface of how powerful Quattro Pro's built-in functions really are.

CHAPTER 14

Changing the Display and Appearance of Data

Corel Quattro Pro provides you with a WYSIWYG—What You See Is What You Get—view of your data. If you change the on-screen appearance of a Quattro Pro notebook, those changes will also be reflected in any printed reports you produce. In addition, Quattro Pro 8 now includes a new editable Page view feature that enables you to easily view and change margins, headers, and footers on-screen. In this chapter, you learn how to use the commands that control the appearance of data, both on-screen and in printed reports.

Producing clear and concise information from raw data can be as important as calculating correct answers. To make data understandable, you can control the format, style, and alignment of data. These commands change only the way data appears, not the value of the data when you customize its format.

Adjust column and row characteristics

You learn how to use column width and row height adjustments to make your Quattro Pro data much easier to read and understand.

Remove the excess

See how you can remove unwanted columns, rows, or sheets from the notebook without destroying your data.

Lock data on-screen

Make it easy to see exactly which data you're using by keeping important information visible as you scroll to different areas of the notebook.

Change the appearance of data

Apply the available formats to improve the appearance of your data.

Use additional appearance improvements

Further enhance the appearance of your Quattro Pro data using fonts, label alignment options, lines, colors, and shading.

Changing the Display

The Quattro Pro display is extremely flexible, allowing you to select screen preferences. For example, you can zoom in to enlarge the on-screen appearance of a notebook on small screens. You can also control whether screen elements such as the toolbar, the Property Bar, or the Application Bar are displayed. These options exist for your convenience, but they don't really have much effect on the display of data or reports.

Some other options, such as adjusting the width of each column, or locking rows or columns on-screen as you scroll, directly affect your Quattro Pro notebooks. Column widths, for example, determine whether numbers are displayed properly. Locked titles enable you to scroll the display to different locations in the notebook without losing track of which type of data should be entered in the individual cells. These options are covered in the following sections.

Adjusting Column Widths and Row Heights

When you start a new notebook, all the columns on each sheet are set to the default column width of approximately nine characters. All the row heights are set to a default height of 12 points (one-sixth of an inch).

NOTE Column widths are stated in characters, but are only valid for nonproportional (or fixed-pitch) fonts. Most Windows fonts are proportional fonts, allowing each character to have a different width, which is based on the actual space necessary to display a character. For example, the letter *m* requires more space than the letter *i*. In a proportional font, several *i*'s will fit in the space required for a single *m*.

If columns are too narrow to display numeric data, asterisks may appear, rather than the numbers. If columns are too narrow for the length of labels and the cell to the right contains data, the labels are truncated. If columns are too wide, you may not see all the columns necessary to view the complete data, and you may not be able to print reports on the number of pages you want.

By default, Quattro Pro columns automatically widen to fit the numbers you enter in cells. If this doesn't happen when you enter numbers, the Fit-As-You-Go feature may not be enabled. To enable this feature, choose Tools, Settings; then click the General tab, select Fit-As-You-Go, and click OK (see Figure 14.1).

Quattro Pro automatically adjusts row heights to fit different fonts and point sizes, vertical orientation, or word wrap, but you can override the default to create special effects or to add emphasis. You can also adjust row heights in Quattro Pro to make notebook entries easier to understand and more attractive.

Figure 14.1 shows why you must sometimes adjust column widths or row heights. Cells A1 and B4 contain the same number, 1,234,567,890. Both cells are formatted to display the number using the comma numeric format with two decimals. Because column A is set to the default width, asterisks appear in place of the number in cell A1. The width of column B was adjusted to correctly display the number.

FIG. 14.1
Sometimes you must adjust column widths or row heights.

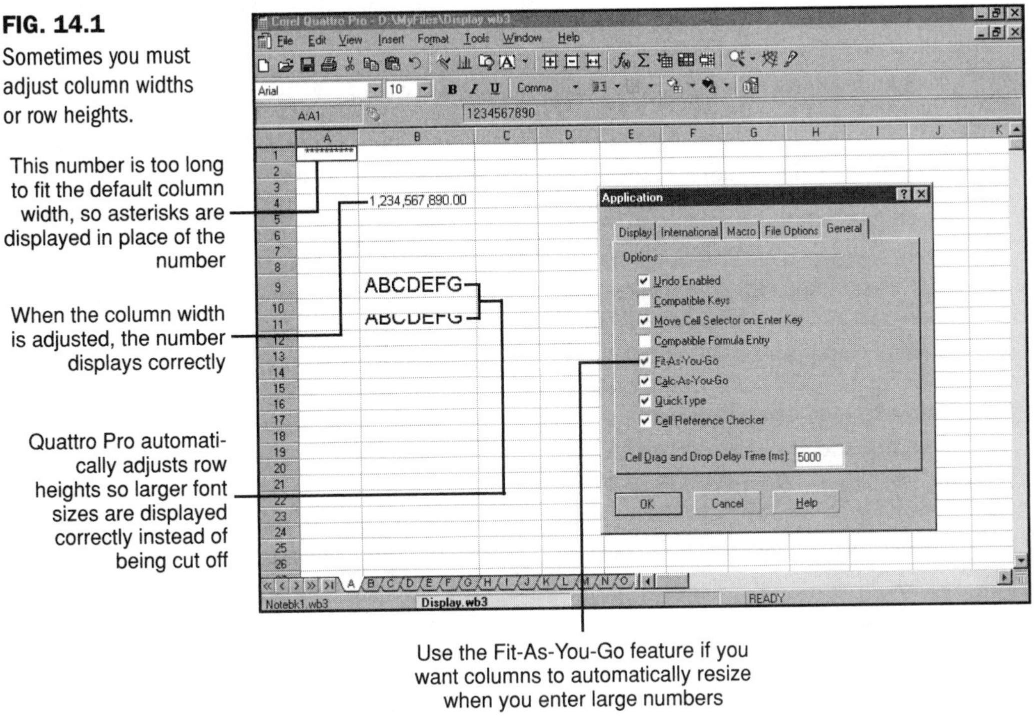
This number is too long to fit the default column width, so asterisks are displayed in place of the number
When the column width is adjusted, the number displays correctly
Quattro Pro automatically adjusts row heights so larger font sizes are displayed correctly instead of being cut off
Use the Fit-As-You-Go feature if you want columns to automatically resize when you enter large numbers
1,234,567,890.00
ABCDEFG
Application
Undo Enabled
Compatible Keys
Move Cell Selector on Enter Key
Compatible Formula Entry
Fit-As-You-Go
Calc-As-You-Go
QuickType
Cell Reference Checker
Cell Drag and Drop Delay Time (ms): 5000
OK
Cancel
Help

Even though Quattro Pro automatically adjusts row heights to fit different fonts and point sizes, as shown in row 9 of Figure 14.1, you can make manual adjustments, too. In the figure, the height of row 11 was adjusted to show how Quattro Pro cuts off the tops of characters if a row is too short.

Setting Column Widths Whether a number fits in a cell depends on the column width, the numeric format, the font type, and font size. If a number appears as a series of asterisks, you need to enable the Fit-As-You-Go feature (as described in the preceding section), or change the column width, numeric format, font type, font size, or some combination of these factors.

> **TIP** Column widths you set manually do not change if you later change the default column width for the sheet.

You can change the width of a single column or a group of columns. When you are adjusting the column width, Quattro Pro displays a dashed line to indicate the position of the new column border. If you move the right column border to the left of the left border, you hide the column.

There are several methods you can use to set column widths. You can select the Active Cells dialog box, click the Fit button, or drag a column width using the mouse. Each method may be useful, depending on your needs.

To change column widths by dragging with the mouse, follow these steps:

1. If you want to adjust more than one column at a time, select the columns you want to adjust by pointing to the column letter in the notebook frame and clicking the left mouse button (drag the mouse pointer to select adjacent columns). If the columns are not adjacent, hold down the Ctrl key as you select the columns.
2. Point to the column border to the right of the column letter (in the spreadsheet frame). The mouse pointer changes to a horizontal double arrow.
3. Press and hold the left mouse button.
4. Drag the column border left or right until the column is the width you want. Notice that the Application Bar lists the current column width as you drag the column border. Release the mouse button.

TIP To reveal columns once they have been hidden, select the columns that surround the hidden columns, right-click, select Column Properties, select the Row/Column tab, select Reveal in the Column Options area, and click OK.

To change column widths using the Active Cells dialog box, perform the following steps:

1. Select a block of cells containing each column whose width you want to adjust. You can use the keyboard or the mouse to select adjacent columns, but you can only select nonadjacent columns using the mouse.
2. Right-click inside the selection to activate the QuickMenu, and then select Cell Properties to display the Active Cells dialog box (see Figure 14.2).

TIP You can also press F12 to activate the Active Cells dialog box.

3. Select the Row/Column tab, if necessary.
4. If you want to enter the column width in Inches or Centimeters rather than Characters, choose the appropriate option button under Units of Measure in the Column Options area.

FIG. 14.2
You can use the Active Cells dialog box to change column width settings.

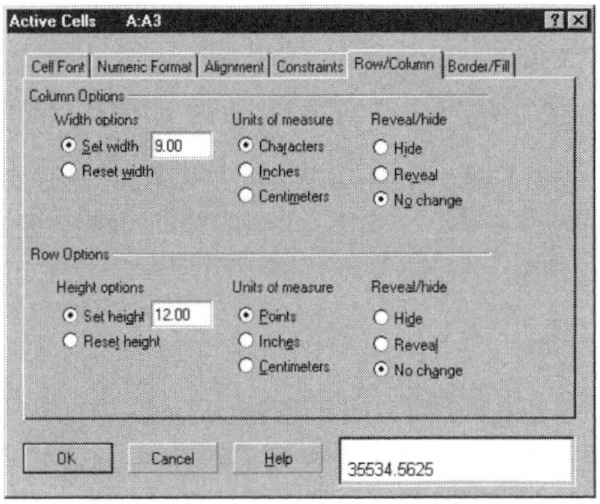

5. If you want to reset the column width, select Reset Width to return the selected columns to the sheet default column width.
6. If you want to specify the column width, type the value in the Set Width text box.
7. Click OK to confirm the dialog box.

You also can click the Fit button on the toolbar to adjust the widths of columns automatically. The width of columns set using the Fit button depends on the number of rows that are selected when you adjust the width. If you select a single row, the column width adjusts to fit the longest data below the cell selector in the entire column. If you select more than one row, the column width adjusts to fit the cell with the longest data below the cell selector in the same column.

TIP The Fit button can only be used on contiguous blocks.

Setting the Default Column Width for a Sheet If you find yourself setting the column widths for most columns on a sheet, you can change the default column width for the entire notebook sheet. To select a new default column width for a sheet, follow these steps:

1. Right-click the sheet tab and select Sheet Properties to display the Active Sheet dialog box.
2. Select the Default Width tab and enter the new default width in Characters, Inches, or Centimeters, depending on which Unit option button you choose.
3. Click OK to confirm the dialog box.

Each sheet in a notebook has its own default column width setting. You change the default column width setting for each sheet individually.

TROUBLESHOOTING

Some columns don't adjust when a new default column width is set for a notebook sheet. Column widths you set using the Fit button remain at the current setting even when the length of data in the column changes. If you want the column width adjusted to fit new data, you must click the Fit button again.

Setting Row Heights You can adjust row heights in Quattro Pro to make notebook entries easier to understand and more attractive. As you change fonts and point sizes, or apply vertical orientation or word wrap, Quattro Pro automatically adjusts row heights to fit the data. However, you can override the default to create special effects or to add emphasis.

You can set the row height for an individual row or a group of rows at one time. You also can hide rows by setting their height to zero. You can set row heights using the Active Cells dialog box, or by dragging the row height using the mouse. Because Quattro Pro automatically adjusts row heights to fit cell data, there is no equivalent to the Fit button for row heights.

To adjust the height of rows by dragging with the mouse, follow these steps:

1. Select the rows you want to adjust. If the rows are not adjacent, hold down the Ctrl key as you select the rows.
2. Point to the row border just below the row number (in the spreadsheet frame). The mouse pointer changes to a vertical double arrow.
3. Press and hold down the left mouse button.
4. Drag the row border up or down until the row is the height you want. Notice that the Application Bar lists the current row height as you drag the row border. Release the mouse button. When you are adjusting the row height, Quattro Pro displays a dashed line to indicate the position of the new row border. If you move the lower row border above the top border, you hide the row.

TIP To reveal rows once they have been hidden, select the rows that surround the hidden rows, right-click, select Row Properties, select the Row/Column tab, select Reveal in the Row Options area, and click OK.

To change the height of rows by using the Active Cells dialog box, follow these steps:

1. Select the rows you want to adjust. If the rows are not adjacent, hold down the Ctrl key as you select the rows using the mouse. If you want to adjust the height of

adjacent rows, place the cell selector in the first row you want to adjust, hold down the Shift key, and move the cell selector to select each of the rows you want to adjust.

2. Right-click inside the selection to activate the QuickMenu, and select Cell Properties to display the Active Cells dialog box (refer to Figure 14.2).
3. Select the Row/Column tab.
4. If you want to enter the row height in Inches or Centimeters rather than Points, select the appropriate option button under Units of Measure in the Row Options area.
5. If you want to reset the row height, choose Reset Height to return the selected rows to automatic.
6. If you want to specify the row height, type the value in the Set Height text box.
7. Click OK to confirm the dialog box.

Removing Columns, Rows, or Sheets

Sometimes you may want to delete sections from a notebook. Perhaps you made extra copies of some data while you were creating the notebook, or maybe you simply rearranged a notebook and have some unsightly gaps you'd like to eliminate.

TIP Don't forget to use Edit, Undo immediately if you delete the wrong data in error.

You can remove part or all of a notebook in several ways. Any data that you remove is cleared from the notebook in memory but does not affect the notebook file on disk until you save the notebook file. Edit, Undo can restore the data if you use the command before making any other changes.

Some Quattro Pro commands, such as Edit, Cut; Edit, Clear, Cells; or Edit, Clear, Values erase cell contents, but leave behind blank cells. In contrast, after you delete a row, column, or sheet, Quattro Pro deletes the row, column, or notebook sheet and moves remaining data to fill the gap created by the deletion. Cell addresses in formulas are also updated when you delete a row, column, or sheet.

To delete a row, column, or sheet, follow these steps:

1. Choose Edit, Delete. Quattro Pro displays the Delete dialog box (see Figure 14.3).
2. In the Cells text box, specify the cells you want to delete. You can type the address, select cells, or preselect the cells.
3. Select the Columns, Rows, or Sheets option button.

4. Select the Entire or Partial option button.
5. Click OK to confirm the dialog box and delete the block.

FIG. 14.3
Use the Delete dialog box to select the cells you want to delete.

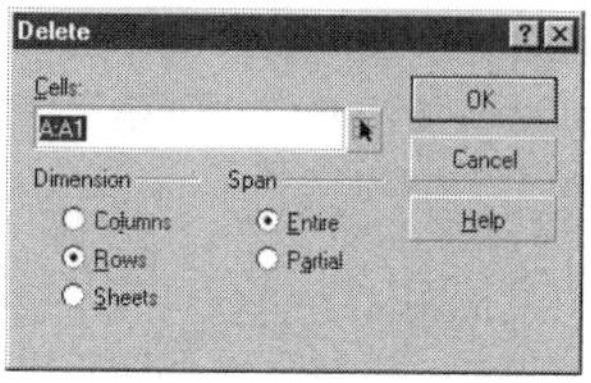

NOTE Deleting a column, row, or sheet does not reduce the number of columns, rows, or sheets in the notebook. Quattro Pro replaces the deleted columns, rows, or sheets at the end of the sheet or the notebook, so each sheet continues to have 256 columns and 8,192 rows, and each notebook has 256 sheets.

When you delete an area, Quattro Pro moves data to fill the gap created by the deletion. If you delete a row, data below the deletion moves up on the current sheet. If you delete a column, data to the right of the deleted column moves to the left. If you delete a sheet, data on following sheets moves forward in the notebook.

Formula references adjust to reflect the new addresses of the data. If you delete rows 5 and 6, for example, the formula @SUM(A1..A10) becomes @SUM(A1..A8). If a formula refers specifically to a deleted cell, however, the formula returns ERR.

If you delete rows, columns, or sheets that are part of a named block, the block becomes smaller. If you delete a row, column, or sheet that contains one of the block borders, the block becomes undefined and any references to the block return ERR.

You don't have to delete an entire row, column, or sheet. You may want to delete only part of a row, column, or sheet, and move remaining data to fill the gap. To accomplish this task, choose the Partial option button. When you specify Partial as the span, Quattro Pro does not remove data from surrounding rows, columns, or sheets.

Inserting Columns, Rows, or Sheets

You also can insert rows, columns, or sheets anywhere in the notebook. After you insert a row, column, or sheet, all existing data below, to the right, or on subsequent notebook sheets moves to create room for the new data. Cell references in formulas and block names adjust automatically, but explicit cell addresses in macros do not adjust. If you make an insertion in the middle of a block, the block expands to include the new rows, columns, or sheets. Formulas referring to that block automatically include the added cells.

NOTE Inserting a column, row, or sheet does not increase the number of columns, rows, or sheets in the notebook. Each sheet continues to have 256 columns and 8,192 rows, and each notebook has 256 sheets. If Quattro Pro cannot delete the columns, rows, or sheets at the end of the sheet or the notebook because data would be lost, an error message is displayed and the insertion fails.

To insert a row, column, or sheet, perform the following steps:

1. Move the cell selector to the cell where you want to begin inserting.
2. Select the number of rows, columns, or sheets you want to insert.
3. Choose Insert, Cells. In the Insert Cells dialog box, select Columns, Rows, or Sheets.

NOTE If you selected *entire* rows, columns, or sheets in step 2, Quattro Pro automatically performs the insertion without displaying the Insert Cells dialog box.

4. To insert a partial row, column, or sheet, select the Partial option button.
5. Click OK to confirm the dialog box and make the insertion.

Locking Data On-Screen

Notebook sheets often are too large to display all the data at one time. As you move the cell selector to display different areas of the sheet, data scrolls off the opposite edge of the display. This can make it difficult to understand data, because you can't see the labels describing the data. To prevent titles from scrolling off the screen, you can lock a number of rows and columns so they remain on-screen as you move the cell selector.

Before you lock rows or columns to keep them on-screen, you need to position the cell selector to tell Quattro Pro which rows or columns you want to remain visible. If you are locking horizontal titles, place the cell selector in the row below the last row you want locked. If you are locking vertical titles, place the cell selector in the column to the right of the last column you want locked. If you are locking both horizontal and vertical titles, place the cell selector in the row just below and the column just right of the intersection of the rows and columns you want to lock.

After you position the cell selector properly, choose View, Locked Titles. Quattro Pro displays blue lines to indicate the position of the locked titles. As you scroll the worksheet, data above and to the left of the blue lines remains on-screen.

Figure 14.4 shows a Quattro Pro notebook containing an address database. In this figure, the cell selector was placed in cell B2 before issuing the View, Locked Titles command. The cell selector was then moved to cell H46, the last cell in the database. Column A and row 1 remain visible, enabling you to more easily understand the data, because you can see both the field names (row 1) and the value contained in the LAST_NAME field (column A).

FIG. 14.4
Titles locked on-screen can make data easier to understand.

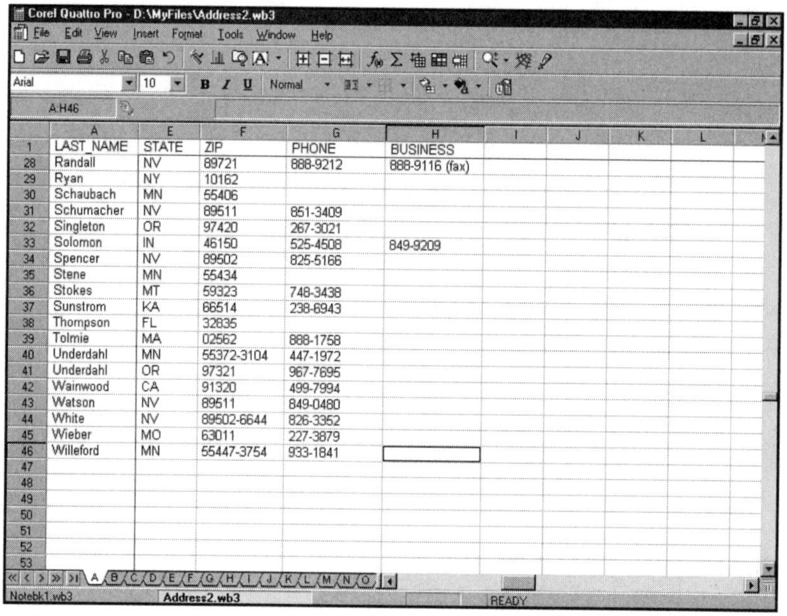

When rows or columns are locked on-screen, pressing the Home key moves the cell selector to the position below and to the right of the titles rather than to cell A1. You can use the mouse or the navigational keys to move the cell selector into the locked titles, however.

Changing the Appearance of Data

How your data appears in a notebook or in a report really doesn't affect the data, but it can have a major effect on how well people understand the data. Appearance can also make quite a difference in how people perceive your business. A well-prepared financial statement, for example, might not guarantee you that small business loan, but you'd probably feel more comfortable presenting your banker something that looked professional and polished.

A few simple steps can greatly improve the appearance of data. Simply applying the proper numeric format can change 1234567 into $1,234,567.00—changing raw data into a value anyone can quickly understand. In addition to numeric formats, you can use alignment, different fonts, borders, and shading to turn an ordinary report into something that is much more. The following sections show you some of the options you can use to improve the appearance of your Quattro Pro notebooks.

Using Numeric Formats

You can display data in a cell in a variety of different numeric formats. Quattro Pro offers a wide choice of numeric formats, which you access through the Active Cells dialog box. Most formats apply only to numeric data, although Text format can apply to string formulas, and Hidden format can apply to any type of data.

Formatting changes the appearance but not the value of data. The number 7892, for example, can be displayed as 7,892, $7,892.00, or 789200.0%, as well as many other formats. No matter how Quattro Pro displays the number in a cell, the actual value remains the same.

To change the numeric format of a cell or block, follow these steps:

1. Select the cell or block.
2. Choose Format, Selection; or right-click the cell or block and select Cell Properties from the QuickMenu.
3. Select the Numeric Format tab. If no numeric format has been assigned, the default General format is selected, as shown in Figure 14.5. Select the desired numeric format.
4. If you chose Fixed, Scientific, Currency, Comma, Percent, or Accounting, enter the number of decimal places in the spin control that appears after you choose one of these formats. Quattro Pro suggests a default of two decimal places, but you can type another number between 0 and 15.
5. Click OK to confirm the dialog box and apply the format to the selected cell or block.

FIG. 14.5
Select a numeric format from the Active Cells dialog box.

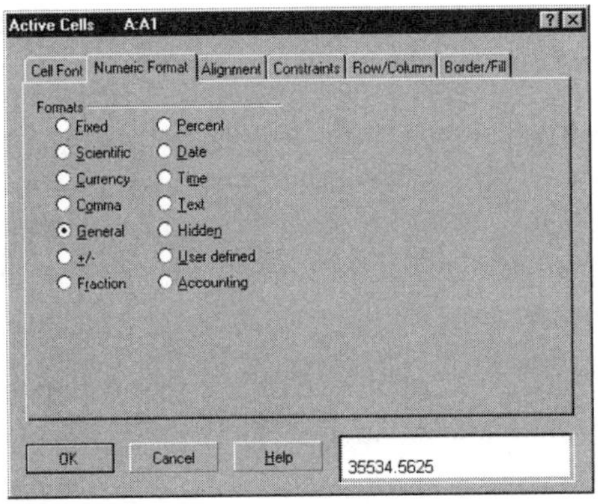

The following sections briefly describe Quattro Pro's numeric format options.

TROUBLESHOOTING

After formatting a block, some cells display asterisks instead of the values. If you apply a numeric format to a cell, the column width must be wide enough to display the cell's data in the format. Otherwise, asterisks display in the cell rather than the formatted value. You may need to adjust the column width to fit the new format.

Fixed Format You use the Fixed format when you want to display values with a specified, fixed number of decimal points. Quattro Pro displays values with up to 15 decimal places. Negative numbers have a minus sign, and decimal values have a leading zero. No punctuation is used to denote thousands.

Scientific Format You use the Scientific format to display very large or very small numbers. Such numbers usually have a few significant digits and many zeros.

A number in scientific notation has two parts: a mantissa and an exponent. The *mantissa* is a number from 1 to 10 that contains the significant digits. The *exponent* tells you how many places to move the decimal point to get the actual value of the number.

If a number has more significant digits than the cell can display using the specified number of decimal places, the displayed value is rounded, but the stored value is used in calculations.

Currency Format Currency format displays values with a currency symbol, such as a dollar sign ($), or the British pound sign (£), and punctuation, depending on the current international settings. When you select the Currency option in the Active Cells dialog box, a list box appears from which you can select the name of the country. When you click the name of a country, the Preview box displays how the number will appear. If you specify a currency symbol, the column width needs an extra position to display each character in the currency symbol. Values formatted as Currency can have from 0 to 15 decimal places. Thousands are separated by commas, periods, or spaces according to the current international settings. Negative numbers appear in parentheses.

Comma Format Like the Currency display format, the Comma format displays data with a fixed number of decimal places and thousands punctuation. The thousands separator and the decimal point depend on the current international settings. Negative numbers appear in parentheses, and positive numbers less than 1,000 appear the same as Fixed display format.

If a value has more decimal digits than the cell can display using the specified number of decimal places, the displayed value is rounded but the stored value is used in calculations.

General Format General format is the default format for all new notebooks. Numbers in General display format have no thousands separators and no trailing zeros to the right of the decimal point. A minus sign precedes negative numbers. If a number contains decimal digits, it contains a decimal point. If a number contains too many digits to the right of the decimal point to display in the current column width, the decimals are rounded in the display. If a number is too large or too small, it appears in Scientific display format.

+/- Format The +/- format displays numbers as a series of plus signs (+), minus signs (-), or as a period (.). The number of signs equals the integer portion of the value. A positive number appears as a row of plus signs, a negative value appears as a row of minus signs, and a number between -1 and +1 appears as a period.

Fraction Format You use the Fraction format when you want to display a value as a fraction, such as $^3/_4$. If the number can be confused as a date, however, you should format the cell before you enter the number. The Fraction format also enables you to choose whether or not Quattro Pro should reduce the fraction for you; in addition, you can specify a set denominator for the fraction.

Percent Format Percent format is used to display values as percentages with 0 to 15 decimal places. The number appears with its value multiplied by 100, followed by a percent sign (%). The number of decimal places you specify is the number displayed in the percent, not the number of decimal places in the value.

If a value has more decimal digits than the cell can display using the specified number of decimal places, the displayed value is rounded but the stored value is used in calculations.

Date Format Date formats display date serial numbers as dates rather than numbers. Quattro Pro stores dates as serial numbers starting with January 1, 1600 (which is -109571) and increases the number by one for each whole day. December 31, 1899 is counted as 1. The latest date Quattro Pro can display is December 31, 3199, with a serial number of 474816.

If the number is less than -109571 or greater than 474816, a date format appears as asterisks. Date formats ignore decimal fractions; 34876.55 with a short international date format appears as 6/26. The decimal portion of a date serial number represents the time as a fraction of a 24-hour clock.

Quattro Pro gives you a choice of five different Date display formats. Both Long Date Intl. and Short Date Intl. depend on the current international date format set using the Application dialog box.

Time Format You use the Time formats to display date serial numbers as times. The decimal portion of a date serial number is a time fraction. The time fraction represents a fraction of a 24-hour day. For example, the time fraction for 8 a.m. is .33333..., the time fraction for noon is .5, and the time fraction for 3 p.m. is .675. When you use a Time format, Quattro Pro displays the fraction as a time.

If a date serial number is greater than 1, the time formats ignore the integer portion. Both .5 and 33781.5 display 12:00:00 p.m.

Quattro Pro gives you a choice of two different Time display formats. Both Long Time Intl. and Short Time Intl. depend on the current international time format set using the Application dialog box.

Text Format You use Text format to display the text of formulas rather than their results. Numbers in cells formatted as Text appear in General format. Unlike long labels that appear in blank cells to the right, formulas formatted as Text are truncated if they are too long to display in the column width. Quattro Pro continues to use the value of formulas when you format them as Text.

Hidden Format A cell or block formatted as Hidden always appears blank. You use Hidden format for intermediate calculations that you don't want to appear in a final report, or for sensitive formulas you don't want displayed. The contents of a Hidden cell appear in the input line when you select the cell, so Hidden format offers little security.

User-Defined Format Quattro Pro enables you to define and apply your own numeric formats. User-defined formats can include many different elements. For example, you can include text, the names of days or months, or leading zeros. For more information on creating your own numeric formats, see "User-Defined Formats" in the Quattro Pro Help system.

Accounting Format The Accounting format is nearly identical to the Currency format discussed in an earlier section. The primary difference is the location of the currency symbol. In the Accounting format (depending on which country you choose), the symbol may appear left-justified in the cell rather than immediately preceding the number. Therefore, this format would be easier to read if you are working with multiple columns of currency data.

Avoiding Apparent Errors with Formatting Some formats display a number in rounded form. Even when the displayed number appears rounded, however, Quattro Pro still stores and uses the exact value in calculations. If you format the value 1.5 as Fixed with zero decimal places, Quattro Pro displays the number as 2 in a cell, but uses the actual value of 1.5 in calculations. This can make it seem as though Quattro Pro is making arithmetic errors, such as 2+2=3. In fact, Quattro Pro is correct, because the two values it is adding are 1.5 and 1.5, so the formula is actually 1.5+1.5=3. This apparent error is caused by rounding the display but not rounding the values.

CAUTION

You easily can create apparent rounding errors—especially when you produce cross-tabulated reports. To avoid apparent rounding errors, you need to round the actual value of the numbers used in formulas, not just their appearance or format. To round the values used in a formula, use the @ROUND function to round each value before the value is used in the formula.

Aligning Data

Just as Quattro Pro offers a very broad range of numeric format options, it also provides quite a few choices you can use to align labels and values. By default, labels are aligned to the left side of cells, and values are aligned to the right side of cells. These default alignments are easily changed. You can change alignment for both labels and values.

You can align labels and values to the left or right side of cells, or center them in a cell or across a block. You can also align them to the top, center, or bottom of the cell, and indent them from the edge of the cell. You can orient labels and values horizontally or vertically. Finally, you can wrap text on multiple lines in a single cell, and join multiple cells to form a single cell.

TIP

You can also change horizontal alignment using the Alignment button on the Property Bar.

To change the label alignment for existing labels or values, follow these steps:

1. Select the cell or block.
2. Right-click the selection, and select Cell Properties from the QuickMenu.
3. Select the Alignment tab in the Active Cells dialog box (see Figure 14.6).
4. In the Horizontal Alignment area, choose General to reset the alignment to the sheet default; or choose Left, Right, Center, Center Across Block, or Indent.
5. In the Vertical Alignment area, choose Top, Center, or Bottom.
6. In the Text Orientation area, choose whether you want Horizontal, Vertical, or Rotated text. If you choose Rotated, specify the degrees to rotate the text in the spin box that appears when you choose this option.
7. In the Cell Options area, select the Wrap Text check box to wrap labels on multiple lines within a single cell; select Join Cells if you want to merge the selected cells into a single cell.
8. Click OK to confirm the dialog box and apply the selected alignment options.

FIG. 14.6
Use the Alignment section of the Active Cells dialog box to specify data alignment.

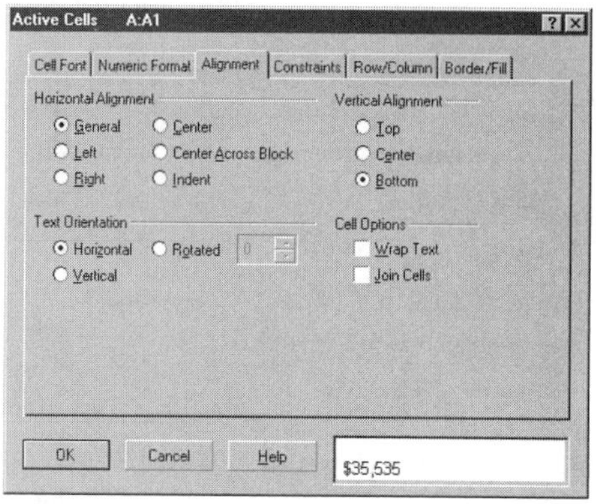

Figure 14.7 demonstrates the various horizontal and vertical alignment and orientation options.

FIG. 14.7
Quattro Pro offers many horizontal and vertical alignment and orientation options.

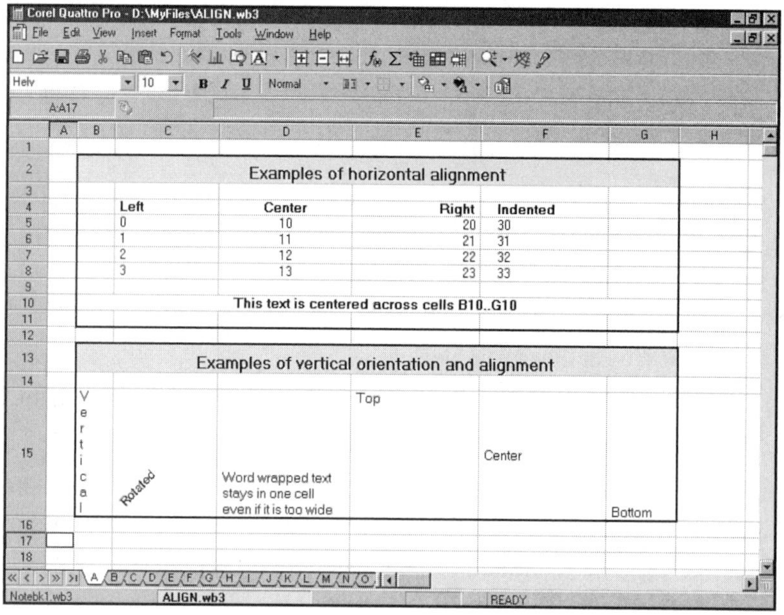

Changing Fonts

Quattro Pro applies the term *font* to the combination of typeface, point size, and attributes used for the characters displayed in your notebooks. A *typeface* is a type style, such as Arial, Courier New, or Times New Roman. Typefaces are available in a number of point sizes that represent character height. A standard 10 character-per-inch (cpi) size usually is considered equivalent to a 12-point type size. Typefaces also have different attributes, such as weight (normal or bold) and italic.

You can use the Cell Font tab in the Active Cells dialog box to choose different fonts. You can also use the Font and Font Size buttons on the Property Bar to make these two selections, and the Bold, Italic, and Underline buttons to apply any of these attributes.

Several factors determine which font options are available. If you have installed additional fonts on your system, you'll be able to select from a larger list of options. Scaleable fonts, such as TrueType fonts, greatly improve the quality of your reports. Corel includes more than 1,000 additional fonts on the Corel WordPerfect Suite 8 CD-ROM, which you can install using Custom install and selecting True Type Fonts under the Corel WordPerfect Suite Setup install option.

If you increase font size, Quattro Pro enlarges the row height to fit the selected fonts. Column widths do not adjust automatically, however, so numeric data may not fit in a cell after you change the font, and the data may display as asterisks. Adjust the column widths as needed to display the data correctly. Figure 14.8 shows how several different typefaces, point sizes, and attributes change the appearance of your data. (You probably will have a different selection of fonts installed on your system.)

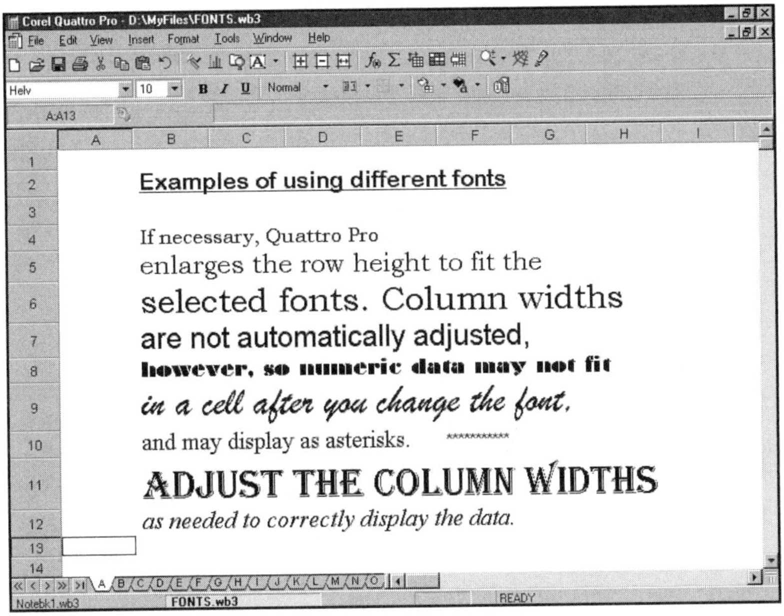

FIG. 14.8
Different fonts change the appearance of data in your notebooks.

Adding Borders and Shading

If you really want to add a professional touch to your notebooks, borders and shading can do the trick. *Borders* are lines around a cell or block. *Shading* is a background tint within a cell or block.

You can use borders to effectively isolate groups of data, making it easy to see all related data. You can also use borders as separators between report sections. Shading is most often used for emphasis, or to make certain report data cannot be altered without the alterations being immediately apparent.

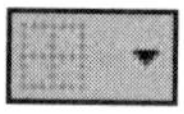

Adding Borders to Cells or Blocks You can use the Border/Fill tab in the Active Cells dialog box to draw lines above, below, on the sides, and around cells and blocks. You can also use the Line Drawing button on the Property Bar to draw lines at the bottom of cells or blocks. Borders can be single lines, double lines, or thick lines.

To draw borders within or around a cell or block, follow these steps:

1. Select the cell or block.
2. Right-click inside the selection and choose Cell Properties from the QuickMenu.
3. Select the Border/Fill tab (see Figure 14.9).
4. Select the placement options you want using the Line Segments, All, Outline, and Inside options.
5. Select the Border Type you want.
6. Select the Border Color you want.
7. Click OK to confirm the dialog box and add the selected borders.

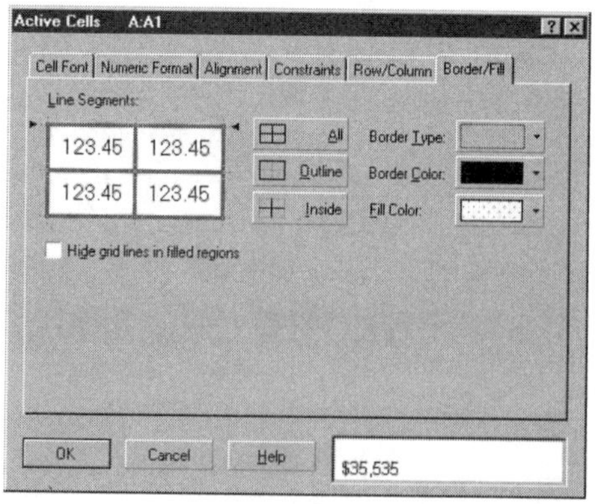

FIG. 14.9
Use the Border/Fill options in the Active Cells dialog box to add borders to cells or blocks.

Adding Shading to Cells or Blocks You can draw attention to cells or blocks by adding shading, a special effect that changes the background from white to a color. When you select shading, you also can select the blend of two colors.

To add shading, follow these steps:

1. Select the cell or block.
2. Right-click inside the selection and choose Cell Properties from the QuickMenu.
3. Select the Border/Fill tab, then select the Fill Color option and click More from the drop-down palette.
4. In the Shading dialog box (see Figure 14.10), select Color 1, Color 2, and Blend (shading pattern). Quattro Pro enables you to select from 16 colors for both the background and the foreground, and from seven different blends.
5. Click OK to confirm the Shading dialog box; then click OK on the Border/Fill tab to apply the shading.

FIG. 14.10
Use the options in the Shading dialog box to add shading to cells or blocks.

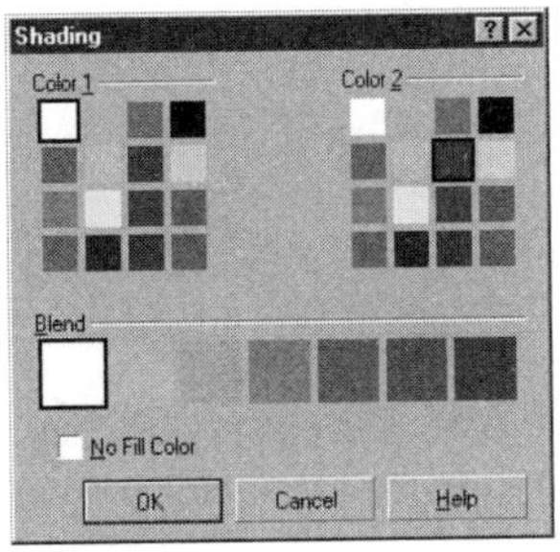

> **CAUTION**
>
> Not all printers can properly print text on a shaded background. Test printing shades on your printer.

Any borders or shading you add to cells or blocks print with the labels and values in a report. It's generally best to use light shading in cells or blocks containing values that must be visible in a printed report, or one that must be photocopied.

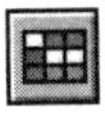

Quattro Pro also has several predefined formats that enable you to quickly set combinations of numeric and text formatting, lines, and shading. Click the Apply a Predefined Format to the Selection button on the toolbar to view the SpeedFormat dialog box, which enables you to select from the available SpeedFormat options.

CHAPTER 15

Analyzing Data

Raw data is the foundation of every business report, but the most effective reports are those that effectively analyze that data. Corel Quattro Pro provides you with a powerful suite of data analysis tools that enable you to solve complex problems, analyze results, produce cross-tabulation summaries, and work directly with external data. These tools are the subject of this chapter.

The concepts introduced in this chapter show you a glimpse of some of the more complex tools in the Quattro Pro tool bag. Several of the functions provided by some of these tools were formerly available only in specialized and high-cost, stand-alone programs. These programs were not only specialized, but they were complex, usually difficult to use, and often required advanced training before you could use them effectively. As a part of Quattro Pro, these tools are much easier to learn and use. This ease of learning and use hasn't come at the expense of power, though. The data analysis tools in Quattro Pro provide the same level of powerful functions available in those stand-alone programs, but you don't have to pay extra to use them. ■

Find the best answers to problems

Use the Optimizer and Solve For tools to find the answers you need to solve complex and difficult problems.

Use what-if tables

Use what-if tables to work with variables whose values are unknown.

View complex relationships in data

Use the new Cross Tabs feature to view the complex and find hidden relationships in your data.

Access external database information

Use the Database Desktop to access external data in Paradox and dBASE files.

Using the Optimizer and Solve For

The Optimizer and Solve For tools are powerful utilities that help you create *what-if* scenarios with notebook data. What-if scenarios are a common way to analyze problems, using many different values for a set of variables to find optimal answers. What-if scenarios can be quite time-consuming, especially if done manually, because even problems with a limited number of variables have many possible solutions.

TIP Use Solve For when you want to find an answer by changing one variable.

The Optimizer tool can analyze problems with up to 200 variables and 100 constraints to determine the best answer. The Solve For tool modifies a single variable to find a specified answer to a problem.

Solving Complex Problems Using the Optimizer

You use the Optimizer to determine a series of possible answers to a specific problem, and to select the answer that best fits your criteria. You can use the Optimizer, for example, to find the production mix that produces the highest profit, to analyze investment portfolios, to determine the least costly shipping routes, and to schedule your staff.

Each Optimizer problem must have one or more *adjustable* cells. Adjustable cells contain the variables that the Optimizer changes while searching for the optimal answer—and can contain numbers only. Adjustable cells might include production quantities, numbers of employees, or capital invested in a project.

Constraints are conditions that serve as problem limits, such as the range of acceptable values. Constraints are expressed as logical formulas that evaluate to true or false, and all constraints must be met before an answer is considered acceptable. Constraints might include limits on production levels, a requirement to produce a profit, or an obligation that at least one employee be on duty.

A *solution cell* contains the formula that defines the problem, and is optional. If you do not include a solution cell, the Optimizer finds answers that meet all the defined constraints. Solution cells might include formulas that calculate profits, overall costs, or the amount earned from different activities.

Using a Production Scheduling Notebook

Figure 15.1 shows a sample notebook that represents the costs involved in producing three different products. In this example, it is assumed that the factory can produce

50,000 total parts per month and that the production can be divided among the three parts in the most profitable manner.

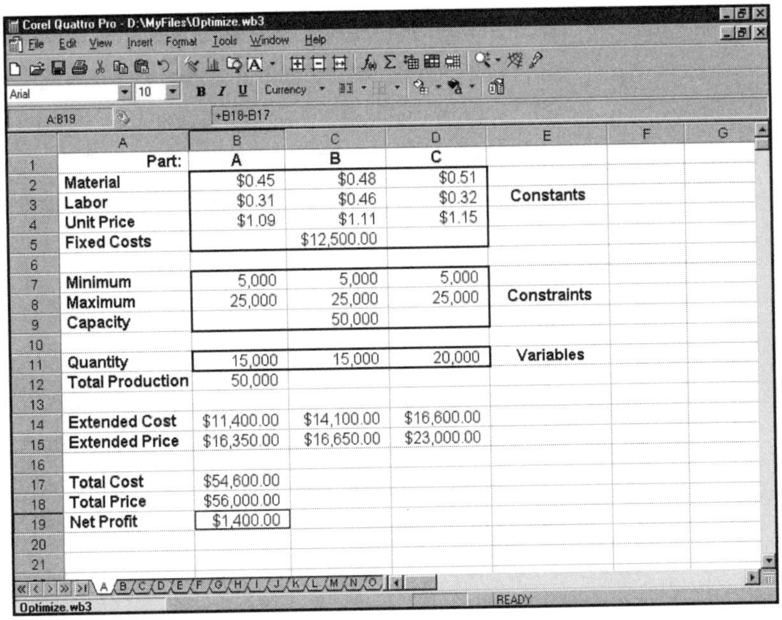

	A	B	C	D	E
1	Part:	A	B	C	
2	Material	$0.45	$0.48	$0.51	
3	Labor	$0.31	$0.46	$0.32	Constants
4	Unit Price	$1.09	$1.11	$1.15	
5	Fixed Costs		$12,500.00		
6					
7	Minimum	5,000	5,000	5,000	
8	Maximum	25,000	25,000	25,000	Constraints
9	Capacity		50,000		
10					
11	Quantity	15,000	15,000	20,000	Variables
12	Total Production	50,000			
13					
14	Extended Cost	$11,400.00	$14,100.00	$16,600.00	
15	Extended Price	$16,350.00	$16,650.00	$23,000.00	
16					
17	Total Cost	$54,600.00			
18	Total Price	$56,000.00			
19	Net Profit	$1,400.00			

FIG. 15.1
We'll use this notebook to compute an optimal product mix.

TIP Optimizer will find a solution more quickly if the initial values in the adjustable cells are a reasonable solution to the problem.

Several factors affect the final profit. As shown in row 11 of Figure 15.1, the production manager has scheduled the production run at 15,000 each for parts A and B, and 20,000 of part C. The net profit with this mix is $1,400. Of course, it would be possible to try other sets of values for each product's production quantity. Because each of the three values can vary between 5,000 and 25,000, however, the number of possibilities would be enormous.

CAUTION

Don't use logical (or Boolean) functions in Optimizer problems; they can make a solution very difficult or impossible to find.

To use the Optimizer to find a better solution, follow these steps:

1. Choose Tools, Numeric Tools, Optimizer to display the Optimizer dialog box.

2. To make the production quantities of the three parts adjustable in the notebook, enter the cell addresses in the Variable Cell(s) text box. In this example, you enter **B11..D11**.

   Next, define the constraints that the Optimizer must satisfy in solving the problem.

3. Select Add to display the Add Constraints dialog box.

   The quantities of the parts (cells B11..D11) must be equal to or greater than the minimum quantity shown in cells B7..D7.

4. Enter **B11..D11** in the Cell text box, select the >= (greater than or equal to) option button in the Operator area, and enter **B7..D7** in the Constant text box.

5. Select Add Another Constraint to enter additional constraints.

   The quantities of the parts (cells B11..D11) must be less than or equal to the maximum quantity shown in cells B8..D8.

6. Enter **B11..D11** in the Cell text box, select the <= (less than or equal to) option button in the Operator area, and enter **B8..D8** in the Constant text box.

7. Select Add Another Constraint to enter the last constraint.

   Cell B12 (total production) must be less than or equal to the value in C9 (capacity).

8. Enter **B12** in the Cell text box, select the <= (less than or equal to) option button in the Operator area, and enter **C9** in the Constant text box.

9. Choose OK when all constraints have been entered.

10. Select the Solution Cell text box in the Optimizer dialog box and enter **B19**, the address of the formula cell. The dialog box should now look like Figure 15.2.

11. Click Solve to instruct the Optimizer to calculate the solution, and then click Close to close the Optimizer dialog box. Figure 15.3 shows the result in the production mix example.

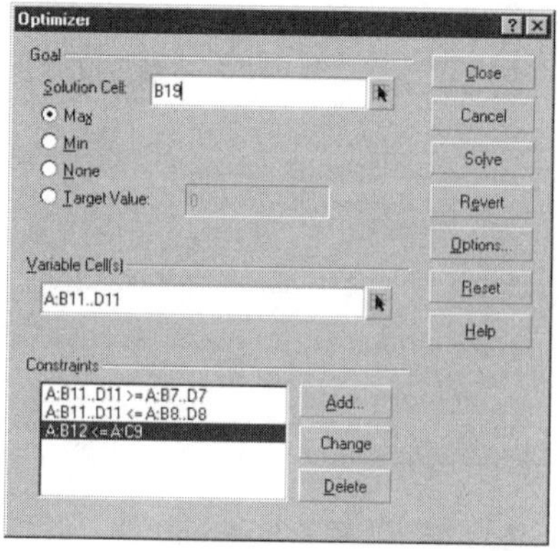

FIG. 15.2
The Optimizer dialog box shows the completed entries.

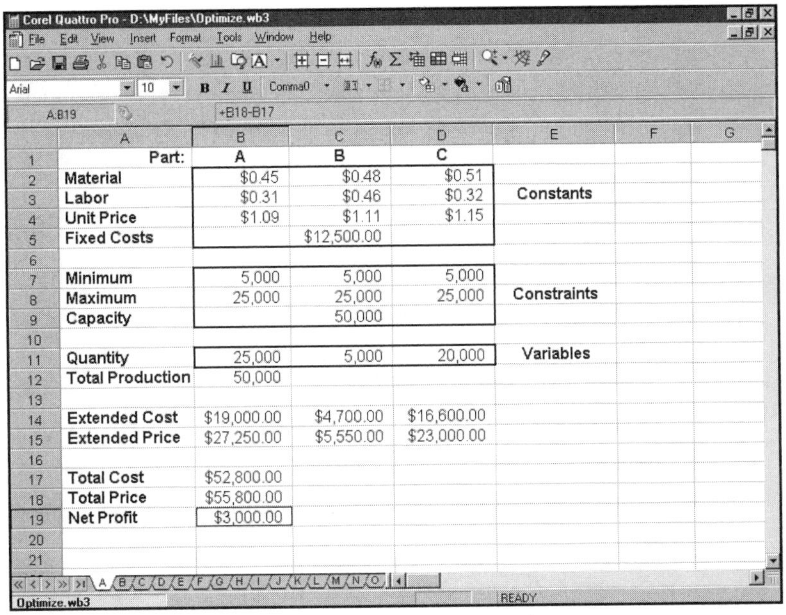

FIG. 15.3
The notebook shows the optimal solution for the product mix example, as determined by the Optimizer.

The Optimizer found a much different solution than the one proposed by the production manager. After redistributing the production quantities shown in row 11, the total monthly profit jumped from $1,400 to $3,000. Although this example did not take all possible factors into account, it clearly demonstrates the value of applying the Optimizer to a what-if scenario.

TROUBLESHOOTING

Optimizer is unable to find an optimal solution to a complex problem, or it sometimes produces different results when solving the same problem a second time. Try to supply initial values for the variables that you feel will be somewhat close to their final values. Optimizer usually has better success when it can start with a reasonable solution.

I can't tell whether the Optimizer's solution is the best solution to my problem. Use the Tools, Numeric Tools, Optimizer, Options, Reporting command to create an answer report. This report shows the values Optimizer used to find its solution.

Solving for a Known Answer Using Solve For

Sometimes you know the answer you want, but don't quite know how to get there. The Solve For tool is a Quattro Pro analysis utility that you use to find the value of a variable when you are seeking a specific goal. Rather than calculating an optimum answer by adjusting a block of variables, the Solve For tool adjusts a single variable to produce an answer you specify.

For example, suppose that you know you can afford $325 as a monthly payment on an automobile, but you don't know how large a loan you can receive for such a payment. The Solve For tool makes it easy to make this type of reverse calculation, where you already know the answer, but don't know the key to finding the answer.

To use Solve For to find the loan amount, follow these steps:

1. Create a Quattro Pro notebook that uses the @PMT function to calculate the loan payment on a loan. For this example, enter a loan amount of **$10,000** in cell C2, **9%** interest in cell C3, a term of **60** months in cell C4, and the formula, **@PMT(C2,C3/12,C4)** in cell C6.
2. Choose Tools, Numeric Tools, Solve For.
3. Specify **C6** in the Formula Cell text box. This is the cell that contains the formula whose value you want to specify.
4. Specify **325** in the Target Value text box. This is the value you want to achieve in the goal cell.
5. Specify **C2** as the Variable Cell, the cell whose value Solve For will adjust. Your screen should now appear similar to Figure 15.4 (in this figure, cells were formatted to display numbers correctly).
6. Click OK to execute the command and return to the notebook. Figure 15.5 shows the notebook with the solution.

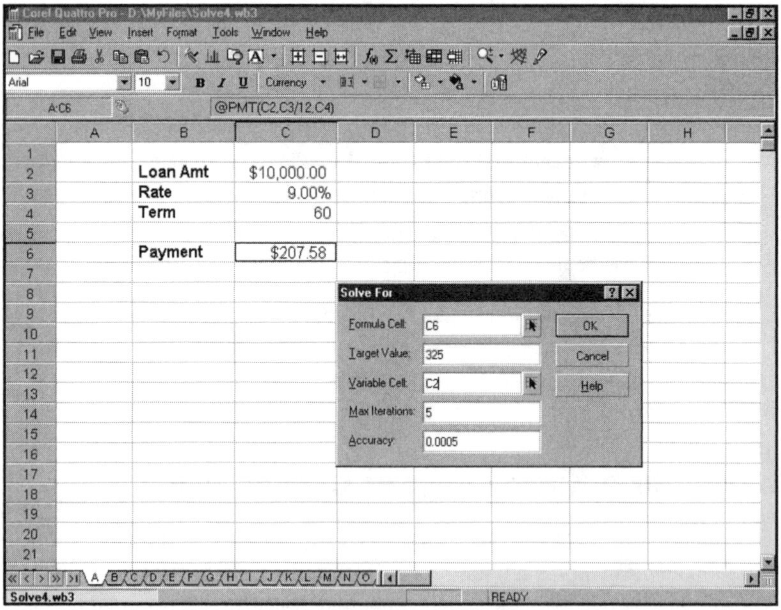

FIG. 15.4
The Solve For dialog box is completed and ready to find the solution.

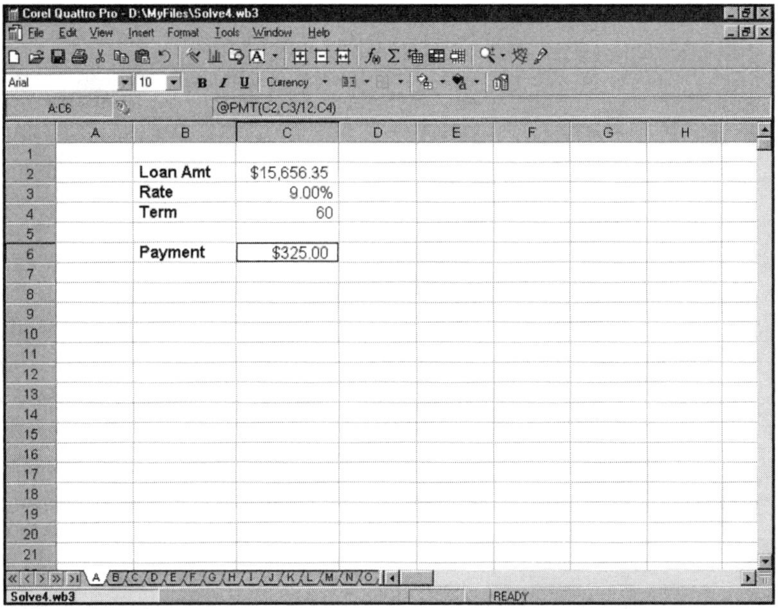

FIG. 15.5
The solved problem shows the answer you seek, in cell C2.

Your $325 monthly budget allows for payments on a loan of $15,656.35. Although you could probably find an answer close to this by trying several different values in cell C2, using Solve For makes the process both simple and fast.

TIP Save the notebook before you use Solve For so you can easily revert to the original values if necessary.

When you use Solve For, the adjustable value is permanently changed in the notebook. You can return to the previous value if you immediately choose Edit, Undo.

Using What-If Tables

In most notebook models, the variables your formulas use are known quantities. What-if tables enable you to work with variables whose values are unknown. Models for financial projections often fall into this category. For example, next year's cash flow projection may depend on prevailing interest rates or other variable costs you cannot predict exactly.

With the Tools, Numeric Tools, What-If command, you can create tables that show the results of changing one variable in a problem or the combined effect of changing two variables simultaneously. Another function of the Tools, Numeric Tools, What-If command is to create *cross-tabulation tables.* A cross-tabulation table provides summary information categorized by unique information in two fields, such as the total amount of sales each sales representative makes to each customer.

Creating a What-If Table

A *what-if table* is an on-screen view of information in a column format with the field names at the top. A *variable* is a formula component whose value can change. An *input cell* is a notebook cell used by Quattro Pro for temporary storage during calculation of a what-if table. One input cell is required for each variable in the what-if table formula. The cell addresses of the formula variables are the same as the input cells. The formulas used in what-if tables can contain values, strings, cell addresses, and functions, but you should not use logical formulas because this type of formula always evaluates to 0 or 1, which is usually meaningless in a what-if table.

TIP Use One Free Variable What-If tables when you need to see the results from more than one formula.

You can build two types of what-if tables in Quattro Pro. They differ in the number of variables and the number of formulas that can be included. A One Free Variable What-If table can contain one variable and can have one or more formulas. A Two Free Variables What-If table can contain two variables, but only one formula. In a One Free Variable What-If table, you place the formulas in the top row of the table. In a Two Free Variables What-If table, you place the formula at the intersection of the top row and the left column of the table.

A common use for a One Free Variable What-If table would be to calculate both the interest and principal portions of each payment on a loan. A Two Free Variables What-If table might be used to calculate monthly payments on a given loan amount at different combinations of interest rates and terms.

Figure 15.6 shows a typical Two Free Variables What-If table. This table calculates monthly payments on a given loan amount at different combinations of interest rates and terms.

To create a similar what-if table, follow these steps:

1. Enter the loan amount of **$15,000.00** in cell B1.
2. For documentation purposes, place identifying labels in column A. In this case, enter **Loan Amt** in A1, **Interest rate** in A2, and **Term** in A3.
3. Enter the formula **@PMT(B1,B2/12,B3)** in cell A5. The formula will show ERR because it refers to blank cells, but Quattro Pro will correctly calculate the what-if table.

FIG. 15.6
This completed What-If table of loan payment amounts uses Two Free Variables.

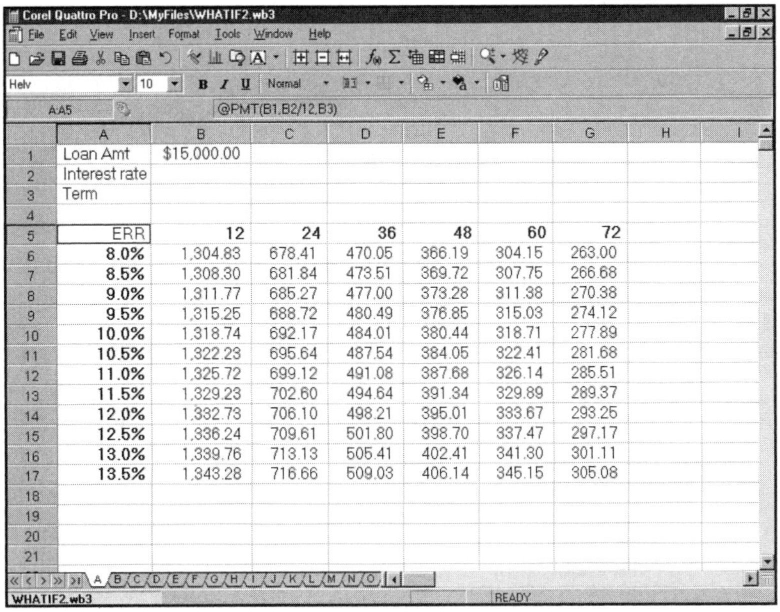

	A	B	C	D	E	F	G
1	Loan Amt	$15,000.00					
2	Interest rate						
3	Term						
4							
5	ERR	12	24	36	48	60	72
6	8.0%	1,304.83	678.41	470.05	366.19	304.15	263.00
7	8.5%	1,308.30	681.84	473.51	369.72	307.75	266.68
8	9.0%	1,311.77	685.27	477.00	373.28	311.38	270.38
9	9.5%	1,315.25	688.72	480.49	376.85	315.03	274.12
10	10.0%	1,318.74	692.17	484.01	380.44	318.71	277.89
11	10.5%	1,322.23	695.64	487.54	384.05	322.41	281.68
12	11.0%	1,325.72	699.12	491.08	387.68	326.14	285.51
13	11.5%	1,329.23	702.60	494.64	391.34	329.89	289.37
14	12.0%	1,332.73	706.10	498.21	395.01	333.67	293.25
15	12.5%	1,336.24	709.61	501.80	398.70	337.47	297.17
16	13.0%	1,339.76	713.13	505.41	402.41	341.30	301.11
17	13.5%	1,343.28	716.66	509.03	406.14	345.15	305.08

4. Enter the interest rates in A6..A17. The fastest method of entering these rates is to enter **8%** in A6, **8.5%** in A7, select A6..A17, and click the QuickFill button. (To improve the appearance of the table, format A6..A17 as Percent, 1 decimal.)
5. Enter the loan terms in B5..G5. Once again, you can use QuickFill.
6. Select the table block A5..G17.
7. Choose Tools, Numeric Tools, What-If.
8. Select Two Free Variables.
9. Type **B2** in the Column Input Cell text box, and then type **B3** in the Row Input Cell text box.
10. Click Generate to calculate the what-if table values.
11. Click Close to confirm the dialog box and return to the notebook.

TIP You can also use PerfectExpert to automate several types of analysis in your Quattro Pro notebooks. See Chapter 30, "Integrating Your Work with PerfectExpert," for more information.

TROUBLESHOOTING

What-if tables don't display new values when the formula variables are changed. What-if tables don't recalculate when values change because the tables don't contain formulas. Choose Tools, Numeric Tools, What-If, Generate to recalculate the what-if table values.

Creating a Simple Cross-Tabulation Table

Crosstabs (or cross-tabulation tables) are tables that summarize the values in a database. For example, an address list showing customers in many different states might include information you could use to determine where you get most of your business, and therefore, where you should plan to spend your advertising dollars. You might also use a crosstab to see a sales summary by salesperson for each product line. Quattro Pro can even generate a chart to quickly display the results of the analysis.

▶ **See** "Creating a Simple Chart," **p. 318**

The structure of a what-if table block for a cross-tabulation analysis is similar to the structure for a what-if analysis. If you are analyzing the effects of one variable, the upper-left cell may be empty, the top row contains the formula(s) that are to be evaluated, and the left column contains the sample values. If you are analyzing the effects of two variables, you place the formula in the upper-left cell of the table, and the two sets of sample values in the top row and left column of the table. In most cases, the formulas contain one or more database functions.

In addition, you must create one or two input cells, depending on the number of variables in the crosstab. For a crosstab analysis, you must place the input cells directly below cells that contain the corresponding database field names.

You also use the Tools, Numeric Tools, What-If command to create a cross-tabulation table. The sample values in the left column, or in the left column and top row, are used to select the values displayed in the crosstab. The sample values for a cross-tabulation analysis are the values or labels that you can use as *criteria* for the analysis.

TIP If your data changes, remember to use the Tools, Numeric Tools, What-if, Generate command to recalculate the results.

After the what-if table has been calculated, each cell in the results block contains the result of the formulas. The formulas have been applied to those database records that meet the crosstab criteria.

Figure 15.7 demonstrates a crosstab analysis of a sales database. In this case, the crosstab is analyzing sales totals for each product line broken down by salesperson. The @DSUM database function in cell E10 is used to perform the analysis. Figure 15.8 shows how Quattro Pro can quickly create a graphical representation of the crosstab analysis.

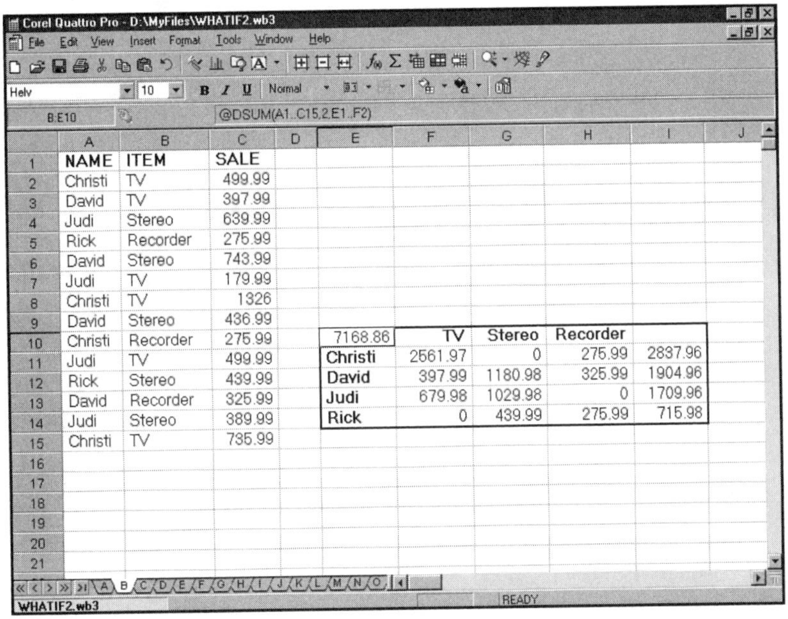

FIG. 15.7
A cross-tabulation displays an analysis of data.

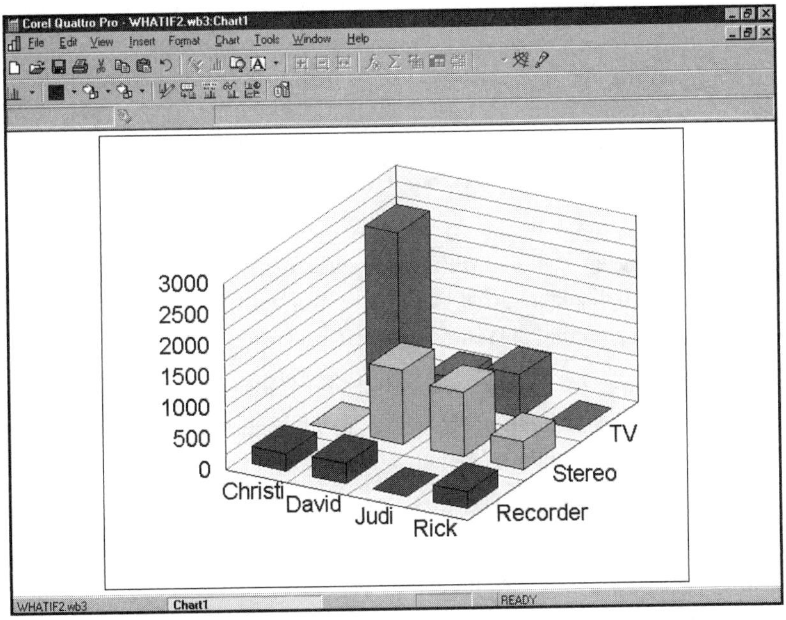

FIG. 15.8
Quattro Pro displays a chart of the cross-tabulation analysis.

You use nearly the same steps to create a crosstab with the Tools, Numeric Tools, What-If command as you do to create a what-if table. Notice the similarities between the what-if table in Figure 15.6 and the crosstab in Figure 15.7. In both tables, the formulas are evaluated based upon the values of the variables. The primary difference between the two types of tables is the data source. A what-if table generates new data, while a crosstab evaluates existing database data.

Using the Cross Tabs Feature

By now you can see that crosstabs can be a very effective data analysis tool. A crosstab can often display data relationships you might not otherwise be able to grasp quickly. Unfortunately, creating a crosstab takes some planning and a lot of work. Not only that, but crosstabs created with the Tools, Numeric Tools, What-If command aren't too flexible—once you create a crosstab, it's difficult to change so you can see different data relationships.

Quattro Pro includes a new integrated tool, the Cross Tabs feature, which enables you to manipulate data easily and create detailed crosstab reports. This tool is flexible, and it's fun to use, too.

NOTE In addition to the Cross Tabs feature, Quattro Pro 8 also includes the Data Modeling Desktop, a separate application that provided the only method of creating crosstabs in Quattro Pro 7. You may still want to use the Data Modeling Desktop in certain instances, such as when you need to summarize data from an external database file.

Understanding the Cross Tabs Feature

Up until now, whenever you've created a crosstab, the finished crosstab was static and unchanging. You determined the data relationships you wanted to view and created a crosstab displaying that view. If you wanted to see a different view, you had to go back to the beginning and start over.

The Cross Tabs feature provides a much different approach to crosstab generation. Instead of a static and unchanging crosstab, the Cross Tabs feature creates a crosstab you can quickly modify to display additional data relationships.

The Cross Tabs feature analyzes data by using certain data sets as row or column labels, and a single numerical data set as the data being analyzed. The labels are used as selection criteria to determine which values to include at the intersections of the labels. For example, if your database contains sales information, you might place the names of the salespeople as labels along the left side of the workspace and items along the top. The intersection of the labels "John" and "Computers" would show the total of all computers sold by John.

Simple crosstabs, such as the above example, really don't show the true power of the Cross Tabs feature. Adding even one additional piece of data to the picture, though, really complicates matters. Suppose that you decide to add time period data to the crosstab. You track sales by date, so you'd like to analyze how well each salesperson did each month, but you want to know how well they did in each product line, too. Now your crosstab is considerably more complicated, and you've only scratched the surface. Imagine that you'd rather change the focus and see how well each product line did each month rather than each salesperson. The Cross Tabs feature enables you to quickly make such changes in focus so that you can find the hidden relationships in your data.

Summarizing Data in a Cross Tabs Report

To analyze data using the Cross Tabs feature, you must organize the data—using a layout identical to a typical Quattro Pro notebook database. Data must be in tabular format, with each record in a single row and field names in the top row.

To summarize data in a Cross Tabs report, follow these steps:

1. Select the notebook database block—the block containing the data you want to analyze (see Figure 15.9).

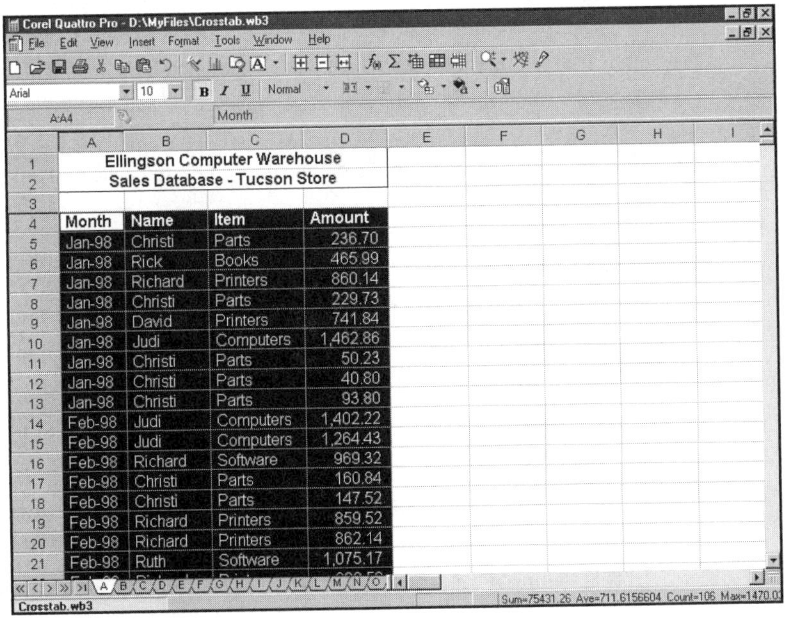

FIG. 15.9
This Sales database includes fields for Month, Name, Item, and Amount.

2. Choose Tools, Data Tools, Cross Tabs to display the Cross Tabs dialog box (see Figure 15.10).

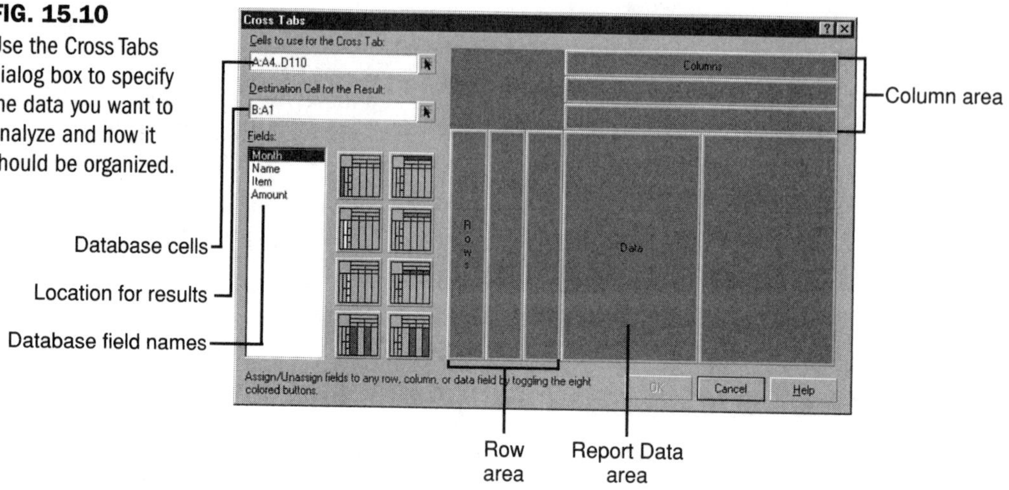

FIG. 15.10
Use the Cross Tabs dialog box to specify the data you want to analyze and how it should be organized.

3. If necessary, edit the block address that appears in the Cells to Use For the Cross Tab text block. Then type the address of the top left cell where you want the crosstab results to appear. (In this example, the default entries for these two text boxes are acceptable.)

NOTE Use the Row and Column areas in the Cross Tabs dialog box to specify the database fields you want to analyze. Usually, these data categories include labels or dates, such as a month, item, or sales representative's name. The Report Data area in the Cross Tabs dialog box includes the summary data. In this example, you want to summarize the sales for each month, showing which sales representatives sold which items. The data categories you add to the Report Data area should contain numeric data that can be summarized mathematically, such as the sales totals.

4. In the Fields list box, select the field you want to use for the row labels; then click the button with the red row label area. (This button is the top button, just to the right of the Fields list box.)

   In this example, select Month in the Fields list box, and then click the red button. Notice that Month is removed from the Fields list box and now appears as a red bar in the Row area.

5. In the Fields list box, select the field you want to use for the column labels; then click the button with the blue column label area.

   In this example, select Item in the Fields list box, and then click the blue button. Notice that Item is removed from the Fields list box and now appears as a blue bar in the Columns area.

6. Select any other remaining fields you want to add to the Row or Column areas, and click the appropriate colored button beside the Fields list box.

   In this example, select Name in the Fields list box, and then click the yellow button. The Row area now contains two field labels, with the Name field displayed to the right of the Month field.

TIP Always add text data to the Column or Row label areas and numeric data to the Report Data area.

7. In the Fields list box, select the field containing the values you want to summarize in the main body of the report; then click the button on the left with the green data area.

   In this example, select Amount in the Fields list box, and then click the green button on the left (the bottom left button in the group of colored buttons). The dialog box is now completed and looks like Figure 15.11.

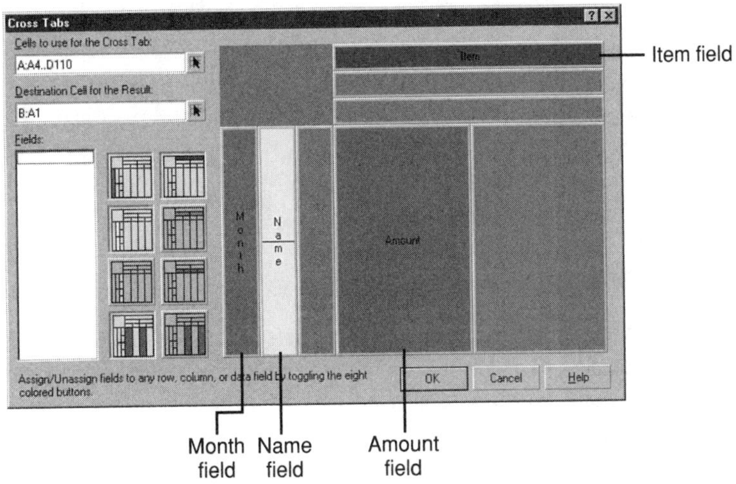

FIG. 15.11 The completed Cross Tabs dialog box shows how the Cross Tab report will be organized.

TIP At this point, you can click one of the bars in the Rows, Columns, or Report Data area in the Cross Tabs dialog box if you want to change the type of value that Quattro Pro reports for the specified field (such as sum, average, count, percent, or string).

8. Click OK to close the Cross Tabs dialog box and create the crosstab report.

   The initial crosstab report appears as shown in Figure 15.12. For this example, line borders and other basic formatting has been applied manually to the report, to make the data easier to read.

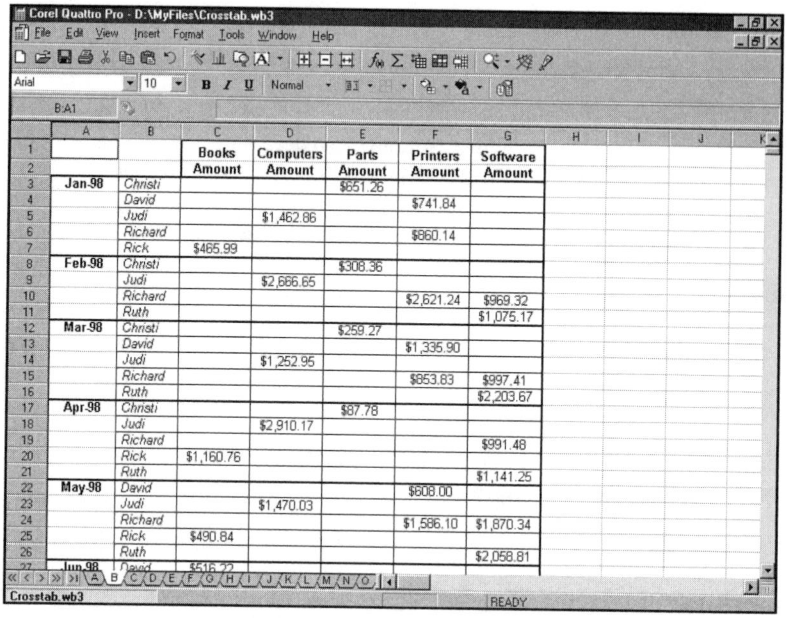

	A	B	C	D	E	F	G
1			Books	Computers	Parts	Printers	Software
2			Amount	Amount	Amount	Amount	Amount
3	Jan-98	Christi			$651.26		
4		David				$741.84	
5		Judi		$1,462.86			
6		Richard				$860.14	
7		Rick	$465.99				
8	Feb-98	Christi			$308.36		
9		Judi		$2,666.65			
10		Richard				$2,621.24	$969.32
11		Ruth					$1,075.17
12	Mar-98	Christi			$259.27		
13		David				$1,335.90	
14		Judi		$1,252.95			
15		Richard				$853.83	$997.41
16		Ruth					$2,203.67
17	Apr-98	Christi			$87.78		
18		Judi		$2,910.17			
19		Richard					$991.48
20		Rick	$1,160.76				
21		Ruth					$1,141.25
22	May-98	David				$608.00	
23		Judi		$1,470.03			
24		Richard				$1,586.10	$1,870.34
25		Rick	$490.84				
26		Ruth					$2,058.81
27	Jun-98	David	$516.22				

FIG. 15.12
The completed crosstab report now has basic formatting applied to the data.

To rearrange the data that appears in a crosstab report, repeat the steps above, but choose a different arrangement of field items for the Row, Column, and Report Data areas in the Cross Tabs dialog box. Remember to select a different destination cell if you want to keep previous crosstab results and avoid overwriting existing data.

TROUBLESHOOTING

Numbers appear in one of the label areas instead of being shown in the Report Data area. Always add numeric data to the Report Data area and the identifying data labels to the Row and Column areas. If you add numeric data to the Row or Column area, or labels to the Report Data area, your report will be meaningless.

Using the Database Desktop

By now you've learned that Quattro Pro provides many options for analyzing your notebook data. Sometimes, though, you may want to use Quattro Pro to analyze data that isn't already in a notebook file. For example, you may want to use data contained in a dBASE or Paradox database file. In this case, you should use the Database Desktop feature in Quattro Pro to access the external data.

Understanding the Database Desktop

NOTE The Database Desktop feature does not install in the Typical installation of WordPerfect Suite 8. If the Insert, External Data, Database Desktop command is dimmed, use the Corel WordPerfect Suite 8 Custom installation program to install the Database Desktop.

Quattro Pro can open many database file types directly, treating them as though they were actually Quattro Pro notebook files. This isn't always the best option, though, and if the database file is very large, it may not be possible. To use a Quattro Pro notebook, it must be loaded completely into your computer's memory. Database managers, such as Paradox, access database files differently. Instead of loading an entire database into memory, Paradox loads a few records into memory, leaving the rest of the records in the database file on disk. Because only a small portion of the database must fit into memory, disk-based databases can be much larger than databases in a Quattro Pro notebook.

The Database Desktop is a companion program to Quattro Pro that enables you to access information in dBASE and Paradox database files. Through the Database Desktop, you can query a database, add new records to a database, modify existing records in a database, create a new dBASE or Paradox database, modify the structure of an existing database file, or delete records from a database.

Using Database Files

To load the Database Desktop into memory, choose Insert, External Data, Database Desktop. Your system briefly displays a message informing you of its progress loading the program, and then displays the Database Desktop (see Figure 15.13). If only the Database Desktop title bar appears, or if the Database Desktop does not fill the screen, click the Maximize button or select Maximize from the Database Desktop Control menu to provide the largest possible work area.

TIP Queries enable you to select the database records you want to see.

Rather than opening a database table and viewing the complete set of records, you often may want to view a subset of those records that you select by using specified criteria. For example, you may want to search for records for a single customer, for records applying to sales over a specified amount, or for customers in a certain group of states. You use the Query commands in the Database Desktop to select specified records. You can then save the query and use the saved query from Quattro Pro to add the selected records into a Quattro Pro notebook.

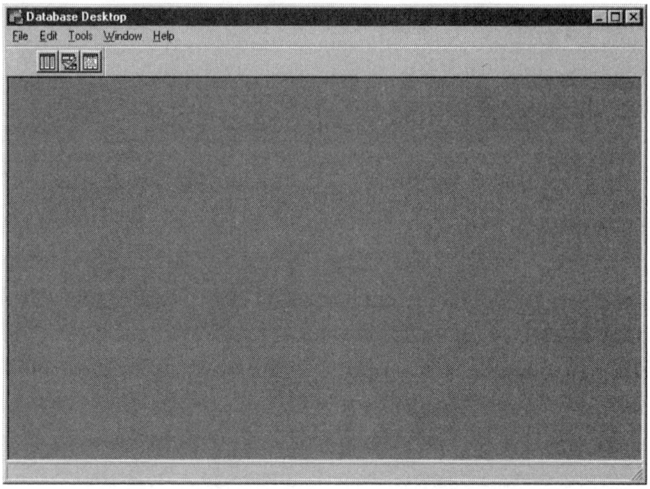

FIG. 15.13
Use the Database Desktop to access disk-based database tables.

To create a new query, choose File, New, QBE Query and choose the database table whose records you want to view. After you select a database table, the Database Desktop Query Editor appears. The Query Editor uses *Query by Example (QBE)* to build a database query; you place example values in the fields displayed in the Query Editor, and records are selected based on these values.

To build a query, you use symbols, operators, and reserved words. Query Editor *symbols* indicate the fields you want included in the answer table, whether to include duplicate values, and the default sort order. *Operators* select field values based on criteria you specify. The >= operator, for example, selects records that contain a value in the selected field greater than or equal to a specified value. *Reserved words* perform special database operations, such as inserting and deleting records. To run the query, choose Query, Run Query or press F8.

Figure 15.14 shows an example of a query that selects customers from a database. In this example, the query specifies that only those customers living in Washington state should be selected. The results of running the query appear in the answer table.

In this case, the answer table shows that the database contains two customers living in Washington. By changing the comparison value and rerunning the query, you can produce different sets of answers. To reuse the same query in the future, use the File, Save or File, Save As command before you close the query or the Database Desktop. Queries you create in the Database Desktop are saved in text files that use the extension QBE. You can use such saved queries in the Database Desktop, Paradox, or through the Quattro Pro Insert, External Data, Table Query command.

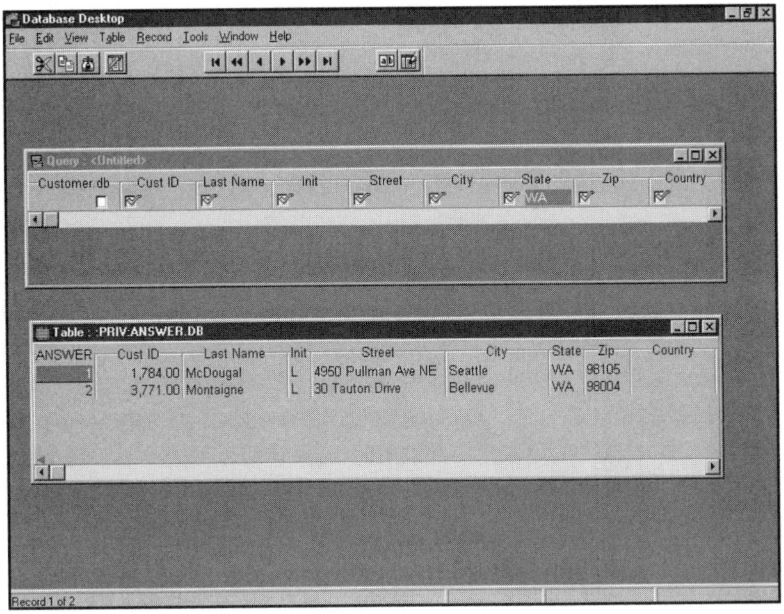

FIG. 15.14
A query selects specific database records.

TIP If you want to save the results of a query, use the Query, Properties, Table Name command and save the results in a table other than ANSWER.DB.

Sharing Results with Quattro Pro

The Database Desktop stores the current answer in a temporary file called ANSWER.DB in your working directory. You can import this file into a Quattro Pro notebook, but when you do, the imported information is static and is not updated when the database changes.

A better way to share database information between the Database Desktop and Quattro Pro is to use the Database Desktop QBE file along with the Quattro Pro Insert, External Data, Table Query command. In this way, the information in your notebook is updated to reflect changes in the database. You can, for example, create and refine a database query, and then execute your fully developed query from within a notebook application.

To run a saved query from within a Quattro Pro notebook, follow these steps:

1. Choose Insert, External Data, Table Query to display the Table Query dialog box.
2. Select Query in File to execute a query in a QBE file, or Query in Selection to execute a query that you previously imported into a notebook block (remember, QBE files are text files).

3. If you select Query in <u>F</u>ile, specify the name of the QBE File. If you select Query in <u>S</u>election, specify the QBE <u>B</u>lock that contains the query.

4. Specify the <u>D</u>estination—the upper-left corner of the notebook block—where you want to place the database records.

5. Click OK to confirm the dialog box and execute the query.

The Database Desktop serves as a tool for creating more powerful Quattro Pro applications that feature easy access to dBASE and Paradox database files. You could use a saved query to automatically update the information in a Quattro Pro notebook to include the latest data—especially if you use shared database files on a network and need to make certain your notebooks are up to date. ●

CHAPTER 16

Using Charts

Create charts

Learn how to create colorful charts from data in a notebook.

Select different chart types

Learn how you can use the many different chart types available in Corel Quattro Pro.

Enhance a chart

See how you can make changes to the appearance of your charts to greatly enhance their effectiveness.

Corel Quattro Pro's presentation graphics features help you present data in an easy-to-understand manner. Instead of trying to understand countless rows and columns of data, a well-executed chart can enable you to see and analyze large amounts of information quickly. The most effective reports are those which appropriately analyze that data.

Quattro Pro includes many powerful graphics capabilities. Because many of these graphics features are built into the Chart Expert, you will find that creating sophisticated graphics within Quattro Pro is quite easy. You don't need to use a separate, dedicated graphics package to produce charts of your Quattro Pro data. ■

NOTE Previous versions of Quattro Pro used the term *graphs* to describe what Quattro Pro now refers to as *charts*.

Creating a Simple Chart

You can create sophisticated, complex, and stunning charts with Quattro Pro. You can even create on-screen slide shows that automatically change from one chart to the next at specified intervals using fancy effects such as dissolves, fades, wipes, or spirals. For most of us, a relatively simple chart that effectively displays our data is a much more reasonable goal, so that's where you start—by learning how to create a simple chart.

Although most of your work in Quattro Pro is done in the spreadsheet, Quattro Pro also provides a Chart window that gives you much more power and control over charting. The Chart window provides you with specialized commands and toolbars that are designed to help you enhance a chart. Before you can access the Chart window, however, you first must create a chart.

Starting a Basic Chart

The data you want to chart must be in a tabular format, similar to a typical Quattro Pro notebook database. The requirements for data you want to chart aren't quite as strict as they are for a database, though, because you can use either rows or columns for similar data. A *crosstab table* is often a very good choice for the layout of data you want to chart, because a crosstab has labels identifying the groups and the elements in your data.

▶ **See** "Using the Cross Tabs Feature," **p. 308**

Figure 16.1 shows a notebook containing the annual sales report for a fictitious company. You use this notebook to demonstrate the steps in creating a Quattro Pro chart.

Choose Insert, Chart to create a chart. By default, Quattro Pro names the first chart Chart1, the second Chart2, and so on. After you create a chart, you have access to several commands on the Chart menu for enhancing the chart. The Chart menu appears only when you have activated a chart. In addition, the Property Bar changes to include buttons that help you to modify the chart. You'll learn more about this later in the section "Enhancing a Chart."

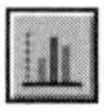

Quattro Pro uses the currently selected spreadsheet block as the block to be charted. If you don't select a block, but the cell selector is located within a block of data, Quattro Pro uses the entire block. If the block you want to chart is contained within a larger block of data, select the block of data to chart before choosing Insert, Chart. You can also click the Create a Floating Chart button on the toolbar to insert a chart directly onto the notebook.

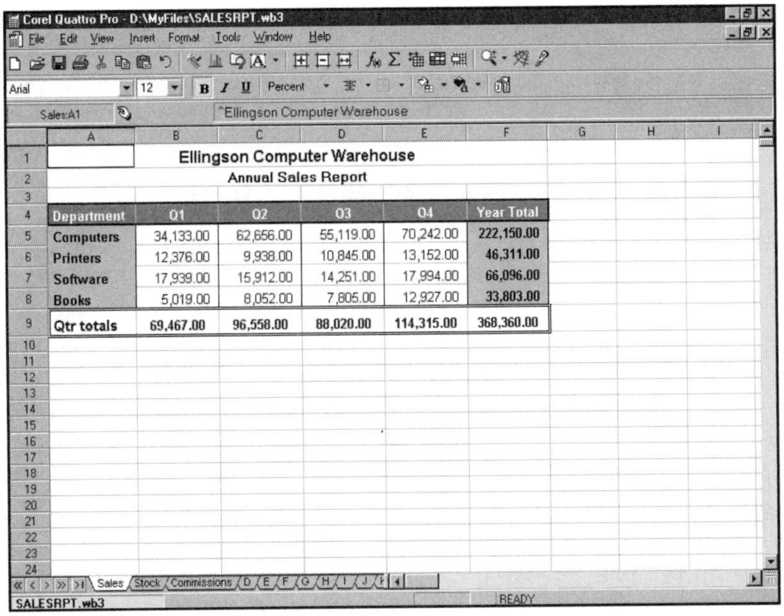

FIG. 16.1
A sample sales data notebook can be used for creating charts.

To chart information from the sales data notebook, you need to know which data you want to plot and which data you want to use in labeling the chart. In Figure 16.1, time-period labels are listed across row 4. Category identifiers are located in column A. The numeric entries in rows 5 through 9, as well as the formula results in row 9 and column F, are suitable for charting as data points. For this example, however, the totals in row 9 and column F are not included in the charted data, because including these totals would make the other data very difficult to see by comparison. In this example, you should select the block A4..E8 before choosing Insert, Chart. The column and row labels can be used to label the points on the chart.

To create a chart using the Chart Expert, follow these steps:

1. Select the block you want to chart, then choose Insert, Chart. The Chart Expert - Step 1 of 5 dialog box displays (see Figure 16.2).
2. If necessary, adjust the block shown in the Chart Data text box. A preview of the chart appears on the left side of the dialog box. If you want to plot your chart data in a different order, you can select one or both of the Swap Rows/Columns and Reverse Series check boxes. The chart preview automatically updates to reflect your selections.

   In this example, Swap Rows/Columns is selected because it improves the appearance of this chart.

FIG. 16.2
Use the Chart Expert - Step 1 of 5 dialog box to create a new chart.

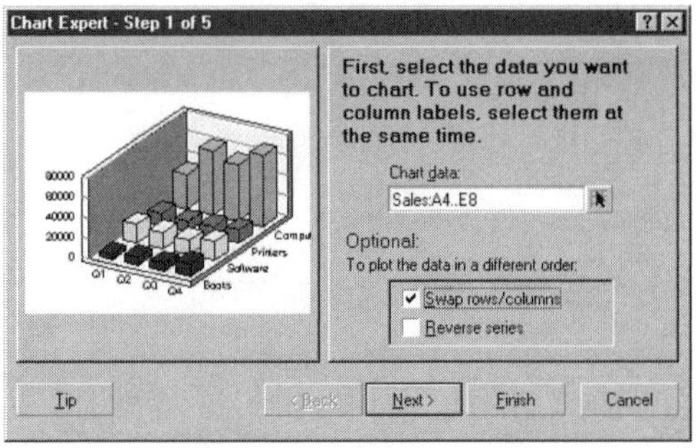

3. Click Next to display Step 2 of the Chart Expert (see Figure 16.3). Click the button representing the general chart type you want to create, such as Bar or Pie; or, if you want Quattro Pro to make this choice for you (based on the data you've selected), click the Expert's Choice button.

FIG. 16.3
Use the Chart Expert - Step 2 of 5 dialog box to choose the general chart type.

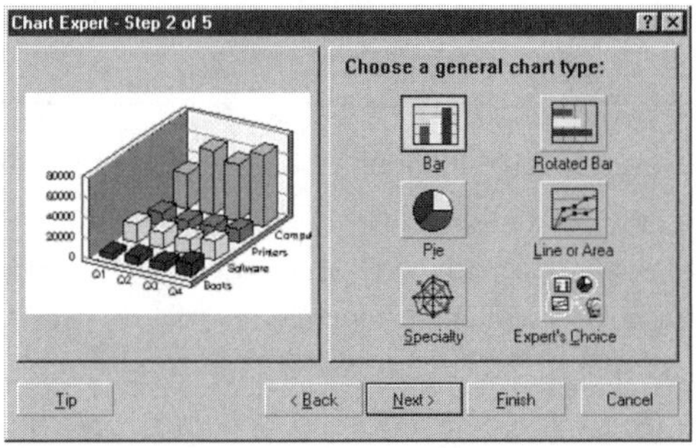

4. Click Next to display Step 3 of the Chart Expert (see Figure 16.4). Click the button representing the specific chart type you want to use. The buttons that appear vary depending on the general chart type you chose in the previous step.

FIG. 16.4
Use the Chart Expert - Step 3 of 5 dialog box to choose the specific chart type.

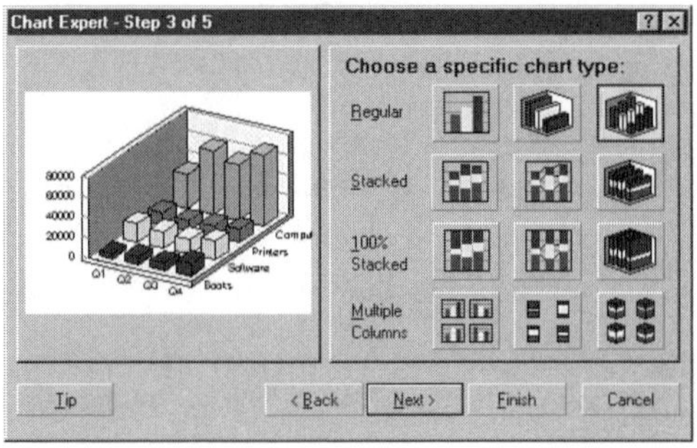

5. Click Next to display Step 4 of the Chart Expert. In the Choose a Color Scheme list box, select the color scheme you want to use in your chart. The chart preview on the left side of the dialog box shows what the selected color scheme will look like. In most cases, you may prefer to use the default colors that Quattro Pro has chosen for you.
6. Click Next to display Step 5 of the Chart Expert. If you want to include titles with your chart, type the title(s) in the appropriate text boxes (see Figure 16.5). Then choose the destination for your chart—the Current Sheet or the Chart Window.

TIP To place your chart on a separate sheet, select Chart Window; otherwise, select Current Sheet to place it on the current sheet with your data.

FIG. 16.5
Use the Chart Expert - Step 5 of 5 dialog box to type the chart titles and select the destination for the chart.

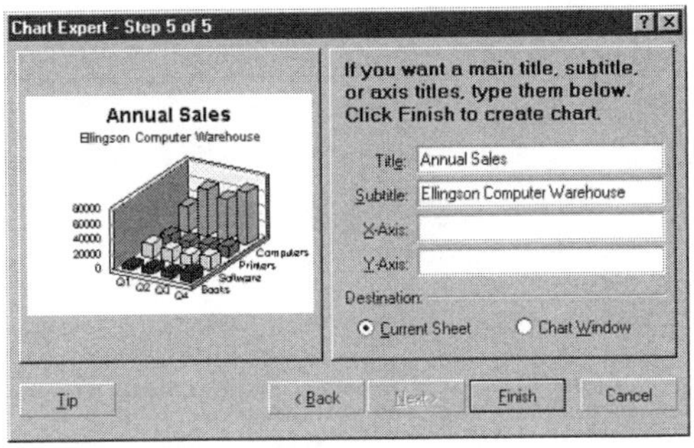

7. Click Finish. Quattro Pro displays a mouse pointer in the shape of a mini-chart. Click in the worksheet where you want the upper-left corner of the chart to appear.

   Quattro Pro places the chart in the current sheet as shown in Figure 16.6 (or in the Chart window, depending on your selection in the previous step). You learn how to modify the basic chart to improve its appearance in "Enhancing a Chart," later in this chapter.

NOTE You can easily move or resize the chart in the current sheet. To do so, click a border of the chart to select it (if it isn't already selected–black handles surround a selected chart). To resize the chart, position the mouse pointer on a black handle and drag to the desired size. To move the chart, position the mouse pointer on a border of the chart (but not on a black handle); a four-headed arrow pointer appears. Drag the chart to the desired position.

TROUBLESHOOTING

The new chart includes data I don't want to chart. Select the block you want to chart before you choose Insert, Chart. Otherwise, Quattro Pro includes the entire current block of data in the chart.

continues

continued

Most of the data values on a chart can't be determined because the Y-axis goes too high. Quattro Pro automatically scales the Y-axis to show the largest values in the chart. You may need to select a smaller data block that doesn't include the largest values, or change the chart to a 2-D chart and chart the largest values on the second Y-axis.

FIG. 16.6
The completed chart appears in the notebook.

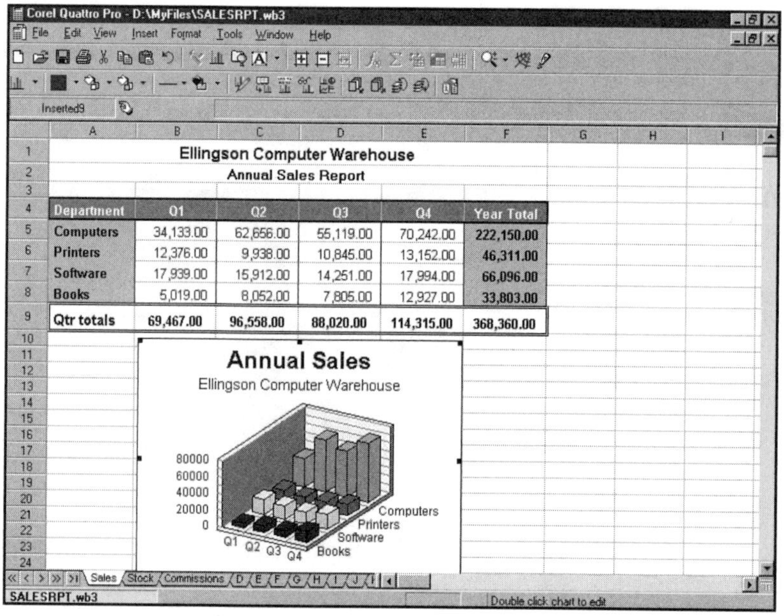

Understanding Common Chart Terms

Most charts (except for bullet charts, text charts, pie charts, and doughnut charts) have a *Y-axis* (a vertical left edge), and an *X-axis* (a horizontal bottom edge). In rotated charts, the Y-axis is the bottom edge, and the X-axis is the left edge. Quattro Pro automatically divides each axis with tick marks and scales the numbers on the Y-axis, based on the minimum and maximum numbers in the associated data block. The intersection of the Y-axis and the X-axis is called the *origin*. The origin is zero unless you specify otherwise.

A chart is made up of one or more *data series*, each of which reflects a category of data. The first category of data is always series 1, the second is series 2, and so on. Some chart types use a limited number of data series; for example, pie and doughnut charts use one data series, and XY charts use two or more. Other chart types, such as line charts, can chart multiple data series.

Legends are text placed beside or below a chart that explain the symbols, colors, or fill used to denote each data series. *Titles* are text placed above the chart and along the horizontal and vertical axis that provide information about the overall chart. *Labels* are text entries used to explain specific data items or entries in a chart.

Understanding Chart Types

Several types of charts are available in Quattro Pro: Area/Line, Bar, Stacked Bar, Pie, Specialty, and Text. Each of the chart types also offers several variations.

Selecting a Different Type of Chart

You can change a chart to a different type several different ways, but you can only change a chart's type if the chart is displayed in the Chart window, or if you first select the chart if it is displayed in a notebook.

To select a new chart type for a chart that is displayed in the Chart window or which has been selected in the notebook, point to an area in the chart outside any chart objects, and click the right mouse button. Choose Type/Layout from the QuickMenu to display the Chart Types dialog box (see Figure 16.7). You can also display this dialog box by activating the chart and choosing Chart, Type/Layout.

NOTE If your chart is displayed in the worksheet, you need to activate the chart before you can access the Chart main menu. To activate a chart, click an area in the chart that is outside any chart objects (but inside the chart border). An activated chart displays a thick border with diagonal lines. Click outside the activated chart to return to the default Quattro Pro main menu.

FIG. 16.7
Use the Chart Types dialog box to select the type of chart to display.

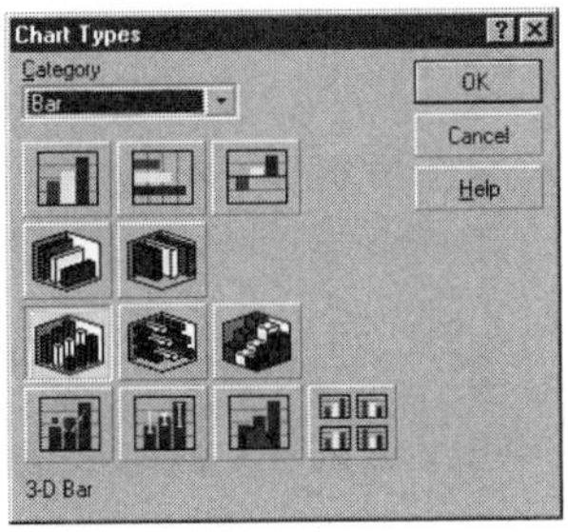

As you select each basic type of chart from the Category drop-down list box—Area/Line, Bar, Stacked Bar, Pie, Specialty, or Text—small samples of each of the optional variations are shown in the dialog box. As soon as you select a new chart type and click OK, your chart is changed to the selected type. The following sections briefly describe the basic chart types.

Understanding Variations within Chart Categories

Quattro Pro offers many different variations within the different chart categories. These include 2-D (two-dimensional) charts, 3-D (three-dimensional) charts, rotated charts, and combination charts. To make the best choice of a chart for your needs, you should understand these variations.

Understanding 2-D Charts Two-dimensional (2-D) charts are the most common type of business charts. In this chart, data is plotted using an X-axis and a Y-axis or, in the case of column and pie charts, using no axis at all. If you want to chart some data using the second Y-axis, you must use a 2-D chart.

Understanding 3-D Charts A 3-D chart plots data in a three-dimensional perspective. Instead of just using an X-axis and a Y-axis, a 3-D chart adds a Z-axis. In some cases, 3-D charts do a better job than 2-D charts of showing the complex relationships between groups of data items. You may want to experiment with the Chart, Perspective settings to change the view of 3-D charts.

Understanding Rotated Charts Sometimes you can create a more stunning visual effect by rotating a chart. *Rotated* charts place the X-data series along the left vertical axis and the Y-data series along the horizontal axis. Values are plotted as horizontal distances from the left axis instead of vertical distances from the lower axis. Don't overdo the use of rotated charts. Most people find rotated charts harder to interpret.

Understanding Combo Charts Quattro Pro enables you to mix chart types so that you can compare different sets of data. You can combine a bar chart and a line, area, or a high-low chart. You also can display multiple columns, 3-D columns, pies, 3-D pies, or bar charts. Charts that combine a bar chart and a line, area, or a high-low chart, are used to display data that is related, but that requires different types of plotting to best show different data series.

Charts that show multiple columns, pies, or bars show several different data series plotted as individual charts, but include each individual chart within a single-named chart in the notebook. When you use multiple columns or pies, each column or pie is the same size. You can compare how the data items within each data series relate as a percentage of the total of the data series, but you cannot determine the relative values of data items between series.

Understanding Area/Line Charts

Quattro Pro offers several variations on the theme of area and line charts. These include the following types.

Line Charts Line charts are the most common type of chart and one of the easiest to understand. Line charts plot values using individual lines to connect the data points for each data series.

Standard line charts plot data values using the height of the line above the bottom of the chart to indicate differences. *Rotated* line charts plot data value variations as distances from the left side of the chart.

TIP If one data set in a line chart has much higher values than the remaining data sets, consider plotting the out-of-proportion data set against the secondary Y-axis. Right-click the line plotting the data set, select Line Series Properties, and Secondary.

Area Charts Area charts emphasize broad trends. Area charts plot the first data series closest to the X-axis and stack additional data series above each other. Each data series line represents the total of the data series being plotted plus all lower data series. Area charts are filled between the origin and the plotted lines.

Area charts can also be displayed using either standard or rotated orientation, depending on your needs.

3-D Area Charts 3-D area charts are quite similar to 2-D area charts, except that 3-D area charts appear to have depth. This third dimension is not used to plot data, but rather to provide a more substantial appearance. 3-D area charts plot the first data series closest to the X-axis, and stack additional data series above each other. Each data series line represents the total of the data series being plotted plus all lower data series. 3-D area charts are filled between the origin and the plotted lines. Figure 16.8 shows a 3-D area chart of the sales data in the Chart window, after the Row/Column Swap check box in the Chart Series dialog box was selected.

TIP To change the emphasis of your chart, select the Row/Column Swap check box in the Chart Series dialog box. Right-click an empty area in your chart and select Series from the QuickMenu to display this dialog box.

3-D Unstacked Area Charts 3-D unstacked area charts plot values using lines (which are stretched to add depth) to connect the data points for each data series, while filling the area between the lines and the origin. Because larger values in a 3-D unstacked area chart can hide lower values plotted behind them, this type of chart is best suited to displaying sorted data.

Ribbon Charts Ribbon charts are similar to 3-D unstacked area charts; they plot values using lines (which are stretched to add depth) to connect the data points for each data series. Ribbon charts, however, do not fill the area between the lines and the origin. Ribbon charts are better than 3-D unstacked area charts at displaying unsorted data because larger values are less likely to hide lower values plotted behind them in a ribbon chart.

FIG. 16.8
Use 3-D area charts to emphasize trends in your data.

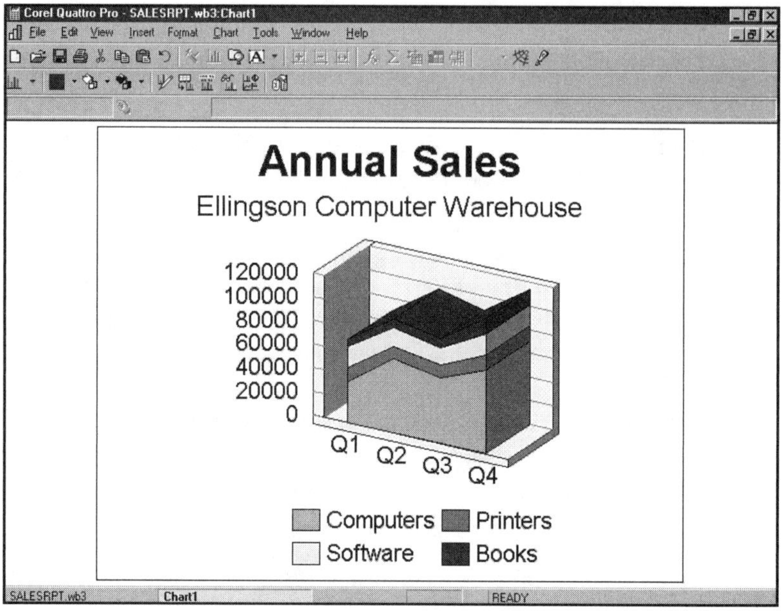

3-D Floating Marker Charts 3-D floating marker charts are also similar to 3-D unstacked area charts. Instead of using lines to connect the data points for each data series, however, small floating blocks are used to represent the data points. 3-D floating marker charts are quite good at displaying unsorted data since the floating blocks are unlikely to hide lower values plotted behind them. Figure 16.9 shows a 3-D floating marker chart of the sales data.

FIG. 16.9
The floating blocks in 3-D floating marker charts are unlikely to hide lower values plotted behind them.

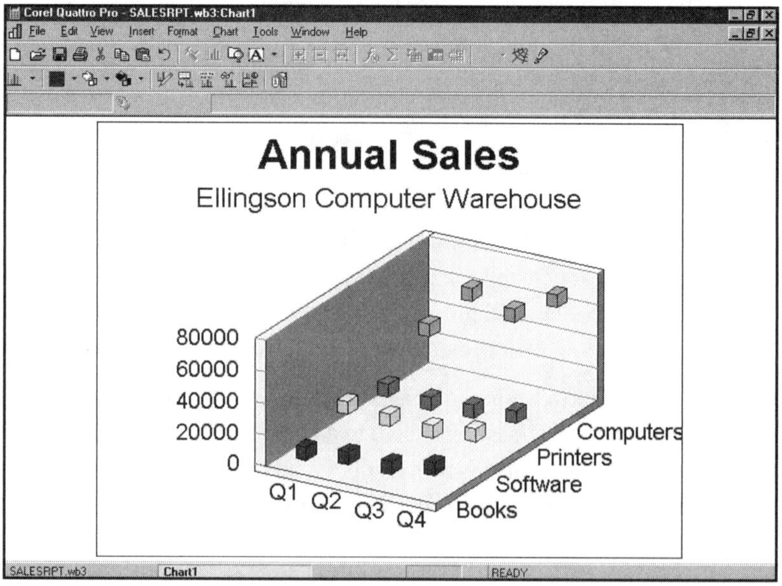

CAUTION

It may be difficult to see small differences in data values in 3-D floating marker charts.

Understanding Bar Charts

Quattro Pro offers several variations of bar charts. These include 2-D, 2.5-D, 3-D, and several combo chart types.

Bar and Rotated 2-D Bar Charts A bar chart shows data as a series of bars drawn next to each other. This type of chart is useful for showing how data categories compare over time. In addition to standard bar charts which plot data values as height above the X-axis, rotated 2-D bar charts plot data values as the distance from the left axis.

TIP In rotated charts, the left axis is the X-axis and the bottom axis is the Y-axis.

Variance Charts A variance chart is similar to a bar chart, except that the origin is adjustable to show how data varies from a specified value. Initially, a variance chart has the origin set to 0, and so the chart appears identical to a standard 2-D bar chart. After you create the basic variance chart, adjust the origin by pointing to the chart Y-axis values, clicking the right mouse button, and choosing Y-Axis Properties, or by choosing Chart, Axes, Primary Y-Axis. Select the Zero Line At text box in the Scale tab of the Y-Axis dialog box, and enter a new value for the origin. Figure 16.10 shows the sales data plotted on a variance chart with the origin adjusted to 30,000.

TIP Use variance charts to emphasize data that falls below targeted values.

2.5-D Bar Charts 2.5-D bar charts show data as a series of deep bars drawn next to each other. A 2.5-D bar chart is not a true 3-D chart, because it does not use depth to portray a Z-axis value, but instead to add a third dimension to the bars. This type of chart is useful for showing how data categories compare over time.

Rotated 2.5-D bar charts are similar to standard 2.5-D bar charts with the data plotted as distances from the left chart axis.

3-D Bar Charts 3-D bar charts show data as groups of bars plotted on a three-dimensional grid. Often a 3-D bar chart provides an easier-to-understand display of the relationship between the plotted data series than a 2-D bar chart can.

3-D bar charts can also be plotted using either standard or rotated orientation. Rotated 3-D bar charts may be more difficult to understand.

FIG. 16.10
Use a variance chart to plot data with a non-zero origin.

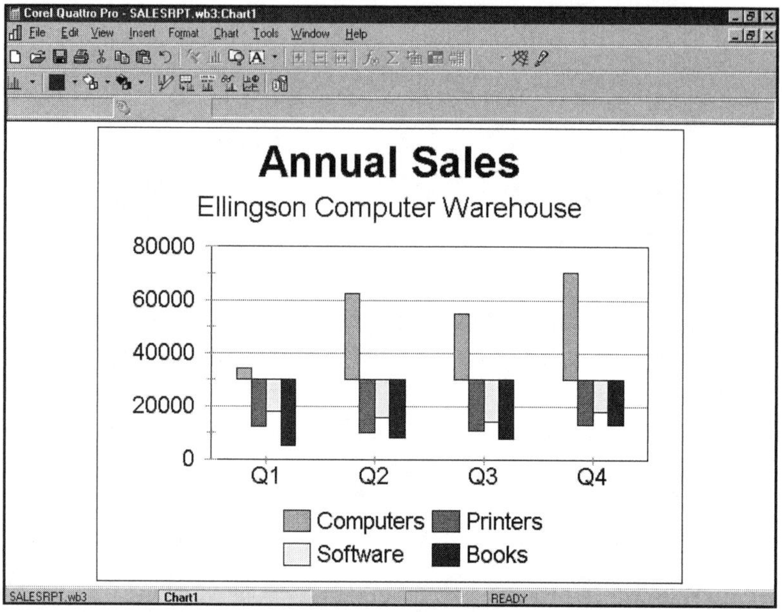

TIP A 3-D bar chart may hide smaller values behind large values. Arrange the data series with the largest values first and the smallest values last. If this is not possible, consider using a 2-D chart to prevent data from being hidden.

3-D Step Charts 3-D step charts are nearly identical to 3-D bar charts, except that the bars in a step chart touch. Step charts are most useful for displaying data that changes in regular increments, rather than data that may change abruptly in either direction. Figure 16.11 shows the sales data plotted as a 3-D step chart.

Combo Bar Charts Quattro Pro provides several types of charts that combine bars and other types of data markers:

- *Line-Bar.* Plot some data as lines and the rest as bars. This type of chart can be handy for showing trends such as temperature variations over a period of time.
- *High Low-Bar.* Plot some data using High-Low markers (see the section "Understanding Specialty Charts" later in this chapter) and some as bars. This chart variation is often used to plot stock market data.
- *Area-Bar.* Combine area charts and bar charts. These charts can be used to display data that exceeds predictions, such as sales which are higher than expected. Because the area chart typically hides bars which fall below the level of the area chart, this type of combo chart can be more difficult to use than line-bar charts.

- *Multiple-Bar.* Display each data series in a separate bar chart. Each chart uses the same scale, so large values in one data series may reduce the size of the bars in the remaining charts.

FIG. 16.11
3-D step charts use bars, which touch each other to plot data.

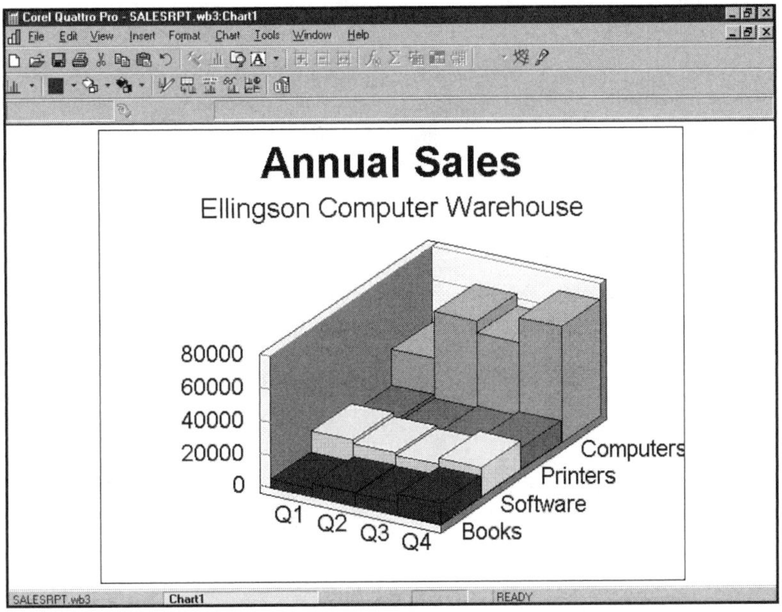

TIP All data series in multiple-bar charts are plotted against the primary Y-axis so each individual bar chart uses the same scale.

Understanding Stacked Bar Charts

Stacked bar charts are quite similar to area charts because all data is plotted together in a bar, which represents the sum of the data values. There are several variations of stacked bar charts.

Stacked Bar Charts A stacked bar chart shows data as a series of bars stacked on top of one another. This type of chart is useful for showing the portion that data categories contribute to a whole, as well as comparing changes in those contributions over time. Stacked bar charts not only show how each data item varies over time, but also how the total of all data items varies over the same time period.

Comparison charts are variations of stacked bar charts. For these chart types, the boundaries between the data segments in each bar are connected to the corresponding boundaries between the data segments in the next bar. These connecting lines can help you to spot trends more easily, but they may be difficult to understand if the bars contain too many data segments.

Both stacked bar charts and comparison charts can be displayed in standard or rotated format. Figure 16.12 shows the sales data plotted on a rotated 2-D comparison chart.

FIG. 16.12
Rotated 2-D comparison charts use lines to connect the data segments on each of the bars.

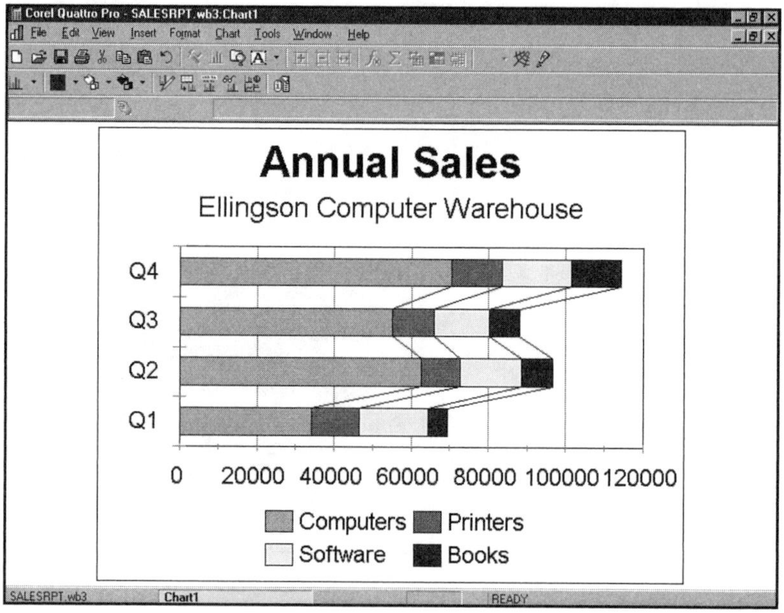

100% Stacked Bar Charts A 100% stacked bar chart is a variation of the stacked bar chart; in this type of chart, the bar is always full height, and the individual data items are shown as their percentage of 100 percent. In addition, 100% stacked bar charts quickly show percentage comparisons between the different data series.

100% stacked bar comparison charts are also a variation of stacked bar charts. For these chart types, the bar is always full height, the individual data items are shown as their percentage of 100 percent, and the boundaries between the data segments in each bar are connected to the corresponding boundaries between the data segments in the next bar.

3-D Stacked Bar Charts Similar to regular stacked bar charts, 3-D stacked bar charts work best with small amounts of data in comparing sets of data over time. A 3-D stacked bar chart shows data as a series of 3-D bars stacked on top of one another. This type of chart is useful for showing the portion that data categories contribute to a whole, as well as comparing changes in those contributions over time. 3-D stacked bar charts not only show how each data item varies over time, but also how the total of all data items varies over the same time period.

3-D 100% stacked bar charts show the data as a percentage. Both 3-D stacked bar charts and 3-D 100% stacked bar charts can use either standard or rotated orientation. Neither 3-D stacked bar charts nor 3-D 100% stacked bar charts are truly 3-D charts because neither uses the Z-axis to plot data.

Understanding Pie Charts

All pie chart variations compare values in a single set of data that contains only positive numbers. Each value appears as a slice of the pie, column, or doughnut and represents a percentage of the total. You can plot only one row or one column of numeric data in a pie chart unless you use the multiple pie or column chart options.

Each of the pie chart types can be displayed in 2-D or 3-D variations. Pie and column charts can also be plotted as multiple 2-D or 3-D charts if you need to display more than one data series.

Pie Charts Pie charts plot data as wedges or pie slices in a circular chart, with each section representing one data value. You can *explode* a pie chart section to make it stand out from the pie by right-clicking the section you want to explode, choosing Pie Chart Properties, and typing the Explode Distance as a percentage of the radius in the text box.

TIP If you attempt to plot too many data items, the wedges of the pie chart become too small to understand easily. Use column charts to plot data series with large numbers of individual items.

Doughnut Charts A doughnut chart is a variation of a pie chart; unlike a pie chart, however, a doughnut chart has a center ring cut out. You use a doughnut chart exactly as you use pie charts.

Column Charts A column chart compares values in a single set of data that contains only positive numbers. Each value appears as a section of the column and represents a percentage of the total. You can plot only one row or one column of numeric data in a single column chart. Column charts are very similar in function to pie charts, but column charts are more effective when you want to plot a large number of data items.

A *3-D column chart* compares values in a single set of data that contains only positive numbers. Each value appears as a section of the column and represents a percentage of the total. You can plot only one row or one column of numeric data in a 3-D column chart. 3-D column charts are very similar to 2-D column charts, except that the column is displayed with a third dimension: depth.

TIP Use multiple column or pie charts to plot more than one data series.

Understanding Specialty Charts

Specialty charts provide you with several chart types that can plot certain types of data more effectively than any of the other types of charts.

Understanding XY Charts The XY chart, often called a *scatter chart*, is a variation of a line chart. Like a line chart, an XY chart has values plotted as points in the chart. Unlike a line chart, an XY chart has its X-axis labeled with numeric values instead of labels.

Quattro Pro always plots the independent variable (data you can change or control) on the X-axis, and the dependent variables (data you cannot control or change, and which is dependent on the independent variable) on the Y-axis; thus, the independent data should be in the first row or column, and the dependent data should be in the second and succeeding rows or columns. Figure 16.13 shows an XY chart of the sine function for X-axis values from 0 to 360 degrees.

FIG. 16.13
XY charts plot the independent variable on the X-axis and the dependent variables on the Y-axis.

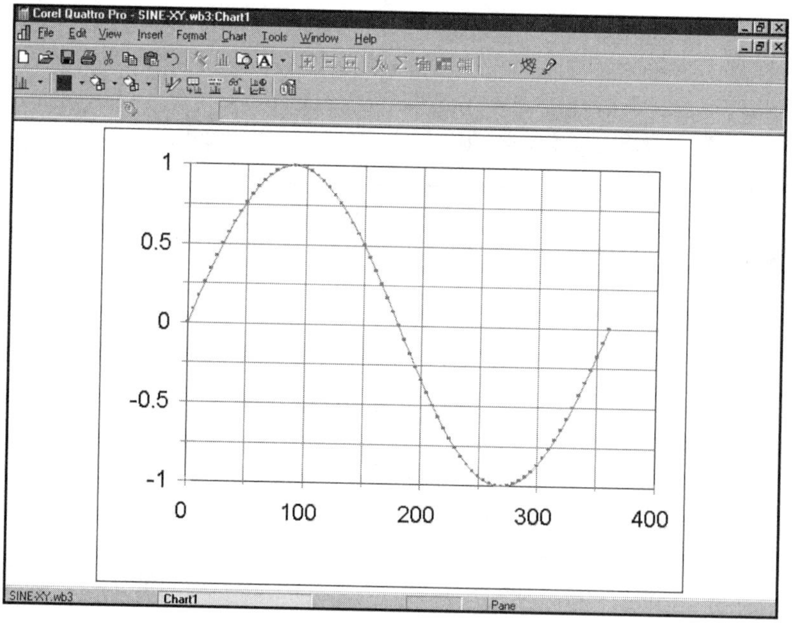

High-Low Charts High-low charts are sometimes called *HLCO charts*, which stands for *high-low-close-open*. A high-low chart is especially useful for charting data about the price of a stock over time. The HLCO figures represent the stock's highest and lowest price in the given time period, stock's price at the end of the time period, and stock's price at the start of the time period.

Each set of data normally consists of four figures representing high, low, close, and open values. The set of data is typically represented on the chart as a vertical line with tick marks. The line extends from the low value to the high value. The close value is represented by a tick mark extending to the right of the line, and the open value is represented by a tick mark extending to the left. The total number of lines on the chart depends on the number of time periods included. If you have a fifth data series, it is plotted as a volume series against the second Y-axis.

Radar Charts A radar chart plots data radiating from a single center point. X-axis values appear as spokes in a wheel, and Y-axis data is plotted on each spoke. Radar charts may make spotting trends easier, depending on the type of data being charted.

3-D Surface Charts 3-D surface charts display data as lines connecting the data items for each series. The line for each data series is connected to the line for the next data series, and the area between the lines is filled in with different colors.

3-D Contour Charts 3-D contour charts are very similar to surface charts, except in the method used to color the surface plot. Instead of coloring the segments between each set of lines with a distinct color, contour charts apply color to show how far the surface lies above the origin. Contour charts can be used to show elevations, as in contour maps.

3-D Shaded Surface Charts 3-D shaded surface charts are another variation on surface and contour charts. The shaded surface chart uses a single color to create the surface, but applies different shading to show the slope of the surface between data points. Shaded surface charts may reproduce better than surface and contour charts on black-and-white printers.

Understanding Text Charts

Text charts are unlike the other types of Quattro Pro charts because they are not used to display numerical data. There are two types of text charts: bullet charts and blank charts.

Bullet Charts Bullet charts are a special type of chart often used in presentations. Instead of charting numerical data, bullet charts display notebook text in a special format. In a bullet chart, a title line is followed by one or more levels of bulleted text, usually presenting information in an outline style format.

To create a bullet chart, you use a block of text either two or three columns wide in the notebook as the source of chart data. The first column contains the chart title, the second contains the first level of bulleted text, and the third contains an optional second level of bulleted text.

Blank Charts Blank charts are another special type of Quattro Pro chart. Instead of plotting notebook data, blank charts enable you to create graphics objects that you can place anywhere you like in a notebook. Blank charts can contain text, objects you create using the drawing tools available in the Chart window, and imported graphics.

TIP Use the Chart and Drawing Tools toolbar to draw floating objects directly on a notebook page rather than using a blank chart. That way, the chart pane won't cover your data.

You can also use the tools on the notebook window Chart and Drawing Tools toolbar to draw floating objects directly on a notebook page. Floating objects drawn on the notebook page are very similar to the objects you draw in a blank chart, except that floating objects drawn on the notebook page do not have an opaque chart pane to obscure other objects on the page. For example, if you draw an arrow directly on a notebook page, objects under the arrow's path are not covered by a rectangular box as they would be by an arrow drawn in a floating chart and then added to the page.

Enhancing a Chart

Quattro Pro offers several options for improving the appearance of your charts and producing final-quality output suitable for business presentations. After you have created the basic chart, you use the Chart menu commands to change the selection of chart blocks, types and orientation; data labels and legends; X-, Y-, and optional second Y-axes; borders and grids; colors; hatch patterns; fonts; and lines.

Changing the Chart Orientation

The initial orientation Quattro Pro selects for the rows and columns of data may not always be the optimal choice. A different chart layout may be more effective in representing your data.

By default, Quattro Pro assumes that the first row or column of your data with labels contains the X-axis labels (the labels along the bottom of the chart that group the data series in comparable sets). To change the orientation of the data series, choose Chart, Series; then select the Row/Column Swap check box in the Chart Series dialog box.

Adding Titles

When you chart data from a notebook, you can specify the titles with the Chart Expert, or after you create and view the chart. With the Chart, Titles command, you can create a Main Title, a Subtitle, an X-axis Title, a Y1-Axis Title, and a Y2-Axis Title (see Figure 16.14).

You use the Main Title and Subtitle text boxes to create the first and second titles; they appear centered above the chart, with the first title in larger type above the second title.

You use the X-Axis Title, Y1-Axis Title, and Y2-Axis Title text boxes to add titles for the chart axes. You can move the main and subtitles, but you cannot move the X- or Y-Axis titles.

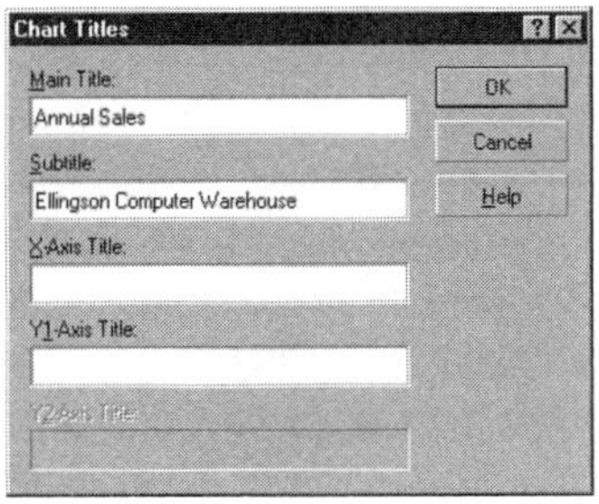

FIG. 16.14
Use the Chart Titles dialog box to add titles to your charts.

You can edit the titles and notes by choosing Chart, Titles and changing or editing the contents of the text boxes. When you have finished entering or editing the titles, click OK. You also can change the color, font, and text attributes of any title by right-clicking the title you want to change, and choosing the Title Properties option.

TIP Right-click any chart object to see the many properties you can change in your charts.

Quattro Pro offers many different options for enhancing charts. These sections have shown only a few of the possibilities. You'll also want to explore some other options such as changing the viewpoint for a 3-D chart, changing the fonts used to display text objects in a chart, and even using bitmaps (pictures) as backgrounds in your charts. To see the many possibilities, right-click an object, such as a data series, the chart background, or a title, and choose the object's Properties selection. You'll find that the resulting dialog boxes provide hundreds of options you can use to fully customize your Quattro Pro charts.

Printing Charts in the Notebook

Quattro Pro can print a chart from the Chart window or as part of a notebook sheet. In many cases, though, you'll find that adding a chart directly into a notebook sheet will be much more effective.

Whenever you plan to print a chart, you should first preview it by choosing File, Print Preview. You might, for example, find that you need to adjust the size of charts added to the notebook. Figure 16.15 shows a print preview of a notebook with a chart added to the notebook. To print the notebook and chart, click the Print button.

FIG. 16.15
A print preview of a chart added to a notebook block shows how your report will print.

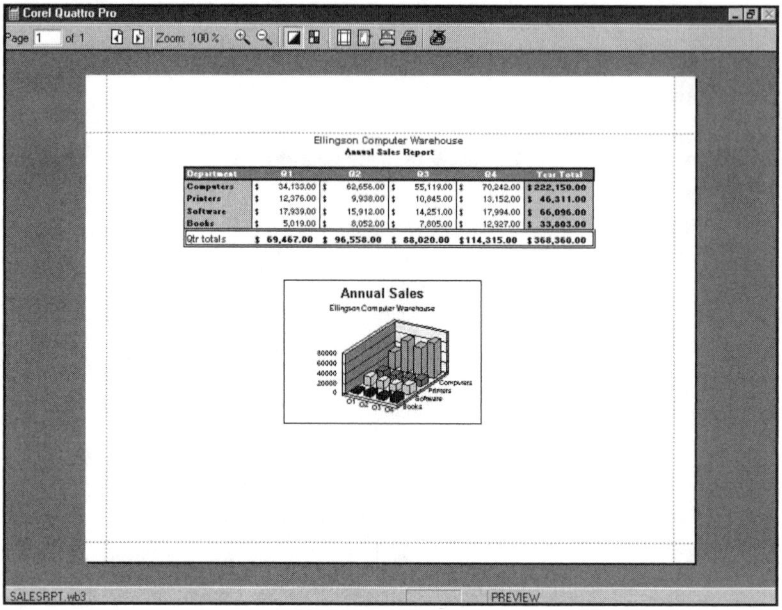

CHAPTER 17

Printing Reports

The final step in creating a useful Corel Quattro Pro notebook is to produce an effective, printed report. This step enables you to make good use of the data in your notebook and database files by sharing it with other people. This chapter introduces the commands and procedures you use to print Quattro Pro reports.

Print reports

Learn how to print your Corel Quattro Pro reports using the printing commands.

Preview reports

See how you can view your reports in print preview mode so that you can discover and correct any problems before printing them.

Enhance reports

Learn how to improve your reports with headers and footers.

Control print margins

Learn to exercise more control over the final appearance of your reports by using the margin setting options.

Select your printer

See how to choose between the available printers on your system.

Setting Up a Report

Setting up a report in Quattro Pro can be quite simple. A very basic report, for example, requires only a few mouse clicks or commands to print. Usually, though, an effective report is a little more thought out. Quattro Pro has many options that enable you to customize your printed reports so that they look professional and convey the information properly.

The following sections show you how to print reports quickly and efficiently. Whether your report is a short report of a page or less or a longer multiple-page report, you'll find the process is quite similar.

Selecting the Print Block

If you don't specify a block to print, Quattro Pro automatically sets the entire *active area* of the current notebook sheet as the print block, so it's important to understand how Quattro Pro determines the active area of a notebook sheet. The active area of a sheet is defined as the rectangular area between cell A1 and the intersection of the last column and the last row that contain entries. Figure 17.1 demonstrates how this works. In this figure, the active area extends from A1 to E14. Cell E14 does not contain any data, but is at the intersection of the last column and the last row used in the notebook. If you print the notebook shown in Figure 17.1, but don't specify a print block, Quattro Pro will print the block A1..E14.

Printing a Single Block If you preselect a block, the selected block becomes the print block. When a print block has been specified, Quattro Pro remembers the specified block and uses the same block as the print block unless you specify a different block. If you forget to preselect the block to print, you can specify the block in the Selection text box of the Spreadsheet Print dialog box. You can select the block with the mouse or the keyboard, or you can type the block addresses.

TIP If you don't want to print the entire active area of the notebook, be sure to preselect the desired print block.

To print a specified print block, follow these steps:

1. Select the block you want to print.

2. Choose File, Print or click the Print a notebook or chart button to display the Spreadsheet Print dialog box (see Figure 17.2).
3. Select the Print tab if necessary, and then click Print.

FIG. 17.1
Quattro Pro automatically prints the active area of the current sheet if you don't specify a block.

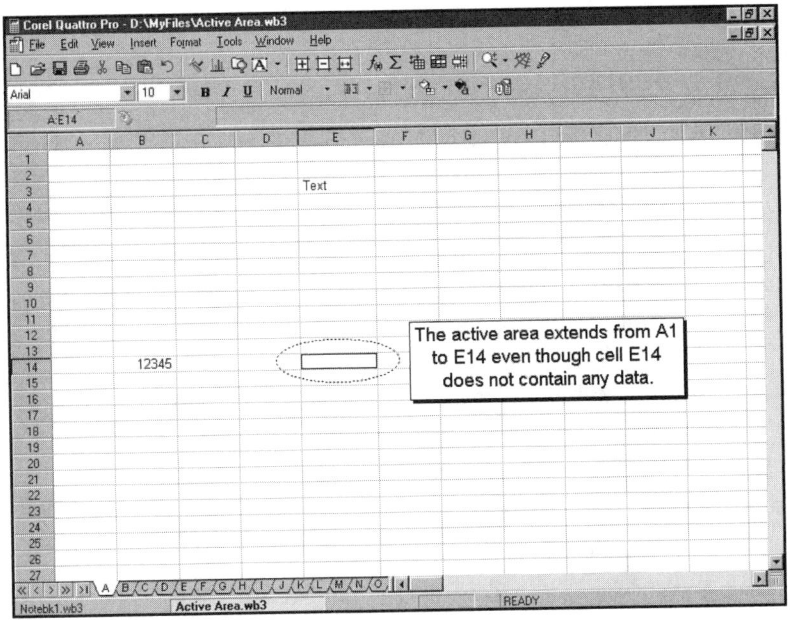

TIP If your printer doesn't print in color, be sure the Adjust Image To Print Black And White check box on the Details tab is selected before you print.

FIG. 17.2
Use the Spreadsheet Print dialog box to specify what you want to print.

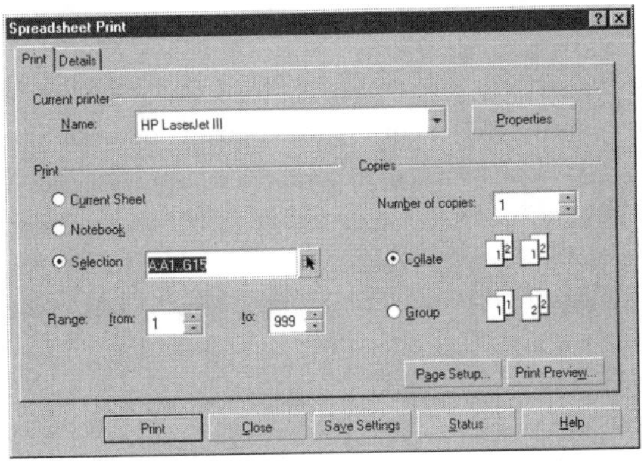

TROUBLESHOOTING

Even though the correct print block is selected, text is cut off when a report prints. Long labels can spill over into empty cells to the right. If a label spills over to a cell outside the print block, only the text within the block is printed. Extend the print block to the right to include all the text, or adjust the width of the rightmost column of the print area to include the entire label.

The printed report includes blank pages. If the print area selection is Notebook, all pages will print even if some pages are blank. Use the Selection text box to specify the exact areas to print.

Printing Multiple Blocks For many reports, a two-dimensional block—a single rectangular area on one notebook sheet—is all you need to print. Sometimes, though, you may need to print three-dimensional blocks or multiple two-dimensional blocks contained on one or more notebook sheets.

A three-dimensional print block includes the same block on two or more notebook sheets. You specify a three-dimensional print block by preselecting the block or by entering the block address or name in the Selection text box of the Spreadsheet Print dialog box—the same way you specify a two-dimensional block. After you have selected the block on the first sheet, hold down the Shift key and click the notebook sheet tabs to move to the final sheet of the block. When you have selected a three-dimensional block, Quattro Pro draws a thick line under the sheet tabs to show the sheets that are included in the block.

See "Using Blocks," **p. 251**

Multiple print blocks are two or more blocks that may be on the same or different notebook sheets. You can use multiple print blocks when you want to print part of the information on a sheet, but you don't want to include certain information that may be between the blocks you do want to print. To specify multiple print blocks, select the first block, then press and hold down the Ctrl key while you select additional blocks. To type the names or addresses of multiple print blocks, enter the first block name or address in the Selection text box of the Spreadsheet Print dialog box, type a comma, and type the next block.

TIP When you specify multiple print blocks, previewing the printed output is always a good idea, so you may want to choose File, Print Preview; or File, Print, Print Preview. Press Esc or click the Close the Print Preview window button to close Print Preview.

Figure 17.3 shows a notebook with two print blocks selected, and Figure 17.4 shows the result of selecting File, Print Preview to preview the printed output. Press Esc to return to the notebook display.

FIG. 17.3
If you want to print only selected areas of your notebook, preselect the print blocks before printing.

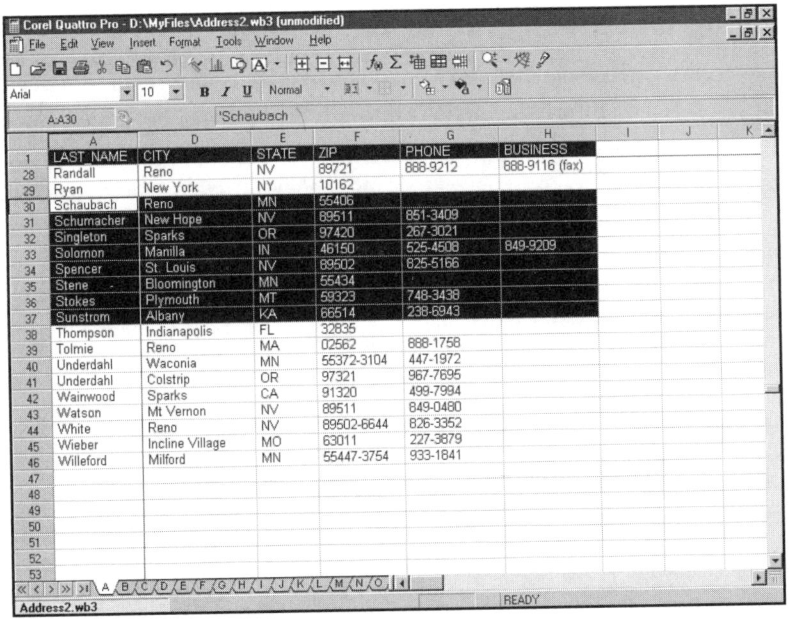

FIG. 17.4
Print Preview shows that the printed report will contain only the preselected print blocks.

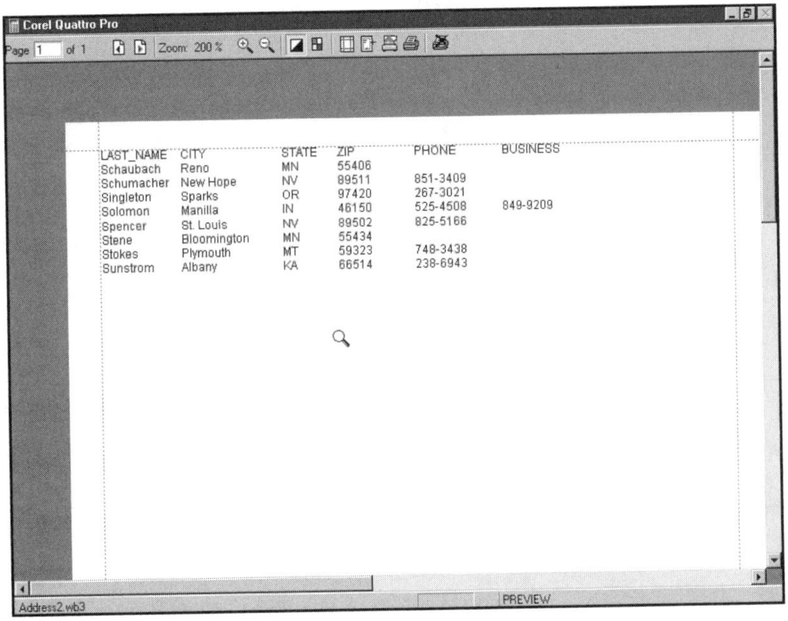

You can specify any combination of two- and three-dimensional print blocks. Quattro Pro prints the blocks in the order that you select the blocks or enter the block names or addresses.

Adding Enhancements to the Report

You can use Quattro Pro's options to enhance your reports in many different ways. You select many printing options through the Spreadsheet Page Setup dialog box, which displays when you choose File, Page Setup or File, Print, Page Setup. The Spreadsheet Page Setup dialog box includes tabs for specifying paper type, a header and footer, margins, print scaling, named print settings, and other options (see Figure 17.5).

NOTE Use the Save Defaults button to save your settings so that Quattro Pro will automatically use them in the future. Use the Load Defaults button to return all settings to their default settings.

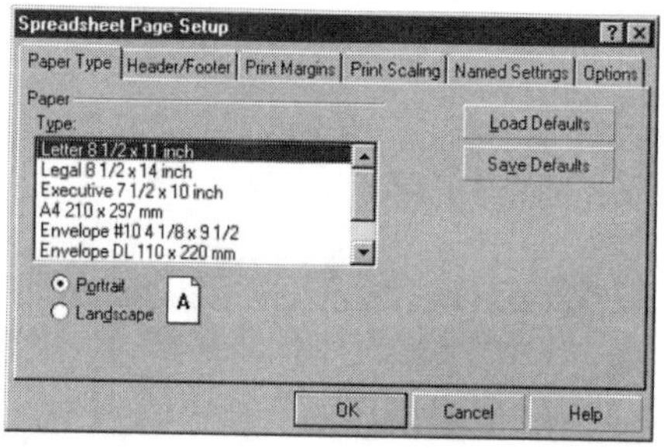

FIG. 17.5
Use the Spreadsheet Page Setup dialog box Paper Type tab to specify the size and orientation of your paper.

Selecting the Type of Paper The Paper Type tab of the Spreadsheet Page Setup dialog box shown in Figure 17.5 enables you to select the type of paper and whether the report will print in Portrait or Landscape orientation. The Portrait selection prints with the paper tall and narrow; the Landscape selection prints with the paper short and wide. The Type list box displays the paper sizes available for the selected printer.

NOTE You may have to change the paper in your printer if you select a different paper size. The Type list shows the paper sizes your printer can use, not the sizes loaded into your printer.

Printing a Header or Footer A *header* is information printed in one or two lines at the top of each page of a report. A *footer* is information printed in one or two lines at the bottom of each page of a report. You specify a header or footer in the Spreadsheet Page Setup dialog box Header/Footer tab (see Figure 17.6).

TIP Include the name of your Quattro Pro notebook in the header or footer to make it easy to remember which notebook produced the report.

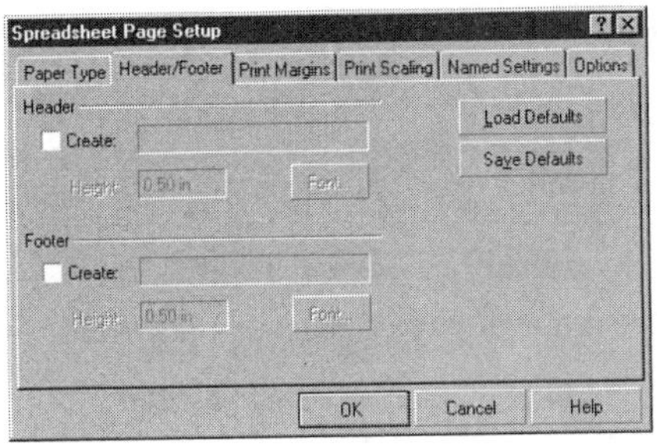

FIG. 17.6
Use the Spreadsheet Page Setup dialog box Header/Footer tab to specify report headers and footers.

Each line of a header or footer can have up to three parts: a left-aligned, a centered, and a right-aligned section. When you enter header or footer text, separate the segments with a vertical bar (|). Segments that precede the first vertical bar are left-aligned; segments following the first vertical bar but preceding the second vertical bar are centered; and segments following the second vertical bar are right-aligned. To place the remaining segments of the header or footer on a second line, use **#n** in the header or footer at the point where you want to create the line break.

Table 17.1 describes the symbols you use to display information in headers and footers. You also can instruct Quattro Pro to include the contents of a cell by entering a backslash (\) followed by the cell address or block name.

Table 17.1 Header and Footer Formatting Symbols

Symbol	Description
#	Current page number
#d	Current date in Short International format
#D	Current date in Long International format
#ds	Current date in standard Short format
#Ds	Current date in standard Long format
#f	Notebook name
#F	Notebook name with path
#n	Prints balance of text on new line
#p	Current page number
#P	Total number of pages in printout
#p+*n*	Current page number plus the number *n*

continues

Table 17.1 Continued

Symbol	Description
#P+*n*	Total number of pages in printout plus the number *n*
#t	Current time in Short International format
#T	Current time in Long International format
#ts	Current time in standard Short format
#Ts	Current time in standard Long format
@	Current date
|	Left-, center-, or right-aligned text

Setting Print Margins Print margins are the distance between the edges of the paper and the beginning of the area where Quattro Pro can print. The Spreadsheet Page Setup dialog box Print Margins tab enables you to change margins (see Figure 17.7).

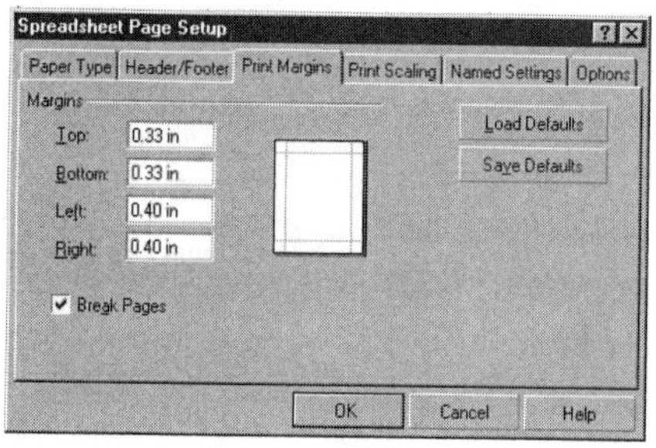

FIG. 17.7
Use the Spreadsheet Page Setup dialog box Print Margins tab to specify the size of margins.

TIP Most laser and inkjet printers cannot print to the edge of a sheet of paper. See your printer manual to determine the minimum acceptable margins. If you are outside the printable margin, you will usually get a message box alerting you.

By default, Quattro Pro reserves a margin that cannot be used for any printing: 0.33 inches at the top and at the bottom of each page, and 0.4 inches at each side of the page. In addition, another 0.5 inches are reserved between the top and bottom margins and any data for headers or footers.

The Spreadsheet Page Setup dialog box Print Margins tab contains four different text boxes you can use to set the page margins: Top, Bottom, Left, and Right.

Use the Break Pages check box to specify whether Quattro Pro should print continuously, regardless of margin settings, or start new pages on a new sheet observing the margin settings. This option applies only to printers using continuous forms that can print to the edge of the paper. If the Break Pages check box is not checked, any header will print only on the first page, and any footer will print only on the final page.

TIP Quattro Pro 8 includes a new Page view that displays your notebook sheets the way they will look when printed. To access this view, choose View, Page. While in Page view, you can change margins on-screen by dragging the dotted blue lines to the desired location. In addition, you can move hard page breaks by dragging the solid blue lines that separate each page.

You also can access the Page Setup dialog box while in Page view by double-clicking in the margin area. To return to the normal view when you are finished, choose View, Draft.

Setting Print Scaling You can reduce or enlarge the size of a printed report by using *print scaling*. This option enables you to specify an exact percentage, or to have Quattro Pro automatically reduce the size of the print enough to fit the entire report on the number of pages you specify. You use the Print Scaling tab of the Spreadsheet Page Setup dialog box to specify print scaling (see Figure 17.8).

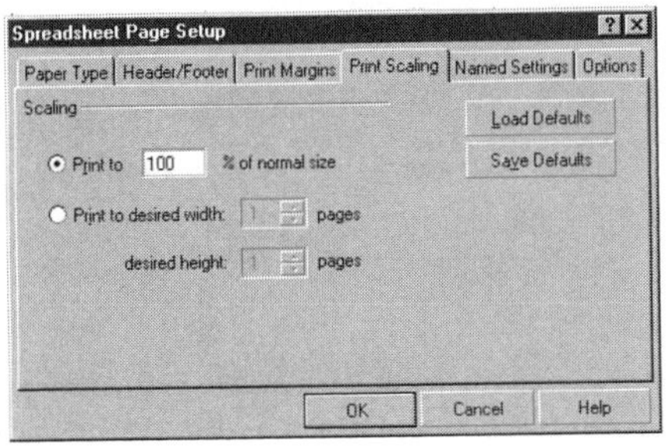

FIG. 17.8 Use the Spreadsheet Page Setup dialog box Print Scaling tab to reduce or enlarge the scale of the printed report.

TIP If you use Print to Desired Width and Desired Height, choose File, Print Preview before printing to preview the printed report. This enables you to verify that the report will not be reduced to an unreadable size.

To fit all the printed output on a specified number of pages, select the Print to Desired Width and Desired Height option. Then type the number of pages for the width and height, or use the spin boxes to select the number of pages you want. Quattro Pro attempts to reduce the size of the print enough to fit the entire report on a single page. If the report still doesn't fit a single page, Quattro Pro uses the maximum compression on all pages.

To control the exact level of compression, select the Print to % of Normal Size option and enter a percentage in the text box. To reduce the size of print by one-half, for example, type **50** in the text box. You can expand the print also by entering a number larger than 100. To print the report three times the normal size, type **300** in the text box.

TROUBLESHOOTING

Reports printed using Print to Desired Width and Desired Height print much too small, and leave large blank spaces at the right or the bottom of the page. Be sure to specify the print block. Quattro Pro is probably printing the entire active area of the current notebook page.

Even though the correct print area is specified, the printed report is still too small to read. You may need to specify an exact percentage in the Print to % of Normal Size check box rather than using the Print to Desired Width and Desired Height option. Your report may require more pages, but at least you'll be able to read it without a magnifying glass.

Using Named Print Settings You can save current print settings under a unique name, recall the settings with this name, and reuse the settings without specifying each setting individually. You use the Named Settings tab in the Spreadsheet Page Setup dialog box to create or use named print settings (see Figure 17.9).

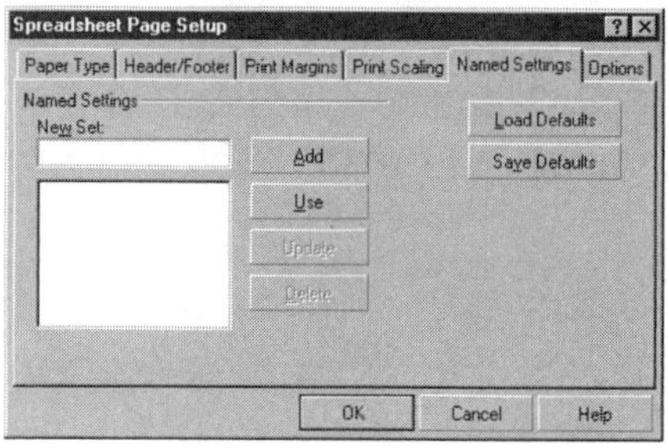

FIG. 17.9
Use the Spreadsheet Page Setup dialog box Named Settings tab to save or reuse groups of print settings.

To assign a name to the current print settings, enter the name in the New Set text box and select Add. This will enable you to reuse the same group of print settings without going through all the steps to select each option. To change an existing named print setting, highlight the setting you want to change, and select Update. To remove a named setting, select the setting you want to remove, and select Delete. To use an existing named setting, highlight the setting you want to use, and select Use.

Printing Row and Column Headings Multiple-page reports can be difficult to understand. This is especially true when you cannot easily determine the correct column or row for data on pages after the first page. One improvement that can make multiple-page reports easier to understand is to include row or column headings, so each printed page includes the descriptive text that explains the data being presented. Setting headings in a printout has an effect similar to freezing titles on a notebook sheet.

CAUTION

Don't include any rows you designate as a Top Heading and any columns you designate as a Left Heading in the print block—they'll be printed twice.

You use the Options tab in the Spreadsheet Page Setup dialog box to include row or column headings (see Figure 17.10). For the Top Heading, select one or more rows of labels to print above each page of data. For the Left Heading, select one or more columns of data to print at the left of each page of data.

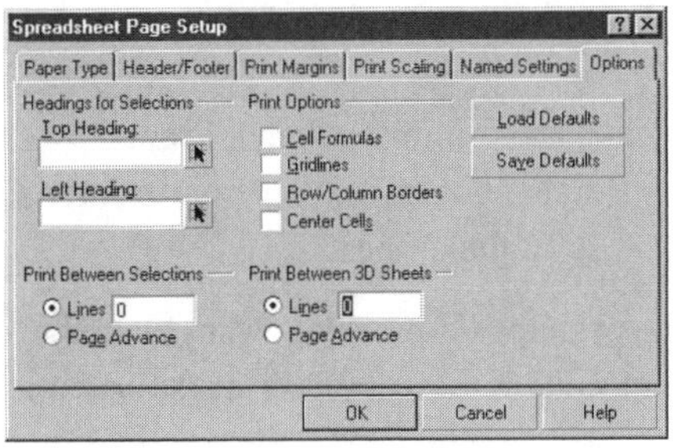

FIG. 17.10 Use the Options tab of the Spreadsheet Page Setup dialog box to specify row or column headings and several other print options.

Using Additional Print Options The Spreadsheet Print Options dialog box has several additional settings you can use to enhance your printed reports. These include:

- *Cell Formulas.* Prints cell formulas instead of the calculated results. This option is primarily for notebook documentation purposes.
- *Gridlines.* Prints the spreadsheet gridlines. This makes your report look more like the on-screen notebook sheet.
- *Row/Column Borders.* Includes the spreadsheet frame in your printed report. This is useful when you are developing a notebook, because the printouts show the location of data on the notebook sheet.
- *Center Cells.* Prints the report centered between the page margins.

You use the Print Between Selections and Print Between 3D Sheets options to specify the separation you want between multiple or 3-D blocks.

Selecting Your Printer

To select or configure a printer, or to redirect print output to a file, choose File, Print, and then click the Details tab (see Figure 17.11). The available choices that appear in the Name drop-down list depend on your system configuration.

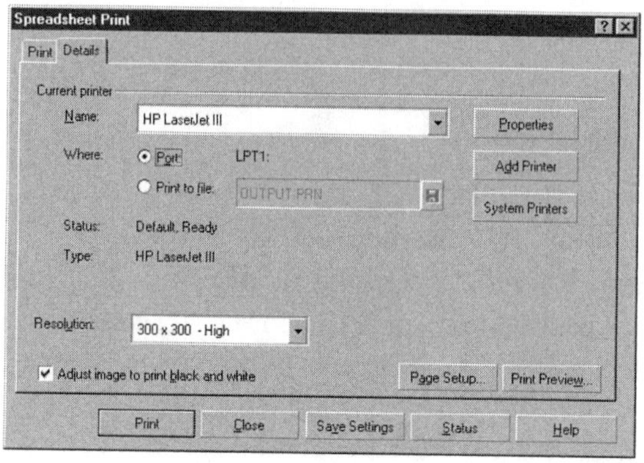

FIG. 17.11
Use the Details tab of the Spreadsheet Print dialog box to select your printer.

To configure your printer, select the printer and click Properties. When you make this selection, Windows displays a dialog box specific to your printer. Click OK to return to the Details tab of the Spreadsheet Print dialog box.

If you want to delay printing, perhaps because you want to create a report you'll print on a printer that is temporarily unavailable, select the Print to File option and specify a name for the print file. The print file will contain instructions specific to the selected printer and will probably not print correctly on any other type of printer.

PART IV

Using Corel Presentations

CHAPTER 18

Getting Started with Corel Presentations

This chapter introduces Corel Presentations 8, a program you can use to create professional quality overhead, paper, 35mm slide, or on-screen presentations. In this chapter, you learn how to start Corel Presentations 8 and create a slide show. You also learn the basic steps to entering and editing slide information, and a variety of ways to view the slide screen. ■

Start a new presentation

Learn about the Corel Presentations 8 screen and how to allow Presentations to walk you through the process of creating a new presentation.

Change views of the Corel Presentations 8 screen

See how you can zoom the presentation, show it in Draft mode if you have a slower computer, or show margins on your drawing window.

Use Outliner to create a presentation

Learn about Outliner view and how it permits you to type text into Corel Presentations 8, just as if you had a steno pad. Understand how to specify whether the text is automatically formatted as bullet slides or other slide types.

View slides in the Slide Editor

Find out how the Slide Editor allows you to select individual elements of your slide and format them, or add new slide elements as needed.

Arrange slides for a presentation

Learn to rearrange your slide show or specify transition effects if you are showing the presentation electronically using these two views.

Starting Corel Presentations 8

You start Corel Presentations 8 like you start any of the applications in Corel WordPerfect Suite 8—by clicking the Start button, then choosing Corel WordPerfect Suite 8, Corel Presentations 8 from the menu. Additionally, you can start Corel Presentations 8 from the Corel WordPerfect Suite 8 DAD (Desktop Application Director) by clicking the Corel Presentations 8 button on the taskbar.

The Corel Presentations 8 screen displays the PerfectExpert New dialog box that puts you to work immediately. You can create a new presentation drawing or a slide show, build one based on a template, or work on another existing document or project.

If you choose to create a new slide show, Presentations helps you by letting you choose a master slide format made up of various colors, patterns, and graphic lines that make your slides attractive and professional looking. The master slide style also defines the contents of each slide—bullets, charts, or text, for example—and how each element is to be displayed.

NOTE If you want to create a drawing such as a poster, a graphic image, or a sign, choose Presentations Drawing from the list. In fact, when you choose Insert, Graphics, Draw Picture in WordPerfect, Presentations becomes the tool you use to draw the picture. For information on how to use Presentations for drawing, see Chapter 20, "Adding and Enhancing Objects."

Selecting a Presentation

When you start Corel Presentations 8, the New dialog box appears, as shown in Figure 18.1. From this dialog box, choose to Create New project or to Work On an existing document or project.

FIG. 18.1
You can choose to open or create a file, set preferences, or exit the program in the New dialog box.

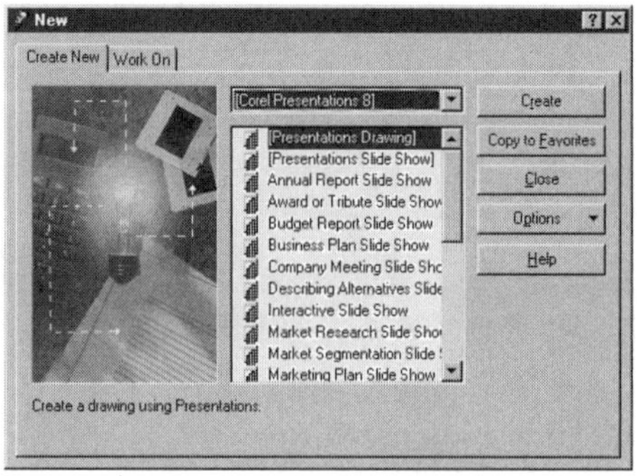

Among the options available to you for creating a new project are:

- *Presentations Drawing.* You can create posters, signs, banners, flyers, and even your own clip art images.
- *Presentations Slide Show.* This option enables you to combine text, graphics, and charts with attractive backgrounds and color schemes to produce professional slides, electronic presentations, or printed handouts.
- *PerfectExpert Projects.* You can choose from several predefined PerfectExpert projects, each of which helps you through the process of creating a specific type of presentation document.

To begin a new project, simply click the project type you want to create and choose Create.

Using the Master Gallery

If you choose to create a new slide show, Presentations first takes you to the Startup Master Gallery dialog box where you can choose the background for all the slides in your slide show (see Figure 18.2).

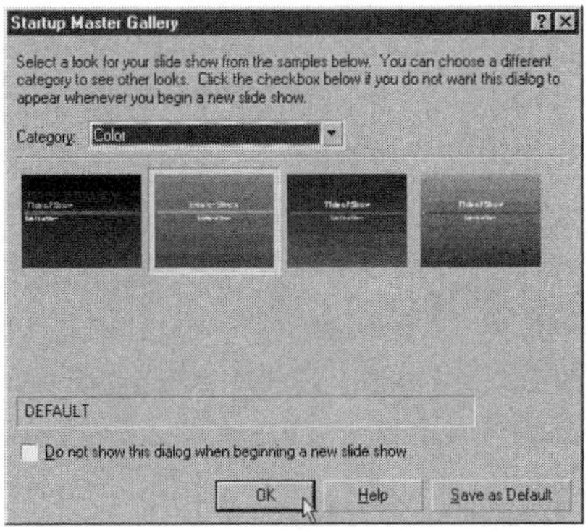

FIG. 18.2
In the Startup Master Gallery dialog box, you choose the master that Corel Presentation will use consistently throughout all your slides.

A *master* is a background for the slide show that you can apply to one or all slides. Normally, you apply the same master to all slides in the show to create consistency in the presentation. Although you can create your entire show using the default background and change that background later, you may prefer to choose a different background before you begin.

While in the Startup Master Gallery, you can:

1. Choose one of the master styles you see displayed on the screen.

   Additionally, the dialog box contains two important option buttons you can use:

   - *Category.* Choose to see the set of masters appropriate to your presentation mode: Color, Design, Nature, Theme, or Business (for color printers and electronic presentations), Printout (for printing with black-and-white printers), and 35mm (for sending to a slide service).
   - *Browse.* Look at the Insert Master dialog box and browse to a masters file you would like to open.

2. Choose a master from the Master Gallery and click OK. The Master Gallery dialog box closes and takes you to the main Presentations editing screen where you can begin work on your slide show (see Figure 18.3). If you change your mind later, you can always change the master while working on a slide show by choosing Format, Master Gallery, and then by using this same simple process.

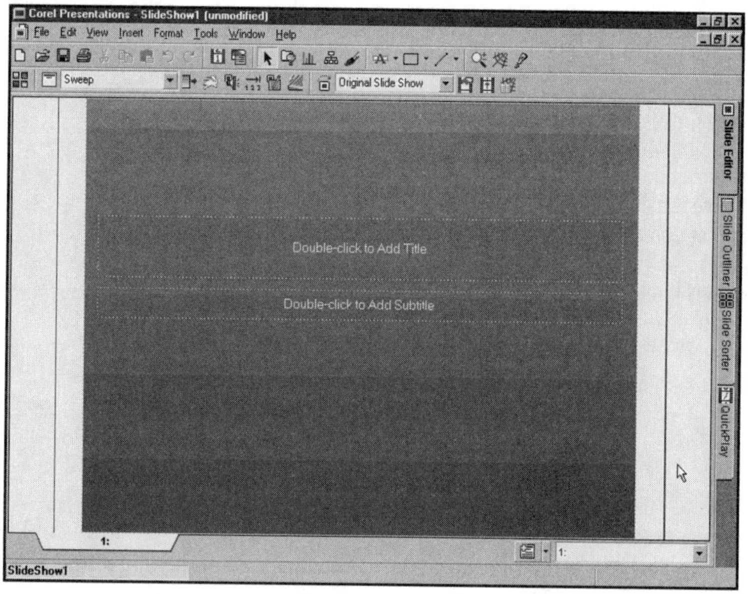

FIG. 18.3
Presentations starts your slide show with a default background and layout style, including title, subtitle, and so on.

NOTE In this and other chapters on Presentations, keep in mind that we are talking about artistic creativity—something that is up to you, the creator. Although we can make suggestions, you should always feel free to experiment with shapes, colors, or layouts, and to ultimately decide what looks and works best for you.

Selecting a Slide Layout

You next choose the slide layout or template you want to use for the first slide. When you click the Select Layout button on the Slide Show Property Bar, a pop-up list appears, as shown in Figure 18.4.

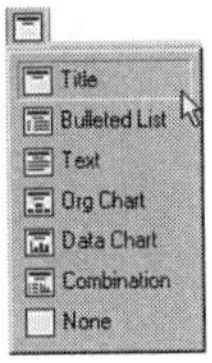

FIG. 18.4
You can choose from among seven slide layouts or templates for your first slide from the Select Layout pop-up list.

Select a slide type. Table 18.1 describes the slide types.

Table 18.1 Slide Types

Type	Description
Title	Background with formatted area for a title and subtitle.
Bulleted List	Background with formatted area for a title, subtitle, and a list of bulleted text.
Text	Background with formatted area for a title and paragraph text.
Org Chart	Background with formatted area for a title and an organizational chart.
Data Chart	Background with formatted area for a title and a data chart.
Combination	Background with formatted area for a bulleted list and a data chart.
None	Background colors and lines only, no text boxes.

Click the type of slide you want to use, and Presentations applies the layout to the slide on-screen.

NOTE When you first create a *drawing*, the screen that is brought up automatically is blank, like a white sheet of paper ready for you to fill with your ideas. When you create a *slide show*, you normally work with a background of some sort. To choose to have no background at all, similar to the draw screen, you must choose Format, Slide Properties, Appearance; click the blank background; and choose OK. You still have to choose a slide layout, even when you have no background. ■

TIP The slide layout you choose applies only to the first slide; you select each additional slide's layout each time you add a slide. The background, on the other hand, remains the same for all slides.

Viewing the Corel Presentations 8 Screen

The Corel Presentations 8 screen includes many screen elements to help you complete your work. In addition to the common Windows 95 features—title bar, menu bar, minimize/maximize buttons, and so on—Corel Presentations 8 offers a toolbar and a Property Bar to help you perform commands quickly, format your presentation, add elements, and move around your presentation with ease.

In addition to screen elements that help you in your work, Presentations offers a variety of views, or *zooms*, that enable you to look at your work in the best view for you. Although the default view is Full Page or Slide view, you can, for example, zoom into a specific part of the slide for a closer look. Figure 18.5 shows the Corel Presentations 8 screen in Full Page view, with the screen elements labeled, including the optional Tool palette.

FIG. 18.5
Initially, you see the first slide in Slide view, which is valuable for selecting and editing specific elements on a slide. The Tool palette does not display initially.

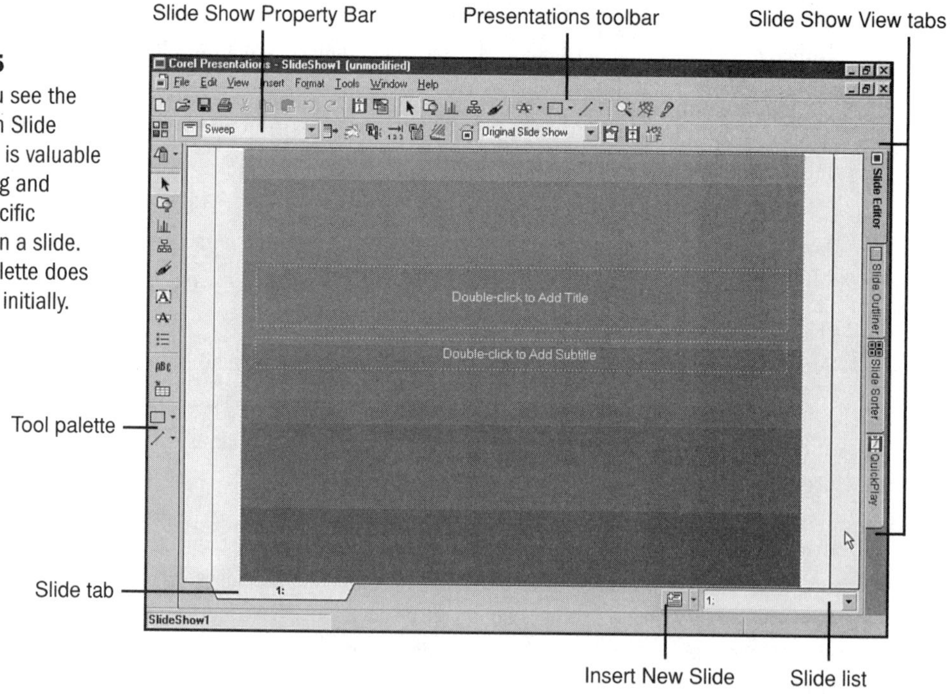

Using the Toolbar, Property Bar, and Tool Palette

The various icon bars and tabs on the Corel Presentations 8 screen help you complete your work by providing formatting, command, and navigating shortcuts you use every day in your work. By using the Slide Tabs, for example, you can move quickly to any slide in the presentation; the Property Bar can be used to change the slide layout type; and so on.

Toolbar Table 18.2 identifies the toolbar icons, or *buttons*, specific to Corel Presentations 8, and describes their uses.

Table 18.2 Toolbar Buttons

Button	Name	Function
	Play Show	Displays the Play Slide Show dialog box; choose Show Options and play the show.
	Slide Appearance	Defines the slide layout, background, and other properties.
	Selection Tool	Selects objects.
	ClipArt	Inserts a clip art image.
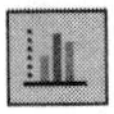	Chart	Inserts a data chart.
	Organization Chart	Inserts an organization chart.
	Bitmap	Creates a bitmapped graphic object.
	Text Object Tools	Creates an area in which you can place one or more lines of text.
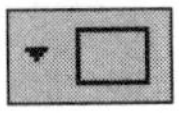	Closed Object Tools	Adds graphics shapes such as rectangles, circles, arrows, or polygons.
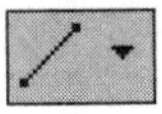	Line Object Tools	Adds open lines, arcs, or bezier curves.
	Zoom Options	Choose how much of your screen you want to see.
	Web Browser	Launches your Web browser to access the Internet or your local intranet.
	PerfectExpert	Help feature that displays on the left side of the screen and assists you through the slide show creation process.

Property Bar The *Property Bar,* located directly below the toolbar, also enables you to format text and other objects, and edit slides. However, it is quite different from the toolbar in that it changes automatically to offer you tools that match whatever you happen to be working on. There are some 20 different Property Bars, and more than 100 different icons. Figure 18.1, shown in the next section, illustrates the basic slide show Property Bar.

TIP If you're not sure what a button on the Property Bar actually does, simply point at the button with the mouse, and after a second or so, a Quick Tip box appears describing the name and purpose of the button.

Tool Palette The *Tool palette* (refer to Figure 18.6) is another set of tools you can use while creating your slide show. To activate the Tool palette, choose View, Toolbars and from the Toolbars dialog box, choose Tool palette. The Tool palette displays along the left side of the screen. Many buttons on the toolbar also appear on the Tool palette, but you also find additional buttons such as a special Graphics menu, separate text tools, and buttons to insert bulleted lists, TextArt, or spreadsheets.

By itself, the Graphics button, which enables you to manipulate various graphic objects on your screen, makes it worth displaying the Tool palette. To use this button, click it and choose from the menu of choices that appear.

The Selection tool enables you to click graphic objects on the screen to select and manipulate them.

To use the next seven tools—ClipArt, Chart, Org Chart, Bitmap, Text Box, Text Line, and Bulleted List—click the button, then use the mouse to drag an area where you want to insert the type of object you have chosen.

The next two buttons—Text Art and Insert Spreadsheet—actually start up other programs that create special objects to add to your slide show.

Finally, the Closed Objects and Line Objects tools enable you first to select an object type by clicking the drop-down arrow on the right of the icon button (see Figure 18.6).

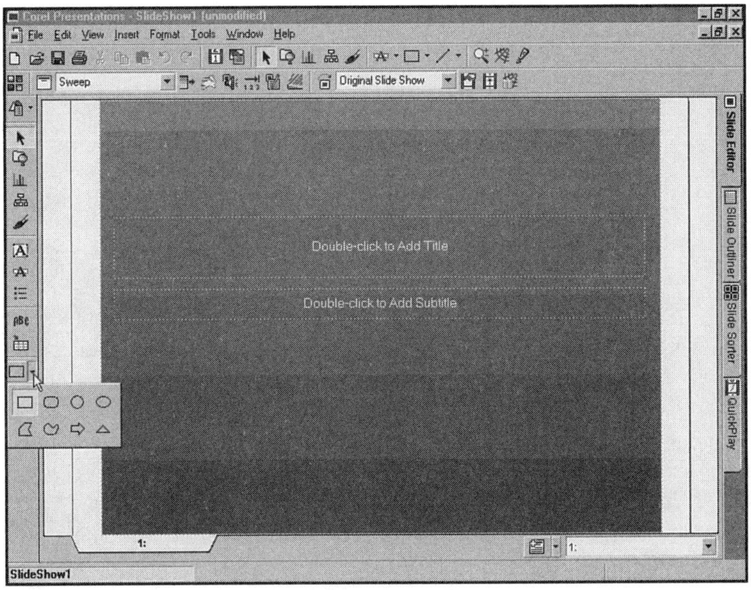

FIG. 18.6
Some Tool palette buttons offer a palette of choices when you click the drop-down arrow next to them. Others simply enable you to select an object type and drag the area on the screen where you want to place them.

Viewing the Presentation

The default view in Presentations Slide Editor is Margin Size view. You also can change the view to various magnifications. When you zoom or change views, the actual size of the objects, pages, text, and so on does not change; only the view of what you see on-screen changes.

To change the view, choose the Zoom Options button on the toolbar. A submenu appears. Table 18.3 describes each of the available views (except specific percentage views) and lists the shortcuts you can use to switch views.

Table 18.3 Changing Screen Views

Screen Views	Description
Zoom to Area Ctrl+Shift+F5	Magnifies the view of a selected area; drag the magnifying glass, thus drawing a rectangle, across the area you want to enlarge.
Margin Size Alt+F5	Displays the margins in the drawing window.
Full Page Shift+F5	Displays the entire document.
Screen Size	Displays the page as it will look when you play the slide show.

continues

Table 18.3 Continued

Screen Views	Description
Selected Objects	Magnifies the view of the selected objects.
Previous View Ctrl+F5	Displays the last view before you used Zoom. This can be handy to toggle between a close-up view and a full-screen view.

Figure 18.7 shows the screen at Margin Size view with the Zoom Area tool preparing to zoom to a specific part of the screen.

FIG. 18.7
You can define an area to zoom with the magnifying glass Zoom Area tool in a Corel Presentation slide.

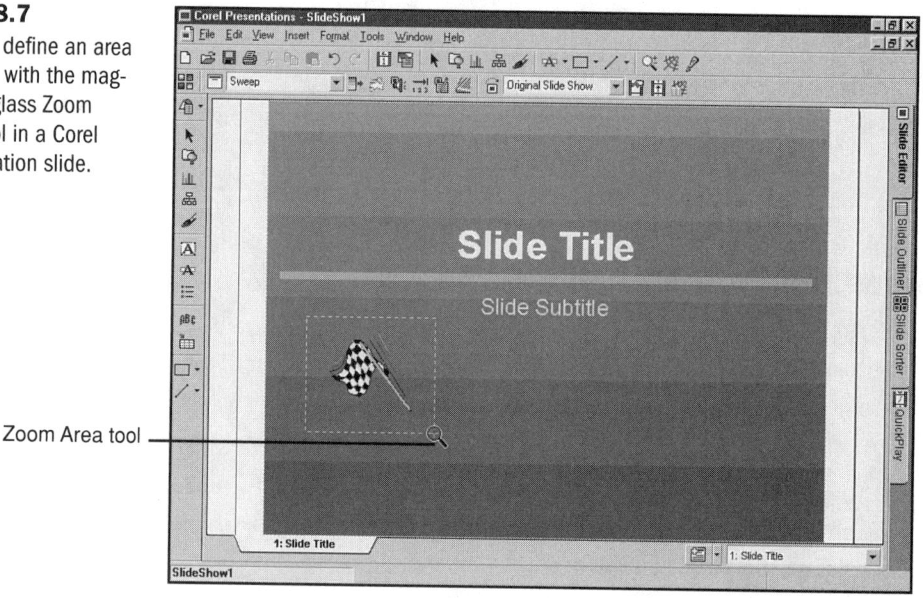

NOTE Another view option is *Draft mode*, found at the top of the View menu. You can choose Draft with any of the Zoom views. Draft view presents the slides without background color and objects with outlines instead of fill colors, patterns, and other attributes. Use Draft view to speed editing. To select Draft, choose View, Draft. A bullet mark appears beside the command in the View menu. To turn Draft off, choose View, Page; Presentations displays once again the background and complete objects.

TIP You can quickly zoom in or out a little bit at a time by pressing Shift+Page Up (zoom in, or magnify 20 percent each time), or Shift+Page Down (zoom out, or reduce 20 percent each time).

Using Outliner

Slide Outliner view is useful for entering text into your slide show. You can add slides and create titles, text, bullets, and so on in Slide Outliner view. Using Slide Outliner view enables you to plan and organize the slide show, rearrange slides, and perfect the show before transferring it to slides, especially if your slide show contains many bullet or text slides.

To change to Slide Outliner view, click the Slide Outliner tab at the right side of the Presentations screen, or choose View, Slide Outliner. Figure 18.8 shows Slide Outliner view.

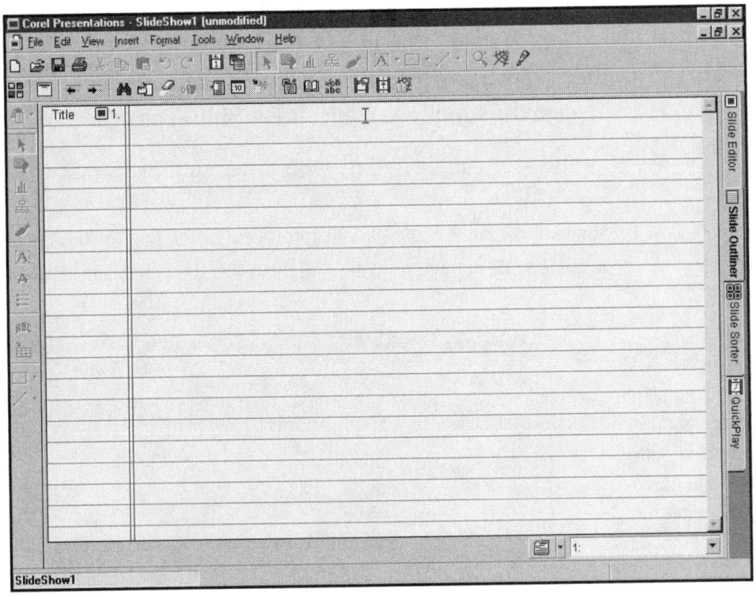

FIG. 18.8
Slide Outliner view looks like a ruled sheet of paper on which you can organize your presentation.

Part IV Ch 18

TIP In addition to entering your Corel Presentations outline in Slide Outliner view, you also can prepare an outline in Corel WordPerfect and insert it into the Presentations Slide Outliner. Choose Insert, File and select the document that contains an outline.

Entering Text and Assigning Levels

Enter the text for your slides in Slide Outliner so you can easily view, edit, and rearrange the slides before viewing them in Slide Editor view. As you enter the text, or even after entering it, you can assign various levels to the text such as title, subtitle, bullets, and so on.

To enter text in Slide Outliner:

1. Position the insertion point and type the text.
2. The first line of any slide type is a Title. Press Enter to create a subtitle.
3. Press Enter again to create bullets. Each time you press Enter after creating the first bullet line, Slide Outliner adds more bullets on the same level.

To change a level:

- Press Tab to move down one level (to the right); or click the Next level button on the Property Bar. You can create up to six levels of bullets by pressing the Tab key five times.

- Press Shift+Tab to move up one level (to the left); or click the Previous level button on the Property Bar. For example, to change a bullet to a subtitle, press Shift+Tab. To change the subtitle to a title, press Shift+Tab again.

Figure 18.9 shows a sample outline with titles, subtitles, and two levels of bullets.

NOTE You can use many customary word processing editing tools while editing an outline, including cut, copy, and paste, and even the spell checker.

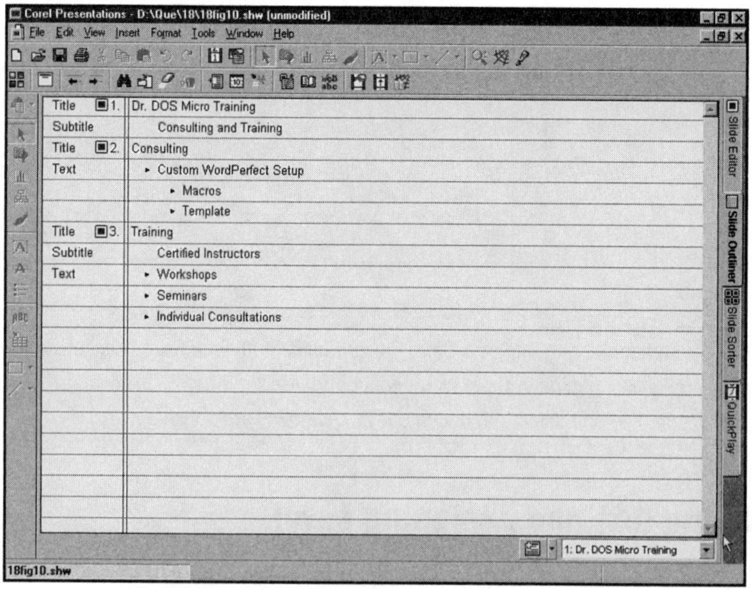

FIG. 18.9 You can create an outline of your slides with titles, subtitles, and bullets in Slide Outliner, and easily arrange and rearrange the levels of the slide contents.

Adding Slides

You can add slides while in Slide Outliner view by using the menu, Insert Slide button, or keyboard. Additionally, you can delete slides if you choose. When you add a slide in Corel Presentations 8, you choose the slide type; alternatively, you can choose to add more than one slide at a time and choose the slide type as you enter the text for each slide.

To add a slide to a presentation, follow these steps:

1. In Slide Outliner view, choose Insert, New Slide. The New Slide dialog box appears, as shown in Figure 18.10.

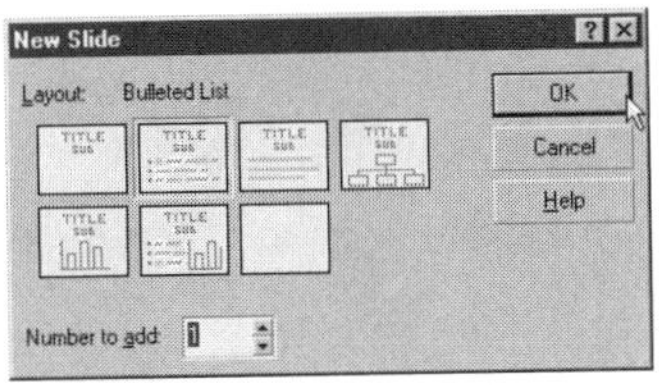

FIG. 18.10
Add a slide to the slide show in Slide Outliner view through the New Slide dialog box.

2. In Number to Add, enter or select the number of slides you want to add.
3. In the Layout area, choose the type of slide you want to add.
4. Click OK to close the dialog box and add the slide(s).

If you want to add just one slide, you can click the Insert Slide button next to the Slide List box at the lower-right of the screen, or you can simply press Ctrl+Enter. If you click the drop-down list at the right side of the button, you can choose the type of slide you want, while pressing Ctrl+Enter or clicking the button automatically assigns the current slide layout to the new slide.

NOTE If you add two or more slides, they will all be the same type–Title, for example. You can change the type by clicking the slide number in the Slide Outline and then clicking the Select Layout button on the Property Bar and choosing a layout type.

CAUTION

If you add too many slides or change your mind after adding, you can click the line in Slide Outliner for the slide you want to delete, and choose Edit, Delete Slides. Presentations displays a message asking if you are sure you want to delete it permanently; click Yes to delete or No to cancel. When you delete a slide, you delete the entire outline family, including all sublevels.

Rearranging Slides

As you create your outline, you can rearrange the slide order of the presentation in Slide Outliner view. Change the slide order by dragging the slide to a new position. All of the slide's text follows the title when you move it.

To move a slide:

1. Position the mouse pointer over the slide icon until the pointer changes to an arrow.
2. Drag the slide up or down to the new position. As you drag, the mouse pointer changes to a drag icon. Additionally, the screen will scroll up or down if you drag the icon past the window borders.
3. Drag the slide icon pointer to a line that holds another slide title. A short, horizontal line appears above the slide title to indicate the new slide will position ahead of it.
4. When you release the mouse button, the slide and the entire outline family slips into its new location.

Figure 18.11 illustrates a slide in the process of being moved to a new location.

FIG. 18.11
Move a slide and its contents by dragging it to a new position.

Line indicates placement

Mouse pointer with slide icon

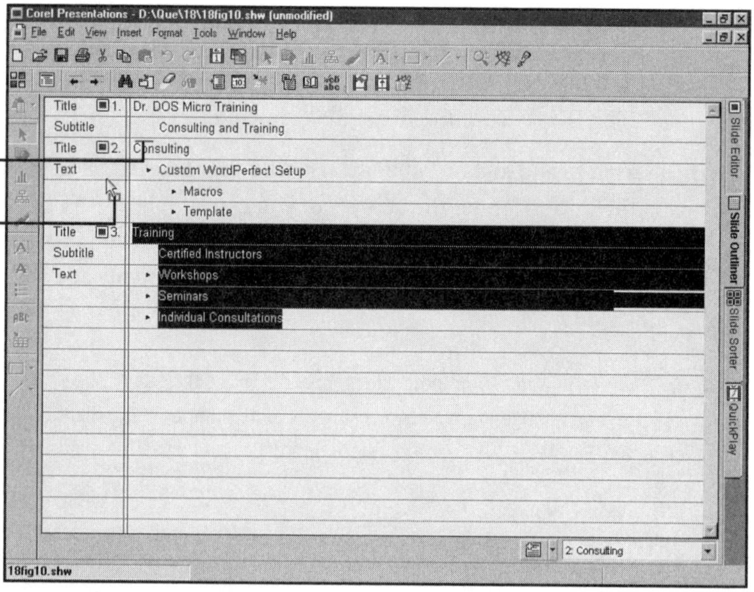

Using the Slide Editor

You use the Slide Editor to view each individual slide as it will look in the slide show or when printed. You can switch to the Slide Editor after using Slide Outliner to enter your text, or you can create the text and other objects for the presentation directly in Slide Editor view.

To switch to Slide Editor view, choose View, Slide Editor, or click the Slide Editor tab at the right side of the screen to quickly switch views.

TIP Click the numbered Slide tabs at the bottom of the editing screen to quickly move to other slides as you work with the presentation. You also can click the Slide List pop-up list and jump directly to another slide.

Adding Text

In Slide Editor view, text box outlines appear which enable you to enter titles, subtitles, bullets, and so on. You can enter, edit, and format the text in a text box. Additionally, you can move the text box or resize it.

To enter text into a text box:

1. Double-click the box. The box changes to a text box with a blinking vertical cursor and a grayed outline (see Figure 18.12).
2. Type the text.
3. When you are finished entering text, click outside the text box.

To edit the text in a text box, double-click the box, and the cursor appears in the text box.

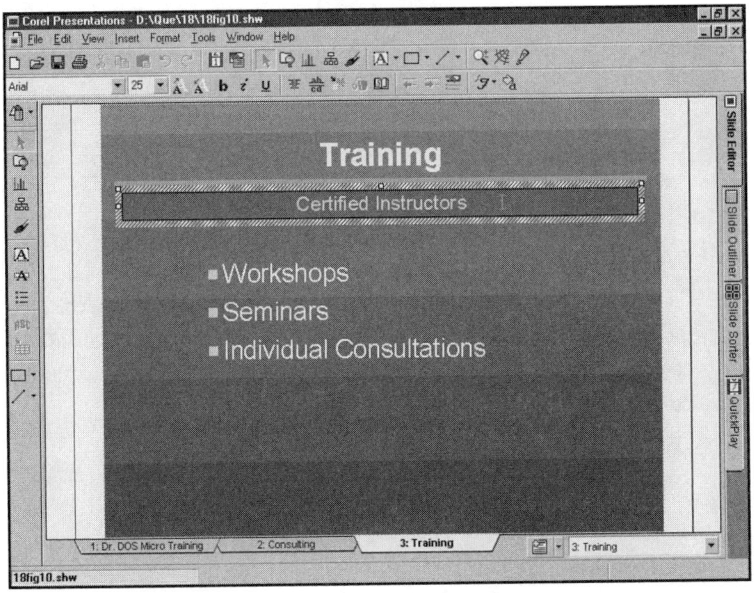

FIG. 18.12 You enter and edit all kinds of text—titles, subtitles, bulleted items, and body text—in the text box.

TIP When you are finished typing in a text box, press the Esc key to indicate you are finished typing. The box remains selected for moving or resizing.

To move or resize a text box, follow these steps:

- Click the box once to select it; small handles appear on the corners of the text box. Drag the box to a new position to move it.
- To resize the box, position the mouse pointer over any handle; the pointer changes to a double-headed arrow (see Figure 18.13). Drag the handle towards the center to make the text box smaller, or away from the center of the box to make the box larger.

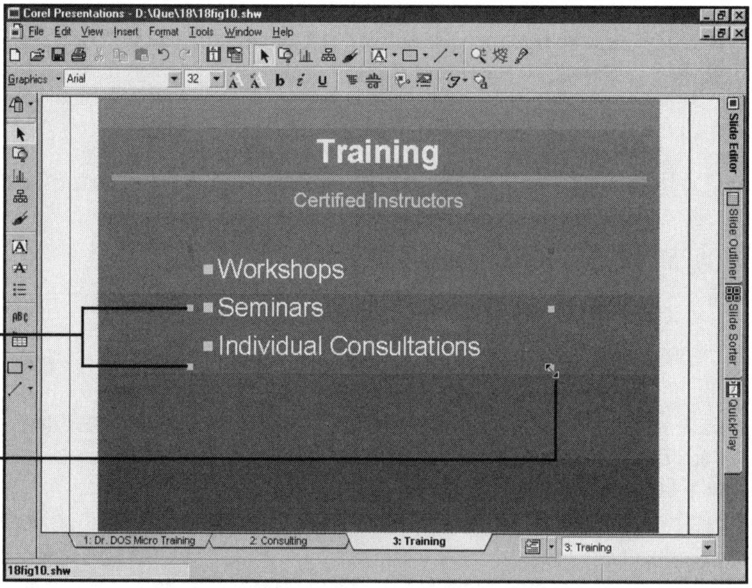

FIG. 18.13 When you resize or move a selected text box with its handles, the pointer changes to a double-headed arrow.

CAUTION

Changing the size of some text boxes (for example, a title box) also changes its font size, thus making the box text inconsistent with other similar boxes. To change the size of the box without changing its content, double-click the box and use the corner and side sizing handles to change the shape of the box.

To create a new text box:

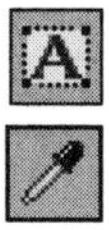

1. Click the Text Line or the Text Box tool and position the tool in the work area of the slide. The tool for the text box looks like a hand holding a rectangle, and the tool for the text line looks like large crosshairs.
2. Drag the hand to create the width of the multi-line text block you want to create, or click at the location you want to begin a single line of text.

   When you release the mouse button, the new text box appears with a blinking cursor, ready to receive text.
3. To close either type of box, press Esc.

Formatting Text

You format the text in a text box similar to formatting any text in other Corel WordPerfect Suite 8 applications, with one exception. In Corel Presentations 8, you must first double-click the text box and then drag the mouse to select the text; merely selecting the text box will not enable formatting of the text. After selecting the text, choose a font, size, or attribute.

After selecting the text:

- Use the various buttons on the Property Bar to change font and size.
- Choose Format, Font to format text in text boxes.

Figure 18.14 shows the Font Properties dialog box where you can choose which options to apply to your selected text.

TROUBLESHOOTING

I switched from Slide Outliner view to Slide Editor view, and the text in my titles is too long, thus overlapping other text. You can do any of three things to solve the problem: Change the font size, edit the text, or move the text box on the page so the text does not overlap other text. However, it's better not to crowd too much text into one slide; rather, divide your slides into smaller logical groups of information.

I can't move to another slide in Slide Editor view. You may be creating a drawing rather than a presentation. A drawing only has one "slide"; a presentation can have several. You need to create a new presentation, rather than a new drawing.

FIG. 18.14
Choose the font, size, and attributes all at one time in the Font Properties dialog box.

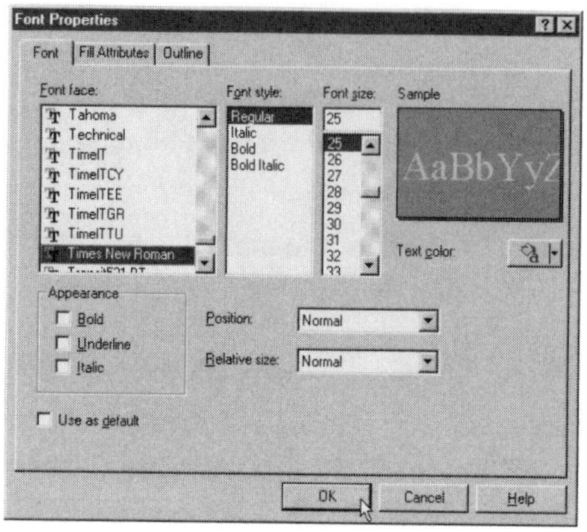

Sorting Slides

Presentations includes another view—Slide Sorter—for you to use when creating and organizing your presentation. You will most likely use this view when you are preparing to play a slide show.

Slide Sorter shows a mini-gallery of each slide so you can visually organize them.

Using Slide Sorter to Rearrange Slides

Slide Sorter view displays the slides in your presentation as small slides so you can see the visual impact of the overall presentation. In addition, you can change the order of the slides in Slide Sorter view. To change the view to Slide Sorter, choose View, Slide Sorter, or click the Slide Sorter tab at the right side of the screen. Figure 18.15 shows the Slide Sorter view.

In Slide Sorter view, you can click and drag a slide to a new position. Additionally, you can select more than one slide to move:

- To select consecutive slides, click the first slide, hold the Shift key, and click the last slide in the consecutive set of slides.
- To select non-consecutive slides, click the first slide, press the Ctrl key, and click the other slides you want to move.

Drag the selected slides to a new position to complete the move.

TIP To edit a slide from Slide Sorter view, you can double-click the slide, and the slide appears in Slide Editor view.

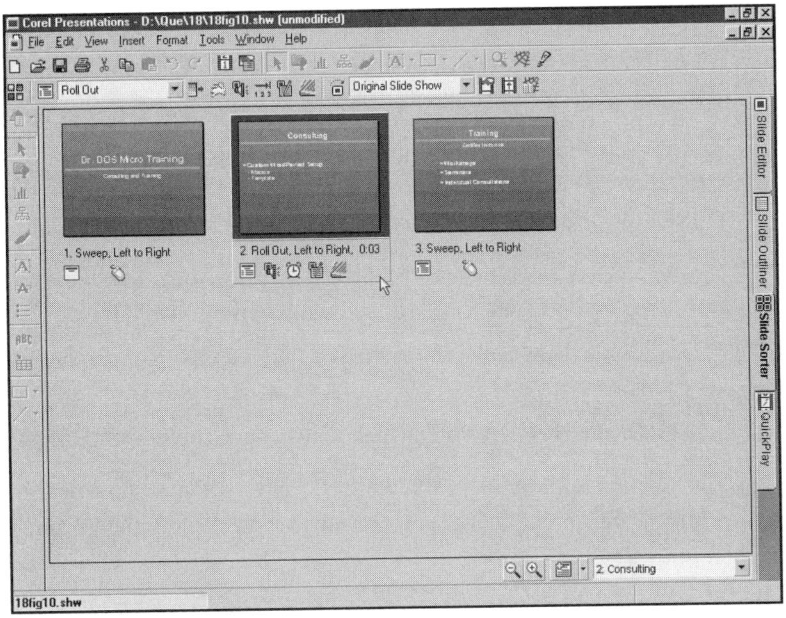

FIG. 18.15
Slide Sorter view is handy for preparing your slide show. You can easily change the order of your slides, and see what kinds of special effects you have added to them.

Understanding Slide Sorter Information

Beneath each slide, Presentations lists any transition effects you added, and also displays icons that represent special properties that you add (see Figure 18.16). These include:

- An icon showing the type of slide (such as a bullet or title).
- A mouse or a clock, to indicate whether the slide is advanced by a mouse click or after a specified amount of time.
- A speaker, if you added sound.
- A notepad, if speaker notes were added.
- A keyboard, if you assigned QuickKeys.

▶ **See** "Creating an Electronic Slide Show," **p. 422**

Customizing the Presentations Startup Screen

If you don't want to see the New or the Startup Master Gallery dialog boxes each time you start up, you can turn them off. For example, while in the New dialog box, choose Options, Show This Dialog at Startup. The next time you start up Presentation, the Slide Show option starts automatically. To turn off the Startup Master Gallery dialog box, while in that dialog box simply check Do Not Show This Dialog When Beginning a New Slide Show.

To make these dialog boxes appear again upon startup, you have to make a change to the settings in Presentations. First, of course, you have to get to the Presentations main editing screen to see the menus.

To change the settings in Presentations, simply choose Tools, Settings, and double-click the Environment icon, as shown in Figure 18.16. In the Startup tab of the Environment dialog box, you can choose various startup options. These include:

- Display Document Selection (New) dialog box, the default, but which you may have turned off from the Options button of the New dialog box.
- Create New Slide Show, whereby no dialog box is displayed before starting a new slide show.
- Create New Drawing, which takes you to the draw editing screen.

In addition to these three mutually exclusive options, you can also choose to display the Master Gallery each time you choose to create a new slide show.

FIG. 18.16
Choose how you want Presentations to start using the Environment dialog box.

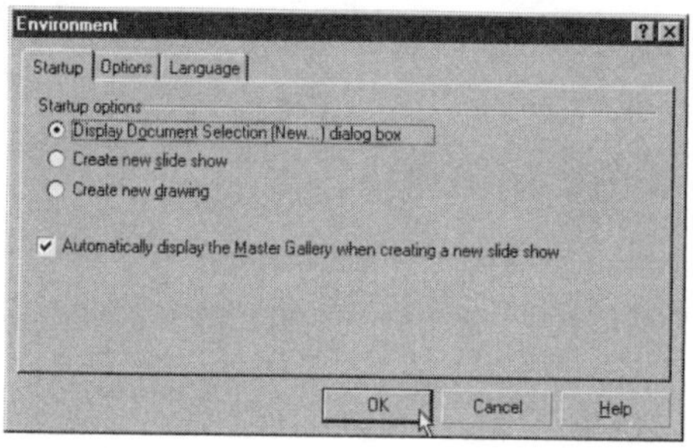

CHAPTER 19

Working with Data Charts

Create a data chart

Present information in your slides using bar, pie, and other types of charts. Enter data, import it from Corel Quattro Pro, and edit it using the datasheet.

Change chart types and layouts

Find out which type of chart is best for different applications, and how you can easily switch your chart from one type to another.

Add and edit titles, data labels, and legends

Learn how to quickly change the color, font, fill, or box around different chart elements, as well as set the scale for your chart's Y axis.

An effective presentation furnishes facts, figures, and brief statements that are quick to read and easy to understand. Strong titles and subtitles, descriptive bulleted lists, and interesting graphics (such as data charts) create a powerful, professional presentation. Data charts present information clearly by comparing parts to the whole, tracking trends over a period of time, or displaying the uniformity of data. ■

Creating a Data Chart

A data chart is a chart created using figures you enter in a *datasheet*—similar to a table or spreadsheet. The chart visually represents the figures, contained in the datasheet, using column bar, pie pieces, lines, and so on. The chart type you choose depends on the data and how you want to represent it; comparing data, for example, is a common use for pie and bar charts.

N O T E Although we are adding a chart to a slide show, you also can add a chart to a Presentations drawing using the procedures described in this chapter. ■

Inserting a Chart

Before you create a chart, you must first choose a chart type. After you make your selection, you will enter the data. You can create a chart using the Data Chart slide type, the Insert menu, or the Chart Object Tool button on the Icon Bar. Following is a summary of the three methods of inserting a chart into a presentation:

■ Define a slide as a data chart type, then double-click in the Add Data Chart; the Data Chart Gallery dialog box appears (see Figure 19.1).

FIG. 19.1

When you create an area for the chart, the Data Chart Gallery dialog box appears.

Data Chart slide type name

Graphic representation of Data Chart slide type

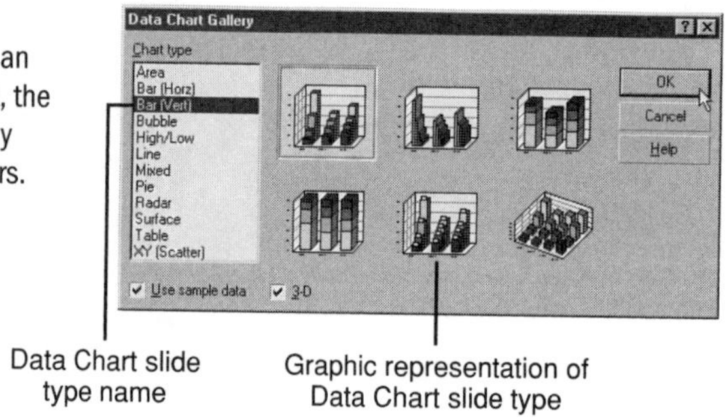

■ Choose Insert, Chart. The mouse pointer changes to a hand holding a frame. Drag the hand on the slide or drawing to indicate the area designated for the chart. When you release the mouse button, the Data Chart Gallery dialog box appears.

TIP To create a chart that fills the entire screen, just single-click the mouse in the slide area.

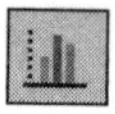

■ Click the Chart button on the toolbar or on the Tool Palette. The mouse pointer changes to a hand. Drag the hand on the slide or drawing to create the area for the chart. When you release the mouse button, the Data Chart Gallery dialog box appears.

TIP You can change the chart type at anytime by clicking the Data Chart Gallery button on the toolbar.

Choosing the Chart Type

You choose the Chart Type in the Data Chart Gallery dialog box. The type of chart you choose depends on the type of data you are planning to use and how you want to present it. Table 19.1 describes the chart types available in Presentations and their common uses.

Table 19.1 Data Chart Types

Chart Type	Description
Area	A chart that shows the height of all values with the area below the line filled with color or patterns. Use an area chart to compare several sets of data or trends over a period of time.
Bar	A chart that represents data by the height or length of the columns or bars; you can create horizontal or vertical bars. Use a bar chart to compare one item to another or to compare different items over a period of time.
Bubble	A chart that displays x, y, and z data on two axes with the bubble size representing the values. For example, you could plot units sold (x-axis data) versus gross profit (y-axis data) and you could make the bubble size represent net profit.
High/Low	A chart that shows the high and low values compared over time using lines and bars. Use High/Low charts to track fluctuating data (stocks, commodities, and so on) over a period of time.
Line	A chart consisting of a series of data elements at various points along the axis; the points are connected by a line that indicates a trend or rate of change over a period of time.
Mixed	A chart that combines parts from a line, bar, or area chart so you can plot data in two forms on the same chart. Use a mixed chart to show a correlation between two or more data series.
Pie	A circular, pie-shaped chart with each piece (wedge) showing a data segment and its relationship to the whole. Use a pie chart to sort data and compare parts of the whole.
Radar	A chart that starts from the center using a grid to represent the various data. Use a radar chart to show data over a period of time and to show variations and trends.

continues

Table 19.1 Continued

Chart Type	Description
Surface	A chart that represents values to look like peaks and valleys, or landscape. Solid areas contour to the data, which is useful in tracking profits or losses.
Table	Not a graphical chart, but a representation of the data in rows and columns, similar to the datasheet.
XY (Scatter)	A chart that plots two sets of data, placing a marker at each point where the data intercept. Use a scatter chart when there are extremely large amounts of data you want to plot along an interception course.

To choose a chart type in the Data Chart Gallery dialog box, first choose an option in the Chart Type list. When you do so, the appropriate graphic views of the chart will be displayed. From the graphic views, select the view of the chart that will best represent your data to your audience (see Figure 19.2). Additionally, you can choose to make a chart three dimensional by selecting the 3-D check box at the bottom of the dialog box. Click OK to accept the chart type and close the dialog box. When you close the dialog box, the datasheet appears.

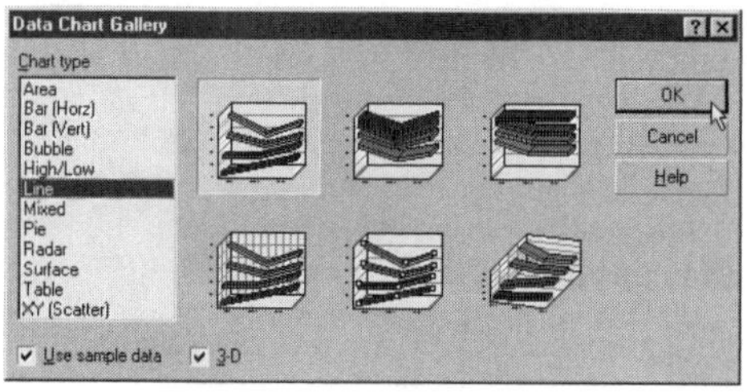

FIG. 19.2 Select chart type options from the Data Chart Gallery dialog box. Note the difference in the graphic representation between the Line type here and the Bar chart type in the previous figure.

TIP Radar charts, Bubble charts, and Tables cannot be created in 3-D.

NOTE When you close the Data Chart Gallery dialog box, the datasheet appears with sample data already entered, by default. You can clear this data to enter your own, or you can de-select the Use Sample Data option in the Data Chart Gallery dialog box. If the option is not checked, a blank datasheet appears.

Entering Data

After you choose the chart type, the datasheet appears with sample data (unless you chose to not display the sample data). Figure 19.3 illustrates the datasheet, sample data, and the chart created from the data. Additionally, the Data menu is added to the menu bar.

The Range Highlighter dialog box also appears. You can use this dialog box to change the color of the Legend, Labels, or Data areas of the datasheet. Normally, you just close this dialog box to get it out of the way.

FIG. 19.3
The datasheet looks and acts like a spreadsheet.

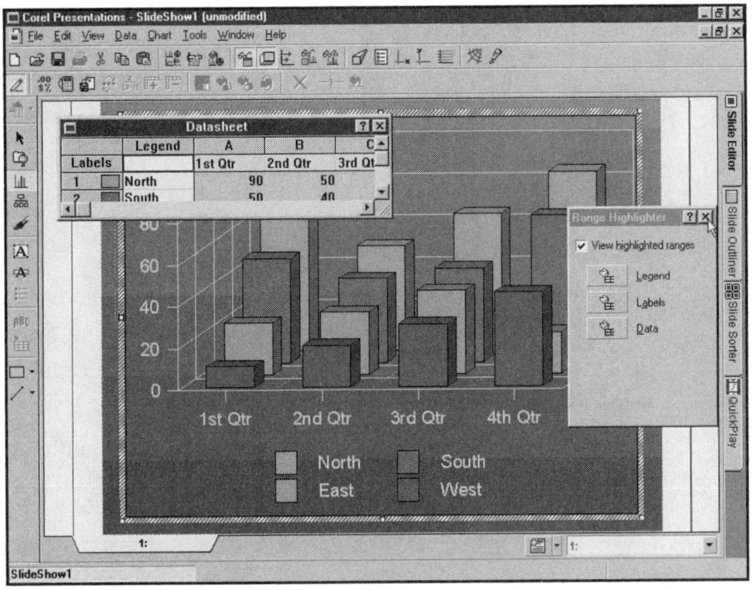

TIP If you cannot see all of the data, you can enlarge the datasheet by positioning the mouse pointer over a corner of the sheet and dragging to enlarge the window.

Inputting Data To enter data in the datasheet, follow these steps:

1. Select the cells containing sample data by clicking the Select All button (see Figure 19.4). Notice how the mouse pointer changed into a combination right and down arrow.
2. Choose Edit, Clear; or press the Delete key. The Clear dialog box appears with the Data option selected (see Figure 19.5).
3. Click OK. The data in the datasheet is deleted.
4. To enter the values, enter the legend text, the data labels, and then the values.

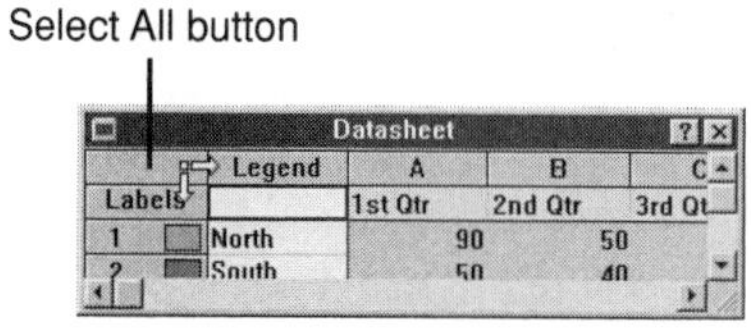

FIG. 19.4
The Select All button on the datasheet permits you to quickly select all information in the datasheet to apply new formatting or for deletion.

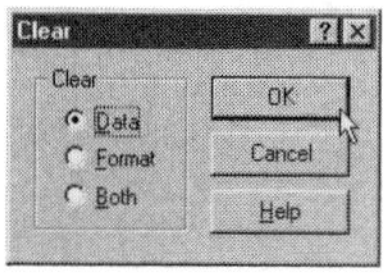

FIG. 19.5
Clear the data from the datasheet and fill in your own.

5. The *legend* text will appear in a box near the chart and tell what each color or symbol in the chart's *data series* represents.

   The data series is a range of values in a worksheet and each data series is represented by a marker; for example, a column in a bar chart is a marker, as is a wedge in a pie chart. Data labels are names put along the vertical (Y-axis) or horizontal (X-axis) axis to describe the data, such as the year, quarter, dollar amounts, and so on.

   Figure 19.6 illustrates a sample datasheet and the resulting chart after the text and values are added.

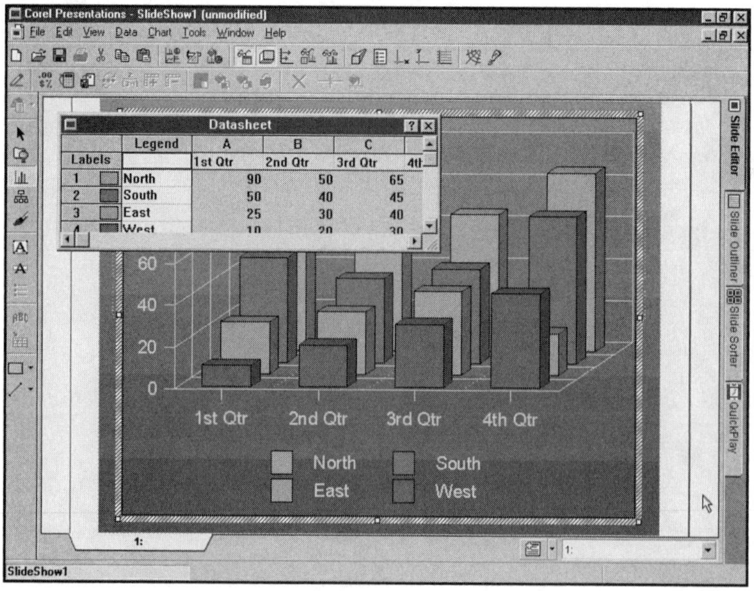

FIG. 19.6
The Bar chart displays the text and values after they have been entered into the datasheet.

6. When you are finished entering the data, click outside the chart area to close the datasheet window and to leave the chart editing mode. You see the finished chart in your slide, with handles around it indicating that it is selected.

TIP You can edit the data in the datasheet at anytime by clicking the View Datasheet button in the toolbar.

NOTE The first time you create a chart using your own data, it might be a good idea to take a few minutes and see what your data looks like displayed in different data chart types. Then compare each chart against its description in Table 19.1. Make sure to try each chart type in both 2-D and 3-D. This will give you a better understanding of how each chart type displays your data, and a better idea of which chart types most effectively present the concepts you want to convey to your particular presentation audience. To change the chart type easily, click the Data Chart Gallery button on the toolbar.

Importing Data You can import data into the datasheet from a spreadsheet program, such as Corel Quattro Pro, by following these steps:

1. Select the cell in the datasheet where you want to import the data.

CAUTION

Make sure any cells that will be filled with data do not contain important data that you want to keep. (If there is existing data in the destination cells of the datasheet, it will be written over.)

2. Choose Data, Import. The Import Data dialog box appears (see Figure 19.7).

FIG. 19.7
Use the Import Data dialog box to import part or all of a spreadsheet.

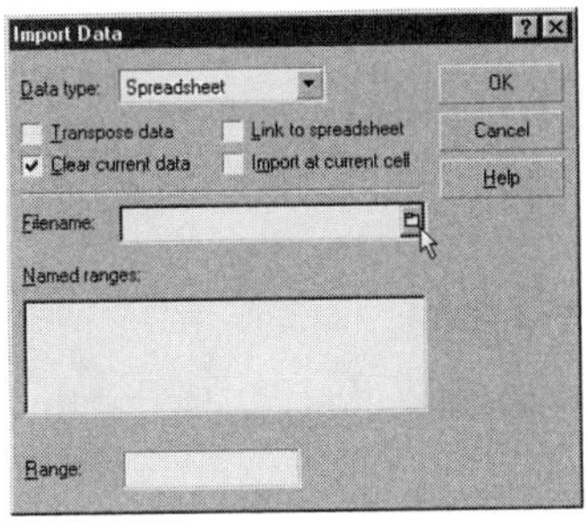

3. Choose the type of data you will import from the Data Type list.
4. Enter the path and file name in the Filename text box.
5. Specify a Range, or you can import the entire worksheet.

6. Select Import at current cell if you want the new data to begin where you currently are in the datasheet.
7. Choose any other options you need (refer to Figure 19.7). These include:
   - *Transpose Data*. Enables you to import row data to columns, and column data to rows.
   - *Clear Current Data*. Clears current speadsheet data.
   - *Link to Spreadsheet*. Updates the resulting chart if the spreadsheet changes.
   - *Import at Current Cell*. Does just that, instead of at the upper-left corner of the datasheet.
   - *Named Ranges*. Brings in selected areas of the spreadsheet, based on named ranges specified in the spreadsheet itself.
   - *Range*. Enables you to import just a specific area of the spreadsheet.
8. Click OK. The specified data imports to the selected cell in the Chart Datasheet.

Editing a Chart

You can easily edit chart data or other chart options by double-clicking the chart. When you double-click the chart, the chart's border appears as a screened line to indicate it's selected. Additionally, the datasheet containing the charting data appears, the Data menu appears, new options appear on the menu bar, and several new buttons appear on the toolbars and Property Bar that pertain only to charts (refer to Figure 19.6). Unless you turned it off, the Range Highlighter also appears.

Editing Data

To edit the data in a chart, double-click the chart. The datasheet appears, unless you closed the datasheet previously. If you did, simply click the View Datasheet button on the toolbar. Click the cell you want to edit and type the text or value. Press Enter and the chart changes to reflect the new data.

In addition to entering new text or editing text, you can format the values in the chart and sort the data in the cells of the datasheet.

Formatting Values You can format a cell in a datasheet to contain specific data types, such as numeric, currency, or text. To format values, do the following:

1. Select the cells you want to format and choose Data, Format, or right-click the cells, then choose Format from the QuickMenu. The Format dialog box appears (see Figure 19.8).

FIG. 19.8
Format the data in selected cells using the Format dialog box.

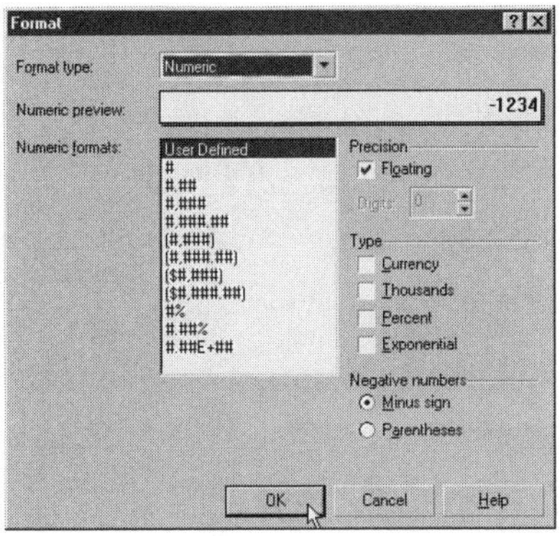

2. In Format Type, choose either General, Numeric, or Date. If you choose General, there are no options; otherwise, the options change depending on the Format Type.
3. Select the format you want to use and other options appear. The Numeric and Date options are described in Tables 19.2 and 19.3.

Table 19.2 Numeric Options

Option	Description
Numeric Preview	Displays the selected numeric format.
Numeric Formats	Choose a format to display the numbers.
Precision	Choose only one option.
Floating	Decimal points and places appear only if needed.
Digits	Specify the number of decimal places; this option is only available if Floating is not selected.
Type	Choose any or all options.
Currency	Displays values with a dollar sign.
Thousands	Displays commas to indicate thousands.
Percent	Displays the percent sign with the number.
Exponential	Displays the exponent of the values.
Negative Numbers	Choose only one option.
Minus Sign	Displays a minus sign to indicate negative numbers.
Parentheses	Displays negative numbers in parentheses instead of with a minus sign.

Table 19.3 Date Options

Option	Description
Date Preview	Displays the selected date format.
Date/Time Formats	Choose a format to display date and/or time.
Custom	Create your own date format.

4. Click OK to close the dialog box.

TIP The numeric format you choose in the Format dialog box changes the axis labels in your chart to the format you select.

Sorting Data You can sort the data in a datasheet in a descending or ascending alphabetical or numerical order. Sorted data is more organized than data that is not sorted, and therefore, sorted data makes a chart easier to read.

To sort in a datasheet, follow these steps:

1. Select the text or values in the datasheet to be sorted.
2. Choose Data, Sort; or right-click the cells, then choose Sort from the QuickMenu. The Sort dialog box appears (see Figure 19.9).

FIG. 19.9
You can Sort data by rows or columns of the datasheet, and in ascending or descending order.

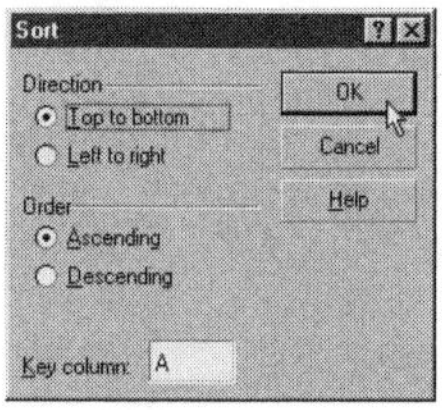

3. In the Sort dialog box, choose to sort the data Top to Bottom (Rows), or Left to Right (Columns) and in either Ascending or Descending order. The Key Column or Row (the column or row by which the data will be sorted) shows the letter or number of the selected column by default, so you should not need to change this.
4. Click OK to close the dialog box and sort the data. Changes are reflected in the data chart.

CAUTION

Undo is not available in the datasheet, so be careful before you perform a sort on datasheet data. If you click outside the chart area and then choose Undo from the Presentations menu, the chart and data do revert to their original order. However, any other formatting changes you made to the chart also are undone.

Changing Chart Types

After you create a chart, you may decide a different chart type would better represent the data. You can change the chart type to pie, line, area, or any other available chart. To change a chart type, double-click the chart to open the Chart Editor. Choose Chart, Gallery to view the larger variety of chart types, or choose Chart, Layout/Type to quickly select a type and edit the properties of the chart. Alternatively, click the Data Chart Gallery button on the toolbar (see Figure 19.10). Choose the chart type you want and the selected chart changes.

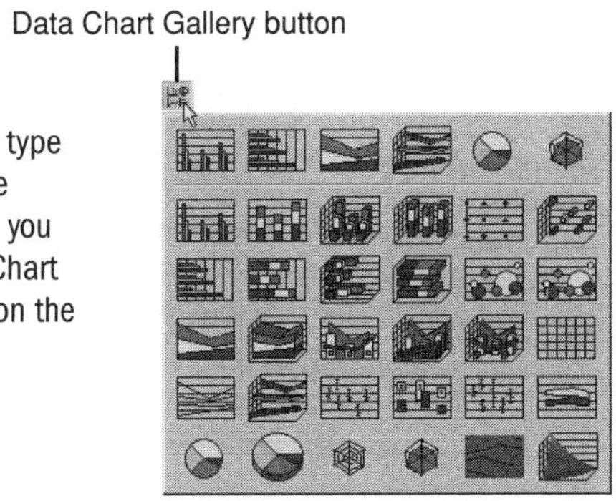

FIG. 19.10
Choose a chart type from the palette displayed when you click the Data Chart Gallery button on the toolbar.

TIP You can choose the Show Table button on the toolbar to add the data to your chart in table format.

Modifying Layout and Series Options

You can edit the layout and the series of a selected chart to further modify the way the data is represented. *Layout* refers to the style, width, size, and general appearance of the chart's markers. The Layout options change depending on what type of chart you are working on. The Series options refer to each individual data series. You can change the color, type, and even the shape of each series in the chart to further represent the chart's data.

Changing Layout To change the layout of the chart, perform these steps:

1. Open the chart in the Chart Editor by double-clicking it.

2. Choose Chart, Layout/Type, or click the Layout button on the toolbar. The Layout/Type Properties dialog box appears (see Figure 19.11). The specific options you see depend on the type of chart selected.

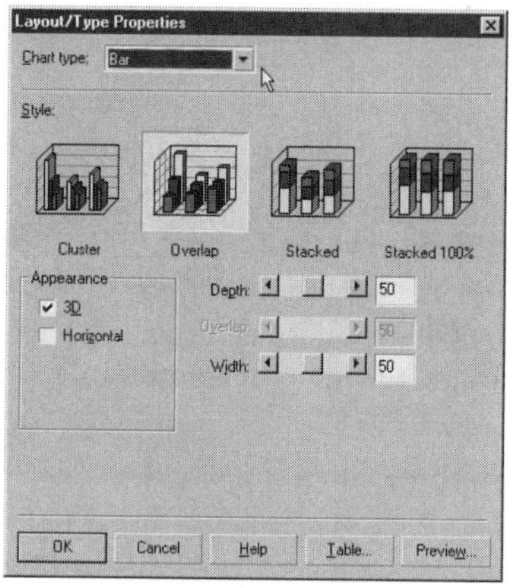

FIG. 19.11
The Layout/Type Properties dialog box allows you to both select the type of chart you want and set properties for the chart.

3. Change any of the options in the dialog box as described in Table 19.4. (The options that are available depend on the chart type that is selected, and not all the options in the table will be available at once. Some options are available for more than one type of chart.) Click the Preview button to view the change before accepting it. Click OK to accept the changes.
4. Click OK to accept the changes and close the dialog box.

CAUTION

Save your presentation *before* you modify the layout of a chart in case you change your mind about the changes; you can always revert back to the saved copy. Additionally, use the Preview button in the Layout/Type Properties dialog box before accepting the changes you make. If you make many changes, you may never be able to undo them all and the changes may not look good in your chart. If you use the Preview button first, you have the option of canceling the changes and trying again.

TIP When using the Preview button in the Layout/Type Properties dialog box, click and drag the title bar of the dialog box to move it for a clearer preview.

Table 19.4 Layout/Type Properties Options

Option	Description
Area Charts	
Overlap	Overlaps the markers.
Stacked	Stacks the markers on top of each other.
Stacked 100%	Stacks the markers so they are even along the top and bottom.
3-D	Applies a three-dimensional look to the markers in the chart.
Horizontal	Changes the direction of the markers from vertical to horizontal.
Depth	Sets depth percentages (only in 3-D).
Bar Charts	
Cluster	Groups each section of markers together so they can better be compared.
Overlap	Overlaps the markers.
Stacked	Stacks the markers on top of each other.
Stacked 100%	Stacks the markers so they are even along the top and bottom.
3-D	Applies a three-dimensional look to the markers in the chart.
Horizontal	Changes the direction of the markers from vertical to horizontal.
Width	Sets width percentages.
Depth	Sets depth percentages (only in 3-D).
Height	Sets height percentages (not Area charts).
Overlap	Sets overlap percentages (only in 2-D bar charts).
High/Low Charts	
Line	Changes markers to lines.
Bar/Error Bar	Changes markers to bars with error indicators.
Error Bar	Changes markers to bars with top and bottom error markers.
Area	Changes markers to area markers.

continues

Table 19.4 Continued

Option	Description
Pie/Exploded Pie Charts	
Pie	Displays data as pie slices.
Column	Changes pie slices to bar or column markers.
3-D	Applies a three-dimensional look to slices in the pie.
Proportional	If using two or more pies, the pie sizes are proportional to their total value.
Sort Slice	Changes the positioning of the exploded slice(s).
Explode Slice	Specifies which slide to explode and how much distance to place between pie and exploded slide.
Link Pie 2 to Slice	Indicates with lines how one pie two relates to a specific slice of pie one. This enables the user to show visually the details of one slice of pie.
Depth	Sets the thickness of a pie chart (3-D only).
Size	Sets the size of the pie.
Angle	Rotate the slices.
Tilt	Sets orientation (3-D only).
Radar Charts	
Overlap	Overlaps the markers.
Stacked	Stacks the markers on top of each other.
Stacked 100%	Stacks the markers so they are even along the top and bottom.
Line	Displays lines instead of filled areas.
Area	Displays filled areas along with lines.
Radial	Displays on a radial grid (Stacked 100% only).
Linear	Displays on a linear grid (Stacked 100% only).
Separate Y axis	Both series of data are displayed on their own Y axis.
Surface Charts	
Outline	Sets the color for the outline of the chart.
Outline Contours	Draws an outline around each area.

NOTE Each of the Layout/Type Properties chart types includes the Table button. The feature enables you to combine a data table along with the chart. See "Inserting and Formatting Tables" in Chapter 20 for more information on working with data tables.

Changing Series A *series* is a row of data in a chart. A series is represented by a column, pie slice, line, or other chart element, also called a *marker*. You can change how the series looks by setting series options.

TIP Not all series options are available for all chart types. However, you can mix series types in the same chart. For example, one row of data could be represented by Area markers, while another could be represented by Line markers.

To change the series options, follow these steps:

1. Choose Chart, Series, or click the Series button on the toolbar. You also can right-click the series marker on the chart itself and choose Series Properties from the QuickMenu. The Series Properties dialog box appears, as in Figure 19.12.

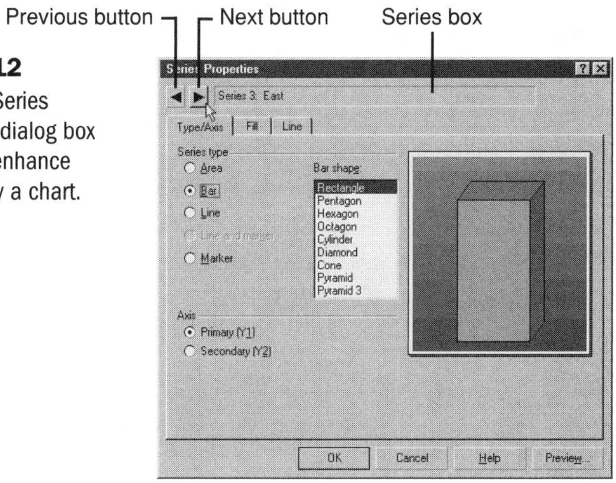

FIG. 19.12
Open the Series Properties dialog box to further enhance and modify a chart.

TIP Nearly any element of a data chart can be modified by double-clicking that element. For example, to modify a series, double-click the marker for that series to display the Series Properties dialog box.

2. In the Series box at the top of the dialog box, choose the Next or Previous button to select the series you want to edit.
3. On the Type/Axis tab, choose your Series Type (Area, Bar, Line, Marker, and so on), and the style or Bar Shape of the Series Type (Rectangle, Cylinder, Pyramid, and so on). Also, choose whether to use the Primary (Y1) or Secondary (Y2) Y axis.

TIP Click the Preview button at any time to see how the change looks.

4. On the Fill tab, choose Pattern, Gradient, Texture, or Picture to display a palette of fill choices. Select a new choice to apply to the current series. You also can reverse the colors in a two-color pattern or gradient fill, and also set which of the two colors is transparent, allowing what's behind the marker to show through.
5. In the Line tab, choose the Color, Width, and Style as desired.
6. Use the Next or Previous buttons, if desired, to choose another series, then repeat steps 3 through 6.
7. Click OK to accept the options and close the dialog box.

TROUBLESHOOTING

I made changes to the Series of the selected chart, and I don't like the changes. Click the Cancel button before closing the Series Properties dialog box. Alternatively, you can deselect the data chart and click the Undo button on the toolbar to reverse the changes. Don't depend on this method, however, since you might undo more than you expected.

Changing the Grid and Axis

The chart's grid is formed by the horizontal and vertical lines behind the chart's markers. The grid enables you to better see the markers in conjunction with the axes labels and therefore, the lines make the data easier to read. You can add two grids to a chart: the major grid and minor grid. The minor grid further divides the values so you can better read the numbers.

A chart's axes are lines used as reference points for the chart data. The X-axis represents the horizontal line and the Y-axis represents the vertical. You can change axis options to help you define the data on the chart.

Changing the Axis To change the axis options, follow these steps:

1. In the Chart Editor, select the axis you want to change. Handles appear at either end of a selected axis. Choose Chart, Axis, then select X, Primary Y, or Secondary Y. The Axis Properties dialog box appears (see Figure 19.13).

TIP Alternatively, double-click the axis you want to modify to display the Axis Properties dialog box.

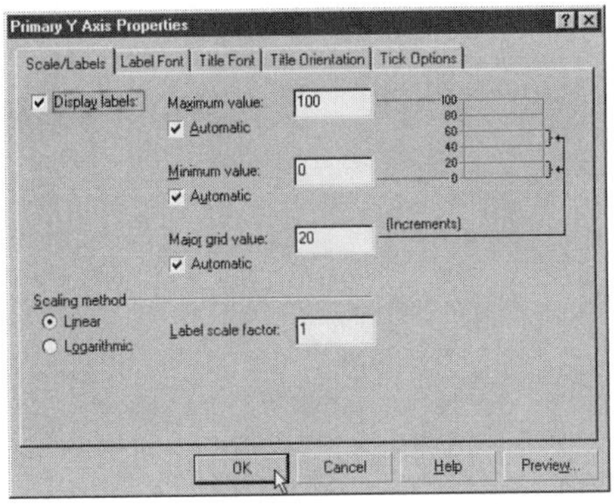

FIG. 19.13
Double-click the axis to display the Scale/Labels tab of the Primary Axis Properties dialog box for that axis.

2. In the Labels tab (X-Axis), choose to display your labels in a variety of ways. This can make your chart readable if you have many labels, or if your labels are long.

   Alternatively, in the Scale/Labels tab (Y-Axis), choose the Maximum and Minimum values for the axis.
3. Click the Label Font tab to specify the font and size for your labels.
4. In the Title Font tab, enter the title for your axis, and the font for that title. Change the orientation of the title, if desired, in the Title Orientation tab.
5. Ticks are short lines that are used to mark off values, such as dollars, distances, and so on. Major ticks are those lines that fall on a label and minor ticks are lines that fall between labels. Set options for the ticks in the Tick Options tab, then click OK.
6. Select the other axis in the Axis area and set options for that axis, if desired.

TIP If you change the font style on one axis, your chart will look more readable and professional if you change to the same style on the other axis.

Changing the Grid The grid in a data chart consists of horizontal and/or vertical lines that help to measure distance between the markers.

To change the grid options, do the following:

1. Select the chart, then choose Chart, Grids. The Grid Properties dialog box appears (see Figure 19.14).
2. On the Line Attributes tab, choose appearance options for the vertical and horizontal grids.
3. On the Line Ratio tab, choose how many vertical and horizontal grids you want to display.
4. Click OK to accept the changes and close the dialog box.

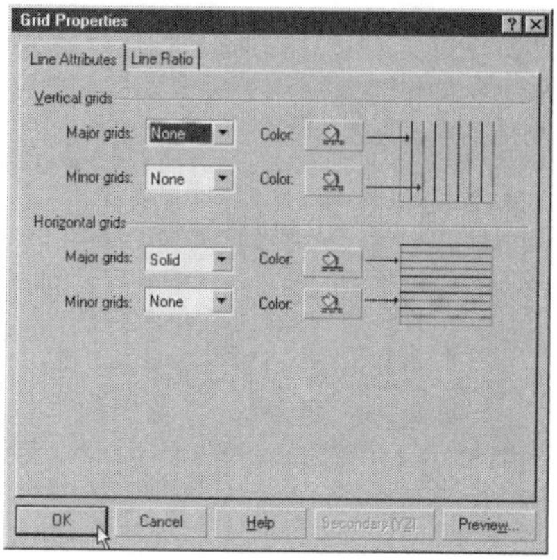

FIG. 19.14
Open the Grid Properties dialog box to change the appearance of the chart's grids.

TROUBLESHOOTING

I cannot see if I have made changes in the Axis Properties dialog box when I click the Preview button. Some options in the Axis Properties dialog box are codependent on options you set in the Grid Properties dialog box. Set grid and tick options and then come back to the Axis Properties dialog box.

After I make changes in the Grid Properties dialog box, the axis changes do not look right. Switch back to the Primary Y Axis Properties dialog box and change some of the options back to automatic by clicking the check box in front of the Minimum Value, Maximum Value, and Major Grid Value options.

Working with Titles and Legends

You can add and edit chart titles, a legend, and data labels to help identify the data in the chart. Titles name the subject of the chart; you also can add a subtitle and axis titles to your chart. The legend lists the colors, patterns, or symbols used for the chart markers and tells you what each represents. You can choose to show or hide the legend in a chart and if you choose to show the legend, you can set its placement, orientation, and various other attributes. Finally, you can edit the data labels in the chart. The labels show the numeric value, time period, or category of the markers.

Adding and Editing Titles

You can add titles to the chart and format the titles so they are easy to read. Editing titles is also quick and easy.

To add or edit titles, follow these steps:

1. Double-click the chart to open the Chart Editor and choose Chart, Title. The Title Properties dialog box appears (see Figure 19.15).

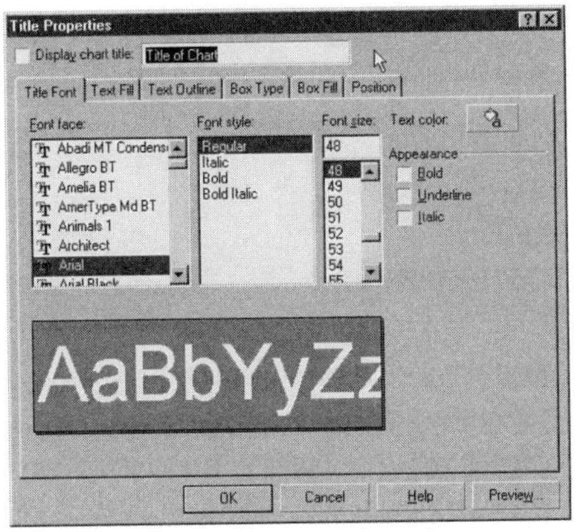

FIG. 19.15 Use the Title Font tab of the Title Properties dialog box to enter the chart's title, and select its font style, size, and other attributes.

2. Check the Display Chart Title box, and type in the title for your chart.
3. Use the tabs of the dialog box to specify the title's font, text fill, text outline, box type (for a box around the title), box fill, and position of the title relative to the chart.
4. Click OK to close the Titles Properties dialog box.

NOTE If you create a chart on a Data Chart slide in a slide show, you may prefer to use the slide's title and subtitle. You need not create titles in both places.

Editing Legends

You can show or hide the legend for the chart. If you choose to show the legend (the default), you can change the position, orientation, box style, and font of the legend box to suit your chart and data.

To modify a legend, follow these steps:

1. Select the chart and choose Chart, Legend. The Legend Properties dialog box appears (see Figure 19.16)

TIP With the datasheet on-screen, double-click the chart's legend to open the Legend Properties dialog box.

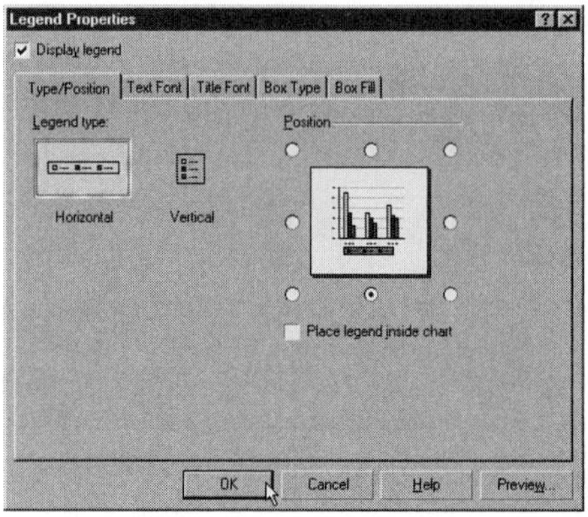

FIG. 19.16
Use the Legend Properties dialog box to modify the legend for your chart.

2. Check the Display Legend check box to display the legend. If you prefer not to show the legend, deselect the Display Legend option in the Legend Properties dialog box so that no check mark displays in the check box.
3. Use the tabs of the dialog box to specify the legend's type and position, font for the legend text, font for the legend title, box type (for a box around the legend), and box fill.
4. Click OK to close the Legend Properties dialog box.

Editing Data Labels

Data labels are tags that identify the tick marks or grid lines in a chart. You can show or hide the data label, plus change attributes, positions, and the fonts of the labels.

To edit the data labels, do the following:

1. Select the chart and choose Chart, Data Labels. The Data Labels dialog box appears as shown in Figure 19.17.

TIP You can double-click a data label in the chart to quickly open the Data Labels dialog box.

2. Check the Display Data Labels check box to display data labels.
3. Use the tabs of the dialog box to specify the data labels' position, font, box type, and box fill.
4. Click OK to close the Data Labels dialog box.

FIG. 19.17
Choose how to display the data labels in the Data Labels dialog box.

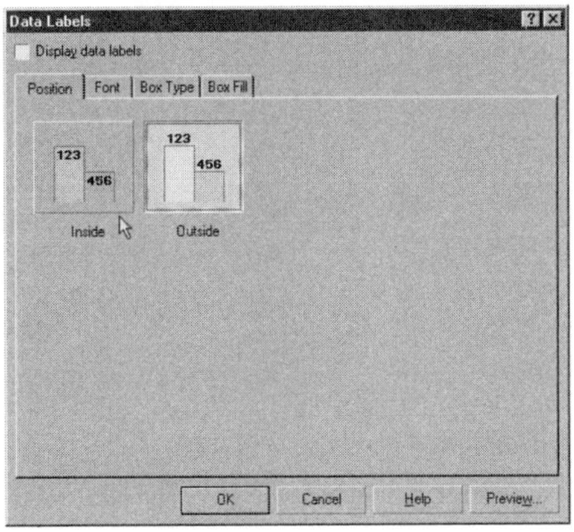

CHAPTER 20

Adding and Enhancing Objects

Presentations or drawings created with Corel Presentations 8—whether printed on paper, overhead transparencies, or on-screen—are effective because of their visual impact. Your presentations are more powerful when you use brief titles and bulleted lists with charts, tables, pictures, and other graphics that are quick and easy to understand, as well as attractive and professional-looking. Presentations enables you to easily and quickly add a variety of graphic objects to your presentations. ■

Add drawing objects

See how you can be artistic and draw your own objects with Corel Presentations 8.

Add lines and borders

Find out how to emphasize areas of your slide with colored lines and borders.

Add pictures and clip art

Learn how to match the medium to the message by adding visual appeal to your slides with pictures and clip art.

Add text from other sources

Understand how to pull in information from other files to cut down on your input time.

Use tables

If you're displaying data, you'll want to see how to create tables in your Corel Presentations 8 slides.

Adding Lines and Borders

You can add a variety of lines and borders to any slide in your presentation to enhance text or other graphics, such as a logo or clip art picture. After adding the lines or borders, you can choose from a variety of line styles, colors, and thickness.

Creating Lines

To draw a line in Presentations, use the Line Object Tools button on the toolbar or on the Tool Palette. You can draw a curved, arced, straight, or freehand line using the tools, and you can select the line, move the line, or change its attributes.

NOTE You can draw objects in either the drawing screen or while working with a slide show. The procedures are identical. You may want to try the examples in this chapter using the drawing screen because it will be easier to see what you're doing without being distracted by the slide background.

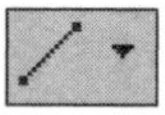

Drawing Lines To create a line, click the Line Object Tools button. You see the pop-up palette shown in Figure 20.1. Move the mouse pointer over the type of line you want to choose and click. Click and drag the tool in the work area to create a line. Each line tool looks like the line type that it creates. You will want to experiment with the tools to get a clear idea of how each works. Table 20.1 describes the Line Object Tools.

FIG. 20.1
Create a variety of lines to enhance text or graphics using the Line Object Tools button on the toolbar or on the Tool Palette.

Line Object Tools Palette

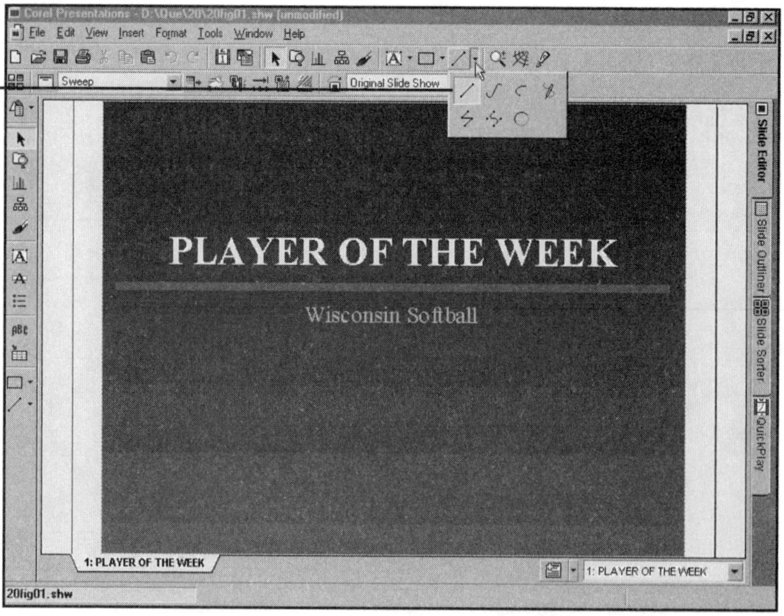

Table 20.1 The Line Object Tools

Tool	Tool Name	Description
	Straight Lines	Create a straight horizontal, vertical, or diagonal line. Click and drag from the beginning to the end of the line.
	Curved Lines	Draw soft curves. Click to begin the curve, and then at each point you want the curve to change directions, click again. Double-click to end the line.
	Sections of Ellipses	Draw arcs that are sections of an ellipse. Drag the tool to begin the arc. Release the mouse button to complete the arc.
	Freehand Lines	Using the mouse, draw a line in any direction. Click and drag the tool as if the mouse were the pencil. Release the mouse button to end the line.
	Angled Lines	Draw a line with several straight line segments. Click to begin the line, and then at each point you want the line to change directions, click again. Double-click to end the line.
	Bezier Curves	Create *Bezier curves*, or curves with sectors you can edit and move independently. Click to begin the curve, then move the pointer to where the curve changes directions and drag the pointer to display the two handles. Move the handle to change the shape of the curve. Double-click the mouse to end the curve. You can go back and select the curve to display handles, then move the handles to edit the curve.
	Sections of Circles	Draw arcs that are circular. Click at the beginning of the arc and hold down the mouse button. Drag the tool to the end of the arc and release the mouse button. Move the pointer to shape the arc, then click again to end the arc shape.

Part IV Ch 20

TIP You can constrain types of line objects with the Shift key. When you constrain a line, for example, you can only draw a vertical, horizontal, or 45-degree line.

Modifying Lines You can change line attributes such as line style, line width, and line color by clicking the appropriate button on the Property Bar. To change line attributes:

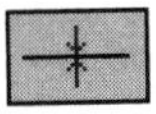

1. Select the line. Click the Line Width button on the Property Bar, then select a line width from the Line Width palette, as shown in Figure 20.2. Notice the More button, which takes you to the Object Properties dialog box (we'll get back to this in a moment).

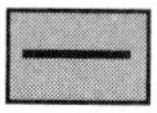

2. Similarly, change the line style by selecting the line, then clicking the Line Style button on the Property Bar, and choosing a line style from the pop-up Line Style palette.

FIG. 20.2
Change the line thickness from the pop-up Line Width palette.

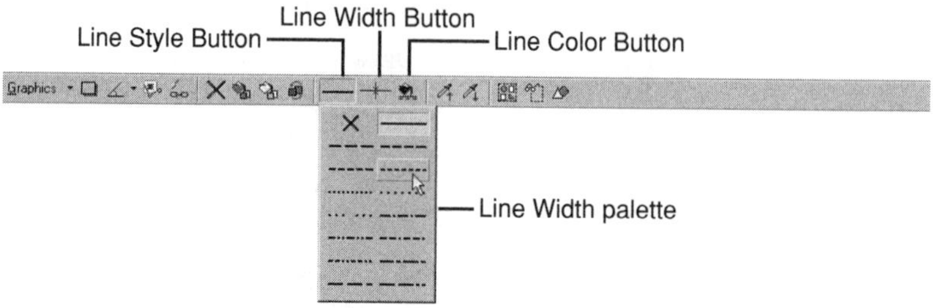

3. Change the line color by selecting the line, then clicking the Line Color button on the Property Bar, and choosing a color from the pop-up Line Color palette.

TIP You can invert certain types of line objects with the Alt key while still holding down the mouse button. When you invert an arc, for example, the arc you are drawing changes from an upward-facing arc to a downward-facing arc.

You also can change line width, style, and color, along with other properties, by using the menu. Follow these steps:

1. Select the line, then choose Format, Object Properties, Line; or right-click the line and choose Object Properties from the QuickMenu. The Object Properties dialog box appears (see Figure 20.3).

TIP If you don't select a line before going into the Object Properties dialog box, the new settings that you choose will become the default for all new lines you draw for the rest of that editing session.

FIG. 20.3
Change line attributes for the selected line in the Object Properties dialog box.

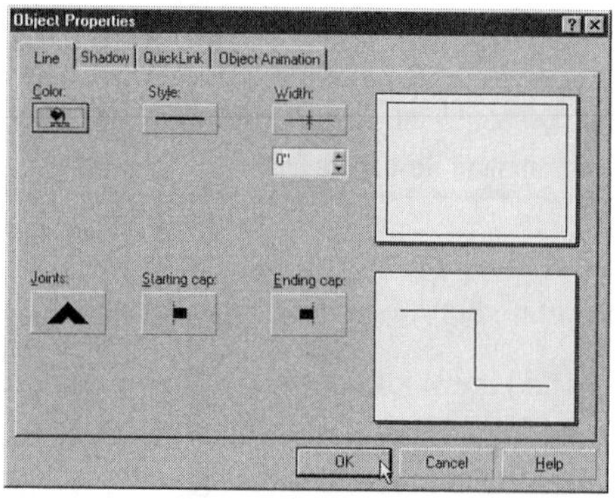

2. On the Line tab, select from the following options. Notice the sample box updated to show you how your line will look.
   - *Color.* If the color you want doesn't appear on the palette, click More to create a custom color.
   - *Style.* Notice that selecting the large x means the line does not display at all.
   - *Width.* Select a predefined width, or in the edit box type the exact measured width you desire.
   - *Joints.* Choose to join two line segments with a Bevel, Miter, or Round edge.
   - *Starting Cap or Ending Cap.* The starting end of your line is where you began drawing. Choose the cap type you want from the palette that appears (see Figure 20.4). Cap types include round, flat, or square ends, and a variety of arrowheads and tails.

TIP The sample box shows you how the line will look as you change its formatting attributes.

FIG. 20.4
You can add arrowheads to lines, as well as specify how line segments are connected and how lines end on the Line tab of the Object Properties dialog box.

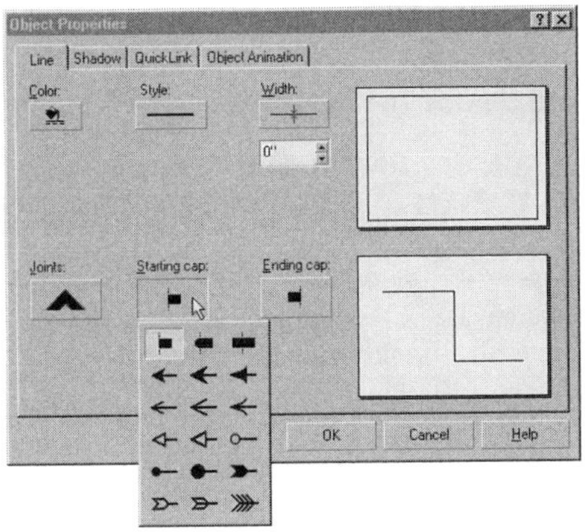

TIP Joints, ends, and arrowheads are more noticeable when the line thickness is greater than .05 inches.

3. When finished with setting the line attributes, choose OK to close the dialog box.

TROUBLESHOOTING

I drew a Freehand line, but it turned out too angled and rough. Freehand lines are very hard to draw smoothly; try using the Bezier Curve Line tool instead. After you draw the curve, double-click

continues

continued

it to edit it, and then select a point (the mouse pointer will turn into a crosshair when it's over a point). Move the handles associated with that point by dragging them.

I drew a line, but can't see it on the screen. Click the Line Style button on the Property Bar and make sure that a line style, rather than the X, is selected.

Creating Borders

Many of the objects you draw—such as data charts, clip art, organizational charts, tables, and so on—enable you to add a border; however, you may also want to add borders to text or to a drawing you create. You can add a border by using the Closed Object tool on the Drawing toolbar.

Drawing the Border To draw a border shape, click the Closed Object Tools button on the toolbar or on the Tools Palette to display the various closed object tools. After drawing a shape, you then can drag one of its handles to change the shape. Table 20.2 describes the Closed Object tools.

Table 20.2 The Closed Object Tools

Tool	Tool Name	Description
	Rectangle	Click the tool and drag to create a rectangle.
	Rounded Rectangle	Click the tool and drag the mouse to create a rectangle with rounded corners.
	Circle	Click and drag the tool to create a circle.
	Ellipse	Click and drag the tool to create an ellipse.
	Polygon	Click to begin the shape and move the pointer to create one edge of the shape. Click, and the shape becomes closed; however, move the pointer to form the second edge and click again. Repeat until the shape is complete. Press the Shift key while drawing to draw exact horizontal, vertical, or 45-degree angles. Double-click to complete the shape.
	Closed Curve	Click once to begin the curved shape, and at each place where the curve changes directions, click again. Double-click to complete the shape.

Tool	Tool Name	Description
	Arrow	Click once to start the arrow, then move the pointer to where the arrow should end and click again. Releasing the mouse button after the second click creates a straight arrow; however, you can drag after the initial click and create a curved arrow shape.
	Regular Polygon	Click the tool and drag to create a five-sided polygon. When you choose Regular Polygon, a dialog box appears that enables you to choose the number of sides your image will use.

TIP Additionally, hold the Shift key while dragging to create a perfect square, circle, or 45-degree angle. Hold the Alt key while dragging to create the object from a center point instead of the edge.

Figure 20.5 shows an example of each of the closed object shapes you can use for a border.

FIG. 20.5
You can use any of these eight closed shapes for borders.

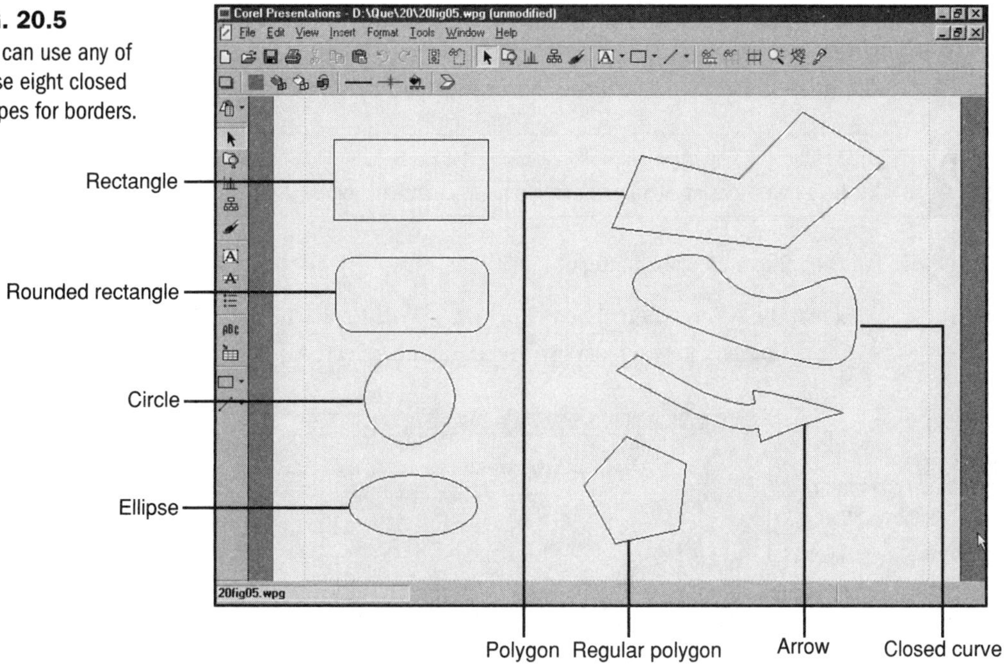

Modifying the Border By default, closed objects appear with a solid color fill. When drawing a closed object, you can choose a fill color and pattern before drawing the object, or draw the object, select it, and then choose the fill and pattern. Additionally, you can change the border line style, color, and thickness before or after drawing the object.

You can create a shape with no fill, so the shape's border line is all you see on-screen and its inside is transparent. Alternatively, you can create the shape with a fill color or pattern and make the fill transparent or opaque. If the fill is transparent, you can use color and still see what's behind the closed shape; if the fill is opaque, it blocks out what is beneath it.

To select a fill or change the fill to None with the Tool Palette:

1. Select the object.

2. Click the Fill Pattern button on the Property Bar. You see the fill pattern pop-up palette shown in Figure 20.6.

FIG. 20.6
Use the fill attributes palette to change the fill type.

3. Choose a fill type, or choose the X to turn off the object's fill.

TIP

Set the color of an object's fill by clicking the Foreground Fill Color button on the Property Bar, then choosing a color from the pop-up palette of colors.

To set the fill to a color or pattern:

1. Select the object, then choose Format, Object Properties, Fill. The Object Properties dialog box now appears with the Fill tab selected, as shown in Figure 20.7.

FIG. 20.7
You can set all Fill types and colors from the Object Properties dialog box.

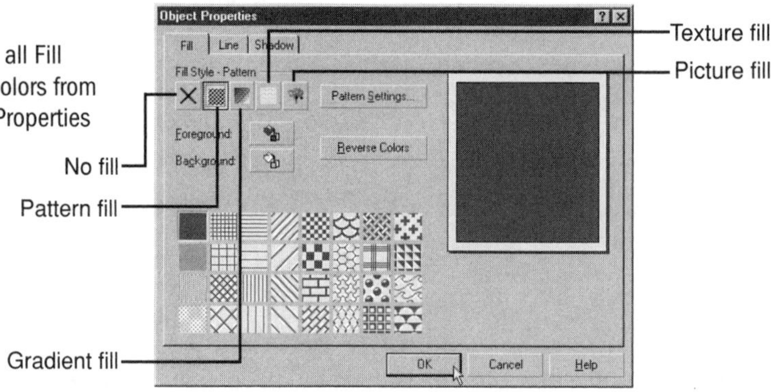

2. In the Object Properties dialog box, choose the X button to remove any fill. Alternatively, choose the Pattern, Gradient, Texture, or Picture buttons. Pattern creates a solid color or pattern, whereas Gradient produces a blend of two colors. Texture and Picture provide you with a selection of textures and pictures that you can fill your objects with.
3. If you chose Pattern, choose the fill pattern from the palette of choices, then choose the Foreground and Background Colors.
4. If you chose Gradient, choose a gradient pattern, then choose the Foreground and Background Colors.
5. If you chose Texture or Picture, choose the Category you want to choose from, then select a specific texture or picture.
6. Click OK to close the dialog box.

Figure 20.8 demonstrates various borders and fills.

FIG. 20.8
Use borders with fills and patterns to attract attention.

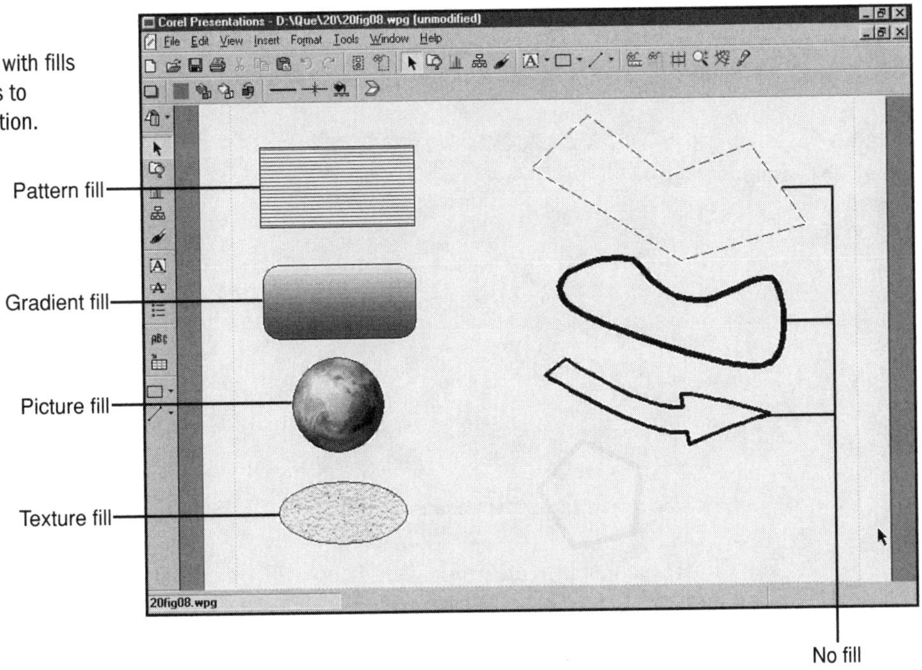

NOTE You can move a border (actually, a closed object with no fill) by selecting and dragging it to a new location. Additionally, you can select two or more items, such as a text box and a border, by holding the Shift key as you click the items.

Adding Pictures

You can add pictures or clip art from the Corel WordPerfect 8 suite of applications, or from other sources. Pictures help illustrate text and make a presentation more attractive. Corel Presentations 8 includes a Scrapbook that provides various categories of clip art, such as animals, architecture, arrows, and so on. Alternatively, you can insert a file from another program, such as a bitmap or Designer file.

Inserting a Presentations Picture

The Presentations Scrapbook provides a limited number of graphics that is installed on your computer when you install the WordPerfect Suite. If you have a CD-ROM drive and the WordPerfect Suite CD is in the drive, you also have access to an additional, very extensive collection of clip art.

To insert a Presentations clip art picture:

1. Choose Insert, Graphics, ClipArt, or click the Clipart button on the toolbar or on the Tool Palette. The Scrapbook dialog box appears (see Figure 20.9).

FIG. 20.9
Insert a picture using the Scrapbook collection of clip art.

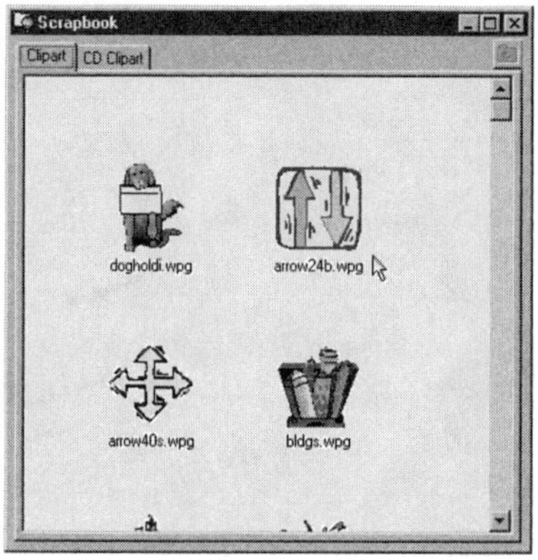

2. The Clipart tab displays the pre-installed clip art figures. Scroll through the scrapbook to find a picture you want to use.
3. If you don't find the image you need, you can access the CD Clipart if you have the WordPerfect Suite CD in your CD-ROM drive. Click the CD Clipart tab, and you see several folders of categories of clip art. Double-click folders to open them. Click the Return button at the upper-right corner of the dialog box to close a folder.

TIP To display more images at once on the screen, right-click the viewing screen and choose View, Small Icons.

4. Select a picture and simply drag it onto the Presentations editing screen. Alternatively, you can right-click the image and choose Copy, then you can paste the image into your Presentations drawing or slide show.

Modifying a Presentations Clip Art Image

You can move, resize, cut and paste, add a border, and otherwise manipulate the picture as you would any object. In fact, when you drag an image onto your screen, more likely the resulting image will be too large. You need to reduce the image by dragging sizing handles on the box until you have the size you want.

TIP To maintain the original proportions of an image, drag the corner handles. If you drag the sides of the image, it will not retain its proportions.

Besides changing its size, you also can modify just parts of the image. Suppose you have an image of a sign and a flower, but you only want the flower. To edit individual sections of the image, follow these steps:

1. Click the image to select it.
2. Click the Graphics button on the Property Bar, and choose Separate Objects. Alternatively, you can double-click the image, which temporarily separates the various parts of the image.

NOTE If you are used to earlier versions of Presentations, you need to look on the Property Bar or on the Tool Palette, not on the menu, for many Graphic menu options.

3. Edit the parts of the image as desired. For example, you could select the parts of the sign and delete them, or even change the color of the flower.
4. Choose the Select tool from the toolbar and drag an area that encompasses the remaining objects of the image. Click the Graphics button on the Property Bar or on the Tool Palette and choose Group. If you double-clicked the image to edit it, simply click outside of the image edit box to regroup the remaining objects.

Separating images and editing them gives you virtually unlimited flexibility in creating the exact image you want without having to create your own original artwork.

Inserting a Picture from Another Program

If you have clip art, drawings, or other pictures you want to use from another program, you can insert them into a presentation slide.

To insert a picture from another program or other clip art collections:

1. Choose Insert, Graphics, From File. The Insert File dialog box appears.
2. In the dialog box, select File Type if you want to narrow the search to a particular type of file (for example, .PCX or .WPG).

NOTE It is usually not necessary to specify the file type. Presentations automatically interprets the file type for you. You will normally only use the file type function when you want to save your file in a format other than .SHW (for slide shows) or .WPG (for drawings).

3. Select the correct folder and then choose the file. Click the Insert button, and the file is inserted into your work area.

Adding Pictures from the Web

You can also add pictures that you find on Web pages to your Presentations drawings or slide shows. The Web has many sites that have public domain images, and as you surf the Web, you may find that you can easily increase your clip art library with these graphics.

CAUTION

While copying images from the Web is technically easy to do, you will usually be in violation of copyright laws if you take images from a public site without permission. Although many people do not know it, you cannot reuse photographs or clip art that you find in public sources without the permission of the creator.

Be sure to e-mail the administrator of the site where you find clip art and ask his or her permission prior to using images you find.

You can take images from a Web site to incorporate into your drawings or slide shows by saving them to your local computer using Netscape. To do so, take the following steps:

1. Using Netscape, browse to the site containing the image you want to use.

   ▶ **See** "Browsing the Web," **p. 450**

2. Right-click the image to be saved, and choose Save Image As. You see a Save As dialog box.

3. Navigate to the folder in which you want to save the image, and choose Save. The image is saved to your local computer.

To import the image, use the procedure outlined in the previous section "Inserting a Picture from Another Program." You then can manipulate the JPG or GIF image as you do other bitmapped images (see "Working with Bitmap Images" later in this chapter).

Inserting and Formatting Tables

You can create a table within Presentations that enables you to display data in rows and columns. Organizing numerical information into a table format makes it easier to read and comprehend. Additionally, you can display any chart data in table format by choosing Table as the chart type; you can change the table back to a chart when it better suits the presentation.

TIP You can also copy a Corel WordPerfect 8 table to the Clipboard and paste it into a Presentation's slide.

When creating a table in Presentations, you can choose from six table formats, including outlined, shaded, and plain table designs. Presentations enables you to add titles, subtitles, and range colors, and otherwise format the data within the table.

Adding a Table

You can create a table within Presentations into which you can enter, edit, and format the text, data, labels, and titles. You can also copy a table or table data from another program, such as Corel WordPerfect 8. After copying the table to the Clipboard, you can paste it into a Presentations slide.

To copy a table from another program, follow these steps:

1. Create the table in the other program (for example, in WordPerfect 8). You can format the table text and alignment; however, Presentations does not retain the formatting when it is pasted into a slide.
2. Select the entire table and choose Edit, Copy.
3. Switch to the Presentations program and display the slide in which you want to paste the table.
4. Choose Edit, Paste, and the table is embedded on the slide.

NOTE When you embed a table in this way, it is created as an OLE 2.0 object in your slide show or drawing, which means you can easily update the table. To find out more about OLE 2.0 objects (including how to edit them), see the section "Learning Techniques for Linking and Embedding" in Chapter 31.

To create a table within Presentations, follow these steps:

1. Choose the Chart button from the toolbar or from the Tool Palette. The mouse pointer changes to a hand holding a square.
2. Drag the hand across the slide page to define the area for the table.

NOTE The area required for a table is much larger than the table itself. Instead of dragging an area for the table, you may find it easier to single-click the editing screen, which gives you a full screen table. You then can size the table later as needed.

3. Release the mouse button. The Data Chart Gallery dialog box appears.
4. In Chart Type, choose Table. Six table formats appear from which you can choose, as shown in Figure 20.10.
5. Choose a table format and click OK. The dialog box closes, and the datasheet window appears next to the table in your slide, as shown in Figure 20.11.

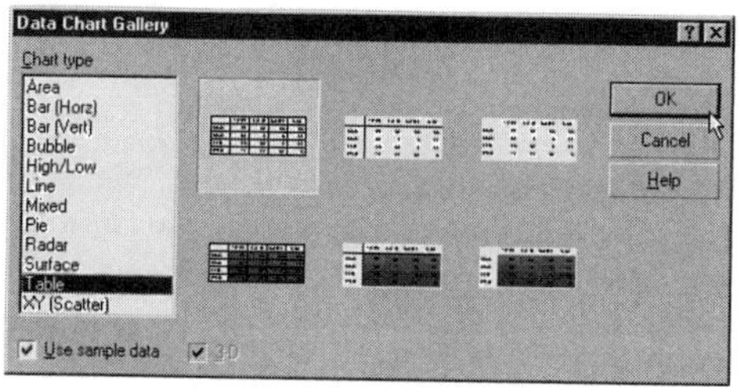

FIG. 20.10
Choose Table as the chart type in the Data Chart Gallery dialog box to view various table formats.

6. Enter the data into the datasheet as you did when creating charts.

   ▶ **See** "Entering Data," **p. 375**

7. Close the datasheet by clicking outside the hatch border that surrounds the chart object. The table appears in the designated area (see Figure 20.12).

Editing a Table

You can edit the information in a Presentations table at any time by editing the data in the table's datasheet. To edit the data in a table, ensure that the table is not selected, then double-click the table to activate it. When active, the table's defining box displays a hatch border, and you may see the table's datasheet.

FIG. 20.11
Use the datasheet to define a table's contents in Presentations.

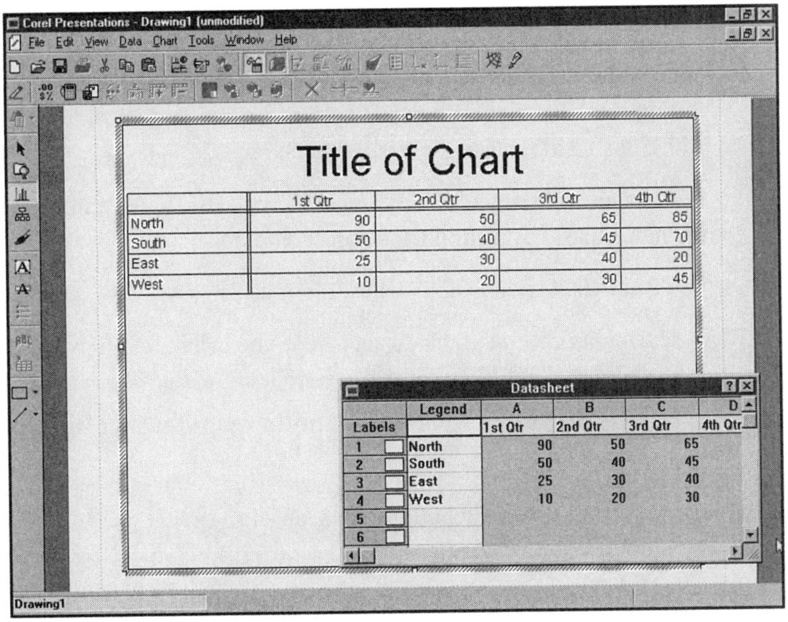

FIG. 20.12
The table appears in the slide or drawing when you close the datasheet after entering your data. The table object displays handles, indicating that it is selected.

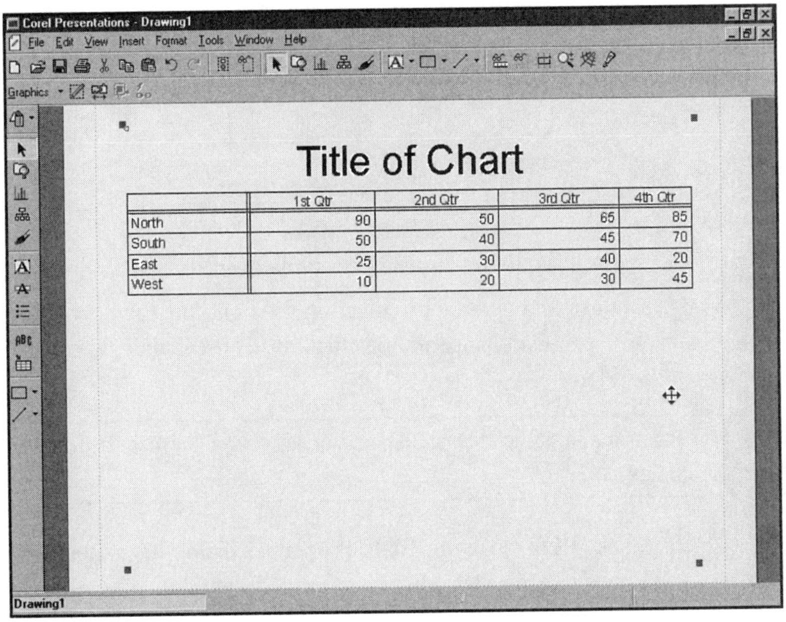

Part IV
Ch 20

If the datasheet is not displayed, you can view it by clicking the View Datasheet button on the toolbar. The datasheet then appears. When you are finished editing, click outside the table editing area to close the datasheet, as well as the Chart Editor.

Enhancing a Table

You can format the text and data in a table so that the text is large enough to easily read during a presentation. When you format the text or data within the table, all of the text within the table reflects the formatted changes.

Additionally, you can add titles and subtitles to the table, and you can change the color of the table lines, background, font, and so on.

To format the text in a table, follow these steps:

1. Double-click the table to activate it, then click the View Datasheet button to close the datasheet, if you prefer to have it out of the way.
2. Choose Chart, Layout/Type. The Table Properties dialog box appears, as shown in Figure 20.13.

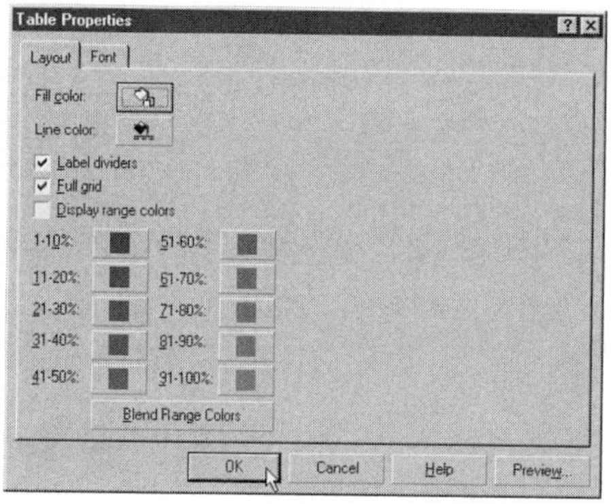

FIG. 20.13
Use the Table Properties dialog box to change the font and other table options.

3. In the Layout tab, choose options as described in Table 20.3.
4. Choose font options by selecting the Font tab, then choosing the font face, style, size, color, and appearance attributes. The Sample box shows you how your fonts will look.

TIP Change the type size to at least 36 points or even larger so it can easily be read in the presentation slide.

5. Click OK to close the Table Properties dialog box; alternatively, you can choose Preview to view the change before accepting it.

Table 20.3 Table/Surface Options

Option	Description
Display Range Colors	Shows or hides the selected colors to the table cells; this option fills each cell with the selected colors in the Range Colors area of the dialog box (see the "Applying Range Colors" section).
Blend Range Colors	Allows you to blend a color chosen for the minimum with a color chosen for the maximum of the range (see the "Applying Range Colors" section).
Label Dividers	Shows or hides the table's formatted gridlines in a table.
Full Grid	Shows or hides all gridlines in the table.
Fill Color	Choose one color to use for the table background.
Line Color	Choose one color to use for all gridlines.

Applying Range Colors

Presentations includes a useful feature that enables the reader to quickly discern the data in a table: *range colors*. Each range color represents a different value in the table; the range color is applied as background color for each cell. The lowest values, for example, may be represented in a red cell, whereas the highest values could be represented in a yellow cell. Using range colors enables the viewer to quickly see the number of high and low values on the table.

TIP Use grays if you are printing in black and white; use colors if your presentation is on-screen.

You choose the range colors in the Table Properties dialog box from among the various shaded percentage buttons. You can blend colors or select specific colors for each range.

To blend colors, click the 1-10% box and a palette appears; choose the color to represent the first range in the table. Similarly, choose a color for the 91-100% box. Click the Blend Range Colors button to automatically fill in the remaining ranges with a blend of the two colors your selected.

TIP Don't use too many colors on a slide, as it clutters it and obscures the information you're trying to convey. Be careful of dark colors that will hide the text/numbers in each cell of the table.

Figure 20.14 shows the table with a blend of grays applied to the ranges. Note that you must turn on the Display Range Colors option.

FIG. 20.14
Blend colors in the Table Properties dialog box to create the variation of grays shown in this table.

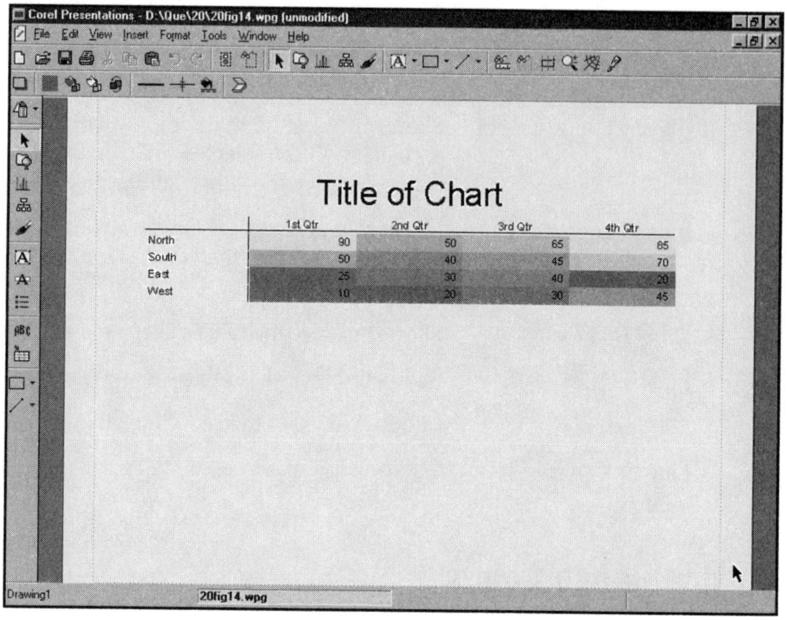

Alternatively, you can choose a color for each range block by clicking the block and choosing a color from the palette.

TIP Keep the colors light enough so you can read all of the data in the table cells. Try making the text bold if it's hard to read. Also, keep the text style simple; stay away from italic and other fancy styles, especially if you will be using the tables in a presentation.

Adding Titles

Presentations enables you to add titles to your table. You can even format the title, if you want. When you create a table in Presentations, it adds `Title of Chart` at the top of the table. Using the Title Properties dialog box, you can enter your own title or delete the title text altogether.

To add a title, follow these steps:

1. Double-click the chart to open the Chart Editor.
2. Double-click `Title of Chart`. The Title Properties dialog box appears (see Figure 20.15).

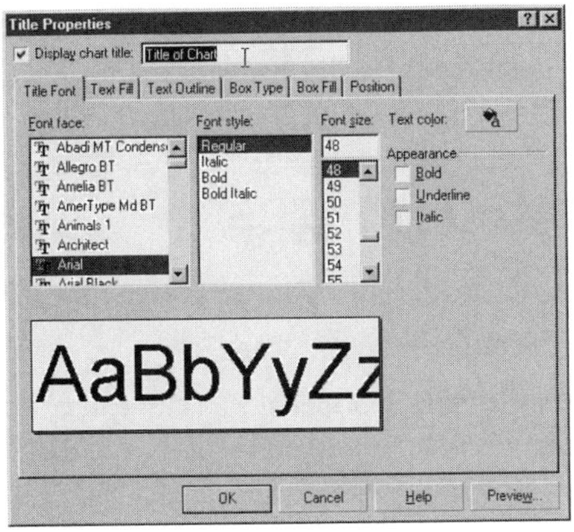

FIG. 20.15
Use the Title Properties dialog box to add titles.

3. Enter the title in the Display Chart Title text box.
4. To format the title font, ensure that you are in the Title Font tab, and then choose the appropriate font options.
5. Choose the Text Fill or Text Outline tab to change the fill from solid to a pattern, or to specify the outline around the title letters. In the Text Outline tab, you need to choose a Line Style before other controls have any effect.
6. Choose the Box Type or Box Fill tabs to change the type of box, or the pattern, gradient, fill, or texture that will fill the box. You need to deselect the No Box check box in the Box Type tab before other controls become available. The Box Type tab is shown in Figure 20.16.

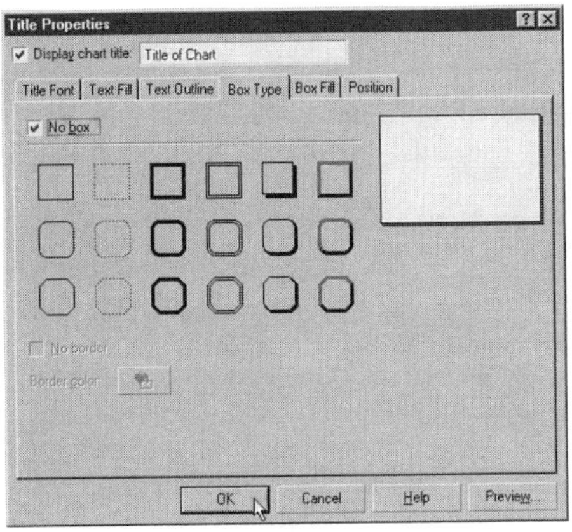

FIG. 20.16
Choose from a variety of boxes for your title in the Box Type tab of the Title Properties dialog box.

Part IV
Ch 20

7. On the Position tab, choose whether to put your title at the top, left, center, or right of the chart.

8. Click OK to close the Title Properties dialog box; then click the slide outside of the selected chart area to deselect the chart and close the datasheet.

Working with Bitmap Images

There are two types of graphic images that you can incorporate in your documents: vector images and bitmap images.

A *vector image* is stored as a formula. For instance, a circle might be stored as several codes that specify the shape (a circle), the location of the center point, the diameter, the line width, style, and color. Vector images can be stored very efficiently because there is very little information to store. They can also be resized and moved very easily because you merely need to alter one or two elements in the stored formula. All the drawing objects you have worked with in this chapter so far are vector images, and vector images are the only type of images that many popular presentation packages can work with.

A *bitmap image* is stored as a series of dots (technically called *pixels*). When you scan a photograph into your computer, you are scanning (and saving) dots, not formulas. Thus, scanned images are stored as bitmaps. While bitmaps are important to be able to work with, they have limitations. They take up much more space, and resizing them is much more problematic because they're not stored as a formula.

Programs that manipulate bitmap images are often called *paint programs*; programs used to manipulate vectors are often termed *drawing programs*. The types of tools used in paint programs are different than the ones in drawing programs. For instance, paint programs contain tools like *paintbrushes*, which spread a swath of color on your image (by changing the color of the pixels that you use the tool on). Other tools include *air brushes* that let you smooth colors gradually on an image—for instance, to "air brush" a smooth complexion on a scanned image of a face.

The default drawing type in Presentations is the vector drawing. However, you can create and edit both vector *and* bitmap images, and even change your bitmap image to a vector image with a function that traces the bitmap and creates formulas that describe it.

Creating a Bitmap Image

To add a bitmap image to a slide, click the Bitmap Image button on the toolbar or Tool Palette. The mouse pointer changes to a hand. Drag the hand across the slide work area to create a box for the image. (If you single click, the bitmap editing area fills the whole screen.) The view changes to Bitmap Editing view (see Figure 20.17), and the toolbar, Tool Palette, and Property Bar all have different tools on them.

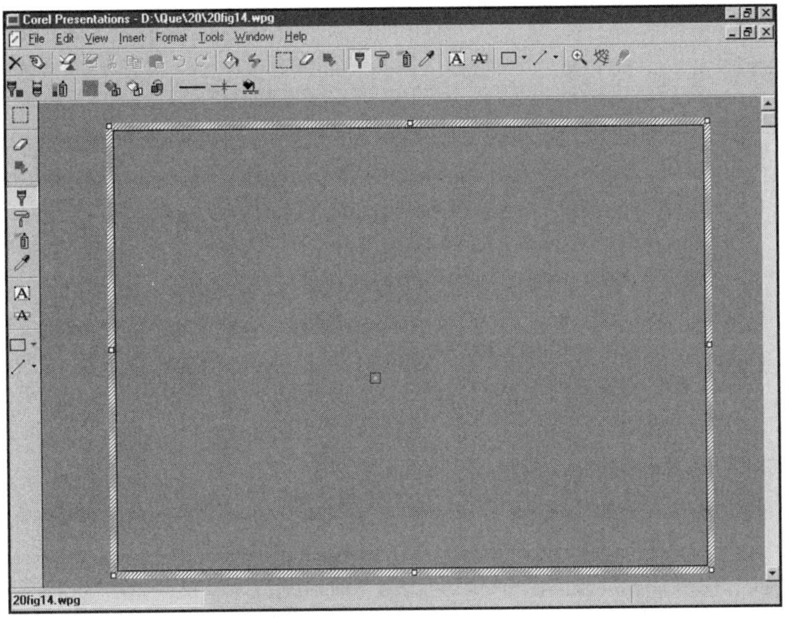

FIG. 20.17
Presentations includes a complete bitmap editor where you can work with graphics at the pixel level.

Use the Text Object, Closed Object, and Line Object tools to create your bitmap image just as you use them to create a vector image. In addition, you can use Paint and Eraser tools to enhance your bitmap images.

To paint a swath of color in your image, select the Paintbrush tool. Select a color with the Foreground Fill color button, and change the brush shape and brush width with buttons on the Bitmap Property Bar, if desired. Your mouse pointer looks like the shape of the brush you have selected. Click and drag the paintbrush over the area of the slide to be painted.

Use the Airbrush tool in a way similar to that used with the Paintbrush. Choose the tool, select the appropriate color, and change the brush shape and width, if desired. Repeatedly swipe the airbrush over the area to be colored to apply the color, just as you would with a real can of spray paint.

Use the Roller tool to flood-fill an entire area of one color with the selected color. For example, you can replace a white background with a blue background.

CAUTION

By default, bitmap drawings have a transparent background, which means only the drawing itself covers other objects in your slide. If you fill the background with a color, then the entire bitmap image, including the rectangular background, covers other images.

TIP You can choose Edit, Undo to undo your last action. If you want the action you undid to come back, you can then choose Edit, Redo.

Use the Eyedropper tool to "dip into" a color to make it the active color. To use this tool, select it, then click an area of the drawing that has the color you want to duplicate. The color becomes the active foreground color, and you can use one of the other tools to apply it to other areas of your drawing.

The Erase tool erases the parts of the image that you drag it over.

When you are finished with your bitmap image, choose File, Close Bitmap Editor; or right-click the image and choose Close Bitmap Editor from the QuickMenu. Your bitmap image is inserted into your slide or drawing.

Editing an Existing Bitmap Image

To edit an existing bitmap, double-click it. If the image was created in Presentations, you will see the same bitmap editing screen that you saw when you created the image.

Tracing a Bitmap Image

You can trace a bitmap image to transform it into a vector image. This can be useful when you want to be able to size the image, as you might with a scanned signature.

To trace a bitmap image, click it once in the drawing or slide to select it. Choose Tools, Trace Bitmap. The image is transformed into a vector drawing.

Saving Graphic Objects as Separate Files

Until this point, we have explored the use of graphic objects as they add to or enhance a slide presentation. On occasion, you might need to save a specific object for use in other situations—in another slide show or as part of a Web page, for example.

Presentations makes it easy to select the image you want to save, and then to save it in a native WPG (WordPerfect Graphics) format, or to export it (convert it) to some other format such as BMP (Windows bitmap), GIF (CompuServe Graphics Interchange Format), or JPG (Joint Photographics Export Group).

Suppose you create a graphic image that you want to post on your own home page. In order to do so, it must be saved in a GIF or JPG format. To do this, follow these steps:

1. Select the object you want to save.
2. Choose File, Save As; indicate in the dialog box that you want to save the selected item(s); and choose OK.
3. In the Save As dialog box, supply the desired file name in the File name box, then change the File Type to .gif or .jpg. Presentations adds the appropriate file name extension to the file name. Choose Save.
4. Presentations displays the Export dialog box (see Figure 20.18). Unless you really need to change anything, such as the size of the image, simply choose OK and Presentations exports the image to the format you chose.

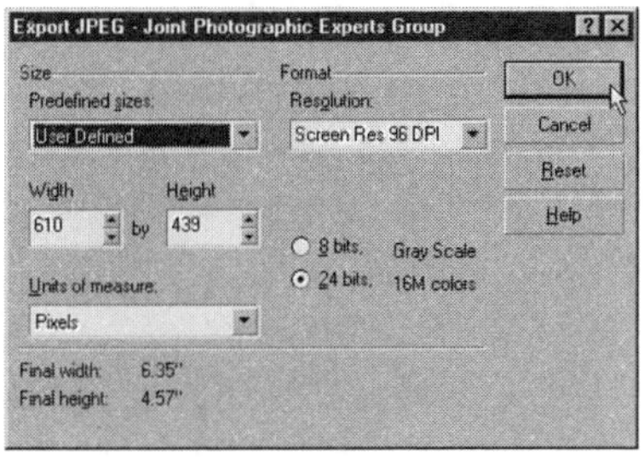

FIG. 20.18
By using the Save As option, Presentations enables you to export graphic images you create to Web-ready formats, such as JPG and GIF images, and to determine their exact size and resolution.

CAUTION

Exporting an image does not save that image in the WPG format. If you intend to use Presentations to edit this image again in the future, you should also save the image as a WordPerfect Graphic.

CHAPTER 21

Printing and Displaying Your Presentation

Print the presentation

Learn how to preview your presentation so you won't waste paper, then select a printer and print presentation elements.

Create an electronic slide show

Find out how to present your presentation electronically.

Add transitions and animation

Learn about spicing up your electronic slide show with a variety of special effects, including transitions and animation.

When you're ready to show your presentation to others, you have several options. You can print the slide show itself to paper, film, or transparencies. Additionally, you can print handouts, the outline, drawings, and other documents from the screen.

You may also want to show the presentation on-screen. Corel Presentations 8 enables you to run the show automatically, setting timing and transitions between the slides. ■

Understanding Printed Slide Show Options

Whether you decide to print your presentation, make transparencies or slides, or present it as an electronic slide show, you may want to have Speaker Notes, handouts, or audience notes to accompany it. *Speaker Notes* are pages that have one or more slides, along with notes that remind you of what you want to say while the slide is displayed. *Audience notes* are similar pages, but instead of notes, they display blank lines like those in Figure 21.1.

FIG. 21.1
Audience notes have blank lines where the audience members can write down important points as they listen to the presentation.

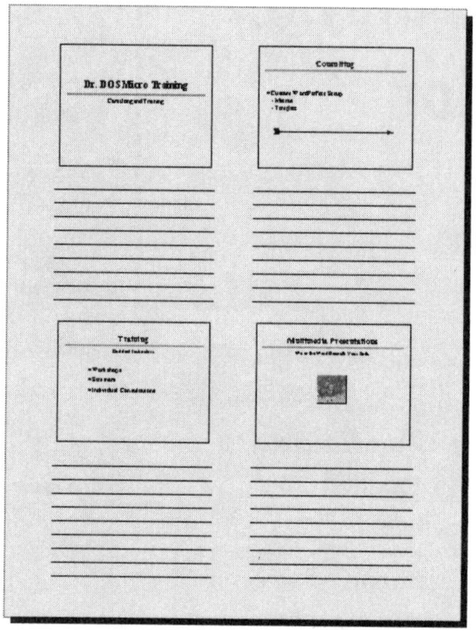

Handouts are merely pages with one or more slides printed on them, like the one shown in Figure 21.2.

Audience notes and handouts can be printed at any time after you have created your slides. Because Speaker Notes have additional text, you need to create them as a separate operation. To create Speaker Notes:

1. Open your presentation and choose Format, Slide Properties, Speaker Notes. The Slide Properties dialog box appears (see Figure 21.3).

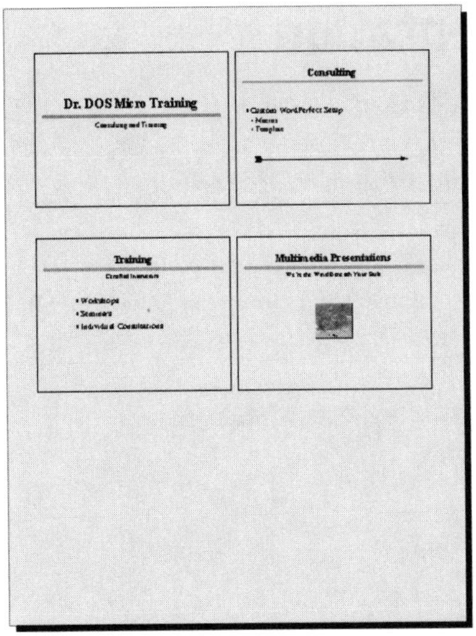

FIG. 21.2
Handouts have just the slides, with no lines or notes.

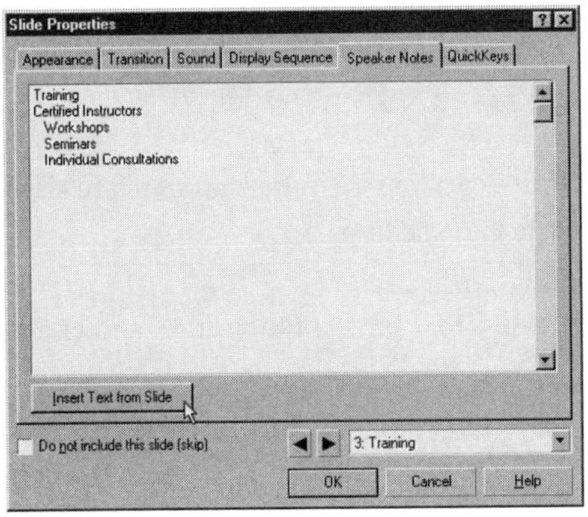

FIG. 21.3
Enter comments and notes on the presentation in the Speaker Notes tab of the Slide Properties dialog box; simply click Insert Text from Slide for quick Speaker Notes.

2. Using the drop-down list in the lower-right corner of the dialog box, select the slide to which you want to add notes.
3. In the text box, enter the notes. Check the Insert Text from Slide button if you want to include the text of the slide in your notes.
4. Repeat steps 2 and 3 to enter notes to additional slides without closing the dialog box.
5. When you are finished, choose OK to close the dialog box.

Printing the Presentation

When you are ready to print, you can choose which presentation element you want to print—such as slides, Speaker Notes, and so on—and you can choose the number of copies, binding offset, and other options before printing.

To choose printing options:

1. Choose File, Print, and ensure the Print tab is selected. You see the Print dialog box shown in Figure 21.4.

FIG. 21.4
Choose print options in the Print dialog box.

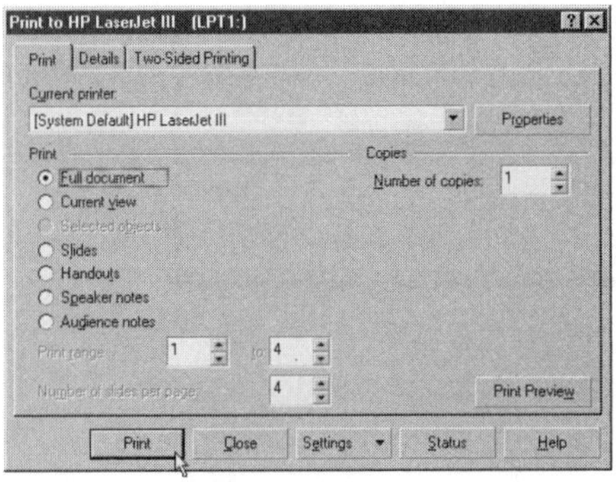

TIP Choose Print Preview in the Print dialog box as you select options to see how your printout will look. Press the Esc key to return to the Print dialog box.

2. Begin by choosing the printer you want to print to and change the printer properties, if necessary.
3. In the Print area, choose the element you want to print:
   - *Full Document.* Prints the full document.
   - *Current View.* Prints only what you see on-screen; for example, if you are in a magnified view (zoom), Current view prints only that which is showing.
   - *Selected Objects.* Prints only those objects you have selected from a slide.
   - *Slides.* Prints all or part of the slide show.
   - *Handouts.* Prints the slide show as thumbnails on handout pages so that viewers can make notes as they watch the show. Enter the number of slides you want on each page in the Number of Slides per Page text box.
   - *Speaker Notes.* Prints thumbnails, or small pictures, of each slide with any notes you entered as Speaker Notes (choose Format, Slide Properties, Speaker Notes).

- *Audience Notes*. Prints thumbnails along with lines so that the audience can take notes as you talk.

4. Select how much of your slide show you want to print (the range of slide), the number of copies, and (for more than one copy) whether you want to collate or group the copies, and whether to print in normal or reverse order. The options to collate or group copies appear only if you specify more than one copy.
5. If you are printing handouts or Speaker Notes, choose how many slides to print per page.
6. Choose to Print Slide Title, or Print Slide Number as a footer or caption beneath the printed slide.
7. If you want, you can click Print Preview to see how your document will look when it is printed.

You can also set other printing options from within the Print dialog box. By selecting the Details tab, you can choose from among these options:

- Choose the printer and printer port you want to print to, or add a new printer.
- Choose the Resolution—whether to print in high, medium, or low quality.
- Choose whether to Print in Color or black and white. If you don't have a color printer, you can't choose that option. You can choose to let your printer try to guess how to print the colors in black and white, or let Presentations Adjust the image to print black and white. On black-and-white printers, it often helps not to print the background of the slide.

TROUBLESHOOTING

I want to stop the print job after I choose Print in the Print dialog box. Presentations displays the Printing dialog box until the print job leaves the print buffer in Presentations. You can cancel the print job by clicking the Cancel button in this dialog box. After that, you can return to the Print dialog box (choose File, Print) and choose Status. From the list of current and past print jobs, click the document you want to cancel and choose Document, Cancel Printing.

If you cancel a print job from Presentations that is partially completed, and you aren't able to delete it from the print queue, then a partial print job will come out of the printer. Alternatively, you can click the Printer icon on the taskbar to display the Printer dialog box after the print job has spooled to Windows, then highlight the print job and choose Printer, Purge Print Jobs.

My color graphics and text look an overall gray when I print to a black-and-white printer. Choose the Details tab in the Print dialog box, then choose the Adjust Image to Print Black and White option. If you are still unhappy with the results, return to the presentation and select the

continues

continued

colored graphics you want to change. From the color palettes, you can choose from a variety of grays to assign text, chart markers, lines, fills, patterns, and so on. You may need to experiment with the grays to get the results you want.

NOTE If you have an HPGL plotter or a film recorder connected to your printer, you can print to either the same way you print to a printer. Using the Print dialog box, select the Print tab, then choose the printer you need from the Current Printer drop-down list. Choose any other options as you did before and click Print.

Creating an Electronic Slide Show

With Corel Presentations 8, you can create a slide show and display that show on your computer's screen—or project it from your computer via a data display panel or projection device—for customers, employees, or students.

Electronic slide shows provide you a much greater opportunity to enhance the presentation by adding transitions between slides, having bullets appear one at a time, animating slide elements, or including sound and video to create a multimedia presentation.

Arranging Your Slides

When you print your slide show, the arrangement of slides is not critical. You can shuffle your slides around and print them in any order that you desire. For electronic slide shows, however, you will need to ensure that your slides are arranged in the order that you intend to show them.

TIP If you have an initial slide that lists all your topics, consider copying this slide so that it is displayed before you start each new topic. This way, the audience will see how each topic fits into the presentation as a whole.

To rearrange your slides, switch to Slide Sorter view by clicking the Slide Sorter tab at the right side of the screen. You see thumbnails of each of the slides in your slide show. Select a slide by clicking it, or select several adjacent slides by clicking the first, then holding down the Shift key while you click the last. Drag the slide(s) you want to move to their new location. As you drag them, you see a vertical line that indicates where the slides will be placed, as shown in Figure 21.5.

FIG. 21.5
Rearrange slides by dragging them in Slide Sorter view.

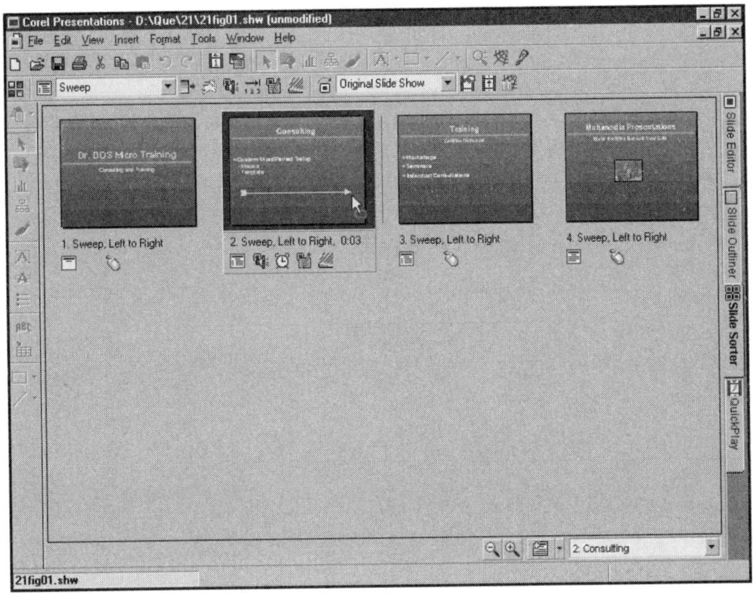

TIP Quickly copy a slide by holding down the Ctrl key while you drag it to its new position.

Adding Slide Transitions

The first option you will probably want to set for your electronic slide show is the transition you will use from one slide to another. You can specify that Presentations should go from one slide to the next when you press a key or click the mouse; or you can set Presentations to move from one slide to another after a specified amount of time. You can set transitions and timing for all slides or separately for each slide, if you like.

TIP If you use too many different types of transitions, the audience may become distracted. Set one transition for all slides, then vary it judiciously for a few slides in the presentation, if needed or for emphasis.

To set transitions:

1. Open your presentation and choose Format, Slide Properties, Transition; or right-click the slide and from the QuickMenu choose Transition. The Slide Properties dialog box appears (see Figure 21.6). (If you select the Slide Appearance toolbar button, you need to then select the Transition tab.)

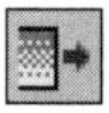

TIP A quick way to select just the transition you want is to click the Direction drop-down list from the Property Bar. As you point with the mouse at each transition type in the list, Presentations displays an animated preview box to show what the transition looks like.

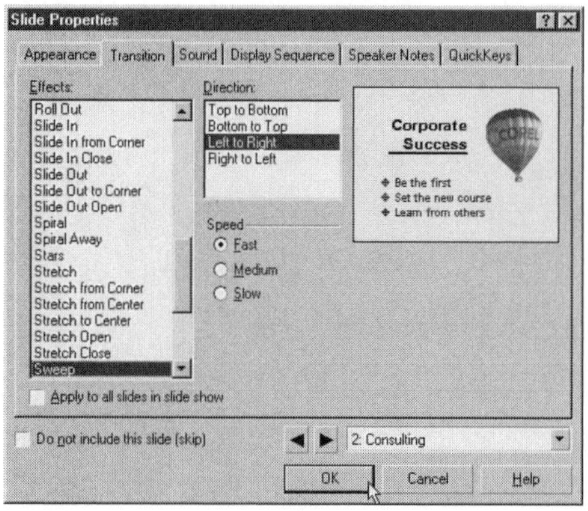

FIG. 21.6
In the Slide Properties dialog box, you can choose from a variety of transition effects that govern how one slide moves to the next.

2. From the list at the lower-right of the dialog box, select the slide for which you want to set options, or check Apply to All Slides in Slide Show.

TIP If you have multiple slides selected before displaying this dialog box, then the right/left arrows don't appear to the left of the slide number.

3. Select the transition type from the Effects list. You see how the effect works in the preview window. Depending on the transition you select, you may also choose the Direction that it will occur. Also, choose the speed for the transition.
4. Move to the next slide to which you want to add a transition, then repeat step 3 as needed.
5. When you are finished setting transitions, choose OK to return to your slide show.

▶ **See** "Playing Your Slide Show," **p. 430**

TIP If you are using Slide Sorter view, Presentations displays the type of transition you have set for each slide, as well as other icons to indicate timing, sound, Speaker Notes, and so on.

Adding Slide Timings

Normally, you want to manually advance from one slide to another so that you can spend as much or as little time needed on each slide.

Sometimes, however, you will want to have your slides advance automatically after a specified number of seconds. You may even want your slide show to loop continuously, as when you play it at a store entrance or convention table to advertise a product or service.

In this case, you will want to set timings for your slides. You can do so as follows.

To set timings:

1. Open your presentation and choose Format, Slide Properties, Display Sequence; or right-click the slide and from the QuickMenu choose Display Sequence. The Slide Properties dialog box appears with the Display Sequence tab selected (see Figure 21.7).

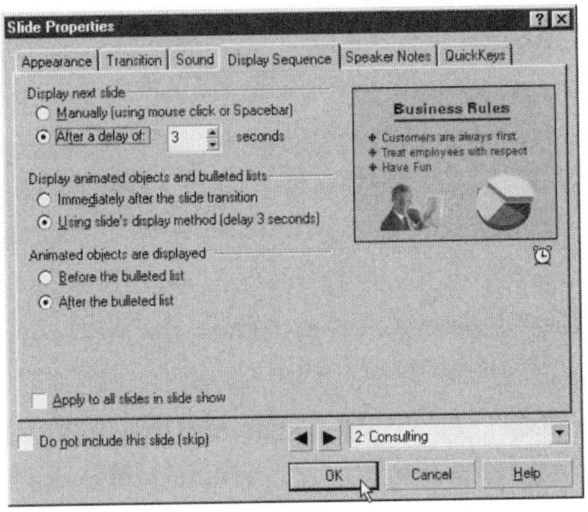

FIG. 21.7
You can have your slides advance from one to the next automatically after a specified number of seconds by setting options in the Slide Properties dialog box on the Display Sequence tab.

2. From the list at the lower-right corner of the dialog box, select the slide for which you want to set options, or check Apply to All Slides in Slide Show.
3. If you want to automate the slide timing, choose After a Delay Of, and specify the number of seconds between slides.
4. Choose options for any animated objects you have on your slide. If you select Immediately After Slide Transition, the animated object appears immediately after the slide has been drawn on screen. If you choose Using Slide's Display Method (Manually), the animations and bullets are displayed manually or after a delay, depending on the option you selected.

   ▶ **See** "Animating Slide Elements," **p. 426**

5. Move to the next slide to which you want to add a slide timing, and then repeat steps 3 and 4 as needed.
6. When you are finished setting timings, choose OK to return to your slide show.

Part IV Ch 21

TIP Set the seconds to delay higher for slides with a lot of information on them, so the viewer is sure to have enough time to read the information.

NOTE You can add sound to a slide show by using MIDI, digital audio, or CD audio sound files to one or more slides, if you have the sound hardware for the job. See the section "Including Multimedia Effects" later in this chapter.

Animating Slide Elements

You can animate your slides further by having bullets appear one by one, with old bullets becoming dim. You can also have drawing objects fly in from the side, giving an animated appearance to your slide show.

To animate your bullets in bullet slides:

1. Choose Slide Editor view by choosing View, Slide Editor, or by clicking the Slide tab at the right side of the screen. (You cannot animate bullets unless you are in Slide Editor view.)
2. Choose a slide that has bullets you want to animate, and click the bulleted list to select it.
3. Choose Format, Bulleted List Properties, and in the Bulleted List Properties dialog box choose the Bullet Animation tab. Alternatively, you can choose Format, Object Properties, Object Animation to see the dialog box shown in Figure 21.8.

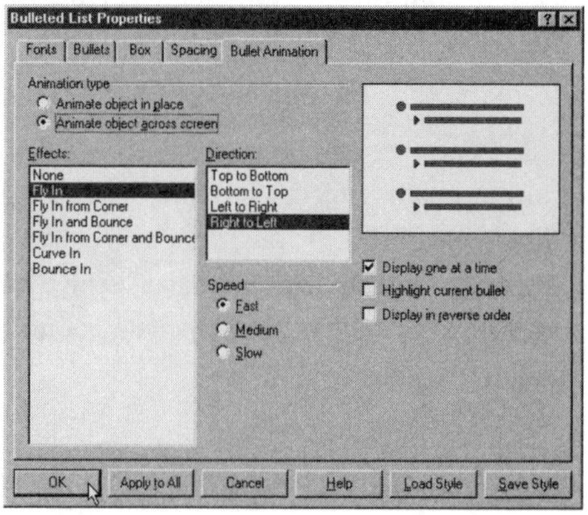

FIG. 21.8 Animate bullets with special effects to add pizzazz to your presentation.

4. Select the type of animation you want to use from the Effects list, and set the Direction and Speed. If you want previous bullets to become dim, choose Highlight

Current Bullet. You can also choose to display one bullet at a time, and to do so in reverse order if you like.

5. Click OK to exit the dialog box.

If you would like to animate drawing objects or QuickArt that you've placed on your slide, do the following:

1. Select the first object to be animated—the object which should appear first after the slide displays.
2. Choose Format, Object Properties, Object Animation; or right-click the object and choose Object Animation from the QuickMenu. You see the Object Animation Properties dialog box shown in Figure 21.9.

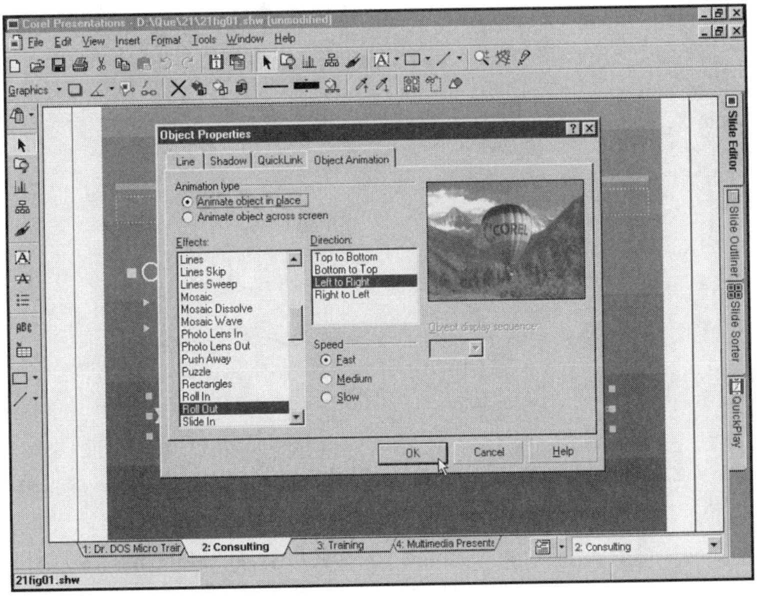

FIG. 21.9
In the Object Animation tab of the Object Properties dialog box, you can animate objects on your slide to have them fly onto the slide.

3. Choose the specific animation or transition effect you want to use, and the direction and speed, if needed.
4. Click OK to return to the slide.
5. Select the next object to be animated, and repeat steps 2 through 4. If you need to reorder the animated object, change its Object Display Sequence number.
6. Continue with this until all objects are animated.

Including Multimedia Effects

You can take your slide show one step further by adding sounds to it, or even video files (if your hardware supports sound or video).

Insert Sounds on Your Slide You can add short bursts of sound, like clapping hands, or longer melodies that you can play during the entire slide show, or during the display of one or more specific slides.

To add sound to your presentation, do the following:

1. Open your presentation and choose Format, Slide Properties, Sound; or right-click the slide and choose Sound from the QuickMenu. The Slide Properties dialog box appears with the Sound tab selected, as shown in Figure 21.10.

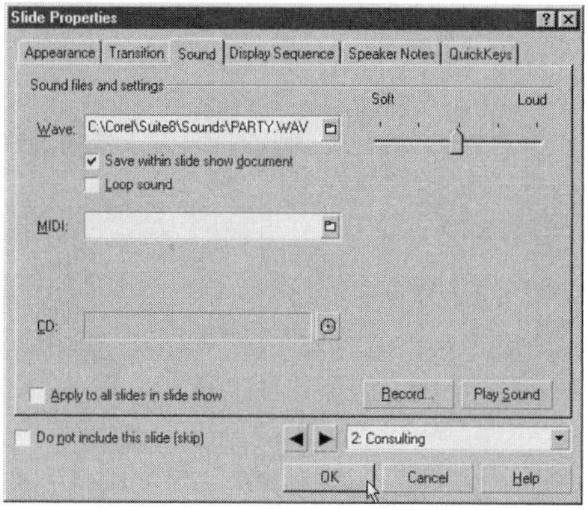

FIG. 21.10
You can add sound to your slides to make a multimedia presentation by using the Sound tab of the Slide Properties box.

2. From the list at the lower-right corner of the dialog box, select the slide to which you want to attach the sound.
3. Select the type of sound you want to use, then click the folder button to browse the folders and find the right sound file.

   Sound options include:

   - *Wave.* Digitized sound files. Usually they are quite large when saved to disk, but can be recorded and even edited with standard Windows audio tools.
   - *MIDI.* Considerably smaller and have much higher quality sound, but also require special equipment to record. However, most Windows systems play MIDI files without any problem.
   - *CD.* Use any sound recording on CD to play along with your slide show. You can even specify which track to play and where to begin and end on that track.

4. If you would like the sound to loop and keep repeating, choose Loop Sound. You can set the volume (for example, louder for the introductory slide, but softer for the slide where you'll be speaking). Click Play Sound to preview how it will sound.
5. If you have a microphone attached to a sound board in your computer, you can choose Record and add your own narration to your slides.
6. Choose OK to close the dialog box and return to your slide show.

TIP To play a sound throughout your presentation, attach the sound to slide 1 and loop the sound.

Add Video Clips to Your Slide Show You can use two methods to insert video clips into a Presentations slide show. The first uses Corel's method and works better with some of its Internet publishing capabilities. The second method depends on OLE (Object Linking and Embedding), and although it's more limited in what it can do, generally it works with a wider variety of movie file types.

To add a video clip to your slide show using Corel's method, do the following:

1. Switch to Slide Editor mode by clicking the Slide Editor tab, and click the tab of the slide you want to attach your video clip to.
2. Choose Insert, Movie. Browse to find the movie file you want and choose Insert.

If you get an error message with the preceding method, then try using OLE. To insert a movie using the OLE method, follow these steps:

1. Switch to Slide Editor mode by clicking the Slide Editor tab, and click the tab of the slide you want to attach your video clip to.
2. Choose Insert, Object. You see the Insert Object dialog box (see Figure 21.11).

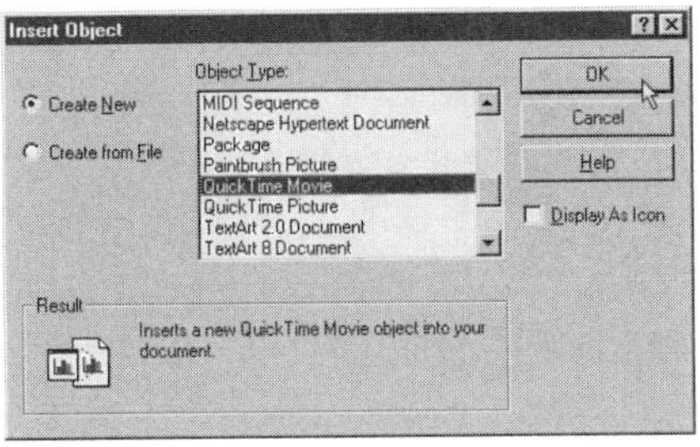

FIG. 21.11 Use the Insert Object dialog box to add a video clip or other multimedia object to your presentation only if Insert, Movie doesn't work.

3. Choose Create from File, then click the Browse button. You see the Browse dialog box.
4. Navigate to the video file you want to use, then double-click it. You return to the Insert Object dialog box. Click OK to return to the slide show.

Using either method, the video clip appears as an object on the appropriate slide. You can position and size the clip just as you do any other object. When the slide show reaches that slide, click the movie clip to play it.

Playing Your Slide Show

When you're ready to play your slide show, Presentations offers you options for moving from slide to slide, using mouse pointers and highlighters to draw attention to aspects of your slide, and saving your show as a Quick File to eliminate pauses in your slide show.

> **CAUTION**
>
> In the first release of Presentations 8, a dialog box appears if you do not have DirectX installed. This dialog box suggests that you go to the Corel Web site and download DirectX, a program from Microsoft that can assist in making slide transitions faster and smoother. Unfortunately, DirectX can also cause some rather severe problems by not interacting properly with your video hardware. Furthermore, once installed, you cannot remove DirectX from your system.
>
> You can ignore this message each time by choosing Continue, or you can download and install the DirectX program. If DirectX does cause problems, you can disable DirectX in Presentations 8 by choosing Tools, Settings, Display, and the unchecking Take full advantage of video memory for smoother transitions.

Playing a Slide Show When you run the slide show, Presentations clears the screen of tools, windows, menus, and everything except each slide.

To play a slide show:

1. Open the slide show. Choose View, Play Slide Show, or click the Play Slide Show button. The Play Slide Show dialog box appears, as shown in Figure 21.12.

FIG. 21.12
Choose to play the slide show, and Presentations offers you options as to how you can present your slide show.

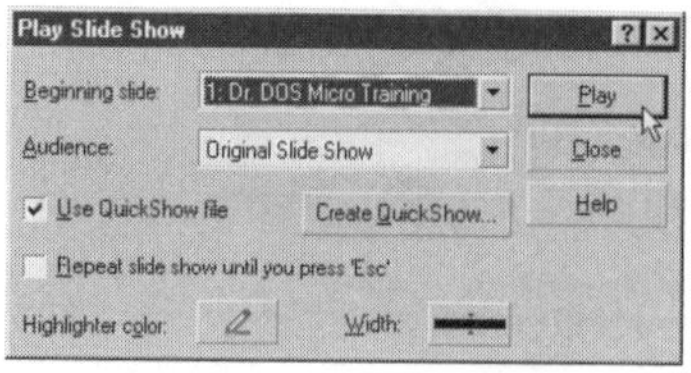

2. From the Beginning Slide list, choose the slide you want to start the presentation with.

3. You can use the mouse to highlight slides as you present them. Choose the Color and the Width of the marker you want to use during the presentation.

TIP Draw on the slide by clicking and dragging with the mouse. Don't just click the mouse, because that will cause the slide show to advance to the next slide.

4. Choose Repeat Slide Show Until You Press 'Esc' if you want the show to run continuously.
5. Choose Play to start the show.

Play Options While you are playing your slide show, you have several options.

If the show is set to Manually advance the slides:

- Click the left mouse button, or press the right arrow or down arrow to advance to the next slide.
- Press Esc to cancel the show at any time.
- Click the right mouse button for a QuickMenu that enables you to jump to the first, last, next, or previous slide; end the sound; or increase or decrease the volume. Keystroke equivalents also are listed on the QuickMenu.

To show the cursor during your slide show, move the mouse pointer. The cursor appears on your slide.

To highlight an area of your slide with an underline, move the mouse pointer to where the underline should start, and then drag the mouse pointer to draw an underline.

Creating a QuickShow File Create a QuickShow file of your slide show to speed up the display. When you create a quick file, you save the slide show as bitmap and thus the display is much quicker; however, the file is much larger than a slide show, so make sure you have enough room for the show on your disk.

To create a quick file, choose View, Play Slide Show. The Play Slide Show dialog box appears. Choose Create QuickShow. If you haven't saved your file, you will be prompted to do so before the QuickShow is created. You see a Making QuickShow dialog box as the file is created.

When you play your slide show in the future, you can choose to use the QuickShow file by checking the Use QuickShow file box in the Play Slide Show dialog box.

TROUBLESHOOTING

I made a change in one of the slides, and now the slide show seems slower. If you saved the slide show as a quick file and then made a change to the show, you must create a quick file again to speed up the display.

I am saving a copy of the slide show to a floppy disk, but I am worried the show is too large to fit on one disk. You can usually fit one slide show onto a high-density 3 1/2 or 5 1/4 floppy disk; however, if your show file is larger and fills up the disk, Presentations prompts you to insert a second disk.

Making a Runtime Slide Show

Making a runtime slide show means to copy the show with all necessary program files to a disk so you can run the show on another computer that does not have Corel Presentations 8 installed.

To make a runtime file:

1. Open the slide show or save the current show.

2. Choose File, Show on the Go. The Show on the Go welcome screen appears (see Figure 21.13). The options that appear may be those from the last time a Show on the Go file was created.

FIG. 21.13
The Show on the Go option allows you to copy your presentation to a disk so that it may be run from a computer that does not have Corel Presentations 8 installed.

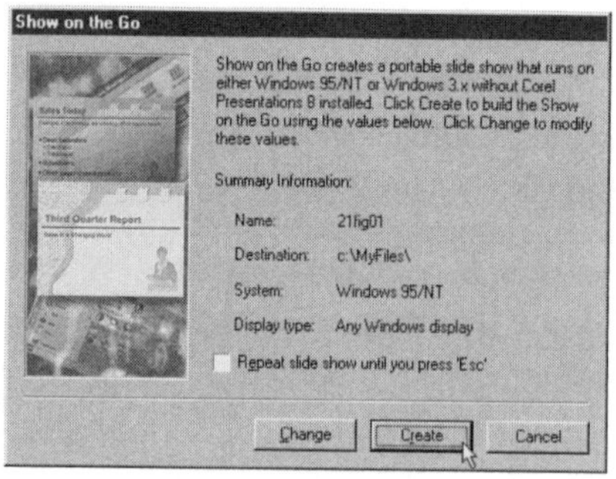

3. Choose Change. You see the second step of the Expert shown in Figure 21.14. Select the drive or folder where you want to create the Show on the Go file, then choose Next. (If you choose a folder that does not exist, you will be asked if you want the Expert to create it.)

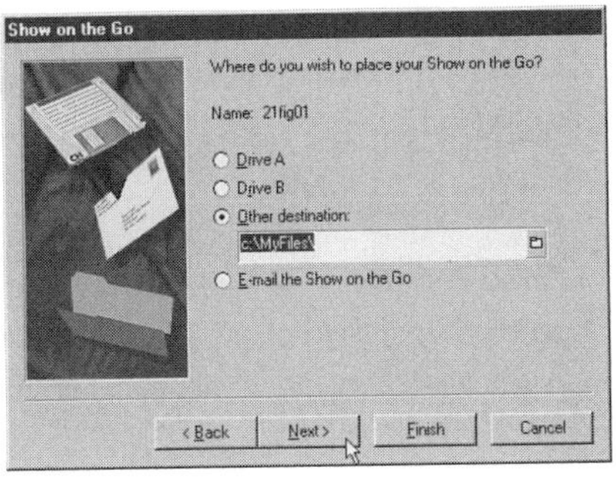

FIG. 21.14
Choose whether to save your runtime slide show to a floppy disk or to a folder on your hard drive.

4. In the third step of the Expert, select whether your show will be played on a Windows 95/NT system or on both Windows 3.x and Windows 95/NT systems (see Figure 21.15). Choose Next.

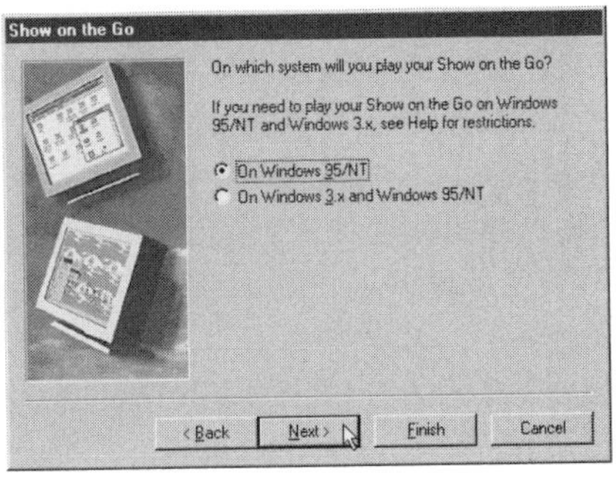

FIG. 21.15
Tell Presentations on what kind of system you plan to play your slide show.

5. In the fourth step of the Expert, select whether the display of the system you will play your slide show on matches yours, or whether it should be able to be played on any Windows display. Choose Finish.

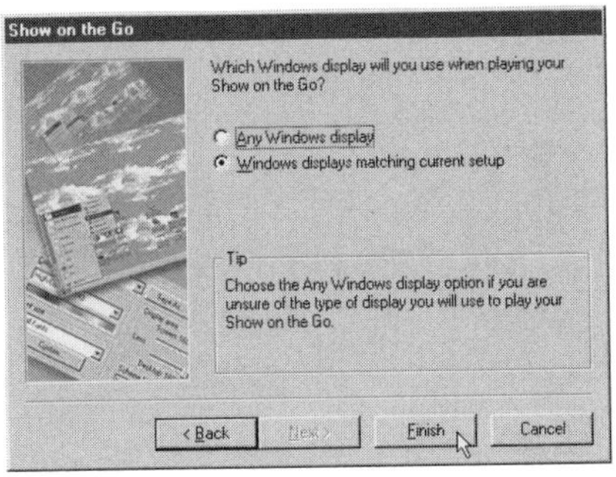

FIG. 21.16
Tell Presentations on what kind of display you plan to show your slide show.

6. The final step shows the choices you have made (refer to Figure 21.13). If any are incorrect, choose Change Again to revisit previous steps. If they are correct, choose Create. You see the Making Runtime dialog box as your show is converted, then you return to the main Presentations window.

NOTE If you choose to save the show so that it can be played both in Windows 95 or Windows 3.1, you will experience certain limitations. All transitions will be immediate, and animation will be removed. Slides with cascading bullets, however, will still play normally. Quicklinks and OLE objects also will not work.

PART V

Using Internet Applications

CHAPTER 22

Using Corel WordPerfect Suite on the Internet

The Internet is a network comprised of millions of computers and computer networks spanning the globe. Because of its global reach, and because so many computers are connected to it, people increasingly find it to be an indispensable business tool, as well as a wonderful vehicle for home use. ■

Understand Internet Basics

Find out what all those funny terms mean: Internet, intranet, World Wide Web, URLs, browsers, and more.

Recognize implications of publishing on the Internet

When you publish to the Internet, the whole world can see it! Find out tips and tricks you should use.

Use the Netscape browser

Learn how to "Surf the Web" with Netscape Navigator, and how to "pull" information off the Web.

Get online help

Help on the Internet, Netscape, and Corel WordPerfect Suite is available on the Internet. Find out how to access it quickly and easily.

Understanding Internet Basics

People use the Internet in many ways to increase their productivity in business and to access a wealth of information:

- *To communicate.* Internet e-mail programs allow people to send and receive e-mail with anyone else who has an Internet connection, anywhere in the world. There are no long-distance telephone charges for this; the only cost is your normal fee for connecting to the Internet. The Internet is also used for public discussions on topics ranging from using WordPerfect to sugarless baking recipes.
- *For information.* Computers on the Internet store a wealth of information. While some of it is private or for-fee, much is free to the public. You can access things including the Library of Congress card catalog, a nationwide telephone directory, maps to go from anywhere in the U.S. to anywhere else, the *Commerce Business Daily*, encyclopedias, dictionaries, and literally millions of other sources of data.
- *For commerce.* Increasingly, businesses are creating a presence for themselves on the Internet. Corporations advertise new products, provide customer support, and even sell products via the Internet.

NOTE Secure communication methods are just beginning to make their debut. Many companies allow you to purchase items with your credit card; unfortunately, security is not yet as tight as it might be, and cases of credit card fraud are becoming more common.

- *For business.* Businesses are using the Internet to create wide area networks, in which regional offices are connected together using the Internet rather than dedicated phone lines.

Physically, the Internet is comprised of a backbone of mainframe computers that are tied together with high-speed optical fiber cables. Networks "hook into" the backbone with fiber optic, copper, and even regular telephone lines. The Internet constitutes a complex web of these computers, where information may go from one place to another through any of thousands of routes, automatically bypassing computers that are out of service, or where the load is too heavy.

These Internet computers are often called *hosts* or *servers*, because they are the "hosts" for users, and "serve up" databases and other applications. Hosts and servers actually have technical meanings, but in general conversation they are used to refer to the Internet computers you log on to and link to.

NOTE If you're on a network, your Internet connection will provide faster or slower response time depending on how much "bandwidth" (or simultaneous information) your connecting line into the Internet supports. The slowest dedicated lines are 56K lines; they barely support one or two connections to the Web. Faster lines are T1, and T3 connections are even faster. If you're connecting to an Internet Service Provider via a modem, the speed of the modem is the limiting factor.

Computers on the Internet communicate by using *protocols,* or agreed-upon ways of transferring information. The Internet is comprised of many types of computers, and these computers do not "speak each other's language" easily. Thus, they need to transfer information in a lowest common denominator—protocols that they can all adhere to. One of these basic protocols is TCP/IP, which is a way of breaking down information into small chunks (called packets) that can be easily transmitted over the network. Another protocol you will learn about in this chapter is HTTP—a way of transmitting files that contain graphics, sound, or video over the Internet.

What Is the World Wide Web?

The World Wide Web is a part of the Internet that supports graphic and multimedia files. The protocols used on the Internet support only the transmission of ASCII text files, not the complex binary files that make up applications and data files like WordPerfect documents.

To get around this shortcoming, complex coding systems have been developed to translate programs and data files into plain text. One of these mechanisms is HyperText Markup Language, or HTML. Using HTML, bold text is denoted by *tags*—ASCII codes that denote, for example, `<b>` as the beginning of bold and `</b>` as the end of bold. Similarly, `<H1>` denotes the Heading 1 style, and `</H1>` denotes the end of it.

NOTE HTML is actually a subset of a much more complex protocol called SGML (Standard Graphics Markup Language). SGML also uses tags to format ASCII text, but in addition supports rules that determine which text elements can follow which others (for example, a Heading 1 must immediately be followed by Heading 2) and the like.

WordPerfect supports SGML, although using SGML is beyond the scope of this book. If you are interested, Que's *Special Edition Using SGML* is an excellent and comprehensive treatment of this topic.

▶ **See** "Creating Web Documents," **p. 496**

HTML has one other important feature. It allows you to define *links*—highlighted areas of a document that, when clicked, take you to another document elsewhere on the Internet.

See "Adding Links and Bookmarks," **p. 501**

The World Wide Web—often referred to as WWW or the Web—is comprised of Internet servers that support HTML. These servers constitute a web, because they are not hierarchically organized. The links on one HTML document may take you to a variety of others, and the combined links resemble a spider web more than a hierarchical organizational chart.

When you publish a series of interlinked HTML documents on the Web, they become a *Web site*, and each HTML document, once it has been uploaded to the Web, is called a *Web page*. The main page on your site that a person would usually go to first is called the *home page*.

See "Copying Documents to Your Web Server," **p. 508**

What Are Intranets?

The Web, in an earlier form, was originally begun by the United States government Department of Defense to permit contact between its departments and universities. As it grew, other universities and government agencies, and later corporations and other organizations, realized the power of the Web to communicate externally and to tie together remote offices.

The next logical idea that occurred to people was: If the Web could be used to communicate externally, why not use it to communicate *internally* as well? Intranets were born. An intranet is an internal Web, comprised of one or more Web servers that are connected to each other, but are not accessible to the larger Internet community. In effect, an intranet is just like a piece of the World Wide Web, except that outsiders generally cannot access the intranet (often, you must be physically logged on to a computer at the site), and access to the Web from inside the intranet is sometimes limited as well.

Why have an intranet? Many organizations do not have standards for hardware and software. Employees often will use a variety of software packages, so that putting a document up on a network is no guarantee that others will be able to read it or edit it. Similarly, if an organization has a variety of computers—Apples, PCs, UNIX-based computers, and Sun workstations, they may not be able to even access the same network to begin with. You can access the World Wide Web from virtually any type of computer, running almost any type of operating system. Thus, by setting up an internal Web—an intranet—the communication problem is solved.

The growth of corporate intranets is expected to be one of the biggest trends in computer use over the next two to three years. It is for this reason, as well as the ability to publish documents to the Internet, that Corel has built HTML functionality into all its major products. It has also developed Barista—a technology that permits publishing documents in Java on intranets or the Internet.

▶ **See** "Publishing Documents with Barista," **p. 511**

▶ **See** "Publishing Spreadsheets with Corel Barista," **p. 518**

▶ **See** "Publishing Corel Presentations with Barista," **p. 537**

NOTE Java is a programming language that creates simple applications (called applets) that can be included in Web pages. Assuming that your browser supports Java, the applet is automatically downloaded when you access a Web page that contains it.

The first and simplest Java applications were ones that created animated figures or sound. Newer Java applets create interactive games on Web pages, allow you to search a database on the Web server that isn't stored as an HTML document, or show complex document formatting without the document being written in HTML.

Connecting to the Internet

There are two main ways you connect to the Internet: by logging into a local area network (LAN) that is connected to the Internet, or individually through an Internet Service Provider (ISP).

Connecting via a Network If you work at an organization that has a LAN, it is probably connected to the Internet, or will be within a year or two at most. Alternatively, your LAN may be connected to a corporate intranet, which offers the same functionality (other than connecting to the rest of the Internet). In any case, if you are on a LAN, connecting to the Internet or an intranet is a simple matter of talking to your system administrator. They will tell you what (if any) connections are available, and how to access them.

Connecting via an Internet Service Provider If you are not on a network, you can still access the Internet and the World Wide Web. To do so, you will need four things: a modem, a telephone line, software to access the Web (a Web browser), and an account with an Internet Service Provider (ISP).

A *browser* is an application that is used for looking at ("browsing") Web pages. Browsers do more than this, however. If you are like most people, your primary connection to the Internet will be via the Web, and your browser is your main tool for connecting to the Web. You can look at Web pages; move across links to other Web pages; save Web pages or download linked files to your local computer; or print Web pages. Browsers also include e-mail programs to send and receive e-mail over the Internet, and newsreaders to participate in public discussions called *newsgroups*.

One of the most popular browsers today is Netscape Navigator. Netscape Navigator 3.0 (or its latest version, called Communicator) is included as part of the Corel WordPerfect Suite 8.

Different browsers support slightly different HTML feature sets, and earlier versions of browsers do not support as many HTML features as later versions of even the same browsers. For instance, some browsers support tables and forms; others do not.

When you use the WordPerfect Suite to publish HTML documents, you should recognize that these documents may look slightly different in various browsers, and that some features may not be supported at all. Web page creators often will put a note on their Web page saying something like "This page is best viewed in Netscape 3.0 or later versions."

CAUTION

If you have access to different browsers, it's a good idea to look at documents you produce in each one to ensure that it can be read by the greatest number of people possible.

An ISP (Internet Service Provider) is a company that has a computer connected to the Internet (an Internet host) and modems that subscribers can connect to. ISPs sell subscribers UserIDs with which they log on to the Internet host computer, and thereby access the Internet.

There are many different ISPs that service various regions of the country. Some are nationwide, offering local telephone numbers in major cities throughout the U.S. for those who travel.

TIP Many ISPs provide you with free browser software with which to access the World Wide Web. The most common browser that is offered is Netscape Navigator.

Some are value-added ISPs, offering technical support, giving interesting information to subscribers on Web sites, or providing automated processes for creating your own Web sites.

What About Other Online Services?

Many households are connected to online services, such as America Online (AOL) or CompuServe Information Services (CIS). These services originally started as completely separate networks that could be accessed from virtually anywhere in the U.S. Within the last two years, they have offered access to the Internet, and eventually may migrate entirely *to* the Internet, becoming sites that can be accessed for a fee, rather than maintaining a separate network infrastructure.

Online services offer a host of easy-to-use features and a friendly interface designed to help the novice get online and feel comfortable getting started. They are also much more expensive to use, if you are online extensively.

As of this writing, subscribers to online services use proprietary software to access them and, through them, to the Internet. Such proprietary software often does not support the full range of features found on many Web pages.

Your ISP will give you several items of information that you will need to connect to the Internet. These include your UserID and password, and several technical items required when you configure Windows 95 to dial to your ISP. You don't need to know what these mean, but you do need to get the following information: the phone number to dial, a primary and secondary Domain Name Server (DNS) address, an SMTP outgoing mail server name, a POP incoming mail server name, and the news server name.

The mail and news server names are used to configure your browser for e-mail and newsgroups, discussed in Chapter 23, "Communicating on the Internet."

Alternatively, your ISP may give you a disk or CD that has a setup program that will not only install a browser, but will configure Windows 95 for you.

NOTE If you are on a LAN that is connected to the Internet, you probably have a fairly high-speed connection, and you see graphic pages loading rather quickly (1-3 seconds, or even faster). If you use a modem to connect to the Internet, the connection is between 5 and 50 times slower than a LAN connection. Complex graphic pages may take as long as five minutes to load, although most will load in 5 to 30 seconds.

TIP Remember that many people have slower Internet connections when you make your own Web pages. If you use too many graphics, many people will find your site too slow and thus unattractive.

Understanding Internet Addresses

Before you start "surfing the Web" or sending Internet e-mail, you will want to know the addresses of sites you want to visit, or people with whom you'd like to exchange mail. It's easiest to do this by starting with e-mail addresses.

E-Mail Addresses A person's Internet e-mail address consists of three parts: their UserID, the "@" symbol, and the name of the host computer on which they have an e-mail account. Typical e-mail addresses include:

bill.bruck@marymount.edu

bbruck@phoenix.marymount.edu

bruck@concentric.net

bill@purple.tmn.com

Notice that in all these addresses, there is a UserID, the @ symbol, and the name of a host computer.

The UserID is created by the rules (or vagaries) of the system administrator, and most often follows one of four conventions: full name, separated by a period (bill.bruck), first initial and last name (bbruck), last name only (bruck), or first name only (bill). This latter is for very small systems, or for the system administrators themselves, who most often get first choice of UserIDs.

The host name is comprised of two or more parts. The suffix, for Internet hosts in the U.S., refers to the type of organization: com (commercial), edu (educational), org (non-profit organization), net (network), gov (government), or mil (military). If the host is in another country, the suffix refers to a country code: ca (Canada), uk (United Kingdom), and so forth.

The name preceding the suffix is usually the name of the organization: marymount (Marymount University), concentric (Concentric Corporation), tmn (The MetaNetwork), and so on.

An organization sometimes will have several Internet hosts. In this case, they may specify the name that the system administrator has given to the computer that your UserID is on: purple, phoenix, and so on. (System administrators have notoriously weird senses of humor, so be prepared for some unusual computer names.)

Note that all names are lowercase in these examples. Most names will be lowercase, but in any case, depending on the Web server, names may be case-sensitive. However you see the name, be sure to type it exactly that way, just in case.

Internet Site Addresses A site on the Internet to which you may go will also have an address. This address is technically called a Uniform Resource Locator, and is most usually referred to by its initials, URL, and spelled out or pronounced "earl."

Typical URLs include:

http://www.wordperfect.com

http://home.netscape.com

http://www.tmn.com/personal/bruck/bb&a.html

The first term in these URLs—http—indicates that the site is an HTML file, or a Web page. (http stands for Hypertext Transport Protocol, and is used to refer to HTML documents in an URL.) Occasionally, you will access other types of sites, such as ftp:// or gopher://. These are used for older, pre-Web ways of accessing information on the Internet. Don't worry, your browser will still handle them.

The next term, **www.wordperfect.com**, is the name of the server that you are accessing. Although you don't see this, your browser looks for the files "index.html," "index.htm," "default.html," "default.htm," "home.html," or "home.htm" and displays whichever file it finds.

Sometimes, you will browse to a specific directory on a server, like the /newfeatures/ directory in the third example. Again, the browser looks for the files index.html, index.htm, home.html, or home.htm in the specified directory.

TIP The newest version of popular browsers such as Netscape does not require that you type the "http://" part of the URL any more. Thus, you can just type **www.corel.com** rather than the longer http://www.corel.com.

Occasionally, you will browse to a specific file in a specific directory on the server, such as the bb&a.html file in the last example.

TIP URLs can be confusing, but don't worry about them. Usually, you will merely click a highlighted term to browse to a location. If you need to go to a specific URL, however, be sure to type it exactly as it was given to you, because URLs are case-sensitive on many servers.

Understanding the Implications of Publishing on the Internet

Creating a Web page can be technically easy, but there's far more to it than that from a legal and marketing perspective, so don't be naïve about it. Literally, the *whole world* is watching and can see what you put out there.

Several issues must be considered in publishing information on the Internet. One of these issues concerns taking information from another site and republishing in your own documents—to the Internet or an internal intranet.

- There are blatant copyright infringement implications (either individual or corporation/company ones) if another's information is copied onto your Web documents and published to another site. Copyright is automatically implied and does not require registration for all pages on the Web. It's much better to link to a site than copy it into your own documents.
- Even if you are publishing on an internal intranet site, that information could still be taken by someone else and used on their site or in a brochure. For instance, say you see a great tip for using a product on the company's Web site. You cut and paste this tip into a document on Tips and Tricks. This is an internal document just for those in your company to view, so you don't see the need to worry about copyright issues. The Public Relations department sees your document, and decides that the best idea in there is the tip that you happened to get from the company itself. They pull that idea out and put it in one of their advertising brochures, which goes out to the world at large including, of course, to the company. The company then sees that their information was used and, at worst, another lawyer can meet his or her rent that month or, at best, customer confidence in your firm is jeopardized.
- The validity of the information that's out on the Internet may be hard to verify. Care should be taken as to how and when it is used. References to where it was obtained should always be included so that readers can make up their own minds as to its "truth" or accuracy.
- Another issue concerns linking to other sites. There is a matter of company policy and image. Say a company is a child-oriented entertainment company with their primary market being families with children under five years of age. This company has advertised that they are "family sensitive" and that their Web sites are "safe" for children. If someone within the company publishes a page with a link to a site that has material that is legal, but would be unacceptable for viewing by small children, the company might be financially or legally liable for damages by lawsuits of the families for false advertising, or more. Or, worse, the word could get around about the connection and the company's business could suffer because of word of mouth that they were not following the "values" that they had said they would. For this reason, many organizations have policies about clearing Web pages with the public relations, marketing, or legal department before posting information.

- You may also want to think about issues surrounding privacy of information. A phone book listing employees' work and home numbers may be customarily distributed in hard copy throughout the organization. If this same information is put on a Web site accessible to the world, the privacy of employees may be impinged on.

While the issues above are all real and important, they are by no means comprehensive. Many other similar issues exist, and would-be Web publishers need to think about legal, ethical, and practical considerations prior to uploading files that the whole world can see.

NOTE The fact that the Internet is composed of many types of computers has one other practical implication for publishing documents on the Internet. You should save your documents using DOS naming conventions (eight characters, no spaces). This eliminates problems that users of other computers have (such as Windows 3.1-based systems) with reading long file names, and with trying to figure out truncated file names.

Introducing Netscape Navigator

Netscape Navigator is one of the most powerful and popular browsers you can buy—and you get it free with Corel WordPerfect Suite 8.

NOTE The WordPerfect Suite 8 comes with Netscape Navigator version 3.0. Future releases of the suite may ship with Netscape's replacement for Navigator– Netscape Communicator. Information on Communicator will be available at Que's Web site:

http://www.quecorp.com

Because the name most people use for the Netscape Navigator browser is "Netscape," the browser is referred to in this chapter as Netscape (which is actually the company name, not the name of the product).

Using Netscape, you can access World Wide Web pages and follow links from one Web site to another (this is called "browsing" or "surfing" the Web). You can also save files you browse on your local computer or print them if you want. Additionally, you can download program or data files directly to your disk.

Netscape even has an e-mail program that allows you to exchange mail with people worldwide, and a newsreader that allows you to participate in public discussion groups. (These two features are discussed in the next chapter.)

TIP You can access Netscape directly from your Corel WordPerfect Suite applications by clicking the Browse to Web button available on toolbars in WordPerfect, Presentations, and Quattro Pro.

Learning the Navigator Screen

Figure 22.1 shows the Navigator screen. You can turn certain screen elements on and off, including the toolbar, location bar, and directory buttons, by choosing the appropriate option from the Options menu. Sometimes you will access Web pages where you cannot see the entire page from top to bottom, and the page is an integrated whole (not one you want to scroll through). In this case, turn off the display of one or more of these items to see the entire Web page.

FIG. 22.1
Your browser allows you to access the Web and view and download files from it.

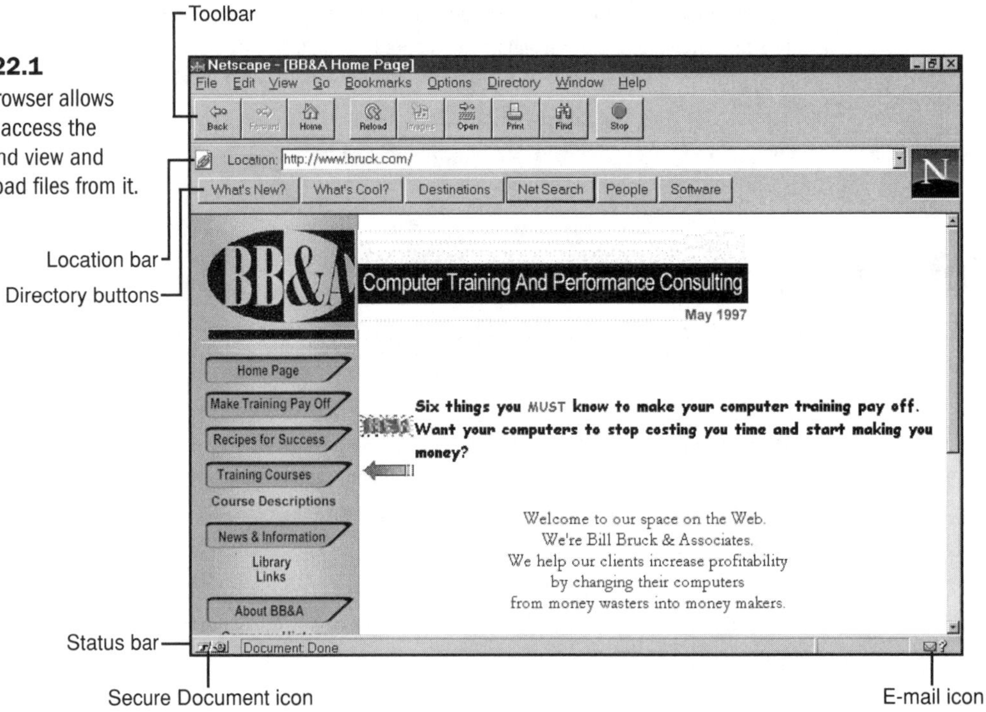

The screen elements that follow will help you browse the Web.

Learning the Navigator Screen Elements

The Toolbar contains buttons that permit you to easily accomplish the most common tasks you will do in Netscape:

- *Back.* Becomes active after you have moved through a link. It allows you to go back to the page from which the link originated.

- *Forward.* Becomes active after you have moved back through a link. It allows you to go forward through the same link without having to locate the link and click it.
- *Home.* Takes you to the site that you access by default when you open Netscape.
- *Reload.* Reloads the site. This can be useful if the page has changed, or if you interrupt the loading process before the page has loaded completely.
- *Images.* Loads the images at the site. (Netscape allows you to load the text portion of sites alone, which can be useful if you access graphics-intensive sites with a slow modem.)
- *Open.* Shows you an Open Location dialog box, where you can type in the URL of a site you want to go to.
- *Print.* Opens the Print dialog box, which allows you to print the current Web page.
- *Find.* Searches the currently loaded Web page for text you specify.
- *Stop.* Halts the loading of the page that is currently being accessed.

The Directory buttons allow you to connect to Netscape's home page, which has a number of resources that list new or "cool" sites and interesting destinations, help you find topics or people on the Web, and allow you to order and download Netscape software products.

The Net Search button is a particularly useful one. It allows you to search for keywords that appear in any page throughout the Web, giving you instant access to information worldwide by using a variety of popular searching programs called *search engines.*

TIP Search engines are one of the most powerful tools on the Web, but each one prioritizes the information it finds differently. Therefore, it's useful when searching to try several different engines for the most thorough search.

Similarly, the Directory button takes you to a Web page listing several available directory services. You can use these services to locate people throughout the world that have Internet e-mail accounts or Web sites.

Other elements that help you browse the Web are:

- *Location bar.* Shows you the URL of the site you are currently viewing. You can type the URL of a new site directly in the location text box and press Enter to go to that site.
- *Secure Document icon.* Informs you whether the document you are viewing is encrypted, or a document is sent openly (in which case hackers or system administrators could more easily intercept the transmission).

- *Status bar messages*. Tell you the process of a document that is being loaded, and when the loading is done.
- *E-mail icon*. Takes you to the e-mail program that allows you to exchange e-mail with others on the Internet. This function is discussed further in Chapter 23, "Communicating on the Internet."

Browsing the Web and Specifying Destinations

Browsing is the process of moving from one Web page to another through links on Web pages. You can actually go from one Web page to another in three different ways: by browsing (following links), by specifying the URL of a Web page you want to go to, or by using *bookmarks*.

TIP Web pages are dynamic, not static. Corporations change their Web pages regularly to improve readership. Thus, many Web pages are here today, gone or changed tomorrow—without notice. The best surfing philosophy is if you see it and need it, grab it and print it or download it, as it may not be there the next time you go out.

Browsing the Web

Most Web pages contain *links*—codes that specify another location on the Web. Some links are text, in which case the text appears in a different color. Others are graphical—often icons or small pictures.

When you move your mouse pointer over a link—whether the link is text or a graphic image—the mouse pointer changes to a hand, as shown in Figure 22.2. The address to which the link points is also displayed in the status bar. When you click the link, the new page appears on your screen.

To browse the Web using links, click the link. You are taken to the Web page that the link points to.

To go back to the Web page from which you came, click the Back button. If you want to go through the link again, click the Forward button.

You can also go back to the default Web page—your *home* location—by clicking the Home button at any time.

FIG. 22.2
When you are on a link, the mouse pointer changes to a hand.

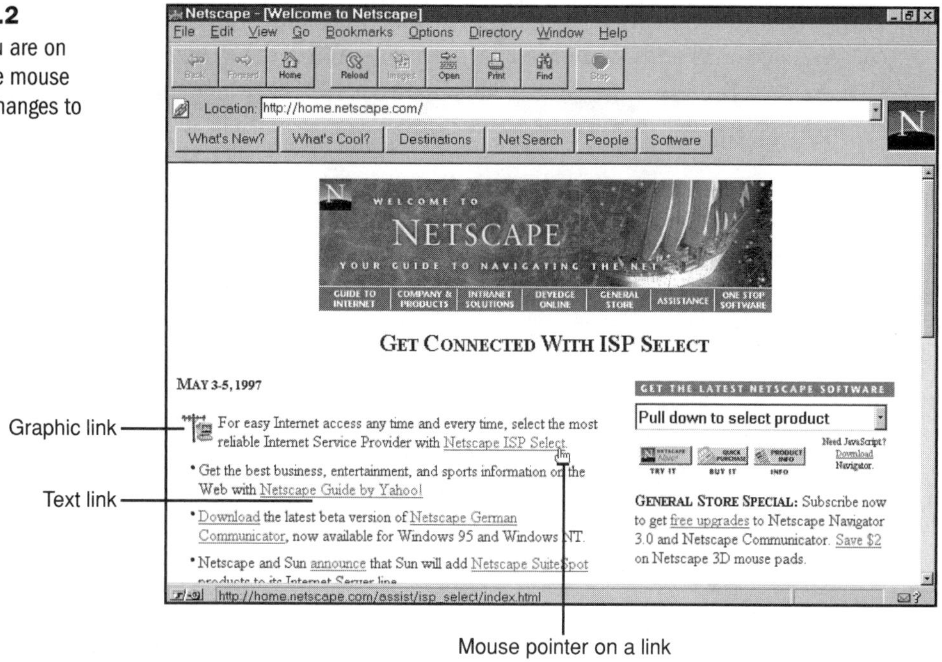

Going Directly to Web Pages

The second way to browse the Web is to go directly to a Web page by specifying its address—technically, its Uniform Resource Locator, or URL.

To go to a specific Web page, choose File, Open Location. You see the Open Location dialog box shown in Figure 22.3. Type in the URL and choose Open. You are taken directly to that location on the Web.

FIG. 22.3
Go directly to a Web page by specifying its URL.

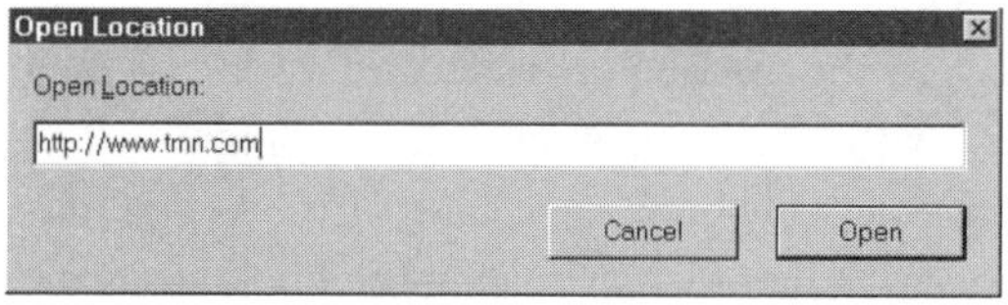

> **TIP** You can also click the Location box, edit the URL there or type in a new one, and press Enter to go to a specific address.

If you have Web pages stored on your local or network drive, you can access them via Netscape as well. This can be very helpful when you are creating pages with the

WordPerfect Internet Publisher and want to see how they will look in Netscape. To open a Web page on your disk, choose File, Open File. You see the Open dialog box shown in Figure 22.4. Browse to the folder containing your Web page, and then double-click it to open it in Netscape.

FIG. 22.4
You can open Web documents stored on your disk from the Open dialog box.

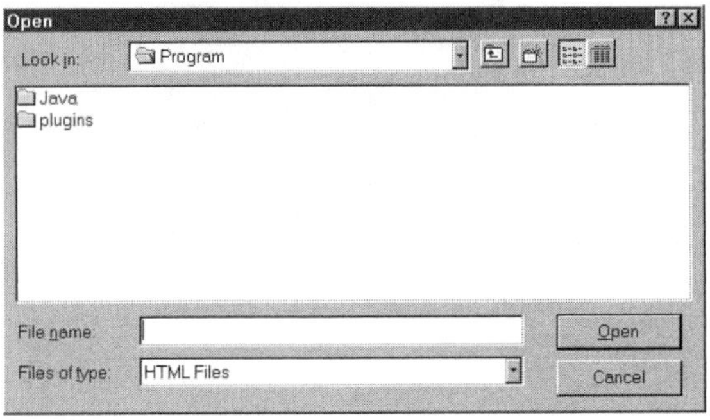

Using Bookmarks

After you've used the Web for a while, you will find certain sites that are particularly valuable and that you'd like to be able to go back to quickly. Typing in URLs is a tedious process, and you can easily make a mistake.

For this reason, Netscape allows you to save the names and addresses of your favorite sites in a list of *bookmarks.*

NOTE The term "bookmark" has a different meaning in Netscape and in WordPerfect. In Netscape, bookmarks are favorite sites, saved in a file named bookmark.htm. In WordPerfect, a bookmark is a marked place in a document that you can quickly jump to.

Using Existing Bookmarks To go to a location for which a bookmark already exists, choose Bookmarks. You see the Bookmarks menu, listing all the bookmarks you have created, or that come with Netscape. Some of the bookmarks have arrows to their right, indicating that they are actually bookmark categories. As you move your pointer over a category, you see a cascading menu showing the bookmarks in that category (see Figure 22.5).

Click the bookmark for the site you want to browse. Netscape accesses that site and, assuming it's not out of service, you are taken to it.

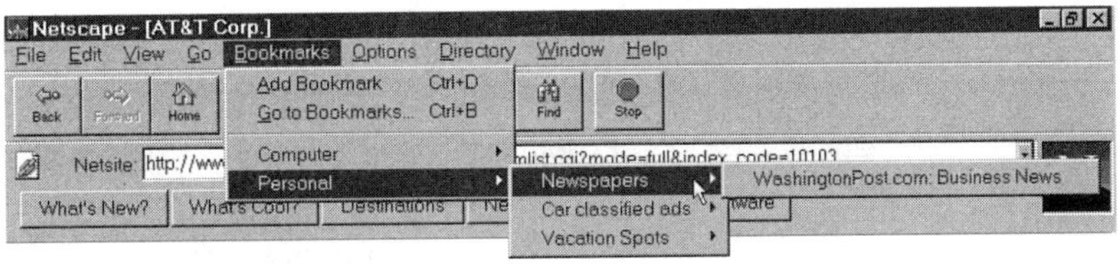

FIG. 22.5
Go back to your favorite sites quickly by using bookmarks that you have created.

> **TIP** If you have more bookmarks than will display on the screen, More Bookmarks is the last entry in the list. Click it to see the rest of your bookmarks.

Creating New Bookmarks To create a new bookmark, browse to the desired site using any of the methods discussed previously.

While you are at the site, the URL for the site appears in the Location box of Netscape. Choose Bookmarks, Add Bookmark. Your new bookmark is added to the end of the bookmark list, and you can access it whenever you want.

NOTE Your bookmarks are stored in an HTML file (a Web page type of file) named BOOKMARK.HTM. By default, it is stored in a subfolder of the Netscape\Users folder.

Editing Bookmarks To edit your bookmark list, choose Bookmarks, Go to Bookmarks. You see the Bookmarks dialog box shown in Figure 22.6.

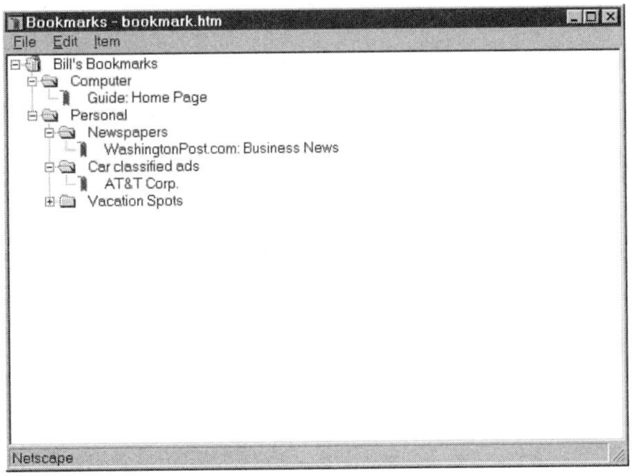

FIG. 22.6
You can create new category folders for your bookmarks, or move them from one folder to another in the Bookmarks dialog box.

Edit your bookmarks as follows:

- Delete a bookmarkby selecting it, and then pressing the Delete key.

- Move a bookmark from one folder to another, or to another place on the bookmark list, by selecting it and dragging it to its new location.
- Create a new category folder for your bookmarks by selecting the bookmark below the new folder to be created, and then choosing Item, Insert Folder. You see the Bookmark Properties dialog box shown in Figure 22.7. Type the name for your new folder, and then click OK.

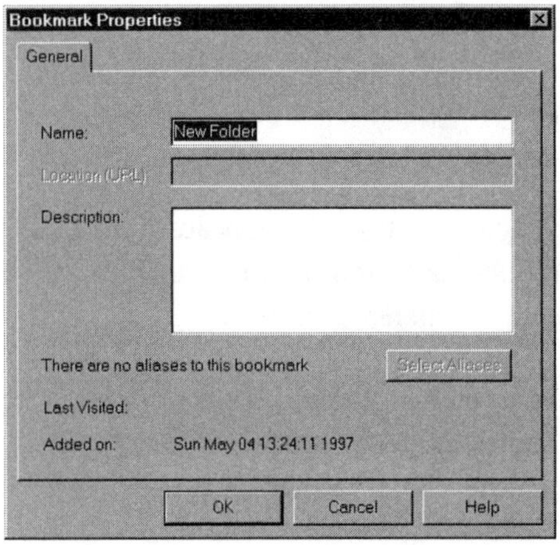

FIG. 22.7
Create new category folders to organize your bookmarks in the Bookmark Properties dialog box.

- Insert a separator line underneath the current folder by choosing Item, Insert Separator. You see a Separator icon below the folder, and when you list your bookmarks again from the Netscape Bookmark menu, you see a separator line underneath that folder.
- Combine another bookmark file with the current bookmark file by choosing File, Import. You see the Import Bookmarks File dialog box (see Figure 22.8). Browse to the folder containing the bookmark file you want to import, and then double-click it.

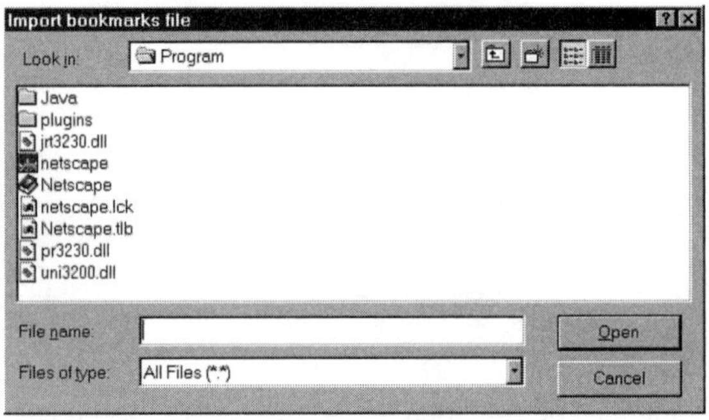

FIG. 22.8
Combine two bookmark files by importing one into the other in the Import Bookmarks File dialog box.

Printing, Downloading, and Executing Files

After you've browsed to a Web site containing useful information, what's next? You may want to print the information, save it to a file on your own computer, or even execute certain types of applications.

Printing Files

To print a Web page, you merely need to browse to it, and then choose File, Print. You see the Print dialog box shown in Figure 22.9.

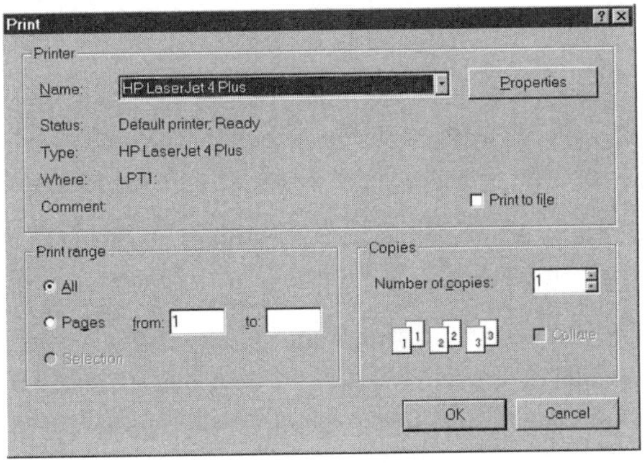

FIG. 22.9 Print your Web pages, including graphics, using the Print dialog box to maintain them in hard copy if desired.

Your Web page is printed to the selected printer, including graphics that are on the page.

Downloading Files

You will often access the Web to obtain information. When you do, you may want to save the files you find to your local computer.

You can do this in two ways: saving Web pages that you browse to, and saving data files that Web pages point to.

Saving Web Pages When you want to save a Web page, do so as follows:

1. Browse to the page in Netscape.
2. Choose File, Save As. You see the Save As dialog box (see Figure 22.10).

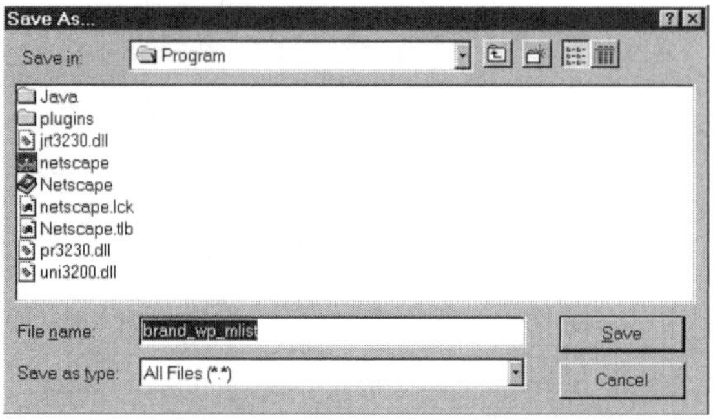

FIG. 22.10
Save Web pages directly to your local computer through the Save As dialog box.

3. Navigate to the folder in which you want to save the Web page, enter a name in the File Name box, and choose Save. Your file is saved in the designated folder.

When you save a Web page, it is saved in HTML format. You can open this file in Word Perfect and edit using WordPerfect's Internet Publisher. You can even upload it back on to the Web, if you have the necessary permissions to upload files to that Web site.

For more information about editing Web documents, see Chapter 24, "Integrating Corel WordPerfect 8 with the Internet."

Saving Data Files When you visit a Web site, there often will be links to data files or even programs that you can download. If the data files are not in HTML format, your Web browser may not be able to view them directly—especially if the browser does not have an add-on viewer that is configured for that type of file.

When you click a link to a program file or a data file that your browser cannot view, you can opt to download it into your computer, where you can open it with the proper application or even (in the case of a program file) execute it.

Customizing Netscape to Your Preferences

You usually will not need to change options in Netscape. Occasionally, however, you may want to fine-tune your installation.

One set of preferences you may want to set controls Netscape's appearance. To set these preferences, choose Options, General Preferences, Appearance. The most common options you might want to set in the Appearance tab shown in Figure 22.11 include the following:

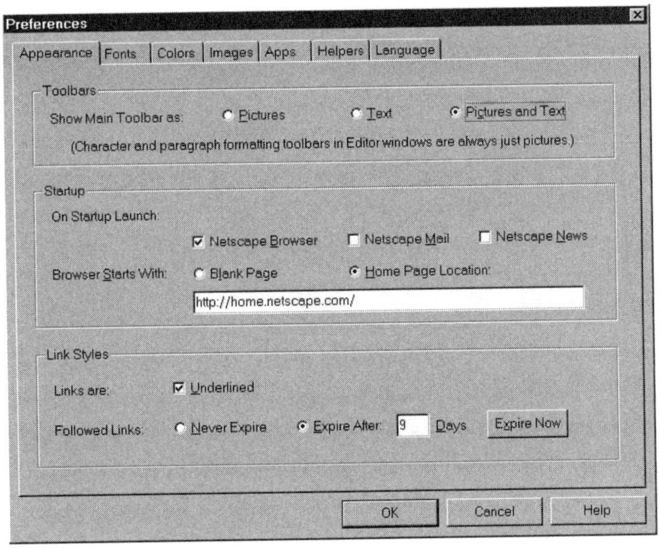

FIG. 22.11
The Appearance tab of the Netscape Preferences dialog box allows you to choose which options are in force and which applications start when you open Netscape.

- *Toolbars*. Showing the toolbar as text only can give you more area to see your Web pages.
- *On Startup Launch*. If you check your mail whenever you enter Netscape, you might consider checking Netscape Mail to launch the mail application automatically.
- *Browser Starts With*. Specifies the Web site that you see initially when you open Netscape. By default, it is **home.netscape.com**, but you may prefer to see a page from a favorite news service, your corporate home page, or even a personal startup page you create that includes links to your favorite sites.
- *Followed Links*. Allows you to specify how long a link stays colored after you follow it. Having the links you have followed appear in color helps you to find your way around the Web; it's a little like leaving a trail of bread crumbs!

You can also select the Fonts or Colors tab to change the font and color of text and backgrounds in the Web documents you browse to.

Another preference you may want to set is the amount of cache you use for saving old Web pages. If you are connecting via modem, graphic-intensive pages take a long time to load. For this reason, you can save pages you have visited in a cache—a place on your disk where temporary files are stored. This way, if you go back to a graphic-intensive page soon after visiting it, you may not need to reload it. Netscape will load it from your disk (which is very fast) rather than your modem (which is relatively slow). The price you pay, however, is that you are using up disk space.

To set your cache size, choose Options, Network Preferences, Cache. You see the Cache tab shown in Figure 22.12

FIG. 22.12
Set your cache on the Cache tab of the Netscape Preferences dialog box to enable you to reload sites from your computer's disk rather than the Internet.

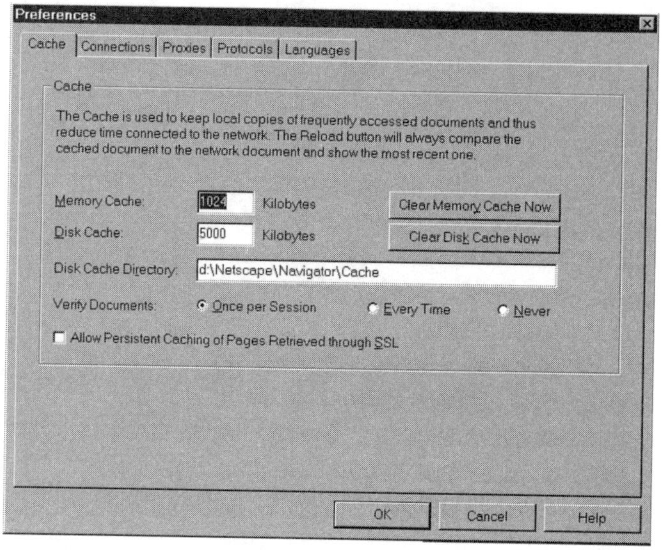

To make reloading Web pages as fast as possible, set your memory and disk caches to the maximum size that allows you to maintain enough free memory and disk space for other applications, and then click OK to close the dialog box and save your changes.

Finding Help on the Internet

You may want to get help on Netscape, on other Corel products, or on subjects unrelated to Corel software.

▶ **See** "Using Help," **p. 22**

To obtain help in using Netscape, choose Help, Handbook. You see the Netscape Navigator Handbook shown in Figure 22.13. The handbook is actually a number of linked HTML pages that are obtained from the Netscape Web site, as you can see from the URL displayed in the figure.

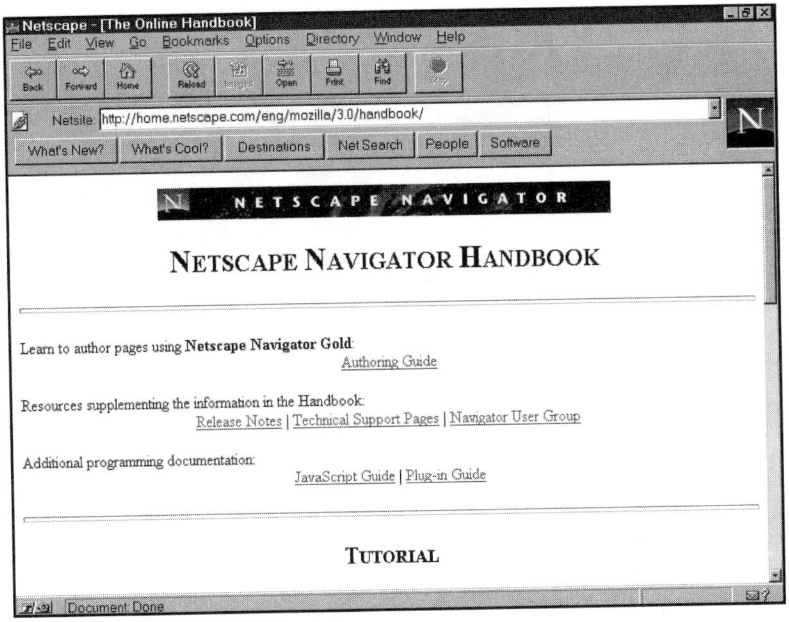

FIG. 22.13 The Netscape Navigator Handbook is obtained from the Netscape Web site.

NOTE Netscape does not maintain extensive help files on your disk. Instead, when you need help, you are connected to the version of the handbook maintained at the Netscape Web site; thus, you connect to the Internet to always see the latest version of the handbook.

Browse through the contents to see help on all aspects of using Netscape.

TIP Click the Destinations button for sites, news, and events on the Internet; or click the Software button to obtain other Netscape products.

If you'd like to search the Web for help with virtually any other question you might want to ask, the Web has powerful tools called *search engines* that can assist you. Want to know the difference between a cocktail and a highball? The name of Dudley Dooright's horse in *The Rocky and Bullwinkle Show*? Search the Web to find out.

Click the Net Search button on the Directory bar to access a Web page that lists popular search engines. You are taken to the Net Search page. Its exact appearance changes regularly, but it will resemble the site shown in Figure 22.14.

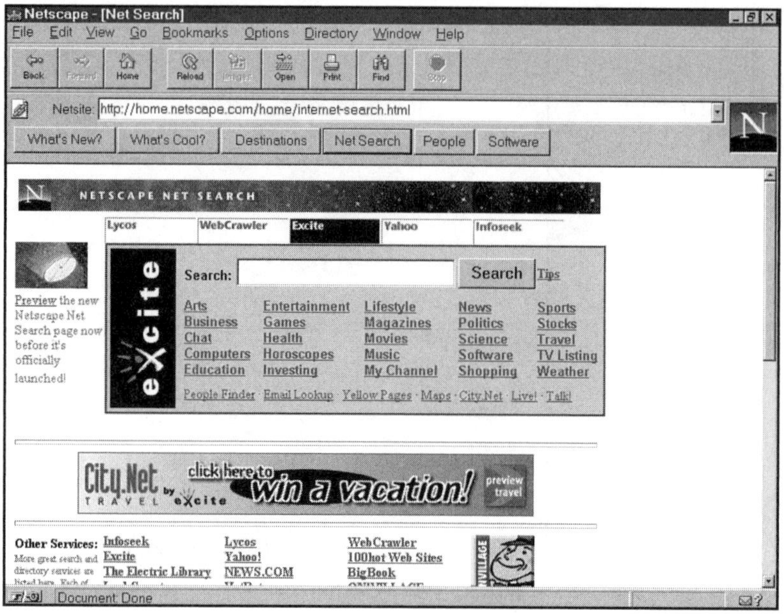

FIG. 22.14
Net Search allows you to search the Web for information of interest.

There are several major search engines that compete for your business. Although they are free to you, you see advertisements for different vendors when you use them; this pays for the service.

The search engines shown in Figure 22.14 include Excite, Yahoo!, Infoseek, Lycos, and Magellan. Each time you access Net Search, you will see a different one of these engines, randomly chosen. In Figure 22.14, it's Excite.

Choose the search engine you want to use; if it is not displayed, click its button. Type the words you are searching for in the text box, and click the Search button.

Millions of documents on the Web are searched, and within a few seconds, you see a list of the documents that best match the terms you searched for (see Figure 22.15).

FIG. 22.15
Search engines show you the documents that best match the terms you searched for.

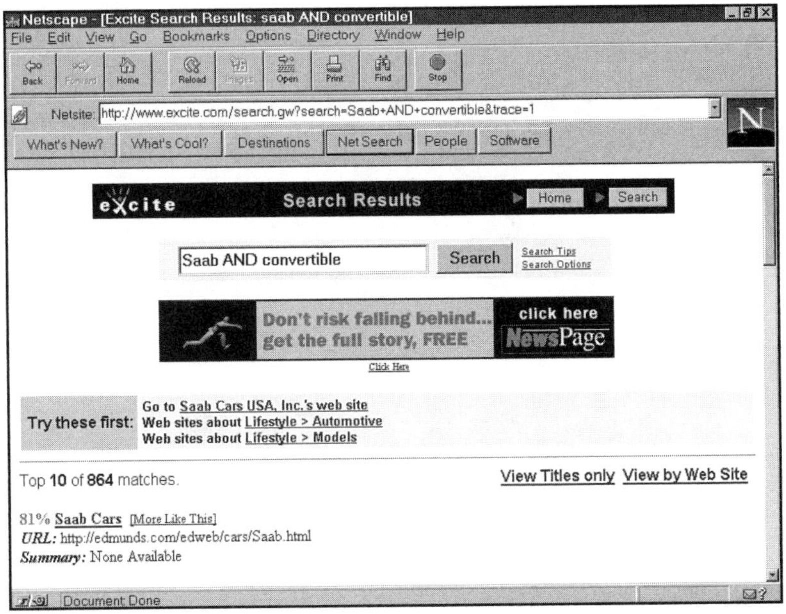

TIP Different search engines often produce different results. As you start, use several of them with the same terms. You will eventually settle on one or two that best meet your needs.

CHAPTER 23

Communicating on the Internet

Use netiquette

Learn about the correct and not-so-correct ways of communicating in the new world of instant online messaging.

Use Netscape Mail

Learn how to send and receive mail and attachments, and maintain an address book for frequent contacts.

Join a mailing list

Find out how to use your Netscape Mail to participate in on-going discussion groups.

Subscribe to newsgroups

See how to use the News Reader to subscribe to on-going newsgroups.

The main use of the Internet is still for communication between people and organizations. Netscape enables you to speak privately with an individual or group via electronic mail, or e-mail. Mailing lists bring public discussions to your e-mail inbox. Newsgroups enable you to participate in on-going conversations that are categorized by topics and responses. This chapter will teach you how to use all three methods to communicate on the Internet. ■

Understanding Netiquette

Netiquette stands for ***network etiquette***, and concerns rules of politeness or "correct behavior" when communicating electronically. The basic rule of netiquette is the same as the basic rule of etiquette: Be considerate of the other party.

Some netiquette rules apply to all communication; others are more specific to the type of communication (private e-mail conversations versus public mailing list and newsgroup conversations) you may have. See the section "Participating in Mailing Lists" later in this chapter. Some netiquette rules that apply to all communication include:

- Keep paragraphs short and to the point, and double-space between paragraphs. It is very hard to read long paragraphs if there is little or no white space in the text.
- DON'T SHOUT! Capitalized text is considered shouting. It's hard to read, and inconsiderate to your reader. Rather, use *asterisks* to emphasize points, or _underline at the beginning and ending of emphasized characters_ for such things as book titles.
- Would you say it to a person's face? This question is asked by Virginia Shea in her online book *Netiquette*. It serves as a nice criterion for whether you are being impolite.
- Use abbreviations and emoticons (*smiley faces*) judiciously. Several abbreviations have become part of the "language" of the Internet; others are more obscure. Use only the abbreviations and emoticons that your recipients are likely to understand. Common abbreviations include IMHO (in my humble opinion), FYI (for your information), BTW (by the way), and PMFJI (pardon me for jumping in). The most common emoticon is :) which represents a smile, but there are many variants on this.

TIP In Netscape, click the Search button, then search for **emoticon** to find sites that have entire pages filled with cute smileys.

NOTE Because the name most people use for the Netscape Navigator browser is "Netscape," the browser is referred to in this chapter as Netscape (which is actually the company name, not the name of the product).

- Don't flame. *Flaming* happens when content-oriented discussions take on a personal, ad hominem, flavor. Often, they resemble the feeding frenzy of sharks as more and more people are drawn into the fray. Watch out for sarcasm and other forms of hostile humor; they don't translate well into print.

- Wait before responding in sensitive instances. It is *so* easy to respond with e-mail that people often do so without thinking through what they are saying and the impact it will have. If you receive an e-mail that causes you to have a negative response, the best thing to do is to send the answer to yourself. Then wait several hours or overnight and reread it. If it still sounds okay, send it. But in many instances, you may find that you will want to reword it before you hit the Send button. Remember that what you write does not necessarily translate to how you would have actually said something. Emphasis, de-emphasis, and sarcasm are hard to feel in an e-mail.

Understanding E-Mail Netiquette

E-mail is a private communication between you and one or more persons. Additional netiquette rules that apply to such mail include the following:

- Always enter a subject. When there is no subject in an e-mail message, the reader must open the message to see what it's about. Many people receive scores of messages each day, and often want to open just the urgent ones when they only have a few minutes.
- Use quote-backs sparingly. Netscape, by default, inserts the entire original message in your reply. Making a person wade through their own words to see your response is impolite. If there's a specific question or point you are responding to, quote that sentence or paragraph—not the whole message. A method of incorporating relevant phrases that you want to respond to is described in the section "Reply to Mail" later in this chapter.
- Attribute things properly. It's easy to cut a person's words out of an e-mail message or a Web site and include them in your e-mail. If you do not attribute them to their source, it is impolite at best and illegal (if the site is copyrighted) at worst. Similarly, be careful about forwarding personal mail someone sends you or posting it to public mailing lists or newsgroups.

There are a few other rules that you might want to consider when you're sending business e-mail:

- Business e-mail is a business communication. Use the same degree of formality or informality as you would in any other mode of written business communication, like a letter or a memo.
- Consider using a *signature block*. If you do, this is a short (no more than three-line) trailer at the end of your message that identifies who you are, your company, and alternative ways of contacting you. Long signature blocks or promotional signature blocks are rude.

- Focus your recipient list. Sending a promotional e-mail to several thousand people who are not selected on any basis other than availability may be good business, but it may generate more ill will than sales.
- Weigh formality. The Internet makes doing business internationally easy, but remember, many people find Americans overly informal in their use of first names. When in doubt, err on the side of formality.
- Keep it short. Try to keep general correspondence to two screens, or put your most important summary data up front. People tend to read a couple of screens and then decide they'll read the rest later—sometimes not getting back to it for quite a while, if at all.
- Don't spam. *Spamming* is sending unwanted messages, most often ones that are self-promoting, off-track, or sent to hundreds of people.

Although we usually think of netiquette as rules of politeness between us and our e-mail recipients, there are also some netiquette rules regarding our e-mail and our system administrator that are cited by Arlene Ribaldi in *The Net: User Guidelines and Netiquette.* These include:

- Check e-mail daily and respond as promptly as possible.
- Delete unwanted messages immediately because they take up disk storage, and remain within your limited disk quota.
- Keep messages remaining in your electronic mailbox to a minimum.
- Mail messages can be downloaded or extracted to files, then to disks for future reference.
- If you are using e-mail at work, remember that the e-mail system and the e-mail itself are the property of the organization; they are not yours. They are like any other work product you produce for hire. Abide by the guidelines and rules of your organization regarding e-mail.
- Never assume that your e-mail can be read by only yourself; others may be able to read or access your mail. Or, someone may forward your e-mail to others with your posting information still visible. Never send or keep anything that you would mind seeing on the evening news.

Understanding Public Conversation Netiquette

Public conversations, like mailing lists, have a few different netiquette rules, because of the nature of the communication. Here are some of the most important ones:

- Monitor the list. When you first join a conversation, listen for a while before jumping in. Often, you'll find that many of your questions are answered within a week or so by just listening to the on-going flow of conversation. This will also give you a sense of the social atmosphere of the conversation—how personal or formal it is, whether long or short postings are encouraged, and so on.

- Combine public and personal modes. If you have a response to someone's remarks that pertains to him or her only, consider responding by e-mail rather than publicly. Conversely, if a person asks a question to which you know the answer, and you suspect that others might benefit as well, post the answer in public.
- Know what to ignore. If remarks are off the subject or personal in nature, resist the temptation to jump in. This only adds to the fire (for personal remarks) or the amount of off-the-subject text.
- Have tolerance. If newcomers ask questions you regard as elementary, or mistakenly send a private message to an entire group of people, be tolerant. You probably made some of the same mistakes when you were starting out.

Set Mail and News Preferences

Before you can start using mail or newsgroups, you need to identify yourself and your Internet server. To do so, obtain the following information from your system administrator or your Internet service provider (ISP):

- Your UserID
- Your Outgoing Mail (SMTP) server name
- Your Incoming Mail (POP) server name
- Your e-mail address
- Your News (NNTP) server name

Then, set up Netscape for mail and news as follows:

1. Open Netscape.
2. Choose Options, Mail and News Preferences, and select the Servers tab.
3. Fill in the Outgoing Mail (SMTP) Server, Incoming Mail (POP3) Server, POP3 User Name (your UserID), Mail Directory, News (NNTP) Server, and News RC Directory.
4. Choose the Identity tab.
5. Fill in your name, e-mail ID, reply-to address, and organization, as shown in Figure 23.1.
6. Click OK when you are finished.

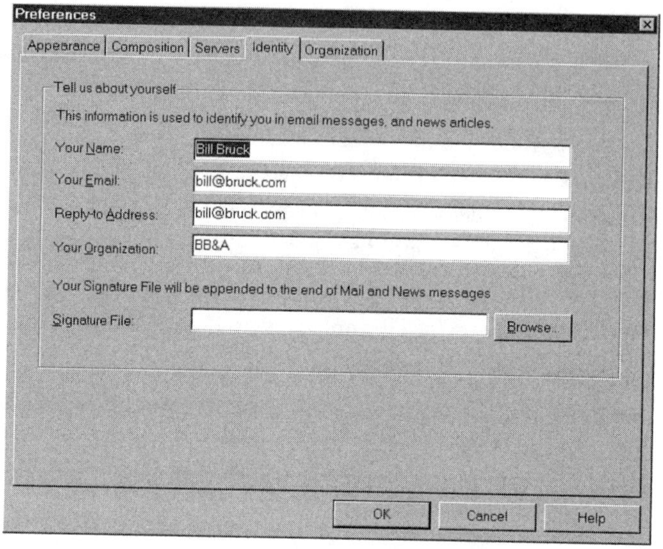

FIG. 23.1
Finish setting mail preferences by filling in information about yourself in the Identity tab of the Preferences dialog box.

Using Mail

After Netscape is configured, you can send and receive e-mail to and from anyone in the world via the Internet.

To access Mail, choose Window, Netscape Mail, or click the Mail icon at the bottom right of the Netscape window. The first time you enter Mail, you are prompted to enter a password. Enter the appropriate password and choose OK. You see the Mail window shown in Figure 23.2.

From the Mail window, you can send, receive, and organize mail into folders. Before learning how to send mail, however, you'll want to know how to maintain a list of your frequent correspondents in the Address Book.

Using the Netscape Address Book

The easiest way to address mail is to store recipients' addresses in the *Address Book*. You can access the Address Book from either the main Navigator window or the Mail window by choosing Window, Address Book. You see the Address Book window shown in Figure 23.3.

NOTE The Netscape Address Book is a file containing e-mail addresses, used only in Netscape. This is different from Corel Address Book 8, which is a stand-alone application.

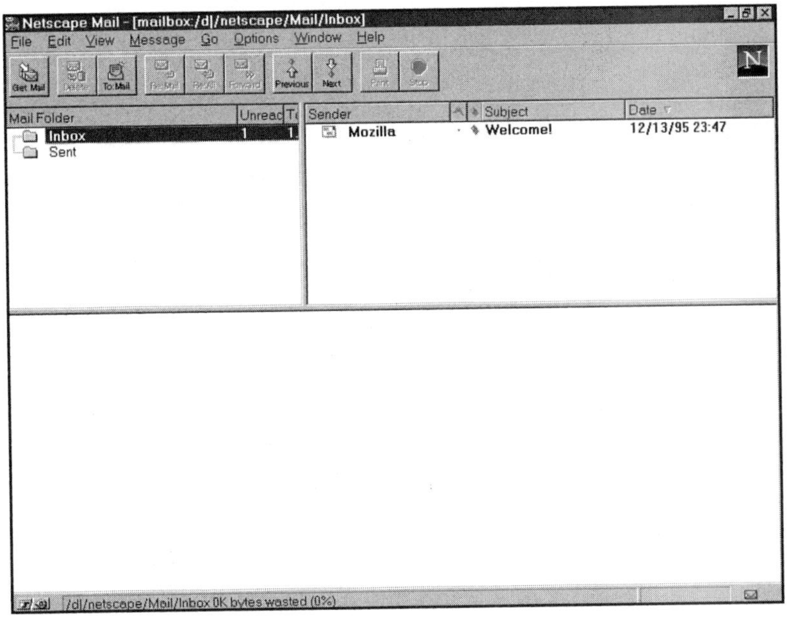

FIG. 23.2
The Mail window allows you to send and receive e-mail, as well as store it in a folder that you create.

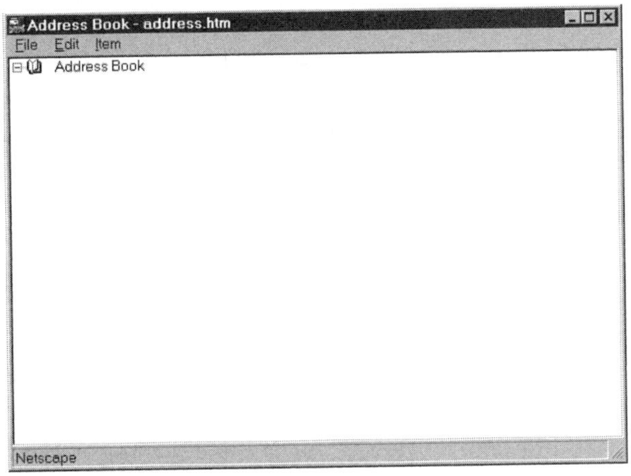

FIG. 23.3
The Address Book window allows you to create lists of your e-mail recipients.

To add a user to your Address Book:

1. Choose Item, Add User. You see the Address Book dialog box shown in Figure 23.4.
2. In the Nick Name box, insert an optional nick name, ensuring that you use only lowercase letters. Put the person's name as you want it to appear in your messages in the Name box, and his e-mail address in the E-Mail Address box.
3. Click OK when you are finished.

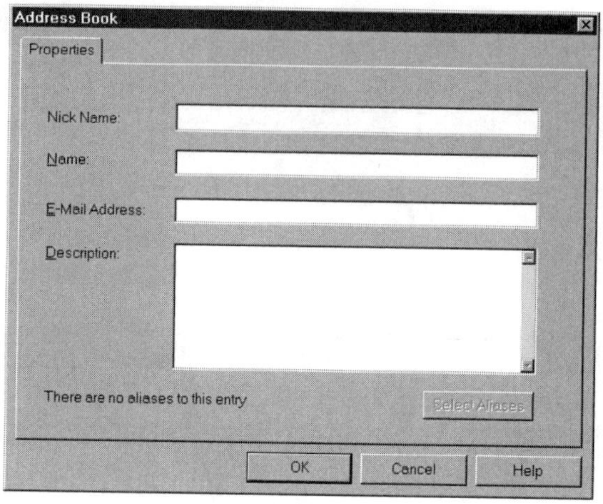

FIG. 23.4
With the Properties tab of the Address Book dialog box, you can add a nickname to each user and make sending mail easier.

You can also create a list of users to whom you often send mail by making a folder for the list, then dragging names into the folder. To create the folder:

1. Choose Item, Add List. You see a similar Address Book dialog box, except that the E-Mail Address box is grayed out.
2. Enter an optional Nick Name and a name for the list.
3. Click OK. The folder is created in your Address Book, as shown in Figure 23.5.

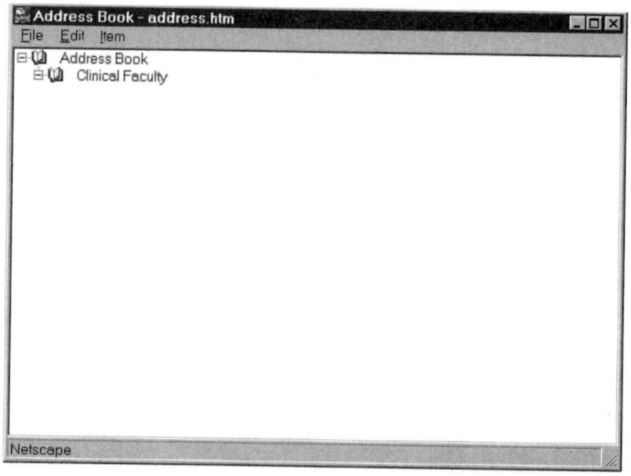

FIG. 23.5
The Address Book dialog box shows the folders that contain lists of the users to whom you send mail.

To put users in the list, copy them into the folder. From the Address Book dialog box, hold down the Ctrl key, and drag the user's icon on top of the folder icon. The user appears in the folder, as shown in Figure 23.6.

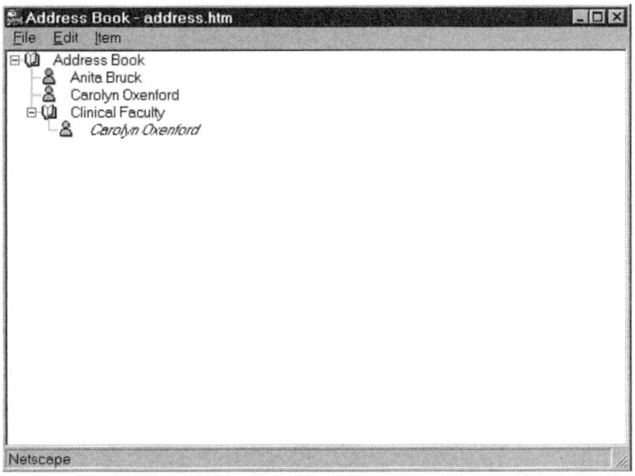

FIG. 23.6
The names of users that you add to the list by dragging them onto the folder will appear underneath that folder.

When you are finished editing your address book, click the Close button (the X in the upper-right corner) to close the Address Book window.

Reading Mail

To see any new messages you have received, click the Get Mail button on the toolbar. You see a message indicating that Navigator is connecting with your mail server on the status bar, and then subject lines for your new messages appear in the right pane of the Mail window, as shown in Figure 23.7.

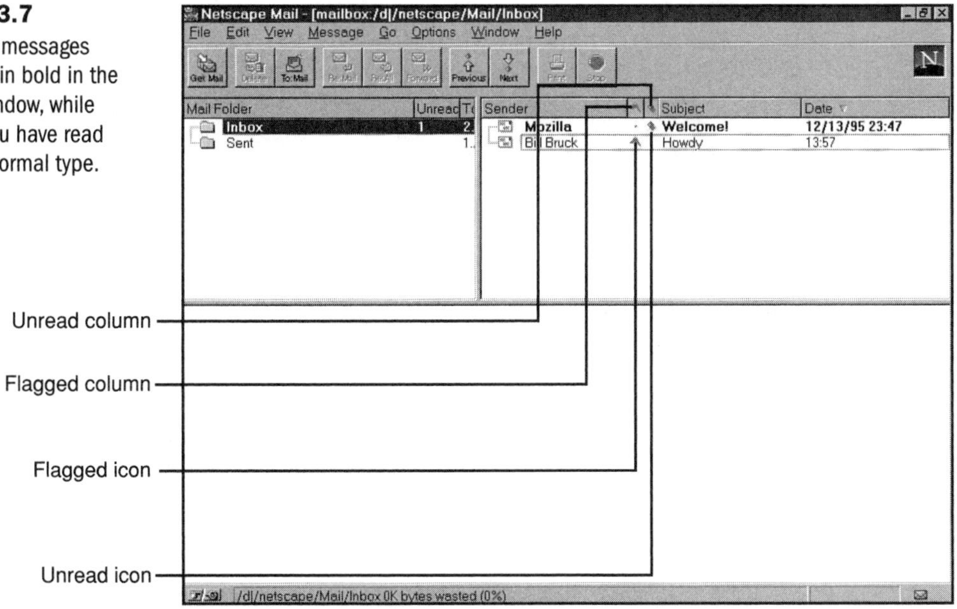

FIG. 23.7
Unread messages appear in bold in the Mail window, while ones you have read are in normal type.

Messages you have not read appear in bold, with a small green icon in the Unread column, while ones you have read are in normal type. The text of the selected message appears at the bottom of the screen. You can use the scroll bars to scroll through the message titles or through the text of the selected message.

TIP You can also mark a message as unread by clicking it in the Unread column—this is the column in the Sender pane with a small green icon as the column heading.

Save or Print a Message While Navigator stores messages internally until you delete them, you will occasionally want to save a message in your regular filing system. In addition, you may occasionally need to have a hard copy of a message to take into a meeting or give to a colleague who doesn't have e-mail.

To save a message:

1. Select its subject line so the message can be read in the lower window.
2. Choose File, Save As. You see the Save Messages As dialog box shown in Figure 23.8.

FIG. 23.8
You can save a message to your regular disk filing system in the Save As dialog box.

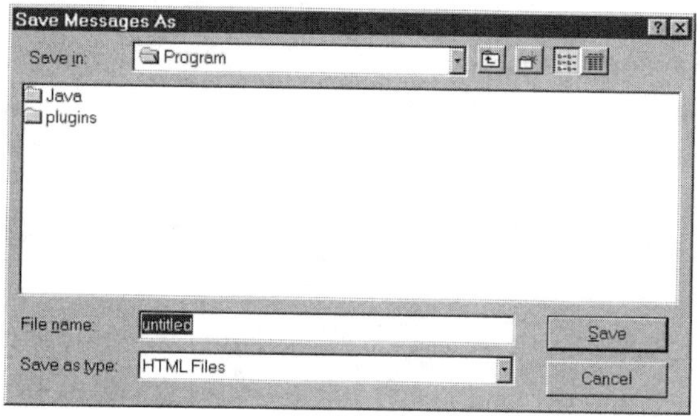

3. Browse to the folder in which you want to save the file, and give the file a name.
4. Click Save.

Printing your message is just as simple. With the message showing in the lower window, click the Print button, or choose File, Print. You see a Print dialog box similar to the one shown in Figure 23.9.

TIP You can also select several messages by clicking one, then holding down the Ctrl key and clicking additional ones, before you click the Print button.

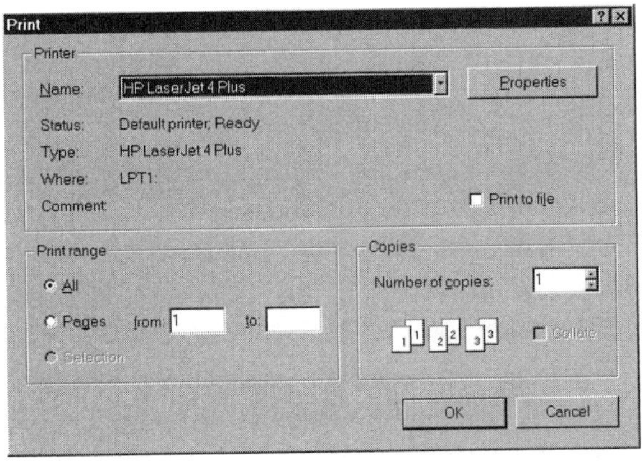

FIG. 23.9
You can print one or more messages (if you need hard copy) through the Print dialog box.

Add Name to Address Book When you are reading your e-mail, it's a great time to add a name to the Address Book if you think you'll be corresponding with that person in the future. To add a name to the Address Book, choose Message, Add to Address Book. You see the Address Book dialog box. The sender's name and e-mail address already appear in appropriate boxes. Enter a lowercase nickname, if desired, in the Nick Name box and choose OK. The name is added to the address book.

Read Attachments If you receive an attachment to your e-mail message, it will usually appear at the bottom of the message in a box like the one shown in Figure 23.10.

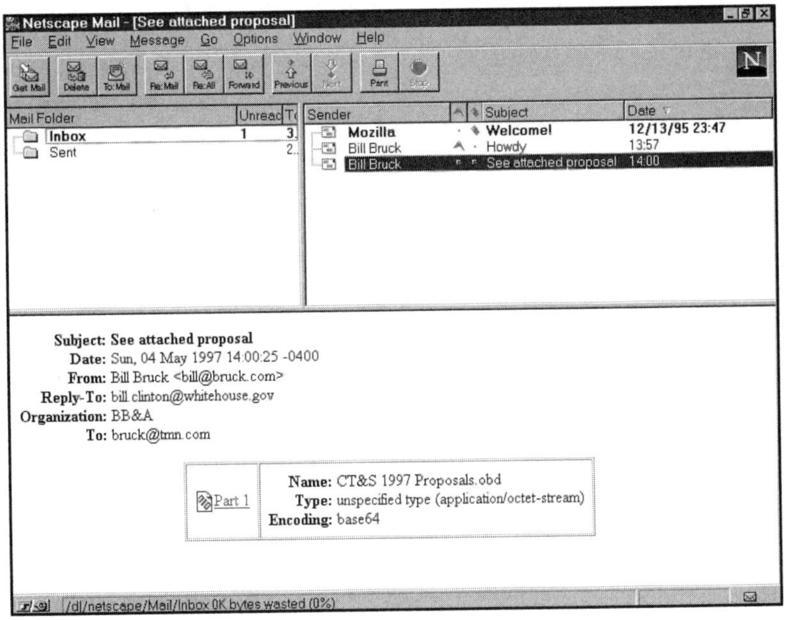

FIG. 23.10
Attachments appear at the bottom of the Mail window. You can save attachments to your disk, then open them later with the appropriate application.

To save the message, click it. You see a Save dialog box. Determine the folder you want to save your message in, then click Save.

NOTE Occasionally, you may receive a message that looks garbled, with pages of codes and characters you can't read. You can download a program from the Internet like Stuffit to decode such files.

Reply to Mail Many times when you read your e-mail, you'll want to reply to it or, less often, forward it to someone else.

To reply to a piece of mail:

1. Select the e-mail you want to answer.
2. Click either option:
    - The Reply button (Re: Mail) to reply only to the original sender.
    - The Reply to All button (Re: All) to reply to all recipients of the mail message.

   You see the Reply window, with the sender's message copied with > signs in front of each line (denoting that these lines were from the original message).
3. Delete the parts of the original message (the quote-back) that can be eliminated in your reply, then type your reply before or after the quote-back.
4. Click the Send button.

If you prefer, you can delete the original message first. The fastest way is to press Ctrl+A to select the entire message, then press Delete.

Alternatively, some people like to insert their reply as paragraphs between paragraphs of the original message, so that you can respond to specific points made by the original sender. To keep your e-mails shorter and more easy to read, it is always advisable to delete any material not related to your response before sending.

Forward Mail To forward mail you receive to another participant:

1. Select the received message.
2. Click the Forward button. You see the Forward window shown in Figure 23.11.
3. The subject of the forwarded message is the word `Fwd:` followed by the subject of the original message. The original message is included as an attachment to the forwarded message. Fill in the Mail To: box.
4. Send the message off, as is described in the next section.

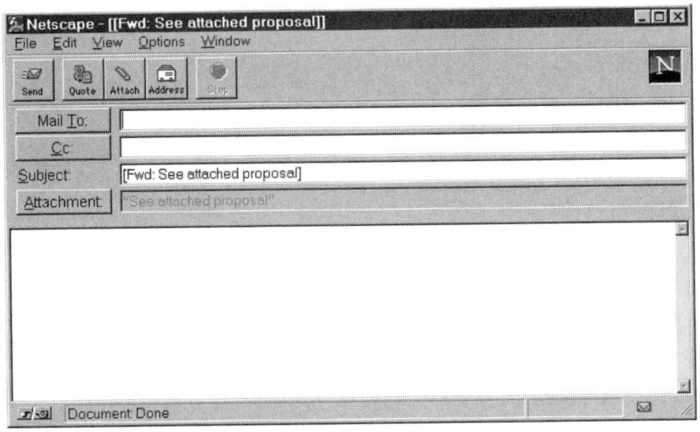

FIG. 23.11 You can forward your mail to someone else, in which case the original message becomes an attachment to the forwarded message.

Sending Mail

To send a message, do the following:

1. Open Netscape Mail.
2. Click the To: Mail button. You see the Message Composition dialog box shown in Figure 23.12.

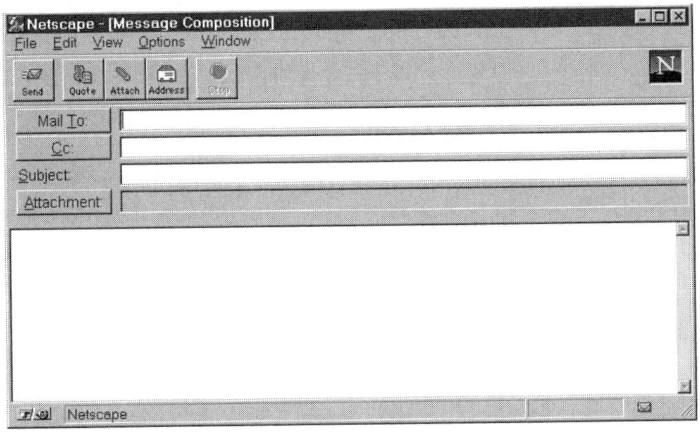

FIG. 23.12 Send mail to anyone with an Internet address throughout the world by using the Mail To: dialog box.

3. Type a valid Internet mail address in the Mail To: box, or click the Mail To: button. You see the Select Addresses dialog box in Figure 23.13.
4. Select an addressee and click To:.
5. Repeat this process for any additional addressees.
6. Click OK when you are finished. You return to the Mail To: dialog box.

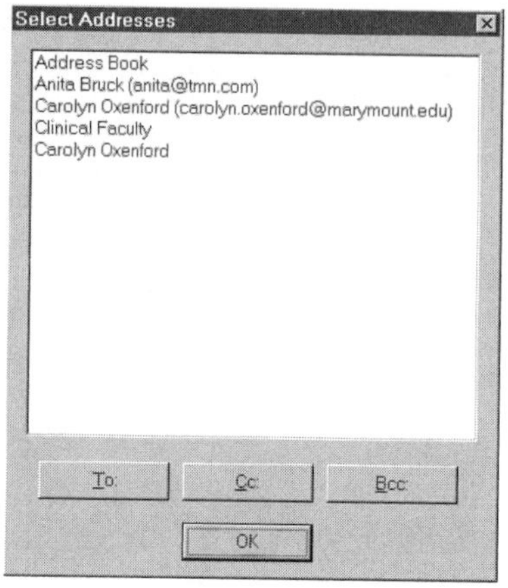

FIG. 23.13
Send mail to anyone in your Address Book with the Select Addresses dialog box.

7. Use the procedure in steps 3 through 6 to select CC: (carbon copy) recipients, if desired.
8. Fill in a Subject for your message.
9. Type the text of your message in the message box. Use standard Windows formatting and text editing commands.

TIP You can cut and paste text from other applications into the text of your message, if desired.

10. Add an attachment if desired, as described in the next procedure.
11. Click the Send button to send your message.

You can attach binary files to your message, such as WordPerfect documents, Presentations slide shows, and the like.

Encoding Files

You can think of two types of files: *text files* (called *ASCII files*), which contain nothing but text; and *binary files*, which can be programmed files or data files containing formatting codes and the like. When you save a WordPerfect document, Quattro Pro spreadsheet, or Presentations slide show, it is saved as a binary file.

Unfortunately, the Internet does not directly support binary files; it only supports text files. However, it is possible to encode a binary file into a text file. This encoding process is done automatically by Navigator, and incoming encoded files are automatically decoded. This process works best when both parties are using standard Internet browsers such as Navigator or Microsoft Explorer. When one party is accessing the Internet via America Online or CompuServe Information Services, the encoding/decoding process often goes awry.

To attach binary files to your mail:

1. Access the Message Composition dialog box as described in the previous section.
2. Click the Attachment button. You see the Attachments dialog box shown in Figure 23.14.

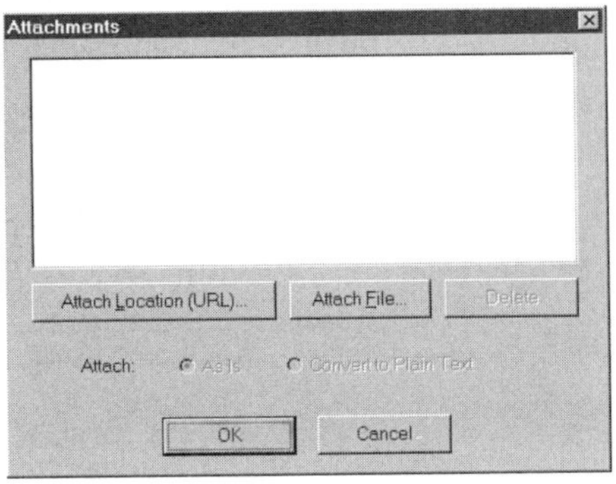

FIG. 23.14 The Attachments dialog box of Netscape makes it easy to attach a WordPerfect, Quattro Pro, or Presentations file to your e-mail message.

3. Click the Attach File button. You see the Enter File to Attach dialog box shown in Figure 23.15.

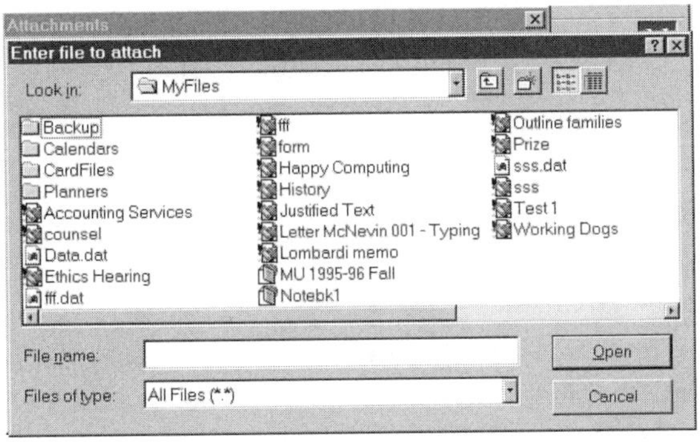

FIG. 23.15 In the Enter File to Attach dialog box, browse to the file you want to attach, then double-click it.

4. Browse to the file you want to attach, then double-click it. You return to the Attachments dialog box and see your file listed.
5. Repeat this step if you want to attach additional files, or click OK to return to the Message Composition dialog box.

Organizing Your Mail

After a while, your mail will tend to pile up. Not only will this make it harder for you to find particular messages, but you will also start using up a lot of disk space. For this reason, Netscape offers you several tools to organize your mail.

Delete Mail One of the best organizing tools is the Delete key. To delete a message, select its subject line and press Delete. The first time you delete a message, a new Trash folder is created. Deleting a message causes it to be moved to the Trash folder.

Emptying the Trash folder deletes the messages completely. Empty the Trash folder by choosing File, Empty Trash Folder. You should do this periodically to keep your messages from piling up and taking up disk space.

TIP To view items in trash, click the Trash folder in the Mail Folder pane. To undelete a message, drag it from the Trash folder to another folder.

Flag Mail You can flag a message for further attention by clicking the Flag column of the message. Once you have flagged messages, you can quickly move between them:

- Choose Go, First Flagged to go to the first flagged message.
- Choose Go, Next Flagged to go to the next flagged message.
- Choose Go, Previous Flagged to go to the previous flagged message.

These options are grayed out if there are no flagged messages.

TIP You can also choose Go, then First Unread, Next Unread, or Previous Unread to move between messages marked as Unread.

Sort and Thread Mail You may find it easier to find mail messages if they are sorted—either by date or by sender. You may also prefer to see replies linked to the original messages. This is called *threading messages*.

To sort your mail, choose View, Sort. You see the pop-up window shown in Figure 23.16, and can sort by a number of different categories.

TIP You can also sort by Sender, Subject, or Date by clicking the appropriate column header.

To thread your messages, choose View, Sort, Thread Messages. You will see replies linked to their original message in an outline format like the one shown in Figure 23.17.

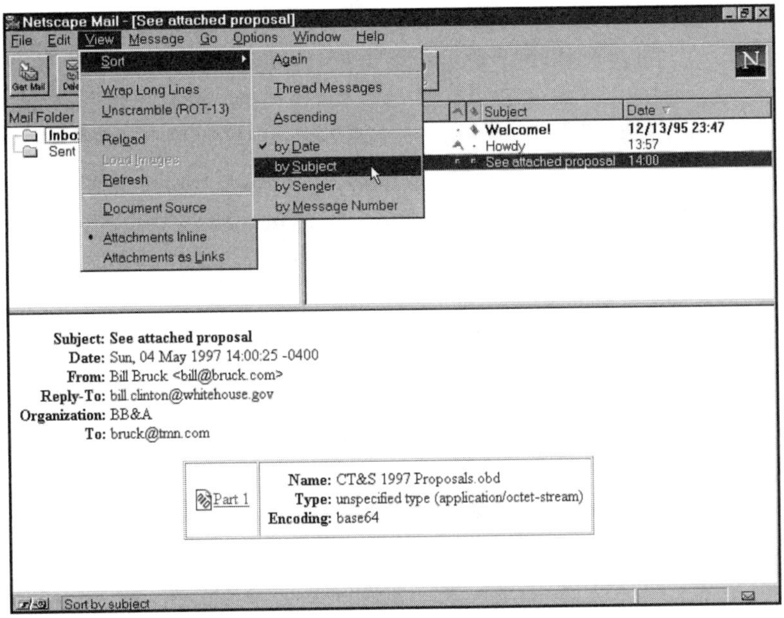

FIG. 23.16
With the Sort drop-down menu, you can sort messages by Date, Subject, Sender, or Message Number.

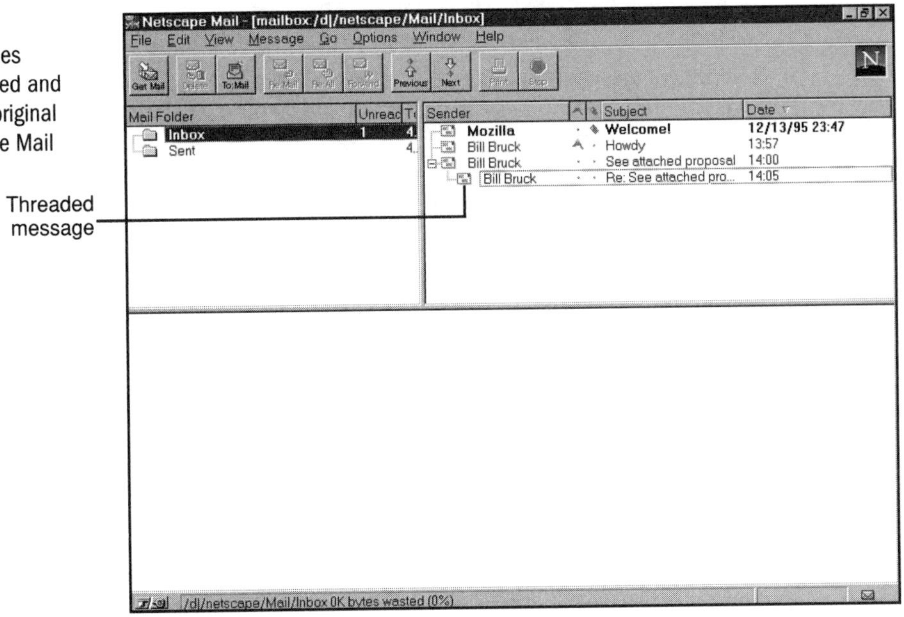

FIG. 23.17
Threaded replies appear indented and linked to the original message in the Mail window.

Using Folders When you first start using Netscape Mail, there is only one folder for incoming mail: the *Inbox*. This folder initially contains all your incoming messages. After you send mail, you will see a Sent folder containing copies of messages you have sent. When you delete messages, a Trash folder is created containing those messages.

Folders are excellent organizational tools for your e-mail. You can create any number of folders and move your mail into them. The mail messages you see in the right pane of the Mail window are the subjects of mail messages contained in the folder selected in the left window.

There are four main actions that are most used with folders:

- To create a new folder, choose File, New Folder. You are prompted to add the name for your new folder. Enter a name, then press Enter. You see the new folder in your folder list.
- To move a message into a folder, drag the message icon (the envelope to the left of the message) to the folder you want. The message disappears from its current folder, and is displayed when you click the icon of the destination folder.
- You can also copy a message into a folder by holding down the Ctrl key while you drag it to the destination folder. The message then appears in both the original folder and the destination folder.
- To delete a message from a folder, select it and press the Delete key. To delete a folder, delete all the messages in it, then select the folder in the left pane and press the Delete key.

Compress Folders If you want to keep a historical record of important messages in a particular folder, you will not want to delete them. However, recognizing that they do take up disk space, you may want to periodically *compress* a folder, thus reducing its size. While compressing a folder saves space, it does not affect how you read its messages.

To compress a folder, click its icon in the left window pane. Choose File, Compress this Folder. The items in the folder are compressed, thus saving disk space.

Change Column Width You can change the width of the columns in both the folder list and the message list. To do so, move your mouse pointer to the edge of one of the column headers. The mouse pointer changes to a resizing pointer. Drag the pointer right or left to resize the column, as shown in Figure 23.18.

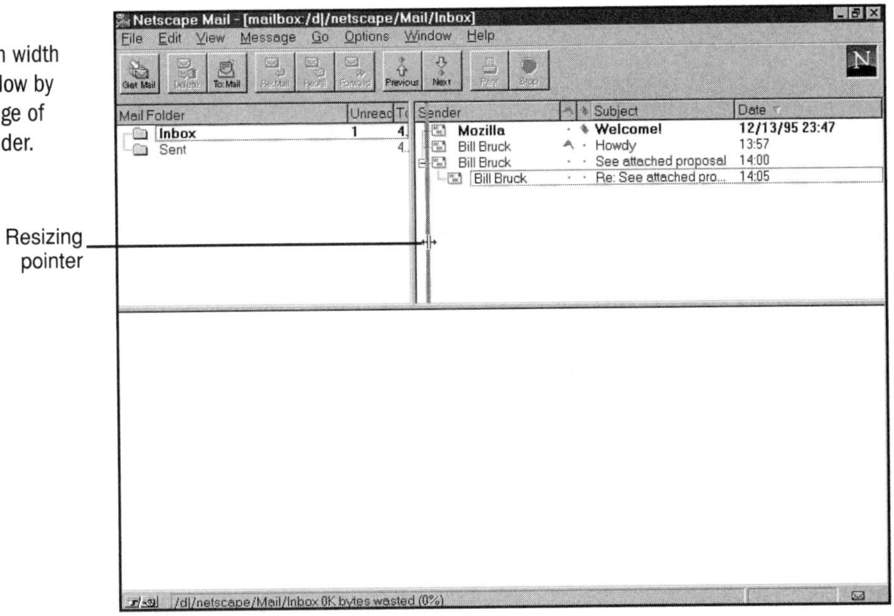

FIG. 23.18 Resize a column width in the Mail window by dragging the edge of the column header.

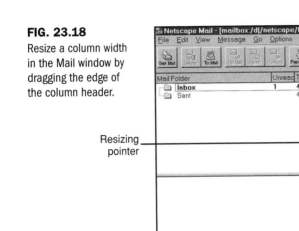

Participating in Mailing Lists

One of the earliest ways that groups used Internet e-mail to communicate was by creating *automated mailing lists*. When you send a message to such a mailing list, you are sending an e-mail to everyone on the list.

NOTE There are several programs that automate mailing lists on the Internet. Listserv is a popular mailing list program, used primarily on IBM mainframe computers. Majordomo is another such program, running primarily on UNIX servers. Some mailing lists are served by the MailList program. In common terms, however, many people tend to refer to all mailing lists as *listservs*, just as they often call facial tissues Kleenex.

The discussion in this section will deal with listservs; however, the procedure for subscribing, unsubscribing, and sending mail is the same in all major automatic mailing list programs.

When you subscribe to a listserv, you are adding your name to the mailing list. You will receive a copy of any mail addressed to that listserv. When you send mail to the listserv, everyone who has subscribed to that listserv will get the message you post. Therefore, even though you are sending e-mail, you are engaging in a public conversation with any number of people all across the world.

CAUTION

Belonging to a listserv can fill up your mailbox very quickly. Many listservs get between 10 and 200 messages per day. It's easy to turn a clean mail system into a nightmare, in which you must wade through hundreds of messages to get to your personal e-mail.

Some people arrange to have a second e-mail ID and join all listservs with this ID, thus separating their personal mail from their listservs. Others are merely more selective about which listservs they join.

Subscribing and Unsubscribing to Listservs

You may already know of a listserv you would like to join, or you may want to find listservs where people have conversations about areas of interest to you. You can find a list of listservs by choosing Search in Netscape and looking up the word **listserv**.

ON THE WEB

As of this writing, this excellent site lists all available listservs by category and alphabetically, and allows you to search the site for keywords:

http://tile.net

The name of a listserv will have two parts: the listserv name itself and the name of the computer where it is maintained (the host name). You'll want to know both of them.

Once you know the name of the listserv you're interested in, you will want to know how to *subscribe* to it (join it) and *unsubscribe* to it.

When you subscribe or unsubscribe to a listserv, you send a piece of e-mail to **listserv@server_name**—that is, a user named "listserv" at the computer that's hosting the listserv you're interested in. The body of the message will say:

```
SUBSCRIBE listname first_name last_name
```

or

```
UNSUBSCRIBE listname
```

For example, if Sam Williams were interested in a listserv called ponies that is hosted at **horse.equestrian.com**, he would subscribe to the listserv by sending an e-mail. The To: line would have the following address:

listserv@horse.equestrian.com

The body of the message would simply say:

```
SUBSCRIBE ponies Sam Williams
```

Conversely, if he found that after a while he no longer wanted to be part of the listserv, he would send another e-mail to **listserv@horse.equestrian.com**. The body of this message would say:

```
UNSUBSCRIBE ponies
```


NOTE If the ponies mailing list were maintained by majordomo rather than listserv, the subscribe command would be mailed to **majordomo@horse.equestrian.com**, as would other commands.

Setting Listserv Options

After you have subscribed to a listserv, you can set several options on the listserv. All of the options assume you are sending e-mail to **listserv@server_name**, as you did in the previous section:

- *Query.* Returns information about your options on the listserv. Put **Query *listserv_name*** in the body of the message.
- *Review.* Returns a description of the listserv, the owner of it, and a list of members. Put **Review *listserv_name*** in the body of the message.
- *Register.* Registers your full name with a listserv server. Any listserv hosted on that computer will then use the name you register. Put **Register *First_Name Last_Name*** in the body of the message.

Responding to Listservs

Once you have subscribed to a listserv, you will receive all mail that anyone sends that is addressed to that listserv. It will appear in your inbox just like any other mail message.

TIP To stop listserv mail from driving you crazy, create a folder for each listserv you belong to and be sure that you move the listserv mail to the appropriate folder regularly.

To respond and participate in the listserv "conversation," you can merely reply to any message you receive. It will automatically be posted to the listserv.

If you want to manually address mail to a listserv, address it differently than when you are sending commands to the listserv. When you are sending commands, you are talking to the listserv program, so you address the mail to **listserv@*server_name***. When you are participating in the conversation, you are addressing the ***people*** in the listserv. You thus address your mail to **listname@*server_name*.**

Thus, in the prior example, to post a response to the ponies listserv, you would address it to **ponies@horses.equestrian.com**. Everyone who has subscribed to ponies will see your message.

TIP Remember the distinction between sending commands to the listserv and participating in discussions. No one likes to keep reading "unsubscribe" commands that are accidentally sent to the entire list.

Participating in Newsgroups

A newer way to hold public conversations is via newsgroups. *Newsgroups* are structured conversations that are displayed as items with associated responses. After a newsgroup receives a certain number of responses, the oldest responses are discarded. Depending on how active the newsgroup is, you may be able to see a few days or a few weeks of conversation when you access it.

You read and participate in newsgroups via a ***newsreader***. Netscape provides a newsreader called *Netscape News*.

There are thousands of newsgroups on the Internet for people who want to talk about virtually anything. To participate in newsgroups, you will want to know how to use the newsreader to list newsgroups, subscribe to ones you're interested in, read postings, and respond to them. Some newsgroups are moderated, and only certain postings are allowed; others are unmoderated, and anyone can join and post to them.

Before learning newsreader commands, however, it's important to understand the structure of newsgroups and how they maintain conversations. Your newsreader and newsgroups organize conversations in a hierarchical manner, as can be seen in the Netscape News window shown in Figure 23.19.

The top level of the hierarchy is the ***news server***. This is the name of the computer (server) that maintains some or all of the newsgroups in storage, ready for you to access. Normally, you will only see one news server, which is the folder in the top left window pane of the screen.

NOTE Some servers maintain all available newsgroups, while others do not make certain adult-oriented newsgroups available to the public. Ask your ISP if you are unsure about the "news feed" that they support.

FIG. 23.19
The newsreader allows you to view and participate in on-going conversations.

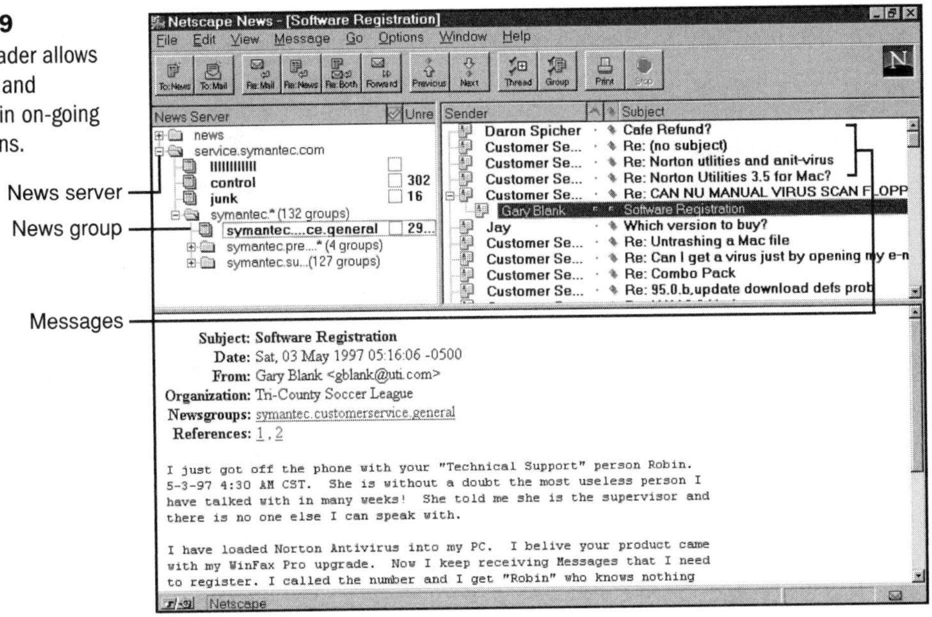

▶ **See** "Connecting to the Internet," **p. 441**

The next level of the hierarchy is a *news category*—a group of related newsgroups that share the same prefix, noted by folders in the left window pane. For instance, one of the largest categories of newsgroups is the "alt" newsgroups, which are unmoderated.

TIP When you first access the newsreader, you will only see three newsgroups. To see all available newsgroups, choose Options, Show All Newsgroups. Depending on the speed of your Internet connection, retrieving all the newsgroups may take a few minutes.

The third level of the hierarchy is an *individual newsgroup*—a series of conversations about a specific topic. These are denoted by icons representing sheets of paper.

Each newsgroup contains a series of messages. The subject lines of the messages for the selected newsgroup are shown in the right-hand pane. By default, these messages are *threaded*—that is, responses to a message are shown underneath the message. The text of the selected message is shown in the bottom window.

NOTE Messages do not remain in newsgroups forever. They scroll off periodically, and you cannot retrieve them once they are gone. The length of time a message stays in a newsgroup depends on how many new messages are added each day. ■

Subscribing to Newsgroups

You will usually not want to see the entire list of 20,000+ newsgroups. Instead, you will probably want to display only specific newsgroups you are interested in, by *subscribing* to these newsgroups.

To subscribe to newsgroups, do the following:

1. From Netscape, choose Window, Netscape News. You see the newsreader. Maximize the window if needed.
2. Show all newsgroups by choosing Options, Show All Newsgroups. You may need to wait a few minutes, then all newsgroups appear in the left window pane.
3. Position your mouse pointer on the right edge of the left window pane until it becomes a double-pointed arrow, then size the window like the one shown in Figure 23.20. You can now see the additional columns: the subscribe column (denoted with a check mark), the unread column showing how many unread messages are in the newsgroup, and the total column, showing how many total messages are in the newsgroup.

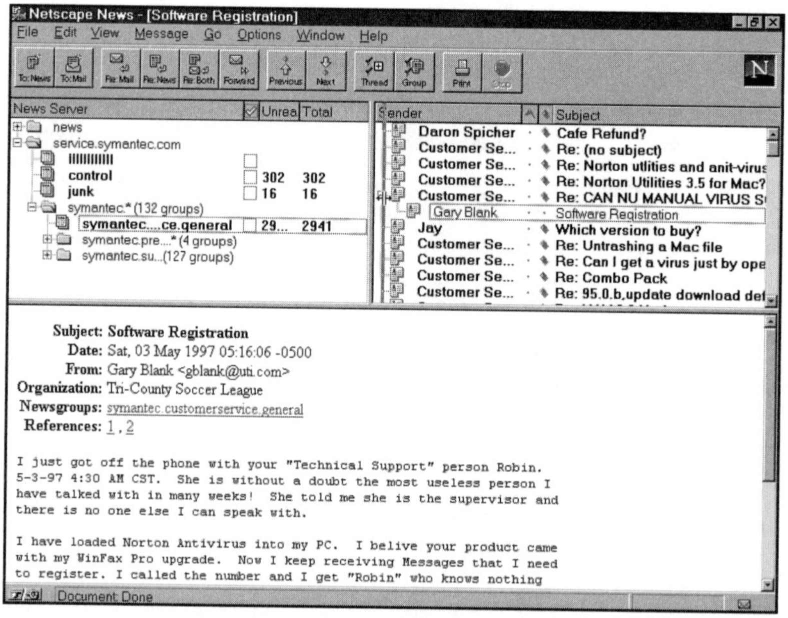

FIG. 23.20
Size the newsgroup window pane to see the columns allowing you to subscribe to newsgroups.

4. Expand newsgroup categories you may be interested in by clicking the plus sign to the left of the folder icon. You see the subcategories and newsgroups contained in them.

5. In the column with a yellow check mark (the Subscribe column), check the boxes of the newsgroups you want to subscribe to.
6. When you have finished subscribing to newsgroups, choose Options, Show Active Newsgroups to show only the newsgroups you have subscribed to that have unread items. Alternatively, choose Options, Show Subscribed Newsgroups to show *all* newsgroups you have subscribed to, whether or not they have unread items.

NOTE Subscribing to a newsgroup is different than subscribing to a listserv. Listservs actually have your name on a mailing list. You have to request to have your name on the list, and request it to be taken off. When you subscribe to a newsgroup, you are just checking which newsgroups you want your computer to display, but your name isn't really on a list anywhere.

Joining In a Newsgroup

After you have selected your newsgroups, you will want to participate, either by reading the postings of others or by posting messages yourself.

To participate in newsgroups, open Netscape News. To read the messages in a newsgroup:

1. Click the newsgroup you want to follow in the left pane. You see the messages headers in that newsgroup in the right pane.
2. Click a message header you want to read. The message is loaded, and displays in the bottom pane.
3. Use the scroll bar in the message pane to scroll through the message.

TIP Resize the three panes as needed by dragging the border between the panes. Similarly, resize the columns in the message header window if needed by dragging the edge of the appropriate column heading.

To mark a message as unread, click in the column with the green icon. The green icon denotes that the message has not been read.

Similarly, flag a message by clicking the column with the red icon. You can use the Go menu to move to the next or previous unread or flagged message.

To post a reply to a message:

1. Select the message you want to reply to.
2. Click the Re: News button. You see a dialog box like the one shown in Figure 23.21. The subject of your message is filled in, and you see the original message quoted back, with a > symbol at the beginning of each line.

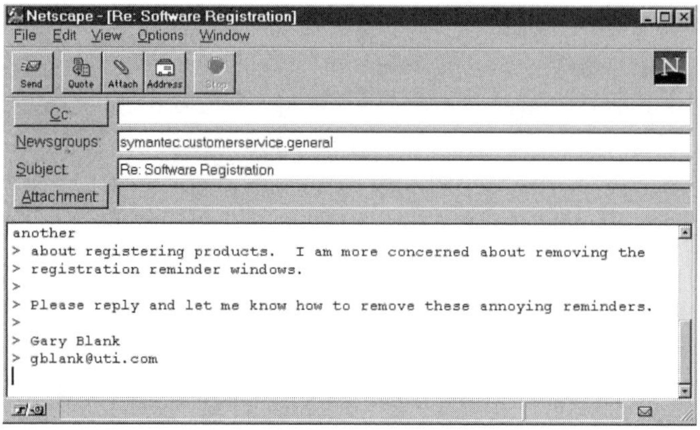

FIG. 23.21

Reply either publicly
to the newsgroup or
privately to the
individual who sent
the original message.

3. Delete as much of the original message that does not need to be repeated.

4. Type your reply in the message box.

5. Click the Send button. Your reply is posted to the newsgroup.

Posting a new message is similar to replying. Click the To: News button. You see a dialog box without a message subject. Enter a subject and the text of your message, then click the Send button.

You can also reply privately to a posting by selecting the message, and then clicking the Re: Mail button. In this case, the automatic address of your message is not the newsgroup, but the individual who sent the message.

Similarly, if you use the Re: Both button, a reply is sent both privately via e-mail and posted publicly to the newsgroup. ●

PART VI

Web Publishing with Corel WordPerfect Suite 8

CHAPTER 24

Integrating Corel WordPerfect 8 with the Internet

WordPerfect helps you extend your desktop into the Internet or corporate intranet by allowing you to browse the Web, download text and images from the Web into your WordPerfect documents, create active links from your documents to the Web, or even publish your documents to the Web in a variety of ways.

If you are not familiar with the Web and Web documents, you might consider reading Chapter 22, "Using Corel WordPerfect Suite on the Internet," before you read this chapter. Even if you have experience with the Web, this chapter may have useful information of which you are not aware.

Publishing on the Internet

Learn what word processing information to publish on the Internet along with some of the limitations of Internet publishing.

Using information from the Web

Learn how to pull information off the Web to incorporate into your word processing documents.

Create Web documents

Find out how to use the Internet Publisher to create complex Web documents with familiar WordPerfect commands.

Publish Web documents

Learn to view your Web documents in a Web browser or upload them to the Internet.

Convert Web documents

Understand how to convert WordPerfect documents into HTML and HTML documents into WordPerfect.

Publish documents with Barista

See how WordPerfect can be converted into a Java applet that can be viewed with Web browsers, yet retains your formatting information.

Browsing the Web from WordPerfect

The first way that you can extend your desktop is by browsing the Web from WordPerfect. Whenever you want to access the Web, click the Change View button. You see the Internet Publisher toolbar shown in Figure 24.1.

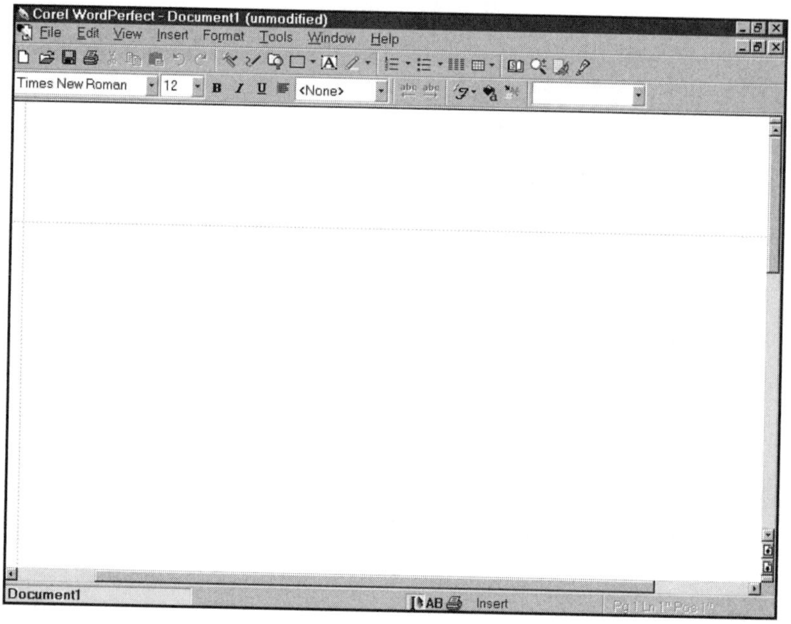

FIG. 24.1
The Internet Publisher toolbar has buttons for browsing the Web and for converting your current document to a Web page.

Click the Browse the Web button. You are taken into Netscape (or your default browser) and from there automatically to Corel's site. From there, you can obtain assistance with Corel products, or jump to anywhere else on the Internet.

Using Information from the Web in Your Documents

You not only can reach out *to* the Web from WordPerfect, but you can also bring information *from* the Web into your WordPerfect documents.

Whether it's recipes, technical support instructions, or IRS instructions, you will find it useful to be able to capture text from Web sites to integrate into WordPerfect documents you create.

Of course, if your Web is a corporate intranet, you may find many documents that are stored on your Web expressly *for* your use. Sections from corporate capability statements, resume information, or the annual report can easily be incorporated into proposals or other documents you create in WordPerfect.

CAUTION

The information contained on Web sites is often copyrighted and will in any case be protected by relevant copyright laws. Always attribute quoted text, and strongly consider establishing a company policy regarding use of information obtained from the Internet after advice from legal counsel.

See "Understanding the Implications of Publishing on the Internet," **p. 445**

There are three ways you can incorporate text from Web pages into your documents:

- Save Web documents to your local disk, and then convert them to WordPerfect.
- Copy information from a Web page to your WordPerfect document.
- Create a link from your WordPerfect document to information on a Web page.

Saving and Converting Web Documents

The first way to incorporate information from the Web into your WordPerfect document is to save and convert the Web document. You can do this by first browsing to the document using Netscape, and then choosing File, Save As to save it to your local disk.

You can then convert the Web page into a WordPerfect document. After the document is converted into WordPerfect, you can edit it or copy or move sections of it into another WordPerfect document you are working on.

See "Browsing the Web," **p. 450**

See "Downloading Files," **p. 455**

Copying Web Information into a Document

Alternatively, you can copy selected text directly from a Web document into your Word-Perfect document. To do so, use Netscape to browse to the document you want to copy text from.

See "Browsing the Web," **p. 450**

When you are looking at the desired document, drag with your mouse over the text you want to select, and then choose Edit, Copy to copy the text to the Clipboard. Switch to Corel WordPerfect, click where you want the text to appear, and then choose Edit, Paste.

CAUTION

Viruses can be downloaded in program, data, and macro files. Be very careful about indiscriminately downloading files from the Web. The wrong virus can make every single file on your computer unusable. Practice "safe computing" by getting a virus protector (for individual machines or on a network) before getting set up to go out on the Web.

Using Hypertext Web Links

You can create links in your WordPerfect document that will take you to specific sites on the Web when you click them. For example, you might have a WordPerfect document on the network that discusses current industry trends. As you make points in your report, the supporting evidence can be links that readers can follow to see the Web-based data that led you to your conclusions.

▶ **See** "Adding Links and Bookmarks," **p. 501**

CAUTION

Web sites change frequently. If you are responsible for WordPerfect documents that contain links to Web pages, be sure to check the links regularly to make sure that they still work.

Understanding About Web Publishing

Everyone who has electricity has heard about the Internet now, and most people in business are sure it's a "good thing." But many people still do not honestly know why they might want to create Web documents.

There are two types of Webs that you might publish documents to, and they each have different purposes: the World Wide Web, which is part of the Internet; and private, corporate Webs called intranets.

Publishing to the World Wide Web

The World Wide Web is part of the global Internet. Information published on it is available to the public. There are many types of WordPerfect documents you may want to put where the public can see them.

▶ **See** "Understanding Internet Basics," **p. 438**

Individuals create *personal Web sites* that are a little bit like a telephone "white pages" listing, except that they tell the public more about you. Personal Web sites often contain information about your interests, your family, your work, and ways to contact you. Personal Web sites can be created using WordPerfect templates.

Companies create *corporate Web sites* on the Internet as a matter of public relations. They not only can establish a corporate presence on the Internet, they can sell products, deliver technical information, or provide white papers on topics of interest to their industry. WordPerfect is not the best software to create a sophisticated *home page* (the initial page you see at a company's site, often with sophisticated graphics). It is excellent, however, for creating the other Web pages, because technical information, white papers, and more, often already exist in WordPerfect.

A key to Web publishing is understanding that it is a public pronouncement. It's like standing on a box in the middle of Times Square and telling passers-by what your opinions are. You don't know who is going to read it, and it may be more permanent than you think. Even if you change what's on a Web page, someone else may well have saved the original version to their disk.

Publishing to a Corporate Intranet

Corporations are increasingly using intranets as the method of choice to publish internal documents. The nature of the intranet means that only corporate employees can access it. The nature of the Web, however, also implies that employees with many different types of computers can see Web documents with all their formatting, allowing for inexpensive cross-platform integration.

For these reasons, corporations are publishing WordPerfect documents to their intranets such as:

- *Internal Corporate Documents.* All sorts of corporate documents, such as employee manuals, insurance application instructions, corporate policies, and the like are being published to intranets from their original WordPerfect format. Often, they are no longer being produced in hard copy to save money.
- *Knowledge Bases.* Because search tools can search the text of all documents published to the intranet, more technical files, resume files, and historical documents are being published to internal Webs to create searchable "knowledge bases" that can be accessed by personnel.

▶ **See** "What Are Intranets," **p. 440**

WordPerfect provides two different ways to publish your documents:

- Creating HTML Web documents that can be uploaded to the Internet or a corporate intranet
- Creating Java applet Web documents with Barista

Creating Web Documents

The Web is a part of the Internet that supports graphic and multimedia files written in HTML format. What's this all about?

The Internet only supports the transmission of text files, not the complex binary files that make up applications and data files and contain complex format coding (such as WordPerfect documents).

To get around this shortcoming, complex coding systems have been developed to translate programs and data files into plain text. One of these mechanisms is the HyperText Markup Language (HTML). Using HTML, bold text is denoted by tags—ASCII codes that denote `<b>` as the beginning of bold and `</b>` as the end of bold. Similarly, `<H1>` denotes the Heading 1 style and `</H1>` denotes the end of it.

NOTE ASCII is a fancy name for the characters on a typewriter keyboard—A-Z, 0-9, and a few others. When you read ASCII, you can generally substitute "plain text."

In the past, you had to learn HTML codes to create documents that could be published on the Web. Now, the Internet Publisher takes care of this for you, and you merely need to format your document using familiar WordPerfect commands.

Internet Publisher is a part of the WordPerfect program. It is a set of functions that allow you to create Web documents, save them in HTML format, and even convert existing WordPerfect documents to HTML and vice versa. You can create an empty Web document or use PerfectExpert to create a simple Web home page for yourself. In addition, the Internet Publisher allows you to add and format text, create links, insert graphics, and add tables to your Web document.

When you publish a series of interlinked HTML documents on the Web, they become a Web site, and each document is called a Web page. The main page on your site that a person would usually go to first is called the *home page*.

For ease of writing, however, the following terms are used in this chapter to mean identically the same thing: HTML document, Web document, and Web page.

NOTE Java is another, newer, coding system with which Web pages can be created. For creating Java applet pages from WordPerfect documents, see the section, "Publishing Documents with Barista," later in this chapter.

Making a Basic Web Document

To start making a Web page, do the following:

1. Choose File, Internet Publisher. You see the Internet Publisher dialog box (see Figure 24.2).

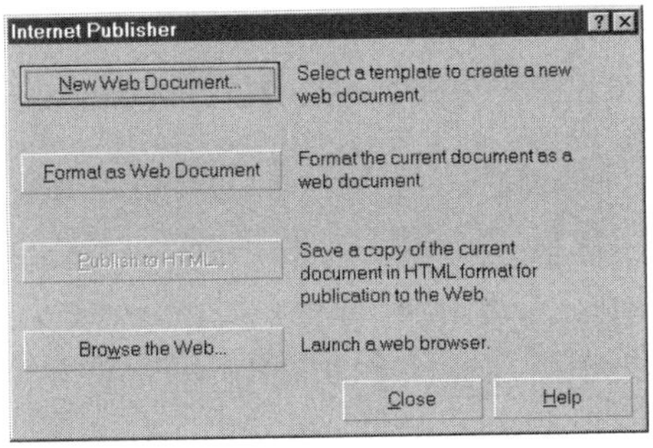

FIG. 24.2
You can click the New Web Document button in the Internet Publisher dialog box to create Web documents, such as home pages for yourself or your business.

2. Click the New Web Document button. You see the Select New Web Document dialog box shown in Figure 24.3.

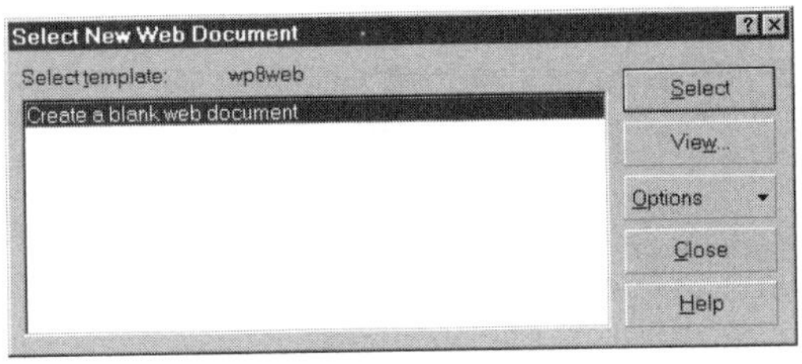

FIG. 24.3
You can create a blank Web document using familiar WordPerfect tools.

3. Select Create a Blank Web Document.
4. Choose Select. You see a blank editing screen.

From here, you can add text, graphics, tables, styles, and other elements to the Web page. After you save your document in HTML format, you can then upload it to the Web. These steps will be described in the following sections.

Adding and Formatting Text

After you have created a Web page, you will want to add text to it and format the text so that it appears attractive when seen in a Web browser such as Netscape. With the Internet Publisher, you not only can do this easily, but you can also copy text into your Web page from other WordPerfect documents.

Adding Text To add text to your Web page, type it in as you would in any other WordPerfect document. All the normal editing commands are available to you, just as they are in any other WordPerfect document. Move around the document with your mouse or keyboard, insert and delete text as you normally would, and even cut and paste text from one part of the document to another.

Copying Text To copy text into your Web document, open the document containing the text, select it, and then choose Edit, Copy. Switch back to your Web document, place your insertion point where you want the text to appear, and choose Edit, Paste. The text is copied into your Web document, just as if you had copied it into any other WordPerfect document.

Formatting Text When you are in the Internet Publisher, only the formatting features supported by HTML (the underlying "language" that Web documents are written in) are available to you. Notice that the toolbar and Property Bar change, as shown in Figure 24.4. Menu items that are not supported in HTML are removed, as well.

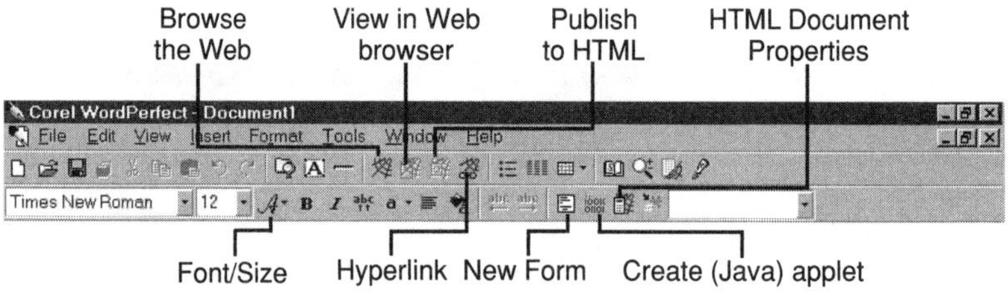

FIG. 24.4 When you create Web pages, your toolbar and Property Bar change to provide you with specialized options for your Web document.

Format your text as you normally would, recognizing that not all the formatting commands you are accustomed to will be available. To bold a sentence, for instance, you highlight it and click the Bold button. To create a bulleted list, click the Bulleted list button at the beginning of a new line, and then type the bulleted items.

Inserting Horizontal Lines

The simplest graphic element that you can use to spice up your Web page is a horizontal line. To insert a horizontal line into your Web page, position your insertion point where you want the line to appear, and then click the Horizontal Line button. You see a line in your Web document.

You can also edit the appearance and attributes of horizontal lines. To do so, select the line to be edited, right-click it, and choose Edit Horizontal Line. You see the Edit Graphics Line dialog box (see Figure 24.5).

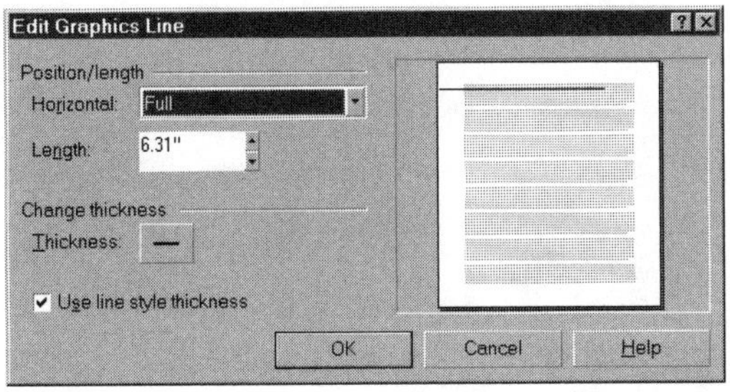

FIG. 24.5
Specify the position, length, and thickness of horizontal lines in your Web document.

Specify the Horizontal position of the line (left, center, right, or full), the line's Length, the Thickness of the line, and then click OK.

Many Web pages contain other types of graphic elements—either clip art or fancy bullets, buttons, and the like. You can import all of these into your Web pages with the Internet Publisher.

Inserting Clip Art

To insert clip art into your Web page, click the Clipart button. You see the Scrapbook window.

Select the Clipart or CD Clipart tab, navigate to the folder containing the image you want to use, and drag the image to your WordPerfect editing window. You see the image in your document (see Figure 24.6). Close the Scrapbook window.

NOTE The Web only supports images saved in two formats: GIF and JPG. Your image will be converted to GIF format when you publish your work as an HTML document.

To move your image, select it by clicking it so that you see handles around it. Position your mouse pointer inside the image; the pointer changes to a four-way arrow. Drag the image to its new location. Notice that you cannot move it anywhere on the page, as you can in WordPerfect, because of the limitations imposed on HTML documents.

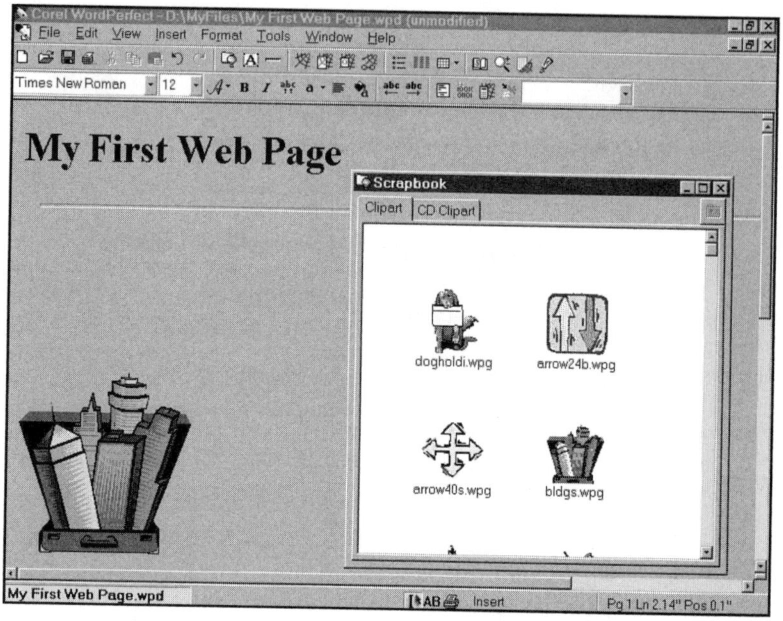

FIG. 24.6
Images appear in your document when you select them, and they are automatically converted to GIF format when you save your document as an HTML file.

Similarly, you can size the image by selecting it, and then positioning your mouse pointer on one of the handles. The mouse pointer becomes a two-way arrow. Drag the handle to resize the image.

TIP You can't wrap several lines of text around a graphic like you can in a WordPerfect document. The box moves with the words in the line. You can change the position of the box on the line, but you can't change how several lines of text wrap.

To edit the image, you can double-click it. You see the Presentations menu options in your WordPerfect document (unless you are using a different default graphics editor for this type of file). Alternatively, you can right-click it to bring up the QuickMenu and use the same image editing tools you use for other images in WordPerfect documents.

When those browsing the Web are in a hurry, they sometimes choose the option to have their browser not automatically load graphics. This can decrease the amount of time it takes for their system to load the information on the page so that they can view more pages faster. Additionally, some users do not have a browser that will permit the viewing of graphics of any sort, so they can only see text.

If you would like to specify text that will display when users do not use a graphical browser, or when users do not choose to automatically load graphics, do so as follows:

1. Select the image, and then right-click it. You see the QuickMenu.

2. Choose HTML Properties. You see the HTML Properties dialog box shown in Figure 24.7.
3. Type the text in the Alternate Text box, and then click OK.

NOTE Users who are familiar with HTML documents can also use this box to add ISMAP images–images that activate links when a specific part of the image is clicked by selecting the Map Link option.

FIG. 24.7
In the HTML Properties dialog box, you can specify text that will display in place of the image box if a user is not using a graphical browser.

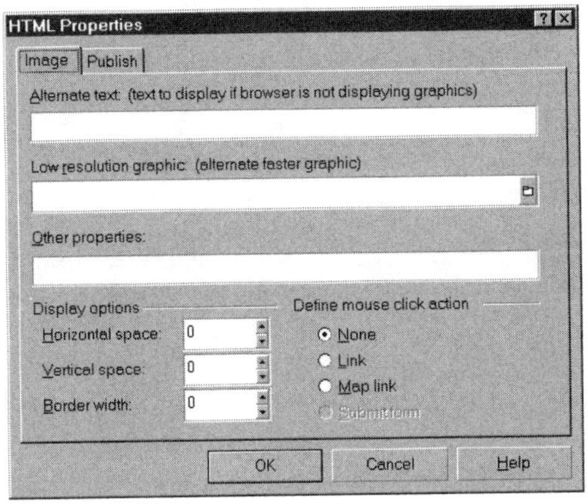

Adding Links and Bookmarks

Your document becomes a full-fledged member of the Web when it provides links to other documents. You can easily add links to other documents, or to specific bookmarks within these documents. The links can be highlighted terms, or they can be small graphics that the user will click.

NOTE The link feature is used most often in conjunction with the Internet Publisher. It is, however, a part of WordPerfect itself. Thus, you can create links from *any* WordPerfect document using the procedures described in this section.

Creating and Editing Links To create a link to a document on your disk or the Web, follow these procedures:

1. Open the document where you want the source of the link to be located.
2. Select the term that should be displayed for the text link or included in the link button.

3. Click the Hyperlink button on the toolbar, and choose Create Link. You see the Hyperlink Properties dialog box (see Figure 24.8).

4. In the Document box, type the name of the file you want to link to. If it is a document on the disk, use the full path to the document, such as C:\Myfiles\Web\Index.htm. If it is a document on the Web, use a complete URL, such as **http://www.corel.com/index.htm**.

   Alternatively, click the Browse Web button. Your default browser will be launched, and you can navigate to the Web site that you want to link to. When you switch back to WordPerfect, the URL for the Web site will appear in the Document box.

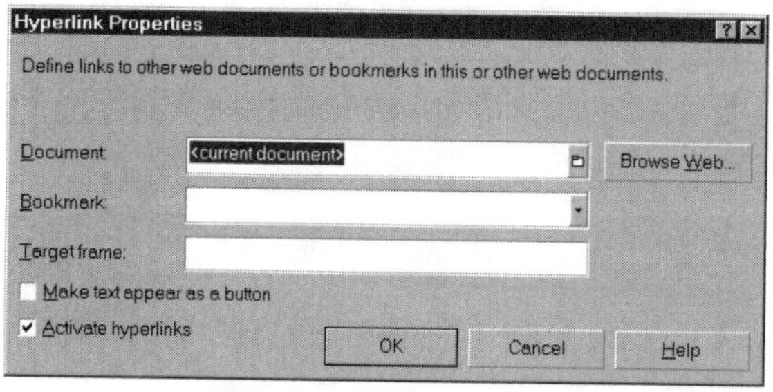

FIG. 24.8
In the Hyperlink Properties dialog box, you can quickly create hypertext links to documents on your disk, your local intranet, or the Internet.

> **CAUTION**
>
> Be careful about using links to Internet documents that you don't control. You may link to an URL that is here today and gone tomorrow, so you need to think about how long the document created with a link will be available. You also need to be willing to check regularly to make sure that links in your documents are still working.

5. If you want the link to take you to a specific bookmark in the destination document, type the name of the bookmark in the Bookmark box. (Creating bookmarks is discussed in the next section.)
6. If you would like the link to be a button, click the Make Text Appear as a Button option button.
7. Click OK. You return to your Web page and see the link term in blue; or you see the link button.

> **TIP** Many Internet servers are case-sensitive. To get to an URL on these servers, you must type in the link with the correct case. Because you don't know which servers are or are not case-sensitive, it's good practice to always use the exact case that you see.

You can edit the link after it's created by right-clicking it and choosing Edit Hyperlink. You see the Hyperlink Properties dialog box, which has identical functionality to the Create Hyperlink dialog box discussed earlier.

Creating Bookmarks A bookmark is a specific position or section of text in a document that has a name. You can use bookmarks to go directly to a specific place in a document. You can create bookmarks in your Web documents—or in regular WordPerfect documents—so that links can take you to a specific place in your document, rather than merely to the beginning of the document.

In Web page design, a long Web page will often have a table of contents at the top, then bookmarked positions throughout the document. Clicking the table of contents link terms will take you to specific sections of the document.

TIP You can go to a bookmark in a document by pressing the GoTo shortcut key Ctrl+G and specifying the bookmark you'd like to go to.

To create a bookmark, do the following:

1. Open the WordPerfect document or Web page that you want to put a bookmark in.
2. Click at the position you want to bookmark, or select the text you want to bookmark.
3. Click the Hyperlink button, and then choose Insert Bookmark. You see the Create Bookmark dialog box shown in Figure 24.9.

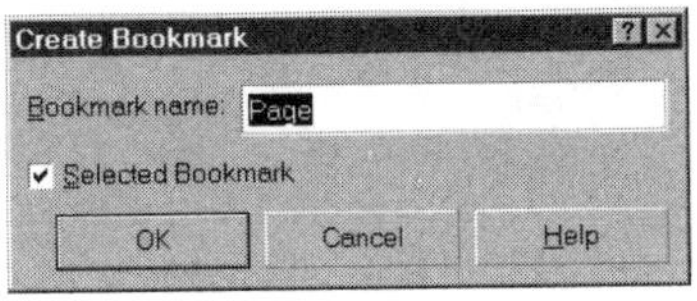

FIG. 24.9 Web documents are even more friendly when you create bookmarks so that links can take the user a specific place in the document.

6. Type the name of the new bookmark in this dialog box, and then click OK. You return to the document.

To use the bookmark, create a link to the appropriate file, including the bookmark, as was discussed in the previous section.

TIP There is no visible prompt that a bookmark has been created. However, you can press Alt+F3 to see the bookmark in Reveal Codes, if you like.

Including Tables

Web pages increasingly are being used to provide data to clients, customers, and employees. Catalogues and other similar information is often best displayed in a table. With

WordPerfect's Internet Publisher, you can insert a table into your Web page in the same way you would into a document.

To insert a table into your Web document using Internet Publisher, do the following:

1. Open the Web page and position your insertion point where you want the table to appear.

2. Click the Tables button on the toolbar, and drag down to the appropriate cell for the number of rows and columns you want in your table. You see the table in your document, as shown in Figure 24.10.

FIG. 24.10
With the Internet Publisher, you can put tables in your Web page to display a variety of information.

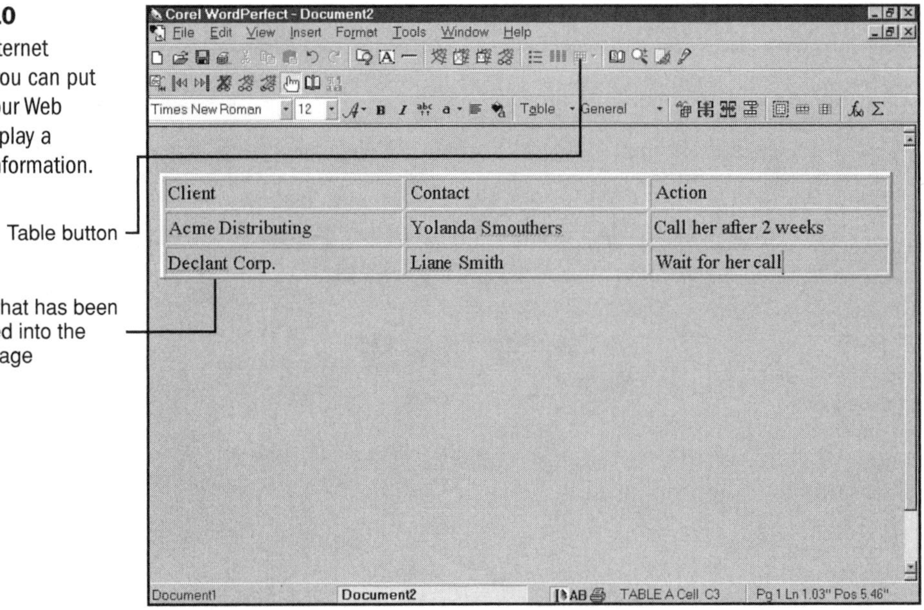

3. Enter data in the table. Press the Tab key to advance to the next cell and Shift+Tab to go to the previous one. If you press the Tab key at the last cell in the table, a new row will be created.
4. To format your table:
   - Select the appropriate cells or columns, click the Table button on the Property bar, and then choose Format.
   - Alternatively, right-click in the table and choose Format.

You see the HTML Table Properties dialog box (see Figure 24.11).

FIG. 24.11
In the HTML Table Properties dialog box, you format your table by cell, column, or entire table.

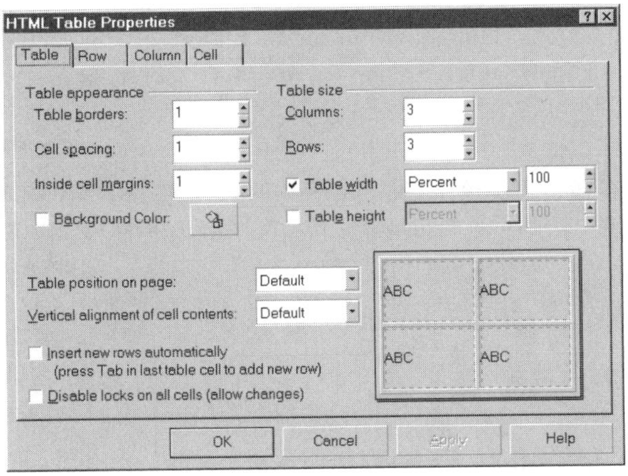

Adding Forms

You may want to insert a form into your Web page to collect information from people who browse to your Web site. The Internet Publisher allows you to do this quickly and easily.

To create a form, click in your Web page where you want the form to appear, and then click the New Form button on the Property Bar. You see two yellow icons—the Form Begin and Form End icons—with your insertion point positioned between them. The Property Bar changes to display form tools, as shown in Figure 24.12.

FIG. 24.12
Internet Publisher provides a variety of tools to enable you to quickly create forms in your Web pages.

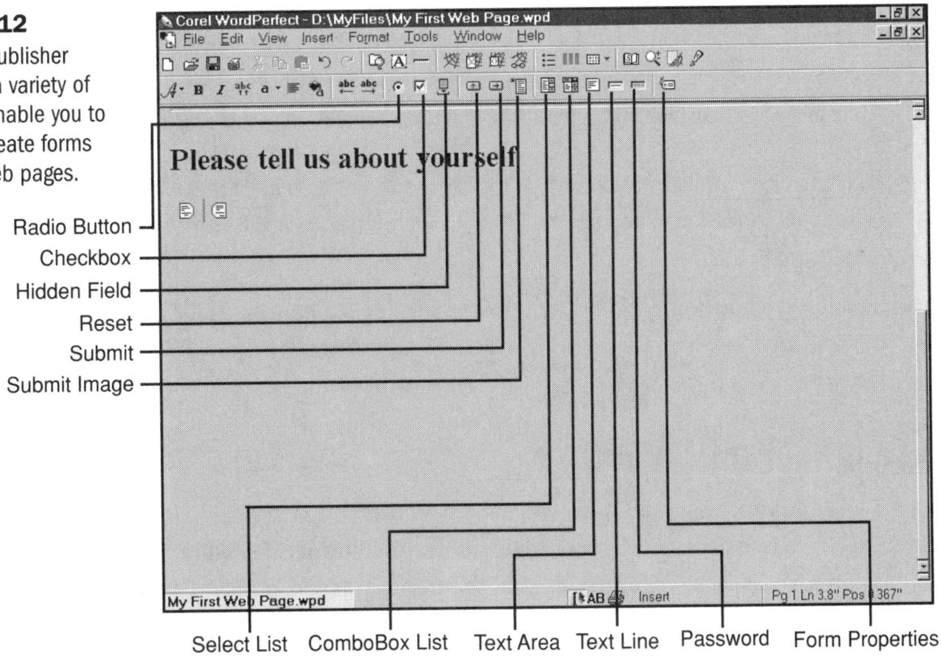

Insert form fields by clicking the appropriate button. You can find out more about what each type of field does by looking up Forms, Web Document in the WordPerfect Help system.

NOTE You will also need to specify how the form transmits information to you or to a database. This is done through an Action URL or Mime Script, which can be specified by clicking the Form Properties button. Discuss how to fill in this dialog box with your system administrator or Internet Service Provider, because the requirements will depend on your specific system.

Publishing HTML Documents

After you have created and edited your Web page using WordPerfect's Internet Publisher, the result is still a WordPerfect document, *not* an HTML (or Web) document. To publish it on the Web, you need to save it as an HTML document. You may also want to save another version of it as a WordPerfect document, so that you can more quickly open it and edit it, without needing to convert it from HTML into WordPerfect when you open it.

NOTE There are two meanings of the term "publish." The normal usage of the term—for example, "publish a Web document"—means to *place* a document on the Web where people can see it. WordPerfect uses the term publish, however, in a different sense, to mean *converting* a WordPerfect document to HTML.

When used in this latter sense, the document will still reside on your disk rather than on the Web, and you will still need to copy it to the Internet so that people can see it.

The meaning of the term in this book can be derived from the context in which it's used.

In any case, publishing your document means saving it as HTML. When you do this, the Internet Publisher converts the binary WordPerfect file into an ASCII text file with HTML codes in it.

Before you do that, however, you might want to see how the HTML document will look in a real Web browser. (Remember, what WordPerfect shows you is *close* to how the document will look in a browser, but not necessarily exact.)

Viewing Your Document

You can view your document whenever you want to, as you build it up and add more features to it. When you view your document, the Internet Publisher converts it to HTML and saves it as a temporary file, and then opens the file in your default Web browser.

To view your document, click the View in Web Browser button. Netscape (or your default browser) opens, and you see your Web page as it will look when it is published (see Figure 24.13).

NOTE Web documents can appear differently, depending on the browser used to access them. For instance, some older versions of standard browsers would not recognize a center code or an underline code. Many problems like this have been cleared up in the newer browser versions, but some people still have older browsers that have been purchased second-hand or passed down to them when new equipment was purchased for others. It is important to know who your most important customers are and the level of technology they have, and then set up pages to that standard.

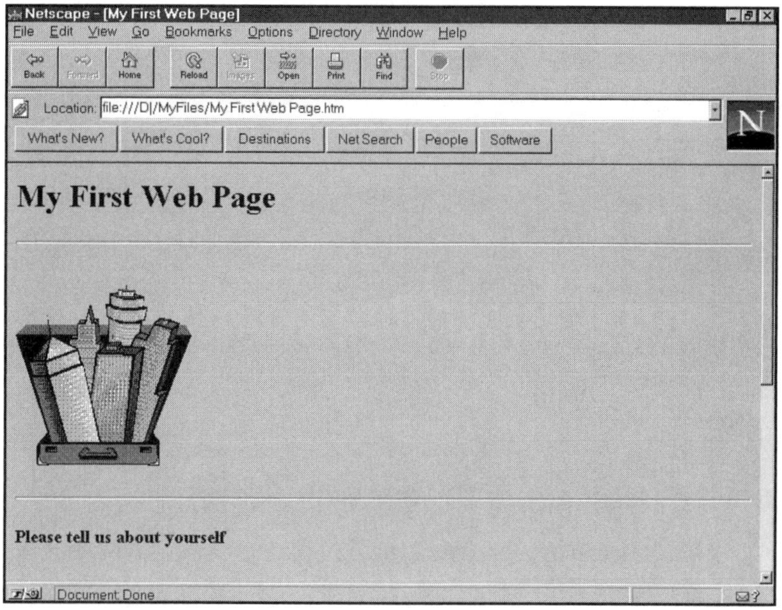

FIG. 24.13 You can view your Web page in your default browser before you publish it to ensure that it looks the same in the browser as it does in the Internet Publisher.

Saving Documents as HTML

Saving your document as HTML creates a new file with an .htm extension. It is an ASCII text file, with HTML codes in it. If you have figures in your document, a folder is created with the same name as the document, and the figures are stored in this folder.

When you are satisfied with the Web page you have created, and you want to convert it to an HTML document, do the following:

1. Save the document as a WordPerfect document so that you can more easily edit it by opening the original WordPerfect document later, and so that you will have a

backup of the file in case something happens to the version you will be putting on the server.

2. Click the Publish to HTML button on the toolbar. You see the Publish to HTML dialog box (see Figure 24.14). If you have previously saved your document, you see the same document name, but with an .htm extension rather than a .wpd extension as the default choice.

NOTE The Publish to HTML dialog box also has a text box where you can specify where graphics and sound files will be saved.

3. Edit the name that appears in the Publish To box or accept the default name, and click OK. A copy of the document is saved as an HTML file, with the extension .htm.

FIG. 24.14
Use the Publish to HTML dialog box to save your document in HTML format.

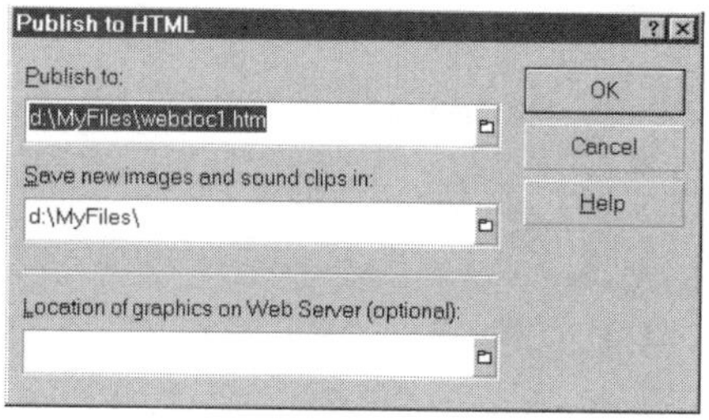

Interestingly, you do not see the HTML file on your screen. You still see the WordPerfect version of the file, as you can see by examining the title bar, which still shows the WPD file.

Copying Documents to Your Web Server

The last step in publishing your Web page is to copy it to the Web server where it will reside.

Uploading Files to the Internet An Internet server is often a UNIX-based computer that you cannot copy files directly to. Because UNIX is a different operating system than Windows, it is very likely that you cannot use a tool like Windows Explorer or WordPerfect's File, Save As and specify the disk drive of your Internet Server as a destination for your files.

You may want to talk to your Internet Service Provider (ISP), your System Administrator, or your Webmaster about the best way to upload files to the Internet. At the very least, these individuals will need to tell you where to upload them, and what permissions are needed.

A common way to upload files to the Internet is to connect to the location of your Web site via File Transfer Protocol (FTP), which you can do through Netscape. If this protocol is supported, then you can upload files to the appropriate workspace on the Internet Server.

To view the list of existing files and folders of your FTP site, type **FTP://** in front of the URL location in your Web browser (you can obtain the URL for your site from your system administrator). Figure 24.15 shows an example of an FTP site as seen through a browser.

To upload your files to the server, do as follows:

1. Open Netscape.
2. Choose File, Open Location, and specify the FTP address of the location to which you want to upload your files. (You will probably need to get the FTP address from your system administrator.) You see a list of files in your FTP directory.

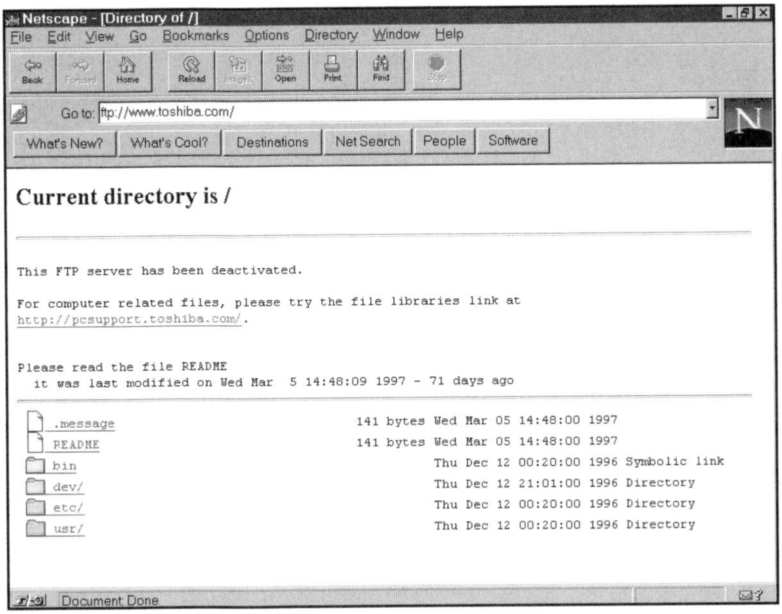

FIG. 24.15
By connecting to an FTP site through your browser, you can see the names of the files and folders located at the site.

3. Choose File, Upload File. You see the File Upload dialog box shown in Figure 24.16.
4. Navigate to the folder containing the file to be uploaded, and then double-click the file. You return to the main Navigator screen, and the file is uploaded to the specified directory.
5. After the upload is complete, you see the file listed in that directory by typing in your FTP site URL as you did previously to view the list of existing files and folders of your FTP site.

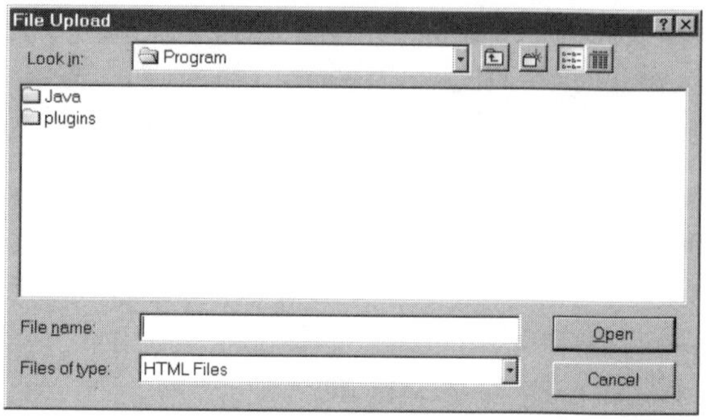

FIG. 24.16
Choose a file to upload to your FTP site from the File Upload dialog box.

Uploading Files to an Intranet Similarly, if you are publishing to a corporate intranet, the intranet might be running on Windows 95, but more likely it is running on Windows NT, Novell NetWare, or UNIX. Directories where Web pages are located usually have limited access. You will want to talk to your system administrator about the best way to upload files to the intranet server. If you have sufficient permissions, you may be able to merely save your document to the intranet server with WordPerfect; or Netscape's File, Upload command (as discussed in the previous section, "Uploading Files to the Internet") may work in your particular situation.

Converting HTML into WordPerfect

WordPerfect's Internet Publisher not only helps you to create *new* Web documents, but you can also convert HTML documents into Corel WordPerfect documents and edit them.

To convert an HTML document into a WordPerfect document, you first need to save it from the Web to your network or local computer. Just do the following:

1. Open Netscape.
2. Choose File, Open Location, and specify the URL of the Web document you want to copy, as shown in Figure 24.17. For more information about using Netscape, see Chapter 22, "Using Corel WordPerfect Suite on the Internet."

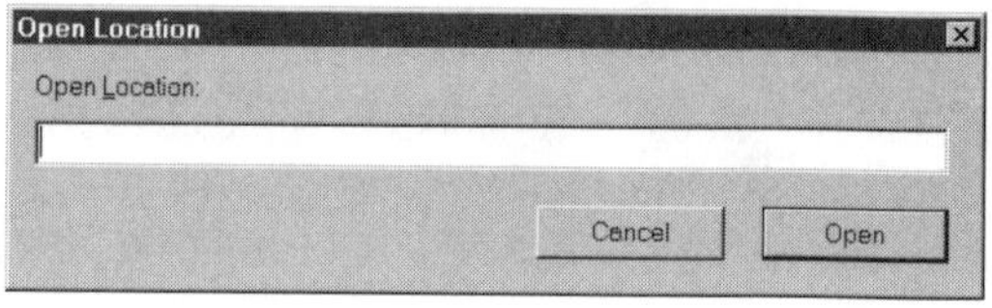

FIG. 24.17
Use Netscape to save files from the Internet or a corporate intranet to your local computer.

3. Choose File, Save As. Navigate to the folder in which you want to save the document, and then click the Save button. The file is saved to your local computer or network drive.

After the file has been saved to a local drive, you can convert it to WordPerfect format by opening it as you would other documents:

1. In WordPerfect, click the Open button. Navigate to the folder containing the Web document to be opened.

TIP Web documents will have an icon to the left of them that represents your default Web browser.

2. Double-click the HTML file to be opened. You see the Convert File Format dialog box, and HTML appears in the Convert File Format From box.
3. Click OK. The file appears on your screen. You can now edit the file using the Internet Publisher as described earlier.

NOTE Using the preceding procedure, your document is still formatted using only WordPerfect functions supported in HTML. If you want to format the document as a true WordPerfect document, choose File, Internet Publisher, Format as WP Document.

Converting WordPerfect into HTML

WordPerfect's Internet Publisher not only helps you to create new Web documents, you can also convert your present WordPerfect documents into HTML.

To do this, open the WordPerfect document, and then choose File, Internet Publisher, Format as Web Document.

You see the menus and toolbars of the Internet Publisher, and your document loses any formatting features that are not supported in HTML.

You can now publish your document in HTML by clicking the Publish to HTML button as described previously, so you can upload it to the Web.

Publishing Documents with Barista

Corel WordPerfect Suite 8 incorporates a new feature called *Barista*—a technology that permits publishing documents in Java on intranets or the Internet.

Java is a programming language that creates simple applications (called applets) that can be included in Web pages. Assuming that your browser supports Java, the applet is automatically downloaded when you access a Web page that contains it.

Barista takes pages exactly as they are and makes Java applets out of them, putting in HTML code required to run the applet.

Barista is an alternative to the Internet Publisher for publishing your WordPerfect documents to the Web. The advantage is that the Java applet approach transcends the rigid, limited coding of HTML and permits documents to be created that look much more like the original WordPerfect document than is possible with standard HTML codes.

The disadvantage is that the files are larger and take longer to download and, because a Java applet is used, additional time is taken in processing the Java "program" that builds the page.

When you publish a page with Barista, two files are created. An HTML file is made, which calls the Java applet. The Java applet is contained in a second file called a "class file." Both files must be copied to the Web server for the page to be seen.

The conversion process also allows you to choose whether to publish a multi-page document to several different Web pages, or to one long one.

The process of publishing a file using Barista is very straightforward:

1. Create or open the WordPerfect file to be converted.
2. Choose File, Send To, Corel Barista. You see the Send to Corel Barista dialog box (see Figure 24.18).

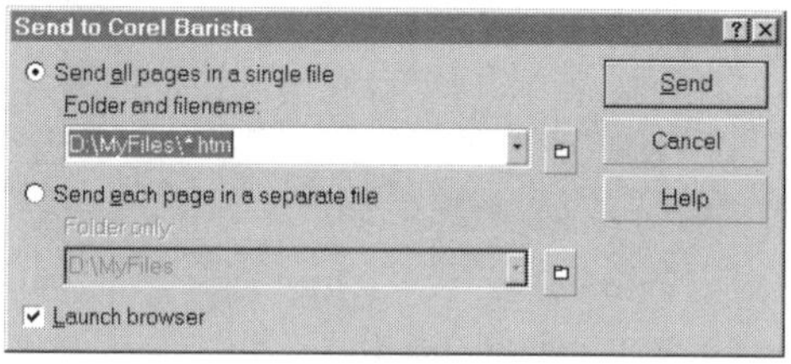

FIG. 24.18 Corel Barista allows you to publish complex documents to the Web and retain their formatting.

3. Choose whether to send All Pages in a Single File or send Each Page in a separate file.
4. Specify a folder and file name for your Web page(s), and then choose Send. Your Web pages are created and, if Launch Browser was checked, your Web browser will be launched so that you can see them.

CHAPTER 25

Using the Internet with Corel Quattro Pro

Create files for the Internet

Learn what you can do to save Corel Quattro Pro files for use on the Internet.

Obtain information from the Internet

See how you can access information on the Internet from Corel Quattro Pro.

Sharing information is one of the best ways to use the Internet. This chapter shows you how to use the Internet with Corel Quattro Pro 8. You learn how to publish Quattro Pro files to the Internet, access Internet files directly from Quattro Pro, find Help information on the Internet, and automatically update Internet links in your notebooks.

If you are just getting started with the Internet and the World Wide Web, or if you want to learn more general information on using Corel WordPerfect Suite 8 with the Internet, you may want to refer to Chapter 22, "Using Corel WordPerfect Suite on the Internet," before you read this chapter. ■

Publishing Corel Quattro Pro Files

Let's start by looking at the ways you can share, or ***publish***, your Quattro Pro files on the Internet. By doing so you can provide easy access to information in your Quattro Pro notebooks.

NOTE Technically, Quattro Pro cannot publish files on the Internet. In fact, not even WordPerfect can really publish files on the Internet. For that, you'll need a *Web server*–the combination of a computer connected to the World Wide Web (commonly just called the Web) plus special software that enables users to access the information.

Fortunately, you usually don't have to worry about setting up your own Web server. If your company has its own Web server, you also have someone who administers the Web server. If an outside company provides your Internet connection, they probably also administer the Web server. If you do have to create and administer your own Web server, you'll find these Que books useful: *Running a Perfect Website with Windows* and *Webmaster Expert Solutions*.

▶ **See** "Understanding the Implications of Publishing on the Internet," **p. 445**

Saving Files in HTML Format

One reason the Internet has become so popular is that standards have developed that enable people using different types of computers and different types of software to all view the same information. *HTML*—HyperText Markup Language—is one of those standards. By saving documents in HTML format, you can make certain that other Internet users will be able to read your documents.

▶ **See** "Creating Web Documents," **p. 496**

In addition to the many standard spreadsheet formats it supports, Quattro Pro can save notebooks in HTML format. When you've saved your Quattro Pro notebooks in HTML format, you can then send the HTML file to your Web site administrator to be included on your Web site. To save a Quattro Pro notebook file in HTML format, choose File, Save As, and select HTML from the File Type drop-down list box (see Figure 25.1). Enter the correct file name in the File Name text box and choose Save.

NOTE When saving files for use on the Internet or on a company server that may not be able to correctly handle long file names, be sure to use file names that follow the DOS 8.3 file-name conventions. This will help prevent any confusion that may result if the server shows only shortened file names.

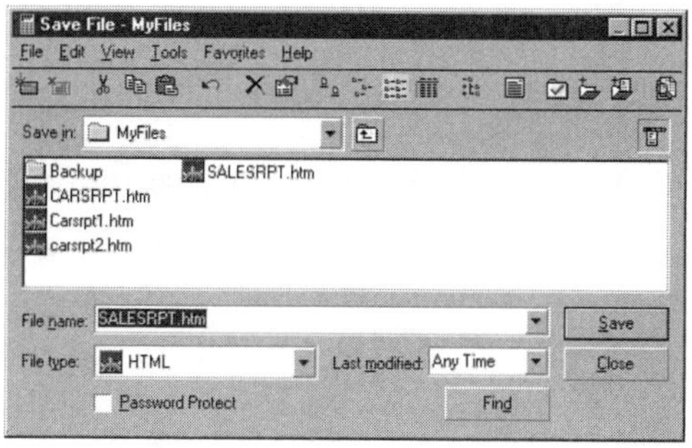

FIG. 25.1
Select HTML from the File Type list box to save your Quattro Pro notebook in HTML format for publishing on the Internet.

TIP Save your Quattro Pro notebook in Quattro Pro 8 format first to make certain you save all the formatting and features unique to Quattro Pro 8.

When you attempt to save a Quattro Pro notebook in a format other than a Quattro Pro WB3 file, features that are unique to Quattro Pro 8 can be lost. This is certainly true when you try to save a Quattro Pro notebook in HTML format. Therefore, you must always make sure to save any changes to a file as Quattro Pro v7/v8 before saving the file as an HTML file. Because of this potential for lost features, Quattro Pro displays an information box (see Figure 25.2) which informs you that certain formatting or features may be lost if you don't save the file as a Quattro Pro 8 file. Because you do want to save the file as an HTML file, choose HTML to continue.

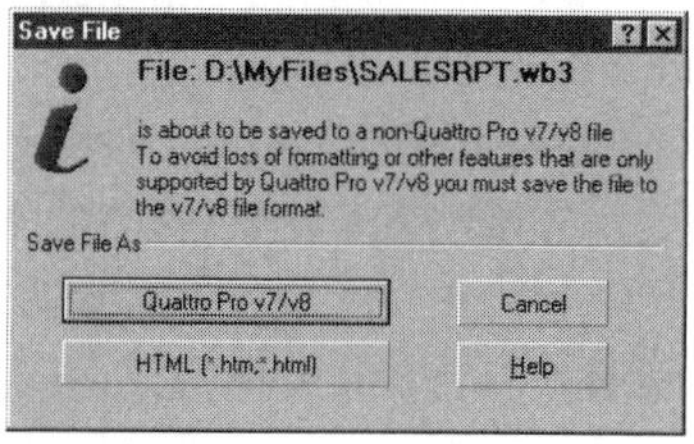

FIG. 25.2
If you save your Quattro Pro notebook in HTML format, you may lose formatting or features unique to Quattro Pro 8.

TIP View your HTML files by opening them in your Web browser (such as Netscape Navigator or Internet Explorer) to see how they'll appear on the Internet. To do so, click the Open button in your Web browser, and then specify the path of the HTML file that you saved while in Quattro Pro. You don't need to connect to the Internet to view your HTML files.

Understanding the Limitations of HTML Format

Although HTML is a true standard allowing easy exchange of information, it was never designed for the complexities of something like a Quattro Pro notebook. Indeed, when you save a Quattro Pro notebook in HTML format, you lose quite a bit of what makes a Quattro Pro notebook useful, such as charts and linking information. Figure 25.3 shows a typical warning you'll see when you attempt to save a Quattro Pro notebook in HTML format. The exact warning you'll see depends on the structure and makeup of your Quattro Pro notebook.

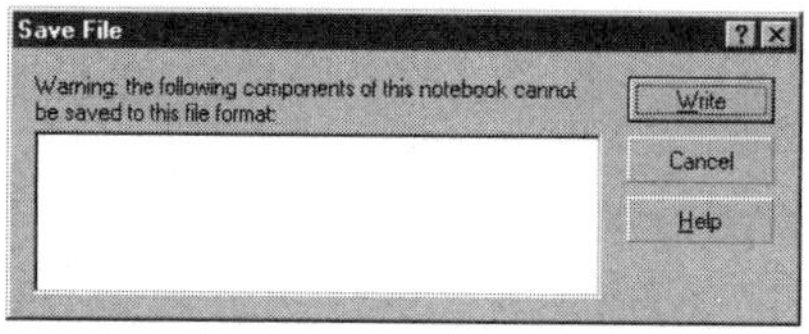

FIG. 25.3
Quattro Pro will warn you about some of the features you'll lose when you save your Quattro Pro notebook in HTML format.

CAUTION

Quattro Pro notebooks saved in HTML format lose a number of elements that may not be listed in the warning in the Save File dialog box. Be sure you save the file in Quattro Pro format before saving to HTML format.

Unfortunately, the dialog box shown in Figure 25.3 really doesn't tell the whole story. In addition to losing all pages except the current page and any charts, you also lose any formulas, special formatting, macros, and links to other Quattro Pro notebooks. For example, Figure 25.4 is a simple Quattro Pro notebook that shows a sales report and a chart. To improve the notebook's appearance, the titles were centered across the columns of the report, different size fonts were used, some text was set to bold, lines and shading were added to make data stand out, and formulas were created to summarize the data.

When you save the Quattro Pro notebook in HTML format, many changes occur. Figure 25.5 shows the same Quattro Pro notebook after it was saved in HTML format and opened in Netscape Navigator. As you can see, the basic information appears, but the appearance is not nearly the same as the notebook's appearance in Quattro Pro.

Although totals for each column and row are listed in the HTML document, if a number is changed anywhere in the column or row, the total will not be updated in the totals cells because the formulas for calculation have been stripped from the notebook during the process of saving to HTML.

Because of the limited capability of HTML, you need to think of your HTML page as a snapshot of your spreadsheet at a given moment in time. The spreadsheet will no longer function as a "living document" on a Web site. Updating it will require saving the next version of the Quattro Pro notebook each time it changes.

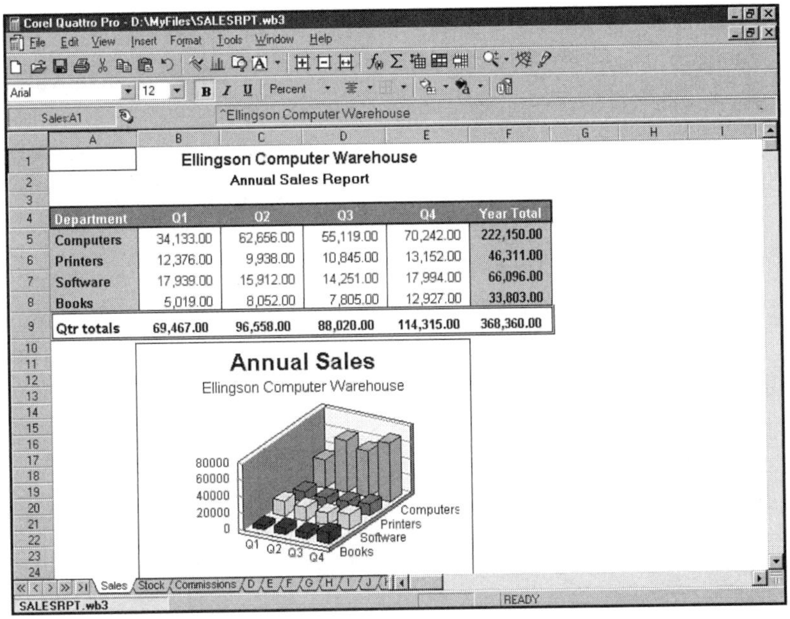

FIG. 25.4 A Quattro Pro notebook as it appears in Quattro Pro includes a number of formatting elements to improve the notebook's appearance.

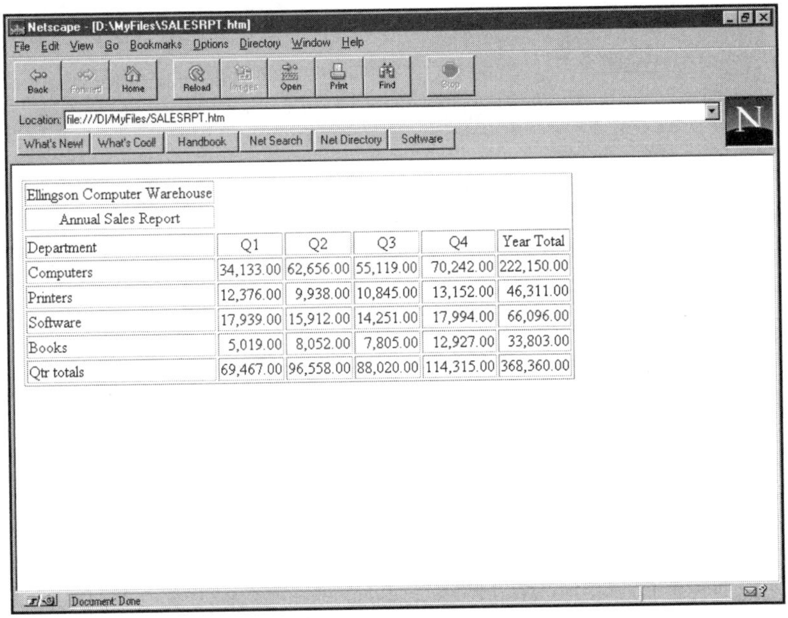

FIG. 25.5 After being saved in HTML format, a Quattro Pro notebook looks much different after losing a number of formatting elements, including the chart.

NOTE Don't forget that saving a Quattro Pro notebook in HTML format saves only the first sheet of the notebook. If you want to save other notebook sheets in HTML format, move them to the front of the notebook before saving the file.

Publishing Spreadsheets with Corel Barista

Although Quattro Pro by itself doesn't produce very good-looking HTML files, there is a way to improve your image as a publisher of Quattro Pro documents on the Internet. An add-in called Corel Barista enables you to create Java applets from your Quattro Pro notebooks that look much more like the actual Quattro Pro notebooks than a standard HTML file would. Barista creates Java applets from your Quattro Pro notebooks so that such features as charts, fonts, and formatting are maintained.

Barista uses *Java*—a programming language used to create applications on the Internet—to improve the appearance of Web pages, including those created from Quattro Pro notebooks.

About Java

Java is a programming language based on C++. It is used to create small applications that enhance Web pages with features not available in standard HTML documents. Barista creates Java applets that include the HTML codes required to run the applet. These applets enable you to display your Quattro Pro notebook on the Internet with an appearance very similar to the way Quattro Pro itself displays the notebook.

Further coverage of Java topics is beyond the scope of this book. If you are interested in learning more about this interesting technology, extensive coverage can be found in *Special Edition Using Java 1.1*, Third Edition, published by Que.

TIP Barista saves the display of notebook gridlines. If you don't want these gridlines to appear in your Web browser, remove their display from your Quattro Pro notebook sheet before you use Barista. To do so, right-click the sheet tab and choose Sheet Properties; then click the Display tab and uncheck the Horizontal and Vertical Grid Lines check boxes.

To use Barista to save a Quattro Pro notebook in Java format, choose File, Send To, Corel Barista to display the Publish the Current Document in Java Format dialog box (see Figure 25.6).

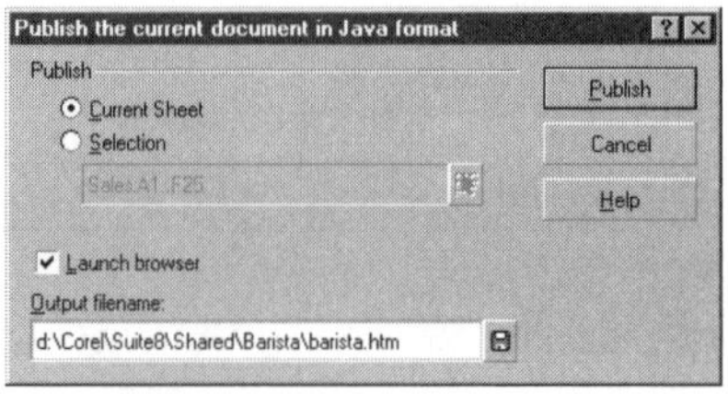

FIG. 25.6 Use the Publish the Current Document in Java Format dialog box to save your Quattro Pro notebooks in a much richer Java format.

Specify whether you want to save the entire Current Sheet or the current Selection. Enter the name for the Web page file in the Output Filename text box. To see how your Quattro Pro notebook appears when it has been saved using Barista, make certain the Launch Browser check box is selected (this is the default). When you have completed your selections, click the Publish button to save the file.

TIP To obtain more information on Barista in the Help system, choose Help, Help Topics; then click the Index tab and type **Barista:Publish To**.

CAUTION

Make certain you save your files in Quattro Pro 8 format before you publish them with Barista. If you attempt to open a file that was created by Barista in Quattro Pro, you'll find Quattro Pro will display a blank notebook because Quattro Pro doesn't understand the Java file code created by Barista.

Figure 25.7 shows how your Quattro Pro notebook appears in a Web browser when you use Barista to save the file. Although the file still cannot include multiple sheets, formulas, or macros, it can include important appearance items such as text formatting, lines, and even charts.

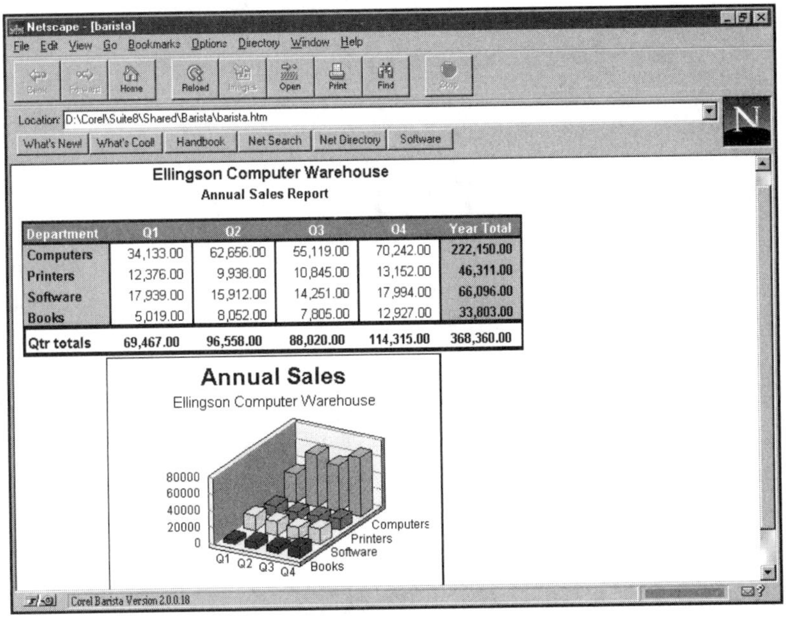

FIG. 25.7
A Quattro Pro notebook saved using Barista includes many of the formatting elements you used to improve the notebook's appearance.

Publishing Documents with Envoy

You can also publish your Quattro Pro notebooks using Envoy, Corel's *portable document format*, which enables users to view documents in their original format even if they lack the application that produced the document. When you save your Quattro Pro notebooks using Envoy, other users will be able to view those notebooks even if they don't have Quattro Pro.

To publish your Quattro Pro notebooks using Envoy, choose File, Send To, Envoy. Your notebook is sent to an Envoy file by the Envoy printer driver. For more information on the capabilities and uses of Envoy, see Chapter 27, "Using the Envoy Viewer."

ON THE WEB

If the Envoy option is dimmed on the File, Send To menu, you need to download the Envoy print driver from the Internet. For more information, refer to the following Web site:

http://www.corel.com/products/wordperfect/envoy7

CAUTION

Because Envoy files are intended to display a large amount of document formatting on-screen, you may find that the files are too large to print on certain printers. Laser printers, for example, must load the entire page into memory before printing and may experience memory overflow problems when attempting to print Envoy files.

Using Internet Files

Although sharing your information is useful, at some point you'll probably have the desire to get information from other people, too. In this section, we'll look at how you can use Internet files in Quattro Pro.

NOTE You must be connected to the Internet before you can open files on the Internet or update links to Internet files. If you connect to the Internet through a dial-up connection, be sure to open that connection before you attempt to use Quattro Pro to open or link to Internet files.

Opening Files on the Internet

You can easily open Quattro Pro notebooks that are on the Internet. Suppose, for example, that your company has a master Quattro Pro notebook containing the current pricing for all of your products. By making this notebook available on the Internet or a corporate intranet, your sales representatives could easily open the current file when they're visiting a customer and be certain that the pricing they're using is correct.

CAUTION

Unless your Web site administrator implements security measures limiting access to authorized users or implements a corporate intranet, anyone in the world who is browsing the Internet can access files you make available.

See "What Are Intranets," **p. 440**

To open a Quattro Pro notebook file located on the Internet, you must know the correct *Uniform Resource Locator* (URL) for the file. After you know the URL, you enter it in the File Name text box of the Open File dialog box instead of entering the name of a local file. For example, to open a Quattro Pro notebook located on a Web page:

1. Choose File, Open.
2. Enter the URL of the notebook file in the File Name text box.
3. Choose Open to open the notebook file. The notebook looks just like a file you might have opened from your local hard disk.

   See "Understanding Internet Addresses," **p. 443**

Saving Files from the Internet

You cannot save Quattro Pro notebook files to Internet locations. If you attempt to save a notebook, Quattro Pro will advise you that the file is read only and will offer to save the file on your computer. After you save the file on your system, you can use it just like any other local file, but you should remember that the local file will not be automatically updated when the Internet file is updated. To update your local copy, you must once again open the copy located on the Internet and then save it on your computer.

Linking to Internet Files

Rather than opening a complete Quattro Pro notebook file on the Internet, you may want to simply create a link to a cell in a notebook file located on the Internet. You may find this a better choice if you need to both save data you've added to the notebook and still make certain that you are always using the current information from a central source. For example, suppose you need to track how many pieces each customer orders of several different items, but your pricing is very volatile. If your home office maintains a master price list file in an Internet or intranet-accessible Quattro Pro notebook file, you can link the pricing column to that file and simply update the links when you enter an order.

TIP You may find that security is easier if your users link to cells in a master Quattro Pro notebook file on the Internet rather than opening an entire file on the Internet. This is because the master linking file can be considerably more obscure and simply contain data without any identifying labels.

In addition to linking to a Quattro Pro notebook on the Internet, you can create links to Internet information that is not in Quattro Pro format. Suppose that you want to create a notebook you can update periodically with the latest stock quotes from the Internet. You would first open the Internet file into a Quattro Pro notebook, using the procedure discussed in the earlier section titled "Opening Files on the Internet." Then, find the cell in the notebook where the information you want to link to appears. Switch to the notebook where you want the link to appear (or open a new notebook). Finally, type a link formula in the notebook that specifies the Internet site, and the sheet and cell reference. The syntax for this linking formula is:

+[*URL*]*sheet:cell*

The *URL* is the Internet address containing the information you want to link; *sheet:cell* is the sheet name and cell reference where the information appeared when you opened it in the notebook. Of course, you may need to update the URL or the sheet and cell reference in the link formula from time to time, if this information changes.

After this linking formula is in place, you can update the link at any time by choosing Edit, Links, Refresh Links. In addition, Quattro Pro gives you the option to update the link whenever you open the notebook file containing the link.

TIP If you want Quattro Pro to automatically update the Internet links at a specific interval, choose Tools, Settings; then click the File Options tab, select Refresh URLs, and use the spin box to specify how often you want to have the links updated.

Using QuickButtons to Display Internet Documents

Sometimes you want to view information on the Internet rather than using that information within a Quattro Pro notebook. In some cases, a particular Web site (document) might contain information that would be useful in your Quattro Pro notebook, but is not contained in a Quattro Pro notebook.

For example, suppose someone has a Web site where they show the current prices for computer memory, but the Web site is an HTML file. You might want to visit this Web site often while you are working within Quattro Pro, and then manually add the current pricing to your Quattro Pro notebook. One way to automate this process is to use a QuickButton to open the document when you click the QuickButton.

To create a QuickButton to open an Internet document, do the following:

1. Choose Insert, QuickButton.
2. Point to an empty place on the notebook sheet and click the left mouse button.
3. Right-click the new QuickButton and choose Button Properties from the QuickMenu.
4. On the Macro tab, choose Link to URL.
5. Type the URL in the URL text box; then click OK.
6. Select the Label Text tab.
7. In the Enter Text text box, enter a short descriptive label for the QuickButton.
8. Click OK to complete the dialog box and return to the notebook.
9. Click a notebook cell to deselect the QuickButton.

To test your QuickButton, first make certain your Internet connection is open and then click the QuickButton. Your Internet browser will open and display the document specified in the URL text box. You may need to switch to your Internet browser to see the document.

TIP Don't forget that information you copy to a Quattro Pro notebook from an Internet document is static. You may want to update the information just before creating a report.

After the document is displayed in your Internet browser, you can copy information to your Quattro Pro notebook. The exact technique you'll need to use will vary according to which Internet browser you use, but the general steps are as follows:

1. Select the information.
2. Use the Edit, Copy command in the Internet browser to copy the information to the Clipboard.
3. Switch to Quattro Pro and choose Edit, Paste to add the information to the notebook.

CHAPTER 26

Integrating Corel Presentations 8 with the Web

Corel Presentations 8 helps you extend your desktop into the Internet or a corporate intranet by allowing you to browse the Web, download images from the Web into your slide shows, create active links between your slide shows and the Web, or even publish your presentation to the Web in a variety of ways. ■

Publishing on the Internet

Understand some of the best types of presentation information to publish on the Internet, along with some of the limitations of Internet publishing.

Using information from the Web

Learn how to pull information off the Web to incorporate into your presentation slides.

Converting slide shows to Web pages

Find out how to convert your slide show into a series of Internet Web pages.

Four types of Internet publishing

Corel Presentations 8 can publish your data on the Internet in four different ways. Learn what they are and when to use them.

Integrating Presentations with the Web

Corel Presentations is no longer merely a desktop application. It allows you to browse the Web and download material such as clip art into your slide shows or drawings.

If you are not familiar with the Web and Web documents, you might consider reading Chapter 22, "Using Corel WordPerfect Suite on the Internet," and Chapter 23, "Communicating on the Internet," before you read this chapter. Even if you have experience with the Web, these chapters may have useful information of which you are not aware.

NOTE Most of the procedures you learn in this chapter apply only to slide shows created in Corel Presentations 8. To integrate drawings, you first must add them to a slide show.

Using the Web Browser Button

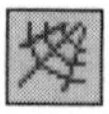

When you click the Web Browser button, you launch Netscape (or your default Web browser) and go automatically to Corel's Web site. You can browse this site for information on Presentations or proceed to somewhere else on the Internet.

▶ **See** "Browsing the Web and Specifying Destinations," **p. 450**

Using QuickLink to Link Slides to the Web

If you are fortunate enough to have an Internet connection available when you play your slide show, you can create links from text or graphics objects in your slide show that jump to specific Web locations in your Web browser.

Suppose, for example, that you have a particular Web site that illustrates one of the points in your bulleted slide. You would follow these steps:

1. Open your slide show and go to the slide where you want to create the link.

2. If you are linking to any object other than an item in a bulleted list, skip to step 3. To create a link to a single item in a bulleted list, you must first create a closed object to cover the bulleted item. For example, select the Closed Object tool, and draw a rectangle over the text area you want to link. You may want to change the fill of the object to None so you can see the text it covers.
3. Right-click the object you want to link and choose QuickLink. The Object Properties dialog box appears showing the QuickLink tab (see Figure 26.1, which shows the link already filled in).

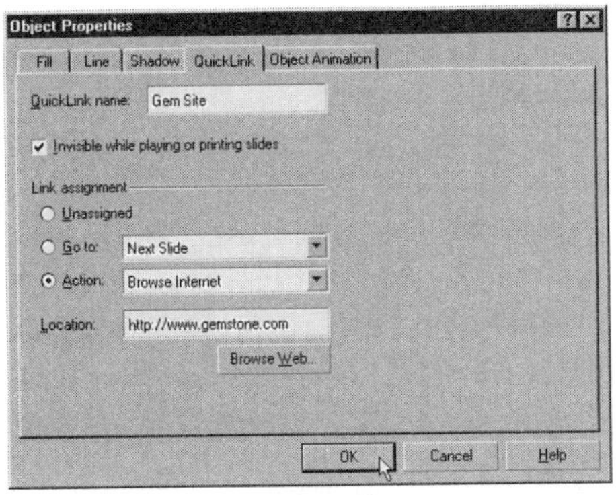

FIG. 26.1
Using QuickLinks, you can create areas on your slides that jump to specific Web sites when you click them.

4. Choose Action and Browse Internet from the drop-down list, then fill in the Location (URL) for the Web site you want to jump to.
5. Give the QuickLink a unique name, and indicate if the object should be invisible when you play the slide show. This is handy if you're using an object laid over another object such as an item in a bulleted list.

Now, when you play the slide, the mouse pointer turns to a hand when positioned over the QuickLinked object. Clicking the object takes you to your browser and the Web site you specified.

Using QuickKeys to Link Slides to the Web

You also can jump to Web sites directly from your slides by defining QuickKey links. For example, you have four items listed on your slide, each referring to a Web site on the Internet. You can assign Web addresses to any alpha or numeric key, and even to many function and control keys. When you press these defined keys, Presentations jumps to your browser and to the address linked to that key.

Suppose you want to jump to the Corel Web site, and you want to press **C** to do so. Follow these steps:

1. Open your slide show and go to the slide where you want to create the QuickKey link.
2. Choose Format, Slide Properties, QuickKeys. Presentations displays the Slide Properties dialog box with the QuickKeys tab selected (see Figure 26.2).

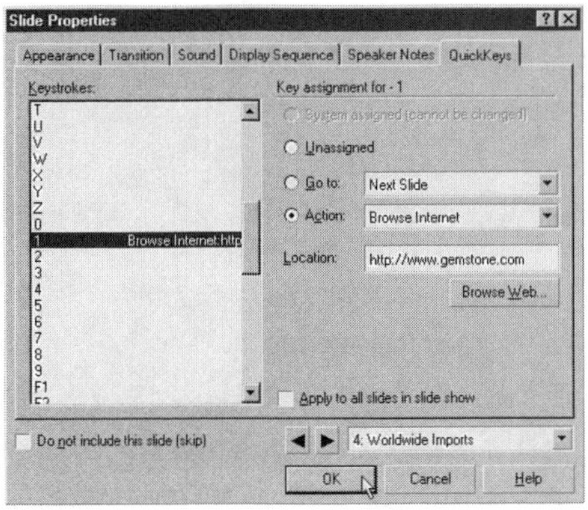

FIG. 26.2
Using QuickKeys, you can assign keys that jump to specific Web sites when you press them.

3. In the Keystrokes list, click the key you want to assign.
4. Choose Browse Internet from the Action drop-down list, then fill in the Location (URL) for the Web site to which you want to jump.
5. If you choose Apply to All Slides in Slide Show, the QuickKey will work while viewing any slide. If not, the QuickKey works only with the current slide, thus enabling you to assign the same key to a different Web site in another slide.
6. When you have made the changes you want, choose OK.

Now when you play your slide show, pressing the QuickKey takes you directly to the Web site you specified.

Using Clip Art from the Web

The Internet can be a rich source for clip art to include in your slide shows. Using Netscape, it's easy to find and save clip art on your local computer, then import it into Presentations.

CAUTION

Images on Web sites are often copyrighted, and will in any case be protected by relevant copyright laws. Be sure to obtain permission from the copyright owner before using images from Web sites, and strongly consider establishing a company or institutional policy regarding use of information obtained from the Internet after advice from legal counsel.

▶ **See** "Understanding the Implications of Publishing on the Internet," **p. 445**

You can find free public domain clip art on the Internet. The easiest way to do so is to search for the term **clip art** using any of the popular search engines.

▶ **See** "Introducing Netscape Navigator," **p. 447**

Once you've found an image you like and have obtained permission to use it, you can copy a Web image into a Presentations slide show easily by following these steps:

1. Open Netscape and browse to the Web site containing the image.

NOTE If you access the Internet through a dial-up service, you first must connect to that service before you can use Netscape or any other browser.

2. Right-click the image. You see a pop-up QuickMenu.
3. Choose Save Image As. You see the Save As dialog box.
4. Specify a folder and file name for the image, then choose Save. The image is saved to your local computer.

From Presentations, you can insert this image into your slide show as you do any other image on your disk. The format of the graphic image, whether GIF or JPEG, converts automatically to a bitmap graphic image in your drawing or slide show.

▶ **See** "Inserting a Picture from Another Program," **p. 404**

Converting Slide Shows to Web Pages

A slide show can be an effective sales tool by presenting your company's mission to the public. Used as a simple type of computer-based training, slide shows can also be a learning tool. It can supplement other text-based Web pages by illustrating points with charts, diagrams, and tables.

Presentations includes a feature that enables you to convert your slide show quickly and easily to one or more Web pages, so you can publish it on the Internet or on a corporate intranet.

▶ **See** "What Are Intranets," **p. 440**

Presentations offers three different methods for publishing your pages to the Web, each with its strengths and limitations:

- *HTML.* This is the standard for Web pages, and all graphics-based browsers can display such pages without special additions or setup.
- *Barista.* This method uses Java to display the slides. It also requires a recent browser version—one that supports Java. But such slides also can be viewed by any program that can run Java applications.
- *Show It!.* This method actually enables users to view slides with sounds, animations, and transitions, just as if you played the slide show yourself. However, this also requires that users have Corel's free ShowIt! plug-in added to their browser.

Understanding HTML Web Page Formats

The most common method for publishing Web pages is by converting your slides to standard HTML. You can use HTML to publish your slide show in four different ways. If your readers will be using a browser that supports frames (such as Netscape Navigator 2.0, Microsoft Internet Explorer 2.0, or later versions of both), you can create Web pages like the one shown in Figure 26.3.

▶ **See** "Introducing Netscape Navigator," **p. 447**

NOTE There are two meanings of the term *publish*. The normal usage of the term, for example, "publish a Web document," means to *place* a document on the Web where people can see it. Presentations uses the term *publish*, however, in a different sense, to mean *converting* a slide show to HTML, preparatory to placing it on the Web.

When used in this latter sense, the document will still reside on your disk rather than on the Web, and you will still need to copy it to the Internet so that people can see it.

The meaning of the term in this book can be derived from the context in which it's used.

FIG. 26.3
You can publish your slide show in Web pages that have frames, if your readers' browsers support this.

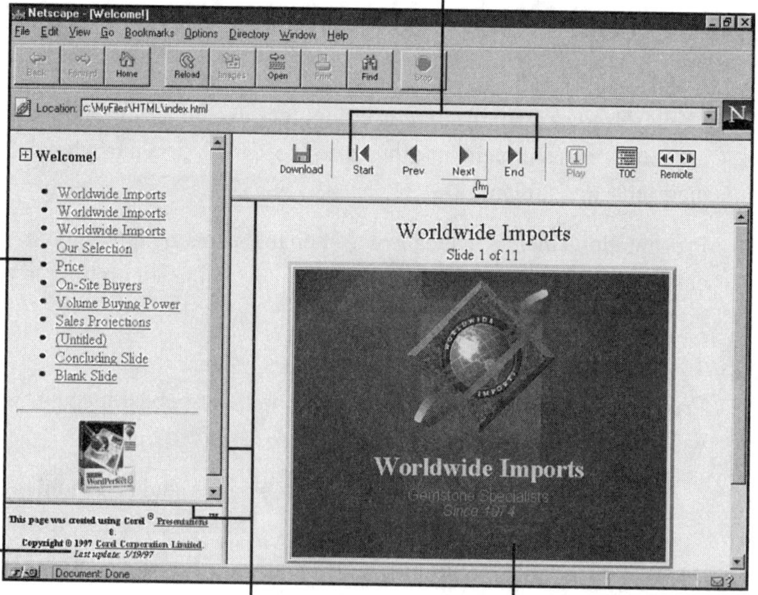

When frames are used, each slide has its own frame that is accessed from the Table of Contents frame or from the Slide Controls frame. In the Table of Contents area, bulleted slides are listed in a collapsible outline format: Click the + to the left of the slide show title to expand the outline and see the slide bullets. In the Slide Controls frame, you have several useful controls for navigating through your slide show. These include:

- *Download.* Clicking this button enables viewers to download the original Presentations slide show. This is particularly useful if they have the Presentations program.
- *Direction Buttons.* These buttons take you to the start (beginning), previous, next, and end slides.
- *Play.* If during setup you choose to make the slide show self-running, the AutoPlay button enables the viewer to start playing the slide show.
- *Table of Contents.* Click this button to hide the Table of Contents frame, or to make it reappear.
- *Remote.* Click this button to turn the slide controls frame into a floating dialog box that you can position anywhere on your screen. Using the remote and also turning off the Table of Contents enables you to see more of your slide on the screen (see Figure 26.4).

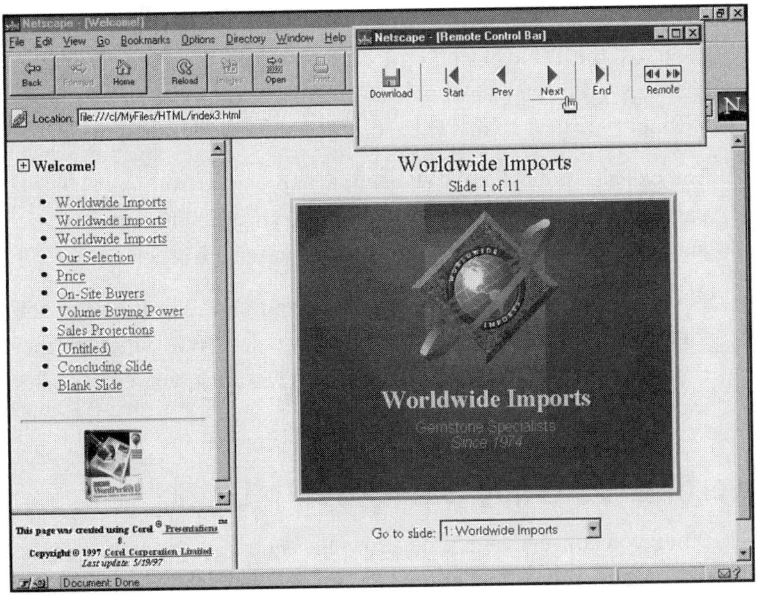

FIG. 26.4
Using the frame version of the Web-based slide show includes several handy tools for helping people browse through your show.

If you want people to be able to read your slide show even if their browser doesn't support frames, you can publish in multiple Web pages, with each slide on its own page, as shown in Figure 26.5.

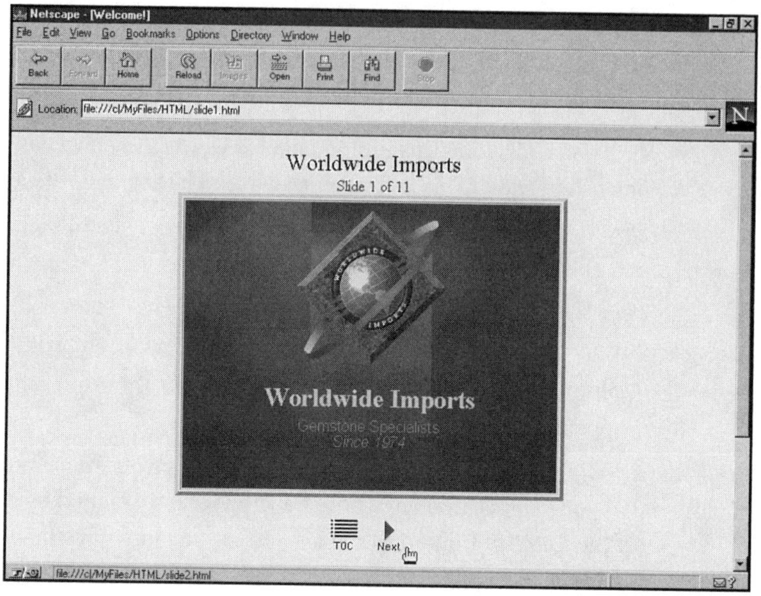

FIG. 26.5
If you are not sure that everyone's browser supports frames, you may want to publish your slide show with individual multiple pages.

With this type of setup, the viewer can click the slide title in the Table of Contents and return to the Table of Contents after viewing each slide. You also can set up the slides so that the viewer has the choice of using next or previous buttons to go on to the next slide without returning to the Table of Contents.

You can also publish your slide show in one long Web page, with all the slides in the same page one after another, like the example shown in Figure 26.6. In this method, the viewer just uses the scroll bar to view one slide after the other.

Finally, you can publish thumbnails of your slide show in one Web page, as displayed in Figure 26.7. You can set this up so viewers just have access to the thumbnails, or so the thumbnails are buttons that the viewers can click, which will take them to a separate page with a larger version of the slide.

Converting Your Slide Show to HTML

When you convert your slide show, Presentations creates a series of files in a folder you specify. You should not try to save more than one slide show in a particular folder, because many of the file names may be duplicates.

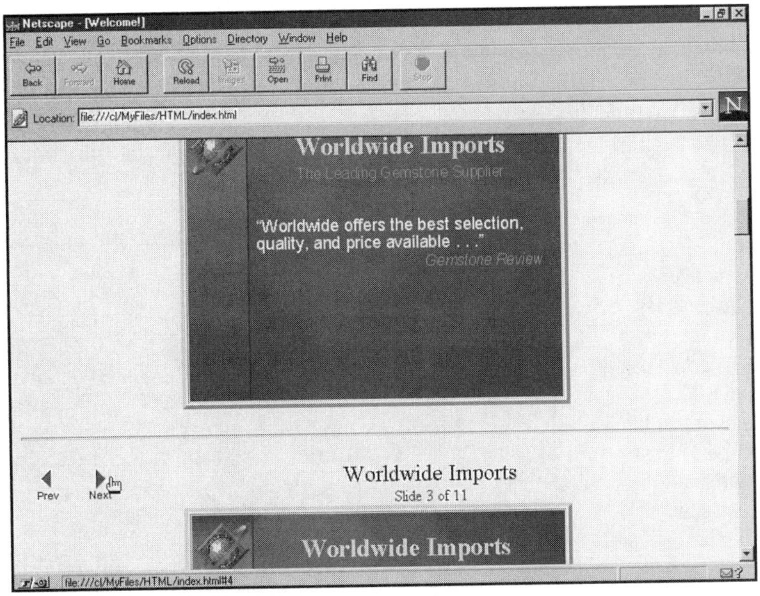

FIG. 26.6
If you prefer, you can put all your slides on one Web page.

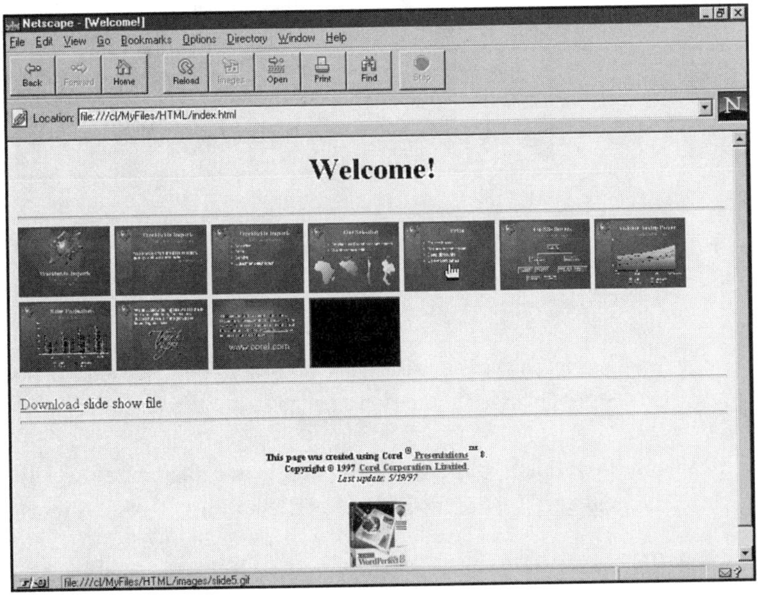

FIG. 26.7
You can also publish thumbnails of each slide; users can double-click a thumbnail to see the slide full size.

To convert your slide show to Web pages, ensure that your slide show has been created, finalized, and saved. Then follow these steps:

1. With the slide show on-screen, choose File, Internet Publisher, or click the Internet Publisher button on the Property Bar. You see the Internet Publisher dialog box shown in Figure 26.8.

FIG. 26.8
The Internet Publisher dialog box enables you to publish your slide show to the Web using standard HTML, Barista (Java), or the ShowIt! plug-in with full sound and animation support.

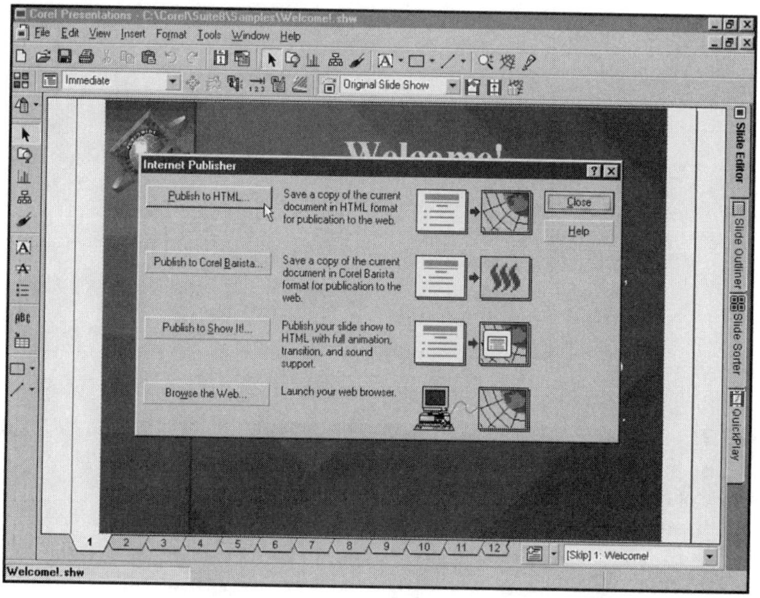

2. Choose Publish to HTML, then choose Use an Existing Layout and select one of the four layout options described earlier: Frame-Enhanced Page, Multiple Pages, Single Page, or Thumbnail Page.

NOTE The option to create a custom layout simply allows you to customize any of the four styles discussed here and to save the style with a unique name.

3. In the Publish to HTML dialog box, you can change the Title of Slide Show, and specify the location you want to Publish Files To (see Figure 26.9).

NOTE As you make your choices, click the Next button to advance to the next screen, and see more options, or the Back button to review and change earlier choices. You can click Finish at any time to accept the normal default settings and create your HTML-based slide show.

By default, the main slide show file is named INDEX.HTML; all other page files have the .HTML extension, and image and sound files are stored in subfolders. To change any of these defaults, click the Advanced button.

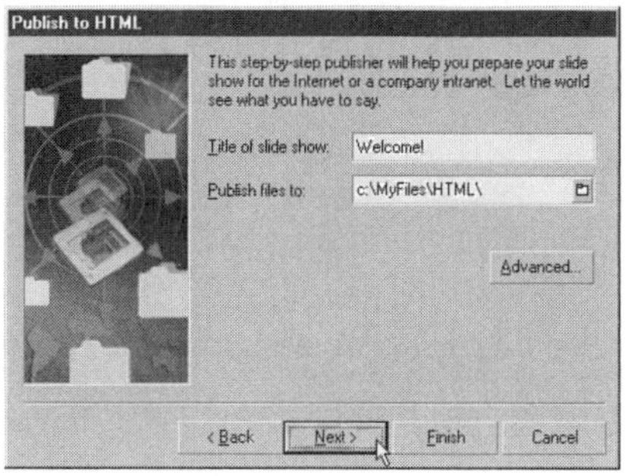

FIG. 26.9 The Publish to HTML dialog box presents several screens to help you publish your slide show to the Web. Here, you can specify the title and the location of the resulting Web page files.

CAUTION

Keep in mind that computers using Windows 3.1 and some networks either cannot cope with long names, or cope with them by truncating them—making identification of individual pages more difficult. For this reason, it is often best to stick with the DOS naming convention of eight-period-three characters.

4. In the next step of the Publish to HTML dialog box, you can change your choice of the particular style you want (see Figure 26.10). Your selections in this screen determine your available choices in the next screens. For example, if you choose the Frame-Enhanced Page style, you have a whole series of navigational tools from which to select (see Figure 26.11).

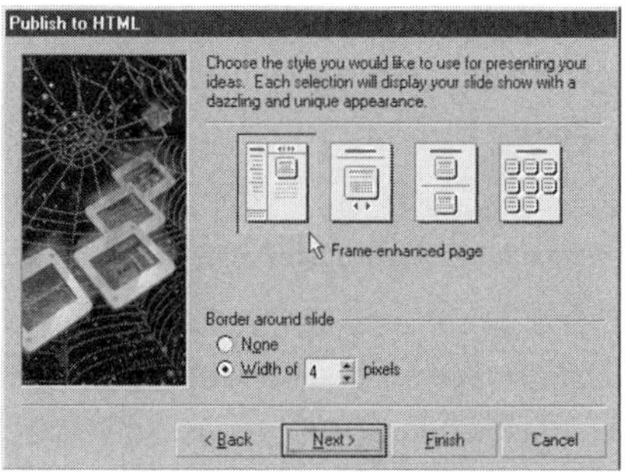

FIG. 26.10 When you publish to HTML, you choose from one of four basic layout styles.

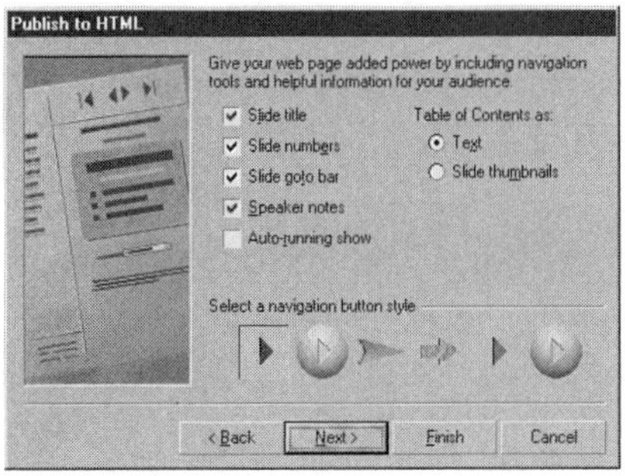

FIG. 26.11
Presentations offers many choices for customizing just how your slide show will appear when you place it on the Web.

Slide show page customization options shown in Figure 26.11 include:

- *Slide Titles.* Put the title of the presentation on each Web page.
- *Slide Numbers.* Put page numbers on each Web page.
- *Slide Goto Bar.* Add a navigation slide bar to the bottom of each slide.
- *Speaker Notes.* Add the Speaker Notes to the bottom of each Web page.
- *Auto-Running Show.* Create a self-running slide show, rather than one with manual advances. The viewer simply clicks the Play button and the show proceeds automatically to the end.
- *Table of Contents As.* Add a table of contents page (for multiple page slide shows) or frame (for frame-enhanced slide shows) that includes either Text (based on the title of each slide) or Slide Thumbnails.

As you click Next and advance to the various Publish to HTML screens, you will see several other options, including:

- *Include Slide Show File for Downloading.* If you mark this check box, a copy of the Corel Presentations 7 slide show file will also be saved in the folder, and a link will be created to the file. In this way, people who visit this Web site and who own Presentations 7 can click the link to download the file to their computer, where they can view it with Presentations.
- *Footer Information.* Indicate the location of your own home page, your e-mail address, the date the page was last updated, and Corel Presentations copyright information.
- *Screen Size and Graphic Type.* Have Presentations create the size slide that looks best on the type screens most viewers will use. You also can specify whether to publish graphics using GIF, JPEG, or PNG (Portable Network Graphics) formats.

CAUTION

If you choose a very high screen resolution, the slides will appear much too large in many viewers. When in doubt, use the lowest common screen size, such as 640×480.

- *Color Options.* Use your browser's default colors, or specify colors for text, links, and so on. Set background colors or use a background wallpaper file.

NOTE Footer information should include Corel Presentations 8 copyright information, your e-mail address (so that viewers may contact you with questions or other information which may be of interest to you), the date the page was last updated (so viewers will know if it has been changed since the last time they looked), and any custom information.

5. Choose Finish when you are done setting options. You see a dialog box showing the process as each slide is converted, and the files are created in the folder you specified. Presentations then asks if you want to launch your browser and view your slide show.

NOTE After you've published your slide show as HTML, you should view it with your browser prior to uploading it to your Web site to ensure that everything is as you want it to be. If the presentation is not right, it's easier to fix it in Presentations and re-publish it, but you can edit the HTML files themselves if you need to. You may want to refer to Que's *Special Edition Using HTML* for further information on editing Web pages.

Publishing Corel Presentations with Barista

Corel Presentations incorporates a new feature called *Barista*—a Corel-developed technology that allows you to publish your presentations in Java on intranets or the Internet. For further information on how to use this technology, see the section "Publishing Documents with Barista" in Chapter 24, "Integrating Corel WordPerfect 8 with the Internet." For in-depth coverage of the Java language, see Que's book *Special Edition Using Java*.

CAUTION

Remember that not all browsers support Java applications such as Barista. Barista might be used safely on an intranet where you are reasonably sure everyone's browser can read the Barista documents. Alternatively, you could create two options for viewers: Barista and standard HTML.

Publishing Corel Presentations with ShowIt!

An exciting new method for publishing your slides to the Web is Corel's ShowIt! program, which actually enables viewers to see your slide shows with animations, sounds, and transitions. You could even present your slide show at a conference or meeting using nothing more than your browser and an Internet connection to your slide show's Web site.

The method for preparing a ShowIt! slide show for the Web is similar to the standard HTML method described earlier in this chapter. You can choose the file names and locations, any additional information you want to add (such as your e-mail address), the size of the display, and the color settings.

Presentations also automatically adds information about how viewers can obtain the free Corel ShowIt! plug-in to add to their Web browser.

After you create the ShowIt! slide show, you play it just like you do a regular slide show (see Figure 26.12).

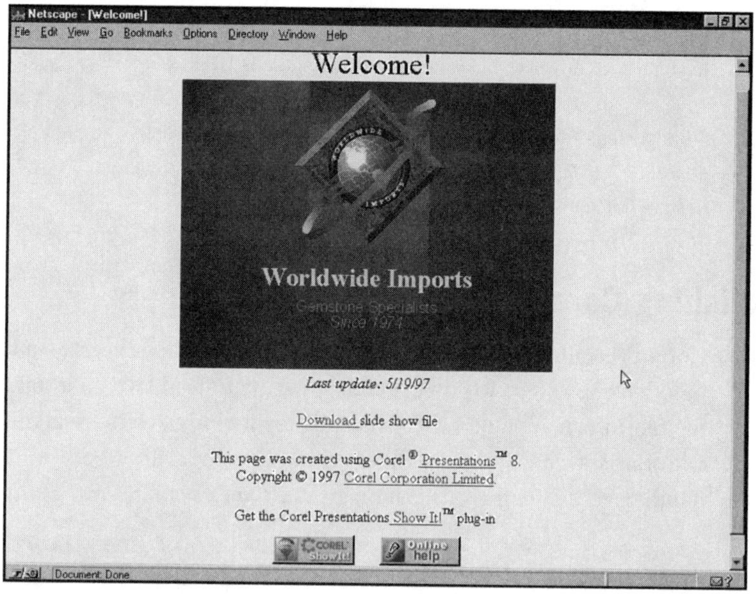

FIG. 26.12 When you publish to ShowIt!, you can play the slide show from your Internet browser just as you usually play your slide show.

While viewing a slide in your browser, you can do the following:

- Click the left mouse button on the slide to advance to the next slide, the next bullet, or an animated object.
- Sound and video files play at their assigned times and locations.
- Click QuickLinks to jump to other Web sites (however, QuickKeys will not work).

- Click the Reload button (or equivalent) in your browser to start the slide show over from the beginning.

Uploading Your Presentation

Before others can see your presentation, you will need to copy it on to the Internet or your corporate intranet. There are a few different applications for doing so.

Copying Your Presentation to the Internet To copy the presentation to the Internet, you need to use programs not included with Corel WordPerfect Suite 8. Thus, this book cannot tell you *how* to do this; however, it is possible to specify *what* needs to be done.

To copy the presentation to the Internet, you must do the following:

- Know the address of the file area to which you will copy the presentation on your Internet server.
- Have sufficient access permission to copy the files.
- Create a subfolder on the Internet server for the presentation. You may also need to create additional subfolders for image and sound files, if you used them in your slide show.
- Copy all files in your Web presentation folder to the appropriate subfolder(s).

You can also create a link from another Web site to your presentation. The link should be of the form:

http://www.*server*.com/*folder*/*subfolder*/index.htm

where ***server*** is the name of your Internet server, ***folder*** is the name of your main folder on that server, and ***subfolder*** is the name of the new subfolder you created for your presentation.

CAUTION

If you have changed the name of your table of contents page, that is the name that should be entered where it says INDEX.HTM in the preceding URL. Also, some servers are very picky about file names. Some require .HTML rather than .HTM as file name extensions. Some are sensitive to upper- and lowercase (Index.html, INDEX.HTML, or index.html could be three different file names).

Copying Your Presentation to a Corporate Intranet Copying your presentation to a local Web site can entail any number of different methods, depending on how your site is set up. The basic procedure, however, is still the same as it is to copy your presentation to the Internet.

You must create a specific subfolder on your Web server exclusively for the presentation, and copy all files from the folder in which you saved your Web presentation to this subfolder.

If files on your Web site are accessible via your Windows 95, Windows NT, or Novell network, you may be able to create the directory (folder) and copy the files via Windows Explorer. More often, you will need to copy the files to a public workspace on your network, and your network administrator or Webmaster will take care of copying them to the appropriate locations on the Web server.

E-Mailing Your Presentation

As you are developing your presentation, you may want to e-mail it to reviewers or your supervisor prior to finalizing it.

If you are using a mail system that supports an e-mail standard called Simple MAPI, such as Novell's GroupWise, you can choose File, Send To, Mail and e-mail your slide show from within Presentations.

N O T E Networks that use compatible e-mail programs sometimes are not configured correctly, and the Send To, Mail option appears grayed. Ask your system administrator to check if the Send item does not appear on your menu. ▦

To e-mail your presentation, have the slide show you want to send on the screen. Choose File, Send To, Mail. You are taken into your e-mail system, and see a Send To dialog box with the slide show automatically included as an attachment to your (blank) message. Fill in the recipient(s), a subject, and a message, and send your message!

If the mail option is not available, go into your e-mail system and use the method appropriate for your system for attaching a file to an e-mail. ●

PART VII

Using Bonus Applications

CHAPTER 27

Using the Envoy Viewer

View Envoy documents

Find out how to read an Envoy document and add annotations to it.

Use bookmarks and links

See how you can make an easily searchable Envoy document by creating a table of contents with bookmarks and hypertext links.

Corel positions the Corel WordPerfect Suite 8 as a total office solution. An important part of this total solution is *document publishing*. Document publishing means distributing a document electronically in a form that is easily readable, no matter what computer is used to read the document.

For many organizations, converting a Corel WordPerfect Suite data file to an HTML file is not the most efficient publishing solution. Often, the document is too complex, and converting it manually takes too much time. Envoy can be an excellent publishing solution in these instances. ■

An Overview of Envoy

Using Envoy, you can create a document that:

- Can be read on both PCs and Macintoshes.
- Cannot be changed by readers.
- Can, however, be annotated by reviewers.
- Includes objects such as sound files or animated pictures.
- Contains bookmarks and hypertext links to help readers move through the document.

For example, you may want to maintain a technical manual that includes text, diagrams, and pictures. It is probably vital that users not make changes to this document, but it is equally important that they be able to jump quickly to procedures of interest.

Alternatively, you may want to route a contract to a variety of attorneys and representatives of the contracting parties for comment. It is important that the original document not be altered, but that reviewers be able to highlight important parts, put "sticky" notes on it, read others' comments, and identify who made which comment.

In any of these cases, Envoy provides the solution.

Envoy consists of two parts: the *printer driver* and the *Viewer*. The Envoy printer driver is used to convert a document from its original format into an Envoy document. This driver enables you to create an Envoy document from any application that can send a job to a Windows printer. It even enables you to embed the original document's fonts in the Envoy document, ensuring that exact formatting is maintained.

NOTE The Standard version of Corel WordPerfect Suite 8 only includes the Envoy viewer. It does not include the Envoy printer driver that enables you to create Envoy files.

CAUTION

You cannot view an Envoy file under Windows 3.1.

The Viewer enables the document to be read and annotated. It provides document security, allowing the creator to choose whether the document can be annotated, printed, or password-protected against even being viewed. The Viewer is also the part of Envoy that enables the document creator to add bookmarks and hypertext links, and permits readers to annotate and/or highlight the document.

NOTE If you have the Envoy printer driver, you can create Envoy documents that include the Envoy Viewer inside them—called the *Runtime Viewer*. The Runtime Viewer allows anyone who has Windows 95 to view Envoy files. If the recipient uses a Mac, the file should be saved as a regular Envoy file, and the recipient should use the Macintosh version of the Envoy Viewer to see the file.

Viewing and Annotating Envoy Files

When you distribute an Envoy file, users may read, print, and/or annotate it, depending on the security options you have specified. Users need to know how to do several things to effectively use the Envoy Viewer:

- Open, close, and print Envoy files
- Set environment options
- Move through the document
- Annotate the document with highlights and notes
- Add bookmarks, hypertext links, and OLE objects to the document

Opening and Closing Envoy Files

You may open an Envoy file from the Windows Explorer or from Envoy itself.

To open an Envoy or a run time Envoy file from the Windows Explorer, navigate to the folder containing the Envoy file, then double-click it.

To open an Envoy file from the Envoy Viewer, follow these steps:

1. Choose Start, Corel WordPerfect Suite 8, Tools, Envoy 7 Viewer. You see the Envoy Viewer shown in Figure 27.1.
2. Choose File, Open or click the Open button. You see the Open dialog box shown in Figure 27.2.
3. Choose the appropriate drive and folder, then double-click the file to choose it. The file is opened in the Envoy Viewer.

▶ **See** "Saving, Opening, and Closing Files," **p. 32**

To close a file, choose File, Close. If you have added annotations to the file, provided there are no security restrictions, you will be asked if you want to save it before closing. If you respond Yes, the file will be saved, replacing the old version with no further prompting.

FIG. 27.1
You can view and annotate Envoy files from the Envoy Viewer.

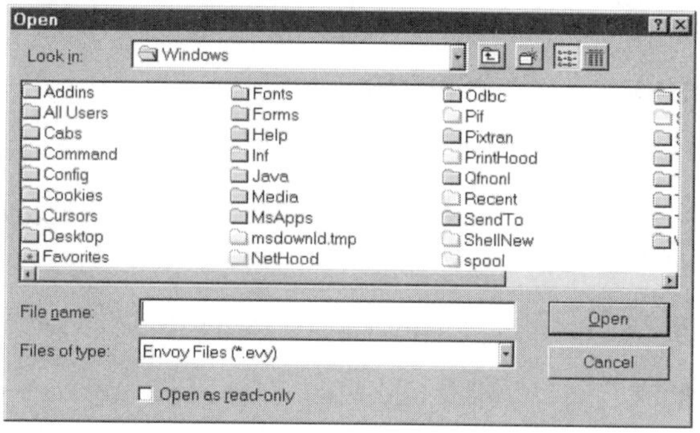

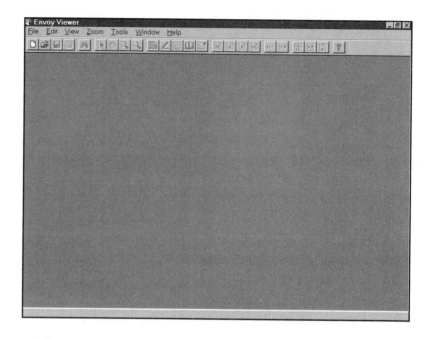

FIG. 27.2
The Open dialog box enables you to open Envoy files.

TROUBLESHOOTING

When I view an Envoy file at home, equations are all messed up. The symbols are showing as boxes. What might be wrong? Apparently, you don't have the fonts at home that were used to create the document at work, and there are no similar fonts. The person who made the Envoy file needs to re-create it, embedding the appropriate fonts in it when it is created.

Printing Envoy Files

To print an Envoy file, follow these steps:

1. Open the file in Envoy, as described in the preceding section.
2. Choose File, Print. You see the Print dialog box (see Figure 27.3).

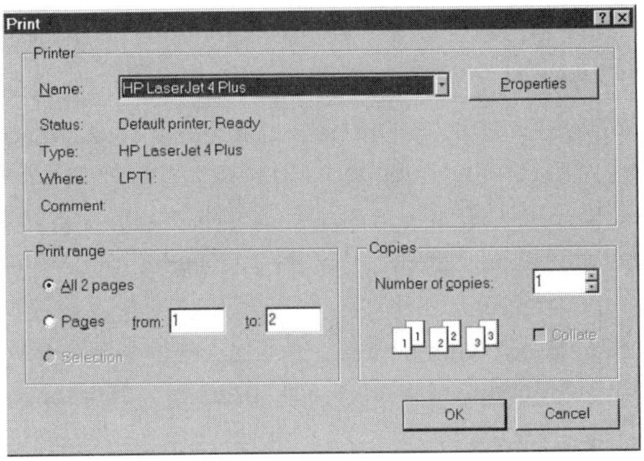

FIG. 27.3
You can print Envoy documents from the Print dialog box of the Envoy Viewer, providing there are no security restrictions against printing.

3. Select the printer, if necessary, in the Name box.
4. Set the Print Range and Number of Copies, if more than one is desired.
5. Click OK to print the document.

Changing the Viewer Environment

You can set environment options that determine how your file will look in the Envoy window, including the zoom factor and display of thumbnails.

Setting the Zoom Factor The *zoom factor* is the degree of magnification that the Envoy file has on-screen. You can show an entire page, or just a few letters.

The quickest way to change the zoom factor is by using the Fit Width and Fit Height buttons on the toolbar:

- The Fit Width button calculates the proper zoom factor to show the entire width of the page from side to side, including the white margins.

- The Fit Height button functions similarly, but shows the entire height of the page from top to bottom, including the white margins.

> **TIP** When you click the Fit Height button, smaller text may be represented by shaded lines rather than letters. Often, the Fit Height button is used to show entire page layout or larger graphics, rather than readable text.

You can also set the zoom factor by choosing Zoom on the Menu bar. You can then choose specific zoom factors, such as 25%, 50%, 75%, 80%, 90%, and so forth.

Finally, you can use the Zoom In and Zoom Out buttons on the toolbar to magnify selected areas of the document in two ways:

- Click the Zoom In or Zoom Out button, and then click the document window. The document will zoom in or out by selected amounts each time you click the button.
- Click the Zoom In button, and then drag a rectangle in the document window. The document will be magnified so that the rectangle you drew occupies the entire window.
- Click the Zoom Out button, then drag a rectangle in the document window. The contents of the document window will shrink to fit into the rectangle that you drew.

> **TIP** After you click the Zoom In or Zoom Out button, the status bar reminds you of the options you have and the current Zoom percentage.

Displaying Thumbnails *Thumbnails* are small representations of each page of a document that can be shown at the top or left of the Envoy screen.

To show thumbnails, click the Thumbnails button on the toolbar. Repeatedly clicking this button scrolls you through the thumbnail display options: The first time you click, thumbnails appear at the top of the window (see Figure 27.4). The second time, they appear at the left. The third time, they disappear.

You may also show the page numbers below the thumbnails while thumbnails are displayed by choosing View, Thumbnails, Show Page Numbers. (If page numbers are already displayed, the last command changes to Hide Page Numbers.)

Moving Through Envoy Files

You can move through Envoy files in several ways by using:

- The scroll bars
- The toolbar or menu
- Thumbnails

- The Scroll tool
- The Find command

Perhaps the easiest way to move through the Envoy document for Windows users is by using the scroll bars.

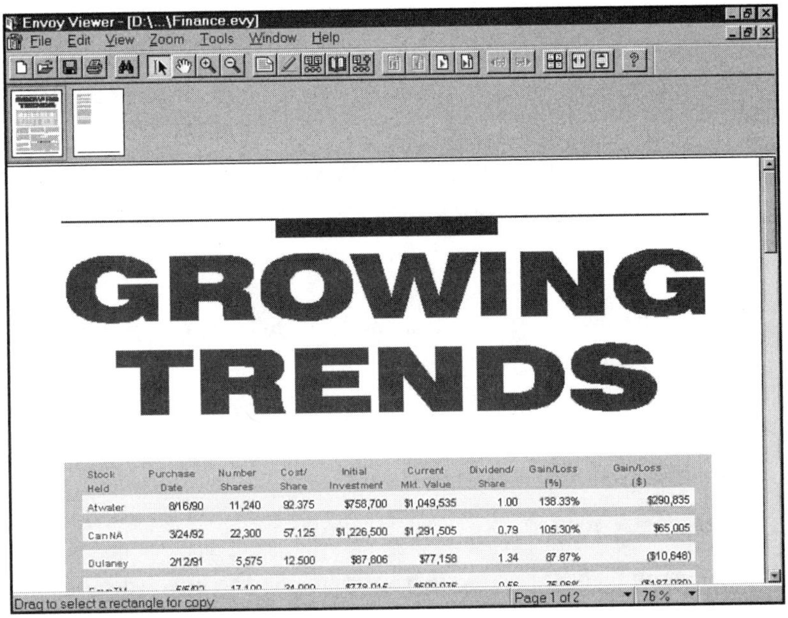

FIG. 27.4
Thumbnails are small pictures of each page. They can appear at the top or left of the Envoy window.

You can also move between pages easily using the First Page, Previous Page, Next Page, and Last Page buttons on the toolbar. Alternatively, you can choose View, then First Page, Previous Page, Next Page, or Last Page.

You can go to a specific page by clicking the page number in the status bar. You see the Go To Page dialog box. Type in the number of the page you want to go to, and then choose OK.

If thumbnails are displayed, you can also go to a specific page by double-clicking the appropriate thumbnail.

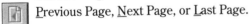

You can also scroll through a document using the Scroll button. When you click the Scroll button, the mouse pointer changes to a hand. You can then drag the page in any direction. Thus, if you drag it down, the text (and/or pages) above the current position starts to show. The Scroll tool is most useful when you want to show a little more of the document than displays in the window.

Alternatively, you can search for specific text within the document or annotation:

1. Choose Edit, Find. You see the Find dialog box (see Figure 27.5).

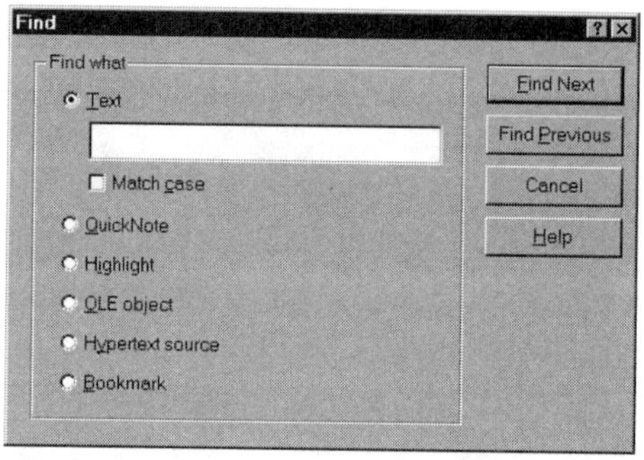

FIG. 27.5
You can search Envoy documents for selected words in the text or in annotations using Find.

2. Choose whether to look for Text, QuickNote, Highlight, OLE Object, Hypertext Source, or Bookmark.
3. Type the text to be searched for in the Find Text box, if you chose Text in step 2.
4. Click Find Next.

Highlighting Text

You can highlight text while you are reading an Envoy document almost like you are doing it by hand with a highlighter.

To highlight text, click the Highlight button on the toolbar. The mouse pointer changes to a miniature highlighter. Drag the mouse pointer over the text to be highlighted. The highlighted text changes color, just as a paper copy would (see Figure 27.6).

Alternatively, you can drag over an area of the document that does not contain text. In this case, a rectangular area is selected.

To clear highlighting:

1. Make sure that the Highlight tool is selected.
2. Click anywhere in an area of highlighted text. The entire highlighted text is selected.
3. Press the Delete key to remove the highlighting.

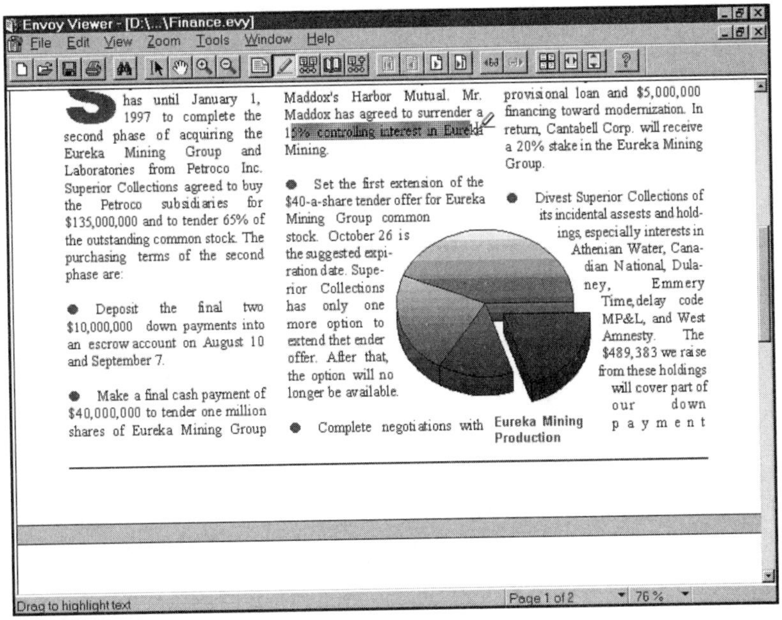

FIG. 27.6
Dragging the Highlight mouse pointer over text highlights it just as it would on paper.

Alternatively, you can right-click the highlighted text, and then choose Clear.

To change highlighting options:

1. Make sure that the Highlight tool is selected.
2. Right-click any area of highlighted text to see a QuickMenu.
3. Choose Highlight Properties. You see the Highlight Properties dialog box (see Figure 27.7).

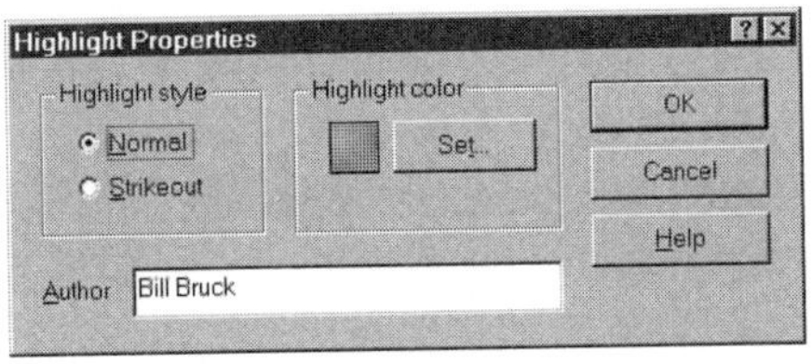

FIG. 27.7
You can change highlighting options by using the Highlight Properties dialog box.

You can change the highlight color or, if your printer prints it better, choose to have highlighted text struck out rather than colored. You can also change the name of the highlight author.

TIP By default, the *highlight author* is the person who logged in (or installed Corel WordPerfect Suite 8, in the stand-alone version).

Any changes you make become defaults affecting the present and future highlighted text—even in future work sessions. They do not, however, affect text that is already highlighted in the document.

Attaching QuickNotes

You can annotate Envoy documents by attaching what look like yellow sticky notes to them, as seen in Figure 27.8. These notes can be any size, and you can move and resize them at will.

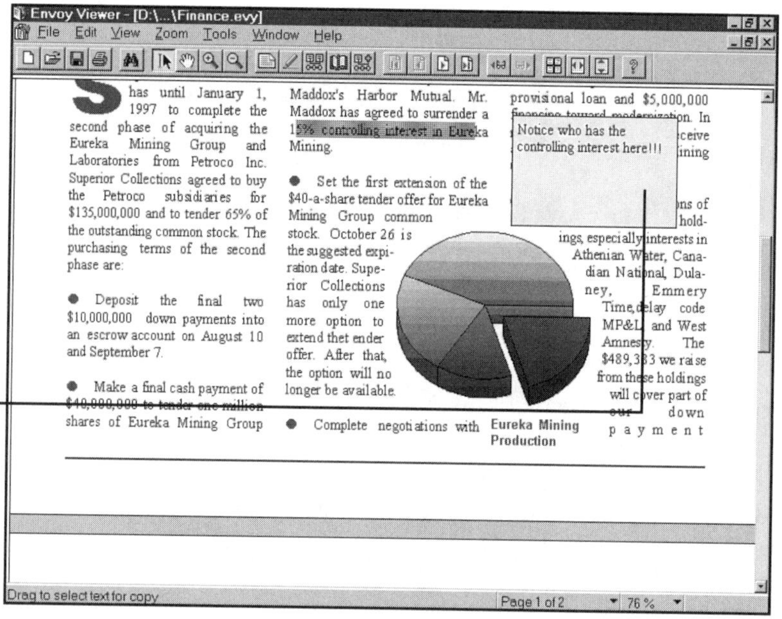

QuickNote

FIG. 27.8
You can attach yellow sticky notes, called *QuickNotes*, to Envoy documents to annotate them.

To create a QuickNote, follow these steps:

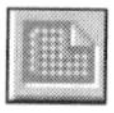

1. Click the QuickNote button on the toolbar. The mouse pointer changes to a note—a sheet of paper with the edge turned over.
2. Click at the position you want the note to appear. A standard size yellow note box appears.

TIP You can create custom size notes by dragging the mouse pointer over the area the note should occupy, rather than clicking where the note should appear.

3. You see a blinking insertion point within the note box. Type the text of the note. Don't worry if there's too much or too little text for the note box—you can resize the box later.
4. When you are finished, click anywhere outside of the note box.

To edit the note, click the Select button on the toolbar. Rapidly double-click the mouse pointer anywhere inside the note box. You see a blinking insertion point, and can edit your text as you desire.

You can also move or resize a note box when it is not currently selected by using the following procedure:

1. Click the Select button on the toolbar.
2. Click anywhere in the note box. You see handles around it (see Figure 27.9).

FIG. 27.9
You can move or resize QuickNote boxes by using their handles.

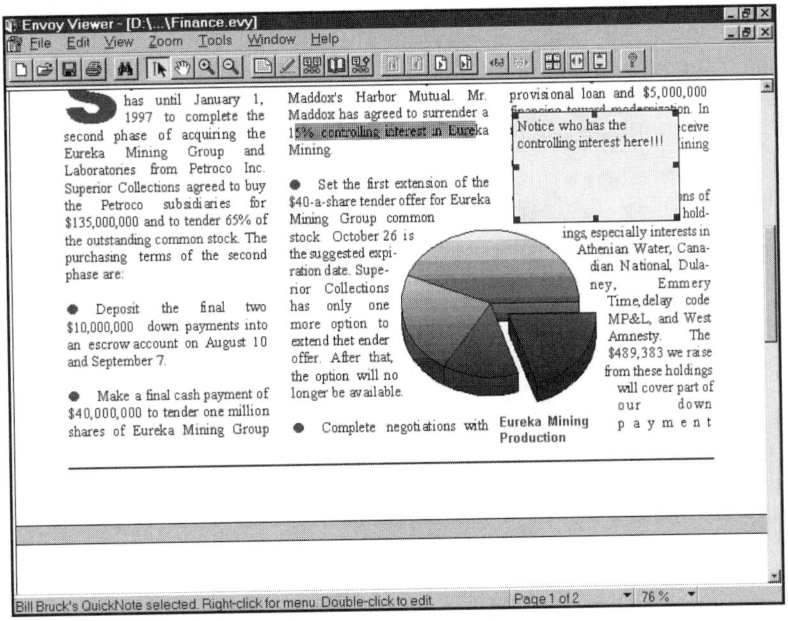

3. Move or resize the note box using the following procedures:
   - To move the note box, position the mouse pointer in the middle of the box, where the mouse pointer changes to a four-headed arrow, and then drag it to its new position.
   - To resize the note box, position the mouse pointer on one of the eight handles, where the mouse pointer changes to a two-headed arrow, and then drag the handle to change the box size.

4. Click anywhere outside of the box to deselect it.

You can also delete a note box. Select the box by clicking it with the Select tool, and then press the Delete key.

CAUTION

There's no Undo command in Envoy. Be careful!

You may not want to see these yellow boxes all over a document you are viewing. You can close a note, leaving only a note icon in the document to indicate where the note is. You can close or reopen a note by using the following procedures:

- To close a note, right-click it with the Select tool, then choose Close QuickNote.
- To open a closed note, double-click the note icon with the Select tool.

To change note box options:

1. Make sure that the Select tool is selected.
2. Right-click the note box to see a QuickMenu.
3. Choose QuickNote Properties. You see the Note Properties dialog box (see Figure 27.10).

You can change the justification, font color of the text, the background color, and the author's name. You can also choose the icon to be displayed when the note is closed.

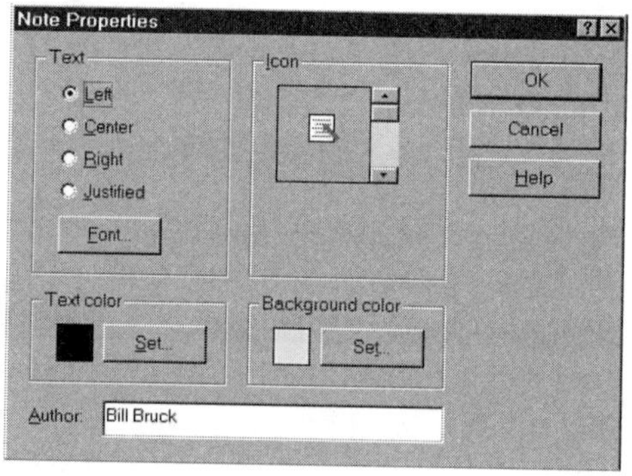

FIG. 27.10 You can reset the default note color, text font and color, and author's name with the Note Properties dialog box.

You can use the color and icons to easily show who is annotating a document. Just make sure that each reviewer uses a unique color (for open notes) and icon (for closed ones). You can easily see who wrote a note by positioning your mouse pointer on it. For example, in a note written by Frank Owen, the status line will say `Click to select Frank Owen's QuickNote. Double-click to edit it.`

NOTE Any changes you make in the Note Properties dialog box become defaults. They will affect future notes written in this document and notes you enter from now on in other documents, until you reset the note properties.

Adding Bookmarks

Bookmarks are an alphabetical list of *jump terms*—terms that enable you to move quickly to predefined places in your Envoy document. The creator of an Envoy document often creates bookmarks prior to saving the document, to assist readers in finding important places quickly.

To effectively use bookmarks, you need to know how to create them, use them, and set bookmark options.

To create a bookmark, follow these steps:

1. Click the Bookmark button on the toolbar. The mouse pointer changes to a bookmark—a book with a place marker in it.
2. Mark the position that you want the user to move to when the bookmark is selected, in one of two ways:
   - Position the mouse pointer inside the text until the bookmark pointer displays an insertion point, then drag over the text to select it.
   - Position the mouse pointer where there is no text until the bookmark pointer displays crosshairs, then drag a rectangle to select the area.
3. You see the Bookmark Properties dialog box (see Figure 27.11). Fill in options as needed:

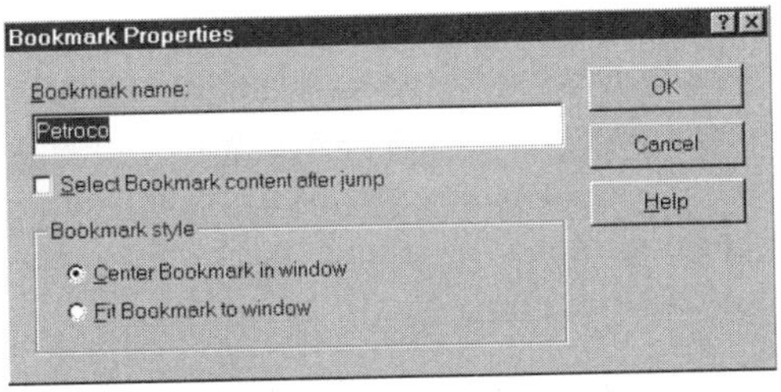

FIG. 27.11 You can change default bookmark options with the Bookmark Properties dialog box.

   - Type a name for the bookmark. (If you selected text, the first words of the selected text will be the label unless you change it.)
   - If you want the content of the bookmark to be selected after you jump to it—perhaps so that the reader can easily copy it to the Clipboard—choose Select Bookmark Content After Jump.

- When you jump to the bookmark, choose whether the bookmark text should be centered in the window (Center Bookmark in Window) or whether the window should zoom to the size needed to fit the bookmark in the window (Fit Bookmark to Window).

4. When you are finished selecting options, click OK.

The bookmark is added to the list, and the mouse pointer remains as a bookmark pointer. Create another bookmark or select a different type of pointer for another action.

To edit the properties of an existing bookmark follow these steps:

1. Click the Bookmark button on the toolbar.
2. Right-click anywhere inside the text of an existing bookmark to display a QuickMenu.
3. Choose Bookmark Properties to display the Bookmark Properties dialog box. You can edit the options of existing bookmarks with the Bookmark Properties dialog box.
4. Change options as needed, then click OK.

To jump to a bookmark, choose Edit, Go To Bookmark. You see a list of available bookmarks. Double-click the desired one. You will jump to the area of the document defined in the bookmark. Alternatively, click the Bookmarks button on the status bar at the bottom of the window, and then click the appropriate bookmark to jump to the defined place in the document.

Adding Hypertext Links

Hypertext links are buttons or jump terms within the document that allow you to jump to predefined places in your Envoy document, such as bookmarks. The creator of an Envoy document often creates hypertext links prior to saving the document. This is most easily accomplished if the original document contains a table of contents, list of figures, index, or other logical place for hypertext links. You can even create hypertext links whenever an unfamiliar term exists in a document—assuming that you have the term defined somewhere else in the document.

To effectively use hypertext links, you need to know how to create them, use them, and set their options.

To create a hypertext link, follow these steps:

1. Click the Hypertext button on the toolbar. The mouse pointer changes to a hypertext pointer.

2. Choose from either of the following procedures, depending on whether you want to create a jump term or a hypertext button:
   - To create a *jump term* (a word or phrase that the user can click to jump through the link), position the mouse pointer inside text until the hypertext pointer displays an insertion point, then drag over text to select it.
   - To create a hypertext button, position the mouse pointer where there is no text until the bookmark pointer displays crosshairs, and then drag a rectangle the size of the button.

   In either case, on the status bar, you see the message `Go to the destination, then drag the link on main view or thumbnails.`
3. Move to the position that you want to jump to, then click the mouse, or drag the mouse over the destination.
4. To set options, right-click in the text, then choose Properties. If you do not want to set options, skip to step 6.
5. Depending on whether you selected text or a rectangle, proceed as follows:
   - If you selected text, you see the Hypertext Properties dialog box shown in Figure 27.12. Select the source text style as Colored Text, Underlined Colored Text, or Underlined Only. Choose the source text color. When you jump through the hypertext link, choose whether the text should be centered in the window (Center Destination in Window) or whether the window should zoom to the size needed to fit the text (Fit Destination to Window). When you are finished selecting options, click OK.

FIG. 27.12
The Hypertext Properties dialog box for text enables you to change the color and underline of jump terms.

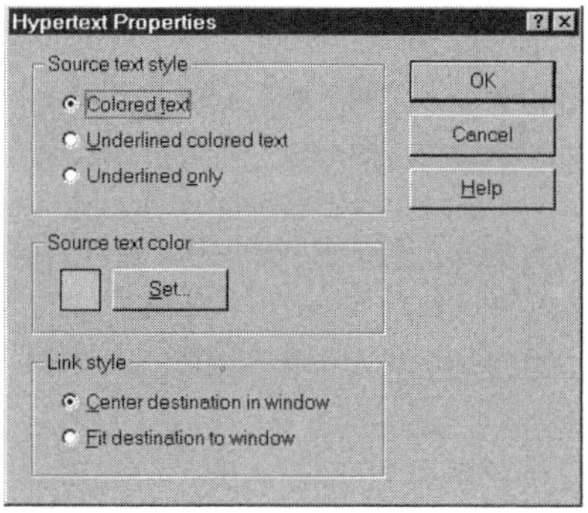

TIP Make jump terms resemble jump terms in Windows help: green and underlined.

- If you selected a rectangle, you see the Hypertext Properties dialog box (see Figure 27.13). Select the source text style as an Invisible Rectangle, Framed Rectangle, or Button. If you chose Framed Rectangle, choose the rectangle color. If you chose Button, use the button scroll bar to choose from predefined button types. When you jump through the hypertext link, choose whether the text should be centered in the window (Center Destination in Window) or whether the window should zoom to the size needed to fit the text (Fit Destination to Window). When you are finished selecting options, click OK.

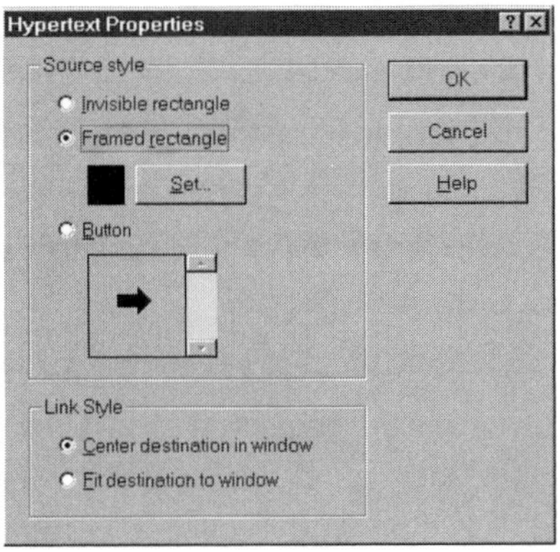

FIG. 27.13
The Hypertext Properties dialog box for rectangles enables you to specify the rectangle as colored, invisible, or a button.

TIP You can choose Invisible Rectangle to make graphic objects in your document into jump terms.

6. The hypertext link is created, and the mouse pointer remains as a hypertext pointer. Create another link or select a different type of pointer for another action.

To edit the properties of an existing hypertext link, follow these steps:

1. Click the Hypertext button on the toolbar.
2. Right-click anywhere inside the text or area of an existing hypertext source. You see a QuickMenu.
3. Choose Properties. You see the appropriate Hypertext Properties dialog box.
4. Change options as needed, and then click OK.

When you are using the Select tool and your mouse pointer is positioned on a hypertext source, it will change to a hand. This is true whether the source is text, a colored box, invisible box, or button.

To jump through a hypertext link, position your selection pointer on a hypertext source. When the mouse pointer changes to a hand, click. You will jump to the area of the document defined in the hypertext link.

Inserting OLE Objects

You can insert objects into your Envoy document—such as sound clips, animated pictures, or links to spreadsheets and databases—by using Object Linking and Embedding (OLE).

▶ **See** "Understanding the Types of Data Transfer," **p. 616**

However, one special consideration applies to using OLE with Envoy documents: OLE enables you to create a link to the object (for instance, to a sound file), or embed the sound file in the Envoy document. When you create a link, the sound file exists on the disk, and when you click the sound file icon in the Envoy document, it reads the file from the disk. When you embed the sound file in the Envoy document, a copy of the sound file is placed in the Envoy document itself.

In most applications, linking is frequently preferred for two reasons:

- Linking keeps the Envoy file relatively small, whereas embedding can make the Envoy file rather large.
- Linking ensures that you are reading the latest version of the file, whereas embedding "locks" the then-current version of the file into the Envoy document.

However, Envoy documents are regularly distributed via the Internet, on a disk or CD to viewers who may have no access to the disk to which an OLE object is linked. If you are creating an Envoy document that will be distributed in this manner, you may want to embed, rather than link, your OLE object.

TIP For you "techies" who are into the details of OLE, Envoy is OLE 2.0-enabled. It is also an OLE 2.0 container, but not a server. For example, you cannot embed an Envoy object into a WordPerfect document.

CHAPTER 28

Using Corel Address Book 8

Corel Address Book 8 is a deceptively simple address list manager. It integrates seamlessly with WordPerfect, allowing you to insert addresses in your WordPerfect documents, and serving as a data source for WordPerfect merges. It also integrates with Microsoft Exchange, allowing you to maintain your Exchange Personal Address Book in Address Book 8, which offers much more functionality. ■

Integrate Corel Address Book 8 with Microsoft Exchange

Maintain your Microsoft Exchange Personal Address Book by using Address Book 8.

Maintain address lists

Use Address Book 8 to maintain multiple address lists for home and business use.

Integrate with WordPerfect

Use Address Book 8 to insert names and addresses in WordPerfect documents and merges.

CAUTION

If Exchange is installed *after* Address Book, then Address Book can error on startup. This occurs because Exchange overwrites information that Address Book modifies on its install. If you have problems integrating the two, try uninstalling Address Book and then reinstalling it (after Exchange has been installed).

Understanding How Address Book Works

Address Book interfaces closely with Microsoft Exchange, and to understand how Address Book works, you need to understand a few things about Exchange.

Understanding Microsoft Exchange Profiles

Exchange is the universal Inbox in Windows 95 that provides a central point for services, including your faxes, Microsoft Mail messages, Internet e-mail, and Microsoft Network e-mail. If you have installed Exchange, you will have one or more of these services installed as well.

These services use address lists. Microsoft Mail uses a Postoffice Address List. The other services can access the Postoffice Address List, but because it doesn't maintain much information, you will usually use the Personal Address Book that is created for you when you install Exchange.

Because more than one person might use a given computer, Exchange supports *profiles.* The Microsoft Exchange help system describes a profile as:

> "...a set of configuration options used by Microsoft Exchange and other messaging applications that contains essential information, such as which information services you are using. This information includes the location of your Inbox, Outbox, and address lists, and the personal folder files available to you for storing and retrieving messages and files."

In short, you can think of a profile as the information needed to support an individual *user* of Exchange services.

Understanding How Address Book Uses Profiles

When you install Address Book, a new Exchange profile—the Corel 8 Settings profile—is created. By default, the service that is set up in this profile includes the Address Book.

Depending on how Exchange was configured when Address Book was installed, the profile may also include your Exchange Personal Address Book, and/or your Microsoft Mail Postoffice Address List.

When you open Address Book, it looks at the last profile you specified. The address books you see will depend on the profile you use. If you create profiles for several people who use the same computer, each person will see only their own address books.

You will usually just use the default Corel 8 Settings profile. If you need to add a profile, or add services to an existing one, you can do so as follows:

1. Right-click the Inbox icon in the Windows 95 desktop, and then choose Properties. You see the MS Exchange Settings Properties dialog box.
2. Choose Show Profiles. You see the Mail and Fax dialog box shown in Figure 28.1.

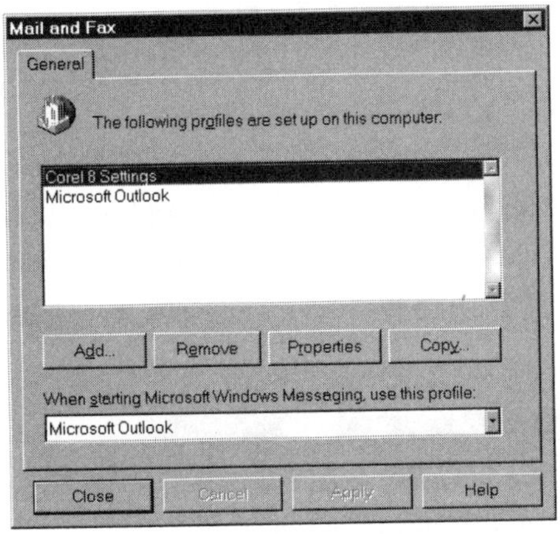

FIG. 28.1
You can create new profiles and add new services to existing profiles.

3. Choose Add to create a new profile or Copy to copy an existing one to a new one. (If you choose Add, you will need to use the Inbox Setup Wizard to configure the different Exchange services you want to include in the new profile.)
4. To add a service to an existing profile, select it, then choose Properties. You see the Corel 8 Settings Properties dialog box shown in Figure 28.2. Select the service you want to add, and then choose Add. The service may be added, or you may need to fill out a properties dialog box for that service.
5. Click OK to add the service.

FIG. 28.2
Add or remove a service from an existing profile with the Corel 8 Settings Properties dialog box.

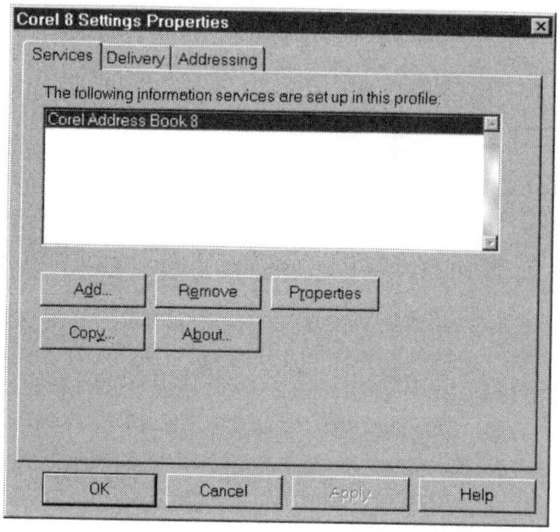

TIP Use this procedure to add the Personal Address Book service to your Corel 8 Settings profile, if you do not see the Microsoft Exchange Personal Address Book as one of your address books in Address Book.

To use a different profile with Address Book 8, open Address Book, and then choose Edit, Settings. You see the Address Book Settings dialog box shown in Figure 28.3. Select the profile you want to use, and then click OK. The new profile will take effect the next time you open Address Book 8.

FIG. 28.3
Address Book Settings allows you to specify the profile you want to use the next time you use Address Book.

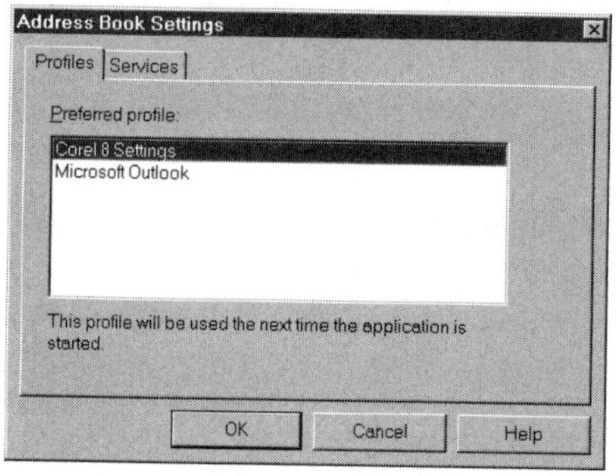

Creating Address Books

You can use just one address book if you prefer, or create as many address books as you like. You may find it useful, for example, to have one address book for personal addresses and another for business contacts.

To create a new address book from the main Corel Address Book window, choose Book, New. You see the New Properties dialog box shown in Figure 28.4. Enter the name of your new address book and click OK. You see a new tab at the top of the Address Book window containing the new address book.

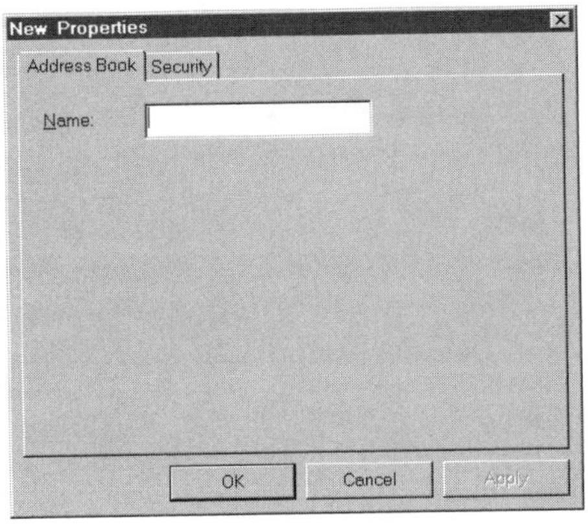

FIG. 28.4
You can create separate address books for your personal and business addresses.

After you have created more than one address book, you can select the appropriate one by clicking its tab.

Adding Contact Information

Address Book maintains two types of records: records for individuals and records for organizations. When you create a record for an individual, you can include their organization as one piece of information about them. If you enter an organization name that is not in the Address Book, a record for that organization is created automatically, containing only the organization name. If, when you create a record for an individual, you specify an organization that is in the Address Book, the person's record is linked to the record for that organization.

To add an organization to your address list, do the following:

1. From the main Address Book window, click the Add button. You see the New Entry dialog box.
2. Select Organization and click OK. You see the New Organization Properties dialog box shown in Figure 28.5.

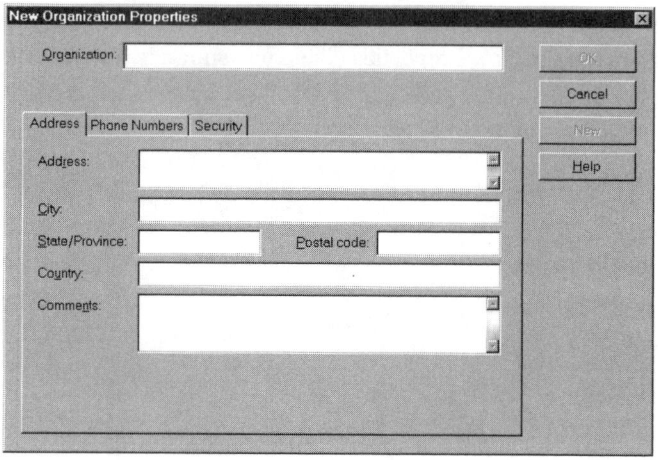

FIG. 28.5
Insert the main number and address for the organization in the New Organization Properties dialog box.

3. Enter information in each field. Press Tab to move to the next field; press Shift+Tab to move to the previous one.
4. When you've finished, click New to add another new record, or click OK to return to the main Address Book window.

Use a similar procedure to enter a new person into the address book:

1. From the main Address Book window, click the Add button. You see the New Entry dialog box.
2. Select Person and click OK. You see the New Person Properties dialog box, which is very similar to the New Organization Properties dialog box.
3. Enter information in each field. Press Tab to move to the next field; press Shift+Tab to move to the previous one.
4. When you've finished, click New to add another new record, or click OK to return to the main Address Book window.

You can edit an existing contact in a similar manner. Select the person or organization whose record you want to change, and then click the Edit button. You see the Properties For dialog box that has the same functionality as the dialog box used to create the record. Make changes in the appropriate fields, and then click OK.

Creating Custom Fields

You can also create custom fields that are maintained for each person or organization. For instance, you might want to have for organizations a field called Web Site, in which you can record the URL for their organization's Web site. To do so, choose Edit, Custom Fields from the main Address Book window. You see the Custom Fields dialog box (see Figure 28.6).

FIG. 28.6
The Custom Fields dialog box allows you to add new fields for persons or organizations.

Choose New. You see the New Custom Field dialog box. Put the name of the new field in the New Field Name box and click OK.

To use custom fields, create or edit a record. You see the Properties dialog box. Click the Custom tab. You see the new fields that you have added. Fill in information as needed.

Importing Contacts

You can also import your contact list from another application. This can be especially handy when you have already created a contact list in another application, and you don't want to have to manually re-enter your entire address list.

The first step is to save your address list in comma separated value (CSV) format. (Corel calls this format ASCII Delimited Text.) The commands you will use for this differ, depending on the program, but commonly there is a File, Export command. Occasionally, you instead will use File, Save As, and specify CSV as the Save As Type. Check the documentation for your particular program for details.

NOTE CSV format puts each record on a separate line, with each field contained in quotes and separated by a comma, as shown here:

```
"Smith","Joe","555-1212"
"Jones","Mary","666-1313"
```

The CSV format is a "lowest common denominator" that most address list programs can all export to and import from.

After you have saved your information as a CSV file, you can import it into Address Book as follows:

1. Choose Book, Import, and ensure that ASCII Delimited Text is selected. You see the first step of the Import Expert, shown in Figure 28.7.

FIG. 28.7
You can import text from other address books by saving them in a common format like comma separated value.

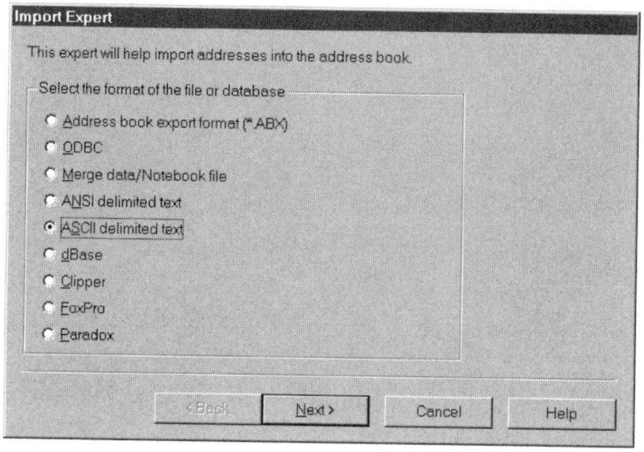

2. Choose Next. In the second step of the Expert, enter the file name in the Select a File box, or choose Browse to select the file from an Address Book Import dialog box.
3. Choose Next. In the third step of the Expert, choose whether the first line of the file contains field names (such as First Name, Last Name) or the first person's information (like John, Jones).
4. Choose Next. In the fourth step of the Wizard, shown in Figure 28.8, specify the Field Separator character as a comma and the Encapsulation Character as a quotation mark.

FIG. 28.8
Specify what character separates fields (usually a comma), and which encapsulation characters should be stripped out of the file (usually quotation marks).

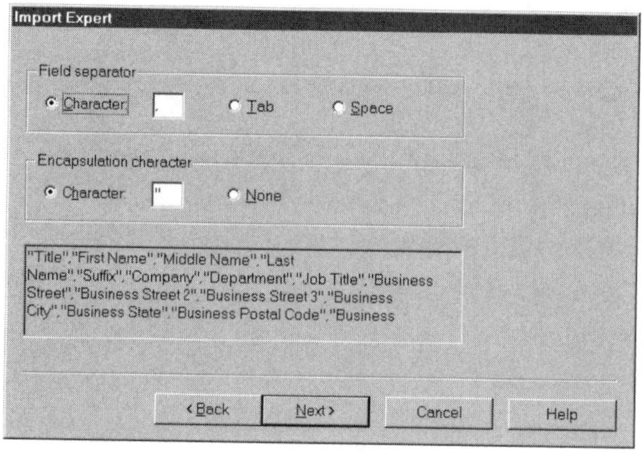

5. Choose Next. In the fifth step, shown in Figure 28.9, you see a list of fields in the database being imported, and you can associate (map) them to the Address Book fields. Fields with the same name are mapped together automatically; fields that don't have a corresponding Address Book name have `IGNORE FIELD`, indicating that they will be ignored unless you specify which field they correspond to. To specify a field that doesn't have a corresponding name, select it in the left column, and then click the field in the right column containing the Address Book fields. Notice that the Corel field name appears in the left column next to the name of the field being imported.

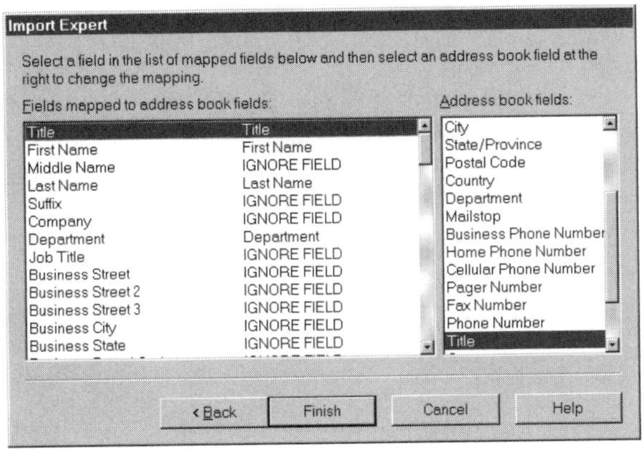

FIG. 28.9
Map fields between the two databases. If fields have the same name, they are mapped together automatically.

6. Choose Finish. The database is imported, and you return to the Address Book main window.

Creating Address Lists

You can create address lists, which are groups of persons or organizations contained in the address book. These groups are part of the address book, and can be created, deleted, edited, or renamed when necessary.

To create an address list, follow these steps:

1. Click the tab of the address book you want to add an address list to.
2. Click the Address List button. You see a new text box at the right of the Corel Address Book window, as shown in Figure 28.10.
3. Select one or more names you want to add to the new address list. To select multiple names, click the first name, and then hold down the Ctrl key while clicking additional names.

FIG. 28.10
You can create address lists to easily send mail to several people.

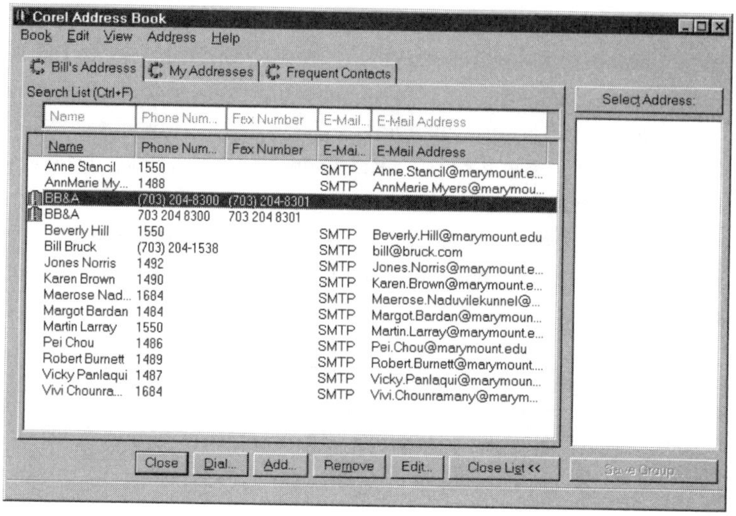

4. Choose Select Address. You see the selected names in the list box at the right side of the Address Book window.
5. If desired, select additional names by repeating steps 3 and 4.
6. Click the Save Group button. You see the Save Group dialog box.
7. Enter a name in the Name box and click OK. The group is added to the Address Book list, denoted by a group icon, as shown in Figure 28.11. You can use a group just as you use any other name in the address list.

FIG. 28.11
Groups and organizations are denoted by special icons in the address list.

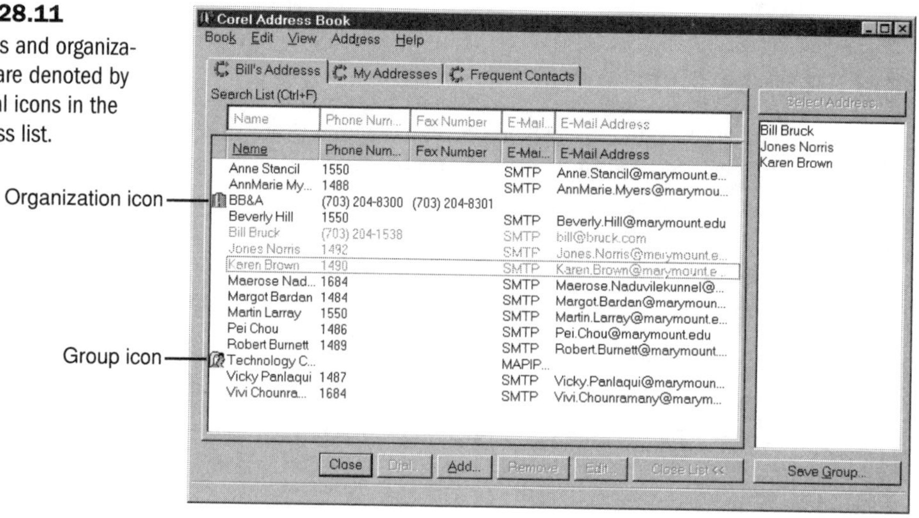

Using Address Book

To use Address Book, you will want to access appropriate records, and edit, delete, or copy records. You may also want to use Address Book in conjunction with WordPerfect, to dial phone numbers from Address Book, or to use Address Book for e-mail addresses.

Finding and Filtering Records

You can arrange the records in Address Book by last name, first name; or by first name, last name. To do so, choose View, Name Format, and then choose First Last; or Last, First. You may need to wait a few seconds, but your list will be resorted by the desired field.

If you want to look up a name by text that exists in any field, click in the column heading of the field in which the text exists, and then type the text. The first name matching the typed letters is selected.

You can also create a filter for your address list that will show only the records meeting specified criteria.

To do so, choose View, Define Filter. You see the Building a Filter dialog box (see Figure 28.12).

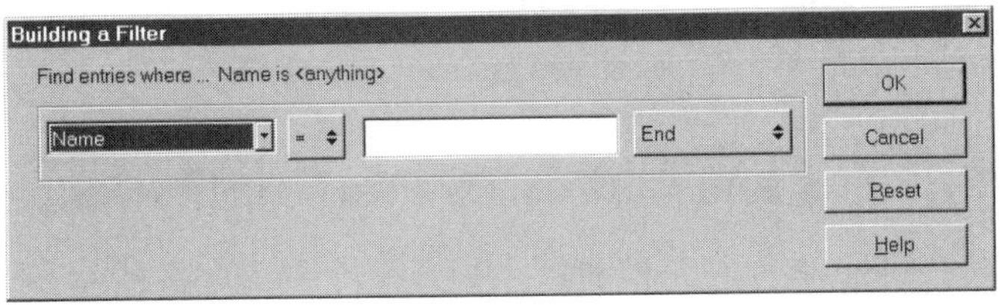

FIG. 28.12
You can create a filter that shows only specified records.

Choose the field you want to filter the list by from the drop-down list, and then choose the operator (by default, it is the equal sign). Type the criterion text in the right text box. If you want to add another criterion, click the End button, change it to And or Or, and enter additional criteria. Click OK when you've finished. You see the filtered list.

Editing, Deleting, or Copying Records

After you have located the appropriate record, you can edit, delete, or copy it. To edit a record, select it, and then double-click it; or choose Edit. You see the appropriate Properties dialog box, where you can make the appropriate changes.

TIP Make sure your filter is turned off by choosing View, Filtering Enabled.

To delete a record, select it, press the Del key or click the Remove button, and then click Yes in the verification dialog box. The record is removed from the address list.

To copy a record, select it and choose Edit, Copy. Switch to the desired address list, if needed, and then choose Edit, Paste. If the operation creates a duplicate record, you will be warned; then the duplicate record will be created.

TIP You may find this to be an easy way to create records for related persons, or persons in the same organization that share many fields of information.

NOTE If you have a modem attached to your computer and a telephone on the same line, you can use Address Book to dial a phone number. You will also need to ensure that the Windows 95 Phone Dialer application is loaded. To dial a person, highlight his or her entry and click the Dial button.

Integrating Address Book with WordPerfect

You may find that you access Address Book more from WordPerfect than you do as a stand-alone application, once you get used to its easy functionality.

Inserting Names and Addresses into WordPerfect

Your address books can be used to quickly insert a name and address into a WordPerfect document, or to serve as the data source for merge operations.

To insert a name and address in a WordPerfect document, open WordPerfect and create or open the document. Position your insertion point where you want the name and address to be inserted, and then choose Tools, Address Book. You see the Corel Address Book window (refer to Figure 28.10).

Choose the appropriate address book, and then select the desired person or organization. Double-click the person's name. You see his or her name and address in your WordPerfect document.

TIP If you select an address group, all the names and addresses will be brought into your document.

If you like, you can specify which fields will be imported into your WordPerfect document. While the Address Book is open, click the Format button. You see the Format Address dialog box (see Figure 28.13). Pick from the four default formats, or add a format that includes just the fields you want by choosing Custom and creating a new format.

▶ **See** "Using Merge," **p. 196**

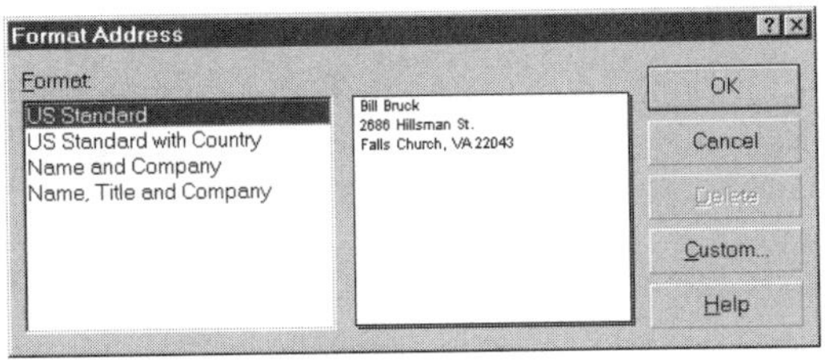

FIG. 28.13
Choose the fields you want to use from the Address Book from the Format Address dialog box.

You can also use your address books as data sources for merge operations. When you choose Tools, Merge in WordPerfect, you see the Merge dialog box shown in Figure 28.14. From this dialog box, you can click the Address Book button to view, edit, or add entries to an address book.

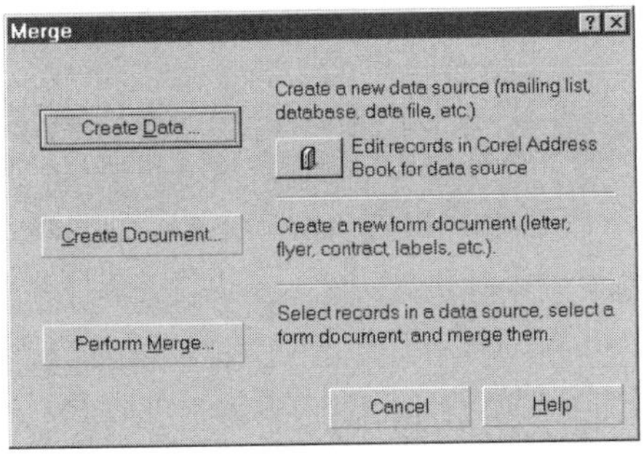

FIG. 28.14
Address books can be used as the data source for WordPerfect merges.

To use an address book as the data source, do not click the Create Data button; this is used to *create* a data source. Instead, choose Create Document. After you choose whether to create the merge file in the active window or a new window, you see the Associate Form and Data dialog box (see Figure 28.15). Select Associate an Address Book, and then choose from existing address books in the drop-down list box that becomes active.

FIG. 28.15
You are given the option of using an address book as the data file when you create the form file.

Using Frequent Contacts

The Frequent Contacts address book is created automatically and updated as you use Address Book to insert addresses into WordPerfect, or as you use your Address Book as a data source for a WordPerfect merge.

The Frequent Contacts address book is shown in Figure 28.16. It can be very useful because it contains copies of the records of people you contact most often and of people you have contacted lately. To sort the list by either one of these fields, drag the appropriate field header (Last Reference or Reference Count) to the left of the header bar. The list is re-sorted by the appropriate field.

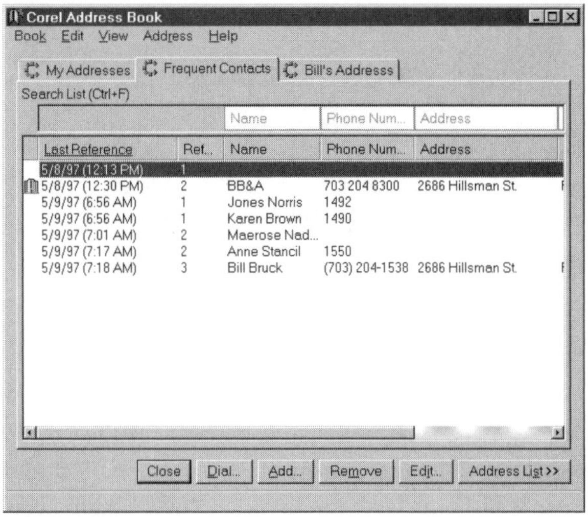

FIG. 28.16
Sort the Frequent Contacts address book by the last contact date, or by the number of contacts.

TROUBLESHOOTING

I entered my personal information the first time I used a template in WordPerfect, and now I want to change it. Choose File, New, and then click Options, Personal Information in the New dialog box. Select your entry in the Address Book, and then click the Edit button. Edit the entry, and then click OK to return to the Address Book. Click Select to return to the WordPerfect New dialog box, and then click Close to return to the main editing window.

Printing an Envelope

WordPerfect's Envelope feature automatically formats and addresses your envelope. If you have already typed the inside address into a letter, and you want an envelope for the letter, just choose Format, Envelope.

To address an envelope after typing a letter, follow these steps:

1. Choose Format, Envelope to open the Envelope dialog box shown in Figure 28.17.

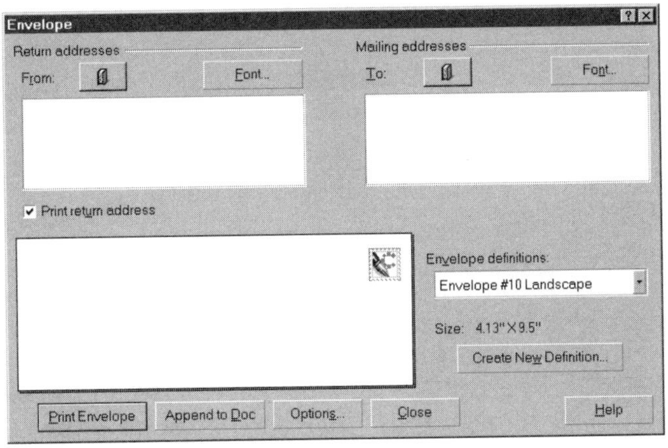

FIG. 28.17 WordPerfect's Envelope feature automatically formats and addresses your envelope.

2. Check Print Return Address. Click the Address Book icon in the From box and select your address for the return address.
3. To change the font face or size used in the return address, click the Font button in the Return Addresses section.
4. To enter or add a mailing address (if the mailing address is not automatically selected), click the Address Book icon in the To box to choose your recipient from Address Book, or type the recipient's name in the To box.

5. As with the return address, you can change the font or point size used in the mailing address.
6. If you want a USPS bar code printed on the envelope, click the Options button, and select whether you want the bar code printed above or below the address.
7. To print the Envelope immediately, click Print Envelope; to add the envelope to the document, choose Append to Doc.

NOTE The font on an envelope is automatically taken from the document initial font (Format, Font, Default Font). To save the document text in the Envelope window, make sure that the document initial font is what you want both for the letter and the envelope.

CHAPTER 29

Using Corel Photo House

Corel Photo House is a special photo-editing program that makes it easy to scan images and photos and to touch them up, add text, or apply other special effects. Photo House also is a bitmap editing program that enables you to create your own original graphic images. Photo House documents can be used in your printed documents or on the Web. ■

Touch up photos

Add special effects, fix problems, or modify scanned or digital photographs.

Create custom bitmap images

Create bitmap images such as geometric shapes, brushstrokes of color, or text. Add such images to your photographs.

Publish bitmap images to the Web

Learn to export photographs and other bitmap images to JPEG or GIF formats for use on the Web.

Understanding Bitmap and Vector Graphics

Computer graphic images fall into two broad categories—bitmap and vector. While you can use either or both in your documents, each has distinct advantages and disadvantages over the other. Understanding these differences helps you choose the right graphics program.

Bitmap Images

In the early days of microcomputers, *bitmap graphics* were commonplace. Paint programs, such as PC Paintbrush, create images that consist of a collection of *bits* or dots, and much like real paint, you cover the screen with brushstrokes. Unfortunately, also like real paint, once it is laid down, you can't really change the pattern without removing the paint or painting over it.

Bitmap images can be resized, but when such images are enlarged, they often appear to have jagged edges. When made smaller, they usually look crisper and cleaner.

In spite of their limitations, bitmap graphics are increasingly necessary once again. Photographs, for example, when digitized for the computer, are bitmap images. Graphic images found on the Web, such as JPEG and GIF images, also are bitmap graphics. In order to publish graphics to the Web, you must convert your images to a bitmap format.

Vector Images

Vector images are defined by points at various locations and then filled in by formulas. For example, a rectangle is defined by four points, then the computer does the calculations to draw lines from one point to the other and to fill in the center if required. Most complex vector graphics actually consist of many images, or *objects*, that lie one on top of the other. These objects can be modified independently of the other objects in the image (for example, you could remove or increase the size of the tail on a donkey).

Generally, if you have a choice, vector graphics offer you greater flexibility. WordPerfect's clip art images, for example, can be sized or modified to come up with just what you need with relatively little effort, while looking very professional.

Unfortunately, you can't convert photographs to the vector format, nor can you use vector graphics on the Web. You can convert vector images to a bitmap format. Once you do, however, you lose the ability to easily modify your image.

Choosing the Right Program

Corel WordPerfect Suite 8 includes two outstanding graphics programs, each with its specific purpose, strengths, and weaknesses.

Presentations is a vector-based program and generally can meet most of your graphics needs. You can combine vector images with bitmap images (these are treated as objects in a Presentations drawing). Further, you can convert Presentations graphics into JPEG and GIF bitmap formats.

Photo House is a bitmap-based program designed to offer a wide variety of special tools just for bitmap graphics. For example, you can touch up photographs by removing the "red eye" look seen so often in amateur photos. You can edit photos by copying the head from one person and pasting onto the shoulders of another!

Which should you use? If you need to create complex original graphic images, use Presentations because it offers you the greatest flexibility in dealing with the various objects in your drawing. You can convert your Presentations graphics to bitmap format when you are finished, and if you keep an original vector version, you can modify the graphic in the future.

If your objective is to prepare photos or other bitmap graphics for publication or for the Web using special effects, consider using Photo House.

Exploring the Photo House Layout

When you first start up Photo House, you see the main screen shown in Figure 29.1. This screen consists of the typical menu bar and toolbar plus a toolbox and Notebook.

Using Menus, the Toolbox, and the Toolbar

The menu bar and the Toolbox always remain visible and provide the basic means of accessing Photo House features. The Toolbox (see Figure 29.1) is particularly important as you work with your bitmap images.

The toolbar offers standard Corel WordPerfect Suite tools (Open, Save, Print, and more), along with special helps such as Zoom, Color Selection, Custom Brush, and Font tools. If you need more screen space for editing, you can turn off the toolbar by choosing View, Toolbar. Choose the same menu command to turn it back on again.

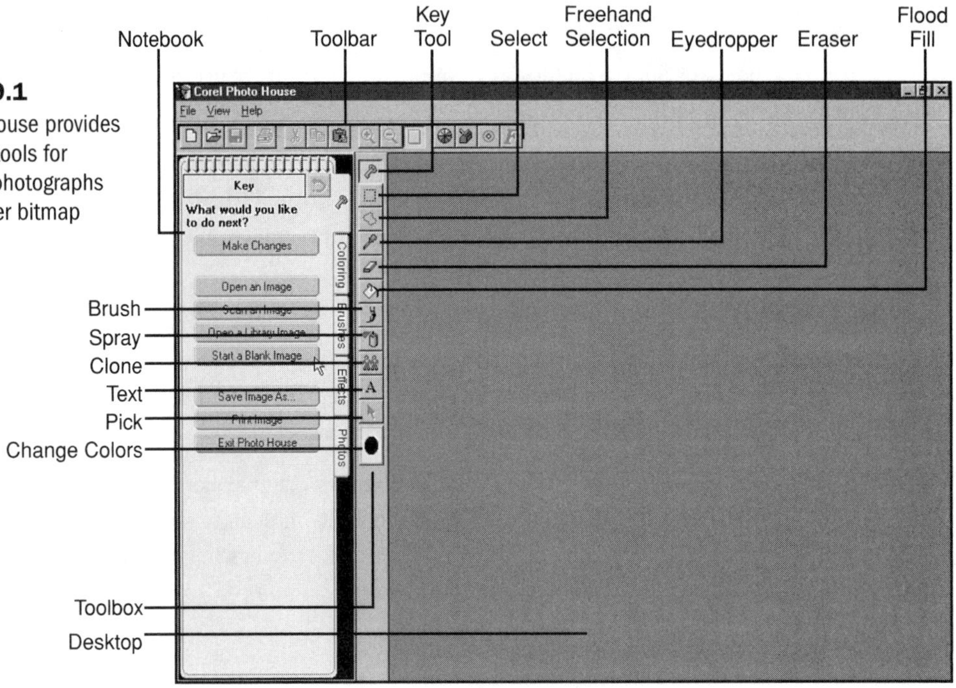

FIG. 29.1
Photo House provides various tools for editing photographs and other bitmap images.

Using the Notebook

The *Notebook* offers useful assistance as you work with your bitmap images. The top level is the Key level, and other sections are marked by tabs on the right side of the Notebook. These include:

- *Coloring.* Select literally any color you want for whatever tool you are using to paint. The color remains active for any tool you use until you change to another color.
- *Brushes.* You can choose from several predefined brush shapes. Some are good for drawing or painting areas, while others are useful for painting a particular shape.
- *Effects.* You apply special effects to your bitmap images, but in particular to your photographs. These include brightness and contrast controls, or features to remove dust, scratches, or red eyes. The Cool & Fun Effects options enable you to convert images to an embossed or blurred look, or even a curled page (see Figure 29.2).
- *Photos.* Even if you don't have your own photographs, Photo House comes with some 250 photos ranging from household objects to wildlife scenes.

FIG. 29.2 Photo House can add attention-grabbing special effects to your photos.

To return to the Key level, click the Key tab, or click the Key Tool on the Toolbox. On any of the tabs, if you need to return to the top page, just click the back arrow at the top of the Notebook.

If you want the screen space for editing an image, you can turn off the Notebook by choosing View, Notebook. Choose the same menu command to turn the Notebook on again.

Creating Bitmap Images

Although you can create entire drawings using nothing more than the bitmap tools in Photo House, you'll probably discover that such tools are better used to add to or modify existing bitmap images. In this section, you learn how to use these tools with an eye toward working with photographs.

NOTE Remember that Photo House is simply a tool to help you express your creativity. Don't be afraid to experiment beyond the simple examples presented here.

Before drawing or editing, you must open an editing screen, using one of the following options:

- To draw on a blank screen, choose File, New; or press Ctrl+N. Alternauvely, you can click the Start a Blank Image button on the Notebook. In the Create New Image dialog box, choose the size and other options you want and choose OK.
- To work on an existing image file, such as a Windows bitmap (BMP) file, choose File, Open; or press Ctrl+O. Alternatively, you can click the Open an Image button on the Notebook. Browse your computer to find the file you want and choose Open.
- To scan an image into Photo House, choose File, Acquire image, Acquire. Alternatively, you can click Scan an Image on the Notebook. Note that you must have a scanner attached and properly set up.
- To use one of the photos that comes with Photo House, choose the Photos tab on the Notebook, double-click a photo category, and then double-click the image you want to open. Note that depending on how you installed Photo House, you may need to have the Corel WordPerfect Suite 8 CD in your CD-ROM drive in order to open Photo House photographic images.

For the following sections, consider opening a new blank screen. We'll work with photographs a bit later.

Selecting the Right Tool

Tools for adding bitmap shapes or images consist of text tools, brush or spray tools, cloning tools, and editing tools such as erasers and select tools. Getting just the right one takes some effort by trial and error, but it doesn't take long to learn which tool to use for which task.

TIP Fortunately, Photo House has Undo and Redo tools that enable you to undo three levels back or redo three levels forward. Experiment with just one part of your drawing before moving on to the next item. That way, you can undo and redo until you're satisfied.

Using the Text Tool Suppose that you want to add text to a photograph. After opening a photo image, as described in the previous section, "Creating Bitmap Images," the following are typical steps you might take:

1. Choose the Text tool from the Toolbox; or on the Notebook Key level, choose Make Changes, then choose Add Text.
2. Click the image where you want to begin your text.

3. If you know what text styles you want, choose Edit, Text Style; or press Ctrl+T; or simply click the Text Styles button on the toolbar and choose the font, size, and other text characteristics you need.
4. If you want a color other than black, click the center of the Color tool on the Toolbox, and from the list of colors, choose the one you want.
5. Type your text. If you type your text first, then want to make text style changes, simply select your text with the mouse or keyboard, then go to steps 3 and 4.

6. When you are finished, click the Pick tool on the Toolbox. Photo House displays the text box with sizing handles (see Figure 29.3).

FIG. 29.3
After creating text, you can size, move, or change its characteristics before merging it with your bitmap image.

7. Use the mouse to size the text or to move it to a new location. If you click the text twice, rotation handles appear, and you can rotate the text to an angle.
8. When you are completely satisfied with your text, choose Edit, Merge Text with Background; or choose the Key tool or any other tool from the Toolbox.

CAUTION

Once you merge text or other objects with the background, they become part of the larger bitmap image and cannot be edited. If this happens accidentally, use Undo immediately to get the editable image back again.

Using Brush Tools and Shapes Photo House offers a variety of brush styles, all intended to help you paint, spray, or otherwise modify your bitmap graphic, especially your photographs.

You begin by selecting the brush style you want, including its color. To do this:

1. Click the Brushes tab on the Notebook and from the extensive list, click the style you want to use.

2. Click the Change Colors tool on the Toolbox to select the color you want to use.

3. Choose the specific tool you want to use to paint with. Use the Brush tool to paint a solid color (as a freshly dipped paint brush), or choose the Spray Can to paint like you do with a can of spray paint—the more you spray, the darker the pattern becomes.
4. Click and drag to paint or to spray. If you just click the image without dragging, the pattern of the brush style you chose appears on the image. See Figure 29.4 for some examples of brush and spray patterns applied to a blank image.

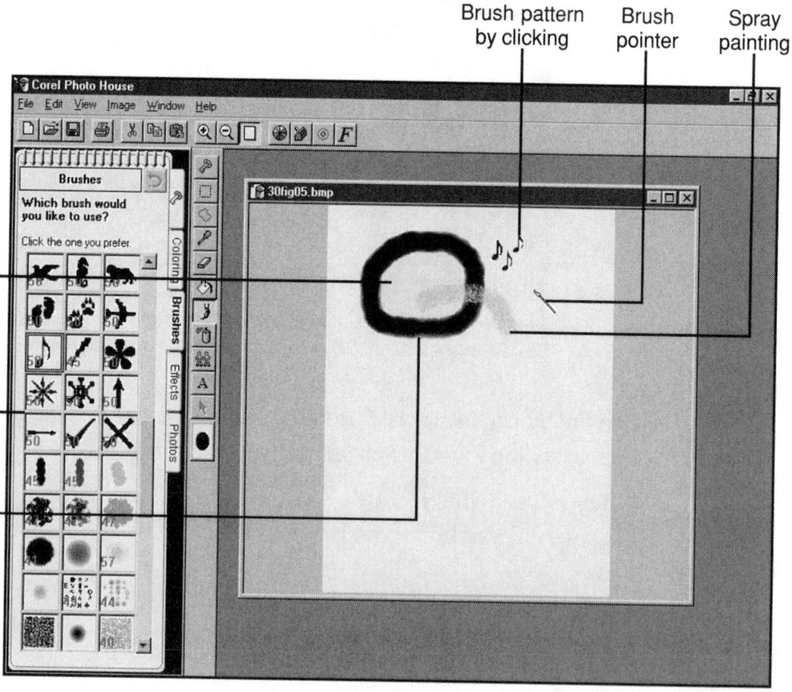

FIG. 29.4
Using the Brush and Spray tools, you can use patterns and colors to touch up your Photo House image.

The mouse is not a very good tool for freehand drawing. If you need to do a lot of freehand drawing, you might consider purchasing a mouse pen or a graphics tablet that enable you to draw more naturally.

Using the Flood Fill Tool Much like the icon that represents it, the Flood Fill tool "pours" color into an area surrounded by other images. If there is a "leak" in the surrounding lines or images, the paint floods out into other areas. This tool is useful for filling an area with a solid color.

To fill an area, first use the Change Colors tool. Choose the fill color, then simply click the Flood Fill tool, position the mouse pointer so the tip of the pouring paint is within the area you want to fill, and click.

If you make a mistake, choose Edit, Undo. For accuracy, you may want to choose View and one of the zoom options to enlarge the area before using Flood Fill.

Using the Clone Tool The Clone tool is more useful with photographic images, but it also works with bitmap images of your own creation.

The idea behind *cloning* is that you specify an area you want to copy, move to the area where you want the copy (clone) to appear, then use the mouse to paint the clone. For example, you want to clone part of a letter from a text image (see Figure 29.5). Follow these steps:

1. Choose the Clone tool from the Toolbox.
2. Choose a brush pattern you want to paint the clone with. For example, if you choose a brush with feathered edges, the edges of your clone also will appear feathered.
3. Position the mouse pointer (crosshairs) exactly at the upper-left edge of the object you want to clone, and click.
4. Move the mouse pointer (the Clone icon) to the exact upper-left corner where you want to create the clone.
5. Click and drag the mouse to paint a copy of the original. You see the clone pointer and the crosshairs pointer moving in synch, and as you drag the crosshairs over the original object, the clone pointer paints the original at the new location. See Figure 29.5 for a glimpse of this feature in action.

You can release the mouse button at any time, move the crosshairs, and click and drag to continue cloning. Until you change the tool you are using, the relative distance between the original and the clone remains constant.

FIG. 29.5
Use the Clone tool to paint a duplicate of an area of your image.

Acquiring Images

If an image you want already is in digital format, you need only open the image in Photo House. Sources for digital images include clip art collections, the Web, or Photo House's own collection of 250 photographic images. If the digital format is something other than the native Photo House CPT format, Photo House automatically converts the image. Vector images also import, making a bitmap copy while leaving the original vector format intact.

TIP You can also drag images from another application or from the Explorer directly to the Photo House desktop.

CAUTION

Images on Web sites are often copyrighted and will, in any case, be protected by relevant copyright laws. Be sure to obtain permission from the copyright owner before using images from Web sites, and strongly consider establishing a company or institutional policy regarding use of information obtained from the Internet after advice from legal counsel.

Modifying Photos

More likely than not, you will use Photo House to touch up or modify your own photographs. You have several options for placing your photos into digital format so that you can touch up or modify them in Photo House:

- If you own or have access to a digital camera, you can take your pictures and save them directly to disk, usually in a number of different formats. Any bitmap format will do. You can then open the photo file into Photo House.
- You can take your photos to many photo developers who can convert your pictures into the Kodak format, and store them for you on a Kodak photo CD.
- You can use a scanner to digitize photographic prints yourself. If the scanner is connected to the computer that is running Photo House, you can choose File, Acquire image. You then can Select source (the scanner type you have), or begin the scanning process by choosing Acquire.

To suggest every way you can use Photo House with photos would be impossible. This section simply explores a few tools you might find useful. You should plan to explore and discover much more on your own.

Applying Standard Touch-up Effects

Even with a good camera, you can have problems with your photos that you'd like to fix. For example, your photo might have scratches, be a bit out of focus, be too light or dark, or display the infamous "red eye" effect.

To touch up your photo, first open it into Photo House. To use a Photo House photo, click the Photos tab on the Notebook, select a category, and then select a photo.

Next, choose the Effects tab on the Notebook. You then choose Touch-Up; Photo House displays the screen shown in Figure 29.6.

The following options are available:

- *Brightness/Contrast/Intensity.* Use this option to make your photo lighter, darker, or richer in color.
- *Deskew Image.* When you scan your image to digitize it, sometimes you skew it just a bit. Assuming you have a plain white border around the photo, you can use this option to straighten the picture.
- *Reduce Speckles.* If a picture from a magazine or videotape is grainy, use this option to correct the problem.

FIG. 29.6
Touch-Up options enable you to fix problems with original photographs.

- *Remove Dust & Scratches.* This option helps clean up photos taken by cameras with dusty or scratched lenses.
- *Remove Red Eyes.* Use this option to correct the "red eye" effect often seen in photographs.
- *Replace Colors.* If you simply don't like the color of something in the photo (a team hat, for example), use this option to change the color.
- *Sharpen.* If the picture is slightly out of focus, use this option to sharpen the image.
- *Simplify Colors.* This reduces the number of distinct shades in a photo, which can be used for special effects.

When you find the touch-up effect you want, just double-click the option, or click and drag the option on top of the desktop image your are working on. If you were to choose the Brightness/Contrast/Intensity option, for example, you would see the screen shown in Figure 29.7.

Move the sliders to change the values. Click the Preview button to view the effect before returning to the image. Click Reset to return to the original settings if you want to start the changes over again.

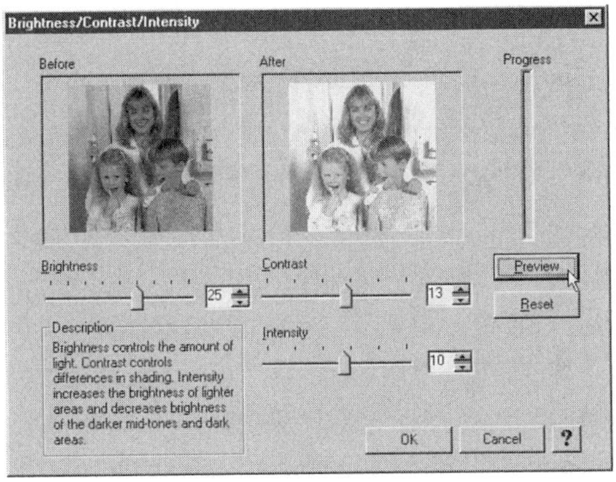

FIG. 29.7
Photo House offers several tools for touching up your photos, such as this one, which enables you to lighten or darken the picture.

In most of the touch-up and special effect dialog boxes, you can click directly on the Before image to zoom in, or right-click it to zoom out. You also can click a zoomed image and drag it to position the portion you want to see in the viewing window.

If you accidentally click OK before you're ready, don't forget that you can use Undo.

Adding Special Effects

Special effects can give your photos a professional look and draw attention to photos that appear in publications or on the Web.

To add effects to an image, first open the photo, then choose the Effects tab on the Notebook. If necessary, click the return arrow at the upper-right corner of the Notebook, then choose Cool & Fun.

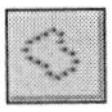

Most effects can be applied to an entire image (photo), or you can use the Select tool on the Toolbox and apply the effect only to the selection. For example, you could use the Freehand Selection tool to outline a hand of a young boy, and use the Motion Blur effect to make it appear that his hand was moving when the picture was taken.

Special effects provided in Photo House include:

- *Add Light Source.* Produces a spot of light that simulates the refraction of light through a camera lens. This option can be used only on high-resolution photos (16 million colors). Other options have similar limitations. When you try to select a special effects option, Photo House will let you know if you cannot use that option.
- *Custom Negative.* Creates a negative image that you can customize, unlike the Photo Negative option which allows only a true negative image.

- *Emboss.* Creates a three-dimensional, carved-in-stone look to the image.
- *Feather.* Blurs the edges of an image to help it blend more easily with a background, or with an image located behind it.
- *Impressionist.* Creates an impressionist painting style, or a rain-covered window effect.
- *Motion Blur.* Creates the illusion of movement in an image.
- *Page Curl.* Rolls a corner back over part of the image. Can be used only with an entire image, not a selection.
- *Photo Negative.* A true negative, without custom options.
- *Psychedelic.* Changes colors in an image to bright, electric, bold colors.
- *Ripple.* Adds the effect similar to dropping a pebble in a pond of water.
- *Sketch.* Makes the image appear hand drawn.
- *Swirl.* Rotates and drags an image in a specified angle.
- *Texture.* Applies paper, linen, or rock patterns to an image.
- *Vignette.* Creates an oval frame around a photo. This option can be used only with an entire image, not on a selection.

The effects you use and the way you use them can result in highly creative images. The more you practice using these effects, the better you will become at getting just what you want.

Cutting and Pasting Portions of Photos

Not that you want to start your own supermarket tabloid, but you can alter photos such that no one will ever know whether the image is real or altered. For example, you could move a face from one person and paste it on the head of another. Or you could simply replace a button that is missing on someone's shirt or blouse.

To cut and paste portions of photos, follow these steps:

1. Choose the Selection tool you want to use—either the Select tool for rectangular selection, or the Freehand Selection tool to select exactly what you want.
2. Drag the mouse on the image over the area you want to select. If you use the Freehand tool, you may want to use the Zoom feature to enlarge the area first so you can drag the area more accurately with the mouse. Release the mouse, and the selection appears surrounded by a dashed line (see Figure 29.8).

FIG. 29.8
By using the Select tools, you can copy or move portions of your image from one location to another.

3. Choose Edit, Copy; or right-click the selection and choose Copy.
4. Click again anywhere else in the document to deselect the copied area.
5. Right-click the image and choose Paste; Photo House places a copy of the selection in the center of the screen.
6. Drag the selection to position it where you want it.
7. Apply any effects you need to make the image blend better with its new surroundings. For example, Feather helps blend it, Brightness/Contrast might help it match better, and so on (see Figure 29.9).

FIG. 29.9
Use touch-up or special effects to blend copies with the background, as in this extended finger.

8. Click anywhere outside of the selection to merge it with the background image; or choose Edit, Merge Selection with Background. If you make a mistake and merge the selection too early, choose Edit, Undo Merge Selection to get the selection back.

Saving, Exporting, and Printing Images

Once you complete the touch-up or modification of your photo, you'll want to save it. You may also need to save the image in a format needed for a specific purpose. For example, if you plan to use the image on the Web, you need to save it in a GIF or JPEG format. If you're going to use it as a Windows wallpaper, the BMP format is required. By default, Photo House attempts to save the image in its original format.

To save your image, simply choose File, Save. Special options may appear in a dialog box, depending on the graphic file format you use. Respond accordingly and choose OK.

If the original came from a CD, or if you want to save the file with a different name, you must choose the Save As option. This is also how you *export* the file to a different format. Follow these steps:

1. Choose File, Save As. Photo House displays the Save As dialog box.
2. Navigate to the folder where you want to save your image.
3. Click the Save as Type drop-down list to choose a graphics format (see Figure 29.10). The formats listed depend partly on the format of the original graphic. For example, if the original was a JPEG file, you cannot save it in the GIF format. You always have the option to save the image in the CPT (Corel PhotoPaint), PCX, TIFF, and BMP formats.

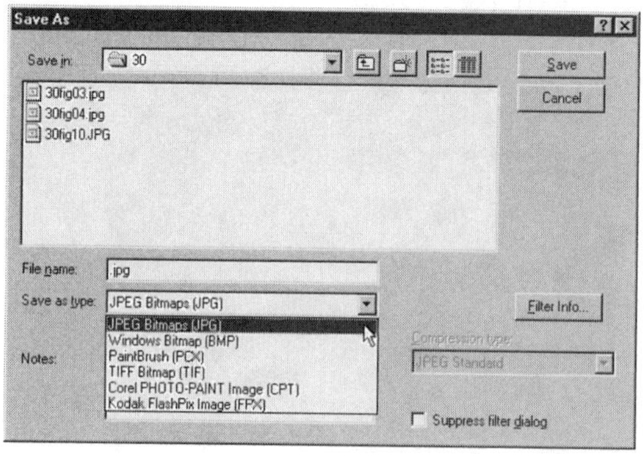

FIG. 29.10
Export Photo House images to other graphic formats using the Save As option.

4. Supply a file name and choose Save.

Depending on your choice of graphic format, you may be given additional choices for customizing the format. For example, for a JPEG file you can choose how much to compress the file, resulting in a smaller file, but also losing some quality of the image.

Finally, if you want to print your image, simply choose File, Print, and in the Print dialog box, choose OK. ●

PART VIII

Integrating and Customizing Corel WordPerfect Suite 8

CHAPTER 30

Integrating Your Work with PerfectExpert

Use PerfectExpert projects

Learn to use PerfectExpert projects to perform over 135 common office and home functions.

Manage PerfectExpert projects

See how to create categories for your PerfectExpert projects, and move or copy your projects to the categories you prefer.

Create PerfectExpert projects

Learn how to easily create projects that integrate with WordPerfect.

Part of what makes Corel WordPerfect Suite 8 the "perfect way to work" is its task orientation. For you, this means that as you use the suite, you should be able to focus on getting your work done rather than on learning specific applications. Instead of focusing on WordPerfect, Presentations, or Quattro Pro features, for example, you can think about the job, or *task*, that you need to accomplish.

The principal feature that integrates applications in the Corel WordPerfect Suite is the Corel PerfectExpert. The suite contains over 135 projects that automate many of your day-to-day tasks. ■

Learning About PerfectExpert Projects

At the heart of Corel WordPerfect Suite 8 is the concept that a suite is more than just a box full of otherwise unrelated products. Suite products need to be *integrated*. In the past, integration meant more work for you. Integrated products could "talk" together, but it was up to you to start the conversation.

Moderating the conversation required you to learn the nitty-gritty details of cross-application communication, such as DDE, OLE 2.0, or in-place editing. Just the terminology is enough to cause a headache.

While most of us enjoy technology, we *use* software to get our work done, not simply for technology's sake. PerfectExpert projects reflect your need to do work rather than merely play with technology.

So what is a PerfectExpert project? It is an automated routine that does work for you. It takes you through the task, step-by-step, from start to finish. Some projects involve two or more applications—but to you it is application-independent. You don't need to know which applications are required. You need not start the applications at all. You simply choose a project, click its button, and the PerfectExpert does the work for you.

Accessing PerfectExpert Projects

You access the PerfectExpert in three different ways:

- You can click the PerfectExpert button on the Desktop Application Director (DAD). When you do, you see a dialog box that contains all the available QuickTasks, shown in Figure 30.1.
- You also can access the PerfectExpert from the Windows 95 Start menu. Choose Start, Corel WordPerfect Suite 8, and select Corel New Project.
- Any time you choose File, New in any Corel WordPerfect Suite 8 application (for example, WordPerfect, Quattro Pro, or Presentations), the PerfectExpert dialog appears to help you start a new project.

NOTE Unless you performed a complete installation of all Corel WordPerfect Suite 8 components, some PerfectExpert projects may not reside on your hard disk. When you attempt to use such projects, you must insert your Corel WordPerfect Suite 8 CD into your CD-ROM drive, or you will not be able to use such projects.

FIG. 30.1
The PerfectExpert dialog box, which you can access from DAD, contains over 135 predefined tasks.

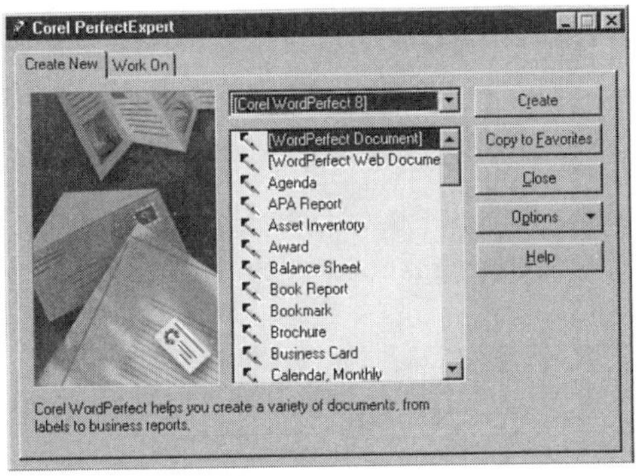

Understanding the PerfectExpert Approach

As you can see, the PerfectExpert dialog box contains two tabs: Create New and Work On. Click the Work On tab and the PerfectExpert displays all recent projects you have worked on, including WordPerfect, Presentations, or Quattro Pro projects (see Figure 30.2). Double-click any of these to resume work already in progress. You need not start up the application first; the PerfectExpert takes care of that for you. If you're not sure you want to open a work in progress, you can check the Preview Document box to see what the project is all about. You can even check the Work In Progress boxes to remind yourself which projects you currently are working on.

NOTE The grayed check box at the bottom of the dialog box does not serve any function other than to remind you to check a box if you want to indicate that it's a work in progress.

FIG. 30.2
The PerfectExpert offers a quick and convenient way to resume work on projects in progress.

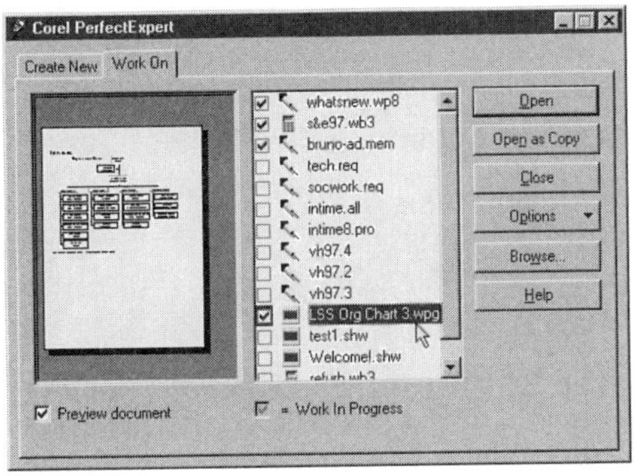

Reviewing Predefined PerfectExpert Projects

Click the Create New tab in the PerfectExpert dialog box to display the PerfectExpert's projects again. These are grouped by Category, such as Auto, Education, or Mortgage.

To display all of the projects in a category, click the drop-down list (see Figure 30.3), click the category you want to see, and click the project you want to work on.

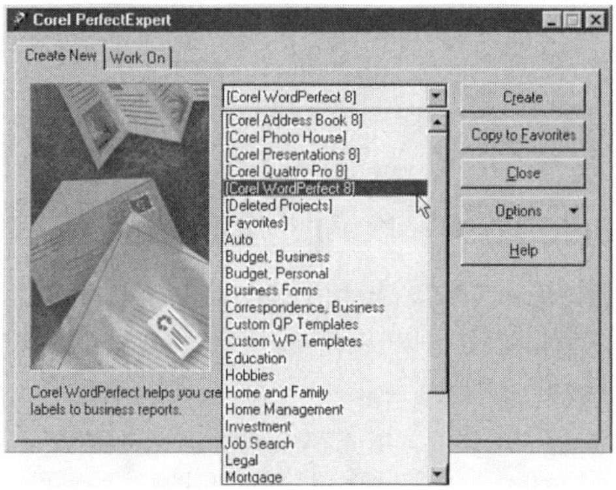

FIG. 30.3
The PerfectExpert helps you with over 135 projects, grouped in task-oriented categories.

TIP Click a project and the PerfectExpert displays a brief description at the bottom of the dialog box.

The list of available projects is extensive—over 135 business and personal projects in all. Projects are grouped by category, as listed in Table 30.1. Some projects appear in more than one category to make it easier for you to find just the right one. In addition, you can create your own categories and group your projects as you please (see "Managing PerfectExpert Projects" later in this chapter.)

Table 30.1 PerfectExpert Projects in WordPerfect Suite 8

Category	Project Name	Application
Auto	Auto expense report	QP
	Auto expense report, monthly	QP
	Buy vs. Lease a Car	QP
Budget, Business	Balance Sheet	WP
	Budget, Cash	QP
	Budget, Trade Show	QP
	Estimating Startup Capital	QP
	Income Statement	WP
	Statement of Cash Flows	QP

Category	Project Name	Application
Budget, Personal	Personal	QP
	Retirement	QP
	School	QP
	Vacation	QP
	Wedding	QP
	Credit Card Log	QP
	Gain on the sale of home	QP
	Kiddie Tax Analysis	QP
	Life Insurance Needs	QP
	Maximum Loan Amount	QP
	Year End Tax Plan	QP
Business Forms	Agenda	WP
	Award	WP
	Balance Sheet	WP
	Company Equipment Receipt	WP
	Conference Room Scheduling	WP
	Daily Time Sheet	QP
	Employee Evaluation	WP
	Employee Vacation Schedule	WP
	Expense Report	QP
	Expense Report	WP
	Fax Cover Sheet	WP
	Fax Cover Sheet, Legal	WP
	Fax Log	WP
	Interview Summary	WP
	Invoice, Sales	WP
	Invoice, Service & Sales	WP
	Invoice, Service	QP
	Invoice, Service	WP
	Job Estimate	QP
	Legal Time Sheet	WP
	Purchase Order	WP
	Report	WP
	Seminar Evaluation	WP
	Telephone Message Form	WP
	Work Schedule	WP
Correspondence, Business	Business Card	WP
	Fax Cover Sheet	WP
	Labels	WP
	Letters, Business	WP
	Memo	WP
	Newsletter	WP
	Press Release	WP

continues

Table 30.1 Continued

Category	Project Name	Application
Custom	(Standard WP Document)	WP
Education	APA Report	WP
	Award	WP
	Book Report	WP
	Bookmark	WP
	Exam Builder	WP
	Grade Schedule	WP
	Grading Sheet	QP
	Graph Paper	WP
	List	WP
	MLA Report	WP
	Multiplication Table	WP
	Report	WP
	Seminar Evaluation	WP
	Speech	WP
	Teaching a Concept Slide Show	PR
	Teaching a Skill Slide Show	PR
	Teaching & Training Slide Show	PR
	Turabian Report	WP
Hobbies	Bookmark	WP
	CD Cover	WP
	Corel Photo House	PH
	Exercise Chart	WP
	Gift Box, Tubular	WP
	Music Sheet	WP
	Recipe Card	WP
	Video Tape Log	WP
Home and Family	Award	WP
	Bookmark	WP
	Calendar, Monthly	WP
	Gift Box, Tubular	WP
	Gift Tags	WP
	Graph Paper	WP
	Hangman Game Sheet	WP
	Journal	WP
	Labels	WP
	Letter, Personal	WP
	List	WP
	Multiplication Table	WP
	Newsletter	WP
	Recipe Card	WP
	Sign	WP
	Tic Tac Toe Game Card	WP

Category	Project Name	Application
Home Management	Asset Inventory	WP
	Home Improvements	WP
	Household Inventory	WP
	Menu Plan and Grocery List	WP
	Telephone Message Form	WP
	Vacation Check List	WP
	Video Tape Log	WP
	Vital Documents Inventory	WP
Investment	401K Planner	QP
	Asset Inventory	WP
	Basic Bond Valuation	QP
	Capital Gains and Losses	QP
	CD Switch Analysis	QP
	Deposits to a Sum	QP
	Mutual Fund Analyzer	QP
	Present Value Annuity	QP
	Present Value of a Lump Sum	QP
	Property and Estate	QP
	Real Rate Calculator	QP
	Real Rate of ROI	QP
	Statement of Net Worth	QP
Job Search	Business Card	WP
	Letter, Personal	WP
	List	WP
	Resume	WP
Legal	Fax Cover Sheet, Legal	WP
	Legal Time Sheet	WP
	Pleading Paper	WP
Mortgage	7 Year Balloon Loan	QP
	Balloon Payment Loan	QP
	Closing Costs	QP
	Home Equity Comparison	QP
	Home Equity Qualification	QP
	Mortgage Amortization	QP
	Mortgage Qualification	QP
	Mortgage Refinancing	QP
	Mortgage, Added Payment	QP
	Mortgage, Biweekly	QP
Publish	Bookmark	WP
	Brochure	WP
	Business Card	WP
	CD Cover	WP

continues

Table 30.1 Continued

Category	Project Name	Application
	Corel Photo House	PH
	Gift Tags	WP
	Labels	WP
	Newsletter	WP
	Recipe Card	WP
Retirement Planning	Budget, Retirement	QP
	Retirement Income Plan	QP
	Retirement Plan Contributions	QP
Slide Shows	Annual Report	PR
	Award or Tribute	PR
	Budget Report	PR
	Business Plan	PR
	Company Meeting	PR
	Describing Alternatives	PR
	Interactive	PR
	Market Research	PR
	Market Segmentation	PR
	Marketing Plan	PR
	Marketing Strategy	PR
	Multimedia	PR
	Persuasive	PR
	Product Launch	PR
	Project Proposal	PR
	Recommending A Strategy	PR
	Teaching a Concept	PR
	Teaching A Skill	PR
	Teaching and Training	PR
	Team Meeting	PR
	Welcome	PR
	Year-End Report	PR
Time Management	Address Book	AB
	Agenda	WP
	Calendar, Monthly	WP
	Calendar, Year	QP
	Journal	WP
	List	WP
	Vacation Checklist	WP
Web Publishing	WordPerfect Web Document	WP

TIP Projects are listed alphabetically. However, recently used projects appear at the top of the category list so that you can access them more quickly.

Taking a Guided Tour of Some PerfectExpert Projects

Enough about how PerfectExpert projects work—or do your work for you. Now it's time to experiment with a few projects. We'll take a guided tour through three specific tasks that automate common things you have to do.

Using the Personal Letter Project

The Personal Letter project guides you through writing a letter from start to finish.

1. Start up the PerfectExpert by clicking the PerfectExpert button on the Desktop Application Director.
2. Click the Home and Family category, and then double-click Letter, Personal. Because this is a WordPerfect project, the PerfectExpert starts up WordPerfect for you.

TIP If you don't remember what category a project falls under, but you remember what type of application it is (for example, WordPerfect), you can choose the Corel WordPerfect 8 category, and choose the project from the lengthy master list of WordPerfect projects.

3. The PerfectExpert accompanies you through the task, appearing at the left side of the screen to coach, guide, and offer options (see Figure 30.4).

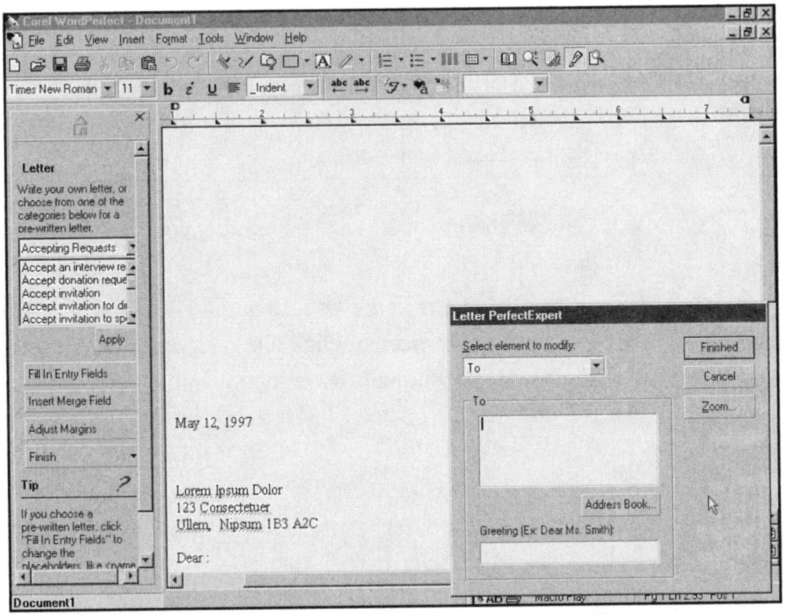

FIG. 30.4 The PerfectExpert assistant appears to help guide you through your projects.

NOTE Some projects automatically use personal information such as your name, your address, or your phone number. The first project you use that requires such information will prompt you to enter your personal information. Fill in the requested information as carefully as possible because, after the first time, the PerfectExpert won't ask you again.

4. The Personal Letter project begins by asking you to whom the letter should be addressed. Fill in the name and address of the recipient, as well as the salutation you desire (for example, "Dear Mr. Steurer"). You also can choose such information from your address book, if you have one. Choose Finished, and the PerfectExpert inserts this information in your letter.

NOTE When starting up a project, be patient. Even on fast computers, it often takes awhile before projects are ready for your use.

5. Choose the type of letter you are writing. Of course you can write your own letter, but the PerfectExpert can help you if you want. For example, from the drop-down list, choose Letters of Recommendation, and then choose Someone Attend School. Double-click or click Apply to insert the predefined paragraphs of information.
6. Some letters include special "fields" or areas needing custom information. For example, in the recommendation letter, you need to provide personalized information about the candidate you are recommending (see Figure 30.5). Click Fill In Entry Fields and the PerfectExpert prompts you to type the required information.
7. Add to or edit the information provided by the PerfectExpert. For example, in the case of the recommendation, only the outline of what needs to be said is provided. You add the rest.

TIP While editing the content or format of the letter, you can hide the PerfectExpert by clicking the X at the upper-right corner of the expert. When you want to resume using the PerfectExpert, simply click the PerfectExpert button on the Toolbar.

8. You also can change or add any formatting you want, such as font, graphic lines, margins, and so on.
9. Check the Tip section at the bottom of the PerfectExpert screen for suggestions on how to use the project, or click the More Help On button for specific ideas for creating a better document (for example, Punctuation of Letters). You may have to scroll down in the PerfectExpert to see the More Help On button.

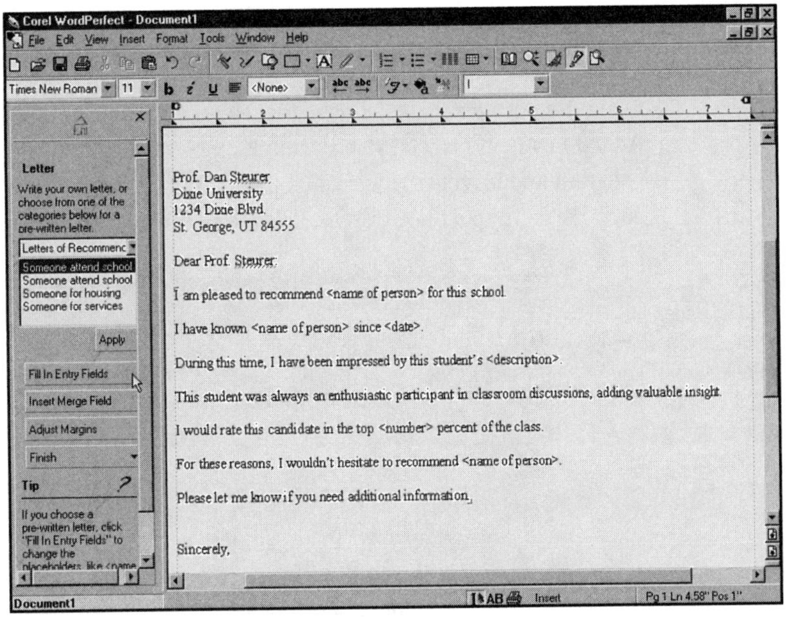

FIG. 30.5
Click the Fill In Entry Fields button to automate the process of filling in form letters.

10. Click the Finish button on the PerfectExpert to choose any or all of the following finishing activities:
    - Check Spelling
    - Print/Fax (print the document, or fax it to someone)
    - Email (send the document as an e-mail attachment)
    - Save
    - Close Without Saving
11. Close the document as you normally would (for example, File, Close). Note that the PerfectExpert reverts to a general WordPerfect document expert. Unless you want to use the expert, simply click the X at the upper-right corner of the PerfectExpert to close it.

Using the Added Mortgage Payment Project

So your forte is word processing and you really don't need some expert telling you how to do it. But what about financial projects? You've heard, for example, that you can save a great deal of money and pay off your loan much sooner if you simply add a little extra to your monthly mortgage payment. But how much, and what effect will it really have? How do you calculate the savings?

Enter once again the PerfectExpert with the Added Payment Mortgage project. To use this project, follow these steps:

1. Open the PerfectExpert, choose the Mortgage category, and select the Mortgage, Added Payment project. The PerfectExpert opens the Quattro Pro spreadsheet program and inserts the worksheet shown in Figure 30.6. As you can easily see, each PerfectExpert is different, tailored to the specific task at hand.

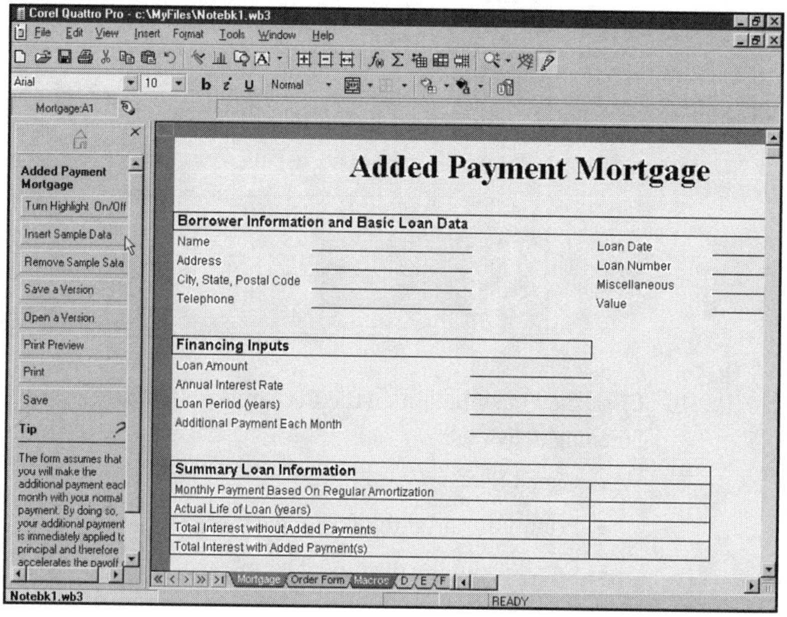

FIG. 30.6 Even if spreadsheets are intimidating to you, the PerfectExpert can make it easy to calculate mortgage payments and more.

2. If you're not sure exactly where you're headed with this project, click the Insert Sample Data button. The PerfectExpert inserts sample information from a fictional loan. Study the results to understand what kind of information you need to provide.
3. Click Remove Sample Data to clear the worksheet.
4. Enter your own data at the appropriate highlighted areas, including the remaining loan amount, the number of years remaining on the loan, the interest rate (for example, enter 9.25% as .0925), and finally the extra amount you intend to add each month.
5. Finish the document by saving it, previewing it, or printing it.

TIP With this project, and with many other financial projects, you don't have to save the file because you may be interested only in the results. However, you still can save different "versions" or scenarios for comparison. Simply click the Save a Version button and provide a version name.

Click Open a Version to retrieve saved versions. You still must save the spreadsheet if you want to keep the results.

Creating a Persuasive Slide Show

You've decided that early mortgage payoff sounds like a good idea, but you don't have quite enough income each month. Perhaps it's time to persuade your company's management to accept your project idea and appoint you team leader, along with an appropriate raise, of course.

You've heard about computer-based slide shows, but you're not sure just where to begin. If you let the PerfectExpert help you, you'll find the perfect slide show. Try these steps:

1. Open the PerfectExpert, and go to the Slide Shows category. Choose the Persuasive Slide Show project. The PerfectExpert opens Presentations and displays the screen shown in Figure 30.7.

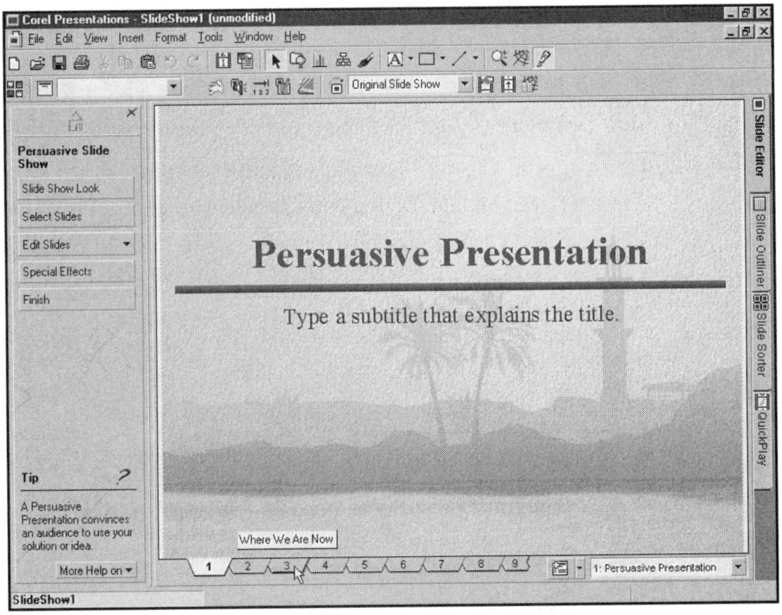

FIG. 30.7 Creating perfect slide shows is a snap when you let the Perfect-Expert help you.

2. Each slide shows you what kind of information is needed. For example, to present the problem, click the Slide 3 tab. Double-click each item shown in Figure 30.8 and replace the information there with your own. Repeat this for each slide in the series.

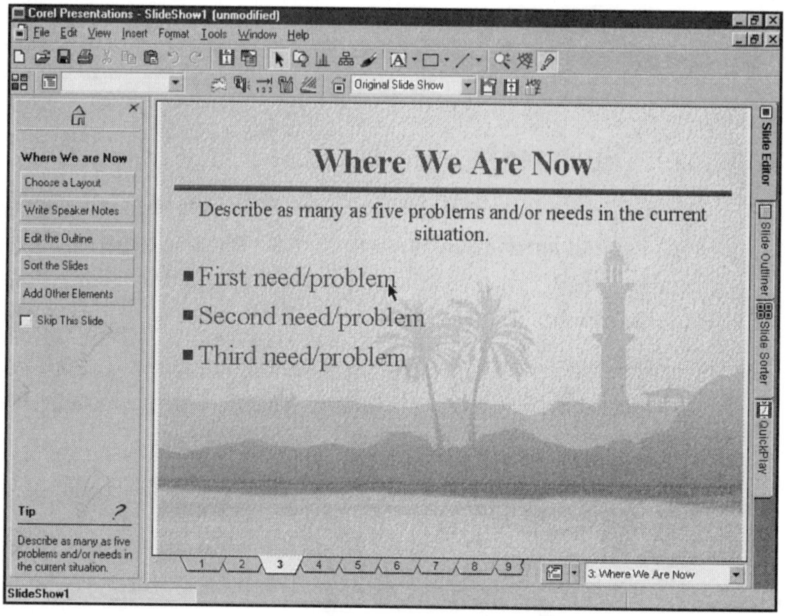

FIG. 30.8
The PerfectExpert helps you build professional slide shows by showing you what to include on your slides.

3. Add Speaker Notes (notes to yourself that you'll refer to during the presentation) or other elements by clicking the appropriate PerfectExpert button.
4. You can return to the "home" PerfectExpert base by clicking the Home button at the top of the expert. There you can add special effects (sound, transitions, or animation), or you can get More Help on what it takes to make a persuasive presentation. You might even want to choose a different layout—one that more closely matches the content or purpose of your presentation.
5. Click the Finish button to save the slide show, to play it or print it, to mail it to someone, or to publish it to the Web.

▶ **See** "Checking Spelling," **p. 114**

▶ **See** "Saving Files," **p. 33**

▶ **See** "Integrating Presentations with the Web," **p. 526**

Managing PerfectExpert Projects

With over 135 available projects, keeping track of them is important if they are to be useful to you. The PerfectExpert enables you to move projects from one category to another, to create your own project categories, and even to create custom projects for your own specific needs.

Copying and Moving

To copy or move a project, first locate the project by opening the category where it is found. Then click the project to select it.

Next, click the Options button on the PerfectExpert dialog box. A pop-up menu appears. When you click or point at the Copy Project or Move Project button, another pop-up menu appears with all the current category names. Click the category name where you want the project to go, and the PerfectExpert copies or moves it to that category.

Removing and Renaming Projects

If you mistakenly place a project in the wrong category, you can remove the project by clicking it and then choosing Options, Remove Project. Choose OK to remove the project.

CAUTION

After you remove a project, you cannot restore it unless you have a copy in another category, or unless you install the project again from the installation CD.

To rename a project, simply select the project and choose Options, Project Properties. In the Modify a Project dialog box, change the Display Name or the Description as you please. Choose OK to save the changes.

Creating New Projects

Suppose that you want to create a custom business card and add it to your PerfectExpert gallery of fine custom documents. Follow these steps:

1. Locate and select the business card you want to use as a model (for example, Publish, Business Card).
2. Choose Options, Edit WP Template. WordPerfect opens up with the project in the WordPerfect template editor (see Figure 30.9).
3. Make any changes you want to the business card, and click the Close button on the Property Bar. Answer Yes when asked if you want to save the changes.

NOTE If you are using a template from your CD drive, WordPerfect will tell you that access is denied because you can't modify the CD. However, WordPerfect does offer to let you save it under a different name.

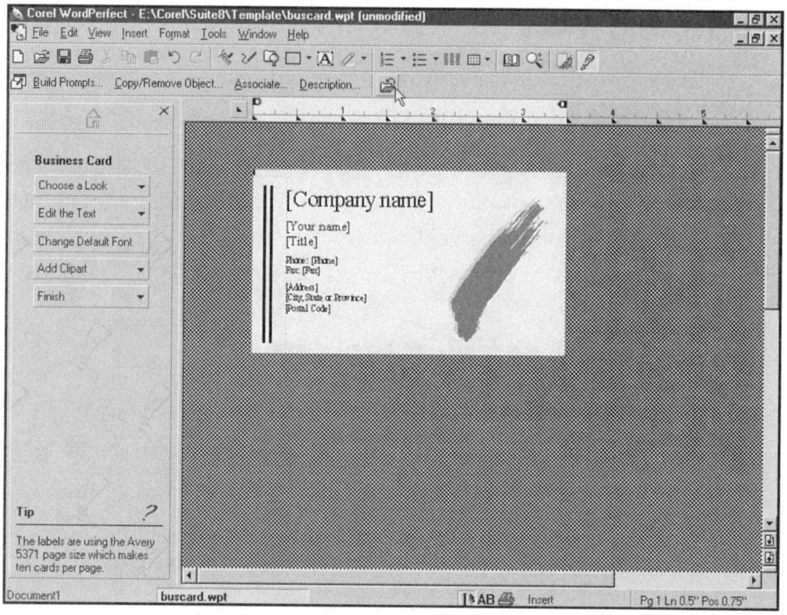

FIG. 30.9
PerfectExpert projects are based on templates, and the WordPerfect Template Editor is a powerful tool for editing existing templates or creating new ones.

4. In the Save As dialog box, provide a new description for the project template, give it a different file name (for example, BUSCARD2.WPT), and choose a category for it to go into (for example, Custom WP Templates). Choose OK.

Now when you return to the PerfectExpert, you find the new Business Card project you just created in your Custom WP Templates category.

NOTE You cannot create new Quattro Pro or Presentations projects, nor can you edit those that appear in the PerfectExpert categories. You only can edit or add WordPerfect-based projects.

Creating New Custom Projects

You can create new custom projects by choosing Options, Create WP Template. The PerfectExpert takes you to the WordPerfect Template editing screen (refer to Figure 30.9).

There you can create an entirely new document, complete with all the formatting and text you want. When you've finished, choose File, Close and choose Yes. In the Save As dialog box, provide a description for the project template, give it a file name (for example, MYDOC.WPT), and choose a category for it to go into (for example, Custom WP Templates). Choose OK to save the project.

You also can use the Build Prompts option to create prompts for information when you use the template. For more information on advanced template features, refer to WordPerfect's on-line help (Template, About). ●

CHAPTER 31

Transferring Data Between Applications

Corel WordPerfect Suite 8's data transferring strategies

See the three ways the Suite permits you to transfer data between applications, and understand the benefits and drawbacks of each.

Moving and Copying Data

Learn how to move and copy data between your applications with ease.

Linking and Embedding

Find out the difference between copying, linking, and embedding data—and when you should do each one.

One of the benefits of working within a suite environment is the ability to think about your work rather than the applications that you are using to get your project done. Behind the scenes, however, data often needs to be transferred between applications for you to obtain a finished result. For instance, a final report may be a Corel WordPerfect document incorporating a Corel Quattro Pro spreadsheet or a Corel Presentations chart.

As you begin to use more than one Corel WordPerfect Suite application and integrate applications to do your work, you'll find that you need more information about what occurs when data is transferred from one application to another.

Before talking about "how to do it," though, it's vital that you understand what's going on with data transfers, and the three very different ways that data is transferred. ■

Understanding the Types of Data Transfer

There are three basic ways that data can be transferred between documents:

- Moving/copying
- Linking
- Embedding

Before you learn the different commands and methods used to transfer data, it's a good idea to get a conceptual understanding of what's happening with the different processes.

▶ **See** "Copying and Moving Text," **p. 64**

Understanding Moving and Copying

Most people are familiar with cut-and-paste, which refers to the moving and copying of data. When you move a sentence from one WordPerfect paragraph to another, or when you move a Quattro Pro cell to another location, you do two operations. First, you cut the data, which removes it from the original location. Then, you paste the data to its new location. Copying works the same way, except that a copy of the data is left in the original location as well. You move data by copying it to the Clipboard, and then you paste it where you want to move it.

NOTE When you cut or copy data, it goes to the Windows Clipboard. This is a temporary storage area that holds the last item that you cut or copied. The data stays in the Clipboard until you either exit Windows or copy something else into the Clipboard.

There are a few important implications:

- The same Clipboard is used in all Windows applications, enabling you to move data from one application to another.
- Because the Clipboard only holds one item, if you put something else in the Clipboard, the first item is erased.
- You can paste the same copy of the data from the Clipboard multiple times—until you copy something else into the Clipboard.

Moving and copying data between applications works the same way as it does within applications. The data is moved or copied to the Windows Clipboard, from which it is retrieved when you paste the data in the destination application.

NOTE When you move or copy data using the drag-and-drop method discussed in previous chapters, the data is not put into the Clipboard, nor are the contents of the Clipboard affected. Therefore, because the data is not in the Clipboard, you cannot repetitively paste multiple copies of it.

Understanding Linking

Linking data adds another dimension to the copying process. For example, when you link a range of spreadsheet cells in Quattro Pro to a WordPerfect word processing document, the spreadsheet information is displayed in the word processing document. This means the word processing document maintains information that specifies where the linked data is to be obtained: the application that created it, the path and file name, and the selected information in that file. When you link data, you thus create a pointer from the file where you want the data to appear to the file in which the data exists.

NOTE You might want to become familiar with the technical terminology used for linked and embedded data (see the following table).

In this chapter, the terminology *source application* and *destination application* are used, rather than *server* and *client*, for clarity.

Term	Refers to
Object	The data that is linked or embedded
Source file	The file from which the object comes
Source application	The application in which the source file is created
Server	Another term for source application
Destination application	The application in which the object appears
Client	Another term for the destination application
Destination file	The file in which the object appears

Because a link consists of a pointer to a source file, when the option for data updating is set to automatic, the object that appears in the destination file is always the latest version. When you or someone else changes the source file containing the object, the object in the destination file is updated with the new information. For example, if someone changes the Quattro Pro file, which affects the cells that are linked to WordPerfect, the spreadsheet cells appearing in your word processing document immediately reflect this change.

Alternatively, you can specify that the link be updated manually. In this case, the object remains static (it retains the old information) unless you manually update it.

TIP When creating a link, first ensure that your source document has been saved so that information about the link can be stored. If the document has not yet been saved, you won't be able to create the link.

Windows applications use different technologies to create links. Three of the most common are DDE, OLE 1.0, and OLE 2.0. DDE, the oldest, stands for Dynamic Data Exchange. It allows for linking, but not embedding. DDE was later subsumed under OLE, Object Linking and Embedding.

The major differences between OLE 1.0 and 2.0 are that OLE 2.0 allows for dragging and dropping data between applications, and it allows you to edit the source data from within the destination application. Corel WordPerfect Suite 8 applications support OLE 2.0 where possible. However, you may have links to other applications that support only OLE 1.0. If you stay in the destination application and the menus change to those of the source application when you double-click a linked object, then the link is an OLE 2.0 link. If, on the other hand, you double-click and the original application opens up, then the link may be OLE 1.0 or 2.0.

NOTE OLE and DDE are quite complex. Usually, the method being used for linking and embedding is immaterial to the user. However, if you *are* interested in the details, Corel WordPerfect 8 is an OLE 2.0 server, meaning that you can link WordPerfect information to Quattro Pro 8 or Corel Presentations 8, for example. It is *not*, however, an OLE 2.0 in-place server. Thus, when you double-click WordPerfect objects that are embedded in Quattro Pro, you will not be able to use in-place editing. ■

Understanding Embedding

Embedding data is like copying it, with one difference: when you embed an object, a copy of it is stored in the destination file, just as it is when you copy it. Because OLE is used to transfer the data, however, you can edit the embedded data using the source application by double-clicking the embedded data. For example, if you have a Quattro Pro spreadsheet embedded into a WordPerfect document, you can double-click the spreadsheet inside WordPerfect, and then use Quattro Pro to edit it.

Depending on the specific applications involved, when you double-click an embedded object to edit it, a window may open enabling you to edit the object using its source application. Alternatively, the title bar, toolbar, and menus may change to those of the source application, enabling you to edit the object in-place from within the destination document.

For instance, when you double-click an embedded Quattro Pro object within WordPerfect, the title bar, menu bar, and toolbar change to those of Quattro Pro, enabling in-place editing. However, when you double-click an embedded WordPerfect object within Quattro Pro, WordPerfect is launched in a separate window, enabling you to edit the WordPerfect object. Because WordPerfect is an OLE 2.0 server, it is not an "OLE 2.0 in-place server" that allows for in-place editing.

Comparing the Methods of Transferring Data

In summary, the differences between the three methods of transferring data can be seen in the following table:

Method	Copies Data to Destination	Allows Editing Using Source Application	Updates When Source Changes
Copying/Moving	Yes	No	No
Linking	No	Yes	Yes
Embedding	Yes	Yes	No

Having looked at the principles behind the three methods of transferring data, let's see how to actually do it.

Learning the Techniques for Moving and Copying

You can use several methods to move or copy data between applications. These include using menus and toolbars, keyboard shortcuts, and drag and drop.

Moving and copying data using the menus, toolbars, and keyboard shortcuts is the same whether you are transferring the data within or between applications:

1. Open the source application, and select the data to be moved or copied.
2. Choose Edit, Cut or Edit, Copy; or click the Cut or Copy button on the toolbar, if they are visible. Alternatively, right-click the data to be moved, and then choose Cut or Copy from the QuickMenu that pops up.

TIP You can also use hotkeys for cutting and pasting: Ctrl+X for cut; Ctrl+C for copy; and Ctrl+V for paste.

3. Open the destination application, and place the insertion point where the data should go.
4. Choose Edit, Paste, or click the Paste button on the toolbar, if it is visible. Alternatively, right-click at the insertion point, and then choose Paste from the QuickMenu.

Learning Techniques for Linking and Embedding

To effectively work with linked and embedded data, you need to be able to:

- Create links and embedding data.
- Edit a linked object.
- Edit the link itself.

Creating Links and Embedding Data

Creating links and embedding data take an extra step than merely copying data, but you'll soon find that you can accomplish them efficiently by following these steps:

1. Open the source application and select the data to be linked or embedded. (If you are going to link the data, the file must be saved before you cut or copy the data.)
2. Cut or copy the data as described previously.
3. Open the destination application, and place the insertion point where the data should go.

> **CAUTION**
>
> In Quattro Pro, you need to clear a space for the information, or the new information could overwrite the old information in the destination cells.

4. Choose Edit, Paste Special. You see the Paste Special dialog box in Figure 31.1.

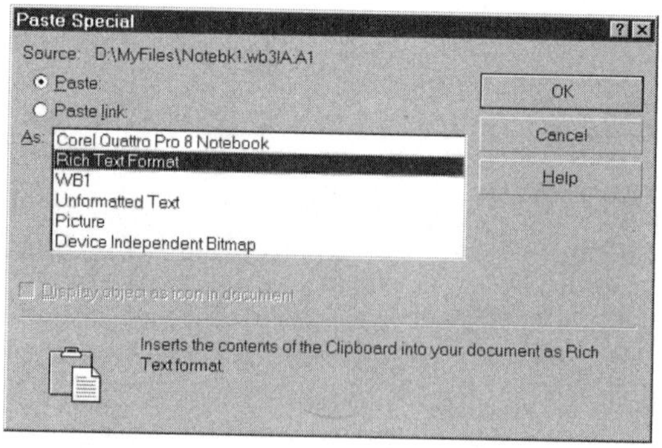

FIG. 31.1
The Paste Special dialog box allows you to both embed and link objects, as well as specify the object type.

5. To embed the data, choose Paste; to link it, choose Paste Link.
6. Select a data type as discussed in the later section "Choosing Data Types," and then click OK. The data appears in your destination application.

Alternatively, if the windows for both applications are simultaneously visible on the Windows desktop, you can drag selected text or objects from one application to another. An easy way to embed an object while keeping it in the source application is to open both application windows, select the data, and then hold down the Ctrl key while dragging the data from one window to another. Just follow these steps:

1. Make sure that both the source application and the destination application are open.
2. Right-click a blank area of the taskbar, and then choose Tile Vertically or Tile Horizontally. Alternatively, move and size the application windows until you can see both the data to be moved in the first application and the destination for that data in the other application.
3. Select the text or object in the source application, and position your mouse pointer inside it.
4. Embed the object and remove it from the source application by dragging it to the appropriate position in the destination application. Or, embed the object and keep it in the source application by holding down the Ctrl key and dragging it to the appropriate position in the destination application.

   Alternatively, link the object by holding down Ctrl+Shift while you drag it to the destination application as shown in Figure 31.2.

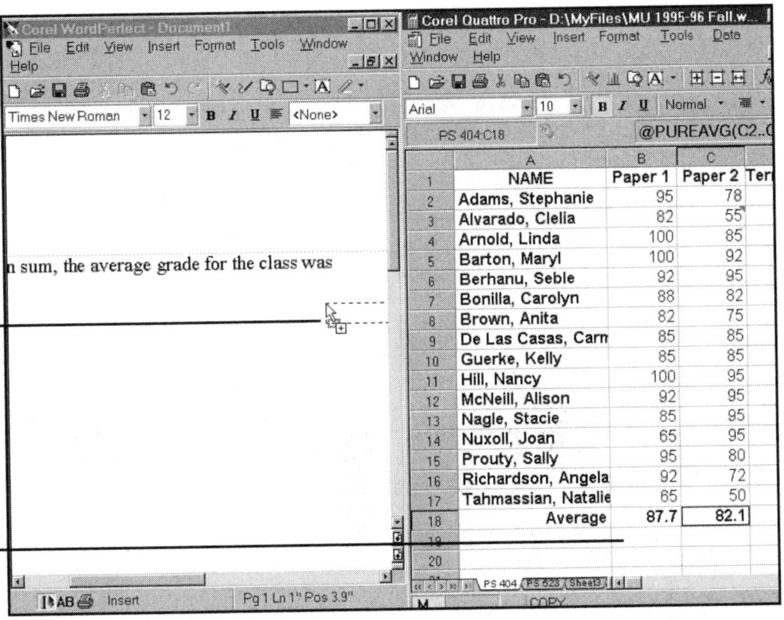

FIG. 31.2
In this example, Quattro Pro data is being dragged into a WordPerfect document.

Destination document with drag-and-drop cursor in place

Source document with selected data that is to be transferred

TROUBLESHOOTING

Why is it that sometimes I can drag text from a non-Corel WordPerfect Suite 8 application into WordPerfect, and sometimes I can't? If the other application is OLE 2.0-compliant, you can drag-and-drop objects into WordPerfect (which is also OLE 2.0-compliant). If the other application is not compliant, you still may be able to cut and paste data using the Edit menu. However, some Windows applications do not use the Windows Clipboard in a standard way. You won't be able to move or copy data from these applications at all.

Choosing Data Types When you are linking or embedding an object in the Paste Special dialog box, you see a number of different object types from which you can choose. The list you see depends on the characteristics of both the source and destination application.

In general, the first data type on this list is the file type of the source application. Thus, when you link or embed a Quattro Pro file into Presentations, the first data type on the list is Quattro Pro 8 Notebook, as you see in Figure 31.3. Similarly, when you link or embed a Presentations drawing into WordPerfect, the first entry on the list is Corel Presentations 8 Drawing. Choosing this option is often advantageous, because it offers full OLE 2.0 functionality.

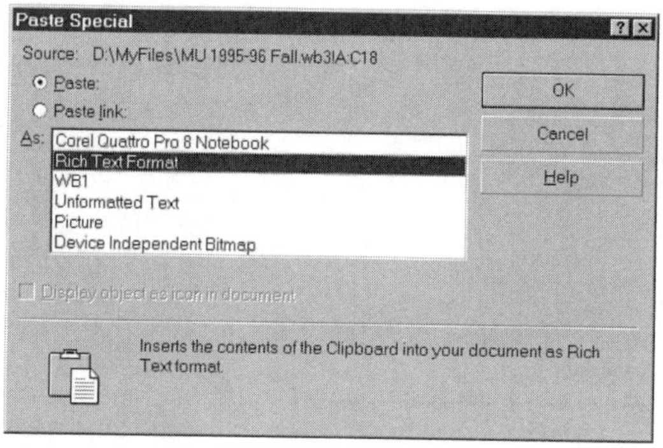

FIG. 31.3
The first data type listed usually provides the best way of linking data. If the Display As Icon option is active, it indicates that the data type provides an OLE 2.0 link.

TIP When you choose OLE 2.0 data types, the Display As Icon option becomes active. This can be particularly useful when you attach sound files or background text files to a document.

Other data types that you can choose may include:

- *Rich Text Format.* This data type is useful in transferring data from one word processor to another, when you want to retain the maximum formatting information possible.

- *Unformatted Text.* This data type is useful in opposite situations, when you want to merely transfer text and no formatting.
- *Picture, Metafile, or Device Independent Bitmap.* These options convert the object into different graphic formats.

When embedding an object, you'll often see options such as Quattro Pro 8 Notebook, Rich Text Format, QB1, or WordPerfect 8 Document. These options allow you to paste the object into your document in a slightly different, often earlier, format than that of the current version of the source application.

NOTE You often have more options when embedding a file with the Paste option than when linking it with Paste Link. This makes sense, because a link usually must be established with the file in its original format.

Inserting Objects You can also embed an object by choosing Insert, Object from the menu of Corel WordPerfect Suite 8 applications such as WordPerfect, Presentations, and Quattro Pro. You see the Insert Object dialog box shown in Figure 31.4.

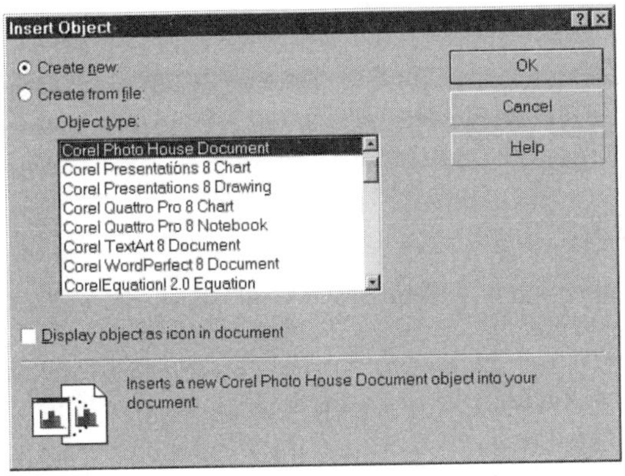

FIG. 31.4 The Insert Object dialog box enables you to create new embedded objects in your file using a variety of OLE-compliant applications, by choosing Create New.

This dialog box provides two choices for embedding an object. If you choose Create New, you see a list of OLE object types that are supported on your system.

TIP If you have installed applications from other vendors that are OLE-compliant, they may also appear on this list.

This option enables you to create a new object using one of the listed types of objects. When you choose an Object Type, the appropriate application opens. If the source application is an OLE 2.0 in-place service, you use in-place editing. Otherwise, it opens in its own window, and you can create the new object there. See the next section for details on editing linked objects.

Alternatively, you may want to embed an object that already exists as a file on the disk. In this case, choose Create from File while you are in the Insert Object dialog box. The dialog box changes to the one shown in Figure 31.5. You can type the name of the desired file, or use the Browse button to see a Corel Office Open dialog box, and then choose the file from there.

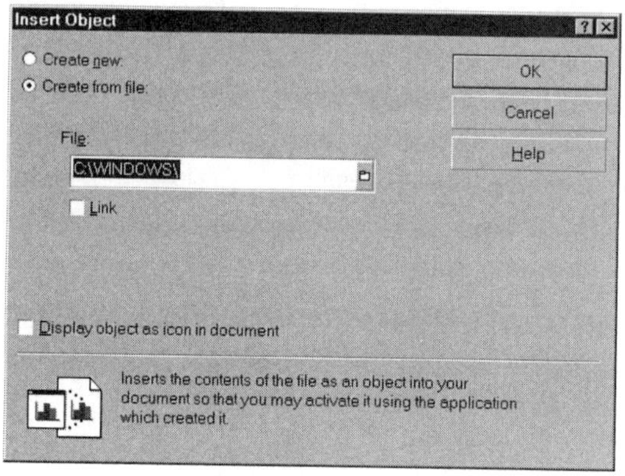

FIG. 31.5 You can embed or link an entire file into your document by choosing Create from File in the Insert Object dialog box.

TIP When you create an object from a file, you have the options of creating it as a link rather than embedding the object or displaying it as an icon.

Editing a Linked Object

One of the nicest things about linking objects is that you can "go back through" the link to edit the source file in the source application that created it.

When you double-click a linked object, another application window opens on-screen. This is the source application that created the object, and you see the source file in that window. Edit the object within the application window and save it as you normally would. When you're finished, choose File. There is an option that enables you to exit and return to the destination application.

Editing a Link

When you have linked one or more objects into your documents, you can edit information about the link. You may want to edit the links in your document for a number of reasons:

- To redefine the link if the source file is renamed or moved.
- To break the link so that the object no longer changes in your document.

- To change the link from automatically updated (whenever the source file changes) to manually updated (when you specify).
- To update a manual link.

To edit a link in WordPerfect or Presentations, choose Edit, Links. The Links dialog box appears (see Figure 31.6). All the links in your document are listed.

FIG. 31.6
The Links dialog box lists all links in your document and allows you to edit them, break them, or specify their update as manual or automatic.

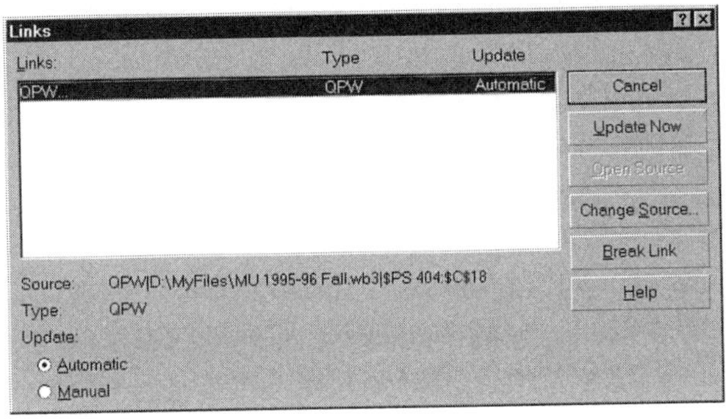

The Links dialog box provides the following options that affect links you have selected:

- *Update Automatic* or *Manual.* Choosing Automatic causes objects to be updated as soon as they are changed. Choosing Manual causes objects not to be updated until an Update command is given.
- *Update Now.* This option causes all selected manual links to be updated—that is, the objects are refreshed from the latest versions of the source files.
- *Open Source.* This option opens the source file in the source application.
- *Change Source.* When you choose this option, the Change Source dialog box appears. You can then change the file name and (in the case of spreadsheets) the cell range.
- *Break Link.* This option breaks the link between the object and its source file.

TROUBLESHOOTING

Why is the Links option grayed out on the Edit menu? The Links option is active only if you have links in your document. If you have embedded objects rather than linked objects, the option is not active.

continues

continued

Why is it that sometimes changes in my source document aren't reflected in my destination document? The source document may not be available, either because it no longer exists, it has been moved, or you cannot establish a connection to it on the network. In this case, the last copy of the object will display in your destination document.

Alternatively, the link may be one that is manually updated, rather than one that is updated automatically. In either case, you can examine the link information and make necessary changes.

CHAPTER 32

Customizing Toolbars, Property Bars, and Menus

Set toolbar preferences

Find out how to display toolbars on any side of the screen, and how to change their display preferences.

Customize toolbars

Learn how to create new toolbars and add and remove buttons from them.

Customize menus

See how to add macros, text scripts, and commands to create your own customized menus.

You can customize Corel WordPerfect Suite 8 to your working preferences by creating and editing toolbars, Property Bars, menus, keyboard definitions, and the Application Bar so that they contain the commands and information that help you do your work.

Depending on the application, you have more or less control over these features. The commands for customizing WordPerfect and Presentations are virtually identical, while you customize Quattro Pro in a slightly different way. (The customization options for Envoy, Site Builder, and other bonus applications are much more limited.) ■

Customizing Toolbars and Property Bars

Corel WordPerfect, Presentations, and Quattro Pro all enable you to customize your toolbars to display the tools you use most frequently. They do so, however, in slightly different ways. To effectively customize your toolbars, you need to know how to:

- Display and hide toolbars
- Select different toolbars
- Access the Toolbar Preferences
- Control toolbar display options
- Position the toolbar in the window

Displaying and Selecting Toolbars and Property Bars

There are several different toolbars you can choose among in each WordPerfect Suite application. Additionally, there are Property Bars that offer additional features for the task you are working on in WordPerfect and Presentations.

In WordPerfect and Quattro Pro, you can display multiple toolbars simultaneously. In Presentations, you can display only one toolbar at a time. In all applications, only one Property Bar can be displayed at a time.

You can control the display of toolbars and Property Bars by choosing View, Toolbars. You see the Toolbars dialog box. Check or uncheck the toolbar(s) or Property Bar to display or hide them.

TIP To quickly hide a toolbar or Property Bar, right-click it and then choose Hide, or uncheck the toolbar or Property Bar entry.

To select a different toolbar to display, ensure that a toolbar is displayed, and then right-click it. You see a pop-up QuickMenu that displays the names of available toolbars. Click the name of the toolbar that you want to display. In Presentations, the selected toolbar will replace the original one. In WordPerfect and Quattro Pro, the selected toolbar will be displayed in addition to the original one.

Customizing Toolbars

To control toolbar display options in WordPerfect, Quattro Pro, or Presentations, or to create, edit, copy, rename, or delete a toolbar, use the following procedure:

1. Make sure that a toolbar is displayed, and then right-click it.

2. Select Settings from the QuickMenu. You see a Customize Settings dialog box in WordPerfect (see Figure 32.1). Ensure that the Toolbars tab is selected.

NOTE In Quattro Pro, choosing Settings from the QuickMenu displays the Toolbar Settings dialog box; in Presentations it is the Customize dialog box. These have similar functionality to the WordPerfect Customize Settings dialog box discussed in this procedure.

FIG. 32.1
You can select different toolbars, as well as create and edit new ones, from the Customize Settings dialog box.

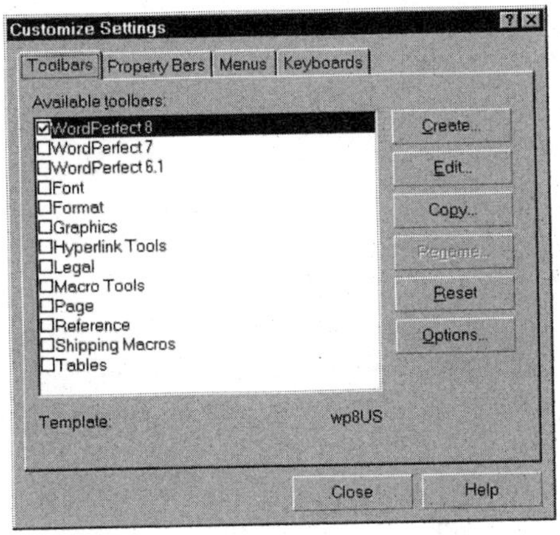

3. Highlight the toolbar that you want to select, edit, copy, rename, or delete.
4. Choose an option from the following list:
   - *Create*. Use this option to create a new toolbar (see "Creating Toolbars and Menu Bars," later in this chapter).
   - *Edit*. Use this option to edit an existing toolbar (see "Editing Toolbars and Menu Bars," later in this chapter).
   - *Copy*. Use this option to copy an existing toolbar. The option works slightly differently, depending on the application (see "Copying Toolbars," later in this chapter).
   - *Rename*. This option enables you to rename an existing toolbar. (You may not be able to rename certain toolbars that ship with the product.)
   - *Reset*. Resets the toolbar to its factory installed condition. This button appears only in WordPerfect and Quattro Pro when you select a toolbar that ships with the suite.
   - *Delete*. Use this to delete a toolbar. Certain default toolbars cannot be deleted. In WordPerfect, the Delete option appears only when toolbars you have created are selected.

- *Options*. This option enables you to set display preferences, as described in "Setting Toolbar Display Preferences" later in this chapter.
- *Help*. This provides context-sensitive help.

5. When you have finished with whichever option you have selected, click OK. You return to your application.

NOTE By default, when you edit the toolbar in Presentations, you will be prompted to make a copy of the <Drawing> toolbar, which is the only toolbar available, and cannot be directly edited. You can, however, edit the copy of the drawing toolbar that you made, and save it with a different name.

Setting Toolbar Display Preferences

You can specify options regarding the appearance and location of your toolbars, although the exact options differ in WordPerfect, Quattro Pro, and Presentations. The selections you make affect any toolbar that you select and are retained in future work sessions until you reset them. To set display preferences, use the following procedure:

1. Access the Customize dialog box as described in the previous section, by right-clicking a toolbar, and then choosing Settings.
2. Choose Options. You see an options dialog box like the Toolbar Options dialog box shown in Figure 32.2.

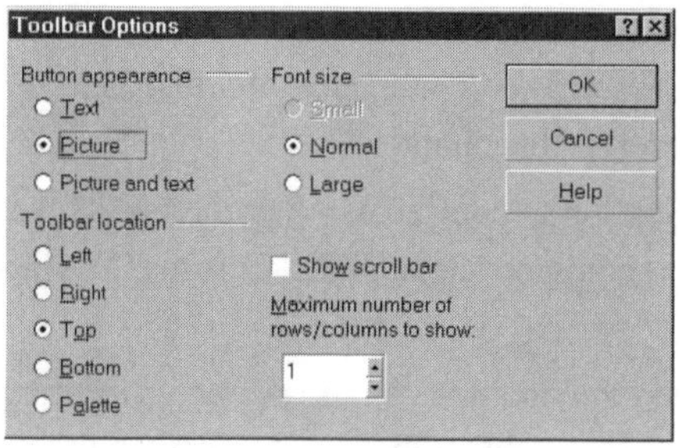

FIG. 32.2
The Toolbar Options dialog box enables you to change the appearance and location of your toolbar.

3. Select display preferences (not all preferences are available in all applications):
   - *Button Appearance*. Toolbars can display Text (text only), Picture (icon only), or Picture and Text.
   - *Font Size*. Choose the text size for toolbars that display text.

TIP If you choose Text or Picture and Text, display your toolbars at the left or right side of the window; otherwise, you will not have room for many buttons.

- *Toolbar Location (Docking Position* in Quattro Pro). You can specify that toolbars display to the Left, Right, Top, Bottom of the window, or as a floating Palette.
- *Show Scroll Bar*. Click this check box to have a scroll bar appear on the toolbar so that you can have more buttons than appear in the window.
- *Maximum Number of Rows/Columns to Show*. You can display more than one row or column of buttons by entering a number greater than 1 in this option.

TIP If you are setting options for a toolbar that is displayed as a floating palette, the Maximum Number of Rows/Columns to Show option will be grayed out.

4. When you have finished selecting preferences, click OK. You return to the Toolbar Preferences dialog box.
5. You can now set further toolbar preferences or choose Close to return to the application.

Moving Toolbars with the Mouse

Another easy way to position toolbars is by moving them with the mouse, as outlined in the following steps:

1. Ensure that the toolbar is visible on-screen.
2. Position the mouse pointer in an area of the toolbar that does not contain buttons—either in the space between buttons or below or after the buttons. The mouse pointer changes to a hand.
3. Drag the toolbar to the desired edge of the window. Alternatively, display the toolbar as a palette by dragging it into the middle of the window.
4. When you release the mouse button, the toolbar moves to its new position.

TIP You can also move a toolbar that appears as a palette in the middle of the screen by dragging its title bar, or close it by double-clicking its Control button.

Copying Toolbars

Copying a toolbar is handled differently by Presentations and WordPerfect. (In Quattro Pro, you do not copy toolbars, you merely create new ones.) In Presentations, you see a Copy Toolbar dialog box that merely asks you for the name of the new toolbar.

In WordPerfect, toolbars are stored in templates. To copy a toolbar, do the following:

1. Display the Toolbar Preferences dialog box as described above.
2. Choose Copy. You see the Copy Toolbars dialog box (see Figure 32.3).

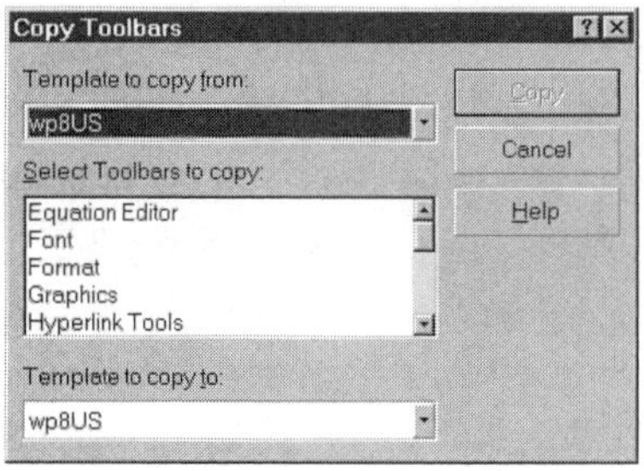

FIG. 32.3
In WordPerfect, you copy a toolbar from one template to another using the Copy Toolbar(s) dialog box.

3. Specify the template containing the toolbar you want to copy.
4. Specify the toolbar in that template to be copied.
5. Specify the template to copy the toolbar to.
6. If the copying operation will result in overwriting the name of an existing toolbar, you are prompted to overwrite the toolbar or provide a new name for it. (You see this prompt, for instance, when you copy a toolbar to the same template it comes from.)
7. Click the Copy button to copy the toolbar.

Customizing Property Bars

The procedures for customizing Property Bars parallel those for customizing toolbars in WordPerfect and Presentations. By right-clicking a Property Bar, you can choose Settings, and see the appropriate customize dialog box, like WordPerfect's Customize Settings shown in Figure 32.4.

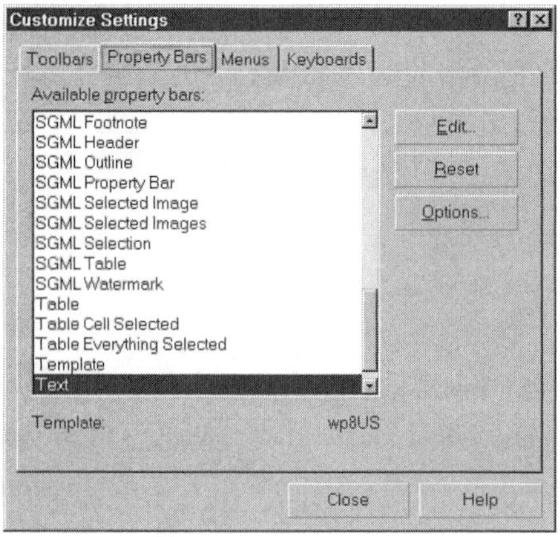

FIG. 32.4
You can customize Property Bars just like you customize toolbars, except that you have fewer customization options.

The only three options you have are Edit (as discussed later in "Editing Toolbars and Menu Bars," Reset (which resets the default settings for the Property Bar), and Options (which controls how the Property Bar is displayed).

Customizing Menu Bars

In WordPerfect and Presentations, you can create multiple menu bars and edit their contents—just as you can with toolbars.

To effectively customize your menus, you need to know how to:

- Select different menu bars
- Access the Menu Preferences dialog box
- Create and edit menus

Selecting Menu Bars

To select a different menu bar to display, right-click the current menu bar. You see a QuickMenu that displays the names of available menu bars (see Figure 32.5). Click the menu that you want to display.

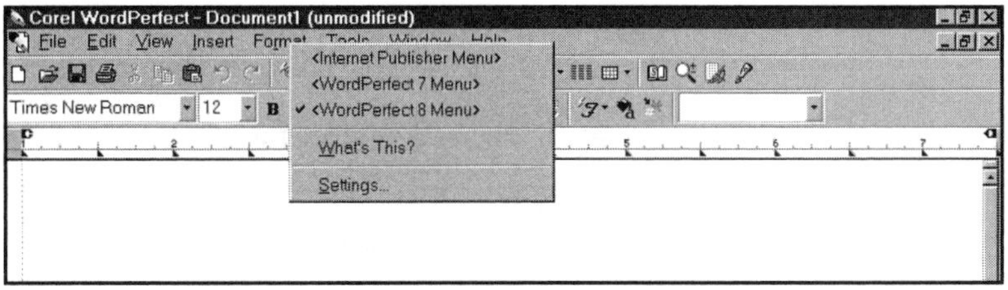

FIG. 32.5 When you right-click a menu bar in WordPerfect or Presentations, you see a QuickMenu enabling you to choose different menus or to set menu preferences.

Setting Menu Preferences

To create, edit, copy, rename, or delete a menu, you must access the Menu Bar Preferences dialog box. To do so, use the following procedure:

1. Right-click the menu. You see a QuickMenu.
2. Choose Settings. You see a Customize Settings dialog box like the one in WordPerfect (see Figure 32.6), or a Customize dialog box in Presentations that offers similar functionality.

FIG. 32.6
The Customize Settings dialog box enables you to customize menus just as you customize toolbars.

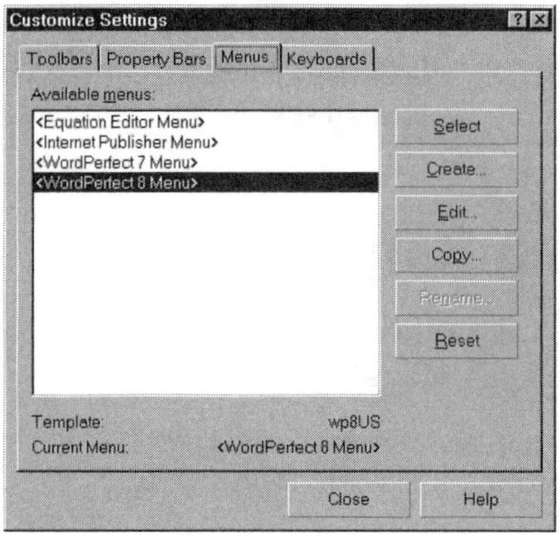

3. Highlight the menu that you want to select, edit, copy, rename, or delete.

TIP Menus that are enclosed in angle braces (<>) are default menus that cannot be edited, renamed, or deleted. You can copy these menus, however, and then edit the copies.

4. Choose an option from the following list:
   - *Select*. Choose this to display the selected menu.
   - *Create*. Choose this option to create a new menu. See the section "Creating Toolbars and Menu Bars" later in this chapter for details.
   - *Edit*. Choose this option to edit an existing menu. See the section "Editing Toolbars and Menu Bars" later in this chapter for details.
   - *Copy*. Choose this option to copy an existing menu. The option works slightly differently depending on the application. See the section "Copying Menu Bars" later in this chapter for details.
   - *Rename*. This option enables you to rename an existing menu if it is not a default menu.
   - *Delete*. Choose this to delete a menu from the list of available menus.
   - *Help*. This option provides context-sensitive help on menus.
5. When you've finished with whichever option you have selected, choose Close. This option completes any operations you have made and returns you to the application.

Copying Menu Bars

Copying menu bars is handled differently by Presentations and WordPerfect. In Presentations, you see a Copy Menu Bar dialog box that merely asks you for the name of the new menu. By default, the new menu has the same entries as the menu selected in the Menu Bars list.

In WordPerfect, menus are stored in templates. To copy a Menu Bar, do the following:

1. Access the Customize Settings dialog box as described above. Choose Copy. You see the Copy Menu Bars dialog box (see Figure 32.7).

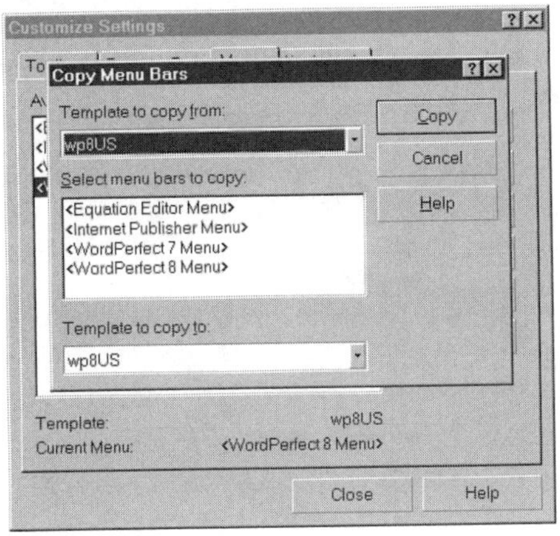

FIG. 32.7
The Copy Menu Bars dialog box in WordPerfect enables you to copy menus from one template to another.

2. Specify the template containing the menu you want to copy.
3. Specify the menu in that template to be copied.
4. Indicate the template to copy the menu to. If the copying operation will result in overwriting the name of an existing menu, you are prompted to overwrite the menu or provide a new name for it. (You see this prompt, for instance, when you copy a menu to the same template it comes from.)
5. Click the Copy button to copy the menu.

Creating and Editing Toolbars and Menu Bars

The process of creating and editing toolbars is almost identical to creating and editing menus. This is because the same elements can be added to toolbar buttons as to menu items. Thus, these are considered here in the same section.

Creating Toolbars and Menu Bars

Creating a new toolbar or menu bar involves two basic steps: giving the toolbar or menu bar a name, and then adding buttons or items to it. To create a new toolbar or menu bar, follow these steps:

1. Right-click the menu or toolbar. You see the QuickMenu.
2. Choose Settings. You see the Customize Settings or Customize dialog box.
3. Choose Create. You see a Create Toolbar or Create Menu Bar dialog box like that shown in Figure 32.8.

FIG. 32.8
The Create Menu Bar dialog box is used to create menu bars.

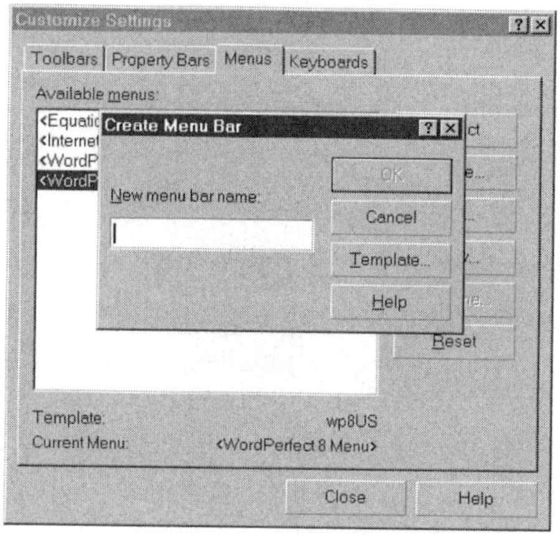

4. Give the toolbar or menu a descriptive name, and then click OK.

NOTE In WordPerfect, toolbars and menu bars are saved in a template rather than as a separate file on the disk. You can specify which template the new toolbar or menu will be saved in by choosing Template from the Create Toolbar or Create Menu Bar dialog box. In the resulting Toolbar or Menu Bar Location dialog box, you can specify either the current document's template or the default template. If you choose the latter, your toolbar or menu will be available in all documents.

5. You see a Menu Editor dialog box similar to the one in Figure 32.9, or a similar Toolbar Editor dialog box.
6. Add, move, and delete buttons as described in the section "Editing Toolbars and Menu Bars" later in this chapter.
7. When you've finished, click OK. You return to the Toolbar or Menu Bar Preferences dialog box. Your new toolbar or menu is on the appropriate list.
8. You can set further preferences or choose Close to return to the application.

FIG. 32.9
After you create a toolbar, you can add buttons to it using the Menu Editor dialog box.

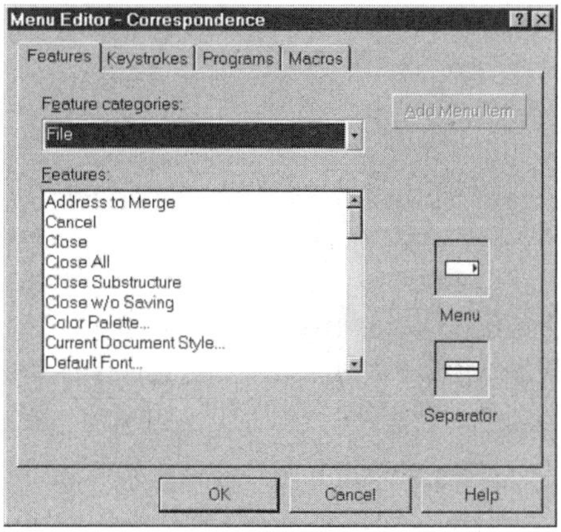

TROUBLESHOOTING

Sometimes I don't know what the toolbar buttons in WordPerfect mean. My office mate's machine gives a little yellow prompt when she puts her mouse pointer on a button. How can I do that? Turn on QuickTips by choosing Tools, Settings, Environment, and then checking the Display QuickTips option in the Interface tab.

Editing Toolbars and Menu Bars

Editing a toolbar or menu bar involves adding, deleting, moving, and customizing buttons or items. To edit an existing toolbar or menu bar, follow these steps:

1. Access the Customize Settings or Customize dialog box as described in the previous section.
2. Select the toolbar or menu to be edited.
3. Choose Edit. You see a Toolbar or Menu Bar Editor dialog box similar to the one shown in Figure 32.10. (The Menu Editor has similar functionality.)
4. Edit the toolbar or menu bar as follows:
   - Add buttons to the toolbar or menu items as described in "Adding Toolbar Buttons and Menu Items" later in this chapter.
   - Move toolbar buttons or menu items by dragging them to a new position on the toolbar or menu.
   - Delete buttons or items by dragging them off the toolbar or menu.

- Customize buttons and items as described in "Customizing Toolbar Buttons and Menu Items" later in this chapter.

5. When you've finished editing the toolbar or Menu bar, click OK. You return to the Customize Settings or Customize dialog box.
6. You can now set further preferences or choose Close to return to the application.

FIG. 32.10
By using the Toolbar Editor dialog box for a specific toolbar, you can add, move, delete, or customize buttons.

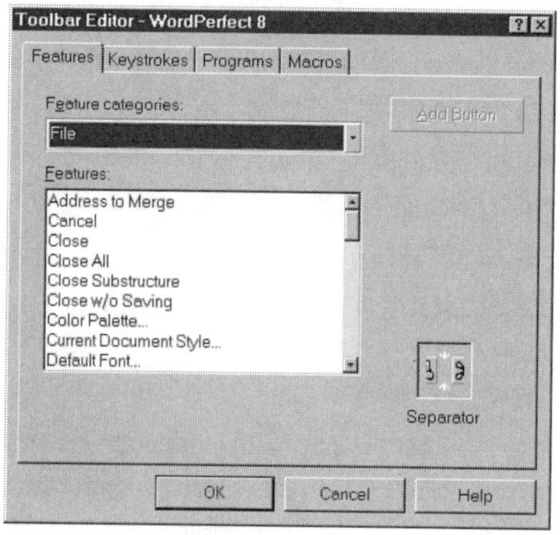

Adding Toolbar Buttons and Menu Items

Toolbar buttons and menu items are extremely powerful. One of their simplest uses is to invoke program features. But toolbar buttons and menu items can perform four different types of tasks:

- *Activate a feature.* Each application has specific features that can be assigned to a toolbar button or menu item. These are the features seen on the default menus of the application. This option enables these menu items to be assigned to toolbar buttons and permits menus to be rearranged to your liking.
- *Play Keystrokes.* You can use a keyboard script to store a sequence of keystrokes. These keystrokes are played back when you click the button or choose the menu item that contains the keyboard script. Keystroke sequences can contain text and extended characters. They can also contain function key and hotkey keystrokes. Thus, you can record simple macros that do anything that can be done by a sequence of keystrokes (but not mouse movements or mouse clicks).
- *Launch a program.* Toolbar buttons and menu items can launch any application on your disk—both WordPerfect Suite and non-WordPerfect Suite programs.
- *Play a macro.* You can also create a button or menu item that will run a macro. (The macro must already have been created and saved on the disk.)

In order to add a button or item to your toolbar or menu, access the Toolbar or Menu Bar Editor dialog box by creating or editing a toolbar or menu as described in the last section. What you do next depends on what type of button or menu item you want to add.

Adding a Feature To add a button or menu item that calls a feature, follow these steps:

1. From the Toolbar Editor or Menu Editor dialog box, choose the Features tab. The dialog box shows options for Feature Categories and Features.
2. Select Feature Categories, and click the down arrow to the right of the Feature Categories text box. You see a list of available Feature Categories (see Figure 32.11). These parallel the main menu options. Some applications may have additional feature categories.

FIG. 32.11
In the Toolbar Editor, you can assign buttons or menu items to application features that parallel default menu items.

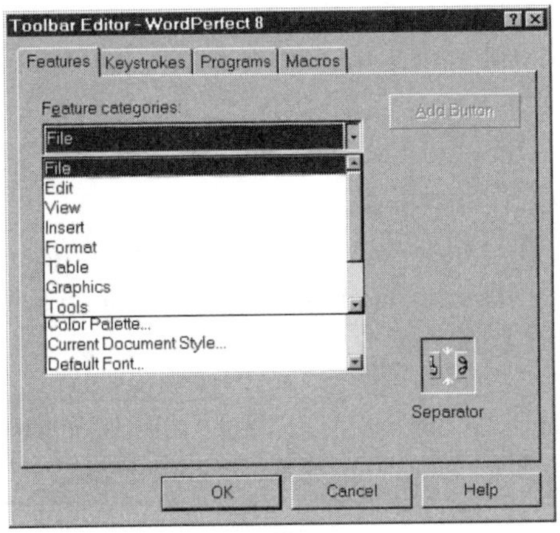

3. Depending on the category you select, a different list of features appears. Select the feature you want to associate with the button, then choose Add Button (or Add Menu Item, if you're editing a menu).
4. A new button or item appears on the toolbar or menu, and you remain in the Edit Toolbar or Menu Editor dialog box so that you can make further additions or accept the change you have made and exit the dialog box by clicking the OK button.

TIP New menu items are added as main selections on the menu bar. Move them by dragging them to their appropriate place on a menu.

Adding a Keystroke Sequence If you want a button or menu item to play a keystroke sequence, follow these steps to create it:

1. From the Toolbar or Menu Bar Editor dialog box, choose the Keystrokes tab. The Keystrokes tab of the Toolbar or Menu Editor dialog box shows a text box for the keyboard script (see Figure 32.12).

FIG. 32.12
In the Toolbar Editor dialog box, you can enter the keystroke sequences that create Toolbar buttons and menu items for text, function keys, or menu choices.

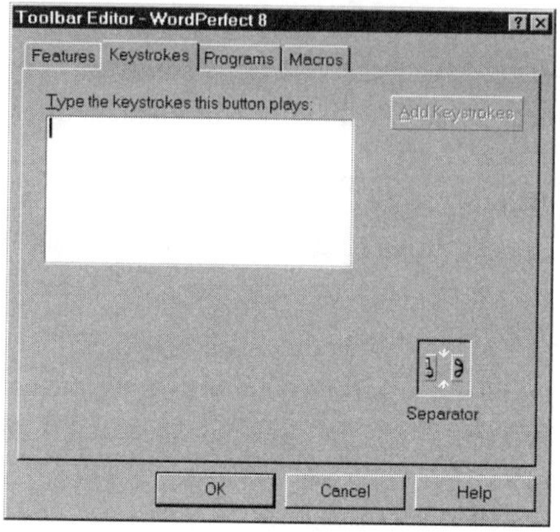

2. Choose Type The Keystrokes This Button (or menu item) Plays. An insertion point appears in the text box.
3. Type the keystrokes that the button should play. Function keys are entered with braces—for example, **{Shift+F7}**.
4. When you've finished, choose Add Keystrokes. A new button or item appears on the toolbar or menu, and you remain in the Toolbar or Menu Editor dialog box so that you can make further additions.

TIP By default, a new keyboard sequence item has the name of the first word in the script. To change this name, double-click the menu item while you are editing the menu bar.

Launching a Program To create a button or menu item that will launch a program, you must know the name of the program file and the folder in which it resides. Then, create the button or item as follows:

1. From the Toolbar or Menu Editor dialog box, choose the Programs tab.
2. Click the Add Program button. You see the Open File dialog box (see Figure 32.13).
3. Navigate to the folder containing the program, and double-click the appropriate program file.

▶ **See** "Saving, Opening, and Closing Files," **p. 32**

A new button or item appears on the toolbar or menu, and you return to the Toolbar or Menu Editor dialog box so that you can make further additions.

TIP By default, a new application launch menu item has the name of the application. To change this name, double-click the menu item.

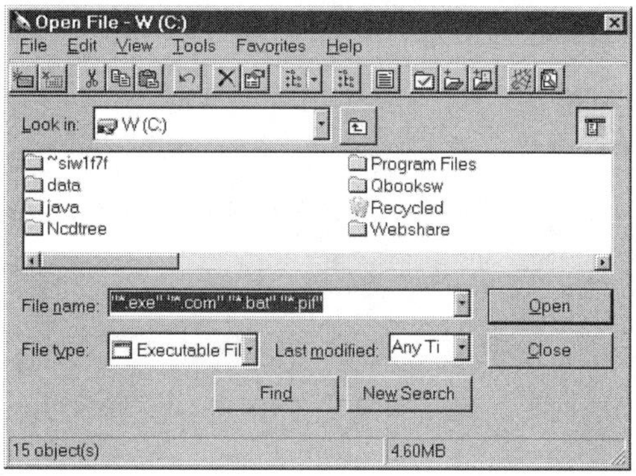

FIG. 32.13
Assign an application to a toolbar button or menu item using the Open File - Programs dialog box.

Running a Macro If you would like to assign a macro to a toolbar button or menu item, use the following steps:

1. From the Toolbar or Menu Editor dialog box, choose the Macros tab.
2. Click the Add Macro button that now appears in the dialog box. You see an Add Macro or a Select Macro dialog box, like the one shown in Figure 32.14, enabling you to choose the macro to be assigned to the button or menu item.

NOTE In WordPerfect, you can also choose Add Template Macro. This adds a macro that is stored in a template to a button or menu item, as opposed to one stored on the disk. In this case, you see a list of macros stored in the current template, and you can choose a macro from this list.

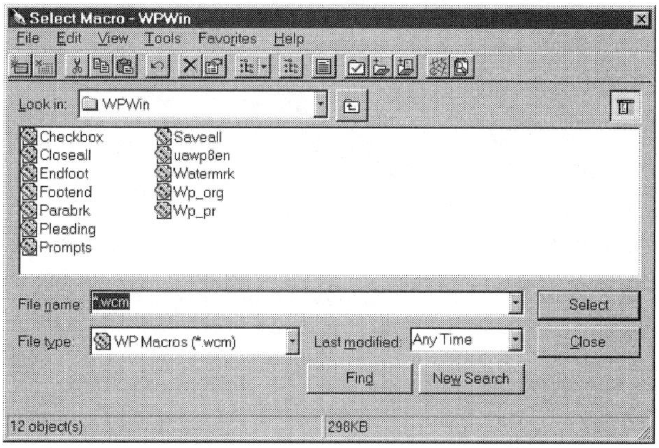

FIG. 32.14
Through the Select Macro dialog box, you can access macros which you can also assign to toolbar buttons and menu items.

3. Navigate to the appropriate folder, and then double-click the macro file. A new button or item appears on the toolbar or menu, and you return to the Edit Toolbar or Menu Editor dialog box so that you can make further additions.

Customizing Toolbar Buttons and Menu Items

You may customize a button or menu item by double-clicking it while you are editing or creating a toolbar or menu bar.

If you double-click a toolbar button, you see the Customize Button dialog box (see Figure 32.15).

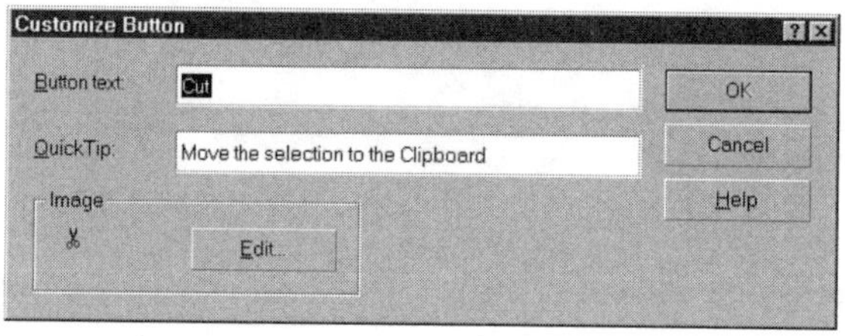

FIG. 32.15
The Customize Button dialog box enables you to change the properties of specific buttons on the toolbar.

If you double-click a menu item, you see the Edit Menu Text dialog box (see Figure 32.16).

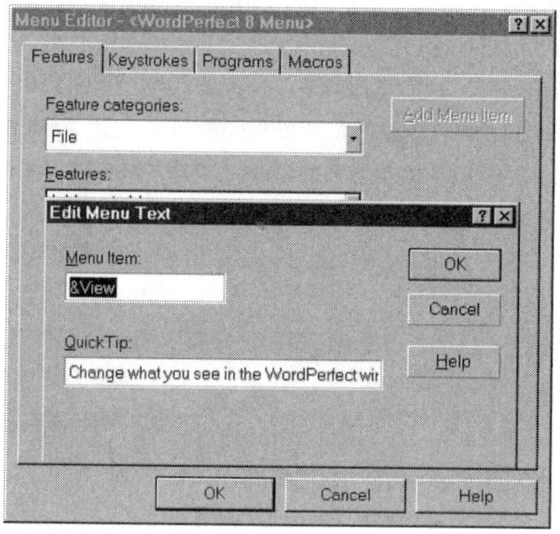

FIG. 32.16
The Edit Menu Text dialog box enables you to change the text of the menu item QuickTip.

These dialog boxes provide options, including:

- *Button Text and QuickTip (for toolbar buttons)*. The text that pops up when you hold the mouse pointer on a toolbar button.
- *Menu Item (for menu items)*. The text of the menu item.
- *Edit (toolbar buttons)*. Enables you to edit the image of the button. Choosing Edit displays an Image Editor dialog box (see Figure 32.17).

If you use the bitmap editor to change the appearance of your toolbar button, you see the following options:

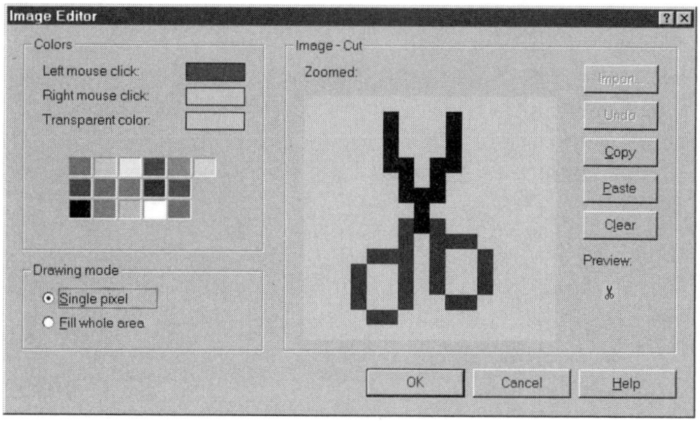

FIG. 32.17
WordPerfect Suite 8 includes a bitmap editor that enables you to change the appearance of toolbar buttons.

- Select the colors that you can paint with the left and right mouse buttons by clicking the appropriate colors with the respective buttons.
- If Single Pixel is selected, click either button to fill small rectangles with the appropriate color, one at a time.
- If Fill Whole Area is selected, clicking a cell changes the color of that cell and all contiguous cells of the same color.
- You can also use the Copy and Paste commands to copy images from one button to another.

Setting Additional Properties

When you edit toolbars and menu bars, and double-click a button or menu item, you may see a Properties button.

This option enables you to change certain aspects of the command invoked by the button or menu item. How it works depends on what the button or menu item does:

- For buttons or menu items that invoke a feature, no Properties option is available. There is also no Properties option available for WordPerfect toolbar buttons that invoke macros stored in the template.
- If the button or menu item plays a keyboard script, choosing Properties displays a Script Properties dialog box that enables you to edit the script.
- Choosing Properties for buttons or menu items that launch a program displays an Application Launch Properties dialog box. You can use this dialog box to specify the Command Line, Working Folder, and whether to Run the program minimized.
- Choosing Properties for buttons that launch macros located on the disk enables you to edit the path and name of the macro.

Index

Symbols

A

B

E

F

G

H

J-K

L

O

P

Q

R

T

X-Y-Z